CORPORATE TAX RATES

If Taxable Income is:		The Tax is:			Of the Amount Over-
Over-	But Not Over-				
$ –0–	50,000			15%	$ –0–
50,000	75,000	$7,500	+	25%	50,000
75,000	100,000	13,750	+	34%	75,000
100,000	335,000	22,250	+	39%	100,000
335,000	10,000,000	113,900	+	34%	335,000
10,000,000	15,000,000	3,400,000	+	35%	10,000,000
15,000,000	18,333,333	5,150,000	+	38%	15,000,000
18,333,333		6,416,667	+	35%	18,333,333

Visit the *Principles of Taxation for Business and Investment Planning* web site at
www.mhhe.com/business/accounting/sjones

Principles of Taxation for Business and Investment Planning
1999 Edition

Sally M. Jones
KPMG Peat Marwick Professor of Accounting
McIntire School of Commerce
University of Virginia

Boston   Burr Ridge, IL   Dubuque, IA   Madison, WI   New York   San Francisco   St. Louis
Bangkok   Bogotá   Caracas   Lisbon   London   Madrid
Mexico City   Milan   New Delhi   Seoul   Singapore   Sydney   Taipei   Toronto

Irwin/McGraw-Hill

A Division of The **McGraw·Hill** Companies

PRINCIPLES OF TAXATION FOR BUSINESS AND INVESTMENT PLANNING, 1999

2 3 4 5 6 7 8 9 0 DOC/DOC 9 3 2 1 0 9 8

ISBN 0-07-303594-7
ISSN 1099-5587

Vice president and editorial director: *Michael W. Junior*
Publisher: *Jeffrey J. Shelstad*
Sponsoring editor: *George Werthman*
Developmental editor: *Marc Chernoff*
Senior marketing manager: *Rhonda Seelinger*
Project manager: *Karen Nelson*
Production associate: *Debra R. Benson*
Freelance design coordinator: *Laurie J. Entringer*
Supplement coordinator: *Rose M. Range*
Compositor: *GAC Shepard Poorman Communications*
Typeface: *10/12 Times Roman*
Printer: *R. R. Donnelley & Sons Company*

http://www.mhhe.com

To Zane, Ward, and Rachael

About the Author

Sally M. Jones is the KPMG Peat Marwick Professor of Accounting at the McIntire School of Commerce, University of Virginia, where she teaches both graduate and undergraduate tax courses. Before joining the Virginia faculty in 1992, Professor Jones spent 14 years on the faculty of the Graduate School of Business, University of Texas at Austin. She received her undergraduate degree from Augusta College, her M.P.A. from the University of Texas, and her Ph.D. from the University of Houston. She is also a CPA. Professor Jones is the author of *Federal Taxes and Management Decisions* (Irwin/McGraw-Hill) and was the first editor of *Advances in Taxation* (JAI Press) and the *Price Waterhouse Case Studies in Taxation*. She has published numerous articles in the *Journal of Taxation, The Tax Adviser,* and the *Journal of the American Taxation Association*. Professor Jones is a frequent speaker at tax conferences and symposia and is a past president of the American Taxation Association.

Preface

Principles of Taxation for Business and Investment Planning is a new approach to the subject of taxation. This text is designed for use in introductory tax courses included in either undergraduate or graduate business programs. The objective of this text is to teach students to recognize the major tax issues inherent in business and financial transactions. The text focuses on fundamental concepts, the mastery of which provides students with a permanent frame of reference for future study of advanced tax topics. Unlike traditional introductory texts, *Principles of Taxation for Business and Investment Planning* downplays the technical detail that makes the study of taxation such a nightmare for business students. Traditional texts are heavily compliance oriented and convince many students that the tax law is too complex and specialized to be relevant to their future careers. This text attempts to do just the opposite by convincing students that an understanding of taxation is not only relevant but critical to their success in the business world.

Principles of Taxation for Business and Investment Planning has its origin in the 1989 White Paper entitled *Perspectives on Education: Capabilities for Success in the Accounting Profession*, published jointly by the Big Eight public accounting firms. The White Paper expressed disenchantment with the narrow technical focus of undergraduate accounting curricula and called for scholastic emphasis on a broad set of business skills necessary for a lifetime of professional success. The Accounting Education Change Commission (AECC), operating under the aegis of the American Accounting Association, embraced the philosophy reflected in the White Paper. In September 1990, the AECC published its Position Statement No. One, entitled *Objectives of Education for Accountants*. This statement reiterated that an undergraduate business education should provide a base on which lifelong learning can be built.

In spite of these calls for reform, many undergraduate tax courses are taught in a traditional manner based on a paradigm developed four decades ago. In the modern (postwar) era of business education, the first generation of tax teachers were practitioners: accountants or attorneys hired as adjunct faculty to initiate students into the mysteries of the newly enacted Internal Revenue Code of 1954. These practitioners taught their students in the same way they trained their employees. In doing so, they created a compliance-oriented paradigm that has survived to the present day. In today's world, this traditional paradigm is an anachronism. Business students don't need to learn how to generate tax information. Instead, they must learn how to use tax information to make good business and financial decisions.

A New Paradigm for the Introductory Tax Course

Principles of Taxation for Business and Investment Planning provides a new paradigm for meeting the educational needs of tax students in the twenty-first century. This paradigm is based on three postulates:

- **Postulate 1: Students should learn the tax law as an integrated component of a complex economic environment.** Students should be aware of the role taxes play in financial and managerial decision making and should understand how taxes motivate people and institutions to engage in certain transactions or activities.

- **Postulate 2: Students should comprehend the tax law as an organic whole rather than as a fragmented collection of rules and regulations.** This postulate dictates that students learn to apply the general tax rules rather than the myriad of exceptions that confuse rather than clarify the general rules. They should appreciate how the general rules apply to all taxpaying entities before they learn how specialized rules apply to only certain entities. Finally, they should learn how the law applies to broad categories of transactions rather than to a particular transaction.

- **Postulate 3: Students who learn fundamental concepts have a permanent frame of reference into which they can integrate the constant changes in the technical minutia of the law.** The rapid evolution of the tax law results in a very short shelf life for much of the detailed information contained in undergraduate tax texts. Yet the key elements of the law—the statutory and judicial bedrock—do not change with each new revenue act passed by Congress. The student who masters these key elements truly is prepared for a lifetime of learning.

As a teacher with almost 25 years of experience, I know that traditional paradigms die hard and educational reform can be both painful and costly. Nevertheless, I also believe that change in the way college and university professors teach tax is both inevitable and extremely worthwhile. Our responsibility to our students is to prepare them to cope in a business world with little tolerance for outdated skills or irrelevant knowledge. My hope is that *Principles of Taxation for Business and Investment Planning* is a tool that can help us all fulfill that responsibility.

Organization and Content

Principles of Taxation for Business and Investment Planning consists of six parts with a total of 17 chapters. The following summaries of each part describe the sequencing and content of the chapters.

Part One, Exploring the Tax Environment, consists of two chapters that familiarize students with the global tax environment. Chapter 1 describes the environment in terms of the legal relationship between taxes, taxpayers, and governments. Definitions of key terms are developed, and the major taxes that businesses routinely encounter are identified. Chapter 2 considers the tax environment from a normative perspective by asking the question: "What are the characteristics of a good tax?" Students are introduced to the notions of tax efficiency and tax equity and learn how contrasting political beliefs about efficiency and equity continue to shape the tax environment.

Part Two, Fundamentals of Tax Planning, concentrates on developing a methodology by which to incorporate tax factors into business decisions. Chapter 3 introduces the pivotal role of net present value of cash flows as the basis for evaluating financial alternatives. Students learn how to compute tax costs and tax savings and how to interpret these numbers as cash flows. Chapter 4 covers the basic maxims of income tax planning. The characteristics of the tax law that create planning opportunities are explained, and the generic techniques for taking advantage of those opportunities are analyzed.

Part Three, The Measurement of Taxable Income, focuses on the quantification of taxable income generated by business operations. Chapter 5 covers the computation of taxable income or loss from ongoing commercial activities, with special emphasis on differences between taxable income and net income for financial statement purposes. Chapters 6 and 7 explore the tax implications of acquisitions and dispositions of business property, while Chapter 8 is devoted to nontaxable exchanges.

Part Four, The Taxation of Business Income, teaches students how to calculate the tax liability on a given amount of business income. Chapter 9 describes the function of sole proprietorships, partnerships, and S corporations as conduits of income, while Chapter 10 discusses corporations as taxable entities in their own right. Chapter 11 builds on the preceding two chapters by exploring the tax planning implications of the choice of business entity. Chapter 12 broadens the discussion by considering the special problems of businesses generating income in more than one tax jurisdiction. This chapter introduces the reader to both multistate and international tax planning strategies.

Part Five, The Individual Taxpayer, concentrates on the tax rules and regulations unique to individuals. Chapter 13 presents the individual tax formula and acquaints students with the complexities of computing individual taxable income and tax liability. Chapter 14 covers compensation and retirement planning. Chapter 15 discusses the tax consequences of investment and rental activities and introduces wealth transfer planning. Finally, Chapter 16 analyzes the tax consequences of personal activities, with particular emphasis on home ownership.

Part Six, The Tax Compliance Process, consists of Chapter 17, which presents the important procedural and administrative issues confronting taxpayers. This chapter covers the basic rules for the payment of tax and the filing of returns, as well as the penalties the Internal Revenue Service may impose on taxpayers who violate the rules. Chapter 17 also describes the judicial process through which taxpayers and the IRS resolve their differences.

Chapter Highlights

The chapters begin with **Learning Objectives** that preview the technical content and alert students to the important concepts to be mastered. These objectives appear again as marginal notations marking the place in the chapter where each learning objective is addressed. The chapters contain numerous **examples** and **cases** illustrating the topic or demonstrating the calculation under discussion. End-of-chapter materials begin with a list of **Key Terms** from the chapter. Definitions of the key terms from all the chapters are compiled in a **Glossary** for the text. The end-of-chapter materials also include four types of problems for instructors to assign for class discussion or for homework.

- **Questions and Problems for Discussion** challenge students to think critically about conceptual and technical issues covered in the chapter. These problems tend to be open-ended and are designed to engage students in debate. Many problems require students to integrate material from previous chapters in formulating their responses.
- **Application Problems** give students practice in applying the technical material covered in the chapter. Most of the problems are quantitative and students must perform a calculation (or a series of calculations) to derive a numeric solution to the problem.

- **Issue Recognition Problems** are designed to develop students' ability to recognize the tax issues suggested by a set of facts and to state those issues as questions. The technical issues buried in these problems typically are *not* discussed in the chapter. Consequently, the students must rely on their understanding of basic principles to analyze the problem, spot the tax concern or opportunity, and formulate the question to be resolved. In short, students must take the first steps in the tax research process to respond to these problems.

- **Tax Planning Cases** give students an opportunity to integrate their tax knowledge into a business planning framework. Most cases involve taxpayers who must decide whether to undertake a certain transaction or who must choose between alternative transactions. Students must assume the role of tax advisor by analyzing the case and recommending a course of action to maximize the after-tax value of the transaction.

Supplemental Materials

An **Instructor's Manual** includes a course outline, topics for class discussion, and teaching hints for a one-semester introductory tax course. The Instructor's Manual also provides suggested solutions to all end-of-chapter problems and cases.

A **Web Page,** prepared by Thomas C. Omer (University of Illinois at Chicago), provides relevant links for each chapter and a series of interactive tutorials.

A **Test Bank,** prepared by Roxanne Spindle (Virginia Commonwealth University), contains multiple-choice, true-false, and short problems requiring analysis and written answers.

Computest is a computerized version of the manual test bank for more efficient use, available in a Windows platform.

Teletest allows users to call a toll-free number, specify the content of desired exams, and have a laser-printed copy of the exams mailed to them.

A **Study Guide,** prepared by Bill Duncan (Arizona State University–West), enables students to review text material and test their understanding. The guide includes a summary of each chapter's highlights, study suggestions, and self-test questions.

Using This Text in a First-Semester Tax Course

Principles of Taxation for Business and Investment Planning is designed for use in a one-semester (15-week) introductory tax course. Instructors can choose which of the 17 chapters in the book deserve a full week's coverage and which can be covered in less than a week. Instructors may even decide to omit chapters that seem less relevant to the particular educational needs of their students. I believe that business students who complete a one-semester course based on this text will be well prepared to function in the current tax environment. If they are required (or may elect) to take a second tax course, they will have a solid, theoretical foundation on which to build. The second tax course typically involves an in-depth study of the taxation of business entities: C corporations, partnerships, and S corporations. Because *Principles of Taxation for Business and Investment Planning* puts so much emphasis on the essential tax consequences of business transactions, students who learn from this text should easily make the transition to an advanced tax course.

The content and organization of this text are highly compatible with the Model Tax Curriculum proposed by the American Institute of Certified Public Accountants in 1996. According to the AICPA, the introductory tax course should expose students to a broad range of tax concepts and emphasize the role of taxation in the business decision-making process. Under the model curriculum, students first learn to measure the taxable income generated by business and property transactions. They are then introduced to the different types of business entity and the tax considerations unique to each type. Individual taxation should be one of the last topics covered in the course, rather than the primary focus of the course. Because *Principles of Taxation for Business and Investment Planning* reflects this recommended pedagogical approach, the text is ideal for courses based on the AICPA Model Tax Curriculum.

This is the second annual edition of *Principles of Taxation for Business and Investment Planning*. I've been a student of the tax law far too long to believe that this edition is free from technical error or includes every relevant topic. I'm certain that adopters of the text will have many excellent suggestions as to how I can improve the next edition. I welcome any and all comments and encourage my fellow teachers to call me (804-924-3483) or e-mail me (smj7q@virginia.edu) with their input.

Acknowledgments

I want to thank the many friends and colleagues who shared their ideas for this project and cheered me on to its completion. I particularly want to acknowledge the contribution of Professor Pat Wilkie and Professor Jim Young at George Mason University. Their article entitled "Teaching the Introductory Tax Course: A Template of the Federal Income Tax Formula, Taxpayer Activities, and Taxpayer Entities" in the *Journal of the American Taxation Association*, (Fall 1997), profoundly influenced my thinking and the final organization of this book. Thanks also to the following individuals who reviewed the manuscript and first edition of the text. Their expert comments were invaluable and the second edition is significantly improved because of their involvement.

Reviewers

Susan Anderson
University of North Carolina at Greensboro

Steven Balsam
Temple University

Robert Bloomfield
Cornell University

Anne L. Christensen
Portland State University

David B. Davidson
California State University– Long Beach

Amy Dunbar
University of Iowa

Terri Gutierrez
University of Northern Colorado

John Janiga
Loyola University–Chicago

Walter O'Connor
Fordham University

Chris Petruzzi
California State University–Fullerton

Elizabeth Plummer
Southern Methodist University

Shelley C. Rhoades
Villanova University

Timothy J. Rupert
Northeastern University

Donald Samelson
Moorhead State University

Roby B. Sawyers
North Carolina State University

Robert A. Scharlach
University of Southern California

Michael Schadewald
University of Wisconsin–Milwaukee

Douglas Shackelford
University of North Carolina

Brian C. Spilker
Brigham Young University

Roxanne Spindle
Virginia Commonwealth University

Toby Stock
University of Colorado at Boulder

Deborah W. Thomas
University of Arkansas

Anne Townsend
University of Texas–Dallas

Don Trippeer
Lehigh University

Patrick Wilkie
George Mason University

William F. Yancey
Texas Christian University

I am very grateful to the entire Irwin/McGraw-Hill team for their professional support. In particular, I want to acknowledge Jeff Shelstad and George Werthman. I'm particularly indebted to Marc Chernoff, who guided me through the entire development and production process. Marc's constant encouragement and unflagging enthusiasm makes him a true partner in this venture. Finally, I want to thank my daughter Rachael, who took over the management of the Jones household so that I could write this text.

Sally M. Jones
University of Virginia

Brief Contents

CONTENTS

Introduction to Students

P*rinciples of Taxation for Business and Investment Planning* explores the role that taxes play in modern life. The book is written for business students who have completed introductory courses in accounting and finance and are familiar with basic business concepts. Those of you who fit this description, regardless of your future career path, will be called on to make decisions in which you must evaluate the impact of taxes. At the most fundamental level, all business decisions have the same economic objective: the maximization of long-term wealth through cash flow enhancement. The cash flow generated by any transaction depends on the tax consequences. Business men and women must appreciate the role of taxes before they can make intelligent economic decisions, whether on behalf of their firm or on their personal behalf.

Taxes as Business Costs

When business professionals are asked to identify the common goal of all business decisions, their immediate response tends to be that the goal is to increase profits. When prompted to think past the current year, most eventually conclude that the long-term goal of business decisions is to maximize the value of the firm. In this text, a **firm** is a generic business organization. Firms include sole proprietorships, partnerships, limited liability companies, subchapter S and regular corporations, and any other arrangement through which people carry on a profit-motivated activity. Firm managers know that short-term profits and long-term value are enhanced when operating costs are controlled. The taxes that firms pay with respect to any facet of their business operations represent out-of-pocket costs. Experienced managers never regard taxes as fixed or unavoidable costs. As you will soon discover, opportunities abound for controlling the tax cost of doing business.

The above observations suggest that tax planning means reducing the tax cost of business operations to maximize the value of the firm. Firms can reduce taxes by implementing any number of strategies. However, tax cost is only one variable that managers must consider in making business decisions. Few strategies affect just one isolated aspect of a firm's overall operation. A strategy that reduces taxes may also have undesirable consequences, such as reducing revenues or increasing nontax costs. Because of nontax variables, the business strategy with the least tax cost may not be the best strategy. Therefore, tax minimization in and of itself may be a short-sighted objective. This point is so elementary yet so important: *effective tax planning must take into account both tax and nontax factors.* When faced with competing strategies, business managers should implement the strategy that maximizes firm value, even when that strategy has a higher tax cost than the alternatives. In other words, managers should never let the tax tail wag the business dog.

Taxes as Household Expenditures

Principles of Taxation for Business and Investment Planning concentrates on the income taxation of business activities and organizations. This concentration does not mean that the tax rules applying to individuals are ignored. Quite to the contrary. For income tax purposes, individuals and the profit-making activities in which they engage are inextricably entwined. As we will observe over and over again, the ultimate taxpayers in every business situation are the people who own and operate that business.

As you study this text, consider your own role as a lifelong taxpayer. Regardless of who you are, where you live, or how you earn and spend your money, you will pay taxes on a regular basis to any number of governments. In fact, in the United States, taxes are the single largest household expenditure. The following pie chart shows that in 1997, a person working an eight-hour day spent almost three hours working to pay local, state, and federal taxes.

Tax Bite in the Eight-Hour Day

State and local taxes: 56 minutes

Federal taxes: 1 hour, 53 minutes

Housing and household operations: 1 hour, 20 minutes

Transportation: 34 minutes

Savings: 22 minutes

Clothing: 20 minutes

Recreation: 25 minutes

Food and tobacco: 49 minutes

Health and medical care: 59 minutes

All other: 22 minutes

Source: Tax Foundation.

People who are clueless as to how taxes work are in a passive role, required by law to participate in a tax system they don't understand and over which they exercise no control. In contrast, if you comprehend how taxes relate to your life, you can assume an active role. You can take positive steps to minimize your personal tax liability to the fullest extent allowed by law. You can make informed financial decisions to take advantage of tax-saving opportunities. You can draw rational conclusions about the efficiency and fairness of existing tax laws and can assess the merit of competing tax reform proposals. And finally, you can change the tax system by participating as a voter in the democratic process.

The Text's Objectives

Principles of Taxation for Business and Investment Planning has three main objectives that motivate the overall design of the text, the selection and ordering of topics, and the development of each topic.

Introducing Tax Policy Issues

The first objective is to acquaint you with the economic and social policy implications of the various tax systems used by governments to raise revenues. Most of the subject matter of the text pertains to the tax environment as it exists today and how successful businesses adapt to and take advantage of that environment. But the text also raises normative issues concerning the efficiency and equity of many features of the tax environment. You will learn how certain provisions of the tax law are intended to further the government's fiscal policy goals. You are invited to evaluate these goals and to question whether the tax system is an effective or appropriate mechanism for accomplishing the goals.

The text identifies potentially negative aspects of the tax environment. It explains how taxes may adversely affect individual behavior or cause unintended and undesirable outcomes. You will be asked to consider whether certain provisions of the tax law favor one group of taxpayers over another and whether such favoritism is justifiable on any ethical grounds. After probing both the strengths and weaknesses of the current tax system, you can draw your own conclusions as to how the system can be improved.

Bridging the Gap between Finance and Tax

The second objective of the text is to bridge the academic gap between the study of financial theory and the study of tax law. Finance courses teach students how to make decisions on the basis of after-tax cash flows generated by the management or investment strategy under consideration. However, these courses give students only rudimentary instruction on determining the tax consequences of transactions and overlook the possibilities for controlling tax consequences to maximize cash flows. In extreme cases, financial models simply ignore tax consequences by assuming that business decisions can be made in a tax-free environment.

Traditional tax law courses err in the opposite direction. These courses teach students to apply statutory rules to well-defined, closed-fact situations and to determine the resulting tax consequences. Correct application of the rule is the learning objective. Students are not required to integrate the tax consequences of transactions into a broad business decision-making framework. In other words, they don't translate tax outcomes into cash flows. Traditional law courses may fail to encourage students to consider how closed-fact situations can be restructured to change the tax outcome and improve the overall financial results. Consequently, students often develop the habit of analyzing transactions from a backward-looking *compliance* perspective rather than from a forward-looking *planning* perspective.

The primary focus of *Principles of Taxation for Business and Investment Planning* is on the common ground shared by financial theory and tax law. The connecting links between the two disciplines are stressed throughout the text. You will learn how effective business planning depends on an accurate assessment of relevant tax factors. Tax rules and regulations are presented and illustrated in the context of an economic decision-making framework. Admittedly, these rules and regulations are tough to master. Two observations should give you reassurance. First, while the detailed structure of the tax law is both extremely technical and complex, the application of the law's underlying principles to business decision making is relatively straightforward. Second, you can learn to appreciate tax planning strategies without becoming a tax-compliance expert.

Teaching the Framework of the Income Tax

The third objective of *Principles of Taxation for Business and Investment Planning* is to teach the framework of the federal income tax, the dominant feature of the modern tax environment. This framework has been remarkably stable over time, even though the particulars of the law change every year. Students who devote their time and energy to understanding the framework needn't worry that their knowledge will be outdated when Congress enacts its next revenue bill.

The federal income tax system has a bad reputation as an impenetrable, intractable body of law. While the whole fabric of the income tax law is every bit as complicated as its critics suggest, its framework consists of a manageable number of basic principles. The principles are internally consistent and underlie many seemingly disparate technical provisions. By concentrating on these principles, you can attain a sufficient level of tax knowledge in a single introductory course. You will not be a tax expert, but you will be tax literate. You may not be capable of implementing sophisticated tax planning strategies, but you will know how those strategies can improve cash flows and maximize wealth.

Because this text adopts a conceptual approach to the tax law, narrowly drawn provisions, exceptions, limitations, and special cases are deemphasized. Details with the potential to confuse rather than clarify the tax principle under discussion are usually relegated to footnotes. When we do examine a detailed provision of the law, the detail should illuminate an underlying concept. Or we may discuss a thorny technical rule just to emphasize the practical difficulties encountered by tax professionals who don't have the luxury of dealing with abstractions.

The conceptual approach should sensitize you to the tax implications of business transactions and cultivate your ability to ask good tax questions. This approach downplays the importance of the answers to these questions. Knowing the answers, or more precisely, finding the answers to tax questions is the job of tax accountants and attorneys who devote long hours in their research libraries to that end. A tax-sensitive business manager knows when to consult these experts and can help formulate the tax issues for the expert to resolve. The text's emphasis on issue recognition rather than issue resolution is reflected in the problems at the end of each chapter. Many of these problems ask you to analyze a fact situation and simply identify any tax concerns or opportunities suggested by the facts. Other problems present you with facts suggesting tax issues with no correct solution.

A Reassuring Word to Accounting Majors.   *Principles of Taxation for Business and Investment Planning* is an ideal introductory text for those of you who are concentrating in accounting and who may even plan to specialize in taxation. You will benefit enormously from mastering the framework of the income tax as the first step in your professional education; this mastery will serve as a foundation for the future study of advanced topics. You will gain a command of basic principles on which to rely as you develop an instinct for your subject—a facility for diagnosing the tax issues suggested by unfamiliar and unusual transactions.

The text's conceptual approach is appropriate for the first tax course because it concentrates on broad themes concerning most taxpayers instead of narrow problems encountered by an isolated few. If you learn these themes, you will be well prepared to expand and deepen your tax knowledge through professional experience. You will understand from the beginning that taxes are only one aspect of the economic decision-making process. Because of this understanding, those of you who become tax professionals will be equipped to serve your clients not just as tax specialists but as valued business advisors.

Conclusion

Hopefully, this introduction has conveyed the message that business men and women who decide on a particular course of action without considering the tax outcomes are making an uninformed, and possibly incorrect, decision. By proceeding with the course of study contained in this text, you will learn to recognize the tax implications of a whole spectrum of business transactions. On entering the business world, you will be prepared to make decisions incorporating this knowledge. You will spot tax problems as they arise and will call in a tax professional before, rather than after, initiating a transaction with profound tax consequences. And finally, you will understand that effective tax planning can save more money than the most diligent tax compliance.

PART ONE

Exploring the
Tax Environment

CHAPTER 1
Types of Taxes and the Jurisdictions That Use Them

CHAPTER 2
Tax Policy Issues: Standards for a Good Tax

1 Types of Taxes and the Jurisdictions That Use Them

Learning Objectives

After studying this chapter, you should be able to:

1. Define the terms *tax, taxpayer, incidence,* and *jurisdiction.*
2. Express the relationship between tax base, tax rate, and tax revenue as a formula.
3. Identify and describe the types of taxes levied by local governments, state governments, and the federal government.
4. Explain why different taxing jurisdictions often compete for revenues from the same taxpayer.
5. Identify the reasons why governments continually modify their tax systems.
6. Describe the three primary sources of federal tax law.

When an explorer plans a journey through unknown territory to a new destination, his preparations include a careful inspection of a map of the territory. The explorer familiarizes himself with topographic features such as major highways, mountain ranges, lakes and rivers, and population centers. He may gather information concerning the climate of the region and the language and customs of its inhabitants. This preliminary knowledge of the environment helps the explorer chart his course and minimizes the danger that his progress will be impeded by unforeseen circumstances.

For students who are just beginning their study of taxation, the tax environment in which individuals and organizations must function is unknown territory. Chapter 1 serves as a map of this territory. The chapter begins by describing the tax environment in terms of the basic relationship among taxes, taxpayers, and governments. It identifies the major types of taxes that businesses routinely encounter and examines how governments with overlapping jurisdictions compete for tax revenues. By reading the chapter, you will gain a familiarity with the tax environment that will serve you in good stead as we journey toward an understanding of the role of taxes in the business decision-making process.

The chapter should alert you to two important features of the tax environment. First, taxes are *pervasive* because they are so widespread, come in so many varieties, and affect virtually every aspect of modern life. Second, taxes are *dynamic* because the tax laws change with amazing frequency. The rate of change reflects the fact that the economic and political assumptions on which tax structures are based are constantly evolving. While these two features make the current tax environment a challenging one for business managers, they also create a vitality that makes the study of tax planning so fascinating.

Some Basic Terminology

Taxes, Taxpayers, Incidence, and Jurisdiction

Objective 1
Define the terms *tax, taxpayer, incidence,* and *jurisdiction.*

Before beginning our exploration of the tax environment, we must define some basic terminology. A **tax** can be defined simply as a payment to support the cost of government. A tax differs from a fine or penalty imposed by a government because a tax is not intended to deter or punish unacceptable behavior. On the other hand, taxes are compulsory; anyone subject to a tax is not free to choose whether or not to pay. A tax differs from a user's fee because the payment of a tax does not entitle the payer to a specific good or service in return. In the abstract, citizens receive any number of government benefits for their tax dollars. Nevertheless, the value of government benefits received by any particular person is not correlated to the tax that person is required to pay. As the Supreme Court explained:

> A tax is not an assessment of benefits. It is . . . a means of distributing the burden of the cost of government. The only benefit to which the taxpayer is constitutionally entitled is that derived from his enjoyment of the privileges of living in an organized society, established and safeguarded by the devotion of taxes to public purposes.[1]

A **taxpayer** is any person or organization required by law to pay a tax to a governmental authority. In the United States, the term *person* refers to both natural persons (individuals) and corporations. Corporations are entities organized under the laws of one of the 50 states or the District of Columbia. These corporate entities generally enjoy the same legal rights, privileges, and protections as individuals. The taxing jurisdictions in this country uniformly regard corporations as entities that are separate and distinct from their shareholders; consequently, corporations are taxpayers in their own right.

The **incidence** of a tax refers to the ultimate economic burden represented by the tax. Most people jump to the conclusion that the person or organization who makes a direct payment of tax to the government bears the incidence of such tax. But in some cases, the payer can shift the incidence of the tax to a third party. Consider the following examples:

> ***Income Tax Incidence.***   Government G imposes a new tax on corporate business profits. A manufacturing corporation with a monopoly on a product in great demand by the public responds to the new tax by increasing the retail price at which it sells the product. In this case, the corporation is nominally the taxpayer and must remit the new tax to the government. The economic burden of the tax falls on the corporation's customers who are indirectly paying the tax in the form of a higher price for the same product.

---

[1]*Carmichael* v. *Southern Coal & Coke Co.,* 301 U.S. 495, 522 (1937).

Property Tax Incidence.   Mr. B owns an eight-unit apartment building. Currently, the tenants living in each unit pay a $6,000 annual rent. The local government notifies Mr. B that his property tax on the apartment building will increase by $2,400 for the next year. Mr. B reacts by informing his tenants that their rent for the next year will increase by $300. Consequently, his total revenue will increase by $2,400. Although Mr. B is the taxpayer who must remit the property tax to the government, the incidence of the tax increase is on the tenants who will indirectly pay the tax through the rent hike.

The right of a government to levy tax on a specific person or organization is referred to as **jurisdiction.** Jurisdiction exists because of some rational linkage between the government and the taxpayer. For instance, our federal government has jurisdiction to tax any individual who is a U.S. citizen or who permanently resides in this country. The government also claims jurisdiction to tax individuals who are neither U.S. citizens nor residents (nonresident aliens) but who earn income from a source within the United States.

U.S. Jurisdiction over Nonresident Aliens.   Mr. K is a citizen of Spain and resides in Madrid. Mr. K owns an interest in a partnership formed under Florida law that conducts a business operation within the state. Even though Mr. K is a nonresident alien, the United States claims jurisdiction to tax Mr. K on his share of the partnership income because the income was earned in this country.

The Relationship between Base, Rate, and Revenue

Objective 2
Express the relationship between tax base, tax rate, and tax revenue as a formula.

Taxes are usually characterized by reference to their base. A **tax base** is an item, occurrence, transaction, or activity with respect to which a tax is levied. Tax bases are usually expressed in monetary terms.[2] For instance, real property taxes are levied on the ownership of land and buildings; the dollar value of the property is the tax base. When designing a tax, governments try to identify tax bases that taxpayers cannot easily avoid or conceal. In this respect, real property is an excellent tax base because it cannot be moved or hidden, and its ownership is a matter of public record.

The dollar amount of a tax is calculated by multiplying the base by a tax rate, which is usually expressed as a percentage. This relationship is expressed by the following formula:

$$\text{tax (T)} = \text{rate (r)} \times \text{base (B)}$$

A single percentage that applies to the entire tax base is described as a **flat rate.** Many types of taxes use a **graduated rate** structure consisting of multiple percentages that apply to specified portions or **brackets** of the tax base.

---

[2]A per capita or head tax requires each person subject to the tax to pay the same amount to the government. This antiquated and very simple type of tax does not have a monetary base.

Graduated Rate Structure.   Jurisdiction J imposes a tax on real property located within the jurisdiction. The tax is based on the market value of the real property and consists of three rate brackets:

Percentage Rate	Bracket
1%	Value from –0– to $100,000
2	Value from $100,001 to $225,000
3	Value in excess of $225,000

Company C owns a tract of real property worth $500,000. The tax liability with respect to this property is $11,750:

1% of $100,000 (first bracket of base)	$ 1,000
2% of $125,000 (second bracket of base)	2,500
3% of $275,000 (third bracket of base)	8,250
Total tax on $500,000 base	$11,750

The term **revenue** refers to the total tax collected by the government and available for public use. Note that in the equation $T = r \times B$, the tax is a function of both the rate and the base. This mathematical relationship suggests that governments can augment revenues by increasing either of these two variables in the design of their tax systems.

Transaction or Activity-Based Taxes

Taxes can be characterized by the frequency with which they are levied. A tax can be **event or transaction based** so that the tax is triggered only when an event occurs or a transaction takes place. A familiar example is a sales tax levied on the purchase of retail goods and services. A second example is an estate tax levied on the transfer of property from a decedent to the decedent's heirs. Potential taxpayers may have some degree of control over the payment of these types of taxes. By avoiding the event or transaction on which the tax is based, a person avoids the tax liability. With certain taxes, such as excise taxes levied on the purchase of liquor and cigarettes, people have total discretion as to whether they ever pay the tax. By choosing not to drink alcoholic beverages or not to smoke, they are also choosing not to pay the excise tax. On the other end of the spectrum, no individual can avoid an estate or inheritance tax levied on the transfer of property at death by indefinitely postponing the event that triggers the tax!

A second category of taxes is **activity based.** These taxes are imposed on the results of an ongoing activity in which persons or organizations engage. Taxpayers must maintain records of the activity, summarize the results at periodic intervals, and pay tax accordingly. An annual income tax is a prime example of an activity-based tax.

An **income tax** is imposed on the periodic inflow of wealth resulting from a person's economic activities. For persons who engage in economic activities consisting of only a limited number or variety of transactions, the measurement of taxable income is relatively simple. For persons who engage in complex activities involving many diverse transactions, the measurement of their income tax base can be a complicated process.

Earmarked Taxes

Still another way to characterize taxes is to link them to specific government expenditures. The revenues from some taxes are **earmarked** to finance designated projects. For instance, revenues from local real property taxes are typically earmarked to support public school systems. Revenues generated by the federal payroll and self-employment taxes fund the Social Security system (Old-Age, Survivors, and Disability Insurance Trust Fund) and Medicare (Health Insurance Trust Fund). Revenues from so-called environmental excise taxes on businesses are appropriated to the Environmental Protection Agency's Hazardous Substance Superfund, which subsidizes the cleanup and disposal of toxic wastes. In contrast to these earmarked taxes, revenues from taxes that pour into a general fund may be spent for any public purpose authorized by the government.

The Pervasive Nature of Taxation

In commenting on the nature of the U.S. tax environment, Supreme Court Justice Potter Stewart made this astute observation:

> Virtually all persons or objects in this country . . . may have tax problems. Every day the economy generates thousands of sales, loans, gifts, purchases, leases, wills and the like, which suggest the possibility of tax problems for somebody. Our economy is "tax relevant" in almost every detail.[3]

Why are taxes so pervasive in our modern world? One reason is the multiplicity of jurisdictions in which people conduct their business activities. Every firm operates in some geographic location falling within the taxing jurisdiction of one or more local governments. Local governments include townships, cities, municipalities, counties, and school districts, all of which have operating budgets financed primarily by tax revenues. Local governments are subject to the authority of state governments, and state constitutions or statutes typically regulate the nature and extent of local taxation.

The governments of each of the 50 states and the District of Columbia levy taxes on firms conducting business within their geographic territory. In turn, the states' taxing jurisdiction is subject to federal constitutional and statutory constraints. The federal government represents still another jurisdiction that taxes business activities conducted within the United States. Consequently, even the smallest domestic enterprise is usually required to pay taxes to support at least three different levels of government. And if a domestic enterprise conducts any business at all in a foreign country, the number of potential taxing jurisdictions is even higher.

Business managers who want to control their firm's tax costs must be aware of any local, state, federal, or foreign tax for which the firm is, or might become, liable. In this section of Chapter 1, we will survey the types of taxes levied by different jurisdictions to finance their governments.

---

[3]*United States* v. *Bisceglia,* 420 U.S. 141, 154 (1975).

Local Taxes

Objective 3
Identify and describe the
types of taxes levied by
local governments.

Local governments are heavily dependent on real property taxes and personal property taxes, which are frequently referred to as **ad valorem** taxes. According to the most recent census data, these two taxes account for more than 75 percent of local government tax revenues.[4]

Real Property Taxes.   All 50 states allow local jurisdictions to tax the ownership of real property situated within the jurisdiction. Real property or **realty** is defined as land and whatever is erected or growing on the land or permanently affixed to it. This definition encompasses any subsurface features such as mineral deposits.

Real property taxes are levied annually and are based on the market value of the property as determined by the local government itself. Elected or appointed officials called **tax assessors** are responsible for deriving the value of realty sited within their jurisdiction and informing the owners of the assessed value. Property owners who disagree with the assessed value of their realty may challenge the value in an administrative or judicial proceeding. A unique feature of real property taxes is that the tax rate is determined annually, based on the jurisdiction's need for revenue for that particular budget year.

> ***Property Tax Rates.***   City G's town council decides that the city must raise $1.2 million of real property tax revenues during its next fiscal year. Because City G's tax assessor determines that the total value of real property located within the city limits is currently $23 million, the council sets the nominal tax rate for the upcoming year at 5.22 percent ($1.2 million ÷ $23 million). This rate can be adjusted each year, depending on the city's future revenue needs and the fluctuating value of its real property tax base.

Local governments may establish different tax rates for different classifications of property. For instance, a township may choose to tax commercial realty at a higher rate than residential realty, or a county might tax land used for agricultural purposes at a higher rate than land maintained for scenic purposes. Governments may grant permanent tax-exempt status to realty owned by charitable, religious, or educational organizations and publicly owned realty. An **abatement** is a tax exemption granted by a government for only a limited period of time. Governments usually grant abatements to lure commercial enterprises into their jurisdiction, thereby creating jobs and benefiting the local economy. From a business manager's point of view, the tax savings obtained through abatements can be significant. Consequently, firms contemplating expansion into new jurisdictions frequently negotiate for property tax abatements before acquiring or beginning construction of realty within the jurisdiction.

> ***Property Tax Abatements.***   According to a recent survey conducted by KPMG Peat Marwick, 51 percent of U.S. companies are receiving some form of property tax abatement or rebate from a state or local government.

---

[4]This and subsequent data are obtained from *Quarterly Summaries of Federal, State, and Local Tax Revenues,* Bureau of the Census, U.S. Department of Commerce.

Personal Property Taxes.   Forty-one states permit localities to tax the ownership of **personalty,** defined as any asset that is not realty. Like real property taxes, personal property taxes are based on the value of the asset subject to tax. However, such value is not usually assessed by local government. Instead, individuals and organizations must determine the value of their taxable personalty and render (i.e., report) the value to the tax assessor.

There are three general classes of taxable personalty: household tangibles, business tangibles, and intangibles.[5] Household tangibles commonly subject to tax include automobiles and recreational vehicles, pleasure boats, and private airplanes. Taxable business tangibles include inventory, furniture and fixtures, machinery, and equipment. The most common form of intangible assets subject to personal property taxation are marketable securities (stocks and bonds).

During the last century, personal property taxation has declined steadily as a revenue source. One reason for the decline is that this tax is much more difficult to enforce than other types of taxes. Personalty is characterized by its mobility; owners can easily hide their assets or move them to another jurisdiction. Any governmental attempt to actively search for personalty, particularly household tangibles, could violate individual privacy rights. Governments have responded to these practical problems by linking the payment of personal property tax to asset registration or licensing requirements.

State Taxes

Objective 3
Identify and describe the types of taxes levied by state governments.

In the aggregate, state governments rely in almost equal measure on sales taxes and income taxes as major sources of funds. Currently, these two kinds of taxes account for approximately 75 percent of total state tax revenues.

Retail Sales, Use, and Excise Taxes.   Forty-five states and the District of Columbia impose a tax on in-state sales of tangible personal property and selected services. (The exceptions are Alaska, Delaware, Montana, New Hampshire, and Oregon.) Moreover, approximately 35 states allow local governments to levy additional sales taxes. Sales taxes have been the great growth taxes of state governments during the past half century.[6] In 1930, only two states had a general sales tax. During the depression era, revenue-starved states began enacting temporary sales taxes as an emergency measure. These taxes proved to be a simple and effective way to generate funds and soon became a permanent feature of state tax systems. Currently, sales taxes produce $133 billion of revenue annually, about one-third of all state tax collections. Sales taxes also have become an important revenue source for local governments, although property taxes remain their primary revenue source.

A **sales tax** is typically based on the retail sale of tangible personalty. State sales tax rates range from 3 percent to 7 percent of the dollar amount of the sales transaction. In those states that allow local sales taxes to be added to the state tax, the combined rate can be higher than 7 percent. Sales taxes are broad based and apply to most types of consumer goods and even to selected consumer services, such as telephone or cable television service.[7] The tax may take the form of a business or privilege tax levied on the seller or, more commonly, a consumption tax levied on the purchaser. Regardless of

---

[5]Tangible property has physical substance that can be perceived by sight or touch. Intangible property has no physical substance.

[6]Hellerstein and Hellerstein, *State Taxation,* vol. II (Boston: Warren, Gorham & Lamont, 1993), p. 12–1.

[7]Many states provide sales tax exemptions for items considered necessities of life, such as foodstuffs and prescription drugs.

the form, the seller is responsible for collecting the tax at point of sale and remitting it to the state government.

Every state that imposes a sales tax imposes a complementary **use tax** on the ownership, possession, or consumption of tangible goods within the state. The use tax applies only if the owner of the goods did not pay the state's sales tax when the goods were purchased. A use tax acts as a backstop to a sales tax by discouraging residents from purchasing products in neighboring jurisdictions with lower sales tax rates. The one-two punch of a sales and use tax theoretically ensures that state residents are taxed on all purchases of consumer goods, regardless of where the purchase was consummated. As a result, merchants operating in high-tax states are not at a competitive disadvantage with respect to merchants operating in low-tax states.

As a general rule, consumers may take a credit for out-of-state sales taxes against their in-state use tax liability.

> ***Use Tax Calculation.***   Ms. T is a resident of State A, which has a 5 percent sales and use tax. While on vacation in State Z, Ms. T purchased a diamond bracelet for $7,600 and paid a $228 (3 percent) sales tax to State Z. Because she did not pay her own state's sales tax on the purchase, she is liable for a $152 use tax to State A. The use tax equals $380 (5 percent of $7,600) minus a $228 credit. If Ms. T had paid a sales tax of more than $380 (i.e., if State Z's sales tax rate was greater than 5 percent), she would not owe any use tax to State A.

Millions of people either are unaware of their responsibility for paying use tax on goods purchased out of state or through mail-order catalogs or they ignore their self-assessment responsibility. States have recently become much more aggressive in collecting use taxes directly from their residents. Forty-four states and the District of Columbia have entered into cooperative agreements to share sales and use tax audit information. Several states have added lines to their personal income tax returns on which individuals are instructed to report the use tax due on their out-of-state and catalog purchases for the year.

An **excise tax** is imposed on the retail sale of specific goods, such as gasoline, cigarettes, or alcoholic beverages, or on specific services, such as hotel or motel accommodations. States may impose an excise tax in addition to or instead of the general sales tax on a particular good or service. In either case, the seller is responsible for collecting and remitting the excise tax. Excise taxes can be extremely heavy. Currently, Connecticut levies a 32-cent excise tax on each gallon of gasoline, Washington levies an 82.5-cent excise tax on one pack of cigarettes, and Tennessee levies a $4 excise tax per gallon of distilled liquor.

Personal Income Taxes.   Forty-three states and the District of Columbia levy some form of personal income tax on individuals who reside in the state and nonresidents who earn income within the state during the taxable year. (The exceptions are Alaska, Florida, Nevada, South Dakota, Texas, Washington, and Wyoming.) The technical details of the computation of taxable income vary considerably from state to state, but the tax rates are uniformly modest. For 1997, the maximum rates varied from 2.8 percent in Pennsylvania to 12 percent in Massachusetts.[8]

---

[8]Massachusetts's 12 percent rate applies to investment income such as dividends and interest. Other income items are taxed at 5.95 percent.

Corporate Income Taxes.   Forty-five states and the District of Columbia tax corporations on their net income attributable to the state. (The exceptions are Michigan, Nevada, South Dakota, Washington, and Wyoming.) Many states allow their cities and counties to tax either the gross receipts or net income of both incorporated and unincorporated businesses operating within the locality.

The computation of corporate taxable income is prescribed by state law. Conceptually, each state could have its own unique set of computational rules, so that one corporation operating in all 46 taxing jurisdictions would be required to make 46 different calculations of taxable income. Fortunately for corporate America, differences in the computations are the exception rather than the rule. All 46 jurisdictions refer to the federal definition of taxable income as the starting point for calculating corporate taxable income for state purposes. "The outstanding characteristic of State corporate net income measures is their broad conformity to the measure of the Federal corporation income tax."[9]

The major advantage of state conformity to federal income tax law is simplicity. State legislatures do not have to reinvent the wheel by drafting and enacting a comprehensive income tax statute. State agencies responsible for administering and enforcing their state's income tax can refer to regulatory and judicial interpretations of the federal law. A second advantage is that state conformity to federal tax law eases the compliance and auditing burdens of corporate taxpayers. The major disadvantage is the states' lack of control over their corporate income tax revenues. Each time the U.S. Congress changes the federal definition of taxable income, the income tax base of conforming states is automatically increased or decreased.

Federal Taxes

Objective 3
Identify and describe the types of taxes levied by the federal government.

The U.S. government depends almost exclusively on the income tax as a source of general revenues. The federal income tax applies to both individuals and corporations, as well as trusts and estates. The structure and operation of the federal income tax is discussed in considerable detail in Parts Three, Four, and Five of this text. At this point, suffice it to say that the federal income tax is predominant in the current business environment.

History of the Income Tax.   The modern income tax does not have a particularly long history in this country. The federal government enacted the first personal income tax in 1861 for the specific purpose of raising money to support the Union armies during the Civil War. Even though Congress allowed the tax to expire in 1872, its revenue-generating capability made a lasting impression on the legislative memory. In 1894, Congress needed a permanent source of funds and decided to resurrect the personal income tax. However, in the landmark case of *Pollock* v. *Farmers' Loan and Trust Company,*[10] the Supreme Court held that the U.S. Constitution did not give the federal government authority to levy a national income tax. Determined to have its way, Congress launched a campaign to change the Constitution, a campaign that ended victoriously on February 25, 1913, when Wyoming became the 36th state to ratify the Sixteenth Amendment:

> The Congress shall have the power to lay and collect taxes on incomes from whatever source derived, without apportionment among the several states, and without regard to any census or enumeration.

---

[9]Hellerstein, op. cit., p. 7–3.
[10]157 U.S. 429 (1895).

Congress immediately exercised its new power by passing the Revenue Act of 1913, and the federal income tax became a permanent feature of American life. In 1939, Congress organized all of the federal tax laws then in effect (income and otherwise) into the first Internal Revenue Code. This compilation was substantially revised as the Internal Revenue Code of 1954 and again as the Internal Revenue Code of 1986.

Employment and Unemployment Taxes. The two largest programs sponsored by the federal government are the Social Security system, which provides monthly old-age, survivors, and disability benefits to qualifying citizens and residents, and Medicare, which provides hospital insurance for the elderly and disabled. These programs are not funded from the general revenues of the income tax. Instead, the revenues from the federal **employment taxes** are earmarked to pay exclusively for Social Security and Medicare. These taxes are based on annual wages and salaries paid by employers to their employees and on the net income earned by self-employed individuals. The details of the computation of these important taxes are discussed in Chapter 9.

The federal and state governments act in coordination to provide monetary benefits to individuals who are temporarily unemployed through no fault of their own. This national unemployment insurance system is administered by the states and financed by federal and state taxes imposed directly on employers. These **unemployment taxes** are based on the annual compensation paid to employees. Virtually every business in this country pays unemployment taxes with respect to its workforce, and significant planning opportunities do exist for controlling this particular cost. Nevertheless, because of the narrow scope of the unemployment taxes, we will not discuss them further in this text.

Other Federal Taxes. The federal government raises general revenues from excise taxes imposed on the retail purchase of specific goods and services such as tobacco products, luxury automobiles, firearms, and telephone calls. The federal **transfer taxes,** which are based on the value of an individual's wealth transferred by gift or at death, are also a source of general revenues. Transfer taxes play a key role in family tax planning and are described in detail in Chapter 15. As Exhibit 1–1 shows, these two types of taxes are a minor source of federal funds. In fiscal year 1997, excise taxes accounted for only 4 percent of federal tax revenues, while transfer taxes accounted for just 1 percent.

Taxes Imposed by Foreign Jurisdictions

The types of foreign taxes that firms encounter when expanding from purely domestic to international operations are as varied as the languages, politics, and cultures characterizing the global business environment. Many foreign taxes have a familiar structure. National governments and their political subdivisions the world over levy income taxes, property taxes, and retail sales taxes. Other taxes may have no counterpart in the United States and are therefore less familiar to domestic companies operating abroad. For instance, many industrialized nations depend heavily on some type of **value-added tax (VAT)** as a source of government revenue. Value-added taxes are levied on firms engaged in any phase of the production or manufacture of goods and are based on the incremental value that the business adds to the goods.

EXHIBIT 1–1

Fiscal year 1997 federal tax revenues

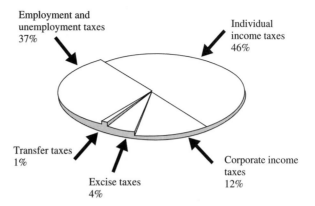

Employment and unemployment taxes 37%

Individual income taxes 46%

Transfer taxes 1%

Excise taxes 4%

Corporate income taxes 12%

> **Value-Added Tax.**   Firm M and Firm W operate in a jurisdiction that imposes a 5 percent VAT. Firm M manufactures small electronic appliances. M's cost per unit for materials, labor, and overhead is $40; and M sells each unit to Firm W, a regional wholesaler, for $46. Firm M's $6 profit represents the incremental value that M added to the production process. Therefore, M must pay a 30-cent VAT (5 percent of $6) for each unit sold.
>
>   Firm W sells the appliances purchased from Firm M to various unrelated retailers for $50 per unit. Firm W's $4 profit on the sale of each unit represents the incremental value that W added to the production process by providing distribution services. Consequently, Firm W must pay a 20-cent VAT (5 percent of $4) for each unit sold.

The above example is extremely simplistic in that it ignores the possibility that both Firm M and Firm W can shift the economic incidence of the VAT by increasing the price at which they sell their product to the next business in the production sequence. To the extent that a VAT is shifted along the entire production sequence to the final purchaser (the customer who buys the product for personal consumption), the VAT resembles a retail sales tax.

Value-added taxes can be very powerful revenue raisers. Even so, Michigan is the only domestic jurisdiction that uses this type of tax. The Michigan Single Business Tax, enacted in 1976 to replace the state's corporate income tax, is a modified VAT applying to both incorporated and unincorporated businesses operating within the state.

Jurisdictional Competition

Objective 4
Explain why different taxing jurisdictions often compete for revenues from the same taxpayer.

Domestic business enterprises that span territorial borders are subject to the taxing authority of multiple state and local governments, as well as to the overall authority of the federal government. Firms that are international in scope may be liable for additional taxes in any number of foreign jurisdictions. Governments understand that their taxing jurisdictions frequently overlap and that, as a result, they are in competition for revenues from the same commercial activities. They also understand that taxpayers are mobile and that business managers make location decisions with an eye on comparative tax costs. Thus, jurisdictional competition creates an interesting tension. On the one hand, a government that fails to diligently protect its jurisdictional turf may lose revenues to more assertive taxing authorities. On the other hand, a government that is overly aggressive and levies taxes without consideration for the fiscal policies of its neighbors runs the risk of driving taxpayers away from its jurisdiction.

In the United States, the competing levels of government have traditionally accommodated each other by relying on different types of taxes as their primary source of funding. As we learned earlier in the chapter, property taxes are the mainstay of local governments, while retail sales taxes are used almost exclusively by state governments. Our federal government does not levy either property taxes or a national sales tax, but instead relies on income and employment taxes for its revenues.

> ***Ready for National Sales Tax?***   A group of business executives organized as Americans for Fair Taxation are publicly campaigning to replace the federal income tax, Social Security and Medicare employment taxes, and transfer taxes with a 23 percent national sales tax. The tax would apply to retail purchases of all goods and services, including food, medicine, and housing. According to AFT, this new tax would raise the same amount of federal revenue as existing taxes, while stimulating economic growth.

Corporations conducting business in more than one state face particularly difficult problems of duplicative taxation. The jurisdictional concerns of corporations engaged in interstate commerce are discussed more fully in Chapter 12. Of course, the potential for jurisdictional conflict is greatest when corporations operate on a global scale. Industrialized nations tend to assume that it is in their self-interest to promote the growth and development of international business operations. These nations understand that if they fail to adapt their tax systems to the needs of the worldwide marketplace, their economies will be at a competitive disadvantage. Consequently, the industrialized nations have created a network of bilateral and multilateral tax treaties designed to minimize the frictions among their respective tax systems and to reduce the impact of duplicative taxation on international businesses. The role of these treaties and other unique features of international tax planning are covered in Chapter 12.

The Dynamic Nature of Taxation

Objective 5
Identify the reasons why governments continually modify their tax systems.

Business managers must understand that taxes are not only pervasive in the modern world but that tax systems are in a constant state of flux. Tax systems are dynamic because they must be attuned to the fiscal condition of their respective jurisdictions. In every jurisdiction, individual citizens and institutions continually reevaluate the nature and the level of services they expect their governments to provide. Governments, in turn, must reassess the tax systems that pay for those services.

Tax Base Changes

Any government dependent on a tax system that no longer raises sufficient revenues will sooner or later be forced to change the system. The loss of revenue-generating power is often attributable to an eroding tax base. For instance, cities that depend on real property taxes experience a decline in revenues when their populations decrease. As families and businesses move away from urban areas, residential and commercial properties located within the city limits lose value. Owners can no longer afford to maintain the properties; and in extreme cases, they may simply abandon them. Cities only worsen this cycle of deterioration if they attempt to bolster revenues by raising their property tax rates. The only solution may be to identify an alternative tax base or a source of nontax revenue.

Legalized Gambling.   One controversial source of nontax revenue is legalized gambling. About 25 years ago, a few states experimented with weekly lotteries as a means of raising money. Lotteries proved so lucrative that the majority of states and the District of Columbia are now sponsoring these betting games. In Maryland, Virginia, and the District, where per capita lottery play is among the highest in the country, lotteries currently rank third behind income taxes and sales taxes as a source of revenue. In the late 1980s, states in the Midwest and the South decided to shore up their tax bases by going into the casino business. Both Iowa and Mississippi agreed to give private gambling corporations legal monopolies to operate within the state. In exchange, these corporations pay as much as 20 percent of their profits to the state treasuries.

Sales and Use Tax Expansion.   State and local governments are increasingly aggressive in exploiting new tax bases that develop in the economy. Historically, state sales taxes applied to retail purchases of tangible property but not to purchases of retail services. Because of the dramatic growth in the service sector over the last several decades, an increasing number of states are adding selected services, such as cable television, parking, and theater tickets, to their sales tax base. In 1987, Florida expanded its general sales tax to apply to a broad range of consumer services, and Massachusetts followed suit in 1991. Public reaction was so negative that both states repealed the sales tax on services within a year.

States are trying to find a way to force out-of-state mail-order companies to collect the state's use tax on sales made to residents of the state. The mail-order industry has enjoyed phenomenal growth in recent years, and millions of consumers have discovered the ease of shopping by catalog. Quite naturally, states take the position that their residents who purchase retail goods through the mail should bear the same tax burden as residents who patronize retail stores located within the state. In 1992, the Supreme Court ruled that state laws requiring mail-order companies with no physical presence in a state to charge in-state customers for use tax were unconstitutional, regardless of the volume of business in the state.[11] State governments were infuriated with this decision and have been lobbying Congress ever since to enact federal legislation permitting states to require use tax collection on mail-order transactions.

Taxes and the Political Process

The very process by which tax law is made contributes to the dynamic nature of taxes. In this country, local, state, and federal tax laws are the result of democratic systems in which elected or appointed representatives decide on the appropriate tax structure. These representatives are naturally sensitive to the political, social, and economic climates of their respective constituencies. As these climates change over time, representatives may decide that the tax structure should change as well. Many of these changes have little to do with the amount of revenues raised. Instead, the changes are philosophic in nature, reflecting a shift in the communal attitude concerning the proper role of taxes in society.

Special interest groups have a significant impact on the tax legislative process. Literally thousands of organizations have pet provisions in the existing law or wish lists of proposals for beneficial new provisions. These organizations use their own emissaries or

---

[11]*Quill Corporation* v. *North Dakota,* 504 U.S. 298 (1992).

hire professional lobbyists to communicate their point of view to government officials. The constant pressure from powerful organizations with competing and even conflicting political objectives certainly adds to the vibrant nature of the tax law.

Regardless of the tax in question or the jurisdiction levying the tax, people don't like paying it. In fact, individuals and businesses are willing to devote considerable money and effort to finding ways to avoid paying tax. Each time taxpayers or their advisors devise a new tactic to reduce their tax burdens, governments respond by enacting a new rule or regulation to render the tactic ineffective. This constant gamesmanship is yet another reason why the tax environment is never still. As humorist Dave Barry explains, "[Tax laws] are constantly changing as our elected representatives seek new ways to ensure that whatever tax advice we receive is incorrect."

Sources of Federal Tax Law

Objective 6
Describe the three primary sources of federal tax law.

Throughout this text, we will constantly refer to the **tax law.** For modern tax systems, this term encompasses three basic sources of authority: statutory law, administrative pronouncements, and judicial decisions. In combination, these sources provide the rules of the game by which both taxpayers and governments must abide. This final section of Chapter 1 describes the primary sources of authority that comprise our federal tax law. In subsequent chapters of the text, you will encounter a considerable amount of technical information originating from this body of law. You should have a much easier time understanding this information if you become familiar with the underlying sources from which the information is derived.

Statutory Authority

In its narrowest sense, federal tax law means the **Internal Revenue Code of 1986,** the voluminous compilation of statutory rules written and enacted by Congress. The Internal Revenue Code itself is a dynamic document; virtually every year Congress passes legislation that adds to, deletes from, or modifies its provisions.

> ***Tax Reform Act of 1997.*** On August 5, 1997, President Clinton signed the Taxpayer Relief Act of 1997 into law. This act included more than 300 new provisions and made more than 800 changes to the Internal Revenue Code of 1986. Virtually every individual and corporate taxpayer is affected in some way by this major tax legislation.

The Internal Revenue Code consists of numerically ordered **sections,** beginning with Section 1 and ending (at last count) with Section 9722. Each section contains an operational, definitional, or procedural rule relating to one of the federal taxes. Code section numbers have become the language in which tax experts communicate, and accountants and lawyers have incorporated many of them into their professional jargon. (Bob, I think our client has a real Section 469 problem.) Sections are divided into subsections, paragraphs, subparagraphs, and so on. In the footnotes to the text, a reference such as §469(f)(3)(B) is citing the precise statutory rule under discussion.

Administrative Authority

Congress has charged the Department of the Treasury with the responsibility of writing regulations that interpret and illustrate the rules contained in the Internal Revenue Code.

These **Treasury regulations** provide a tremendous amount of guidance to taxpayers and their advisors. Literally every week the Treasury publishes new regulations or amends existing regulations in an attempt to keep abreast of legislative developments. While Treasury regulations carry great authority as the government's official explanation of the law, they are not laws in and of themselves. On rare occasions, taxpayers have convinced the federal courts that a regulation was an incorrect interpretation of statute and was therefore invalid.[12]

The citation to a Treasury regulation consists of a sequence of numbers, the first of which identifies the type of federal tax under consideration. For instance, a regulation beginning with 1 is an income tax regulation. The next series of numbers identifies the Code section to which the regulation relates. The last number in the sequence is the number of the regulation itself. The cite Reg. §1.469-4 refers to the fourth Treasury regulation relating to Section 469 of the Internal Revenue Code. Some sections have only one regulation while others have dozens. And some Code sections have no interpretive regulations at all!

The **Internal Revenue Service (IRS),** the subdivision of the Treasury responsible for the enforcement of the law and collection of tax, provides still more guidance in the form of published **revenue rulings and revenue procedures.** These pronouncements explain how the IRS applies current tax law to a particular set of facts and circumstances. While they carry much less authority than the Code and regulations, these pronouncements do represent the IRS's official position and provide valuable insight on specific issues. Rulings and procedures are published in weekly **Internal Revenue Bulletins (IRBs)** that are compiled into semiannual **Cumulative Bulletins (CBs).** Footnote references such as Rev. Rul. 96-13, 1996-23 IRB 12 or Rev. Proc. 89-17, 1989-1 CB 118 are citing these sources of authority.

Judicial Authority

The third primary source of tax law is the federal judicial system. Taxpayers who disagree with the IRS's interpretation of the law as it applies to their own situations may take their cases to federal court. The hundreds of legal decisions handed down every year clarify the correct implementation of the tax law. The weight of authority of a particular case depends on the court that rendered the verdict. Trial court verdicts have less authority than verdicts by an appellate court. Of course, a Supreme Court verdict is the equivalent of law and becomes the final word in any tax dispute. Chapter 17 discusses the process by which a federal judge or jury resolves a controversy between a taxpayer and the IRS. When this text refers to a certain judicial decision, an accompanying footnote provides the complete legal cite of the case. You can use the cite to locate the decision in any law library or commercial tax service.

Conclusion

Business managers engaged in effective tax planning take into account the wide variety of taxes existing in the modern economic environment. When making strategic decisions, managers must consider the impact on their firm's total tax burden rather than on each tax in isolation. A strategy that minimizes the cost of one tax

---

[12]The Internal Revenue Code occasionally empowers the Treasury to write regulations that have the force and effect of law. These so-called legislative regulations have the same authority as statutory law.

could easily increase the cost of another. The primary focus of this text is the federal income tax; as a result, other taxes that affect business and investment decisions will be mentioned only occasionally. Even so, many planning strategies that we will analyze in the context of the income tax are equally valid in other tax contexts. Decision makers should remember that every tax represents a controllable cost of conducting business.

As increasing numbers of U.S. firms expand their operations across territorial boundaries, jurisdictional tax planning becomes crucial. Managers must determine which tax systems result in favorable business climates and which systems are inhospitable to foreign investors. They must be aware of crucial differences between competing tax regimes and how those differences can be exploited to the firm's advantage. In today's tax environment, successful tax planning must be conducted on a global scale.

Key Terms

Abatement 8	Real property tax 8
Activity-based tax 6	Realty 8
Ad valorem tax 8	Revenue 6
Bracket 5	Revenue rulings and revenue
Cumulative Bulletin (CB) 17	procedures 17
Earmarked tax 7	Sales tax 9
Employment tax 12	Section 16
Event or transaction-based tax 6	Tax 4
Excise tax 10	Tax assessor 8
Flat rate 5	Tax base 5
Graduated rates 5	Tax law 16
Incidence 4	Taxpayer 4
Income tax 6	Transfer tax 12
Internal Revenue Bulletin (IRB) 17	Treasury regulation 17
Internal Revenue Code of 1986 16	Unemployment tax 12
Internal Revenue Service (IRS) 17	Use tax 10
Jurisdiction 5	Value-added tax (VAT) 12
Personalty 9	

Questions and Problems for Discussion

1. How do tax payments differ from other types of payments that people or organizations make to governmental agencies?

2. The Green River, which is heavily polluted by industrial waste, flows through State S. Eighty-five companies currently operate manufacturing facilities that border the river. State S recently enacted legislation requiring each of these companies to pay $50,000 annually into a special fund to clean up Green River. Does this payment meet the definition of a tax?

3. Jurisdiction J is considering raising revenues by imposing a $25 fee on couples who obtain a marriage license within the jurisdiction. Does this fee meet the definition of a transaction-based tax?

4. Mr. P owns a residential apartment complex located in a suburban area. During the year, the local jurisdiction increased the property tax rate on the apartment complex. To offset this additional cost of operating the property, Mr. P decreased the amount he usually spends on maintaining the exterior of the building and the

landscaping. Based on these facts, discuss the incidence of the increased property tax.

5. Mr. and Mrs. K pay an annual tuition of $18,000 to a private school for their three children. They also pay $2,300 of property tax on their personal residence to support the local public school system. Should Mr. and Mrs. K be exempt from this property tax?

6. A local government recently imposed a new 2 percent tax on the gross receipts of businesses operating within its jurisdiction. The XYZ Company, which manufactures soap and other toiletries, responded to the tax by reducing the size of its bars of soap and purchasing a cheaper grade of ingredients. By making these changes, XYZ maintained its before-tax level of profits. With respect to the XYZ Company, what is the incidence of the new gross receipts tax?

7. Why is real property a better tax base than personal property?

8. Many local jurisdictions apply a special, low property tax rate to land owned by privately operated golf courses. What is the economic justification for such a preferential rate?

9. University K is located in a small town that depends heavily on real property taxes as a source of revenue. Over the past decade, University K has expanded by purchasing a number of commercial buildings and personal residences and converting them to classrooms and dormitories. In what way could this expansion result in a decline in the town's tax revenues?

10. Why can people generally avoid paying an excise tax more readily than they can avoid paying a sales tax?

11. The Internal Revenue Code and Treasury regulations are two major sources of federal tax law. Differentiate between the Code and the regulations in terms of their relative weight of authority.

12. A municipal government recently increased its local sales tax from 1 percent to 2 percent of the dollar value of consumer goods purchased in the city. However, the city's sales tax revenues increased by only 30 percent subsequent to the doubling of the tax rate. What factors might account for this result?

13. Both the federal government and many states impose so-called sin taxes: excise taxes levied on the retail sale of liquor and cigarettes. Discuss the reasons why sales of these particular items make a good tax base.

14. Does the federal income tax or the federal payroll tax have the broader tax base?

15. Differentiate between a property tax and a transfer tax.

16. One way for the federal government to increase tax revenues would be to enact either a VAT or a national retail sales tax. The U.S. sales tax could be collected in the same manner and at the same time as state and local sales taxes. Which tax would be less costly for the federal government to implement and administer? Which tax would be less likely to cause jurisdictional conflict?

Application Problems

1. During the past year, Company LI built a new light industrial facility in County G. The assessed property tax value of the facility is $20 million. To convince Company LI to locate within its jurisdiction, the county abated its normal 4 percent property tax for the year. Because of the local economic boom created by the new facility, the aggregate assessed value of County G's property tax base (including the LI facility) increased by $23 million. Calculate the net impact on County G's current year tax revenue resulting from the abatement granted to company LI.

2. During the past year, Jurisdiction A decided to raise revenues by increasing its general sales tax rate from 5 percent to 6 percent. Because of the increase, the volume of taxable sales declined from $800 million to $710 million. In contrast, Jurisdiction Z decided to raise revenues from its 5 percent sales tax by expanding the tax base to include certain retail services. The volume of services subject to tax was $50 million. Based on these facts, compute the amount of additional revenue raised by Jurisdiction A and by Jurisdiction Z.

3. Firm H operates its business in Jurisdiction H, which levies a 6 percent sales and use tax. During the year, the firm purchased $600,000 of tangible property in Jurisdiction K and paid $18,000 of sales tax to the jurisdiction. The firm also purchased $750,000 of tangible property in Jurisdiction L and paid $48,750 of sales tax to the jurisdiction. Firm H transported both items of property into Jurisdiction H for use in its business.
   a. Compute the use tax that Firm H owes to Jurisdiction H with respect to the property purchased in Jurisdiction K.
   b. Compute the use tax that Firm H owes to Jurisdiction H with respect to the property purchased in Jurisdiction L.
4. Firm L, which operates a mail-order clothing business, is located in State L. During the current year, the firm shipped $18 million of merchandise to people living in State R who ordered the merchandise from Firm L's current catalog. State R imposes a 6 percent sales and use tax on the purchase and consumption of retail goods within the state.
   a. Are State R residents who purchased Firm L merchandise liable for use tax on their purchases?
   b. If State R could legally require Firm L to collect and remit a 6 percent tax on mail-order sales made to residents of the state, how much additional revenue would the state collect? Explain the reasoning behind your answer.
5. Firm Q and Firm R conduct business in a jurisdiction that imposes a 3 percent VAT. Firm Q produces entertainment videos at a unit cost of $6 and sells the videos to Firm R for $9 per unit. Firm R sells the videos at retail for $10 per unit. During the current year, the combined efforts of Firm Q and Firm R resulted in sales of 12.4 million videos to the public. Based on these facts, compute the VAT liability for each firm.

Issue Recognition Problems

Identify the tax issue or issues suggested by the following situations and state each issue in the form of a question.

1. A local government levies an annual real property tax on the personal residence located at 123 Maple Drive. This tax is assessed on a calendar year basis, and the homeowner must pay the current year tax before December 31. In November, Mr. and Mrs. J received the 1997 tax bill for $2,900. The couple purchased the home from its previous owner on October 6, 1997.
2. Company F operates in a jurisdiction that levies real property tax but no personal property tax. During the current year, the company spent $6 million to add an exterior lighting system and security fences to the parking lot adjacent to its corporate headquarters.
3. Company B, which has offices in six states, owns an airplane that company executives use when they travel from office to office. When the plane is not in use, it is stored in a hangar located in a jurisdiction that does not levy a personal property tax on business tangibles. When the plane is in use, it frequently is stored on a temporary basis in hangars located in jurisdictions that tax business tangibles.
4. For the past 22 years, Mrs. O has contributed part of her salary to a retirement plan sponsored by her corporate employer. Under federal law, Mrs. O is not required to pay tax on the income so contributed. She will, however, pay federal income tax on the distributions received from the plan when she retires. Mrs. O has been a resident of State A for her entire life. Because State A's personal income tax is based on taxable income as computed for federal purposes, Mrs. O has never paid any State A tax on her retirement contributions. In the current year, Mrs. O retires and moves to State K, which has no personal income tax.
5. Business Q orders $500,000 of office furniture from Vendor V. Vendor V ships the furniture by rail from its manufacturing facility located in State V to Business Q's corporate headquarters located in State Q. State V imposes a 6.5 percent sales tax while State Q imposes only a 4 percent sales tax.
6. Acme Corporation was formed under the laws of State X and has its corporate headquarters in that state. Acme operates a manufacturing plant located in State Y and sells goods to customers located in

States X, Y, and Z. All three states impose a corporate income tax. For the current year, Acme's net profit from its tristate operation was $14 million.

7. Mr. W is a professional golfer. During the current year, he played 23 tournaments in 14 different states and earned $893,000 total prize money. When he is not traveling, Mr. W lives with his family in Tucson, Arizona.

Tax Planning Cases

1. The management of WP Company must decide between locating a new branch office in foreign Jurisdiction F or foreign Jurisdiction G. Regardless of location, the branch operation will use tangible property (plant and equipment) worth $10 million and should generate annual gross receipts of $2 million. Jurisdiction F imposes an annual property tax of 4 percent of the value of business property and a 15 percent gross receipts tax. Jurisdiction G imposes no property tax but imposes a 30 percent gross receipts tax. Based solely on these facts, should WP locate its new branch in Jurisdiction F or Jurisdiction G?

2. BKR Company manufactures a tangible product that it sells to the general public. BKR's cost of making each unit of product is $15, and it sells each unit for $25. The company sells an average of 20 million units each year. During the current year, the jurisdiction in which BKR operates increased its net income tax rate by 2 percent. BKR's manager has identified the following three possible responses to the tax increase:

   - BKR could raise its selling price to $26 per unit. The company's marketing department estimates that this price increase would cause annual sales to drop to 18.5 million units.
   - BKR could cut its manufacturing costs to $13.50 per unit. The resulting decrease in quality would cause annual sales to drop to 18 million units.
   - BKR could hold both price and cost steady and simply absorb the tax cut out of net profit.

   Which response to the income tax rate increase would you recommend to BKR's manager and why?

2

Tax Policy Issues: Standards for a Good Tax

Learning Objectives

After studying this chapter, you should be able to:

1. Explain the concept of sufficiency as a standard for a good tax.
2. Differentiate between the income effect and the substitution effect of an increase in income tax rates.
3. Compare the concept of a convenient tax from the government's viewpoint and from the taxpayer's viewpoint.
4. Contrast the classical economic standard of tax neutrality with the Keynesian concept of taxes as a fiscal policy tool.
5. Define horizontal and vertical equity.
6. Differentiate between a regressive, a proportionate, and a progressive tax rate structure.
7. Explain the difference between marginal and average tax rate.
8. Discuss the concept of distributive justice as a tax policy objective.

In Chapter 1, we examined one dimension of the tax environment by describing the various taxes that different jurisdictions use to raise revenues. In this chapter, we will consider a more qualitative dimension of the environment as we identify the *normative* standards by which politicians, economists, social scientists, and individual taxpayers evaluate the merit of a tax.

Governments are cognizant of and influenced by these standards as they formulate tax policy. **Tax policy** can be defined as a government's attitude, objectives, and actions with respect to its tax system. Presumably, tax policy reflects the normative standards that the government deems most important. After reading this chapter, you can draw your own conclusions as to the relative importance of the standards by which tax systems are judged. You will be able to evaluate the current federal tax system in light of these standards. When you are asked as a voter to choose between competing tax policy proposals, the material covered in this chapter will help you make an informed decision.

Business managers and their tax advisors typically share a keen interest in tax policy. They know that many complex technical rules in the Internal Revenue Code have an underlying policy rationale. If they can understand this rationale, the rule itself is easier to interpret and apply. Moreover, business people know that today's policy issues shape tomorrow's tax environment. By paying close attention to the current policy debate, managers can anticipate developments that might affect their firm's long-term business strategies. Their familiarity with policy issues helps them assess the probability of changes in the tax law and develop contingent strategies to deal with such changes.

Standards for a Good Tax

The American jurist, Oliver Wendell Holmes, is quoted as saying, "I like to pay taxes. With them I buy civilization." Few people in modern society seem to share this sentiment. In fact, many people regard taxes as a necessary evil and consider the notion of a good tax as a contradiction in terms. Nonetheless, tax theorists maintain that every tax can and should be evaluated on certain basic standards.[1] These standards can be summarized as follows:

- A good tax should be *sufficient to raise the necessary government revenues.*
- A good tax should be *convenient for the government to administer and for people to pay.*
- A good tax should be *efficient in economic terms.*
- A good tax should be *fair.*

In Chapter 2, we will discuss these four standards in detail. We will also identify the reasons why standards that are easy to describe in the abstract can be so difficult to put into practice.

Taxes Should Be Sufficient

Objective 1
Explain the concept of sufficiency as a standard for a good tax.

The first standard by which to evaluate a tax is its **sufficiency** as a revenue raiser. A tax is sufficient if it generates enough funds to pay for the public goods and services provided by the government levying the tax. After all, the reason that governments tax their citizens in the first place is because governments need revenues to spend for specific purposes. If a tax (or combination of taxes) is sufficient, a government can balance its budget; tax revenues equal government spending, and the government has no need to raise additional funds.

What is the consequence of an insufficient tax system? The government must make up its revenue shortfall (the excess of current spending over tax receipts) from some other source. In Chapter 1, we learned that state governments now depend heavily on legalized gambling as an alternative source of funds. Governments may own assets or property rights that they can lease or sell to raise money. For example, the U.S. government raises minuscule revenues each year by selling energy generated by federally owned dams and mineral and timber rights with respect to federal lands.

Another option is for governments to borrow money to finance their operating deficits. In the United States, both local and state governments as well as the federal government routinely issue debt obligations that are offered for sale in the capital markets. By selling both short-term instruments (such as three-month U.S. Treasury

---

[1]Adam Smith, author of *The Wealth of Nations,* was one of the first economists to suggest such standards. Smith's four canons were that a good tax should be equitable, certain in application, convenient for people to pay, and economical for the government to collect.

bills) and long-term bonds, governments with insufficient tax systems can make ends meet. Debt financing is not a permanent solution to an insufficient tax system. Like other debtors, governments must pay interest on the funds they borrow. As the level of public debt increases, so does the annual interest governments must pay. At some point, a government may find itself in the untenable position of borrowing new money not to provide more public goods and services but merely to pay the interest on its existing debt. In a worst case scenario, a government may be forced to default on its debt obligations, damaging its own credibility and creating havoc in its capital markets.

The Federal Debt

Our federal government's reliance on borrowed funds has increased dramatically over the last three decades. For every fiscal year from 1970 through 1997, the government operated at a deficit. In 1970, the national debt was approximately $5.5 billion. By 1997, the debt had grown to a mind-boggling $5 trillion! In 1970, the government paid $14 billion of net interest on the national debt, an amount representing 7 percent of annual federal expenditures. In 1997, the federal government paid $250 billion of net interest to its creditors, an amount representing 15 percent of annual expenditures and roughly the same amount spent on national defense.

These data suggest that our existing federal tax system is insufficient to support the current level of government spending. Yet politicians continue to tell their constituencies that taxes are too high, and few people seem inclined to disagree. But the arithmetic is inescapable. If we want to pay less tax and at the same time curb the growth of the national debt, the federal government must cut spending. If we want our government to maintain its current level of spending without incurring additional debt, we should be prepared to pay more federal tax.[2]

> ***A Budget Surplus by the Year 1999?***   Because of the robust economy and the resulting surge in tax revenues, the Congressional Budget Office projects that the 1998 federal deficit may be a modest $5 billion (compared to $22 billion in 1997), and that a surplus could be achieved as early as the year 1999. Politicians are already debating whether a future surplus should be used to pay down the national debt, fund new federal programs, or returned to taxpayers in the form of a tax cut.

How to Increase Tax Revenues

Taxing jurisdictions can attempt to increase revenues in at least three ways. One way is to exploit a new tax base. For instance, the legislature of one of the seven states without a personal income tax could enact such a tax. Another way is to increase the rate of an existing tax. A jurisdiction with a 5 percent corporate income tax could hike the rate to 7 percent. Still a third way is to enlarge an existing tax base. A jurisdiction with a retail

---

[2]As another author so eloquently describes the situation, "Elected representatives must eventually confront the political reality of an electorate with an apparently insatiable appetite for 'public goods' that at the same time harbors a deep-rooted intolerance for the levels of taxation sufficient to support its own proclivities." Sheldon D. Pollack, "The Failure of U.S. Tax Policy: Revenue and Politics," 73 *Tax Notes* 341, 348.

sales tax applying to tangible goods could expand the tax to apply to selected personal services, such as haircuts or dry cleaning. Or a jurisdiction that exempts land owned by private charities from real property tax could simply eliminate the exemption.

From a pragmatic perspective, the enactment of a tax on a new base is the most radical, and therefore the most politically sensitive, way to increase revenues. Consequently, elected officials tend to favor the less drastic alternative of enhancing the revenue-raising capability of a tax that people are accustomed to paying. In this situation, an increase in the percentage rate is the more obvious strategy and therefore is likely to anger the greatest number of voters. In contrast, an expansion of the tax base tends to be more subtle and less likely to attract public attention. It is hardly surprising that many significant tax increases in recent years have been accomplished through the base-expansion method.

Social Security Tax Increases.   The 6.2 percent rate for the federal Social Security payroll tax has not changed since 1990. However, the tax base (the annual amount of wages or salary subject to tax) increases every year. In 1990, this "wage base" was $51,300. In 1998, the base is $68,400. In 1990, an employee with a $75,000 salary paid $3,181 of Social Security tax (6.2 percent of $51,300). In 1998, that employee pays $4,241 of Social Security tax (6.2 percent of $68,400).

Static versus Dynamic Forecasting

In Chapter 1, we expressed the amount of tax as an arithmetic function of the tax rate and base: $T = r \times B$. This equation suggests that an increase in the rate should increase government revenues by a proportionate amount. For instance, if the tax rate is 5 percent and the base is $500,000, a rate hike of one percentage point should generate $5,000 additional tax. This straightforward math represents a **static forecast** of the incremental revenue attributable to a change in the rate structure. The forecast is static because it assumes that B, the base variable in the equation, is unrelated to r, the rate variable. Accordingly, a change in the rate has no effect on the tax base.

Economic theory suggests that in many cases the two variables in the equation $T = r \times B$ may be correlated. In other words, a change in the rate actually may cause a change in the base.

Effect of a Rate Change on Base.   For the last 10 years, Jurisdiction J has levied a hotel occupancy tax equal to 10 percent of the price of a room. In the prior fiscal year, this tax yielded $800,000 of revenue:

Total annual hotel receipts subject to tax	$8,000,000
Prior year rate	.10
Prior year revenue	$ 800,000

At the beginning of the current fiscal year, the jurisdiction increased the tax rate to 12 percent. Based on a static forecast, the jurisdiction expected revenue to increase to $960,000:

Forecasted hotel receipts subject to tax	$8,000,000
Current year rate	.12
Forecasted current year revenue	$ 960,000

During the current year, business travelers and tourists reacted to the additional cost represented by the higher room tax by purchasing fewer accommodations from hotels located within Jurisdiction J. Occupancy rates fell, and annual hotel receipts declined by $500,000. Consequently, the room tax yielded only $900,000 of current year revenue.

Actual hotel receipts subject to tax	$7,500,000
Current year rate	.12
Actual current year revenue	$ 900,000

In the above example, the increase in the tax rate resulted in a decrease in the tax base. Because Jurisdiction J failed to anticipate and account for this effect, it overestimated the incremental revenue from the rate increase.

If a jurisdiction can predict the extent to which a change in tax rates will affect the underlying tax base, it can incorporate the effect into its revenue projections. These projections, which assume a correlation between rate and base, are called **dynamic forecasts.** The accuracy of dynamic forecasts depends on the accuracy of the assumptions concerning the correlation between rate and base. In a complex economic environment, a change in tax rates may be only one of many factors contributing to an expansion or contraction of the tax base. Economists may be unable to isolate the effect of the rate change with any degree of certainty or to test their assumptions empirically. Consequently, governments usually rely on static forecasting to estimate the revenues gained or lost because of a tax rate change.

Behavioral Responses to Changes in the Income Tax Rate

In the case of an income tax, the incremental revenue generated by an increase in rates depends on whether (and to what extent) the increase affects the aggregate amount of income subject to tax. Specifically, the increment depends on the ways that individual taxpayers modify their economic behavior in response to higher tax rates.

Objective 2
Differentiate between the income effect and the substitution effect of an increase in income tax rates.

The Income Effect.   An increase in income tax rates might induce people to engage in more income-producing activities. Consider the case of Mr. S, who earns $25,000 a year as a factory worker and currently pays 20 percent of that income ($5,000) in tax. Mr. S spends every penny of his $20,000 after-tax income to make ends meet. How might Mr. S react if the government increases the tax rate to 30 percent, thereby reducing his disposable income to $17,500? Our taxpayer might decide to work more hours or even take a second job to increase his before-tax income to at least $28,600. Under the new rate structure, Mr. S will pay $8,580 of tax on this income, leaving him with $20,020 and the same disposable income he enjoyed before the rate hike. This reaction (akin to running faster just to stay in the same place) has been labeled the **income effect** of a rate increase.[3]

If Mr. S responds to the higher tax rate by working longer to generate more income, the government will enjoy a revenue windfall. A static forecast indicates that the government should collect an additional $2,500 of revenue from Mr. S because of the 10 percent rate hike.

Static Forecast	
Revenue after rate increase	
(30% of $25,000 base)	$7,500
Revenue before rate increase	
(20% of $25,000 base)	(5,000)
Additional revenue from Mr. S	$2,500

However, if Mr. S reacts by increasing his taxable income from $25,000 to $28,600, the government will actually collect $3,580 of additional revenue:

Income Effect	
Revenue after rate increase	
(30% of $28,600 base)	$8,580
Revenue before rate increase	
(20% of $25,000 base)	(5,000)
Additional revenue from Mr. S	$3,580

The Substitution Effect.   If we change the financial circumstances of our hypothetical taxpayer, we might expect a different behavioral response to an income tax rate increase. Assume Ms. H works 60 hours a week as a self-employed management consultant, earning annual income of $350,000. At the current 20 percent tax rate, her after-tax income is $280,000—more than enough to support her comfortable lifestyle. If the government increases the tax rate to 30 percent, Ms. H may devote less time and effort to her income-producing activity. Such a reaction makes sense if the after-tax value of an hour of additional labor is now worth less to Ms. H than an additional hour of leisure. This very different behavioral reaction to a rate increase is called the **substitution effect.**[4]

If Ms. H responds to the higher tax rate by working fewer hours and generating less income, the government will suffer a revenue shortfall. Based on a static forecast, the government is counting on an additional $35,000 of revenue from Ms. H.

---

[3]Musgrave and Musgrave, *Public Finance in Theory and Practice,* 3rd ed. (New York: McGraw-Hill, 1980), p. 663.

[4]Ibid.

Static Forecast

Revenue after rate increase	
(30% of $350,000 base)	$105,000
Revenue before rate increase	
(20% of $350,000 base)	(70,000)
Additional revenue from Ms. H	$ 35,000

But if the business income of Ms. H falls to $325,000 because the tax increase dampened her entrepreneurial spirit, the additional revenue from Ms. H will be only $27,500.

Substitution Effect

Revenue after rate increase	
(30% of $325,000 base)	$97,500
Revenue before rate increase	
(20% of $350,000 base)	(70,000)
Additional revenue from Ms. H	$27,500

The probability of a substitution effect varies across taxpayers. The degree of personal control that individuals exercise over their careers determines the extent to which they can replace an hour of work with an hour of relaxation. Consequently, the substitution effect is more potent for self-employed persons than for salaried employees with rigid 9 A.M. to 5 P.M. schedules. The financial flexibility necessary to curtail work effort is more characteristic of a family's secondary wage earner than of the primary wage earner. Finally, ambitious career-oriented people who are highly motivated by nonmonetary incentives such as prestige and power may be impervious to the substitution effect.

Whether an income tax will goad a person to extra effort or whether it will be a disincentive to work depends heavily on that person's economic circumstances. Theoretically, the income effect is most powerful for lower-income taxpayers who may already be at a subsistence standard of living and don't have the luxury of choosing leisure rather than income-generating labor. The substitution effect becomes more compelling as an individual's disposable income rises and the financial significance of each additional dollar declines. From a macroeconomic viewpoint, these contradictory behavioral reactions have important tax policy implications. Conventional wisdom suggests that governments requiring more revenue should increase the tax rate on people with the greatest tax bases, that is, the highest incomes. But if the tax rate climbs too high, the substitution effect may become so strong that the projected revenues never materialize as more and more people are discouraged from working because the after-tax return on their labor is too small.

Supply-Side Economics.   Faith in the substitution effect is the foundation for **supply-side economic theory,** which holds that a decrease in the highest income tax rates should ultimately result in an increase in government revenues. The logic underlying this theory is that a rate cut increases the value of income-generating activities (work and investment) relative to the value of nonincome-generating activities (leisure and consumption). Accordingly, the people who benefit directly from the rate reduction will invest their tax windfall in new commercial ventures rather than simply spend it. This influx of private capital will stimulate economic growth and job creation. An expanding economy will result in prosperity across the board so that everyone, regardless of income level, indirectly benefits from the tax rate reduction. People will earn more income for the government to tax, and government revenues attributable to this enlarged tax base will swell.

Does this supply-side theory hold true? In 1981, the Reagan administration, acting on its belief in the theory, convinced Congress to enact the Economic Recovery Tax Act. This legislation lowered the highest marginal individual tax rates from 70 percent to 50 percent on ordinary income and from 28 percent to 20 percent on capital gains. The Tax Reform Act of 1986 went even further by reducing the highest marginal rate for individuals to 28 percent. These deep rate cuts were just one of many dramatic factors affecting the U.S. economy during the 1980s. The price of oil dropped by half, and the double-digit inflation of the late 1970s fell to less than 4 percent. Federal spending on many domestic programs declined, but defense spending soared. Congress increased the federal payroll tax rates significantly in an effort to keep pace with the explosive growth in Social Security and Medicare outlays. The government borrowed money at an unprecedented rate, creating structural deficits of record peacetime magnitude.[5]

Economists have engaged in nonstop debate as to whether the supply-side experiment of the 1980s (dubbed Reaganomics by the press) was a success or a failure. Some believe that the Reagan tax cuts fueled the rising level of employment, expansion of the small business sector, and steady growth in the gross domestic product over the last 15 years. Others maintain that the cuts were a financial windfall to the wealthiest American families but did little to enhance the prosperity of the middle- and lower-income classes. There is only one point on which economists seem to agree: disentangling the stimulative effect of the tax cuts from the web of other factors that shaped the Reagan economic era is an impossible task.

Taxes Should Be Convenient

Objective 3
Compare the concept of a convenient tax from the government's viewpoint and from the taxpayer's viewpoint.

Our second standard for evaluating a tax is **convenience.** From the government's viewpoint, a good tax should be convenient to administer. Specifically, the government should have a method for collecting the tax that the majority of taxpayers understand and with which they routinely cooperate. The collection method should not overly intrude on taxpayers' privacy but should offer minimal opportunity for noncompliance. States that levy retail sales taxes use a collection method under which the sellers of taxable goods are legally responsible for collecting the tax from buyers at point of sale and remitting the tax to the state on a periodic basis. This method is effortless for buyers and offers them no opportunity to evade the tax. States can concentrate their enforcement efforts on retail businesses, which are much easier to audit than individual consumers. In contrast, states have yet to develop a workable collection mechanism for use taxes; consequently, these taxes generate almost no revenue.

A good tax should be economical for the government. The administrative cost of collecting and enforcing the tax should be reasonable in comparison with the total revenue generated by the tax. At the federal level, the Internal Revenue Service (IRS) is the agency responsible for administering the income, payroll, excise, and transfer taxes.

---

[5]Isabel V. Sawhill, "Reaganomics in Retrospect: Lessons for a New Administration," *Challenge,* May–June 1989, p. 57.

For its fiscal year ending September 30, 1996, the IRS operated at a cost of $7.4 billion and collected $1,487 billion of tax revenue. Thus, the federal government's cost of collecting $100 of tax was a modest 50 cents.[6]

From the taxpayer's viewpoint, a good tax should be convenient to pay. The convenience standard suggests that people can determine their tax liability with a reasonable degree of certainty. Moreover, they do not have to devote undue time or incur undue costs in complying with the tax law. A retail sales tax receives high marks when judged by these criteria. People can easily compute the sales tax on a purchase and can pay the tax as part of the purchase price with no effort whatsoever!

In contrast, the federal income tax is denounced as both uncertain and costly. Because the income tax laws are so complex and change with such frequency, even tax professionals may be unsure as to how the law should apply to a particular transaction. Millions of Americans are bewildered by the income tax and have no confidence in their ability to compute the amount they owe. As a result, the majority of individual taxpayers pay someone else to prepare their income tax returns. By any measure, the cost to society of complying with the federal tax law is high; according to IRS estimates, taxpayers devote more than 5 billion hours each year to this inconvenient task. In dollar terms, the annual private sector cost of federal tax compliance is estimated at $225 billion.[7]

Taxes Should Be Efficient

Our third standard for a good tax is economic **efficiency.** Tax policymakers use the term *efficiency* in two different ways. Sometimes the term describes a tax that does not interfere with or influence taxpayers' economic behavior. At other times, policymakers describe a tax as efficient when individuals or organizations react to the tax by deliberately changing their economic behavior. In this section of the chapter, we will compare these two competing interpretations of efficiency.

The Classical Standard of Efficiency

Objective 4
Contrast the classical economic standard of tax neutrality with the Keynesian concept of taxes as a fiscal policy tool.

Policymakers who believe that competitive markets result in the optimal allocation of scarce resources within a society define an efficient tax as one that is *neutral* in its effect on the free market. From this perspective, a tax that causes people to modify their economic behavior is inefficient because it distorts the market and may result in suboptimal allocations of goods and services.

The classical economist Adam Smith definitely believed that taxes should have as little impact as possible on the economy. In his 1776 masterwork, *The Wealth of Nations,* Smith concluded the following:

> A tax . . . may obstruct the industry of the people, and discourage them from applying to certain branches of business which might give maintenance and employment to great multitudes. While it obliges the people to pay, it may thus diminish, or perhaps destroy, some of the funds which might enable them more easily to do so.

The laissez-faire system favored by Adam Smith theoretically creates a level playing field on which individuals and organizations, operating in their own self-interest, freely compete. When governments interfere with the system by imposing taxes on

---

[6]IRS 1996 Data Book.
[7]The Tax Foundation, "Compliance Costs of Alternative Tax Systems," 71 *Tax Notes* 1081, 1085.

some type of economic activity, the playing field tilts against the competitors engaging in that activity. The capitalistic game is disrupted, and the outcome may no longer be the best for society.

Of course, every modern economy incorporates some type of tax system, and firms functioning within the economy must adapt to that system. Business managers become familiar with the existing tax laws and make decisions affecting both current and future operations that take those laws into account. To return to the sports metaphor, these managers have adjusted their game plan to suit the present contours of the economic playing field.

When governments change their existing tax structures, firms are forced to reevaluate their tax situations in light of the change. Some may find that they stand to benefit from the change, while others may conclude that the new tax structure puts them at a competitive disadvantage. Managers must reassess how the tax laws affect their particular business operations. They may discover that traditional planning strategies no longer work, but that the efficacy of new strategies is uncertain. In short, every time the government changes its tax structure, the contours of the economic playing field shift. The fact that these shifts are both costly and unsettling to the business community has prompted many an economist to conclude that "an old tax is a good tax."

Taxes as an Instrument of Fiscal Policy

The British economist John Maynard Keynes disagreed with the classical notion that a good tax should be neutral. Keynes believed that free markets are highly effective in organizing production and allocating scarce resources but lack adequate self-regulating mechanisms for maintaining economic stability.[8] According to Keynes, governments must take responsibility for protecting their citizens and institutions against the inherent instability of capitalism. Historically, this instability was manifested by cycles of high unemployment, severe fluctuations in prices (inflation or deflation), and uneven economic growth. Lord Keynes believed that governments could counteract these problems through *fiscal policies* designed to promote full employment, price-level stability, and a steady rate of economic growth.

In the Keynesian schema, tax systems are a primary tool of fiscal policy. Rather than trying to design a neutral tax system, governments should deliberately use taxes to move the economy in the desired direction. If an economy is suffering from sluggish growth and high unemployment, the government could reduce taxes to transfer funds from the public to the private sector. The tax cut should both stimulate demand for consumer goods and services and increase the level of private investment. As a result, the economy should expand and new jobs should be created. Conversely, if an economy is overheated so that wages and prices are in an inflationary spiral, the government could raise taxes. People will have less money to spend, the demand for consumer and investment goods will soften, and the upward pressure on wages and prices will be relieved.

The U.S. government formally embraced its fiscal policy responsibilities when Congress enacted the Employment Act of 1946. This legislation charged the Executive Branch with developing strategies for promoting full employment and a stable dollar and resulted in the formation of the President's Council of Economic Advisors. Over the last 50 years, both political parties have consistently regarded the federal income tax

---

[8]John Maynard Keynes, *The General Theory of Employment, Interest and Money* (New York: Harcourt, Brace, 1936).

system as a legitimate instrument of fiscal policy and have advocated changes in that system to further their respective economic agendas. Changes that seem to have the intended macroeconomic effect are applauded as enhancing the efficiency of the tax system, while changes that apparently have no impact on the national economy are branded as inefficient. Certainly, this Keynesian concept of efficiency is far removed from the classic touchstone of economic neutrality.

Taxes and Behavior Modification

Modern governments routinely use their tax systems to address not only macroeconomic concerns but also specific social problems. Many such problems could be alleviated if people or institutions within the society could be persuaded to alter their behavior. Governments can promote behavioral change by writing tax laws to penalize those who engage in undesirable behavior or reward those who behave in the desired manner. The penalty takes the form of a higher tax burden, while the reward is some type of tax relief.

Some of the social problems that the federal income tax system attempts to remedy are undesirable by-products of the free enterprise system, which economists refer to as **negative externalities.** One of the most widely recognized of these is environmental pollution. The tax system contains provisions enacted to either pressure or entice companies to clean up their act, so to speak. One example of a provision designed to discourage environmentally unfriendly behavior is the excise tax on the sale or use of ozone-depleting chemicals manufactured in or exported into the United States.[9] An example of a provision intended to encourage the private sector to be more environmentally responsible is the lucrative tax break available with respect to the construction of pollution control facilities such as waste water purification plants.[10]

Tax systems may also contain provisions designed to foster activities that are undervalued by the free market but that the government believes are socially desirable. By bestowing a deliberate tax benefit on the activity, the government is providing a financial "carrot." This carrot should induce more taxpayers to engage in the activity and thus result in a greater level of the activity across society. An example of an activity that the federal government wants to promote is the rehabilitation of historic buildings. Accordingly, the law allows firms to reduce their annual tax bills by a percentage of the cost of renovating a certified historic structure.[11] Without this tax break, firms might find it cheaper to build or purchase modern buildings than to invest in historic structures requiring extensive renovation. At the margin, the tax break could be enough of a financial incentive to make the investment in the historic structure the more cost-effective business decision.

Governments use tax breaks to subsidize targeted activities, thereby making those activities less costly or more profitable. An excellent example of such a subsidy is the provision in the Internal Revenue Code making the interest paid by state and local governments on their debt obligations nontaxable to the recipient.[12] Because investors pay no tax on the income generated by these tax-exempt bonds, they are willing to accept a lower before-tax interest rate than if the interest on the bonds were taxable. Consequently, state and local governments can pay less interest than other debtors and

---

[9]This tax is authorized by §4681 (Internal Revenue Code of 1986).
[10]See §169.
[11]See §47.
[12]See §103.

still be competitive in the financial markets. By providing this tax break, the federal government is effectively subsidizing state and local governments by reducing their cost of borrowed capital.

Income Tax Preferences.   Provisions in the federal income tax system designed as incentives to encourage certain behaviors or as subsidies for targeted activities are described as **tax preferences.** These provisions are not in the law because they contribute to the accurate measurement of the tax base or the correct calculation of the tax liability. Tax preferences do not support the primary function of the law, which is to raise revenues. In fact, tax preferences do just the opposite. Because they allow certain persons or organizations to pay less tax, preferences lose money for the Treasury. In this respect, preferences are indirect government expenditures.

Like any other government outlay, a tax preference is justifiable only if the intended result has merit and deserves public support. But a tax preference should be subject to a second level of scrutiny: Is a tax incentive or subsidy the best way for the government to accomplish the intended result or would direct government support be more effective? This question can be hard to answer in any objective manner. Preferences are based on assumptions about how taxpayers react to a specific provision in the law. In a complex economy consisting of well over 100 million taxpayers, measuring the extent to which the predicted reaction occurs is extremely difficult.

The Tax Expenditures Budget.   Opponents to the use of tax preferences maintain that they are too well hidden within the Internal Revenue Code and, as a result, their cost to the government is easily overlooked. In response to this criticism, Congress publishes an annual **Tax Expenditures Budget** that quantifies the revenue loss attributable to each major tax preference.[13] For example, the government loses about $45 billion each year because the law allows individuals to deduct their home mortgage interest payments and another $17 billion because local property taxes on personal residences are deductible in the computation of taxable income.

The Tax Expenditures Budget sheds much needed light on the cost of specific preferences as well as their aggregate cost to the government. However, tax expenditures are not included in the calculation of the annual federal operating deficit. Another troubling aspect of tax preferences is that they add enormously to the length and complexity of the tax law. If the Internal Revenue Code could be stripped of every provision that is not absolutely necessary to measure taxable income and compute tax liability, the income tax would be far simpler to understand and apply.

Taxes Should Be Fair

The fourth standard by which to evaluate a tax is whether the tax is fair to the people who are required to pay it. While no economist, social scientist, or politician in his right mind would ever argue against fairness as a norm, there is precious little agreement as to the exact nature of tax equity. Many people nurture the belief that their tax

---

[13]A tax expenditure is measured by the difference between tax liability under present law and the tax liability that would result from a recomputation of tax without benefit of the tax expenditure. This measurement is static because taxpayer behavior is assumed to remain unchanged for tax expenditure estimate purposes. Joint Committee on Taxation, *Estimates of Federal Tax Expenditures for Fiscal Years 1998–2002,* December 15, 1997.

burden is unfairly heavy, while everyone else's burden is too light. As former U.S. Senator Russell Long expressed it, the attitude of the man on the street concerning tax equity is "Don't tax you, don't tax me; tax the fellow behind the tree." Clearly any meaningful discussion of the standard of fairness must rise above this sentiment.

Ability to Pay

A useful way to begin our discussion of equity is with the proposition that each person's contribution to the support of government should reflect that person's **ability to pay.** In the tax policy literature, ability to pay refers to the economic resources under a person's control. Each of the major taxes used in this country are based on some dimension of ability to pay. For instance, income taxes are based on a person's inflow of economic resources during the year. Sales and excise taxes are based on a different dimension of ability to pay: a person's consumption of resources represented by the purchase of goods and services. Real and personal property taxes complement income and sales taxes by focusing on a third dimension of ability to pay: a person's accumulation of resources in the form of certain types of wealth. And transfer taxes capture yet a fourth dimension: the accumulated wealth that a person gives to others during life or at death.

Horizontal Equity

Objective 5
Define horizontal equity.

If a tax is designed so that persons with the same ability to pay (as measured by the tax base) owe the same amount of tax, that system can be described as horizontally equitable. The structure of certain taxes guarantees their **horizontal equity.** In a jurisdiction with a 6 percent sales tax, every consumer who buys a taxable good with a $50 retail price pays a $3 sales tax. The horizontal equity of taxes with more complex structures may not be so easy to analyze.

Taxable Income and Ability to Pay.   In the federal income tax system, the tax base is annual taxable income. Consequently, the income tax is horizontally equitable if the taxable income calculation accurately reflects ability to pay. Let's explore this notion in more depth by comparing two people, Ms. B and Mr. D, both unmarried, both earning a $40,000 annual salary. Neither has any additional inflows of economic resources. Do Ms. B and Mr. D have the same ability to pay an income tax to the federal government? If we consider only their identical marital status and salaries, the answer must be yes, and the two should pay an equal tax.

But what additional facts might be considered in measuring ability to pay? Suppose that Ms. B suffers from a chronic illness and has $7,000 of uninsured medical expenses for the year while Mr. D is in perfect health. And suppose that Mr. D pays $4,500 of alimony to a former spouse during the year while Ms. B has no such legal obligation. Based on this new evidence, should we still conclude that Ms. B and Mr. D have the same ability to pay an income tax? Asking the question another way, should medical expenses and alimony enter into the computation of taxable income? Certainly our two individuals would argue that it is only fair to consider these variables.

The horizontal equity of the income tax is enhanced by refining the calculation of taxable income to include the significant variables affecting a person's economic circumstances for the year. But perfecting the tax base has its price; every refinement adds another page to the Internal Revenue Code. Increased precision in the measurement of ability to pay may improve the horizontal equity of the federal income tax, but it also increases the complexity of the law.

Annual versus Lifetime Horizontal Equity.   Federal taxable income is computed on a 12-month basis. This annual measurement of ability to pay may bear little or no relationship to a person's lifetime ability to pay.

> ***Annual versus Lifetime Equity.***   A blue-collar laborer wins a $200,000 lottery jackpot and as a result has the same current year taxable income as the scion of a wealthy family who lives off the interest and dividends from a trust fund. Prior to his lucky year and for the rest of his working life, the laborer's taxable income averages $25,000 while the trust fund beneficiary's income averages $200,000. Nevertheless, both individuals owe the same $40,000 tax liability for the current year.

Tax Preferences and Horizontal Equity.   In the previous section of this chapter, we introduced the concept of tax preferences. These income tax provisions are designed as incentives or subsidies and favor people who arrange their affairs to take advantage of the preference. Consequently, the tax benefit represented by preferences is not distributed impartially across taxpayers.

> ***Preferences and Equity.***   Two unrelated individuals, Mr. X and Ms. Y, invested in two different businesses during the year. Both businesses earned a $20,000 profit for their respective investors. Mr. X's business qualifies for several tax preferences, and as a result, Mr. X must report only $14,000 of the profit on his income tax return. In contrast, Ms. Y must report her entire profit. Their business investments increased our two individuals' economic ability to pay by the same $20,000. But because of the tax preferences with respect to Mr. X's business, Mr. X's taxable income is $6,000 less than Ms. Y's.

This example suggests that tax preferences can distort the horizontal equity of the income tax. Certainly the public perception is that the law is riddled with preferences that allow a privileged few to avoid paying their fair share of tax. We will examine the validity of this perception in later chapters of the text. Even if the perception is false and preferences do not materially undermine horizontal equity, the perception nonetheless erodes civic confidence in the fairness of the income tax system.

Vertical Equity

Objective 5
Define vertical equity.

A tax system is vertically equitable if persons with a greater ability to pay owe more tax than persons with a lesser ability to pay. While horizontal equity is concerned with a rational and impartial measurement of the tax base, **vertical equity** is concerned with a fair rate structure by which to calculate the tax on different amounts of base.

Horizontal and Vertical Equity.   A local government enacted a real property tax and established a board of assessors to determine the market values of the properties in its jurisdiction. The board completes its task in a conscientious and unbiased manner so that each resident's tax base (the assessed value of their real property) is fairly established. The property tax system has a two-bracket rate structure:

Percentage Rate	Bracket
2%	Assessed value from –0– to $1 million
1	Assessed value in excess of $1 million

Mr. M owns real property with an assessed value of $500,000; his property tax is $10,000 (2 percent of $500,000). Ms. N owns real property with an assessed value of $1.5 million; her property tax is $25,000 (2 percent of $1 million + 1 percent of $500,000).

This property tax is horizontally equitable because the base is fairly measured, and taxpayers with the same base (assessed value) bear an equal tax burden. The tax is also vertically equitable in that taxpayers with a greater base (such as Ms. N) owe more tax than taxpayers with a lesser base (Mr. M).

Objective 6
Differentiate between a regressive, a proportionate, and a progressive tax rate structure.

Regressive Taxes.   The property tax described in the preceding example meets a strict definition of vertical equity because Ms. N pays more tax than Mr. M: her $25,000 to his $10,000. However, Ms. N's average tax rate is less than Mr. N's average tax rate.

Ms. N: $25,000 tax ÷ $1,500,000 base = 1.667% average tax rate

Mr. M: $10,000 tax ÷ $500,000 base = 2% average tax rate

This inversion in average rates occurs because the property tax has a **regressive rate structure:** graduated rates that decrease as the base increases. Tax policymakers are in agreement that regressive rates violate the standard of equity because they place a proportionally greater tax burden on persons with smaller tax bases. However, the regressive nature of a tax is not always obvious from its rate structure.

Retail sales taxes consist of only a single rate and therefore are not explicitly regressive. Even so, many economists criticize these taxes as regressive in operation, bearing most heavily on people with the least economic resources.

Regressive Sales Tax Rates.   State P has a 5 percent sales tax on all retail purchases. Mr. J earns $20,000 of annual disposable income and spends this entire amount on taxable purchases. Mr. J pays $1,000 of sales tax, and his average tax rate (with respect to disposable income) is 5 percent.

Mr. J: $1,000 tax ÷ $20,000 base = 5% average tax rate

In contrast, Mr. K earns $100,000 of annual disposable income, spends only $75,000, and invests the remaining $25,000. Mr. K pays $3,750 of sales tax, and his average tax rate is 3.75 percent.

Mr. K: $3,750 tax ÷ $100,000 base = 3.75% average tax rate

A 1988 study concluded that "sales and excise taxes everywhere are regressive, often shockingly so; they can create unconscionable hardships for people living in poverty, they represent real financial burdens for middle-income families, and they let the rich, particularly the super-rich, off the hook almost entirely."[14] The majority of states mitigate the inherent regressivity of sales taxes by legislating broad exemptions for groceries purchased for home consumption, prescription medicines, and residential utilities.

Income Tax Rate Structures.   In an income tax system, the simplest rate structure consists of a single, or flat, rate applied to taxable income. To illustrate this **proportionate rate structure,** consider a group of three individuals, A, B, and C, who have respective taxable incomes of $20,000, $45,000, and $100,000. A proportionate income tax of 10 percent results in the following tax liabilities:

Proportionate Rate (10%)

	Taxable Income	Total Tax
Taxpayer A	$ 20,000	$ 2,000
Taxpayer B	45,000	4,500
Taxpayer C	100,000	10,000
		$16,500

Under this rate structure, individual C, who has the most taxable income and presumably the greatest ability to pay, owes the most tax, while B, who has more income than A, owes more tax than A. Despite this result, many tax theorists believe that a flat income tax fails to fairly apportion the tax burden across people with different incomes. They argue that the 10 percent tax levied on C is relatively less of a hardship than the 10 percent tax levied on A and B; and although the tax rate is proportionate, the economic sacrifice is disproportionate.

This argument is based on the theory of the **declining marginal utility of income.** This theory presumes that the financial importance associated with each dollar of income diminishes as total income increases. In other words, people value the subsistence income spent on necessities, such as food and shelter, relatively more than they value incremental income spent on luxury items. According to this theory, a

[14]Citizens for Tax Justice, "Nickels and Dimes: How Sales and Excise Taxes Add Up in the 50 States," March 1988.

progressive rate structure in which the rates increase as income increases results in an equality of sacrifice across taxpayers.[15]

Assume that our individuals A, B, and C compute their income tax under a progressive rate structure consisting of three rate brackets:

Percentage Rate	Bracket
5%	Income from –0– to $20,000
10	Income from $20,000 to $50,000
18	Income in excess of $50,000

This rate structure results in the following:

Progressive Rates

	Taxable Income	Tax Computation	Total Tax
Taxpayer A	$20,000	5% of 20,000	$ 1,000
Taxpayer B	45,000	5% of 20,000 +10% of 25,000	3,500
Taxpayer C	100,000	5% of 20,000 +10% of 30,000 +18% of 50,000	13,000
			$16,500

Note that this rate structure raises the same $16,500 revenue for the government as the 10 percent proportionate rate structure. From the taxpayers' viewpoint, the aggregate tax burden is unchanged. However, A and B are paying fewer dollars while C's tax liability has increased by $3,000.

With respect to our three individuals, is the proportionate or the progressive rate structure the more equitable? And if the progressive rate structure seems somehow fairer than the proportionate structure would a more progressive structure—perhaps with a top rate of 25 percent—be even better? There are no objective answers to these questions. Progressivity has an intuitive appeal to many people, and the U.S. income tax has always used a progressive rate structure. Nonetheless, while it may be plausible that individuals consider money as less meaningful and less enjoyable as their economic resources increase, this proposition cannot be tested empirically. Referring back to our illustration, the taxing authorities have no idea how A, B, or C personally values income, or whether the economic sacrifices they make by paying tax are even remotely comparable. Until economists discover how to measure the utility of income and to

---

[15]See Walter J. Blum and Harry Kalven, Jr., *The Uneasy Case for Progressive Taxation* (Chicago: University of Chicago Press, 1953), for a provocative analysis of the arguments for and against progressive tax rates.

compare utilities across individuals, the extent to which any progressive rate structure achieves equality of sacrifice is a matter of opinion.

Objective 7
Explain the difference between marginal and average tax rate.

Marginal and Average Tax Rates.   Before leaving the subject of income tax rate structures, we need to distinguish between marginal and average tax rates. The **marginal rate** is the rate that applies to the *next* dollar of taxable income. In the progressive rate structure in our example, individual C with $100,000 of taxable income owed $13,000 of tax. If C earns one more dollar of income, that dollar is subject to an 18 percent tax rate. Nevertheless, the fact that C is in the 18 percent marginal tax bracket does not mean she is paying 18 percent of her taxable income to the government. Her $13,000 tax liability divided by $100,000 taxable income is an **average rate** of only 13 percent. Similarly, individual B has a 10 percent marginal rate, but her average rate is 7.8 percent ($3,500 tax liability divided by $45,000 taxable income).

Under a proportionate rate structure, the marginal and average rates are the same for all levels of taxable income. Under a progressive rate structure, the marginal rate is higher than the average rate for taxable incomes in excess of the first rate bracket. The graphs in Exhibit 2–1 illustrate the relationship between marginal and average rate for the proportionate and progressive tax structures in our examples. In both graphs, the marginal rate is represented by a solid line and the average rate is represented by a broken line.

Distributive Justice

Objective 8
Discuss the concept of distributive justice as a tax policy objective.

In a social sense, a tax is equitable to the extent it redresses economic inequities existing in a capitalistic system. A vastly uneven distribution of private wealth across households, characterized by extremes of poverty and affluence, is one such inequity. By definition, taxes appropriate private wealth for public use, and typically appropriate a greater amount from the rich than from the poor. Consequently, taxes become mechanisms for the redistribution of wealth across society. Wealth transfer taxes, such as the federal estate and gift taxes, are prime examples of taxes with strong distributional implications. These taxes were enacted early in this century to allow the government to tap into the immense personal fortunes amassed during America's "gilded age." Some tax policymakers believe that the justification for a progressive income tax is its potential for rectifying distributive inequity. "The case for drastic progression in taxation must be rested on the case against inequality—on the ethical or aesthetic judgment that the prevailing distribution of wealth and income reveals a degree (and/or kind) of inequality that is distinctly evil or unlovely."[16]

Many social commentators view the current distribution of wealth across American households as unjust.[17] These commentators suggest that the federal government could combat this injustice by making the income tax rate structure more progressive. But once again the nagging question arises: How much more progressivity is desirable? Only the most fanatic egalitarian would argue that the tax system should result in a perfectly equal distribution of wealth across households. Although many people agree (to a greater or lesser extent) with the concept of distributive justice, there are those who strongly oppose the notion of Uncle Sam playing Robin Hood. In the final analysis, the

---

[16]Henry Simons, *Personal Income Taxation* (Chicago: University of Chicago Press, 1938), pp. 18–19.

[17]According to recent data, the wealthiest 10 percent of American households control 67 percent of the national net worth. 1992 Survey of Consumer Finances, Congressional Budget Office.

Exhibit 2–1a

Marginal and average tax rates under proportionate rate structure

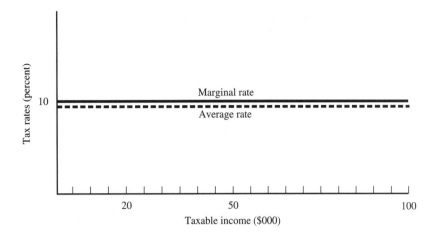

Exhibit 2–1b

Marginal and average tax rates under progressive rate structure

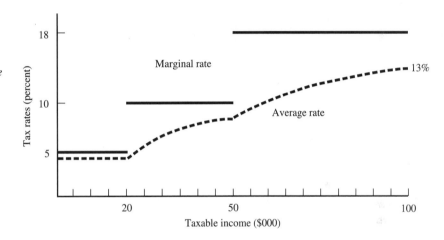

degree of progressivity in the income tax system remains a value judgment—a matter of political taste rather than of natural law.

The Perception of Inequity

The most widespread complaint against the federal income tax system is that it is unfair. Of course, no government has been or ever will be capable of designing a tax that people enjoy paying. As Edmund Burke, the English parliamentarian and social scientist, observed, "To tax and to please, no more than to love and be wise, is not given to man." Nevertheless, the public perception that the federal income tax is unfair has increased dramatically in recent decades.

This perception of inequity has many negative consequences. Research has shown that individuals who are convinced that the income tax system is inherently unfair are more likely to deliberately underreport their taxable incomes than individuals who believe the system is fair. This result suggests that as public confidence in the equity of the federal tax system erodes, the level of compliance will decline. As greater numbers of citizens regard tax evasion as acceptable, and even rational, behavior, the tax system will place an increasingly unfair burden on the honest remainder who continue to comply with the law.

> Taxpayer morale ultimately depends on the belief that taxes are fair. If the basis for this belief comes under suspicion, voluntary compliance with the tax laws is jeopardized. Thus, the perceived lack of fairness of the income tax may be as important as actual complexities, economic distortions, and inequities.[18]

Many individuals believe that the income tax system is unfair because it is so complicated. They are convinced that the system is full of exotic loopholes that benefit only the rich who can afford expert legal advice. As you will learn, this conviction is unfounded. Many of the complexities of the income tax law were designed to ensure that high-income taxpayers cannot manipulate the system to unwarranted advantage. Affluent individuals undeniably use the tax planning strategies discussed throughout this text on a routine basis to maximize the net present value of their business and investment transactions. However, most of these strategies derive from commonplace features of the law rather than from closely guarded secrets known only to tax professionals.

Conclusion

Jack Kemp, the 1996 Republican vice-presidential candidate, provides this summary description of a good tax.

> Surely, a tax code which is simple and fair must generate sufficient revenue so that the federal government may carry out its legitimate tasks. Second, it must not place a tax burden on those members of society least able to bear one. And, perhaps most important of all, it must not restrict the innovative and entrepreneurial capacities of Americans upon which rising living standards and our general prosperity so greatly depend.[19]

This summary touches on the four normative standards discussed in Chapter 2: sufficiency, convenience, efficiency, and equity. In our discussions, we learned that people interpret these standards in different ways and hold diverse opinions as to how each should be implemented.

The standards for a good tax are not necessarily in harmony and reconciling them can be a tricky proposition. A government's attempt to improve the sufficiency of its tax system by raising rates or expanding the base could make the tax less efficient in terms of its impact on the economy. The introduction of a preferential rule to enhance economic efficiency might damage the equity of the tax. Conversely, the enactment of a provision making a tax more fair may add another layer of complexity that makes it more difficult to administer. Tax policymakers are well aware of the potential frictions between the standards for a good tax. They know that trade-offs may be necessary in the design and implementation of the tax system that best serves the needs of their governments.

---

[18]Department of the Treasury, *Tax Reform for Fairness, Simplicity, and Economic Growth,* vol. 1 (Washington, D.C.: U.S. Government Printing Office, 1984), p. 9.

[19]"Unleashing America's Potential: A Pro-Growth, Pro-Family Tax System for the 21st Century," National Commission on Economic Growth and Tax Reform, 70 *Tax Notes* 413, 415.

Key Terms

Ability to pay   35
Average rate   40
Convenience   30
Declining marginal utility of income   38
Dynamic forecast   27
Efficiency   31
Horizontal equity   35
Income effect   28
Marginal rate   40
Negative externality   33
Progressive rate structure   39

Proportionate rate structure   38
Regressive rate structure   37
Static forecast   26
Substitution effect   28
Sufficiency   24
Supply-side economic theory   29
Tax Expenditures Budget   34
Tax policy   23
Tax preferences   34
Vertical equity   36

Questions and Problems for Discussion

1. After reading this chapter, identify the tax policy issue that you believe is the most important in today's society.
2. What evidence suggests that the federal tax system receives a low grade when evaluated on the standard of sufficiency?
3. Identify three ways that governments can alter their tax system to increase revenues.
4. National governments have the authority to print their own currency. Why might governments be reluctant to finance an operating deficit (excess of spending over revenues) by simply printing more money to spend?
5. In each of the following cases, discuss how the taxpayers might respond to a tax rate increase in a manner consistent with the income effect:
   a. Mr. E earns $32,000 a year as an employee and Mrs. E doesn't work.
   b. Mr. F earns $22,000 a year as an employee and Mrs. F earns $10,000 a year as a self-employed worker.
   c. Mr. G earns $22,000 a year as an employee and Mrs. G earns $10,000 a year as an employee.
6. In each of the following cases, discuss how the taxpayers might respond to a tax rate increase in a manner consistent with the substitution effect.
   a. Mr. H earns $125,000 a year as a salaried employee and Mrs. H doesn't work.
   b. Mr. J earns $125,000 a year as a salaried employee and Mrs. J earns $20,000 as a salaried employee.

   c. Mrs. K is single and earns $125,000 a year as a self-employed consultant.
7. Ms. V is a resident of a jurisdiction that levies a 35 percent income tax. Ms. V has $40,000 that she could invest in bonds paying interest of 12 percent a year. She is also considering spending the $40,000 on a new luxury automobile. Ms. V is having a hard time deciding between these two attractive alternatives. Why might her decision be easier if the jurisdiction increases its income tax rate to 50 percent?
8. What nonmonetary incentives affect the amount of time and energy people devote to income-generating activities?
9. The U.S. Congress has occasionally considered enacting a federal tax on the sale of consumer goods and services. This national sales tax would be in addition to any sales tax levied by state and local governments. Would this new source of federal revenue have any impact on the revenues of state and local governments?
10. The federal government levies a gift tax on the value of property that people give away during their life and an estate tax on the value of property that people transfer at death. From the government's perspective, which tax is more convenient?
11. Discuss the tax policy implications of the saying "an old tax is a good tax."
12. Jurisdiction R and Jurisdiction S both impose a personal income tax on their residents. Under Jurisdiction R's system, employers are required to withhold income tax from their employee's

paychecks and remit the tax to the government on their employee's behalf. Jurisdiction S's system has no such withholding requirement. Instead, residents must compute their income tax liability and pay the tax directly to the government on a monthly basis. Which tax system is more convenient for the government and for the taxpayer?

13. The federal income tax is criticized as being both inequitable across individuals and overly complicated. Discuss why equity and simplicity can be considered conflicting tax policy goals.

14. Jurisdiction W has decided to enact a personal income tax on its residents. Policymakers are considering the following alternatives:
    a. No tax on income up to $35,000 and a 15 percent tax on all income in excess of $35,000.
    b. A 10 percent tax on all income.
    c. A 15 percent tax on all income up to $80,000 and no tax on any income in excess of $80,000.
    Identify the rate structure of each of the three alternatives.

15. Corporation R and Corporation T both conduct business in Jurisdiction Q. The corporations' financial records for the last year show the following:

	Corporation R	Corporation T
Gross receipts from sales	$5,000,000	$5,000,000
Cost of goods sold	(3,200,000)	(3,670,000)
Gross profit	$1,800,000	$1,330,000
Annual operating expenses	(1,000,000)	(400,000)
Charitable contributions	–0–	(300,000)
Net profit	$ 800,000	$ 630,000

Jurisdiction Q has decided to enact a tax on corporations conducting business within its jurisdiction but has not decided on the tax base. Identify four different tax bases suggested by the corporations' financial records and discuss each base in terms of horizontal equity.

16. Jurisdiction E spends approximately $7 million each winter on snow removal. The jurisdiction is considering adding a provision to its income tax statute that would allow businesses to deduct the cost of snow removal equipment purchased during the year in the computation of taxable income.
    a. Does this proposed change in Jurisdiction E's tax law meet the definition of a tax preference? Explain briefly.
    b. Jurisdiction E forecasts that the proposed change will decrease its annual income tax revenues by $250,000 but will actually improve the jurisdiction's financial condition by $300,000. On what assumptions is this forecast based?

17. Ms. P is considering investing $20,000 in a new business venture. She projects that this investment should generate $3,000 of income each year. In estimating her tax liability on this future income stream, should Ms. P use her marginal or her average tax rate?

Application Problems

1. Mrs. C, a single taxpayer, earns an annual salary of $28,000 and pays 15 percent of that salary in state and federal income tax. If tax rates increase so that Mrs. C's annual tax rate is 20 percent, how much additional income must she earn to maintain her after-tax standard of living?

2. Mr. and Mrs. J own and operate a florist business that generates $100,000 of taxable income each year. For the past few years, the couple's federal tax rate on this income has been 30 percent. Congress recently enacted a tax hike that increases Mr. and Mrs. J's tax rate for next year to 40 percent.
    a. Based on a static forecast, how much additional tax will the federal government collect from Mr. and Mrs. J in the next taxable year?

b. How much tax will the government collect if Mr. and Mrs. J respond to the tax hike by working harder and earning $118,000 in the next taxable year?

c. How much tax will the government collect if Mr. and Mrs. J respond to the tax hike by working less and earning only $90,000 in the next taxable year?

3. Government G levies an income tax with the following rate structure:

Percentage Rate	Bracket
6%	Income from –0– to $30,000
10	Income from $30,000 to $70,000
20	Income from $70,000 to $200,000
28	Income in excess of $200,000

a. Taxpayer A's income for the current year is $83,000. Compute A's tax liability and average tax rate. What is A's marginal tax rate?

b. Taxpayer B's income for the current year is $310,000. Compute B's tax liability and average tax rate. What is B's marginal tax rate?

Issue Recognition Problems

Identify the tax issue or issues suggested by the following situations and state each issue in the form of a question.

1. County M imposes a 1 percent tax on the gross receipts earned by firms operating within its jurisdiction. For the last year, gross receipts subject to tax totaled $400 million. The county government is considering raising the tax rate to 2 percent because it needs $400,000 additional revenue to make badly needed improvements to its road system.

2. The Internal Revenue Code allows individuals to deduct state income tax payments in the computation of their taxable income for federal purposes. However, state sales tax payments are not deductible. Mrs. F is a resident of a state with a 5 percent personal income tax and a 3 percent sales tax. Mrs. L is a resident of a state with no personal income tax and a 7 percent sales tax. During the past year, both women paid $8,000 of state tax.

3. Four years ago, the citizens of Country C complained that the national tax system was too uncertain because the government changed the tax laws so frequently. In response to this criticism, the government enacted a 10-year moratorium on change: no existing tax law can be modified and no new tax law can be enacted for a decade. In the current year, Country C is experiencing a severe recession. Economic growth is at a standstill, and the national unemployment rate is 18 percent.

4. Two years ago, the government of State P decided to improve the horizontal equity of its individual income tax by allowing families to deduct the cost of heating and air conditioning their homes. This modification to the state's tax laws resulted in an additional tax form and three additional pages of instructions. For the past two years, only one-third of the families eligible for the deduction actually claimed it on their returns.

5. Jurisdiction J wants to clean up its streets, parks, and waterways. It decides to do so by providing a tax break for businesses that assign employees to pick up trash for a minimum number of hours each month. The annual revenue loss from this tax break is $1.9 million.

Tax Planning Case

Jurisdiction B's tax system consists of a 6.5 percent general sales tax on retail goods and selected services. Over the past decade, the average annual volume of sales subject to this tax was $500 million. The juris-diction needs to increase its tax revenues by approximately $5 million each year to finance its spending programs. The taxing authorities are considering two alternatives: a 1 percent increase in the sales tax rate or a new 2 percent tax on the net income of corporations doing business in the jurisdiction. Based on recent economic data, the annual net income subject to the new tax would be $275 million. However, the jurisdiction would have to create a new agency responsible for enforcing and collecting the income tax. The estimated annual cost of the agency is $500,000. Jurisdiction B borders four other taxing jurisdictions, all of which levy a general sales tax and two of which levy a corporate income tax.

1. Based on a static forecast, how much incremental revenue would Jurisdiction B raise under each alternative?
2. Assume that the taxing authorities in Jurisdiction B want a dynamic forecast of the incremental revenues under each alternative. What additional facts would be important in making such a forecast and why?

PART TWO

Fundamentals of Tax Planning

3

Taxes as Transaction Costs

Learning Objectives

After studying this chapter, you will be able to:

1. Given the marginal tax rate, compute the tax cost resulting from an income-generating transaction and the tax savings resulting from an income tax deduction.

2. Integrate tax costs and savings into net present value calculations of after-tax cash flows.

3. Identify the reasons why assumptions concerning future tax costs and savings are uncertain.

4. Explain why a business strategy that minimizes tax costs is not necessarily the optimal strategy for a firm.

5. Explain why the parties to a private market transaction should consider the tax consequences of the transaction to both parties.

6. Distinguish between an arm's-length transaction and a related party transaction.

In the introduction to *Principles of Taxation for Business and Investment Planning,* we established the premise that the overall objective of business decisions is to maximize the value of the firm. The premise is relevant to managers who are employed to make decisions on behalf of the owners of the firm. Managers who make good decisions that enhance the value of owners' equity can expect to be well compensated for their success. Managers who make bad decisions that result in a decline in value can expect to lose their jobs. A variation of the premise holds true for individuals acting in their own economic self-interest. People want to make personal financial decisions that further their goal of wealth maximization.

In Chapter 3, we will explore the business decision-making process. We begin by examining the concept of net present value of cash flows as the cornerstone of this process. The chapter then focuses on how the tax consequences of business transactions affect net present value and how these consequences must be integrated into the decision-making framework. We will consider how managers can structure transactions to control tax consequences and maximize net present value. The chapter concludes by discussing the extent to which the various parties to a business transaction can negotiate to reduce the tax burden on the transaction and to share the tax savings among themselves.

The Role of Net Present Value in Decision Making

Every business operation consists of a series of transactions intended to generate profit and create value for the owners of the firm. Business managers obviously need a method for evaluating whether an isolated transaction or an integrated sequence of transactions will contribute to or detract from the profitability of the operation. The method should be useful to managers who must choose between alternative transactions that accomplish the same functional result for the firm.

Quantifying Cash Flows

Financial theorists agree that the first step in evaluating a business transaction is to quantify the cash flows attributable to the transaction. Some transactions result in the receipt of cash by the firm: the sale of merchandise to a customer or the rental of property to a lessee are examples of transactions generating cash inflows. Other transactions require the firm to disburse cash: the purchase of business assets and the hiring of employees are common transactions involving cash outflows. Of course, many transactions involve both inflows and outflows and must be evaluated on the basis of **net cash flow** (the difference between cash received and cash disbursed).

The various revenue-generating transactions in which firms engage typically result in positive net cash flows that increase the value of the firm. If managers must choose between alternative revenue-generating opportunities, they should choose the opportunity with the greatest positive net cash flow. The various costs that firms incur can be expressed as negative net cash flows. Viewed in isolation, negative net cash flows decrease the value of the firm. However, costs are essential components of an integrated business operation and indirectly contribute to short-term and long-term profitability. If managers conclude that a particular cost is unnecessary because it does not enhance profitability, the cost should be eliminated. If a cost is justified, managers should reduce the negative net cash flow associated with the cost as much as possible.

In summary, managers want to make decisions that enhance profitability by increasing revenues and controlling costs. More precisely, managers want to make decisions that maximize the value of the firm by maximizing positive cash flow or minimizing negative cash flow.

The Concept of Present Value

When cash flows attributable to a transaction occur at different times, the quantification of net cash flow should take into account the **time value of money.** Time value refers to the fact that a dollar available today is worth more than a dollar available tomorrow because the current dollar can be invested to start earning interest immediately.[1] A dollar available today has a present value of a dollar. The present value of a dollar the availability of which is deferred until a future period is based on a **discount rate**—the rate of interest on invested funds for the deferral period. A transaction's **net present value (NPV)** is the sum of the present values of cash inflows and outflows relating to the transaction.

The next several paragraphs provide a quick review of the mathematical derivation of present value. If you are already familiar with this material, please feel free to jump ahead to the discussion of taxes and cash flows on page 53.

---

[1]This proposition is considered the first basic principal of finance. Richard A. Brealey and Stewart C. Myers, *Principles of Corporate Finance,* 5th ed. (New York: McGraw-Hill, 1996).

Present Value.   The algebraic expression of the present value (PV) of a dollar available at the end of one period based on the discount rate (r) for that period is:

$$PV(\$1) = \frac{1}{1 + r}$$

PV Calculation.   At an annual 10 percent discount rate, the present value of $1 to be received at the end of one year is $.9091:

$$\$.9091 = \frac{1}{1.10}$$

If the availability of the dollar is deferred for a number of periods (n) over which the discount rate is constant, the algebraic expression of present value is:

$$PV(\$1) = \frac{1}{(1 + r)^n}$$

PV Calculation.   At an annual 10 percent discount rate, the present value of $1 to be received at the end of three years is $.7513:

$$\$.7513 = \frac{1}{1.331} = \frac{1}{(1.10)^3}$$

In other words, $.7513 invested today to earn 10 percent compounded annually will accumulate to $1 at the end of three years.

Present Value of an Annuity.   A cash flow consisting of a constant dollar amount available at the end of the period for a specific number of periods is called an **annuity.** Examples include monthly rent payments over the term of a lease agreement and equal annual payments to retire the principal of an outstanding loan. The algebraic expression of the present value (PV) of an annuity of one dollar for a number of periods (n) based on the discount rate (r) over the period is:

$$PV(\$1 \text{ for n periods}) = \frac{1}{r} - \frac{1}{r(1 + r)^n}$$

PV of an Annuity.   At a 10 percent annual discount rate, the present value of $1 to be received at the end of years 1 through 4 is $3.1699:

$$PV(\$1 \text{ for 4 years}) = \frac{1}{.10} - \frac{1}{.10(1.10)^4}$$

$$PV(\$1 \text{ for 4 years}) = 10 - \frac{1}{.10(1.4641)}$$

$$\$3.1699 = 10 - \quad 6.8301$$

The present value of the annuity is the sum of the present values of the four $1 payments. Note that this formula only works for a series of *equal* payments.

Present Value Tables.   The algebraic formulas developed in the preceding paragraphs can be used to derive tables of discount factors for computing the present value of cash receipts or payments deferred for any given number of periods. Appendix A of this text is a table of discount factors for computing the present value of $1 available at the end of 1 through 20 years at annual discount rates ranging from 3 percent to 20 percent. Appendix B is a table of discount factors for computing the present value of a $1 annuity for a period of 1 through 20 years at annual discount rates ranging from 3 percent to 20 percent. Throughout the text, computations of the net present value of cash flows are based on factors from these tables.

The net present value of cash flows can also be computed by using a financial calculator or a spreadsheet computer program such as Microsoft Excel or Lotus 1-2-3. Remember that discount factor tables, calculators, and electronic spreadsheets are all means to the same end; business managers use whichever tool is the most convenient for computing net present value.

The Issue of Risk

The quantification of cash flows and calculation of their net present value are necessarily based on assumptions concerning future events. In projecting the cash inflows and out-flows attributable to a proposed transaction, business managers research pertinent industry and economic data, consult professionals who have expertise relevant to the transaction, and rely on their experience with past transactions of a similar nature. Nonetheless, even the most carefully developed projections can be inaccurate, and unexpected events can dramatically alter the actual cash flows associated with new business ventures.

Financial forecasters must accept the possibility that one or more of the assumptions on which their cash flow projections are based will be wrong. Of course, some assumptions are more certain than others. The assumption that the U.S. government will pay the interest on its debt obligations is more certain than the assumption that the value of an initial public offering (IPO) of stock will double in value over the next 12 months. This difference in certainty makes a decision to invest in U.S. Treasury bills less risky than a decision to invest in the IPO.

Business managers must be sensitive to the relative uncertainties and the resultant degree of risk inherent in any proposed transaction. When calculating net present value, they should invoke the financial principle that a safe dollar is worth more than a risky dollar. In other words, the present value of a highly speculative future dollar should be based on a higher discount rate than the present value of a guaranteed future dollar.

Because this text concentrates on the tax aspects of business decisions, the cash flow examples throughout the text incorporate two simplifying assumptions concerning financial risk. First, they assume that the discount rate specified in the example reflects the relative risk of the transaction under consideration. Second, the examples assume that such risk is stable over time so that the appropriate discount rate does not change from period to period.

A Basic Net Present Value Example

Let's summarize our discussion of net present value and its role in business decision making by working through a simple example. Suppose a consulting firm must decide between two lucrative engagements, either of which would require the firm's complete attention for two years. Engagement 1 will generate $150,000 of revenues in each of the two years. The firm estimates that this engagement will require $90,000 of expenses in the current year and $10,000 of expenses in the second year. Engagement 2 will generate $200,000 of revenues in the current year and $125,000 of revenues in the second year. The firm estimates that Engagement 2 will require $65,000 of annual expenses. Based on a 10 percent discount rate and *without considering the impact of any type of tax,* the net present values of the competing engagements are computed as follows:

Net Present Value of Engagements 1 and 2

	Engagement 1	Engagement 2
Current year:		
Cash revenues	$150,000	$200,000
Cash expenses	(90,000)	(65,000)
Net cash flow	$ 60,000	$135,000
Second year:		
Cash revenues	$150,000	$125,000
Cash expenses	(10,000)	(65,000)
Net cash flow	$140,000	$ 60,000
Present value of current year cash flow[2]	$ 60,000	$135,000
Present value of second year cash flow		
(Cash flow × .909 discount factor)	127,260	54,540
Net present value	$187,260	$189,540

The firm now has a rational basis for choosing between the two consulting opportunities. Because Engagement 2 has a net present value greater than that of Engagement 1, the firm should accept Engagement 2.

Taxes and Cash Flows

Objective 1
Given the marginal tax rate, compute the tax cost resulting from an income-generating transaction and the tax savings resulting from an income tax deduction.

Calculations of net present value must reflect all cash flows including any tax costs or tax savings resulting from the transaction. In the business decision-making process, cash flows before tax have no relevance.

Tax Costs.   If a transaction results in an increase in any tax liability for any period, the increase (**tax cost**) is a cash outflow. A tax cost may be incremental to a nontax cost. For instance, a firm that purchases machinery may pay a sales tax; the cash outflow from the transaction includes both the purchase price and the tax. In the context of an income tax, tax cost can be a direct result of the receipt of taxable income; the cash outflow represented by the tax is linked to any cash inflow represented by the income.

> *Income Tax Cost.*   Firm F sells an item of inventory for $50 cash. If the firm's investment in the inventory was $40, the sales transaction generates $10 of taxable profit. If the firm is subject to a 30 percent income tax, the tax cost of the transaction is $3. The sales transaction generates both $50 of cash inflow and $3 of cash outflow, resulting in positive net cash flow of $47.

---

[2]Throughout the text, cash flows in any year are considered available on the first day of the year. Consequently, current year cash flows are not discounted in the net present value calculation.

Tax Savings.   If a transaction results in a decrease in any tax liability for any period, the decrease **(tax savings)** represents a cash inflow. In the income tax system, tax liability is based on net business profits rather than gross revenues. Accordingly, many business expenditures can be subtracted, or deducted, in the computation of taxable income. The **deduction** reduces taxable income and causes a corresponding reduction in tax liability. Hence, the deductible expenditure results in a tax savings.[3]

> *Income Tax Savings.*   Firm F leases office space for a monthly rent of $1,000. Each $1,000 expenditure is deductible in computing the firm's taxable income; in other words, the expenditure shields $1,000 of income from tax. If the firm is subject to a 30 percent tax rate, the deduction causes a $300 tax savings. The monthly rent transaction involves both a $1,000 cash outflow and a $300 cash inflow, resulting in negative net cash flow of $700.

The Significance of Marginal Tax Rate

The income tax cost or savings associated with a particular business transaction is a function of the firm's marginal tax rate. In Chapter 2, we defined marginal rate as the rate that applies to the next dollar of taxable income. When analyzing transactions that either increase or decrease taxable income, the marginal rate is the rate at which the increase or decrease would be taxed. If this rate is constant over the increase or decrease, the computation of the tax cost or savings from the transaction is simple.

> *Constant Marginal Rate.*   Firm F is subject to a progressive income tax consisting of two rates: 15 percent on the first $50,000 of taxable income and 30 percent on taxable income in excess of $50,000. The firm's taxable income to date is $100,000. If Firm F engages in a transaction that generates $10,000 of additional income, the entire increment is subject to a 30 percent tax rate. Therefore, the transaction has a $3,000 tax cost.

The computation of tax cost or savings is more complex if the marginal tax rate is not constant over the change in taxable income.

> *Changing Marginal Rate.*   Firm G is subject to a progressive income tax consisting of two rates: 15 percent on the first $50,000 of taxable income and 30 percent on taxable income in excess of $50,000. The firm's taxable income to date is $44,000. If Firm G engages in a transaction that generates $10,000 of additional income, the marginal rate on the first $6,000 increment is 15 percent and on the next $4,000 increment is 30 percent. Thus, the transaction has a $2,100 tax cost.
>
> If Firm G engages in a transaction that generates a $10,000 deduction, the marginal tax rate on the entire income shielded by the deduction is 15 percent. Thus, the transaction results in a $1,500 tax savings.

---

[3]In the accounting and finance literature, the tax savings from deductible business expenditures are often described as *tax shields.*

Obviously, managers must be keenly aware of their firm's marginal tax rate to accurately compute the cash flows attributable to the tax consequences of a business transaction.

Net Present Value Example Revisited

Objective 2
Integrate tax costs and savings into net present value calculations of after-tax cash flows.

Let's integrate income tax consequences into the net present value example developed earlier in the chapter. Remember that our consulting firm must choose between two engagements that generate different amounts of revenues and involve different amounts of expenses over a two-year period. Now assume that (1) the expenses are fully deductible in computing the firm's annual taxable income and (2) the income tax rate is 40 percent. Based on these additional assumptions, the net present values of the competing engagements are computed as follows:

Net Present Value of Engagements 1 and 2 Revisited		
	Engagement 1	*Engagement 2*
Current year:		
Cash revenues	$150,000	$200,000
Deductible expenses	(90,000)	(65,000)
Before-tax cash flow/taxable income	$ 60,000	$135,000
Income tax cost at 40%	(24,000)	(54,000)
After-tax cash flow	$ 36,000	$ 81,000
Second year:		
Cash revenues	$150,000	$125,000
Deductible expenses	(10,000)	(65,000)
Before-tax cash flow/taxable income	$140,000	$ 60,000
Income tax cost at 40%	(56,000)	(24,000)
After-tax cash flow	$ 84,000	$ 36,000
Present value of current year cash flow	$ 36,000	$ 81,000
Present value of second year cash flow		
(after-tax cash flow × .909 discount factor)	76,356	32,724
Net present value	$112,356	$113,724

The introduction of an income tax reduced the net present value of each engagement but did not change the proportionate difference between the values. With or without the tax, the net present value of Engagement 1 is only 98.80 percent of the net present value of Engagement 2. Because the income tax applies in the same manner to each engagement and because the firm's marginal rate doesn't change over the two-year period, the tax is neutral. In other words, income tax consequences are not a factor affecting the firm's decision as to which engagement to accept. Now let's consider two examples in which the income tax consequences become an important factor in the decision-making process.

Different Tax Treatments across Transactions.   Tax costs are not neutral if the income tax law applies differentially to the two engagements. Assume that the law authorizes a deduction for 100 percent of the expenses incurred in connection with Engagement 1, but it allows the firm to deduct only 75 percent of the expenses incurred in connection with Engagement 2. Observe how the present value computations change.

Different Tax Treatments of Engagements 1 and 2

		Engagement 1		Engagement 2
Current year:				
Cash revenues			$150,000	$200,000
Deductible expenses			(90,000)	(48,750)
Nondeductible expenses			–0–	(16,250)
Before-tax cash flow			$ 60,000	$135,000
Income tax cost:				
Taxable income	$60,000		$151,250	
	.40		.40	
Tax cost			(24,000)	(60,500)
After-tax cash flow			$ 36,000	$ 74,500
Second year:				
Cash revenues			$150,000	$125,000
Deductible expenses			(10,000)	(48,750)
Nondeductible expenses			–0–	(16,250)
Before-tax cash flow			$140,000	$ 60,000
Income tax cost:				
Taxable income	$140,000		$76,250	
	.40		.40	
Tax cost			(56,000)	(30,500)
After-tax cash flow			$ 84,000	$ 29,500
Present value of current year cash flow			$ 36,000	$ 74,500
Present value of second year cash flow				
(after-tax cash flow × .909 discount factor)			76,356	26,816
Net present value			$112,356	$101,316

The fact that the tax law limits the deduction for the expenses associated with Engagement 2 increases the tax cost of the engagement and decreases after-tax cash flow. As a result, the net present value of Engagement 2 is less than that of Engagement 1, and Engagement 1 is the superior opportunity. In this case, tax consequences are a critical factor in the firm's decision.

Different Tax Rates over Time.   Calculations of net present value are sensitive to changes in tax rates over time. To illustrate this point, modify the example again by returning to the initial assumption that the expenses of both engagements are fully deductible. But now assume that Congress recently enacted legislation reducing the income tax rate from 40 percent in the current year to 25 percent in the second year.

Different Tax Rates for Current and Second Year

	Engagement 1	Engagement 2
Current year:		
Cash revenues	$150,000	$200,000
Deductible expenses	(90,000)	(65,000)
Before-tax cash flow/taxable income	$ 60,000	$135,000
Income tax cost at 40%	(24,000)	(54,000)
After-tax cash flow	$ 36,000	$ 81,000
Second year:		
Cash revenues	$150,000	$125,000
Deductible expenses	(10,000)	(65,000)
Before-tax cash flow/taxable income	$140,000	$ 60,000
Income tax cost at 25%	(35,000)	(15,000)
After-tax cash flow	$105,000	$ 45,000
Present value of current year cash flow	$ 36,000	$ 81,000
Present value of second year cash flow		
(after-tax cash flow × .909 discount factor)	95,445	40,905
Net present value	$131,445	$121,905

The fact that a lower tax rate is in effect for the second year decreases the tax cost for that year relative to the tax cost for the current year. Engagement 1 generates a much greater percentage of its total taxable income in the second year than Engagement 2. Consequently, Engagement 1 has a lower overall tax cost and a greater net present value than Engagement 2 and is the superior opportunity.

The Uncertainty of Tax Consequences

Objective 3
Identify the reasons why assumptions concerning future tax costs and savings are uncertain.

A net present value calculation is incomplete unless it includes cash flows stemming from both the current and future tax consequences of the proposed transaction. However, assumptions concerning tax consequences are subject to their own unique set of uncertainties.

Audit Risk.   Oftentimes the correct application of the tax law to some aspect of a proposed transaction is unclear or unresolved. In such case, business managers must decide on the most probable tax consequences to incorporate into their net present value calculations. Whenever a firm enters into a transaction involving ambiguous tax issues, it runs the risk that the Internal Revenue Service (or state and local tax authorities) will challenge the firm's tax treatment on audit. The IRS may conclude that the transaction resulted in a higher tax cost or a smaller tax savings than the manager originally projected. The firm can dispute the unfavorable result of the audit in court. In most civil tax cases, the **burden of proof** is on the taxpayer, not the government. In other words, the firm must convince the court that the IRS's conclusions are wrong. Even if the firm wins its case, the cost of litigation can be substantial. Accordingly, actual cash flows from a contested transaction may be very different than the estimated cash flows used in the net present value calculation.

Managers can take precautions that reduce the risk that the IRS will challenge the tax consequences of their firm's business activities. They can engage a tax professional, such as a CPA or an attorney, to analyze questionable transactions and render an expert opinion as to the proper tax treatment thereof. Managers can even request the IRS to analyze a proposed transaction and to conclude how the tax law should be applied. The IRS will communicate its conclusion in the form of a **private letter ruling** to the firm. Obtaining a private letter ruling can be expensive; firms typically require professional help in drafting a ruling request, and the IRS currently charges a $3,650 fee for a ruling.[4] Despite the cost, a private letter ruling can be invaluable when tax liabilities of thousands or even millions of dollars are at stake. If a firm reports the tax consequences of a transaction in accordance with a private letter ruling, it has a guarantee that the consequences will not be challenged by the IRS upon subsequent audit.[5]

Tax Law Uncertainty.   A second source of uncertainty is the possibility that tax laws may change during the time period involved in the net present value computation. Of course, the potential for change varies greatly with the particular tax under consideration. The federal income tax system is notorious for the frequency with which Congress changes the rules of the game. But even within this volatile tax system, some provisions are quite stable. The tax consequences of a proposed transaction to which a stable tax provision applies are more predictable than the consequences of a transaction subject to a provision that Congress modifies every year. As a result, the net present value of the former transaction can be calculated with greater certainty than the net present value of the latter.

> ***Stable and Unstable Tax Provisions.***   The Internal Revenue Code allows firms to deduct "all interest paid or accrued within the taxable year on indebtedness." This provision was included in the Internal Revenue Code of 1939 and has been substantially unchanged for almost 60 years. In contrast, the provision requiring corporations to pay an alternative minimum tax in addition to regular income tax was added to the Internal Revenue Code in 1986, then substantially amended in 1988, 1990, 1992, 1993, 1996, and 1997.

Marginal Rate Uncertainty.   The estimated tax costs or savings with respect to a transaction are a function of the firm's projected marginal tax rate. The firm's marginal rate may change in future years because the government changes the statutory rates for all taxpayers. The marginal rate may also change because of a change in the firm's circumstances. In the income tax context, a firm's marginal rate depends on the level of its annual taxable income. If the taxable income for a future year is significantly more or less than anticipated, the actual marginal rate for that year may differ from the projected rate. If the actual rate is higher than projected, the tax cost or savings in that year will be more than expected. Conversely, if the rate is lower than projected, tax cost or savings will be less than expected.

---

[4]See Rev. Proc. 98-1, Appendix A, 1998-1 IRB 17.

[5]A taxpayer may rely on a ruling unless the ruling request misstated or omitted material facts concerning the proposed transaction or the actual transaction differs substantially from the proposed transaction. No taxpayer may rely on a ruling issued to another taxpayer. See Rev. Proc. 98-1, Section 12, 1998-1 IRB 17.

Structuring Transactions to Reduce Taxes

The tax consequences of business transactions depend on the legal or financial characteristics of the transaction. Firms can often change the tax consequences by altering or restructuring some characteristic of the transaction. For instance, a firm that needs an additional worker to perform a certain task could hire a part-time employee to meet its needs. As a result of this employment transaction, the firm is liable for federal and state payroll taxes based on the salary or wage paid to the employee. The firm could alter the transaction by engaging an independent contractor to perform the same task.[6] The firm is not liable for payroll taxes on the fee paid to the independent contractor. Thus, by altering the transaction, the firm eliminates the payroll tax cost of adding personnel.

Let's add some numbers to compute the after-tax cost of each alternative.

Cost of Employee.   Firm W plans on hiring an employee to perform a certain task. The firm would pay a $15,000 salary and $1,250 of payroll tax on the salary. Both the salary and the payroll tax are deductible in computing the firm's taxable income. If the firm's marginal income tax rate is 35 percent, the after-tax cost of the transaction is $10,562:

Cash flows:	
Compensation (salary)	$(15,000)
Payroll tax cost	(1,250)
Income tax savings	
($16,250 × 35%)	5,688
Net cash flow	$(10,562)

Cost of Independent Contractor.   If Firm W engages an independent contractor to perform the task and pays the contractor a $15,000 fee, the after-tax cost of the transaction is only $9,750.

Cash flows:	
Compensation (fee)	$(15,000)
Income tax savings	
($15,000 × 35%)	5,250
Net cash flow	$ (9,750)

In this simplistic example, Firm W can eliminate the payroll tax cost without affecting any nontax cash flow (the compensation paid). The income tax applies in the same manner to both alternatives and thus is a neutral consideration. Consequently,

---

[6]An independent contractor is a self-employed individual who performs services for compensation. Unlike an employee, an independent contractor controls the manner in which the services are performed.

Firm W can minimize the after-tax cost of the employment transaction by engaging an independent contractor instead of hiring an employee.

An Important Caveat

Objective 4
Explain why a business strategy that minimizes tax costs is not necessarily the optimal strategy for a firm.

The structural characteristics of a business transaction determine both the tax and non-tax outcomes of the transaction. Business managers who decide to change some aspect of the transaction to reduce tax costs must carefully consider the impact of the change on nontax factors. If a change that saves tax dollars adversely affects other factors, the change may be a bad idea. In financial terms, a business strategy that minimizes the tax cost of a transaction may not maximize net present value and may not be the optimal strategy for the firm.

To demonstrate this important point, reconsider the example in which Firm W needs additional personnel and can either hire an employee or engage an independent contractor. The firm can hire the employee for a $15,000 salary and an after-tax cost of $10,562. But what if the independent contractor demands a $17,500 fee to do the job?

> ***Cost of Independent Contractor***   If Firm W engages an independent contractor to perform the task and pays the contractor a $17,500 fee, the after-tax cost of the transaction is $11,375.
>
> | Cash flows: | |
> |---|---:|
> | Compensation (fee) | $(17,500) |
> | Income tax savings | |
> | ($17,500 × 35%) | 6,125 |
> | Net cash flow | $(11,375) |

Now the alternative that eliminates the payroll tax cost increases the compensation Firm W must pay. As a result, the after-tax cost of engaging an independent contractor ($11,375) exceeds the after-tax cost of hiring an employee ($10,562). Firm W should hire the employee, even though this alternative does not minimize the payroll tax cost of the employment transaction.

Transactional Markets

The extent to which managers can control the tax consequences of transactions depends on the nature of the market in which the transaction occurs. A **market** is a forum for commercial interaction between two or more parties for the purpose of exchanging goods or services. One or both parties may want to customize the terms of the exchange to obtain a certain tax result; their ability to do so depends on the flexibility of the particular market.

Objective 5
Explain why the parties to a private market transaction should consider the tax consequences of the transaction to both parties.

Private Market Transactions.   Many business transactions involve private parties who deal directly with each other. The parties have flexibility in designing a transaction that accommodates the needs of both. The legal and financial characteristics of the transaction are specified in the contractual agreement to which both parties finally consent. In negotiating such **private market** transactions, each party can evaluate the tax consequences not only to itself but also to the other party. By doing so, the parties can work together to minimize the aggregate tax cost of the transaction and share the tax savings between them.

To illustrate this bilateral approach to tax planning, consider the case of Firm M and key employee Mr. G, and their negotiation of a new employment contract. For simplicity's sake, the case disregards payroll tax costs and focuses on the income tax consequences of the prospective contract. Firm M and Mr. G have respective marginal income tax rates of 35 percent and 30 percent. Salary payments are fully deductible to the firm in computing taxable income and fully taxable to Mr. G.

Initial Compensation Package.   Firm M and Mr. G begin their negotiation by analyzing the consequences of a $120,000 salary payment. The firm's after-tax cost of the $120,000 compensation would be $78,000:

Cash flows:	
Compensation (salary)	$(120,000)
Income tax savings	
($120,000 × 35%)	42,000
Net cash flow	$ (78,000)

Mr. G's after-tax compensation would be $84,000:

Cash flows:	
Compensation (salary)	$ 120,000
Income tax cost	
($120,000 × 30%)	(36,000)
Net cash flow	$ 84,000

Firm M knows that Mr. G spends $10,000 each year to pay the premiums on his family's health insurance policy. Mr. G can't deduct this expense in computing taxable income; therefore, the premium payments don't result in any tax savings to him.[7] After this expense, Mr. G's after-tax cash flow is only $74,000:

Mr. G's Net Cash Flow	
Cash flows:	
Compensation (salary)	$ 120,000
Income tax cost	
($120,000 × 30%)	(36,000)
Insurance premium	(10,000)
Net cash flow	$ 74,000

---

[7]The tax consequences of an individual's personal expenses are discussed in Chapter 16.

Both parties know that if Firm M would purchase comparable health insurance for Mr. G as part of a group plan, the firm's premium cost would be only $5,000. Moreover, this premium payment would be fully deductible by the firm. The compensatory fringe benefit (employer-provided health insurance) would be nontaxable to Mr. G.[8] Based on this mutual knowledge, the parties agree to a final compensation package.

Final Compensation Package.   Firm M agrees to pay Mr. G a $110,000 salary and provide health insurance coverage under its group plan. The firm's after-tax cost of this compensation package is $74,750.

Cash flows:	
Compensation (salary)	$(110,000)
Insurance premium	(5,000)
Income tax savings	
($115,000 × 35%)	40,250
Net cash flow	$ (74,750)

Based on this compensation package, Mr. G's after-tax cash flow is $77,000:

Cash flows:	
Compensation (salary)	$110,000
Income tax cost	
($110,000 × 30%)	(33,000)
Insurance premium	–0–
Mr. G's after-tax cash	$ 77,000

By considering the tax consequences to both parties, Firm M and Mr. G modified the initial compensation package to improve both their after-tax positions. Specifically, Firm M decreased the after-tax cost of employing Mr. G by $3,250, and Mr. G increased his after-tax cash by $3,000.

The Arm's-Length Presumption.   An important presumption about market transactions is that the parties to the transaction are negotiating at arm's length. In other words, each party is dealing in its own economic self-interest, trying to obtain the most advantageous terms possible from the other party. In an **arm's-length transaction,** the parties' consideration of the mutual tax consequences is just one aspect of their bargaining strategy. If one party suggests a modification to the transaction that directly reduces its own tax cost, the other party may not agree unless it can indirectly capture some part of the tax savings for itself. To do so, the other party might demand more favorable terms with respect to another aspect of the transaction.

This *quid pro quo* is exemplified in the employment contract between Firm M and Mr. G. The fact that part of Mr. G's final compensation package consists of a nontaxable fringe benefit (the insurance coverage) results in a direct tax savings to him. However,

---

[8]Nontaxable employee fringe benefits are discussed in Chapter 14.

the firm captures part of this tax savings by paying less salary to Mr. G. In the final analysis, Firm M agreed to a compensation package that includes the fringe benefit because the package minimizes the firm's after-tax cost, not because the package saves income tax for Mr. G.

The only interested party worse off because of the final terms of the employment contract is the federal government. The inclusion of a nontaxable fringe benefit in the compensation package costs the Treasury $1,250 in revenue.

Tax Cost to Government	*Initial Package*	*Final Package*	*Increase (Decrease) in Government Revenue*
Firm M's tax savings	$42,000	$40,250	$ 1,750
Mr. G's tax cost	36,000	33,000	(3,000)
Net decrease in government revenue			$(1,250)

In spite of potential revenue loss, the IRS (and state and local tax authorities) generally accept the tax consequences of arm's-length transactions because those consequences reflect economic reality. The IRS understands that parties consummate transactions to further their respective financial objectives and that any favorable tax outcomes are legitimate by-products of these objectives.

Public Market Transactions.   Some business transactions occur in **public markets** that are too large, too impersonal, or too regulated to allow parties to communicate privately and to customize their transactions. Firms entering such markets must accept the terms dictated by the market. For instance, if a firm decides to invest excess working capital in short-term U.S. government bonds, it must purchase the bonds through a federal bank for the prevailing market price. The firm can't negotiate with the selling party (the government) to buy the bonds at a different price. Similarly, the financial characteristics of the bonds such as the interest rate and maturity date are nonnegotiable.

Firms have limited flexibility in tailoring public market transactions to control the tax results. Because buyers and sellers are not involved in direct negotiation, they can't develop a bilateral strategy to improve their joint tax consequences. Any tax planning that does occur must be one-sided.

Objective 6
Distinguish between an arm's-length transaction and a related party transaction.

Fictitious Markets: Related Party Transactions.   The arm's-length presumption is unreliable for transactions between related parties, such as family members or subsidiary corporations owned by the same controlling parent corporation. **Related party transactions** lack the economic tension characteristic of transactions between unrelated parties. In commercial dealings, unrelated parties typically have competing objectives; related parties may have compatible objectives or even share a single objective. Unrelated parties are motivated by self-interest to drive the hardest possible bargain; related parties may be eager to accommodate each other in their negotiations.

If related parties are not dealing at arm's length, no true market exists, and any transaction between them may not reflect economic reality. In this fictitious market setting, related parties are unconstrained by many of the financial considerations that normally drive arm's-length transactions. As a result, related parties enjoy significant flexibility in controlling the tax consequences of their transactions. Taxing jurisdictions are well aware that related party transactions lack arm's-length rigor and regard the tax consequences with suspicion. If the jurisdiction concludes that a transaction is bogus, it may disallow any favorable tax outcome claimed by the related parties.

Let's examine a related party transaction with a favorable tax outcome.

> ***Related Party Transaction.*** Mr. and Mrs. B are the owners of a business the income from which is taxed at a marginal rate of 36 percent. The couple has a 17-year-old son who is interested in taking over the business at some future date. Mr. and Mrs. B decide to give their son some experience by hiring him as a full-time employee. If Mr. and Mrs. B pay their son a $20,000 annual salary, this deductible payment saves them $7,200 a year in federal income tax.[9] Because the son has so little taxable income, his marginal tax rate is only 15 percent. Consequently, his tax cost of the salary is only $3,000. As a result of this related party transaction, the B family saves $4,200 of income tax.

While the federal tax laws don't explicitly prohibit Mr. and Mrs. B from deducting the salary payment to their son, the IRS will carefully scrutinize the employment transaction if and when it audits the parents' tax return. The familial relationship of the transacting parties strongly suggests that the salary was not negotiated at arm's length. If the IRS examines all the relevant facts, it may discover that the son did not actually perform any valuable services whatsoever for his parents' business. In this extreme case, the employment transaction had no purpose other than tax avoidance, and the IRS may recast the $20,000 payment from parents to child as a gift.[10] Consequently, Mr. and Mrs. B lose their $20,000 tax deduction, the son has no salary income, and the family's anticipated income tax savings disappear.

On the other hand, the relevant facts may indicate that the son is an authentic business employee and that his salary is comparable to the salary an unrelated person could have negotiated at arm's length. In this case, the IRS should respect the transaction and allow the favorable tax consequences of the $20,000 salary payment to stand. Whatever the outcome, the lesson from this example should be clear. Whenever related parties transact, they must be aware that the tax authorities may challenge the validity of the transaction. If the related parties can't offer convincing evidence that the terms of the transaction approximate an arm's-length standard, they may forfeit control of the tax consequences altogether.

Conclusion

The estimation of cash flows and the calculation of the net present value of those cash flows are central to the business decision-making process. A manager's ability to determine after-tax cash flows depends on his or her skill in recognizing and quantifying the tax implications of the transaction under consideration. Managers must be familiar with current tax law and must be prepared to make informed assumptions concerning how that law might change in future periods. Managers involved in business negotiations

---

[9]Federal payroll taxes are not an issue in this example because such taxes are not levied on wages paid by parents to their children under the age of 18. See §3121(b)(3)(A).

[10]When a related party transaction is a blatant tax avoidance scheme, the IRS may impose monetary penalties on the taxpayers. See the discussion of taxpayer negligence and fraud in Chapter 17.

should evaluate the tax implications for all parties to the transaction in formulating an optimal tax strategy.

While managers should view all business taxes as controllable costs, they should understand that the transaction with the least tax cost may not be the transaction that maximizes net present value. Business transactions consist of any number of interrelated tax and nontax variables, all of which must be considered in the decision-making process. In the next chapter, we will concentrate on strategies that firms use to manipulate the income tax variable. But as we focus on tax planning ideas, remember the basic lesson of this chapter: profits, costs, and cash flows can't be analyzed in a meaningful way until they are stated as after-tax numbers.

Key Terms

Annuity 51	Private letter ruling 58
Arm's-length transaction 62	Private market 60
Burden of proof 57	Public market 63
Deduction 54	Related party transaction 63
Discount rate 50	Tax cost 53
Market 60	Tax savings 54
Net cash flow 50	Time value of money 50
Net present value (NPV) 50	

Questions and Problems for Discussion

1. Does the net present value of a stream of future cash flows increase or decrease as the discount rate increases?
2. Explain the relationship between the financial risk associated with a stream of future cash flows and the discount rate used in the computation of net present value.
3. Does the after-tax cost of a deductible expense increase or decrease as the taxpayer's marginal income tax rate increases?
4. Firm A and Firm Z are in the same line of business. Both firms considered spending $10,000 in the current year for the exact same business reason. The expense would be a current deduction for both firms. Firm A decided that the expenditure was worthwhile and spent the money but Firm Z rejected the expenditure. Can you provide a tax reason to explain these apparently inconsistent decisions?
5. In what circumstance is the before-tax cost of an expenditure equal to its after-tax cost?
6. Corporation N must decide between two business opportunities that will generate different cash flows over a five-year period. Describe the

circumstances in which the tax cost of the opportunities is a neutral factor in the corporation's decision-making process.
7. Which assumption about the tax consequences of a future transaction is subject to a higher degree of tax law uncertainty: an assumption based on a provision that has been in the Internal Revenue Code for 25 years or an assumption based on a provision that Congress added to the Code two years ago?
8. Which type of tax law provision should be more stable and subject to less uncertainty as to its future application: a provision relating to the proper measurement of taxable income or a provision designed to encourage individual taxpayers to engage in a certain economic behavior?
9. In the U.S. system of criminal justice, a person is innocent until proven guilty. Does this general rule apply to disputes between a taxpayer and the IRS?
10. Identify two reasons why a firm's actual marginal tax rate for a year could differ from the projected marginal tax rate for that year.

11. Firm F is negotiating to purchase a multimillion dollar computer system from the manufacturer. Under applicable state law, Firm F is exempt from sales tax on the purchase. When the manufacturer discovered this fact, it increased its selling price for the system by $25,000. Is this transaction taking place in a private or a public market?

12. Corporation P owns 85 percent of the outstanding stock of Corporation R. During the current year, employees of Corporation R performed extensive management services for Corporation P. In return for the services, Corporation P paid a $250,000 fee to Corporation R, which Corporation P reported as a deductible business expense.
    a. Is the consulting arrangement between the two corporations an arm's-length transaction?
    b. If the IRS challenges the validity of Corporation P's deduction, what facts might the corporation offer as evidence of the validity of the payment?

Application Problems

1. Using the present value tables included in Appendix A and B, compute the net present value of each of the following cash flows:
    a. A payment of $89,000 to be received at the end of six years. The discount rate is 12 percent.
    b. An annual payment of $3,400 to be received at the end of each of the next 15 years. The discount rate is 9 percent.
    c. A 10-year annuity of $5,000 per annum. The first $5,000 payment is due immediately. The discount rate is 6 percent.
    d. An annual payment of $20,000 to be received at the end of years 1 through 5 followed by an annual payment of $13,000 to be received at the end of years 6 through 10. The discount rate is 15 percent.

2. Taxpayer D has $100,000 in an investment paying 12 percent interest per annum. Each year D has $1,500 of expenses relating to this investment. Compute D's annual net cash flow from the investment assuming the following:
    a. D's marginal income tax rate is 15 percent, and the annual expense is deductible.
    b. D's marginal income tax rate is 35 percent, and the annual expense is deductible.
    c. D's marginal income tax rate is 20 percent, and the annual expense is not deductible.
    d. D's marginal income tax rate is 35 percent, and only $1,000 of the annual expense is deductible.

3. Firm E must choose between two alternative business transactions. Transaction 1 requires a cash outlay of $9,000; this expense would be nondeductible in the computation of the firm's taxable income. Transaction 2 requires a cash outlay of $13,500, all of which would be a deductible expense. Determine which transaction has the lesser after-tax cost, assuming:
    a. Firm E's marginal tax rate is 20 percent.
    b. Firm E's marginal tax rate is 40 percent.

4. Firm Q is about to engage in a transaction with the following cash flows over a three-year period:

	Year 1	Year 2	Year 3
Revenue received	$10,000	$12,500	$18,000
Deductible expenses	(3,400)	(5,000)	(7,000)
Nondeductible expenses	(800)	(1,100)	–0–

If the firm's marginal tax rate over the three-year period is 35 percent and its discount rate is 10 percent, compute the net present value of the transaction.

5. Corporation ABC has invested in a project that will generate $60,000 of annual after-tax cash flow in years 1 and 2 and $40,000 of annual after-tax cash flow in years 3, 4, and 5. Compute the net present value of these cash flows assuming:
    a. Corporation ABC uses a 7 percent discount rate.
    b. Corporation ABC uses a 10 percent discount rate.
    c. Corporation ABC uses a 12 percent discount rate.

6. Company DL must choose between two business opportunities. Opportunity 1 will generate $14,000

of before-tax cash in years 1 through 4. The annual tax cost of Opportunity 1 is $2,500 in years 1 and 2 and $1,800 in years 3 and 4. Opportunity 2 will generate $14,000 of before-tax cash in year 1, $20,000 of before-tax cash in years 2 and 3, and $10,000 cash in year 4. The annual tax cost of Opportunity 2 is $4,000 in years 1 through 4. Based on these facts, which opportunity should Company DL choose if the company uses a 10 percent discount rate to compute net present value?

7. M&B Inc. must choose between two business opportunities. Opportunity 1 will generate an $8,000 deductible loss in year 1, $5,000 of taxable income in year 2, and $20,000 of taxable income in year 3. Opportunity 2 will generate $5,000 of taxable income in years 1 through 3. The income and loss reflect before-tax cash inflow and outflow. M&B uses a 12 percent discount rate to compute net present value and has a 39 percent marginal tax rate over the three-year period.

   a. Based on these facts, which opportunity should the corporation choose?

   b. Would your answer change if the corporation's marginal tax rate over the three-year period is 15 percent?

   c. Would your answer change if the corporation's marginal tax rate is 39 percent in year 1 but only 15 percent in years 2 and 3?

Issue Recognition Problems

Identify the tax issue or issues suggested by the following situations and state each issue in the form of a question.

1. Mr. and Mrs. J's taxable income from their business has been very stable for the last five years, and their average federal income tax rate for those years has ranged between 22 and 24 percent. Because of a boom in the local economy, the couple estimates that their business will generate an additional $100,000 of taxable income for the next year. In making their cash flow projections, the couple estimates that their federal income tax cost with respect to this incremental income will be $24,000.

2. Firm V must choose between two alternative investment opportunities. Based on current tax law, the firm projects that the net present value of Opportunity 1 is significantly less than the net present value of Opportunity 2. The provisions in the tax law governing the tax consequences of Opportunity 1 have been stable for many years. In contrast, the provisions governing the tax consequences of Opportunity 2 are extremely complicated and have been modified by Congress several times during the last five years.

3. Company WB is evaluating a business opportunity with very uncertain tax consequences. If the company takes a conservative approach by assuming the least beneficial tax consequences, the tax cost of the transaction is $95,000. If the company takes an aggressive approach by assuming the most beneficial tax consequences, the tax cost of the transaction is only $86,000. If the company takes the aggressive approach, the IRS will certainly challenge the approach on audit.

4. Refer to the facts in Problem 3. Company WB is considering engaging a CPA to prepare a request for a private letter ruling from the IRS concerning the tax consequences of the business opportunity.

5. Ms. O is the chief financial officer for Firm XYZ. The firm's marketing department has requested approval for an $80,000 cash expenditure. The memo from the marketing department points out that the expenditure would be fully deductible in the current year. Therefore, the marketing department concludes that Ms. O would be minimizing Firm XYZ's after-tax cost by approving this expenditure.

6. Earlier in the current year, Mrs. G, a business manager for Company RW, evaluated a prospective business opportunity that could generate $20,000 of additional taxable income for the company. Mrs. G determined that the company's marginal tax rate on this income was 31 percent. Later in the year, a different manager evaluated another opportunity that could generate $100,000 of additional taxable income. This manager referred to Mrs. G's earlier evaluation and used the same 31 percent marginal rate in his analysis of after-tax cash flows.

Tax Planning Case

Firm B wants to hire Mrs. X to manage its advertising department. The firm offered Mrs. X a three-year employment contract under which it will pay her an $80,000 annual salary in years 1, 2, and 3. Mrs. X projects that her salary will be taxed at a 25 percent marginal rate in year 1 and a 40 percent rate in years 2 and 3. Firm B's marginal tax rate for the three-year period is 34 percent.

1. Assuming an 8 percent discount rate for both Firm B and Mrs. X, compute the net present value of (*a*) Mrs. X's after-tax cash flow from the employment contract and (*b*) Firm B's after-tax cost of the employment contract.

2. To reduce the tax cost with respect to her employment contract, Mrs. X requests that the salary payment for year 1 be increased to $140,000 and the salary payments for years 2 and 3 be reduced to $50,000. How would this revision in the timing of the payments change your net present value computations?

3. Firm B responds to Mrs. X's request with a counter-proposal. The firm will pay her $140,000 in year 1 but only $45,000 in years 2 and 3. Compute the net present value of Firm B's after-tax cost under this proposal. From the firm's perspective, is this proposal superior to its original offer ($80,000 annually for three years)?

4. Should Mrs. X accept the original offer or the counter-proposal? Support your conclusion with a comparison of the net present value of each offer.

4

Basic Maxims of Income Tax Planning

Learning Objectives

After studying this chapter, you should be able to:

1. Differentiate between the concepts of tax avoidance and tax evasion.
2. List the four variables that interact to determine the tax consequences of a business transaction.
3. Explain why an income shift or a deduction shift from one entity to another can improve after-tax cash flows.
4. Explain how the assignment of income doctrine constrains income-shifting strategies.
5. Identify the circumstances in which a strategy that defers tax liability may not improve the net present value of a transaction.
6. Explain why the distinction between ordinary income and capital gain is important in the tax planning process.
7. Distinguish between an explicit tax and an implicit tax.
8. Summarize the four basic maxims that firms use to develop tax planning strategies.
9. Describe the three tax law doctrines that the IRS can use to challenge the favorable outcome of a tax planning strategy.

In the preceding chapter, we learned that the concept of net present value plays a key role in the business decision-making process and that the computation of net present value incorporates tax costs as cash outflows and tax savings as cash inflows. With these lessons in mind, we begin Chapter 4 by defining **tax planning** as the structuring of transactions to reduce tax costs or increase tax savings to maximize the net present value of the transaction.

Why does the structure of a business transaction matter in the tax planning process? Specifically, what are the variables that determine the tax outcome of the transaction? These questions are addressed in the first section of the chapter. Our study of the important variables leads to the development of *income tax planning maxims*—basic principles that are the foundation for many specific planning techniques discussed in subsequent chapters. We will analyze how these maxims improve the tax outcomes of business transactions. We will also identify the major limitations on their use in the planning process. In the final section of the chapter, we will consider how managers use the maxims to develop tax strategies for their firms and why managers must be cognizant of how the Internal Revenue Service (IRS) may react to their strategies.

Tax Avoidance—Not Evasion

Objective 1
Differentiate between the concepts of tax avoidance and tax evasion.

Our discussion in this and subsequent chapters is restricted to tax planning ideas that are entirely legal. Legitimate means of reducing taxes are described as **tax avoidance;** illegal means to the same end constitute **tax evasion.** Tax evasion is a federal crime—a felony punishable by severe monetary fines and imprisonment.[1] The qualitative difference between avoidance and evasion is in the eye of the beholder. Many aggressive tax plans involve major questions of judgment; taxpayers eager to implement these plans run the risk that the IRS will conclude that the plan crosses the line between a good faith effort to reduce tax and a willful attempt to defraud the U.S. government. Business managers should always exercise caution and consult a tax professional before engaging in any transaction with profound tax consequences.

Even if tax avoidance strategies are legal, are they ethical? In 1947, federal judge Learned Hand answered this question in the following way:

> Over and over again courts have said that there is nothing sinister in so arranging one's affairs as to keep taxes as low as possible. Everybody does so, rich or poor; and all do right, for nobody owes any public duty to pay more than the law demands: taxes are enforced exactions, not voluntary contributions. To demand more in the name of morals is mere cant.[2]

This spirited defense of the tax planning process makes the point that every person has the civic responsibility of paying the legally required tax and not a penny more. Business managers should be reassured that when they engage in effective tax planning, they are engaging in proper behavior from the perspective of their firm, their government, and society.

What Makes Income Tax Planning Possible?

The federal income tax system applies to every entity conducting a business activity within the United States. If the tax law applied uniformly to every commercial transaction by every entity in every time period, it would be neutral and therefore irrelevant in the business decision-making process. However, as we will observe over and over again, the income tax is anything but neutral with respect to business transactions. The tax system is replete with rules affecting only particular transactions, entities, or time periods. And in every case in which the law applies differentially with respect to a certain dollar of business profit or cost, a planning opportunity is born.

Objective 2
List the four variables that interact to determine the tax consequences of a business transaction.

The tax consequences of a business transaction depend on the interaction of four variables common to all transactions:

1. The entity variable: Which entity undertakes the transaction?
2. The time period variable: During which tax year or years does the transaction occur?
3. The jurisdiction variable: In which taxing jurisdiction does the transaction occur?

---

[1] The civil and criminal penalties for tax evasion are discussed in detail in Chapter 17.
[2] *Commissioner* v. *Newman*, 159 F.2d 848, 850 (CA-2, 1947).

4. The character variable: What is the tax character of the income from the transaction?

We will focus on each variable in turn to ascertain why the variable matters and how it can be manipulated to change the tax outcome of the transaction.

The Entity Variable

In the federal tax system, individuals and corporations are the two primary entities that pay tax on income generated by their business activities. While trusts and estates are also taxable entities, they don't routinely engage in the active conduct of a trade or business. For this reason, this text doesn't address the specialized rules governing the income taxation of trusts and estates. Businesses certainly can be conducted as partnerships or S corporations, but these organizational forms are not taxable entities. Income generated by a partnership or S corporation is taxed to the partners or shareholders. The operation of partnerships and S corporations is examined in detail in Chapter 9.

For the most part, the provisions in the Internal Revenue Code governing the computation of taxable business income apply uniformly across organizational forms.[3] In other words, the *amount of taxable income* generated by a business activity does not depend on the type of entity conducting the business; the tax law is essentially neutral across entities with respect to the tax base. So why do the tax consequences of business transactions depend on which entity undertakes the transaction? The answer lies in the potential difference between applicable *tax rates*.

Section 1 of the Internal Revenue Code provides the tax rate structure for individuals, which currently consists of five income brackets with rates ranging from 15 percent to 39.6 percent. Section 11 provides a completely different rate structure for corporations; the corporate rates range from 15 percent to 39 percent. (The current rates for both individuals and corporations are printed on the inside of the front cover of the text.) Both the individual and corporate rate structures are progressive, so that the tax on a given dollar of business income depends on the marginal tax rate of the entity earning that dollar.[4] An entity facing a lower marginal rate will pay less tax on a dollar of income than an entity facing a higher marginal rate. Consequently, the after-tax value of the dollar is greater to the low-tax entity than to the high-tax entity.

Tax Rate Differential.   Entity H has a 39 percent marginal tax rate while Entity L has a 15 percent marginal tax rate. Both receive $100 cash that represents taxable income. The after-tax cash available to each entity is computed as follows:

	Entity H	*Entity L*
Cash received	$100	$100
Tax cost ($100 income × marginal rate)	(39)	(15)
After-tax cash	$ 61	$ 85

---

[3]The few special provisions applying only to businesses operated in the corporate form are discussed in Chapter 10.

[4]A complete discussion of the intricacies of the corporate rate structure is included in Chapter 10.

A comparison of the tax consequences to Entities H and L suggests our first income tax planning maxim: *Tax costs decrease (and cash flows increase) when income is generated by an entity subject to a low tax rate.*

This maxim is especially important when entrepreneurs are starting a new venture and must decide which organizational form to adopt. The choice of organizational form determines whether the business income will be subject to the individual tax rates or the corporate tax rates. Chapter 11 is devoted exclusively to an in-depth discussion of the tax implications of the choice of organizational form for new businesses.

Income Shifting

Objective 3
Explain why an income shift or a deduction shift from one entity to another can improve after-tax cash flows.

The first maxim implies that tax on the income from an established business activity can be reduced if that income is shifted from an entity with a high tax rate to an entity with a low tax rate. Assume that in the previous example, Entity H could redirect its $100 cash receipt (and the income represented by the cash) to Entity L.

> **Income Shift.** Entity H and Entity L both expect to receive $100 cash that represents taxable income. Entity H arranges to shift its $100 to Entity L. The after-tax cash available to each entity is computed as follows:
>
> | | *Entity H* | *Entity L* |
> | -- | ---------- | ---------- |
> | Cash received | $-0- | $200 |
> | Tax cost (taxable income × marginal rate) | -0- | (30) |
> | After-tax cash | -0- | $170 |

This income shift reduces the tax on the shifted $100 from $39 to $15 and increases the after-tax cash from $61 to $85. However, that after-tax cash now belongs to Entity L rather than to Entity H. From Entity H's perspective, the income shift *reduces* its after-tax cash flow from $61 to zero. Presuming that Entity H makes rational business decisions, this transaction makes sense only if Entity H controls, enjoys, or benefits from the transferred cash in some roundabout manner. One possible explanation is that Entity L is a corporation and Entity H is its sole shareholder. In such case, any cash transferred from Shareholder H to Corporation L increases the value of Corporation L's stock and still belongs indirectly to Shareholder H. Although Shareholder H holds less cash, the entity's wealth (which includes the value of Corporation L stock) increases by the $24 tax savings from the income shift.

Deduction Shifting

Entities with different marginal rates can save tax not only by shifting items of income between them but also by shifting deductible expenses. To illustrate a deduction shift, let's use Entities H and L again.

> **Deduction Shift.** Entity L expects to pay an $80 expense that is fully deductible in computing taxable income. Because Entity L is in a 15 percent marginal tax bracket, the $80 deduction would save $12 in tax and the after-tax cost of the payment is $68.

Cash expended by Entity L	$(80)
Tax savings ($80 deduction × 15%)	12
After-tax cost	$(68)

If Entity H could make the $80 payment on behalf of Entity L and claim the $80 deduction on its own tax return, the tax savings would increase to $31 and the after-tax cost would decrease to $49:

Cash expended by Entity H	$(80)
Tax savings ($80 deduction × 39%)	31
After-tax cost	$(49)

Because the deduction is shifted from the entity with the low tax rate to the entity with the high tax rate, the cash outflow with respect to the business expense decreases by $19. But the shift actually increases Entity H's cash outflow by $49. Entity H would never agree to this strategy unless it derives some indirect economic benefit from the tax savings.

Constraints on Income Shifting

Because income-shifting transactions involve transfers of value from one taxpayer to another, they usually occur between related parties. After the income shift, the parties in the aggregate are financially better off by the tax savings from the transaction. Congress has long recognized that income-shifting techniques lose revenue for the Treasury. Many effective techniques that were once widely used by related parties have been abolished by legislation; in subsequent chapters, we will consider a number of powerful statutory restrictions on income shifting. The IRS is vigilant in policing related party transactions involving beneficial income shifts. If a transaction serves no genuine purpose besides tax avoidance, the IRS may disallow the tax consequences intended by the parties.

Objective 4
Explain how the assignment of income doctrine constrains income-shifting strategies.

The Assignment of Income Doctrine.   The federal courts have consistently held that our income tax system cannot tolerate artificial shifts of income from one taxpayer to another. Almost 70 years ago, the Supreme Court decided that income must be taxed to the person who earns it, even if another person has a legal right to the wealth represented by the income.[5] Thus, a business owner who receives a $10,000 check in payment for services rendered to a customer can't avoid reporting $10,000 of income by simply endorsing the check over to his daughter. In the picturesque language of the Court, the tax law must disregard arrangements "by which the fruits are attributed to a different tree from that on which they grew."

The Supreme Court elaborated on this theme in the case of a father who detached negotiable interest coupons from corporate bonds and gave the coupons to his son as a

---

[5]*Lucas* v. *Earl*, 281 U.S. 111 (1930).

gift.[6] When the coupons matured, the son collected the interest and reported it as income on his own tax return. The Court concluded that the interest income was taxable to the father because he continued to own the underlying asset (the bonds) that created the right to the interest payments. The holdings in these two cases have melded into the **assignment of income doctrine:** income must be taxed to the entity that renders the service or owns the capital with respect to which the income is paid. Over the years, the IRS has frustrated many creative income-shifting schemes by invoking this simple, but potent, doctrine.

The Time Period Variable

Because both federal and state income taxes are imposed on an annual basis, the tax cost or savings with respect to a transaction depends on the year in which the transaction occurs. In Chapter 3, we learned that these costs and savings are a function of the firm's marginal tax rate. If that rate changes from one taxable year to the next, the firm's tax costs and savings fluctuate accordingly. We've also discussed the fact that the technical details of the federal and state income tax systems change periodically. A tax benefit available in one year may disappear in the next. Conversely, a statutory restriction causing a tax problem this year may be lifted in the future. Managers must be aware of annual changes in the tax laws pertaining to their business operations. By controlling the timing of transactions, they may reduce the tax cost or increase the tax savings for their firm.

Even if marginal tax rates and the income tax laws were absolutely stable over time, the cash flows attributable to the tax consequences of business transactions would still vary with the time period during which the transaction occurs. This variation is attributable to the time value of money: in present value terms, a dollar of tax paid in the current year costs more than a dollar of tax paid in a later year. Conversely, a dollar of tax saved this year is worth more than a dollar of tax saved in some future period.

Consider a profitable transaction that takes place over two taxable years. During the first year, Firm R receives $120 of revenues and incurs $40 of deductible expenses. During the second year, Firm R receives $180 of revenues and incurs $80 of deductible expenses. The entire transaction generates $180 of taxable income: $80 in the first year and $100 in the second year. If Firm R faces a 35 percent marginal tax rate each year and uses a 12 percent discount rate, the net present value of the cash flows is $110.

Two-Year Transaction (Original Facts)	Year 1		Year 2	
Revenues		$120		$180
Deductible expenses		(40)		(80)
Income tax cost:				
Taxable income	$ 80		$100	
	.35		.35	
Tax cost		(28)		(35)
After-tax net cash flow		$ 52		$ 65

[6]*Helvering* v. *Horst*, 311 U.S. 112 (1940).

Present value of year 1 cash flow	$ 52
Present value of year 2 cash flow	
($65 × .893 discount factor)	58
Net present value	$110

Now assume that Firm R could restructure the transaction in a way that doesn't affect before-tax cash flows but allows the firm to report the entire $180 of taxable income (and pay the $63 tax thereon) in the second year.[7]

Two-Year Transaction (Deferred Tax Cost)	Year 1	Year 2
Revenues	$120	$180
Deductible expenses	(40)	(80)
Income tax cost:		
Taxable income	$-0-	$180
		.35
Tax cost	–0–	(63)
After-tax net cash flow	$ 80	$ 37
Present value of year 1 cash flow	$ 80	
Present value of year 2 cash flow		
($37 ×.893 discount factor)	33	
Net present value	$113	

The net present value of Firm R's restructured transaction is $3 more than the net present value of the original transaction. This entire increase is attributable to the deferral of a $28 tax from year 1 to year 2; the only difference in the transactions is one of timing. This observation suggests our second income tax planning maxim: *In present value terms, tax costs decrease (and cash flows increase) when a tax liability is deferred until a later taxable year.*

Income Deferral and Opportunity Costs

The restructured transaction in the preceding example represents an ideal situation in which a firm defers the payment of tax without altering the pattern of before-tax cash flows from the transaction. Realistically, firms can defer tax liability only by deferring the taxable income generated by the transaction, which may be difficult to do without affecting cash flows. A tax deferral strategy that changes the pattern of before-tax cash flows may not improve net present value. To illustrate this possibility, assume that Firm R avoids taxable income and tax liability in year 1 by delaying the receipt of $80 of revenues until year 2. Let's recompute the net present value of the transaction based on this assumption:

---

[7]For purposes of computing net present value, before-tax cash flows, tax costs, and tax savings in the same taxable year are assumed to occur at the same point in time.

Two-Year Transaction (Delayed Revenues)

	Year 1	Year 2
Revenues	$ 40	$260
Deductible expenses	(40)	(80)
Income tax cost:		
Taxable income	$-0-	$180
		.35
Tax cost	–0–	(63)
After-tax net cash flow	$-0-	$117
Present value of year 1 cash flow	$-0-	
Present value of year 2 cash flow		
($117 ×.893 discount factor)	104	
Net present value	$104	

In this transaction, the net present value is $6 *less* than that of the original transaction. While Firm R defers a $28 tax for one year, it also delays the receipt of $80 cash. The net result is that Firm R loses the use of $52 for one year at an opportunity cost of $6 ($52 − [$52 × .893 discount factor]).

Instead of delaying the receipt of revenues, what if Firm R could defer taxable income by paying all the expenses relating to the transaction in year 1?

Two-Year Transaction (Accelerated Expenses)

	Year 1	Year 2
Revenues	$120	$180
Deductible expenses	(120)	–0–
Income tax cost:		
Taxable income	$-0-	$180
		.35
Tax cost	–0–	(63)
After-tax net cash flow	$-0-	$117
Present value of year 1 cash flow	$-0-	
Present value of year 2 cash flow		
($117 ×.893 discount factor)	104	
Net present value	$104	

This alternative method for deferring taxable income has exactly the same negative effect on net present value. By deferring a tax of $24 and accelerating the payment of $80 of expenses, Firm R deprives itself of the use of $52 for one year at an opportunity cost of $6. In both transactions, the advantage of tax deferral is overwhelmed by a disadvantageous change in before-tax cash flows. Consequently, we can conclude that our second tax planning maxim holds true only when a tax payment can be deferred independently of before-tax cash flows or when the value of the deferral exceeds any opportunity cost of a coinciding change in before-tax cash flows.

Income Deferral and Rate Changes

Objective 5
Identify the circumstances in which a strategy that defers tax liability may not improve the net present value of a transaction.

The deferral of taxable income into future years creates uncertainty as to the marginal rate that will eventually apply to that income. The value of the deferral could be severely undermined if Congress were to increase the statutory rates or if the firm were to move unexpectedly into a higher tax bracket. The risk that deferred income will be taxed at a higher rate escalates with the length of the deferral period. To illustrate this problem, assume that Firm N, which is in a 35 percent marginal tax bracket, generates $30,000 of profit on a transaction. The firm has the choice of reporting the entire profit as current year income or reporting the profit as income ratably over the next three years at no opportunity cost. The firm implements the deferral strategy based on the following projection (which uses a 9 percent discount rate):

Projected Net Present Value (NPV) of Tax Costs				
	Year 1	*Year 2*	*Year 3*	*Year 4*
Without deferral:				
Taxable income	$30,000	$ –0–	$ –0–	$ –0–
Tax cost at 35%	$10,500	$ –0–	$ –0–	$ –0–
NPV of tax costs	$10,500			
With deferral:				
Taxable income	$ –0–	$10,000	$10,000	$10,000
Tax cost at 35%	$ –0–	$ 3,500	$ 3,500	$ 3,500
Discount factors		.917	.842	.772
		$ 3,210	$ 2,947	$ 2,702
NPV of tax costs	$ 8,859			

Now assume that Firm N's marginal tax rate in years 2 through 4 jumps to 45 percent because of an unforeseen change in the tax law. As a result, the tax costs in years 2 through 4 are much higher than projected:

Actual Net Present Value (NPV) of Tax Costs				
	Year 1	*Year 2*	*Year 3*	*Year 4*
Taxable income	$ –0–	$10,000	$10,000	$10,000
Tax cost at 45%	$ –0–	$ 4,500	$ 4,500	$ 4,500
Discount factors		.917	.842	.772
		$ 4,127	$ 3,789	$ 3,474
NPV of tax costs	$11,390			

Because the value of deferring the tax cost is insufficient to compensate for the higher rate at which the deferred income is actually taxed, Firm N's decision to defer the income *increased* the tax cost of the transaction by $890 in present value terms:

Actual NPV of tax costs	$11,390
NPV of tax cost without deferral	(10,500)
	$ 890

The Jurisdiction Variable

Every domestic business activity is subject to the taxing jurisdiction of the federal government. Therefore, the geographic location of a firm within the United States is essentially a neutral factor in the computation of that firm's federal income tax liability. However, most states and the District of Columbia also tax business income. Because of the structural differences in state tax systems, a firm's aggregate income tax liability (federal, state, and local) is very much a function of the jurisdictions in which it conducts business.

Consider two domestic firms that each receive $5,000 cash, all of which is taxable income. Firm Y operates in State Y, which imposes a flat 4 percent tax on business income. Firm Z operates in State Z, which imposes a flat 10 percent tax on business income. For federal purposes, state income tax payments are deductible in the computation of taxable income.[8] Both firms face a 39 percent federal tax rate. Under these facts, Firms Y and Z have the following after-tax cash flows:

Different State Jurisdictions		
	Firm Y	*Firm Z*
Before-tax cash/income	$ 5,000	$ 5,000
State income tax cost	(200)	(500)
Federal taxable income	$ 4,800	$ 4,500
Federal tax cost		
(Taxable income × 39%)	(1,872)	(1,755)
After-tax cash flow	$ 2,928	$ 2,745

A comparison of these after-tax cash flows gives us our third income tax planning maxim: *Tax costs decrease (and cash flows increase) when income is generated in a jurisdiction with a low tax rate.*

The comparison between the after-tax cash flows of Firms Y and Z would be more complex if these firms operate in any foreign country that taxes business income. Clearly, managers must be aware of the income tax laws of every locality in which their firm operates or plans to operate in the future. Managers should appreciate that they can often minimize the firm's total tax burden by conducting business activities in jurisdictions with favorable tax climates. The intricacies of tax planning in a multijurisdictional setting are the subject of Chapter 12.

---

[8] See §164(a).

The Character Variable

Objective 6
Explain why the distinction between ordinary income and capital gain is important in the tax planning process.

The fourth variable that determines the tax consequences of business transactions is the tax character of the income generated by the transaction. The tax character of any item of income is determined strictly by law; it is not intuitive and may bear no relationship to any financial or economic attribute of the income. In addition, the character of income and the ramifications of that characterization can change with each new tax bill passed by Congress or each new regulation published by the Treasury. Because the character variable is so artificial, it is the hardest one to discuss in a generalized manner.

Every item of income is ultimately characterized for tax purposes as either **ordinary income** or **capital gain.** The income generated by a firm's routine sales of goods or services to customers or clients is ordinary income. The yield on invested capital, such as interest, dividends, and rents, is also ordinary in character. As the label implies, ordinary income is taxed at the regular individual or corporate rates. The sale or exchange of certain types of property, referred to as capital assets, gives rise to capital gain. The term *capital asset* is defined in detail in Chapter 7. Historically, capital gain has enjoyed favorable treatment under the federal tax law, usually in the form of a preferential tax rate. Currently, individuals (but not corporations) pay tax on their capital gains at a 28, 25, 20, or 10 percent rate.[9]

Many items of ordinary income and capital gain have additional characteristics that in some way affect the tax liability on the income. For instance, the ordinary income that a U.S. firm generates on the sale of its products in the international market is characterized as either U.S. source income or foreign source income. As we will discuss in Chapter 12, this special characterization is crucial in determining how much federal income tax the firm must pay on its ordinary income.

To demonstrate the effect of the character variable, let's compare the cash flow consequences of three different items of income received by Mr. T, who is in the highest (39.6 percent) regular tax bracket. Each item consists of $1,000 cash. The first item is ordinary income with no other special characteristic; the second item is capital gain eligible for the 20 percent rate; and the third item is interest on a bond issued by the City of New York. While interest generically is ordinary income, municipal bond interest has a very special characteristic—it is exempt from federal income tax. In other words, municipal bond interest is taxed at a preferential rate of zero.

Cash Flow and Preferential Rates

	Ordinary Income	Capital Gain	Tax-Exempt Income
Before-tax cash/income	$1,000	$1,000	$1,000
Tax cost	(396)	(200)	–0–
After-tax cash flow	$ 604	$ 800	$1,000

The fact that the character of income determines whether the income is taxed at the regular rate or at a special rate suggests our fourth tax planning maxim: *Tax costs*

---

[9]The preferential rates apply only to long-term capital gains. Chapter 15 includes a detailed discussion of the individual capital gains rates.

decrease (and cash flows increase) when income is taxed at a preferential rate because of its character.

Determining the Value of Preferential Rates

The value of a preferential rate to a particular taxpayer can be quantified only by reference to that taxpayer's regular marginal rate. In the above example, the $196 difference between the after-tax cash flow from the ordinary income and the capital gain is due to the 19.6 percentage point spread between Mr. T's regular tax rate of 39.6 percent and the 20 percent preferential rate on the capital gain. If Mr. T's marginal rate on ordinary income is only 31 percent, the 11 percentage point spread between the regular rate and the preferential rate would result in only a $110 difference in after-tax cash flow.

Cash Flow and Preferential Rates	*Ordinary Income*	*Capital Gain*
Before-tax cash/income	$1,000	$1,000
Tax cost (31% regular rate)	(310)	(200)
After-tax cash flow	$ 690	$ 800

Constraints on Conversion

For many years, taxpayers and their advisors have heeded the fourth tax planning maxim by structuring transactions to result in capital gain rather than ordinary income. The more aggressive have devised ingenious techniques for converting the ordinary income potential inherent in a transaction to capital gain. In response, Congress has worked diligently to protect the integrity of the distinction between the two types of income. The Internal Revenue Code contains dozens of prohibitions against artificial conversions of ordinary income into capital gain, many of which we will examine in later chapters. In fact, the preferential treatment of capital gains is responsible for more complexity in the federal income tax system than any other feature. Why then does Congress persist in maintaining the capital gains preference? This intriguing tax policy question is considered in detail in Chapter 15.

Implicit Taxes

Objective 7
Distinguish between an explicit tax and an implicit tax.

A firm's decision to engage in a transaction generating income subject to a preferential rate should be based on the net present value of the transaction rather than the lure of the preferential rate. The tax cost of the transaction may not be the only cash flow affected by the tax-favored character of the income. Suppose that Firm P has $20,000 to invest in either a tax-exempt municipal bond or a corporate bond of identical risk.

The interest from the latter would be ordinary income, subject to the firm's 31 percent marginal tax rate. Let's make an initial assumption that both bonds pay 10 percent interest per annum. A comparison of the annual after-tax cash flows indicates that the municipal bond is the superior investment:

Taxable and Nontaxable Bonds: Equal Before-Tax Yields

	Corporate Bond Interest	*Municipal Bond Interest*
Before-tax cash/income	$2,000	$2,000
Tax cost	(620)	–0–
After-tax cash flow	$1,380	$2,000

The assumption that the two bonds offer identical before-tax yields is unrealistic. State and local governments consistently take advantage of the tax-exempt status of their debt obligations by offering lower interest rates than their competitors in the capital markets. They know that many investors will accept the lower rate because of the tax-favored status of the bonds. Let's change our example by assuming that the municipal bond would pay 8 percent interest on Firm P's $20,000 investment.

Taxable and Nontaxable Bonds: Different Before-Tax Yields

	Corporate Bond Interest	*Municipal Bond Interest*
Before-tax cash/income	$2,000	$1,600
Tax cost	(620)	–0–
After-tax cash flow	$1,380	$1,600

While the municipal bond is still a better investment than the corporate bond, the value of the preferential tax rate to Firm P has decreased because of the difference in the bonds' respective before-tax yields. While Firm P would pay no direct **explicit tax** on the interest from the municipal bond, it must accept a reduced market rate of return to take advantage of the tax preference. In the tax literature, this reduction is referred to as an **implicit tax.**[10]

What if the municipal bond would pay only 6.5 percent interest on the $20,000 investment?

---

[10]This term was popularized by Myron S. Scholes and Mark A. Wolfson in *Taxes and Business Strategy: A Planning Approach* (New Jersey: Prentice Hall, 1992).

Taxable and Nontaxable Bonds: Different Before-Tax Yields

	Corporate Bond Interest	Municipal Bond Interest
Before-tax cash/income	$2,000	$1,300
Tax cost	(620)	–0–
After-tax cash flow	$1,380	$1,300

Now the $700 implicit tax that Firm P would incur by purchasing the municipal bond rather than the corporate bond (the difference between the market yields of the two bonds) is greater than the $620 explicit tax on the interest from the corporate bond. Consequently, the after-tax cash generated by the corporate bond exceeds the after-tax cash generated by the tax-favored municipal bond, and Firm P should invest accordingly.

Municipal bond interest has no inherent financial characteristic that creates a natural immunity to taxation.[11] Congress purposefully granted tax-exempt status to this type of income to help state and local governments compete in the capital markets. The loss in revenues attributable to the tax preference represents an indirect federal subsidy to these governments. Whether this tax preference (or any other preference) is worth anything to a given investor depends on the investor's marginal tax rate and any implicit tax on the tax-favored investment.

Developing Tax Planning Strategies

Objective 8
Summarize the four basic maxims that firms use to develop tax planning strategies.

Our analysis of the variables that determine the tax consequences of business transactions resulted in the following maxims:

- *Tax costs decrease (and cash flows increase) when income is generated by an entity subject to a low tax rate.*
- *In present value terms, tax costs decrease (and cash flows increase) when a tax liability is deferred until a later taxable year.*
- *Tax costs decrease (and cash flows increase) when income is generated in a jurisdiction with a low tax rate.*
- *Tax costs decrease (and cash flows increase) when income is taxed at a preferential rate because of its character.*

The planning strategies that firms use to reduce tax costs and enhance cash flows typically reflect at least one of these maxims. Many business strategies combine two or more maxims working together to minimize taxes. Other strategies may adhere to one maxim but violate another. In such cases, business managers must carefully assess the overall tax consequences to determine if the strategy improves the net present value of cash flows. The following example demonstrates the problem of conflicting maxims.

---

[11]For state income tax purposes, interest on state and local bonds is generally subject to tax.

Conflicting Maxims.   Firm V operates as two separate taxable entities, Entity V^1 and Entity V^2. The firm is negotiating a transaction that will generate \$25,000 of net cash in year 1 and \$60,000 of net cash in year 2. If Entity V^1 undertakes the transaction, taxable income will correspond to cash flow (i.e., Entity V^1 will report \$25,000 and \$60,000 of taxable income in years 1 and 2). If Entity V^2 undertakes the transaction, it must report the entire \$85,000 of taxable income in year 1. Entity V^1 has a 31 percent marginal tax rate while Entity V^2 has a 25 percent marginal tax rate. Firm V uses a 12 percent discount rate to compute net present value.

	Entity V^1		Entity V^2	
Year 1:				
Before-tax cash flow		$ 25,000		$ 25,000
Taxable income	$25,000		$85,000	
	.31		.25	
Tax cost		(7,750)		(21,250)
After-tax cash flow		$ 17,250		$ 3,750
Year 2:				
Before-tax cash flow		$ 60,000		$ 60,000
Taxable income	$60,000		$ –0–	
	.31			
Tax cost		(18,600)		–0–
After-tax cash flow		$ 41,400		$ 60,000
Present value of year 1 cash flow		$ 17,250		$ 3,750
Present value of year 2 cash flow				
(.893 discount factor)		36,970		53,580
Net present value		$ 54,220		$ 57,330

Based on a comparison of net present values, Firm V should undertake the transaction through Entity V^2. This strategy adheres to the tax planning maxim that cash flows increase when income is generated by an entity with a low tax rate. However, the strategy accelerates the firm's entire tax liability on the transaction into year 1, thus violating the maxim that calls for deferral of tax costs for as long as possible.

Additional Strategic Considerations

The four tax planning maxims offer general guidance to the tax planning process. Like all generalizations, each one is subject to conditions, limitations, and exceptions depending on the exact nature of the tax strategy under consideration. Even though the maxims focus on the reduction of tax costs, managers should remember that their strategic goal is not tax minimization per se but net present value maximization. Consequently, they must consider key factors other than tax costs in formulating a winning strategy. One obvious factor is the expense of implementing the strategy. Firms may require professional advice in designing, executing, and monitoring a sophisticated tax plan, and the cost of the advice must be weighed against the potential tax savings from the strategy.

Managers must consider the economic consequences of tax strategies to all parties. In Chapter 3, we learned that firms negotiating in private markets often work together to achieve a coordinated set of tax results that maximize the after-tax value of the transaction to both parties. A manager intent on implementing a unilateral tax strategy may miss an opportunity for effective multilateral planning. Even worse, if a manager fails to consider the repercussions of a strategy on other interested parties, those parties might retaliate in ways that diminish the overall value of the strategy to the firm.

> *Multilateral Planning.*   Corporation F and Corporation D plan to form a joint venture to conduct a new business activity. Corporation F's tax cost with respect to the activity would be minimized if the business is conducted in Germany. Corporation D's tax cost would be minimized if the business is conducted in the United States. Corporation F agree to locate the business in the United States, provided that Corporation F will receive 60 percent of the business profit and Corporation D will receive only 40 percent. While this compromise increases Corporation F's tax cost and decreases Corporation D's before-tax profit, it maximizes the after-tax value of the joint venture to both corporations.

Tax strategies must be evaluated on the basis of flexibility: the extent to which the strategy can be adapted to unforeseen circumstances. Every strategy's anticipated impact on cash flows is based on assumptions about the future. The more uncertain the assumptions, the greater the risk that the strategy could backfire and have a detrimental effect on cash flows. If the firm can quickly modify or even reverse a failed strategy at minimal cost, this risk may be slight. But if the strategy is irreversible or would be extremely expensive to fix, the cost of potential failure may outweigh the benefit of success.

Tax Law Doctrines

Objective 9
Describe the three tax law doctrines that the IRS can use to challenge the favorable outcome of a tax planning strategy.

Managers must be as confident as possible that they have identified and reported the correct tax consequences of the tax strategies implemented by their firm. If a manager makes a technical error in applying the tax law to a critical transaction and the IRS discovers the error on audit, the firm's planning strategy could unravel, with disastrous impact on cash flows. Even when managers are satisfied that a strategy is technically sound, they must consider the government's reaction to the overall propriety of the strategy. Over the years, both the IRS and the federal courts have tried to make taxpayers adhere not only to the letter but also to the spirit of the law. Consequently, three important legal doctrines have evolved in the tax planning area; by invoking these doctrines the IRS can cry foul when a firm seems to be bending the rules to gain a unjustified tax advantage.

The **business purpose doctrine** holds that a transaction should not be effective for tax purposes unless it is intended to achieve a genuine and independent business purpose other than tax avoidance. The lack of any business purpose by the participants can render a transaction meaningless, at least from the perspective of the IRS, even if the transaction is in literal compliance with the law.[12]

---

[12]This doctrine originated with the case of *Gregory* v. *Helvering*, 293 U.S. 465 (1935).

Lack of Business Purpose.   Early this year, Mr. E decided to sell an investment asset. He calculated that the sale would generate $45,000 of gain on which he would pay tax at a 25 percent rate. Mr. E planned to invest the after-tax cash from the sale in his family business. Instead of selling the asset directly, Mr. E formed a new corporation to which he contributed the asset. The corporation immediately sold the asset and paid tax on the $45,000 gain at a 15 percent rate. The corporation then made a long-term loan of the after-tax cash from the sale to Mr. E's family business. If the IRS concludes that Mr. E had no business purpose for creating the new corporation but did so only to reap the benefit of the lower corporate tax rate, it could disregard the incorporation transaction. As a result, the IRS would treat Mr. E as the seller of the asset and would require him to pay tax on the gain at his 25 percent rate.[13]

The **substance over form doctrine** holds that the IRS is entitled to look through the legal formalities to determine the economic substance (if any) of a transaction. If the substance differs from the form, the IRS will base the tax consequences of the transaction on the reality rather than the illusion.[14]

Substance over Form.   The sole shareholder and president of Corporation JKL negotiates a leasing contract with a local businessman. Under the terms of the contract, JKL pays $35,000 for the use of equipment for one year and deducts this payment as a business expense. The revenue agent who audits this return uncovers two additional facts. First, the local businessman who received the $35,000 is a candidate for a state political office and has been enthusiastically endorsed by JKL's owner. Second, the corporation had no apparent need for the leased equipment. If these facts convince the agent that the substance of the leasing arrangement was a disguised political contribution (which is completely nondeductible), JKL may lose its $35,000 deduction and the tax savings therefrom.

The **step transaction doctrine** allows the IRS to collapse a series of intermediate transactions into a single transaction to determine the tax consequences of the arrangement in its entirety.[15] The IRS applies the doctrine when transactions are so obviously interdependent that the parties involved would not have consummated the first transaction without anticipating that the whole series of transactions would take place. Transactions occurring within a short period of time are more vulnerable to the step transaction doctrine than those occurring over a longer interval. As a rule of thumb, the IRS considers transactions occurring within a 12-month period as suspect.[16] Transactions separated in time by more than 12 months are presumed to be independent; in tax parlance, the first transaction is "old and cold" with no connection to the second transaction.

---

[13]See *Paymer* v. *Commissioner*, 150 F.2d 334 (CA-2, 1945).

[14]See *Commissioner* v. *Danielson,* 378 F.2d 771 (CA-3, 1967), *cert. denied* 389 U.S. 858 (1967).

[15]See *Helvering* v. *Alabama Asphaltic Limestone Co.*, 315 U.S. 179 (1942).

[16]See, for example, Treas. Reg. §1.368-2(c).

Potential Step Transactions.   The ABC Corporation sells property to an unrelated purchaser who subsequently resells the property to a wholly owned subsidiary of ABC. If these two sales occur within the same month, the IRS would certainly question their autonomy. Unless ABC could present evidence to the contrary, the IRS could collapse the two transactions into a direct sale of property from ABC to its subsidiary and recast the tax consequences of this related party transaction. On the other hand, if the first sale occurs five years before the second sale, the substantial length of time between the sales should grant them immunity to the step transaction doctrine.

There is considerable overlap in the scope of these three doctrines, and the IRS frequently uses them in combination to challenge an offending transaction. Of course, the courts may or may not uphold the IRS's challenge. Judges or juries may side with the taxpayer by concluding that a transaction has an independent business purpose and an economic substance to match its form. Business managers should understand that the doctrines seem to be the exclusive property of the IRS; taxpayers cannot invoke them to undo the consequences of their own ill-fated tax strategies.[17] Managers should be aware that the IRS's application of these doctrines is extremely subjective. Given the omnipresent threat of the business purpose, substance over form, and step transaction doctrines, managers can never be absolutely certain that a creative tax plan will work, even if it seems to comply with the letter of the law.

Conclusion

Now that you've completed Part Two of *Principles of Taxation for Business and Investment Planning*, you should appreciate how tax planning strategies can reduce tax costs and thereby increase the net present value of business transactions. The framework for a thorough understanding of the tax planning process is in place. Parts Three and Four of the text build on this framework by presenting the basics of the income tax law itself: how firms compute their annual taxable income and the federal tax liability on that income. As you integrate this legal knowledge into your understanding of taxes as financial costs, your appreciation of the tax planning process will progress from the abstract to the specific.

---

[17]See *Durkin*, TC Memo 1992-325.

Key Terms

Assignment of income doctrine 74	Step transaction doctrine 85
Business purpose doctrine 84	Substance over form doctrine 85
Capital gain 79	Tax avoidance 70
Explicit tax 81	Tax evasion 70
Implicit tax 81	Tax planning 69
Ordinary income 79	

Questions and Problems for Discussion

1. For each of the following situations, discuss whether the individual is engaging in tax avoidance or tax evasion.
   a. During the current year, Mr. L performed minor construction work for a number of individuals who paid for his work in cash. Because Mr. L knows that there is almost no chance that the IRS could learn of these payments, he reports only half the payments as income on his federal tax return.
   b. Mr. P, who is in the 39.6 percent tax bracket, recently had the opportunity to invest $50,000 in a new business that should yield an annual return of at least 17 percent. Rather than invest himself, Mr. P made a gift of $50,000 cash to his son, who then made the investment. The son's marginal tax rate is only 15 percent.
   c. Mrs. Q sold an asset during January of the current year; her $12,000 profit on the sale is ordinary income. After preparing her income tax return for the prior year, Mrs. Q realized that her marginal tax rate for the prior year was 31 percent. She also realized that her marginal rate for the current year will probably be at least 36 percent and maybe even 39.6 percent. Mrs. Q decides to report the profit from the asset sale on her prior year return to take advantage of the lower tax rate for that year.

2. Assume that Congress amends the tax law to provide for a maximum 18 percent rate on rental income generated by single-family residences. What immediate impact might this preferential rate have on the market value of this category of real estate?

3. Tax planners often tell their clients that "a tax delayed is a tax not paid." Can you provide a more formal explanation of this bit of wisdom?

4. Mrs. K is about to begin a new business activity and asks you if she can reduce the taxable income from the activity by operating it as a corporation rather than as a sole proprietorship. How do you answer Mrs. K?

5. Is every business organization a taxable entity for federal income tax purposes? Explain briefly.

6. Based on the rates printed on the inside of the front cover, determine the marginal tax rate for:

   a. A corporation with taxable income of $23,000.
   b. A corporation with taxable income of $250,000.
   c. A single (unmarried) individual with taxable income of $75,000.
   d. A single (unmarried) individual with taxable income of $250,000.

7. Assume that the U.S. Congress replaces the current individual and corporate income tax rate structures with a proportionate (flat) rate that applies to both types of taxpayers. Discuss the impact of this change in the federal law on tax strategies based on:
   a. The entity variable.
   b. The time period variable.
   c. The jurisdiction variable.
   d. The character variable.

8. Compare the potential tax savings attributable to an income shift from one taxpaying entity to another if the entities are subject to:
   a. A progressive income tax system with rates ranging from 5 percent to 19 percent.
   b. A progressive income tax system with rates ranging from 10 percent to 50 percent.
   c. A 20 percent proportionate income tax system.

9. Why do income shifts and deduction shifts usually occur between taxpayers who are related parties?

10. Corporation P owns a controlling stock interest in two subsidiaries, Corporation S_1 and Corporation S_2. Corporation P's marginal tax rate for the year is 25 percent. During the year, Corporation P engages in one transaction that shifts $10,000 income from P to S_1. Corporation P engages in a second transaction that shifts a $15,000 deduction from P to S_2. Based on these facts, what conclusions can you draw about marginal tax rates of the two subsidiary corporations?

11. Firm A expects to receive a $25,000 item of income in August and a second $25,000 item of income in December of the current taxable year. The firm could implement a planning strategy that delays the receipt of both items until January of the following taxable year. As a result, the firm would defer the payment of tax on the $50,000 of

income for one full year. After analyzing the strategy, Firm A decides to receive the August payment in the current year (and pay tax on the $25,000 of income in the current year) but delay the receipt of the December payment. Can you offer an explanation for this differential treatment?

12. Identify the reasons why business managers should evaluate the flexibility of a tax planning strategy before implementing the strategy.

13. Assume that in June of the current year the U.S. Congress enacts legislation that increases income tax rates for all entities effective for the next calendar year.

    a. Why might such legislation result in an increase in federal tax revenues for the current year?

    b. In what way would this legislation create a conflict between tax planning maxims?

14. Mr. T is considering a strategy to defer $10,000 of income for five years with no significant opportunity cost. Discuss the strategic implications of the following independent assumptions:

    a. Mr. T is age 24. He graduated from law school last month and has just accepted a position with a prominent firm of attorneys.

    b. Mr. T is age 63. He plans to retire from business at the end of this year and devote his time to volunteer work and sailing.

Application Problems

1. For the current year, Firm A has a 15 percent marginal tax rate while Firm Z has a 35 percent marginal tax rate. Firm A owns a controlling interest in Firm Z. During the current year, the owners of Firm A decide to incur a $40,000 deductible expense that will benefit both firms. Compute the after-tax cost of the expense assuming that:

   a. Firm A incurs the expense.

   b. Firm Z incurs the expense.

2. Firm M and Firm N are related parties. For the past several years, Firm M's marginal tax rate has been 34 percent while Firm N's marginal tax rate has been 25 percent. Firm M is evaluating a transaction that will generate $10,000 of net profit in each of the next three years. Firm M could restructure the transaction so that the income would shift to Firm N. Because of the restructuring, the annual profit would decrease to $9,000. Based on these facts, should Firm M restructure the transaction?

3. Assume that Congress amends the tax law to provide for a maximum 20 percent rate on dividend income. Calculate the annual tax savings from this new preferential rate to each of the following taxpayers:

   a. Mrs. A, who is in the 39.6 percent marginal tax bracket and receives $70,000 of dividend income each year.

   b. Mr. B, who is in the 31 percent marginal tax bracket and receives $15,000 of dividend income each year.

   c. Ms. C, who is in the 39.6 percent marginal tax bracket and receives $8,000 of dividend income each year.

   d. Mr. D, who is in the 15 percent marginal tax bracket and receives $3,000 of dividend income each year.

4. Firm H has the opportunity to engage in a transaction that will generate $100,000 of cash flow (and taxable income) in year 1. How does the net present value of the transaction change if the firm could restructure the transaction in a way that does not affect the before-tax cash flow but results in no taxable income in year 1, $50,000 of taxable income in year 2, and the remaining $50,000 of taxable income in year 3. In making your calculation, assume a 10 percent discount rate and a 34 percent marginal tax rate for the three-year period.

5. What is the effect on the net present value of the restructured transaction in Problem 4 if Firm H's marginal tax rate in year 3 increases to 39 percent?

6. Mr. G has $15,000 to invest. He is undecided about putting the money into tax-exempt municipal bonds paying 7 percent annual interest or publicly traded corporate bonds paying 9.5

percent annual interest. The two investments have the same risk.

   a. Which investment should Mr. G make if his marginal tax rate is 31 percent?

   b. Would your conclusion change if Mr. G's marginal tax rate is only 15 percent?

7. Firm L has $500,000 to invest and is considering two alternatives. Investment A would pay 13 percent ($65,000 annual before-tax cash flow). Investment B would pay 9.5 percent ($47,500 annual before-tax cash flow). The return on Investment A is fully taxable, while the return on Investment B is tax exempt. Firm L forecasts that its current 36 percent marginal tax rate will be stable for the foreseeable future.

   a. Compute the explicit tax and implicit tax that Firm L will pay with respect to Investment A and Investment B.

   b. Based on these facts, which investment results in the greater annual after-tax cash flow?

8. Firm W, which has a 34 percent marginal tax rate, plans to undertake a new business venture that should generate $40,000 annual cash flow/ordinary income for three years. Alternatively, Firm W could form a new taxable entity (Entity N) to undertake the venture. Entity N would pay tax on the three-year income stream at a 25 percent rate. The up-front cost to Firm W of forming Entity N would be $5,000; assume that this cost is not deductible in the computation of either Firm W's or Entity N's taxable income. Based on these facts and assuming an 11 percent discount rate, should Firm W undertake the business venture directly or form Entity N to undertake the venture?

Issue Recognition Problems

Identify the tax issue or issues suggested by the following situations and state each issue in the form of a question.

1. Mr. and Mrs. TR own an investment yielding a 7.2 percent after-tax return. Their friend, Ms. K, is encouraging them to sell this investment and invest the proceeds in a business in which she owns a 40 percent interest. This business takes advantage of several very favorable tax preferences. Consequently, Ms. K's after-tax return on her 40 percent interest is 8.4 percent.

2. Company QP must decide whether to build a new manufacturing plant in Country B or Country C. Country B has no income tax. However, its political regime is unstable and its currency has been devalued four times in as many years. Country C has both a 20 percent income tax and a stable democratic government.

3. Dr. P is a physician who operates his own medical practice. For the last several years, Dr. P's marginal income tax rate has been 39.6 percent. Dr. P's daughter, who is a college student, has no taxable income. During the last two months of the current year, Dr. P instructs his patients to remit their payments for his services directly to his daughter.

4. Mrs. Y owns 1,800 shares of Acme Inc. common stock, which she purchased for $10 per share in 1990. In November of the current year, Mrs. Y needs cash and decides to sell her Acme stock for the current market price of $27 per share, the highest price at which the stock has traded in the last 22 months. Mrs. Y's friend advises her to hold onto the Acme stock until January of the next year so that Mrs. Y's profit from the sale will be taxable in the next year rather than in the current year.

5. In November of the current year, Firm Q was negotiating to sell a tract of land to an unrelated buyer. The buyer refused to close the sale until February of the next year. Firm Q wants to close the sale by the end of the year so that its gain on sale will be taxed at the firm's current marginal rate of 25 percent. Firm Q projects that its marginal rate for the next year will be 39 percent. In December of the current year, Firm Q sells the land to a wholly owned (100 percent) subsidiary corporation; in February of the next year the subsidiary sells the land to the unrelated buyer.

6. Mr. and Mrs. K own rental property that generates $4,000 of gross monthly revenue. For

the current year, the couple is in the 36 percent marginal tax bracket. For Christmas, Mr. and Mrs. K give the uncashed rent checks for October, November, and December to their 19-year-old grandson as a gift.

7. Firm Z is considering implementing a long-term tax strategy to accelerate the deduction of certain business expenses. The strategy has an opportunity cost in that it decreases before-tax cash flows, but the tax savings from the strategy should be greater than this opportunity cost. The strategy is fairly aggressive, and the IRS might disallow the intended tax outcome if it audits Firm Z's tax returns.

8. Ms. LG plans to carefully structure a business transaction as a legal sale of property, even though the economic substance of the transaction is a lease of the property. In Ms. LG's current tax position, the tax consequences of a sale are much more favorable than those of a lease. Ms. LG believes that if her tax position unexpectedly changes so that she would prefer a lease to a sale, she can ignore the legal formalities and report the transaction as a lease.

9. Firm HR is about to implement a very aggressive long-term business strategy consisting of three phases. It is crucial to the success of the strategy that the IRS accepts Firm HR's interpretation of the tax consequences of each distinct phase. The firm could implement the first phase in November of year 1 and the second phase in August of year 2. Alternatively, it could delay the second phase until January of year 3.

Tax Planning Cases

1. Firm DFG wants to open a foreign subsidiary through which to sell its manufactured goods in the European market. The firm must decide between locating the subsidiary in Country X or Country Z. If the subsidiary operates in Country X, the gross revenues from the foreign sales will be subject to a 3 percent gross receipts tax. If the subsidiary operates in Country Z, the profits from the foreign operation will be subject to a 42 percent net income tax. However, Country Z's tax law has a special provision to attract foreign investors: no foreign subsidiary is subject to the income tax for the first three years of operations.

   Firm DFG projects the following annual operating results for the two locations (in thousands of dollars):

	Country X	Country Z
Gross receipts from sales	$110,000	$110,000
Cost of sales	(60,000)	(60,000)
Operating expenses	(22,000)	(15,000)
Net profit	$ 28,000	$ 35,000

   The firm projects that it will operate the foreign subsidiary for 10 years and that the terminal value of the operation at the end of this period will be the same regardless of location. Based on these facts and assuming a 10 percent discount rate, determine which location maximizes the net present value of the foreign operation to Firm DFG.

2. Individual A, who is in the 36 percent marginal tax bracket, must decide between two investment opportunities, both of which require an initial cash outlay of $50,000. Investment 1 will yield $6,500 of before-tax cash flow for three years. This cash represents ordinary taxable income. At the end of three years, A can liquidate the investment and recover his $50,000 cash outlay. He must pay a nondeductible $200 annual fee (in years 1, 2, and 3) to maintain Investment 1.

   Investment 2 will not yield any before-tax cash flow during the three-year period over which A will hold the investment. At the end of three years, A will be able to sell Investment 2 for $70,000 cash. His $20,000 profit on the sale will be capital gain taxed at 20 percent.

   Based solely on these facts and assuming a 9 percent discount rate, determine which investment has the greater net present value.

PART THREE

The Measurement of Taxable Income

5

Taxable Income from Business Operations

Learning Objectives

After studying this chapter, you should be able to:

1. Describe the relationship between a firm's business operating cycle and its choice of taxable year.

2. Explain the realization and matching principles of income measurement.

3. Compare the cash method and the accrual method of accounting as they relate to the measurement of net income.

4. Contrast the principles of conservatism reflected by generally accepted accounting principles (GAAP) and by the tax law.

5. Identify the tax policy objectives that lead to differences in the computation of book income and taxable income.

6. Differentiate between a permanent and a temporary book/tax difference.

7. Define the doctrine of constructive receipt for cash basis firms.

8. Recognize the common differences between the calculation of book and taxable income for accrual basis firms.

9. Explain how the net operating loss deduction allows firms to smooth taxable income over time.

The keynote of the text to this point has been the role of taxes in the business decision-making process. We've been concerned with income and deductions only in the generic sense and have worked through a series of hypothetical transactions demonstrating how income and deductions result in tax costs and tax savings. In turn, these costs and savings have been incorporated into cash flow models for computing the net present value of the transactions.

In Part Three of the text, our attention turns to the statutory, regulatory, and judicial rules governing the measurement of taxable income. Chapter 5 examines the impact of a firm's choice of a taxable year and a method of accounting on the measurement process, with emphasis on the differences between the computation of a firm's financial statement income and the income reported on its federal tax return. In contrast to earlier chapters, this chapter contains numerous references to specific sections of the Internal Revenue Code and Treasury regulations and to court cases pertaining to the computation of taxable income. We will analyze this new technical material in terms of its impact on cash flows and its relevance to the tax planning process. In doing so, we will accomplish one of the main objectives of *Principles of Taxation for Business and Investment Planning*—bridging the gap between finance courses that assume away knowledge of the tax law and traditional law courses that ignore the role of tax outcomes in the larger context of financial decision making.

Business Profit as Taxable Income

The base for the federal income tax is **taxable income,** defined by statute as gross income minus allowable deductions.[1] The Internal Revenue Code defines **gross income** by stating that "gross income means all income from whatever source derived."[2] In the business context, gross income consists primarily of the revenues derived from the sale of goods or performance of services in the regular course of a firm's commercial activity. Gross income also includes revenues generated by a firm's invested capital, such as interest, dividends, and rents. The concept of gross income is broad enough to encompass other, less commonplace, increases in net worth that result from business transactions.

> ***Cancellation of Indebtedness Income.***   Firm C has an $80,000 overdue account payable to a major supplier of the raw materials that Firm C uses in its manufacturing process. The supplier knows that Firm C is having severe cash flow problems and is eager to settle the account as quickly and as advantageously as possible. After some negotiation, both parties agree that Firm C will pay $60,000 cash in full settlement of the account payable. Because Firm C extinguished an $80,000 liability with only $60,000 of assets, its net worth has increased by $20,000, an increase that the firm must account for as current year income.

Firms can deduct most of their routine operating expenses in the computation of taxable income.[3] They can also deduct the various state, local, and foreign taxes incurred in carrying on their business activities.[4] Firms can even deduct the cost of assets acquired for long-term use in their business; however, such cost recovery deductions (such as depreciation) are generally spread over some extended period of years. Cost recovery deductions are discussed in detail in Chapter 6. Because the tax law allows firms to deduct expenses and costs incurred in revenue-generating activities, the federal income tax is imposed on *net profit* rather than gross receipts.

The Taxable Year

A firm must measure its taxable income every year and pay tax on an annual basis. The tax law gives firms considerable latitude with respect to the 12-month period over which to measure income. The general rule is that a firm's taxable year corresponds to its

---

[1]§63(a).

[2]§61.

[3]"There shall be allowed as a deduction all the ordinary and necessary expenses paid or incurred during the taxable year in carrying on any trade or business." §162(a).

[4]§164(a). Firms may forgo a deduction for foreign income taxes paid to claim a credit for these taxes against their federal income tax liability. The foreign tax credit is discussed in Chapter 12.

annual accounting period for financial statement purposes.[5] If a firm keeps its financial books and records on a **calendar year,** it measures taxable income over the same January through December period. If a firm keeps its financial books and records on a **fiscal year** (any 12-month period ending on the last day of any month except December), it uses this fiscal year as its taxable year.[6]

Objective 1
Describe the relationship between a firm's business operating cycle and its choice of taxable year.

The choice of a calendar or fiscal year is usually dictated by the firm's operating cycle; firms want to close their books and calculate their profit at the end of a natural cycle of business activity. A retail clothing store might find that a February 28 fiscal year-end results in the most accurate reflection of an operating cycle that peaks during the holiday season and reaches its lowest point before the beginning of the spring season. A ski resort might use a May 31 fiscal year-end so that its financial statements reflect the profit from a business cycle that ends when the snow finally melts off the slopes.

Changing a Taxable Year

As a general rule, a new business entity establishes its taxable year by filing an initial tax return on the basis of such year.[7] The initial return reflects taxable income or loss from the date business operations began until the end of the year. As a result, an initial return typically reflects a short period of less than 12 months. After establishing a taxable year, a firm can't change its year unless it formally requests and receives permission to do so from the IRS.[8] This requirement has particular significance when an individual begins a new business venture as a sole proprietor and wants to keep records on a fiscal year basis. In all likelihood, the individual has always filed a calendar year tax return. Although the business itself is new, the taxable entity (the business owner) has already established herself as a calendar year taxpayer. Consequently, the individual must request permission from the IRS to change to a fiscal year conforming to the sole proprietorship's accounting records.

When a firm has a sound business reason for changing its annual accounting period, the IRS usually grants permission for the firm to make a corresponding change in its taxable year. If the firm lacks a convincing reason, the IRS may withhold permission for the change. In those cases in which the IRS grants permission, the firm files a **short-period return** to accomplish the change.

> ***Changing a Taxable Year.***   Corporation B, a calendar year taxpayer since 1985, recently developed a new line of business with an annual operating cycle ending in midsummer. The corporation requests and receives permission from the IRS to change to a fiscal year ending July 31. To move from a calendar year to a fiscal year, the corporation files a return for the period January 1 through July 31, a period of only seven months. Corporation B's returns for future years will reflect a 12-month taxable year running from August 1 through July 31. This change in taxable years is illustrated by the following time line:

---

[5]§441(b) and (c).

[6]Firms may also use a 52–53-week year for financial statement and tax return purposes. A 52–53-week year is an annual period that is either 52 or 53 weeks long and that always ends on the same day of the week. §441(f).

[7]Reg. §1.441-1T(b)(2).

[8]§442.

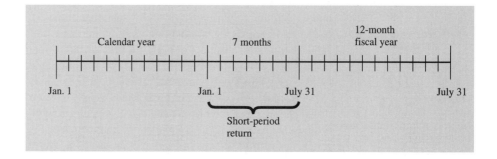

Annualizing Income on a Short-Period Return

Because a short-period return reflects less than a full year of taxable income, the tax liability on that income might be abnormally low. To demonstrate this possibility, assume that Corporation B in the previous example generates $10,000 of monthly income. In a 12-month year, the corporation's average tax rate is 25.04 percent. However, in a taxable year consisting of only seven months, the average tax rate falls to 17.86 percent.

Average Tax Rate on Short-Period Income

	12-Month Year	*7-Month Year*
Taxable income	$120,000	$70,000
Tax on:		
First $50,000 at 15%	$ 7,500	$ 7,500
Next $25,000 at 25%	6,250	5,000
Next $25,000 at 34%	8,500	
Next $20,000 at 39%	7,800	
Total tax liability	$ 30,050	$12,500

12-month year: $30,050 tax ÷ $120,000 taxable income = 25.04%
7-month year: $12,500 tax ÷ $ 70,000 taxable income = 17.86%

The 7.18 percent rate reduction would result in a permanent tax savings to Corporation B of $5,026 ($70,000 × 7.18 percent). The savings results from the application of progressive rates to a truncated tax base.

The federal tax law prevents this serendipitous result when a firm files a short-period return to change its taxable year. The taxable income reported on the return must be **annualized**—mathematically inflated to reflect 12 months of business operations.[9] The tax liability is calculated on the inflated base, then deflated to reflect the actual number of months covered by the return. Let's annualize Corporation B's taxable income on its short-period return and see what happens.

---

[9]§443(b).

Average Tax Rate on Annualized Income	
	7-Month Year
Taxable income	$ 70,000
Multiplied by inflation factor	
(12 months ÷ 7 months)	1.7143
Annualized income	$120,000
Tax on annualized income	$ 30,050
Multiplied by deflation factor	
(7 months ÷ 12 months)	.5833
Total tax liability	$ 17,528
$17,528 tax ÷ $70,000 taxable income = 25.04%	

Corporation B's average tax rate on the short-period return is 25.04 percent, the same rate at which the corporation pays tax on a normal 12-month basis. Because of the annualization requirement, firms reap no tax benefit when they file a short-period return pursuant to a change in their taxable year. The requirement is inapplicable to short-period returns filed because the taxable entity was *in existence* for only a portion of a taxable year.[10] Accordingly, the short-period income reported on the first return filed by a new business entity or the last return filed by an entity going out of business may be taxed at a bargain rate.

Methods of Accounting

After establishing its taxable year, a firm must assign the items of income and deduction from its various business transactions to a particular year. To do this, the firm must adopt a **method of accounting:** a consistent system for determining the point in time at which items of income and deduction are recognized (taken into account) for tax purposes. The term *method of accounting* refers to a firm's overall method for **recognition** as well as to any method applying to only a particular type of transaction.[11]

The tax law acknowledges that "no uniform method of accounting can be prescribed for all taxpayers. Each taxpayer shall adopt such forms and systems as are, in his judgment, best suited to his needs."[12] Moreover, a taxpayer engaged in more than one business may use a different method of accounting for each business.[13] This permissive attitude is tempered by a caveat: "no method of accounting is acceptable unless, in the opinion of the Commissioner [of the IRS], it clearly reflects income."[14] Thus, the IRS reserves the right to satisfy itself that a firm's method of accounting for tax purposes accurately and fairly measures the firm's ability to pay federal income tax for the year.

---

[10]Reg. §1.443-1(a)(2).
[11]Reg. §1.446-1(a).
[12]Reg. §1.446-1(a)(2).
[13]§446(d).
[14]Op. cit., fn. 12.

A firm adopts a method of accounting by using the method to prepare its initial tax return.[15] Once a method is adopted, whether it be an overall method or the accounting treatment of a particular transaction, the firm may not change the method unless it formally requests and receives permission to do so from the IRS.[16] The request must state the reason why the firm wants to change its accounting method and provide a detailed description of the firm's present and proposed method of accounting. The IRS does not rubber stamp these requests. When the IRS does grant permission, it carefully monitors the change to make sure that the firm does not omit income or duplicate deductions in the year it converts to the new method of accounting.

Two Important Accounting Principles

The Internal Revenue Code states that "taxable income shall be computed under the method of accounting on the basis of which the taxpayer regularly computes his income in keeping his books."[17] Firms derive the information for preparing their tax returns from their financial books and records. These records reflect the overall method of accounting by which the firm measures annual net income. Therefore, a good way to begin our discussion of overall methods of accounting for tax purposes is by reviewing two financial accounting principles that are fundamental to the measurement of income.

Objective 2
Explain the realization and matching principles of income measurement.

The Realization Principle.   For financial accounting purposes, firms take revenue into account only when the revenue is realized.[18] **Realization** occurs when a firm completes the earning process with respect to the goods or services it provides by entering into an exchange transaction with a customer or client. The realization principle also dictates that an increase in the value of an asset or property right over time is not recorded as revenue because the increase in value has not been realized. If and when the owner sells the asset or property right to another party, the increase in value is finally realized as a gain and can be measured and reported as revenue.

The Matching Principle.   A second basic principle of financial accounting—the **matching principle**—holds that when a firm realizes and records revenue, it should also record all the expenses that contributed to the generation of that revenue. A proper matching of revenue and expense items results in an accurate measure of the firm's *net* income for that period. With the realization and matching principles in mind, let's examine the two overall methods of accounting that firms use to measure income: the cash method and the accrual method.

The Cash Method

Objective 3
Compare the cash method and the accrual method of accounting as they relate to the measurement of net income.

Under the **cash method of accounting,** firms realize revenue from the sale of goods or performance of services in the year that payment is received, regardless of when the sale occurred or the services were performed.

---

[15]Reg. §1.446-1(e).

[16]§446(e).

[17]§446(a).

[18]This principle is also referred to as the revenue principle. See Libby, Libby, and Short, *Financial Accounting* (Burr Ridge, IL: Richard D. Irwin, 1996), p. 111.

> ***Cash Method for Income.***   Firm CM, a calendar year, cash basis consulting business, completed an engagement late in the year. On December 12, the firm mailed a bill to the client for its $20,000 consulting fee. If the firm does not receive a check in payment of the fee before year-end, it does not realize revenue for the year, even though the services were performed during the year. The receipt of the check in January will be the realization event, and Firm CM will report the $20,000 of revenue from the engagement on next year's income statement.

Under the cash method, firms match expenses against revenues in the year the expense is paid, regardless of when the firm incurred the liability for the expense.

> ***Cash Method for Expenses.***   Firm CM hired a temporary employee to help the secretarial staff with year-end paperwork. The temp completed the assignment on December 28, but the firm didn't issue his $950 paycheck until January 15. The firm incurred the $950 liability in the year when the employee completed the job in a satisfactory manner. Even so, Firm CM will expense the payment on next year's income statement.

The Cash Method and Cash Flows.   The term *cash method* should not be taken too literally. In the first place, the receipt of noncash forms of payment triggers the realization of revenue to the extent of the value of the payment. The fact that no currency is received is irrelevant.

> ***Noncash Receipts.***   Firm CM billed a client for a $12,000 consulting fee and the client settled the bill by transferring $12,000 worth of marketable securities to the firm. Firm CM realizes $12,000 of revenue on the receipt of the securities, even though the transaction did not involve the receipt of cash.

As this example suggests, the net income computed under the cash method does not equate to the net cash flows generated by a firm's business activities. In other words, the terms *income* and *cash* are not synonymous, even for a cash basis taxpayer.

> ***Income and Cash Flow.***   Firm CM lends $25,000 to an unrelated party at a 10 percent annual interest rate. Three years later, the debtor pays $33,275 ($25,000 principal + $8,275 interest) to Firm CM in satisfaction of the debt. The firm's net income and net cash flows with respect to this transaction are as follows:
>
> | | Income/Expense | Net Cash Flow |
> |---|---|---|
> | Year of loan | $ –0– | $(25,000) |
> | Year of repayment | 8,275 | 33,275 |

The Accrual Method

Objective 3
Compare the cash method
and the accrual method
of accounting as they
relate to the measurement
of net income.

Under the **accrual method of accounting,** firms realize revenue when the earnings process with respect to goods or services is complete, regardless of when payment for those goods and services is received.

> ***Accrual Method for Income.***   Firm AM, a calendar year, accrual basis consulting business, performed services for a client during October and November. The firm mailed a bill to the client for its $9,200 consulting fee on December 8 and recorded a $9,200 account receivable from the client and $9,200 of current year revenue. Firm AM realized the revenue in the current year even if it does not receive the client's check until January of the following year.

Under the accrual method, firms match expenses against revenues in the year the firm incurs the liability for the expense, regardless of when the expense is paid.[19]

> ***Accrual Method for Expenses.***   Firm AM hired a plumber to repair some leaky pipes in the executive washroom. The plumber completed the repairs on December 19 and submitted his bill for $550. The firm recorded a $550 account payable to the plumber and a $550 expense. This expense is matched against current year revenues, even though Firm AM does not pay the bill until January of the following year.

Choice of Method for Financial Statement Purposes

Many small businesses use the cash method of accounting to maintain their financial books and records. The cash method has the advantage of being both simple and objective because the measurement of income is tied to cash receipts and disbursements. However, under **generally accepted accounting principles (GAAP),** the cash method does not accurately measure income and only the accrual method of accounting is considered to be conceptually sound.[20] Firms that provide audited financial statements to external users are typically required to use the accrual method of accounting. The Securities and Exchange Commission (SEC) requires every publicly traded corporation to prepare accrual basis financial statements in accordance with GAAP.

The Origins of Book/Tax Differences

If a firm uses the same overall method of accounting to maintain its financial records and to prepare its tax return, shouldn't that firm's annual net income per books equal current year taxable income? The answer to this question is usually no; for most business ventures, book income and taxable income are different numbers. Discrepancies

---

[19]A *liability* is a firm's present obligation to transfer assets or provide services to other entities in the future as a result of past transactions or events.

[20]Generally accepted accounting principles are developed by the Financial Accounting Standards Board (FASB) and adhered to by the public accounting profession.

between the two income computations occur because certain transactions are treated one way under GAAP and another way for tax accounting purposes. One explanation for the inconsistent treatment is the contrast in perspectives on income measurement that shape financial accounting principles and the tax law.

Contrasting Perspectives on Income Measurement

Objective 4
Contrast the principles of conservatism reflected by generally accepted accounting principles (GAAP) and by the tax law.

Business managers have one attitude toward the measurement of income for financial statement purposes and a different attitude toward the measurement of income for tax purposes. Managers typically have incentives to report as much book income as possible. Their compensation and even their job security may depend on the level of earnings reported to existing and potential investors in the firm. However, GAAP is based on a principle of conservatism: when in doubt, financial statements should delay the realization of income and accelerate the realization of losses.[21] In theory at least, GAAP curbs any tendency on the part of management to *inflate* book income by overstating revenues or understating expenses.

In contrast to their expansive attitude toward book income, managers typically want to *deflate* the taxable income (and resultant tax liability) reported to the government. Congress and the Treasury are well aware of this measurement bias. Consequently, the federal tax law also embraces a principle of conservatism, but one that operates to prevent managers from understating gross income and overstating deductions. The contrasting principles of conservatism reflected by GAAP and the federal income tax law lead to many of the book/tax differences described in this chapter and throughout the text.

The natural tension between income measurement under GAAP and income measurement under the Internal Revenue Code exists only for firms that prepare financial statements for external users and income tax returns for the government. Many small, privately owned companies produce financial statements for internal use only. These companies are not required by any state or federal regulatory agency to engage independent auditors to examine their books and records. Because they are not responsible for maintaining their financial accounting records in accordance with GAAP, these companies can conform their records to the method of accounting required for federal income tax purposes. As a result, there may be minimal or even no difference between their book income and taxable income.

Tax Policy Objectives That Transcend Income Measurement

Objective 5
Identify the tax policy objectives that lead to differences in the computation of book income and taxable income.

Another explanation for many differences in the computation of financial statement income and taxable income is that precise measurement of income is not the sole objective of the tax law. Congress wants the tax law to be consistent with public policy and political concerns; the provisions in the law that achieve this consistency have nothing to do with income measurement. For instance, contributions to a political party or candidate for public office, as well as federal or state lobbying expenses, are not deductible in the computation of taxable income.[22] Firms certainly must account for these business expenses in the computation of book income. But because Congress does not want to indirectly subsidize partisan efforts to influence legislative matters, the

---

[21]Jamie Pratt, *Financial Accounting*, 2nd ed. (Cincinnati, Ohio: South-Western Publishing, 1994) p. 192.
[22]§162(e) and §276.

expenses do not reduce taxable income, regardless of the firm's method of accounting for tax purposes.

The tax law may disallow a deduction for certain business expenses because of the public perception that the expenses themselves are in some way inappropriate. Firms cannot deduct fines or penalties paid to a government for the violation of any law, nor can they deduct illegal bribes or kickbacks paid in the course of a business transaction.[23] Congress does not want to soothe the sting of the former or underwrite the latter with the savings generated by a tax deduction.

A prime example of a politically sensitive expense is the cost of business meals and entertainment. Virtually every firm spends money on meals and entertainment for its customers, clients, employees, or investors. This fact suggests that these expenses are necessary, and perhaps crucial, to the success of the business and add value to the firm. Nonetheless, these expenses may result in personal enjoyment for the individuals involved; the "three-martini lunch" has become a catch phrase to describe lavish business meals and entertainment with inordinate potential for pleasure. Middle-income taxpayers (particularly individuals whose occupations don't involve three-martini lunches) have been outspoken in their criticism of the government subsidy resulting from a deduction for meals and entertainment. In response to this criticism, the tax law allows firms to deduct only 50 percent of most meal and entertainment costs.[24] Therefore, a firm facing a 35 percent marginal tax rate must evaluate a $100 expense for a business meal based on an after-tax cost of $82.50 rather than $65.

Book-Tax Reconciliation for Nondeductible Expenses.   During the year, Company PL paid a $2,000 fine for violating a local zoning law, made a $3,500 political contribution to a candidate for state office, and incurred $8,200 of business meal and entertainment expenses. These three expenses are included in the computation of the company's book income. If Company PL's book income before tax is $196,000 *and the company has no other book/tax differences,* its taxable income is computed as follows:

Net income per books (before tax)	$196,000
Nondeductible fine	2,000
Nondeductible political contribution	3,500
Nondeductible meals and entertainment ($8,200 × 50%)	4,100
Taxable income	$205,600

Tax Preferences.   The Internal Revenue Code contains many provisions that purposely deviate from sound income measurement principles to encourage certain economic behaviors or to subsidize certain activities. These tax preferences invariably result in differences between financial statement income and taxable income. In Chapter

---

[23]§162(c) and (f).

[24]§274(n). Code §274 contains a multitude of detailed restrictions on the deductibility of business travel and entertainment expenses.

4, we learned that interest paid on debt obligations issued by state and local governments is exempt from federal income tax. While this interest is recorded as revenue on the recipient's financial statements, it is excluded from the gross income reported on the recipient's tax return. The tax law bestows a similar preference on the proceeds of life insurance policies: gross income does not include amounts received under a life insurance contract if such amounts are paid by reason of the death of the insured.[25] Many firms insure the lives of their officers and top-level executives to protect against the disruption to the business if one of these essential personnel dies unexpectedly. The firm itself (rather than the insured individual's family) is the beneficiary of such **key-person life insurance policies.** When an insured employee dies and the firm receives payment from the insurance company, these dollars are not taxable, even though they are reported as revenue on the firm's income statement.

A corollary to the tax-exempt status of municipal bond interest and key-person life insurance proceeds is that any expenses related to these income items are nondeductible. Accordingly, a firm can't deduct the interest paid on a debt if the borrowed funds were used to purchase or carry tax-exempt bonds.[26] Nor can a firm deduct the annual premiums paid to keep key-person life insurance policies in force.[27] While these rules are certainly logical, they result in additional differences between book income and taxable income.

Book/Tax Reconciliation for Key-Person Life Insurance. During the year, Corporation R paid a $4,000 premium on a key-person insurance policy on the life of the corporation's president. Late in the year, the president died in a plane crash and Corporation R received $500,000 of insurance proceeds. Both the revenue represented by the insurance proceeds and the premium expense are included in the computation of book income. If Corporation R's book income before tax is $2,300,000 *and the firm has no other book/tax differences,* its taxable income is computed as follows:

Net income per books (before tax)	$2,300,000
Nontaxable life insurance proceeds	(500,000)
Nondeductible insurance premiums	4,000
Taxable income	$1,804,000

Permanent versus Temporary Differences

Objective 6
Differentiate between a permanent and a temporary book/tax difference.

The differences between financial statement income and taxable income identified to this point in the chapter have all been **permanent differences.** A permanent difference results when:

- Income or gain is realized for book purposes but is *never* recognized for tax purposes.

---

[25]§101(a).
[26]§265(a)(2).
[27]§264(a).

• Expense or loss is realized for book purposes but is *never* deducted for tax purposes.

A permanent difference also results in the converse situations:

• Income or gain is recognized for tax purposes but is *never* realized for book purposes.
• A tax deduction is allowed that *never* corresponds to an expense or loss for book purposes.

Firms that experience a permanent book/tax difference never recoup the tax cost or repay the tax savings attributable to the difference.

Permanent Book/Tax Difference.   Refer to the facts in the previous example. During the current year, Corporation R realized $500,000 of revenues that were not recognized as taxable income (life insurance proceeds) and incurred a $4,000 nondeductible expense (insurance premiums). At a 34 percent marginal rate, Corporation R's permanent tax savings with respect to the $496,000 net book/tax difference is $168,640.

The next section of this chapter analyzes differences between financial statement income and taxable income that arise because of differences in the firm's method of accounting for book and tax purposes. These differences are **temporary differences:** the same item of income, gain, expense, or loss is taken into account in a different year (or years) for book purposes than for tax purposes. Any current year excess of taxable income over book income caused by a temporary difference turns around as an excess of book income over taxable income in some future year, and vice versa. The current year tax cost or tax savings attributable to the temporary difference is recouped or repaid in the future year when the difference reverses.

Reversal of Temporary Book/Tax Difference.   In year 1, Corporation Q engages in a transaction that generates $100,000 of income for financial accounting purposes. For tax purposes, the transaction generates $60,000 of income in year 1, $35,000 of income in year 2, and $5,000 of income in year 3. The following table shows the computation of the book/tax difference each year and the tax savings (cost) attributable to the difference at a 34 percent rate:

	Book Income	Taxable Income	Difference	Tax Savings (Cost)
Year 1	$100,000	$ 60,000	$ 40,000	$ 13,600
Year 2	–0–	35,000	(35,000)	(11,900)
Year 3	–0–	5,000	(5,000)	(1,700)
Total	$100,000	$100,000	$ –0–	$ –0–

Tax Expense versus Tax Payable.   When a firm experiences temporary book/tax differences, the federal tax expense reported on the firm's income statement is based on book income rather than taxable income. Consequently, federal tax expense per books is different from the actual federal tax liability the firm must pay. The difference between the two tax numbers is recorded as **deferred taxes** on the firm's balance sheet.[28]

Deferred Taxes.   In year 1, Corporation Q's tax expense per books with respect to the transaction described in the previous example is based on $100,000 of book income; at a 34 percent rate, the tax expense is $34,000. However, the firm pays only $20,400 of tax in year 1 with respect to the transaction (34 percent of $60,000 taxable income). The $13,600 difference is credited to Corporation Q's deferred tax account. In years 2 and 3, Corporation Q has no tax expense per books with respect to the transaction. The tax payments in those years are charged against the deferred tax account, which is reduced to zero by the end of the three-year period.

	Tax Expense	Current Tax Payable	Deferred Taxes
Year 1	$34,000	$20,400	$ 13,600
Year 2	–0–	11,900	(11,900)
Year 3	–0–	1,700	(1,700)
Total	$34,000	$34,000	–0–

The deferred tax account in this example reflects Corporation Q's tax savings in year 1 attributable to the $40,000 of financial statement income deferred for tax purposes. Corporation Q repays this tax savings in years 2 and 3 when aggregate taxable income exceeds financial statement income by $40,000.

Accounting Method Issues in Computing Taxable Income

In this section of Chapter 5, we address a number of issues that firms must consider in choosing and implementing a method of accounting for tax purposes. Some issues relate only to the cash method while others relate to the accrual method. Many of the issues involve transactions that must be accounted for differently under GAAP and the tax law.

Cash Method Issues

From a small firm's viewpoint, the cash method of accounting has the advantage of being both simple and objective. The cash method also provides a measure of control over the timing of income recognition.

---

[28]Permanent book/tax differences do not create deferred taxes. The tax cost or savings from a permanent difference is reflected in current year tax expense.

Cash Method Control.   Firm E, a calendar year, cash basis service business, completes all the work required on a major engagement by the end of November. Firm E can control the timing of the recognition of income from this engagement through its billing procedure. If Firm E delays the billing so that the client doesn't remit payment until January, the firm won't recognize taxable income until the following year, even though the income was earned in the current year. The firm's opportunity cost of the deferral is minimal because the receipt of the cash payment is delayed by less than two months. However, Firm E defers paying federal income tax on that income for a full year.

Objective 7
Define the doctrine of constructive receipt for cash basis firms.

Constructive Receipt.   Under the cash method of accounting, income is received when a person has unrestricted access to and control of the income, even if the income item is not in the person's actual possession. Treasury regulations state that this doctrine of **constructive receipt** applies when income is credited to a taxpayer's account, set apart for him, or otherwise made available so the taxpayer can draw on it during the taxable year.[29] For instance, interest accumulating in a savings account is constructively received by the owner of the account on the day she has the right to withdraw the interest; the owner doesn't avoid income recognition merely because she declines to make the withdrawal.

In litigation between cash basis firms and the IRS as to whether the firm was in constructive receipt of an item of income, the courts have generally concluded that constructive receipt occurred if no substantial barrier to the firm's control and possession of the income existed. In other words, a calendar year, cash basis company can't defer income from one year to the next by holding the checks received from its customers in December and cashing the checks the following January.[30]

Accounting for Inventories.   For federal tax purposes, even the smallest sole proprietorship that maintains an inventory of merchandise held for sale to customers must use the accrual method to account for purchases and sales of inventory.[31] This rule means that a firm can't simply deduct the cost of inventory items bought and paid for during the year. Instead, the firm must maintain records of the inventory on hand at year-end and reflect the cost of such inventory as an asset on the balance sheet rather than as a current year expense. When the firm sells an item of inventory, income must be recognized in the year of sale instead of the year that payment is received from the customer. Even though firms must use the accrual method to account for purchases and sales of inventory, they may use the cash method to account for other transactions. As a result, many small companies use this **hybrid method of accounting** for both book and tax purposes.

---

[29]Reg. §1.451-2(a).
[30]*C. F. Kahler*, 18 TC 31 (1952).
[31]Regs. §1.446-1(a)(4)(i) and §1.471-1.

Inventory or Supplies?   Galeridge Construction Inc., an asphalt paving contractor, used the cash method to account for the income from its paving jobs. At the beginning of each day, Galeridge picked up hot asphalt from the manufacturer, hauled the asphalt to the customer's job site, and quickly laid the asphalt while it was still pliable. At the end of the day, Galeridge discarded any unused asphalt, which was rock hard and could not be remelted or returned to the manufacturer. Galeridge deducted the cost of the asphalt as a supplies expense and recognized income with respect to each paving contract only when payment was received from the customer. The IRS contended that the asphalt was "merchandise" and that Galeridge maintained an inventory as part of its business activity. Consequently, Galeridge must use the accrual method of accounting for the purchase and sale of the asphalt. The federal court that heard the dispute disagreed with the IRS by concluding that Galeridge Construction was a provider of services and that the asphalt was a supply consumed in the provision of such services. The company did not maintain inventories and was not required to use the accrual method of accounting.[32]

Prepaid Expenses and Interest.   Under the cash method of accounting, an expense is deductible in the year payment is made. Cash basis firms can create a current deduction by paying an expense before the year in which that expense contributes to the generation of revenues. If the tax savings from the deduction is greater than the opportunity cost of the early payment, the firm has implemented a successful tax planning strategy. This strategy is limited by the well-established rule of law that any expense creating an asset with a useful life extending beyond the close of the year is not deductible but must be capitalized and amortized over its useful life.[33] Both the IRS and the courts agree that, as a rule of thumb, payments for assets to be consumed by the close of the *following* year are fully deductible in the year of payment.[34]

Prepaid Expenses.   On December 29, Firm L, a calendar year, cash basis taxpayer, paid $1,100 for six months' worth of office supplies and $4,200 for a fire and casualty insurance policy on its business equipment. The policy will be in force for the next three calendar years. Firm L can deduct the $1,100 payment because the supplies will be consumed by the end of the next year. In contrast, Firm L must capitalize the $4,200 insurance premium and deduct one-third ($1,400) of the cost in each of the next three taxable years.

For many years, cash basis firms with a bit of excess liquidity toward the end of the taxable year could generate a deduction by making prepayments of interest expense to cooperative creditors. Congress forestalled this popular planning technique by enacting

[32]*Galeridge Construction Inc.,* TC Memo 1997–240.
[33]*Welch v. Helvering,* 290 U.S. 111 (1933).
[34]Rev. Rul. 79-229, 1979-2 CB 210.

a statutory requirement that prepaid interest be capitalized and deducted in the future year or years for which the interest is actually charged.[35]

> ***Prepaid Interest.***   On October 1, Firm W, a calender year, cash basis taxpayer, borrowed $100,000 from a local bank at 8.2 percent interest per annum. On December 19, the firm paid $8,200 to the bank for the first year's interest on the loan. Even though Firm W is a cash basis taxpayer, it can deduct only $2,050 (the interest charged for October, November, and December of the current year). The $6,150 interest charged for the period from January 1 through September 30 of the following year is deductible by Firm W in the following year.

Limitation on Use of the Cash Method by Corporations.   Because the cash method of accounting can be manipulated to result in the deferral of income and acceleration of deductions, Congress limited its use by large corporate taxpayers. The Internal Revenue Code prohibits corporations and partnerships with corporate partners from using the cash method for tax purposes.[36] This prohibition does not apply to **personal service corporations:** corporations that offer professional services (medical, legal, accounting, etc.) performed for the corporation's clients by the corporation's shareholders. Any corporation, no matter how large, that meets this definition may use the cash method to compute its taxable income.

Accrual Method Issues

Objective 8
Recognize the common differences between the calculation of book and taxable income for accrual basis firms.

Large companies that prepare financial statements for external users generally utilize the accrual method to compute income for both financial reporting and tax purposes. In spite of this overall consistency in accounting methods, many isolated differences distinguish the calculation of book and taxable income for accrual basis firms.

Prepaid Income.   Under the accrual method of accounting, income generated by the sale of goods or performance of services is realized when the goods or services are actually provided to customers or clients, even if the customers or clients remit payment in an earlier year. For financial statement purposes, such prepayments are not included in the recipient's income. The Treasury is unwilling to be so patient, preferring to collect tax when firms have the cash in hand to pay. Thus, federal tax law requires that many types of prepaid income be recognized as gross income in the year received.[37]

---

[35]§461(g). This capitalization requirement does not apply to prepaid interest (points) on certain home mortgages.

[36]§448. Any corporation or partnership business that meets a statutory *de minimis test* may use the cash method of accounting for tax purposes. This test is met if the business has average annual gross receipts of $5 million or less for its three most recent taxable years.

[37]Prepaid income for services is subject to a special rule. If the recipient is required by contract to perform the services by the end of the year following the year of receipt, the recipient recognizes the income in the year earned (i.e., under the accrual method). If the recipient could delay performing the services until after the following year, the prepaid income must be recognized in the year of receipt. Rev. Proc. 71-21, 1971-2 CB 549.

Prepaid Income.   Corporation X, an accrual basis taxpayer, leases real estate to a tenant for an annual rent of $30,000. At the beginning of its current taxable year, Corporation X receives a $90,000 payment from the lessee for three years' rent. For financial statement purposes, Corporation X realizes the $30,000 rent earned for the current year and records the $60,000 prepayment in a deferred income account. For tax purposes, the firm must recognize the entire $90,000 of income on its current year tax return. The $60,000 excess of taxable income over book income is a temporary difference; over the next two years the difference will reverse as the firm realizes $30,000 of financial statement income each year without any corresponding recognition of taxable income.

Related Party Accruals.   The parties to a business transaction may use different methods to account for the tax consequences of the transaction. As a result, the two sides of the transaction may be reported in different years.

Different Accounting Methods: Arm's-Length Transaction.   Company AB, an accrual basis taxpayer, hires Firm CB, a cash basis taxpayer, to provide professional services. Firm CB performs the services in year 1 and bills Company AB for $10,000. Company AB pays this bill in year 2. For financial statement purposes, the two parties record the following:

	Year 1	Year 2
Company AB's accrued expense	$(10,000)	–0–
Firm CB's realized income	–0–	$10,000

If Company AB and Firm CB are not related parties, the tax consequences of the transaction are consistent with the financial accounting treatment. Company AB reaps the tax savings from a $10,000 deduction in year 1, while Firm CB bears the tax cost of the $10,000 of income in year 2. In present value terms, the tax savings exceed the tax cost, even if both parties have the same marginal tax rate. Although the Treasury is being whipsawed because of the differences in the parties' accounting methods, the tax law tolerates the result as a natural by-product of the arm's-length transaction.

Now assume that Firm CB owns a controlling interest in Company AB. Because the transaction occurs between related parties, the tax law refuses to let Company AB claim a deduction in year 1. Instead, Company AB must defer the deduction for its $10,000 expense until year 2 when Firm CB recognizes $10,000 of income from the transaction.[38]

---

[38]§267(a)(2). Under this section, a controlling interest is generally more than a 50 percent ownership interest.

Different Accounting Methods: Related Parties.   If Company AB and Firm CB are related parties, Company AB will expense the $10,000 liability for financial statement purposes in year 1 but report a $10,000 tax deduction in year 2.

	Year 1	*Year 2*
Company AB's:		
Accrued expense	$(10,000)	–0–
Tax deduction	–0–	$(10,000)
Firm CB's realized income	–0–	10,000

Business Bad Debts.   When an accrual basis firm sells goods or services and the purchaser doesn't pay cash at the point of sale, the firm records an account receivable for the sales price. The firm simultaneously realizes income because the earnings process with respect to the sale is complete. Firms anticipate that some portion of their accounts receivable will never be collected because of defaults by customers to whom the firm extended credit. According to GAAP, firms should use the **allowance method** to account for bad debts. Under this method, firms estimate the portion of their accounts receivables that will be uncollectible and establish a bad debt allowance or reserve for this portion. The annual addition to the allowance represents the current year receivables expected to go bad. This addition is recorded as a bad debt expense and matched against sales revenue.

Congress and the Treasury are extremely reluctant to allow firms to claim a tax deduction based on the mere expectation of a future event. Accordingly, firms must use the **direct write-off method** for tax purposes. Under this method, firms can deduct accounts receivable (and any other business debts) actually written off as uncollectible during the current year.[39]

Accounting for Bad Debts.   ABC Inc., an accrual basis corporation, began the year with a $298,000 balance in its allowance for bad debts. During the year, the controller concluded that $155,000 of ABC's accounts receivable were worthless and should be written off against this allowance. Based on ABC's year-end accounts receivable, the independent auditors determined that a $173,000 addition to the bad debt allowance was necessary. As a result, the year-end balance in the allowance increased to $316,000.

Beginning allowance for bad debts	$298,000
Actual write-offs during the year	(155,000)
Addition to allowance required by auditors	173,000
Ending allowance for bad debts	$316,000

---

[39] §166(a).

> ABC's financial income statement shows a bad debt expense of $173,000; ABC's tax return shows a bad debt deduction of only $155,000. If ABC's book income before tax is $6,700,000 *and the firm has no other book/tax differences*, its taxable income is computed as follows:
>
> | | |
> |---|---:|
> | Net income per books (before tax) | $6,700,000 |
> | Nondeductible bad debt expense | 173,000 |
> | Deductible bad debt write-offs | (155,000) |
> | Taxable income | $6,718,000 |

Premature Accruals.   Under GAAP, a business liability attributable to current operations must be reflected as an expense even if the liability is not paid until a future year. Consider the case of Company GD, which provides a medical reimbursement plan for its workforce. At year-end, GD routinely estimates the reimbursable expenses incurred by its employees over the past 12 months for which the employees have not yet filed claims. For financial statement purposes, GD must accrue both a current expense and a liability for the estimated amount. But should this accrued expense, which is based on the estimated cost of a future event, be deductible on GD's tax return?

The tax law contains an **all-events test** for determining if an accrued expense qualifies as a tax deduction. The test consists of two basic requirements.[40] First, the liability on which the accrued expense is based must be fixed; in other words, all the events necessary to establish the liability must have occurred. Second, the amount of the liability must be determinable with reasonable accuracy. Referring back to the case of Company GD, does the company's accrual of reimbursable medical expenses pass the all-events test? The Supreme Court, which considered this case, concluded that the accrual failed the test because GD's liability for the reimbursements was not absolutely established until its employees actually filed their completed claim forms.[41] Hence, the company had to wait until the taxable year in which a claim was filed to take a deduction for the medical reimbursement.

For most year-end accruals that result in a proper matching of the accrued expense against current revenues, the all-events test consists of only the two requirements described in the preceding paragraph. But in the case of certain nonrecurring, extraordinary accruals, the all-events test has a third requirement: **economic performance** with respect to the liability must occur before a deduction is allowed. In its most general sense, economic performance means that all activities necessary to satisfy the liability have been completed. Because the technical details concerning economic performance are so many and so complex, let's content ourselves with two examples illustrating the severity of this third requirement.

Economic Performance: Tort Liability.   Mr. D is seriously injured due to the alleged negligence of his employer, Firm V. The independent auditors insist that Firm V accrue its contingent liability for legal damages and report the

---

[40]Reg. §1.461-1(a)(2)(i).

[41]*United States* v. *General Dynamics Corp.*, 481 U.S. 239 (1987).

corresponding expense on its financial income statement. However, Firm V cannot deduct the accrued expense because the fact of the liability has not yet been established. Two years later, the employee has his day in court and the jury awards him $1.2 million in damages. At this point, the first two requirements of the all-events test are satisfied. But for a liability arising out of any tort, economic performance does not occur until Firm V actually makes a $1.2 million payment to the employee.[42] If Firm V delays paying the $1.2 million until the year after the litigation, the $1.2 tax deduction for the expense will be delayed as well.

Economic Performance: Provided Services.   In the current year, accrual basis Partnership PST enters into a binding contract with a legal firm under which the firm agrees to provide future professional services to PST for a flat fee of $500,000. PST will not pay the fee until the services are completed. At the end of the year, PST accrues a $500,000 liability on its books. Because both the legal fact and the dollar amount of the liability are certain, the accrual meets the first two requirements of the all-events test. Nevertheless, economic performance will not occur until the year in which the services are completed. Consequently, Partnership PST cannot deduct the accrued expense until the year of completion.[43]

Even though the all-events test postpones, rather than disallows, a deduction for the *premature* accrual of an expense and therefore affects only the timing of the deduction, the postponement has a real impact on the after-tax cost of the expense. To quantify this impact, let's build on the preceding example involving Partnership PST.

All-Events Test and After-Tax Costs.   Partnership PST contracted for $500,000 of legal services in year 1 but does not pay for the services until they are completed in year 3. Under the all-events test, the partnership cannot deduct the expense until year 3. If the PST partners pay tax at a 39.6 percent marginal rate and use a 9 percent discount rate, the postponement of the deduction from year 1 to year 3 increases the after-tax cost of the expense from $223,000 to $254,284.

	Year 1	Year 3
Current deduction:		
Before-tax cost of legal services	–0–	$(500,000)
Tax savings		
($500,000 deduction × 39.6%)	$ 198,000	–0–
Present value of year 1 cash	$ 198,000	–0–

---

[42]§461(h)(2)(C).
[43]§461(h)(2)(A)(i).

Present value of year 3 cash ($500,000 × .842 discount factor)	(421,000)	
NPV (after-tax cost)	$(223,000)	
Postponed deduction:		
Before-tax cost of legal services	–0–	$(500,000)
Tax savings ($500,000 deduction × 39.6%)	–0–	198,000
		$(302,000)
NPV (after-tax cost) ($302,000 × .842 discount factor)	$(254,284)	

Section 482

When related parties enter into business transactions, the IRS has particular reason to scrutinize the methods of accounting used by the parties to report the tax consequences of the transaction. Congress has given the IRS broad authority to challenge the accounting for related party transactions under Section 482 of the Internal Revenue Code. The section states that in the case of two or more businesses under common ownership or control, the IRS may "distribute, apportion, or allocate gross income, deduction, credits, or allowances" among the businesses to clearly reflect the income of each.

The IRS typically invokes Section 482 when it determines that a method of accounting results in a beneficial shift of income between related parties. The following case illustrates this situation:

Using an Accounting Method to Shift Income. ABC Inc. and XYZ Inc. are owned by the same four shareholders. ABC operates a profitable manufacturing business; XYZ is a regional wholesaler that purchases its inventory from a number of suppliers, including ABC. During the current year, ABC's marginal tax rate is 39 percent and XYZ's marginal tax rate is only 15 percent. As a result, the owners have an incentive to shift income away from ABC to XYZ. They accomplish this shift by having ABC sell its product to XYZ at cost instead of the normal price charged to unrelated wholesalers. When XYZ sells ABC's product to unrelated customers, the entire profit with respect to the manufacture and sale of the product is included in XYZ's income.

In the above example, ABC's unique method of accounting for its sales to XYZ distorts the taxable income of both corporations. If a revenue agent discovers the questionable accounting method during the course of an audit, the IRS could invoke its authority under Section 482. Specifically, the IRS could impose a method of accounting that, in its opinion, clearly reflects the income earned by ABC on its intercompany sales.

Net Operating Losses

In this chapter, we've learned that firms must choose a consistent method of accounting to divide a continuous stream of business income into 12-month segments. The choice of accounting method has very little to do with the measurement of taxable income *over the life* of a firm, but everything to do with the measurement of income for each taxable year. The final section of this chapter focuses on one possible outcome of this annual measurement process: a net operating loss.

The Problem of Excess Deductions

If a firm's business operations for a taxable year result in an excess of deductible expenses over gross income, this excess is labeled a **net operating loss (NOL)** and is reported as such on its tax return. Because it reports no taxable income, the firm obviously incurs no current year tax cost. But a more subtle fact is that the excess deductions yield no current tax savings; the firm has the same zero tax cost with or without these deductions. If the excess deductions are simply wasted because they never reduce the firm's tax cost, the firm's average tax rate *over time* could be distorted.

Excess Deductions and Average Tax Rate.   TUV Inc. conducts a business with a 24-month operating cycle. TUV's most recent operating cycle generated $300,000 of economic profit:

	Year 1	Year 2	Total
Gross revenue	$ 100,000	$ 625,000	$ 725,000
Operating expenses	(300,000)	(125,000)	(425,000)
Economic profit			$ 300,000

If TUV had to report its income and pay a tax based on strict 12-month intervals, it would report a $200,000 NOL for year 1 and $500,000 of taxable income for year 2. At a 34 percent rate, the firm would owe no tax in year 1 and $170,000 of tax in year 2. Thus, TUV's overall tax rate on its economic profit would be 56.67 percent:

$$\$170,000 \text{ tax} \div \$300,000 \text{ profit} = 56.67\%$$

This inflated rate reflects the fact that $200,000 of TUV's deductible expenses (the year 1 NOL) generated no tax savings for the corporation.

Solution: The NOL Deduction

Objective 9
Explain how the net operating loss deduction allows firms to smooth taxable income over time.

The tax law prevents the rate distortion that could result from an inflexible one-year reporting period by permitting firms to smooth their income over time by deducting excess expenses incurred in one year against income recognized in another. Specifically, a firm may carry a current NOL back as a deduction against taxable income reported in the two years immediately before the current year; the deduction must be used in chronological order beginning with the earlier year in the carryback period.[44] Any NOL

---
[44]§172.

in excess of the previous two years' income may be carried forward as a deduction to the next 20 taxable years.

NOL Carryback and Carryforward. In 19X4, Corporation Q generated a $612,000 NOL. The following schedule shows the years in which the corporation used the NOL as a deduction against taxable income.

	19X2	19X3	19X5	19X6	19X7	19X8
Taxable income before NOL deduction	$ 165,000	$ 110,000	$ 138,000	$ 99,000	$ 54,000	$ 125,000
NOL deduction	(165,000)	(110,000)	(138,000)	(99,000)	(54,000)	(46,000)
Taxable income	$ –0–	$ –0–	$ –0–	$ –0–	$ –0–	$ 79,000

Corporation Q used $275,000 of the 19X4 NOL as carryback deductions to reduce 19X2 and 19X3 taxable income to zero. It used the remaining $337,000 NOL as carryforward deductions in 19X5 through 19X8.

A firm reports an **NOL carryback** by filing a one-page form with the IRS showing (1) the NOL deducted against prior year income and (2) the recomputed prior year tax liability. After processing the form, the IRS refunds the prior year overpayment of tax to the firm. A firm reports an **NOL carryforward** as a deduction on future tax returns until the NOL has been fully utilized or until it expires.

Let's incorporate an NOL deduction into the earlier example involving TUV Inc.

NOL Deduction. Assuming that year 1 was TUV Inc.'s first taxable year, the NOL in year 1 is carried forward as a deduction into year 2. The firm's tax returns for the two years show the following:

	Year 1	Year 2
Gross income	$ 100,000	$ 625,000
Deductible expenses	(300,000)	(125,000)
NOL	$(200,000)	
NOL carryforward deduction	└──────────▶	(200,000)
Taxable income		$ 300,000

At a 34 percent rate, TUV owes $102,000 of tax in year 2. Because of the NOL carryforward, TUV's taxable income in year 2 equals the firm's $300,000 profit for the 24-month operating cycle, and the firm's overall tax rate with respect to this profit is 34 percent.

Determining the Value of an NOL Deduction

The value of a deduction equals the tax savings attributable to the deduction. In the case of an NOL deduction, the tax savings (and the impact on cash flows) depends on the year (or years) in which the firm takes the deduction against taxable income. If the NOL can be deducted against prior years' income, the firm enjoys the tax savings immediately in the form of a cash refund.

Cash Flow from an NOL Carryback. Corporation C, which has operated profitably for 12 years, experiences a severe business downturn during 19X5 and closes the year with a $900,000 loss. The corporation carries this loss back as an NOL deduction to 19X3 and 19X4:

	19X3	*19X4*
Taxable income on original return	$ 430,000	$1,600,000
NOL carryback from 19X5	(430,000)	(470,000)
Recomputed taxable income	$ –0–	$1,130,000
Tax on original return*	$ 146,200	$ 544,000
Recomputed tax	–0–	(384,200)
Refund due to Corporation C	$ 146,200	$ 159,800

*Tax computations are based on the current corporate rate schedule.

Corporation C will receive a $306,000 refund of 19X3 and 19X4 taxes, a cash inflow resulting in a 19X5 *after-tax* loss of $594,000 ($900,000 operating loss minus $306,000 tax savings). In other words, the NOL deduction is worth $306,000 to Corporation C.

Now let's modify the example so that 19X5 is Corporation C's first taxable year. Consequently, the corporation can use its $900,000 NOL deduction only on a carryforward basis. In this case, the present value of the deduction depends on the corporation's forecast of its future income stream.

NPV of an NOL Carryforward. Corporation C projects that its business activity will generate $350,000 of annual income over the next three years. Based on a 9 percent discount rate, the value of Corporation C's NOL carryforward is only $268,958:

	19X6	*19X7*	*19X8*
Projected annual income	$ 350,000	$ 350,000	$ 350,000
NOL carryforward from 19X5	(350,000)	(350,000)	(200,000)
Taxable income	$ –0–	$ –0–	$ 150,000

Tax on annual income before NOL deduction*	$ 119,000	$ 119,000	$ 119,000
Actual tax liability	–0–	–0–	(41,750)
Tax savings from NOL	$ 119,000	$ 119,000	$ 77,250
Present value of tax savings	$ 109,123	$ 100,198	$ 59,637
NPV of tax savings	$ 268,958		

*Tax computations are based on the current corporate rate schedule.

Because the tax savings from the NOL deduction are deferred into future years, the present value of the deduction decreases. Therefore, Corporation C's after-tax 19X5 loss is $631,042 ($900,000 − $268,958). Clearly, the longer the period of time over which a firm deducts an NOL carryforward, the less value the deduction has to the firm.

Giving Up an NOL Carryback

An interesting feature of the NOL deduction is that firms can elect to give up the carryback and keep the entire loss as a prospective deduction for future years.[45] In most cases, firms are eager to use an NOL carryback deduction to create immediate cash flow in the form of a tax refund. However, if a firm determines that its marginal tax rate during the two-year carryback period was significantly lower than its projected rate for future years, a decision to forgo the carryback may maximize the value of the NOL deduction.

Giving Up an NOL Carryback.   Corporation JM incurs a $20,000 NOL for its current taxable year. The corporation could carry the NOL back as a deduction against prior year income. However, the marginal tax rate in the carryback year was only 25 percent. Corporation JM projects that its marginal tax rate next year will be 39 percent. If the corporation uses a 12 percent discount rate, the NOL deduction is worth $1,965 more as a carryforward than as a carryback.

Present value of NOL carryforward	
($20,000 × 39% × .893 discount factor)	$ 6,965
Present value of NOL carryback	
($20,000 × 25%)	(5,000)
	$ 1,965

Conclusion

The computation of business taxable income depends on the taxable year and the method of accounting adopted by the firm. Firms often use the same overall method for both financial reporting and tax purposes. Even so, many discrepancies exist between

[45]§172(b)(3).

the computations of book and taxable income. In subsequent chapters, we'll encounter many more of these book/tax differences. To make sense of these differences, it may help to keep the following in mind. The goal of generally accepted accounting principles (and financial statements prepared in accordance with GAAP) is to provide useful and pertinent information to management, shareholders, creditors, and other business decision makers. In contrast, the primary (but certainly not the only) goal of the Internal Revenue Code (and the responsibility of the IRS) is to generate and protect federal tax revenues.

Key Terms

Accrual method of accounting 100	Hybrid method of accounting 106
All-events test 111	Key-person life insurance policies 103
Allowance method 110	Matching principle 98
Annualized income 96	Method of accounting 97
Calendar year 95	Net operating loss (NOL) 114
Cash method of accounting 98	NOL carryback 115
Constructive receipt 106	NOL carryforward 115
Deferred taxes 105	Permanent difference 103
Direct write-off method 110	Personal service corporations 108
Economic performance 111	Realization principle 98
Fiscal year 95	Recognition 97
Generally accepted accounting principles (GAAP) 100	Short-period return 95
	Taxable income 94
Gross income 94	Temporary difference 104

Questions and Problems for Discussion

1. Discuss the choice of a taxable year for a firm operating the following:
   a. Retail plant and garden center.
   b. French bakery.
   c. Chimney cleaning business.
   d. Moving and transport business.
   e. Software consulting business.
2. Corporation DB operates three very different lines of business. Can the corporation elect a different overall method of accounting for each line of business or must the corporation adopt one overall method?
3. Firm LK bought a warehouse of used furniture to equip several of its clerical offices. An employee who was cleaning the furniture discovered a cache of gold coins in a desk drawer. A local court declared Firm LK the rightful owner of the coins, which have a market value of $72,000.

Does Firm LK have realized income because of this lucky event?
4. Discuss the various circumstances in which a firm is required to prepare financial statements in accordance with GAAP.
5. Firm NB, which uses the overall cash method of accounting, recently received two cases of French wine from a client in settlement of a $1,300 bill. As a cash basis taxpayer, does Firm NB avoid income recognition because it received a noncash item as payment?
6. For many years, Mr. K, the president of KJ Inc., took the corporation's most important clients to lunch at Al's Steak House several times a week. However, since the tax law was amended to disallow a deduction for 50 percent of the cost of business meals, Mr. K and his clients patronize this restaurant only once or twice a month. What

does this scenario suggest about the incidence of the indirect tax increase represented by the meals and entertainment disallowance rule?

7. If a corporation purchases insurance on the life of its chief executive officer and the corporation is named the policy beneficiary, the corporation's premium payments are nondeductible. If the officer's spouse and children are named as beneficiaries, the premium payments are deductible. Can you provide a reason for this inconsistent tax treatment?

8. Describe the contrasting treatment of prepaid income under GAAP and under the tax law and explain how each treatment reflects a different principle of conservatism.

9. Describe the book/tax difference resulting from each of the following business transactions:
   a. Firm A spent $110 on a business dinner attended by the firm's vice president and a potential client.
   b. Firm B borrowed $50,000 from an unrelated party and invested the loan proceeds in tax-exempt City of Los Angeles bonds. During the year, Firm B paid $2,800 of interest on the loan and earned $3,500 of interest on the bonds.
   c. Firm C sent its president and several other key employees to Washington D.C. to lobby a group of senators to enact legislation that would have an extremely beneficial impact on the firm's business. The cost of this trip was $7,400. While in the capitol city, the president attended a "$10,000 a plate" fund-raising dinner sponsored by one senator's reelection committee.

10. The manager of Firm Z, a new business enterprise that should enjoy a steady and substantial growth in profits over the next decade, must decide between the cash method and the accrual method as the firm's overall method for tax reporting purposes. She understands that the difference between the two methods is essentially one of timing and that over the life of the firm, either method should result in the same taxable income. What she doesn't understand is why the cash method might improve the net present value of the firm's cash flows over the next decade. Can you provide an explanation?

11. Net operating losses can be carried forward for 20 years, after which time they expire. Why is it unusual for a firm to experience the expiration of a net operating loss?

12. Why do tax preferences often result in differences between the computations of book income and taxable income? Would a book/tax difference attributable to a tax preference be a permanent difference or a timing difference? Which type of difference is more valuable to a firm in terms of net present value?

Application Problems

1. PT Inc., which has been in business since 1980, uses a fiscal year ending June 30 for federal tax reporting purposes. The shareholders recently voted to disband the business and dissolve the corporation under state law. PT ceased operations in September and distributed its remaining assets to its shareholders in October. The corporation's final tax return for the taxable year beginning on July 1 and ending on October 31 reported $80,000 of taxable income.
   a. Based on these facts, compute PT Inc.'s tax liability using the current corporate tax rates.
   b. Assume that PT Inc. operates an ongoing business. The corporation filed the short-period return described above because the IRS granted permission for the corporation to change its taxable year from a fiscal year ending June 30 to a fiscal year ending October 31. How does this change in fact affect the tax computation?

2. Firm B uses the calendar year as its taxable year and the cash method as its overall method of tax accounting. On December 31, 19X7, Firm B made the following cash payments. To what extent does the payment result in a deduction on Firm B's 19X7 tax return?
   a. $3,000 of compensation to an outside business consultant who spent three weeks in January

19X8 analyzing the firm's internal control system.

b. $5,000 to purchase a new refrigerator for the employee's lounge. The refrigerator was delivered on January 8, 19X8.

c. $16,900 of property tax to the local government. The tax is for the first six months of 19X8.

d. $50,000 for a two-year lease on office space. The lease begins on February 1, 19X8.

e. $23,700 of inventory items that Firm B holds for sale to its customers.

3. RTY Corporation is a calendar year taxpayer. On December 12, RTY billed a client $25,000 for services rendered during October and November. The corporation had not received payment of the bill by December 31. On December 10, RTY received a $4,000 check from a tenant that leases office space from the corporation. The payment was for the following year's January and February rent.

a. If RTY is a cash basis taxpayer, how much gross income should the corporation recognize from the above transactions in the current year?

b. If RTY is an accrual basis taxpayer, how much gross income should the corporation recognize from the above transactions in the current year?

4. Firm F, a calendar year taxpayer, owes an $800,000 long-term debt to an unrelated creditor. In December of the current year, the firm paid $72,000 to the creditor as interest for the 12-month period from September 1 of the current year through August 31 of the following year. Compute the firm's current year deduction for this payment assuming that:

a. Firm F uses the accrual method of accounting for tax purposes.

b. Firm F uses the cash method of accounting for tax purposes.

5. Company N, an accrual basis taxpayer, owes $50,000 to Creditor K. At the end of 19X1, Company N's bookkeeper properly accrued $4,100 of interest payable on this debt. The bookkeeper didn't pay this liability until March 3, 19X2. Both Company N and Creditor K are calendar year taxpayers. For each of the following cases, determine the year in which Company N can deduct the $4,100 interest expense.

a. Creditor K is a cash basis taxpayer, and Company N and Creditor K are unrelated parties.

b. Creditor K is an accrual basis taxpayer, and Company N and Creditor K are related parties.

c. Creditor K is a cash basis taxpayer, and Company N and Creditor K are related parties.

6. MG Inc. is an accrual basis taxpayer. In 19X7, the corporation's chief accountant concluded that a $65,000 account receivable was uncollectible and wrote it off as a bad debt. In 19X8, MG received a $65,000 check from the creditor in full payment of the old receivable.

a. What is the effect of the write-off of the receivable on MG's 19X7 financial statement income and taxable income?

b. What is the effect of the collection of the receivable on MG's 19X8 financial statement income and taxable income?

7. EFG Inc., an accrual basis taxpayer, reported $500,000 of net income before tax on its 19X7 financial statements prepared in accordance with GAAP. The corporation's financial records reveal the following information:

- EFG's allowance for bad debts as of January 1 was $58,000. Write-offs for the year totaled $13,800 while the addition to the allowance for the year was $12,500. The allowance as of December 31 was $56,700.

- On August 7, EFG paid a $17,500 fine to the state of Delaware for a violation of state pollution control laws.

- In October, EFG was sued by a consumers group maintaining the corporation engaged in false advertising practices. Although the corporation's lawyers are convinced that this is a frivolous suit that can eventually be settled out of court for a modest sum, EFG's independent auditors insisted on establishing a $50,000 allowance for contingent legal liability and reporting a $50,000 accrued expense on the 19X7 income statement.

Based on the above facts, compute EFG Inc.'s 19X7 taxable income.

8. In 19X9, GT Inc.'s net income before tax on its financial statements was $700,000 and its taxable income was $810,000. The $110,000 difference is the aggregate of a number of temporary book

tax differences. Based on these facts, compute the amount of increase or decrease in GT's deferred tax account if the corporation's tax rate is 35 percent.

9. PSD Inc., an accrual basis taxpayer, reported $320,000 of net income before tax on its 19X7 financial statements prepared in accordance with GAAP. The corporation's records reveal the following information:
   - Late in the year, PSD entered into a five-year licensing agreement with an unrelated firm. The agreement entitles the firm to use a PSD trade name in marketing its own products. In return, the firm will pay PSD an annual royalty of 1 percent of gross revenues from the sale of the product. The agreement required the firm to pay a $50,000 advanced royalty to PSD on the day the agreement was finalized. For financial statement purposes, this prepayment was credited to a deferred income account.
   - At its final meeting for 19X7, PSD's board of directors authorized a $25,000 salary bonus for the corporation's president to reward him for an outstanding performance over the last year. The president received the bonus on January 12, 19X8. The president does not own enough PSD stock to make him a related party for federal tax purposes.
   - PSD was incorporated in 19X6. On its 19X6 tax return, the corporation reported a $13,600 net operating loss.

   Based on the above facts, compute PSD Inc.'s 19X7 taxable income.

10. In 19X7, AS Inc., an accrual basis taxpayer, contracted with a nationally prominent artist to paint a mural in the lobby of the new corporate headquarters under construction. Under the terms of the contract, the artist's commission was $180,000, payable on completion of the mural. Construction was completed in 19X8, and the artist finished her work and received the $180,000 commission in 19X9. AS Inc. has a 35 percent marginal tax rate and uses a 12 percent discount rate to compute net present value.
    a. Compute AS's after-tax cost of the commission if the corporation can deduct the $180,000 accrued liability in 19X7.
    b. Compute AS's after-tax cost of the commission if the economic performance requirement prevents the corporation from deducting the commission until 19X9.

11. Corporation H's auditors prepared the following reconciliation between the corporation's book and taxable income for 19X8:

Net income before tax	$600,000
Permanent book/tax differences	15,000
Temporary book/tax differences	(76,000)
Taxable income	$539,000

Based on this reconciliation and using a 34 percent tax rate, compute:
    a. Federal tax expense for financial statement purposes.
    b. Federal tax liability.
    c. The amount credited to the corporation's deferred tax account.

Issue Recognition Problems

Identify the tax issue or issues suggested by the following situations and state each issue in the form of a question.

1. Corporation DS owns assets worth $550,000 and has outstanding debts of $750,000. One of DS's creditors just informed DS's controller that it is writing off a $15,000 account receivable from DS because it believes the receivable is uncollectible. However, even with this debt forgiveness, DS is insolvent and has no net worth.

2. Two years ago, a professional theater company paid $300 to an antique dealer for an old oil painting that the company used as a prop. This year the company's prop manager was cleaning the painting and discovered an older painting hidden beneath the top coat of pigment. To the company's delight, the older painting was signed by Paul

Cezanne. Two independent appraisers determined that the painting is worth at least $250,000.

3. BL Inc. has been in business since 1990. During the current year, the corporation's new CPA discovered that BL has been using an incorrect tax accounting method for a certain category of business expense. The corporation is willing to change to the correct tax accounting method recommended by the CPA.

4. Company A, a calendar year taxpayer, has always used the cash method of accounting for tax purposes. The company completed an engagement for a major client in November 19X8 and submitted a bill for its $160,000 fee. Because Company A did not receive payment before year-end, it recognized no income from the engagement on its 19X8 tax return. Early the next year, the company requested and received permission from the IRS to change from the cash method to the accrual method of accounting. This change is effective for Company A's 19X9 taxable year. On February 2, 19X9, the company's bookkeeper received a $160,000 check from the client in payment of the prior year bill.

5. Mr. RJ owns and operates a consulting firm that uses a calendar year and the cash method for tax accounting purposes. In November, Mr. RJ billed a client $3,500 for services performed during the previous September. After waiting several weeks, Mr. RJ called the client to remind her of the bill. The embarrassed client promised to telephone Mr. RJ as soon as her bookkeeper prepared a check for $3,500. Mr. RJ left his business office on December 23 and did not return until January 2. A message on his answering machine informed him that he could pick up his check from the client's receptionist. The message was dated December 30.

6. CVB Company, an accrual basis, calendar year taxpayer, operates a chain of 42 retail candy stores. During December 19X1, the company sponsored a contest for its customers called "Guess the Gumballs." Each store displayed a large glass bowl filled with gumballs. Each customer who bought at least $20 of merchandise could write a guess as to the number of gumballs on an entry card, which the store manager kept on file. The contest closed on December 31, 19X1. On January 3, 19X2, each store manager identified the entry card with the most accurate

guess. The 42 lucky winners were notified by telephone that they could come by the store to claim their $2,500 cash prize.

7. The ABC Investment Partnership owns 100 percent of the stock of two corporations, HT Inc. (an advertising firm) and LT Inc. (a commercial real estate development firm). HT Inc. is in a 34 percent marginal tax bracket this year. LT Inc. has an NOL carryforward deduction and will pay no tax this year. HT Inc. recently developed a new advertising campaign for LT Inc. and charged $75,000 for its services.

8. During its 19X7 taxable year, Firm K paid $129,000 of real property tax to Jurisdiction J and deducted the payment in the computation of 19X7 taxable income. In 19X8, the firm's chief financial officer successfully contested the property tax assessment. As a result, Jurisdiction J refunded $18,000 of Firm K's prior year property tax payment.

9. During its 19X6 taxable year, Firm G completed a consulting engagement for a client and received a $200,000 cash payment for its services. In December, the client notified Firm G that it was not satisfied with a particular aspect of the engagement and demanded that Firm G refund $50,000 of the payment. Firm G refused to make any refund and referred the matter to its attorney. In 19X8, Firm G settled the dispute by paying the client $30,000. Firm G's marginal tax rate for 19X6 was 39 percent. Its marginal tax rate for 19X8 was 34 percent.

10. Corporation WJ began business in 19X1 and reported taxable income in both 19X1 and 19X2. In 19X3, the corporation incurred a $25,000 net operating loss. The corporation's controller plans to carry the loss back as a deduction against 19X2 taxable income because WJ's marginal tax rate in 19X2 was higher than its marginal tax rate in 19X1.

11. Corporation BL and Corporation TM are both calendar year corporations. On January 1, 19X9, BL purchased TM's entire business (all TM's balance sheet assets). TM's shareholders then dissolved the corporation under state law. As of January 1, Corporation TM had $190,000 of NOL carryforwards from prior taxable years. Corporation BL's business activity for 19X9 (which includes the business purchased from TM) generated $600,000 of taxable income.

Tax Planning Cases

1. Company Y began business in February 19X1. By the end of the calendar year, the company had billed its clients for $3.5 million of services and had incurred $800,000 of operating expenses. As of December 31, the company had collected $2.9 of its billings and had paid $670,000 of its expenses. It expects to collect the remaining outstanding bills and pay the remaining expenses by March of the following year. Company Y has decided to adopt a calendar year for federal tax purposes. The company may use either the cash method or the accrual method of accounting on its first tax return. The company's treasurer has asked you to quantify the value of using the cash method for the first year; in doing so, assume Company Y uses a 10 percent discount rate to compute net present value.

2. Corporation NVB generated a $350,000 net operating loss for 19X7. The corporation's tax return for the three previous years provide the following information:

	19X4	19X5	19X6
Gross income	$ 150,000	$ 1,890,000	$ 7,810,000
Deductions	(190,000)	(1,830,000)	(7,700,000)
Taxable income (NOL)	$ (40,000)	$ 60,000	$ 110,000

a. Based on the above data, did the corporation derive any tax benefit from its 19X4 NOL? Explain your conclusions.

b. Corporation NVB's chief financial officer forecasts that the corporation will continue to operate at a loss through 19X8 but should generate at least $1 million of taxable income in 19X9. Based on this projection, compute the value of the 19X7 NOL, assuming the corporation deducts the NOL as a carryback and carryforward to the extent possible. In making your calculations, use a 12 percent discount rate to compute net present value.

c. Should Corporation NVB elect to give up the carryback of its 19X7 NOL and use the entire NOL as a carryforward deduction? Support your conclusion with calculations.

6 Property Acquisitions and Cost Recovery Deductions

Learning Objectives

After studying this chapter, you should be able to:

1. Describe the factors that determine if a business expenditure qualifies as a current deduction or a capital cost.
2. Define the terms *tax basis* and *adjusted basis*.
3. Explain why the use of leverage can reduce the after-tax cost of purchased assets.
4. Apply the formula to compute cost of goods sold.
5. Describe the relationship between recovery period, depreciation method, and depreciation convention in the MACRS computation.
6. Explain the benefit of and the limitations on the limited expensing election.
7. Incorporate depreciation deductions into the computation of net present value.
8. Explain how a firm recovers the cost of purchased intangibles through amortization.
9. Distinguish between cost depletion and percentage depletion.

In Chapter 5, we learned that a firm's taxable income equals the excess of gross income recognized over deductible expenses for the year. If a firm has an excess of deductions over gross income, the excess is a net operating loss that may be carried back or forward as a deduction in prior or future years. Of course, not every business expenditure relates solely to current year operations. If an expenditure results in a long-term benefit, the firm generally is not allowed to deduct the entire expenditure against current year gross income. Instead, the deduction is deferred and properly matched against the firm's future income stream.

In Chapter 6, we address this timing issue: In which taxable year or years can a firm deduct its business expenditures against gross income? The chapter begins with a discussion of the tax rules that distinguish between expenditures that qualify as current deductions and expenditures that must be capitalized. The discussion then turns to the concept of capitalized costs as the tax basis of business assets. The relationship between basis and cost recovery deductions is explored, and the impact of this relationship on cash flows is examined. The second part of the chapter focuses on the various methods by which firms recover basis as cost of goods sold or through depreciation, amortization, and depletion deductions.

Deductible Expense or Capitalized Cost?

Objective 1
Describe the factors that determine if a business expenditure qualifies as a current deduction or a capital cost.

When a firm expends resources as part of its income-generating activity, the cost of the expenditure is reduced by any tax savings attributable to the expenditure. In present value terms, the tax savings are usually maximized (and the after-tax cost is minimized) if the expenditure is deductible in the current tax year. The present value of the tax savings decreases if the firm must capitalize the expenditure and postpone its deduction until some future year. For tax accounting purposes, **capitalization** means that an expenditure is recorded as an asset on the balance sheet rather than as a current expense. If the firm is never allowed any tax deduction for the capitalized expenditure, the before-tax cost of the expenditure equals its after-tax cost.

Absent any restrictions, firms would deduct every business expenditure in the current year. However, a basic premise of the federal income tax is that *no expenditure is deductible* unless a specific provision of the Internal Revenue Code authorizes the deduction. The Supreme Court has elaborated on this premise by observing that "an income tax deduction is a matter of legislative grace" and "the burden of clearly showing the right to the claimed deduction is on the taxpayer."[1] These observations are consistent with the tax law's conservative attitude toward the measurement of taxable income.

The Internal Revenue Code does allow firms to deduct all "ordinary and necessary expenses paid or incurred during the taxable year in carrying on any trade or business."[2] Because of this generic rule, firms deduct routine operating expenses in the year the expenses are recognized under the firm's method of accounting. But the Code also prohibits a deduction for payments for "permanent improvements or betterments made to increase the value of any property."[3] As we will learn later in this chapter, the law softens this prohibition by allowing firms to recover many capital expenditures in the form of *future* deductions. In these cases, the difference in the tax consequences of current expenses and capitalized costs is the timing of the deduction for each. Even so, in cash flow terms, future deductions are worth less than current deductions, and firms minimize their cost of operations by deducting expenditures as quickly as possible.

What factors determine whether a particular business expenditure qualifies as a current deduction or a nondeductible capital cost? If the expenditure results in the creation or enhancement of a distinct asset with a useful life substantially beyond the current year, the expenditure must be capitalized.[4] Even if the expenditure does not result in a new asset or enhance an existing asset, the expenditure must be capitalized if it results in a significant long-term benefit to the firm.[5] Moreover, if the tax treatment of an expenditure is uncertain, capitalization is the norm while deductibility is the exception.[6]

[1] *Interstate Transit Lines* v. *Commissioner*, 319 U.S. 590, 593 (1943).
[2] §162(a).
[3] §263(a).
[4] Reg. §1.263(a)-2(a) and *Commissioner* v. *Lincoln Savings & Loan Assn.*, 403 U.S. 345 (1971).
[5] *Indopco Inc.* v. *Commissioner*, 503 U.S. 79 (1992).
[6] Ibid.

The following example quantifies the difference between tax treatments in cash flow terms:

Current Deduction versus Capitalized Cost.   During the past year, Corporation M raised $1 million of new capital by issuing preferred stock to a group of private investors. The corporation incurred $40,000 of legal and other professional fees in connection with this transaction. Corporation M's marginal tax rate is 35 percent. Compare the after-tax cash flows under two different assumptions concerning the tax treatment of the $40,000 expenditure:

	Current Deduction	Capitalized Cost
Proceeds of stock sale	$1,000,000	$1,000,000
Professional fees	(40,000)	(40,000)
Tax savings		
($40,000 deduction × 35%)	14,000	–0–
After-tax cash flow	$ 974,000	$ 960,000

In this example, the $40,000 expenditure did not create a distinct balance sheet asset for Corporation M. However, the federal courts have consistently ruled that expenses related to raising capital or reorganizing a firm's capital structure are for the betterment of the firm's operation for the duration of its existence and are not deductible.[7] Based on this rule of law, Corporation M must charge the $40,000 expenditure against the proceeds of the stock sale, which nets $960,000 for the corporation on an after-tax basis.

Repairs and Cleanup Costs

Every firm that owns tangible operating assets must make incidental repairs and perform routine maintenance to keep the assets in good working order. Repair and maintenance costs that are regular and recurring in nature and that do not materially add to either the value or the useful life of an asset are deductible.[8] In contrast, expenditures that substantially increase the value or useful life of an asset are nondeductible capital improvements. Similarly, the expense of adapting an existing asset to a new or different use must be capitalized as part of the cost of the asset.[9] The distinction between a repair and a capital improvement is not always obvious and is frequently a matter of dispute between taxpayers and the Internal Revenue Service (IRS).

Repair or Capital Improvement?   Out of concern for earthquake safety, the city of San Francisco required the Fairmont Hotel to either remove or replace the concrete parapets and cornices that had decorated the hotel's exterior since 1907.

---

[7]See *General Bancshares Corp.* v. *Commissioner*, 326 F.2d 712 (CA-8, 1964) and *Mills Estate, Inc.* v. *Commissioner*, 206 F.2d 244 (CA-2, 1953).

[8]Reg. §1.162-4.

[9]Reg. §1.263(a)-1(b).

The hotel spent $3 million to replace the old parapets and cornices with replicas made of light-weight fiber glass. The Fairmont Hotel deducted the expenditure as a repair. The IRS concluded that the expenditure was a capital improvement to the building and disallowed the deduction. In court, the Fairmont's owners argued that the $3 million expenditure was necessary to maintain the classical appearance of the building and to preserve its identity as a "grand hotel of the world." Moreover, the expenditure was not voluntary but was required by city ordinance. In spite of these arguments, the court agreed with the IRS that the expenditure materially prolonged the life and increased the value of the Fairmont Hotel and was not deductible.[10]

The business community and the IRS are presently engaged in a debate concerning the proper treatment of environmental cleanup costs. Many firms, either voluntarily or because of government mandate, are spending millions of dollars to clean up pollutants, toxic wastes, and other dangerous substances unleashed on the environment as industrial by-products. These firms argue that these cleanup costs should be currently deductible, while the IRS maintains that many such costs must be capitalized.

Cleanup Costs.   Company NM replaced the asbestos insulation in all its manufacturing equipment with nonhazardous insulation and deducted the replacement expense. The company justified the deduction because the replacement was made to protect the health of its employees and did not improve the operating efficiency or increase the value of the equipment. Furthermore, the replacement expense remedied a historic problem and was not related to the generation of future business income. Upon audit, the revenue agent concluded that the asbestos replacement did, in fact, result in a long-term benefit to Company NM by permanently improving the work environment. Therefore, the IRS required the company to capitalize the replacement expense to the cost of the reinsulated equipment.[11]

As part of the Tax Reform Act of 1997, Congress enacted a provision allowing firms to elect to deduct (rather than capitalize) expenditures incurred to abate or control hazardous substances at targeted contamination sites, commonly described as "brownfields."[12] This new provision should encourage firms to undertake environmental remediation of these sites by reducing the after-tax cost of the remediation.

Environmental Remediation.   AVC Inc. recently purchased a manufacturing plant situated on 25 acres of land qualifying as a targeted contamination site. AVC spent $80,000 to rid the property of toxic chemical substances. If AVC is in a 35 percent marginal tax bracket and elects to deduct its environmental remediation expenditure, the after-tax cost of the expenditure is $52,000 ($80,000 − $28,000 tax savings from the deduction).

---

[10]*Swing Investment Co. v. United States,* 98 F.3d 1359 (CA-FC, 1996).
[11]This example is based on IRS Letter Ruling 9240004 (July 29, 1992).
[12]§198.

Current Deductions of Capital Expenditures as Subsidies

The tax law contains special rules permitting firms to claim deductions for expenditures that clearly should be charged to a capital account. These preferential rules reduce the firm's after-tax cost of the expenditure and thereby represent an indirect federal subsidy. For instance, firms may deduct the first $15,000 of the annual cost of the removal of architectural and transportation barriers from buildings or transportation equipment to make such facilities more accessible to handicapped or elderly people.[13] A more significant preference is the allowance of a deduction for research and experimental costs; this deduction is available even if the research leads to the development of an identifiable asset with an extended useful life to the firm.[14] This valuable preference reflects the federal government's belief that basic research is crucial to the nation's economic growth and should be encouraged through the tax law.

Many preferential deductions benefit only certain industries. For instance, farmers are allowed to deduct soil and water conservation expenditures, which include the cost of leveling, grading, and terracing land, constructing drainage ditches and earthen dams, and planting windbreaks to inhibit soil erosion.[15] Farmers get a second tax break in the form of a deduction for the cost of fertilizers or other materials used to enrich farmland.[16]

Oil and gas producers may deduct **intangible drilling and development costs (IDC)** associated with locating and preparing wells for production.[17] Expenses such as wages, fuel, repairs to drilling equipment, hauling, and supplies that contribute to the development of a productive well undeniably result in a long-term benefit to the producer. By allowing a deduction for such IDC, the tax law provides an incentive for producers to undertake new drilling projects.

Advertising costs are deductible, even though a firm's successful advertising campaign can increase its market share and improve its competitive position for years to come.[18] While the IRS acknowledges that the advertising of a particular product or advertising intended to promote name recognition or goodwill may have some future effect on a firm's profitability, it does not require capitalization of advertising costs except in unusual circumstances.[19]

The Critical Role of Tax Basis

Objective 2
Define the terms *tax basis* and *adjusted basis*.

When an expenditure creates an asset that the firm will use in its future business operations, the capitalized expenditure becomes the firm's **tax basis** in its new asset. Basis can be defined as a taxpayer's investment in any asset or property right—the measure of *unrecovered dollars* represented by the asset. An asset's basis plays a key role in the calculation of cash flows because taxpayers are entitled to recover this basis at no tax cost. This recovery occurs either through a series of future deductions or when the taxpayer disposes of the asset. Cost recovery deductions are covered in this chapter, while the tax consequences of asset dispositions are the subject of Chapter 7.

---

[13]§190.

[14]§174(a).

[15]§175. This preferential deduction may not exceed 25 percent of the gross income derived from farming during the taxable year.

[16]§180.

[17]§263(c).

[18]Regs. §1.162-1(a) and §1.162-20(a)(2).

[19]Rev. Rul. 92-80, 1992-2 CB 57.

Basis, Cost Recovery, and Cash Flow

When a firm is allowed a deduction for a portion of the capitalized cost of an asset, the deduction has two consequences. The first consequence is that the asset's initial tax basis is reduced by the deduction.[20] The reduced basis is called the asset's **adjusted basis**. The second consequence is that the deduction generates a tax savings that reduces the after-tax cost of the asset.

Basis, Cost Recovery, and After-Tax Cost. Firm J pays $5,000 cash for a business asset. The tax law allows Firm J to deduct the capitalized cost of the asset ratably over five years. In the current year and in each of the four subsequent years, the firm deducts $1,000 and reduces its basis in the asset by this deduction. If the firm has a 35 percent marginal tax rate and uses a 9 percent discount rate to compute net present value (NPV), the after-tax cost of the asset (NPV of the cash flows) is $3,516.

| | | | Cash Flows | | | |
Year	Year-End Adjusted Basis	Annual Deduction	Initial Payment	Tax Savings from Deduction	Discount Factor	NPV
1	$4,000	$(1,000)	$(5,000)	$ 350		$(4,650)
2	3,000	(1,000)		350	.917	321
3	2,000	(1,000)		350	.842	295
4	1,000	(1,000)		350	.772	270
5	–0–	(1,000)		350	.708	248
						$(3,516)

Firm J's adjusted basis in its asset at the end of each year is the $5,000 cost less the accumulated cost recovery deductions. By the end of the fifth year, the firm has recovered its entire investment in the asset, leaving the asset with a zero tax basis. A zero tax basis does not imply anything about the continued value of the asset to the firm; it simply indicates that Firm J has deducted the entire $5,000 expenditure that created the asset.

The difference between Firm J's $5,000 before-tax cost and $3,516 after-tax cost results from the stream of tax savings generated by the cost recovery deductions. If the firm could have recovered its tax basis over a shorter period of time, the present value of this stream would increase and the after-tax cost of the asset would decrease. Conversely, if the recovery period were longer, the present value of the tax savings would decrease and the after-tax cost of the asset would increase.[21]

Cost Basis

The majority of the assets reported on a firm's balance sheet have an initial **cost basis**—the price paid to acquire the asset. Cost basis includes any sales tax paid by

---

[20] §1016(a)(2).

[21] This calculation of after-tax cost implies that the asset has no residual value after five years. If the firm could sell the asset for cash, the present value of this after-tax cash would reduce the after-tax cost of the asset. The cash flow implications of asset sales are addressed in the next chapter.

the purchaser and any incidental costs related to putting the asset into production.[22] While many assets are acquired in straightforward cash transactions, firms also acquire assets in exchange for property or services. In such case, the cost basis of the newly acquired asset equals the fair market value of the property surrendered or the services performed.[23]

> ***Cost Basis of Asset Acquired in Exchange for Property.***   BT Corporation, a manufacturer of heavy equipment, sells inventory to an unrelated land developer. BT agrees to let the developer pay for the inventory by transferring five acres of land to the corporation. The inventory has a fair market value of $139,000. The corporation's cost basis in its new asset (the land) is $139,000, the value of the inventory that BT surrendered to acquire the asset.

> ***Cost Basis of Asset Acquired in Exchange for Note.***   Modify the previous example by assuming that BT sold the inventory for the developer's promise to pay $139,000 in three years' time, a promise evidenced by a written interest-bearing note from the developer. The corporation's cost basis in its new asset (the note receivable) is $139,000, the value of the inventory that BT surrendered to acquire the asset.

> ***Cost Basis of Property Acquired in Exchange for Services.***   Firm C, a consulting business, performed professional services for an unrelated corporation and billed the corporation for $17,500. The corporation paid its bill by issuing 1,000 shares of its own common stock to the firm. Firm C recognizes $17,500 of gross income and takes a $17,500 cost basis in its new asset (1,000 shares of corporate stock). This basis represents Firm C's investment in these shares—the dollar amount that the firm can recover tax free when it disposes of the stock.

Leveraged Cost Basis.   When a firm acquires an asset through debt financing, the cost basis of the asset equals its entire cost, not just the firm's equity in the asset. Refer back to the example on page 130 in which Firm J purchased a business asset for $5,000. Assume that the firm financed the purchase by paying $1,500 from its bank account and borrowing $3,500 from a commercial lender. Firm J gives the lender a lien on the asset to secure the debt. Although the firm's initial investment in the asset is only $1,500, its cost basis is the full $5,000 purchase price.[24] The firm's repayment of the debt will create additional equity in the asset but will have no effect on the firm's tax basis in the asset.

---

[22]See, for example, Rev. Rul. 69-640, 1969-2 CB 211.

[23]Fair market value is the price at which property or services would change hands between a willing buyer and a willing seller, neither being under any compulsion to buy or to sell and both having reasonable knowledge of the relevant facts. Reg. §20.2031-1(b). Although this definition is found in the estate tax regulations, it is the accepted definition for income tax purposes.

[24]*Crane* v. *Commissioner*, 331 U.S. 1 (1947)

Objective 3
Explain why the use of leverage can reduce the after-tax cost of purchased assets.

Tax planners refer to the use of borrowed funds to create tax basis as **leverage.** The use of leverage can reduce the purchaser's after-tax cost of the asset. Let's expand on the Firm J example to demonstrate how the after-tax cost of the $5,000 asset is reduced by the firm's use of borrowed funds.

> **After-Tax Cost of Leveraged Purchase.**   Under the terms of its agreement with the commercial lender, Firm J must pay $315 interest (9 percent) at the beginning of each year and repay the $3,500 principal amount at the beginning of the fifth year. The annual interest payments are deductible expenses, while the final principal payment is charged against (and retires) the firm's $3,500 debt. The following table reflects each year's net cash flows with respect to the asset purchase using Firm J's 35 percent marginal tax rate and 9 percent discount rate:

			Tax Savings From				
Year	Initial Payment/ Debt Repayment	Interest Payment	Cost Recovery Deduction	Interest Deduction	Net Cash Flow	Discount Factor	NPV
1	$(1,500)		$350		$(1,150)		$(1,150)
2		(315)	350	110	145	.917	133
3		(315)	350	110	145	.842	122
4		(315)	350	110	145	.772	112
5	(3,500)	(315)	350	110	(3,355)	.708	(2,375)
							$(3,158)

By leveraging its purchase of the business asset, Firm J reduced the after-tax cost of the asset from $3,516 to $3,158. The cash flow data explains this result. Firm J's initial cash outflow to buy the asset was only $1,500; by borrowing the balance of the purchase price, the firm deferred paying $3,500 cash until the fifth year. This beneficial change in cash flows did not affect the firm's $5,000 tax basis in the asset, its annual cost recovery deductions, or the timing of the stream of tax savings from those deductions. The cost of the leverage in years 2 through 5 was $205, the after-tax interest on the note ($315 interest payment − $110 tax savings). However, even considering this additional cost, the leverage saved the firm $358.[25]

Introduction to Cost Recovery Methods

The topics covered in the first part of this chapter all relate to a key tax planning concept: the after-tax cost of a capitalized expenditure depends on the time period over which the firm can recover the expenditure as a deduction. The remainder of the chapter examines the four basic methods of periodic cost recovery: cost of goods sold, deprecia-

---

[25]In this simple example, Firm J's cost of external borrowing and its internal rate of return on productive assets are both 9 percent. If the firm's internal rate of return is higher than 9 percent, this higher rate should be used to compute the present value of the cash flows in years 2 through 5. In such case, the firm's after-tax cost of the asset would be even less. If the internal rate of return is less than 9 percent, the value of the cost recovery deductions might not offset the cost of borrowing. In this case, the after-tax cost of the leveraged purchase could exceed the after-tax cost of the cash purchase.

tion, amortization, and depletion. If none of these recovery methods is applicable, a cost is recoverable only when the firm disposes of the asset to which the cost relates or when that asset ceases to exist.

Inventories and Cost of Goods Sold

In Chapter 5, we learned that firms maintaining inventories of goods for sale to customers are required to account for their inventory on the accrual basis. In other words, firms can't deduct the cost of manufactured or purchased inventory but must capitalize the cost to an asset account. At the end of each year, the firm ascertains how much inventory is still on hand and how much has been sold during the year. The cost of the former is carried on the firm's balance sheet, while the cost of the latter is deducted as **cost of goods sold.**[26] The following formula summarizes this accounting procedure:

Cost of inventory on hand at the beginning of the year
Capitalized cost of inventory manufactured or purchased during the year

Total cost of inventory available for sale
(Cost of inventory on hand at the end of the year)

Cost of goods sold

Objective 4
Apply the formula to compute cost of goods sold.

This formula is based on two assumptions. The first assumption is that all expenditures that contributed to the value of inventory are capitalized to the inventory account. The second assumption is that the total cost of inventory is properly allocated between the inventory on hand at the end of the year and the inventory sold during the year. Let's briefly examine the basic tax rules underlying each of these assumptions.

The Unicap Rules

Firms typically prefer to treat expenditures as deductible *period costs* rather than *product costs* that must be capitalized to inventory. Not surprisingly, the tax law contains explicit rules concerning the types of expenditures that must be included in inventory. These **uniform capitalization (unicap) rules** are as strict as they are complicated.[27] Under unicap, firms must capitalize all direct costs of manufacturing, purchasing, or storing inventory (direct materials and direct labor). They must also capitalize any indirect costs that "benefit or are incurred by reason of the performance of production or resale activities."[28] Examples of indirect costs that must be capitalized *to the extent they relate to a firm's production or resale function* include:[29]

- Officer's compensation.
- Pension, retirement, and other employee benefits.
- Rents paid on buildings and equipment used in a manufacturing process.
- Premiums paid to carry property insurance on production assets.
- Repair and maintenance of production assets.

---

[26]Technically, cost of goods sold is subtracted from gross receipts to compute current year gross income. Reg. §1.61-3(a).
[27]The unicap rules are found in §263A and the accompanying regulations.
[28]Reg. §1.263A-1(e)(3)(i).
[29]Reg. §1.263A-1(e)(3)(ii).

- Cost recovery deductions for the cost of production assets.
- Interest paid on debt incurred to finance the purchase of production assets.

The unicap rules may require firms to capitalize expenditures for tax purposes that are reported as expenses on the firm's financial statements. The resulting book/tax difference is a temporary difference that will reverse in the year or years in which the capitalized expenditures are deducted as cost of goods sold.

Book/Tax Reconciliation for Unicap.   In 19X1, Company MN constructed an inventory item that was on hand at year-end. The firm incurred $100,000 of direct and indirect costs in the construction process. For financial statement purposes, Company MN capitalized $80,000 as inventory product costs and expensed $20,000 as period costs. Under the unicap rules, Company MN capitalized $88,000 of the total costs to inventory and deducted only $12,000 on its 19X1 tax return. In 19X2, Company MN sold the inventory item. For the two-year period, the difference in accounting methods resulted in the following:

	Book		Tax		
Year 1	*Expense*	*Inventory Cost*	*Deduction*	*Inventory Cost*	*Taxable Income in Excess of Book Income*
	$20,000	$80,000	$12,000	$88,000	$8,000
Year 2	*Cost of Goods Sold*		*Cost of Goods Sold*		*Book Income in Excess of Taxable Income*
	$80,000		$88,000		$8,000

Allocating Costs between Inventory and Cost of Goods Sold

The allocation of total costs between ending inventory and cost of goods sold is based on the method of accounting by which a firm tracks the flow of inventory items through its system. If a firm knows the actual cost of each item, it can use the **specific identification method** to value ending inventory and compute cost of goods sold. Real estate developers and antique dealers are good examples of businesses in which specific identification of inventory is feasible.

For manufacturing and retail businesses that deal with thousands, if not millions, of inventory items each year, specific identification of each item is impossible. These firms must use a costing convention that has nothing to do with the physical movement of inventory through the system. The two most commonly used costing conventions are **FIFO** (first-in, first-out) and **LIFO** (last-in, first-out).

A firm's selection of an inventory costing convention may have a substantial impact on the taxable income recognized each year. During a period of rising prices, it is generally to a firm's advantage to adopt LIFO because the convention assumes that the last goods manufactured or purchased are the first goods sold. In an inflationary economy, the most recently acquired goods are the most expensive. If a firm assumes these goods are the first to be sold, it maximizes the cost of goods sold and minimizes the cost of ending inventory. While the LIFO convention can offer substantial tax savings, its popularity is diminished by the fact that any firm electing LIFO for tax purposes must also use it to prepare financial statements.[30] Because of this forced conformity, any reduction in taxable income attributable to LIFO is mirrored by a reduction in accounting income and earnings per share reported to the firm's investors.

Depreciation of Tangible Business Assets

Book and Tax Concepts of Depreciation

Under generally accepted accounting principles (GAAP), firms write off or *depreciate* the capitalized cost of tangible assets over their estimated useful lives.[31] As a result, the cost of a particular asset is expensed over the years in which it contributes to the firm's revenue generating activity. The concept of **depreciation** applies only to wasting assets that:

- Lose value over time because of wear and tear, physical deterioration, or obsolescence.
- Have a reasonably ascertainable useful life.

Nonwasting tangible assets that lack these characteristics, such as land and works of art acquired for display, are nondepreciable. For financial statement purposes, firms may calculate their annual depreciation expense under a variety of methods and may choose the method that results in the best matching of the cost of an asset against income.

Before 1982, depreciation for tax purposes was also based on the estimated useful life of business property. Because the probable useful life of any wasting asset is a matter of conjecture, taxpayers and the IRS were constantly wrangling over the question of asset lives. Firms aggressively argued for the shortest life over which to recover the tax basis of their tangible operating assets, while the IRS asserted that a longer recovery period was more realistic. In 1981, Congress enacted a radically new cost recovery system to replace the old depreciation rules. In 1986, Congress refined this system into the **Modified Accelerated Cost Recovery System (MACRS),** which is in effect today.[32] Under MACRS, the estimated useful life of an asset is irrelevant in the computation of tax depreciation. Because the MACRS computation is independent of the computation of book depreciation, the depreciation deduction on a firm's tax return and depreciation expense on its financial statements are often different numbers.

The MACRS Framework

Objective 5
Describe the relationship between recovery period, depreciation method, and depreciation convention in the MACRS computation.

This section of Chapter 6 presents the MACRS framework: the general rules for computing depreciation for federal tax purposes. Business managers who understand this framework can appreciate the pivotal role of MACRS in the tax planning process. They do not need to master the system's fine technical points; consequently, many of the details of MACRS are omitted from our discussion.

Recovery Periods.   MACRS applies to both depreciable realty (buildings, improvements, and other structures permanently attached to the land) and personalty (any tangible asset not part of a building or other permanent structure) used in a trade, business, or other income-producing activity. Every depreciable asset is assigned to one of 10

---

[30]§472(c).

[31]The depreciable cost is reduced by the asset's estimated residual or salvage value.

[32]§168.

TABLE 6–1   **Recovery Periods for Tangible Business Assets**

MACRS Recovery Period	*Assets Included*
3 years	Small manufacturing tools, racehorses and breeding hogs, special handling devices used in food manufacturing
5 years	Cars, trucks, buses, helicopters, computers, typewriters, duplicating equipment, breeding and dairy cattle, and cargo containers
7 years	Office furniture and fixtures, railroad cars and locomotives, most machinery and equipment
10 years	Single-purpose agricultural and horticultural structures, assets used in petroleum refining, vessels, barges, and other water transportation equipment, fruit- or nut-bearing trees and vines
15 years	Land improvements such as fencing, roads, sidewalks, bridges, irrigation systems, and landscaping, telephone distribution plants, pipelines, billboards, and service station buildings
20 years	Certain farm buildings
25 years	Commercial water treatment facilities, municipal sewers
27.5 years	Residential rental real property (duplexes and apartments)
39 years	Nonresidential real property (office buildings, factories, and warehouses)
50 years	Railroad grading or tunnel bore

recovery periods. Table 6–1 lists these periods and gives examples of assets assigned to each. For the most part, the MACRS recovery period for an asset is shorter than the asset's estimated useful life. The shortened time frame over which firms may deduct their investment in operating assets reduces the after-tax cost of those assets and acts as an incentive for firms to make capital acquisitions.[33]

Depreciation Methods.   The method by which annual depreciation is calculated is a function of the recovery period. Assets with a 3-year, 5-year, 7-year, or 10-year recovery period are depreciated using a 200 percent (i.e., double) declining-balance method. Assets with a 15-year or 20-year recovery period are depreciated using a 150 percent declining-balance method. In each case, the depreciation method switches to straight-line when a straight-line computation over the remaining recovery period results in a greater deduction than the declining-balance method. For these six classes of business personalty, MACRS lives up to its name—depreciation deductions are indeed accelerated into the early years of the recovery period. Such front-end loading of tax depreciation provides a further reduction in the after-tax cost of tangible personalty.[34]

Before 1987, buildings and other types of realty could also be depreciated using accelerated declining-balance methods. Since 1987, properties with a 25-year, 27.5-year, 39-year, or 50-year recovery period must be depreciated using the straight-line method. For real property, MACRS is an accelerated cost-recovery system in name only.

Depreciation Conventions.   The depreciation computation requires some assumption as to how much depreciation a firm may claim in the year of an asset's acquisition or

---

[33]A major exception to MACRS is the set of rules applying to passenger automobiles owned or rented for business use. These rules severely limit the annual deduction for depreciation or lease payments with respect to these assets. §280F.

[34]Under §168(b)(5), taxpayers may elect the straight-line method (rather than an accelerated method) for any class of property placed in service during the year.

disposition. Under MACRS, all personalty (assets with recovery periods from 3 to 20 years) are assumed to be placed in service or disposed of exactly halfway through the year. This **half-year convention** means that in the first year of the recovery period, six months of depreciation is allowed, regardless of when the asset was actually placed in service. The same convention applies in the year in which an asset is disposed of: regardless of the actual date of disposition, the firm may claim six months of depreciation.[35]

The half-year convention is subject to an important exception. If more than 40 percent of the depreciable personalty acquired during a taxable year is placed in service during the last three months of the year, the firm must use a **midquarter convention** with respect to *all* personalty placed in service during the year. Under this convention, assets placed in service during any quarter (three months) of the year are assumed to be placed in service midpoint (one and one-half months) through the quarter. When an asset subject to this convention is disposed of, the disposition is treated as occurring at the midpoint of the quarter in which the disposition occurs.

Half-Year and Midquarter Conventions.   During its current calendar year, Company P made the following purchases of depreciable personalty:

Date Placed in Service	Depreciable Basis
February 27	$ 68,000
July 8	20,000
November 19	55,000
	$143,000

Only 38 percent of the depreciable personalty was placed in service during the last three months of the year. Therefore, Company P will use the half-year convention and calculate six months of depreciation for each asset placed in service during the year.

Now assume that Company P purchases a $19,000 depreciable asset on December 4. In this case, 46 percent of the company's depreciable personalty ($74,000 ÷ $162,000) was acquired in the last three months of the year. For this reason, Company P must use the midquarter convention with the following result:

Quarter Placed in Service	Depreciable Basis	Months of Depreciation Allowed
First quarter	$ 68,000	10.5 months
Second quarter	–0–	7.5
Third quarter	20,000	4.5
Fourth quarter	74,000	1.5
	$162,000	

---

[35]No MACRS depreciaton is allowed for property placed in service and disposed of in the same year. Reg. §1.168(d)-1(b)(3)(ii).

A **midmonth convention** applies to the year in which depreciable realty (assets with recovery periods of 25, 27.5, 39, or 50 years) is placed in service or disposed of. Under this convention, realty placed in service (or disposed of) during any month of the year is treated as placed in service (or disposed of) midway through the month.

Midmonth Convention.   During its current calendar year, Company RS places three buildings into service. The company can claim the following number of months of depreciation for each building:

	Date Placed in Service	Months of Depreciation Allowed
Building 1	April 2	8.5 months
Building 2	June 30	6.5
Building 3	December 18	.5

Comprehensive Examples.   The next two examples illustrate the calculation of the annual MACRS depreciation deduction.

MACRS Calculation.   Firm P, a calendar year taxpayer, buys a computer for $38,000 and places it in service on September 19. The computer has a five-year recovery period, and the firm uses the 200 percent declining-balance method to compute depreciation. Under this method, the straight-line rate of depreciation (20 percent) is doubled and the resulting rate (40 percent) is applied each year to the unrecovered basis of the asset. Firm P will depreciate the computer according to the following schedule:

Year	Unrecovered Basis at Beginning of Year	Recovery Method	Convention	MACRS Depreciation
1	$38,000	40% DB	Half-year	$ 7,600
2	30,400	40% DB		12,160
3	18,240	40% DB		7,296
4	10,944	40% DB		4,378
5	6,566	SL*		4,378
6	2,188	SL		2,188
				$38,000

*$364.78 per month.

- Because only one-half year of depreciation is allowed in year 1, one-half year of depreciation is necessary in year 6 to complete the five-year recovery period.

- The declining-balance method is changed to the straight-line method in year 5 so that the $6,566 unrecovered basis is depreciated ratably over the remaining one and one-half years (18 months) in the recovery period.
- The basis of the computer is reduced to zero; for MACRS purposes, depreciable assets are assumed to have no residual value.

MACRS Calculation in Year of Sale.   Refer to the facts in the previous example but assume that Firm P sells the computer on May 3 in year 4. In this case, the half-year convention also applies in the year of disposition.

Year	Unrecovered Basis at Beginning of Year	Recovery Method	Convention	MACRS Depreciation
1	$38,000	40% DB	Half-year	$ 7,600
2	30,400	40% DB		12,160
3	18,240	40% DB		7,296
4	10,944	40% DB	Half-year	2,189

The computer's adjusted basis immediately prior to sale is $8,755 ($10,944 unrecovered basis at beginning of year 4 − $2,189 depreciation in year 4).

IRS Depreciation Tables.   To allow taxpayers to avoid the MACRS math process, the IRS publishes a set of convenient tables incorporating the MACRS computational rules. The tables consist of a series of annual percentages that are multiplied against the *initial undepreciated* basis of the asset to result in depreciation for the year. Table 6–2 contains the annual percentages for the six recovery periods for business personalty. By referring to this table, Firm P can compute its annual depreciation deductions for its $38,000 computer as follows:

MACRS Tables

Year	Initial Basis	Table Percentage	MACRS Depreciation
1	$38,000	20.00%	$ 7,600
2	38,000	32.00	12,160
3	38,000	19.20	7,296
4	38,000	11.52	4,378
5	38,000	11.52	4,378
6	38,000	5.76	2,188
			$38,000

TABLE 6–2   MACRS for Business Personalty

If the Recovery Year Is:	And the Recovery Period Is:					
	3-Year	5-Year	7-Year	10-Year	15-Year	20-Year
	The Depreciation Rate Is:					
1	33.33	20.00	14.29	10.00	5.00	3.750
2	44.45	32.00	24.49	18.00	9.50	7.219
3	14.81	19.20	17.49	14.40	8.55	6.677
4	7.41	11.52	12.49	11.52	7.70	6.177
5		11.52	8.93	9.22	6.93	5.713
6		5.76	8.92	7.37	6.23	5.285
7			8.93	6.55	5.90	4.888
8			4.46	6.55	5.90	4.522
9				6.56	5.91	4.462
10				6.55	5.90	4.461
11				3.28	5.91	4.462
12					5.90	4.461
13					5.91	4.462
14					5.90	4.461
15					5.91	4.462
16					2.95	4.461
17						4.462
18						4.461
19						4.462
20						4.461
21						2.231

Applicable depreciation method: 200 or 150 percent declining-balance switching to straight-line.

Applicable recovery periods: 3, 5, 7, 10, 15, 20 years.

Applicable convention: half-year.

Note that the table percentage in year 1 is one-half of the 40 percent declining-balance rate. In other words, the half-year convention for the year of acquisition is built into this table. However, the table percentages for the remaining years reflect a full year of depreciation. If an asset is disposed of before it is fully depreciated, the MACRS deduction for the year is only one-half of the amount indicated by the table.[36]

Table 6–3 provides the percentages for computing annual depreciation for 27.5-year recovery property (residential rental properties). Because these properties are depreciated on a straight-line basis, these tables are of limited benefit in any year other than the year of acquisition in which the midmonth convention applies. In all other years, depreciation can be calculated by dividing the original cost of the property by 27.5.

---

[36]The IRS publishes additional tables providing annual percentages for assets subject to the midquarter convention for the first, second, third, and fourth quarters. See IRS Publication 946.

TABLE 6–3   MACRS for Residential Rental Property

If the Recovery Year Is:	And the Month in the First Recovery Year the Property Is Placed in Service Is:											
	1	2	3	4	5	6	7	8	9	10	11	12
	The Depreciation Rate Is:											
1	3.485	3.182	2.879	2.576	2.273	1.970	1.667	1.364	1.061	0.758	0.455	0.152
2	3.636	3.636	3.636	3.636	3.636	3.636	3.636	3.636	3.636	3.636	3.636	3.636
3	3.636	3.636	3.636	3.636	3.636	3.636	3.636	3.636	3.636	3.636	3.636	3.636
4	3.636	3.636	3.636	3.636	3.636	3.636	3.636	3.636	3.636	3.636	3.636	3.636
5	3.636	3.636	3.636	3.636	3.636	3.636	3.636	3.636	3.636	3.636	3.636	3.636
6	3.636	3.636	3.636	3.636	3.636	3.636	3.636	3.636	3.636	3.636	3.636	3.636
7	3.636	3.636	3.636	3.636	3.636	3.636	3.636	3.636	3.636	3.636	3.636	3.636
8	3.636	3.636	3.636	3.636	3.636	3.636	3.636	3.636	3.636	3.636	3.636	3.636
9	3.636	3.636	3.636	3.636	3.636	3.636	3.636	3.636	3.636	3.636	3.636	3.636
10	3.637	3.637	3.637	3.637	3.637	3.637	3.636	3.636	3.636	3.636	3.636	3.636
11	3.636	3.636	3.636	3.636	3.636	3.636	3.637	3.637	3.637	3.637	3.637	3.637
12	3.637	3.637	3.637	3.637	3.637	3.637	3.636	3.636	3.636	3.636	3.636	3.636
13	3.636	3.636	3.636	3.636	3.636	3.636	3.637	3.637	3.637	3.637	3.637	3.637
14	3.637	3.637	3.637	3.637	3.637	3.637	3.636	3.636	3.636	3.636	3.636	3.636
15	3.636	3.636	3.636	3.636	3.636	3.636	3.637	3.637	3.637	3.637	3.637	3.637
16	3.637	3.637	3.637	3.637	3.637	3.637	3.636	3.636	3.636	3.636	3.636	3.636
17	3.636	3.636	3.636	3.636	3.636	3.636	3.637	3.637	3.637	3.637	3.637	3.637
18	3.637	3.637	3.637	3.637	3.637	3.637	3.636	3.636	3.636	3.636	3.636	3.636
19	3.636	3.636	3.636	3.636	3.636	3.636	3.637	3.637	3.637	3.637	3.637	3.637
20	3.637	3.637	3.637	3.637	3.637	3.637	3.636	3.636	3.636	3.636	3.636	3.636
21	3.636	3.636	3.636	3.636	3.636	3.636	3.637	3.637	3.637	3.637	3.637	3.637
22	3.637	3.637	3.637	3.637	3.637	3.637	3.636	3.636	3.636	3.636	3.636	3.636
23	3.636	3.636	3.636	3.636	3.636	3.636	3.637	3.637	3.637	3.637	3.637	3.637
24	3.637	3.637	3.637	3.637	3.637	3.637	3.636	3.636	3.636	3.636	3.636	3.636
25	3.636	3.636	3.636	3.636	3.636	3.636	3.637	3.637	3.637	3.637	3.637	3.637
26	3.637	3.637	3.637	3.637	3.637	3.637	3.636	3.636	3.636	3.636	3.636	3.636
27	3.636	3.636	3.636	3.636	3.636	3.636	3.637	3.637	3.637	3.637	3.637	3.637
28	1.970	2.273	2.576	2.879	3.182	3.458	3.636	3.636	3.636	3.636	3.636	3.636
29	0.000	0.000	0.000	0.000	0.000	0.000	0.152	0.455	0.758	1.061	1.364	1.667

Applicable depreciation method: straight-line.
Applicable recovery period: 27.5 years.
Applicable convention: midmonth.

MACRS and Market Value.   Earlier in the chapter, the point was made that MACRS deductions do not represent cash outflows. Neither do these deductions correlate to any decline in the fair market value of the depreciable asset. While operating assets typically lose value as they age, the annual MACRS deduction in no way reflects such loss. Moreover, firms may claim depreciation deductions for assets that have actually appreciated in value over time.[37] The adjusted tax basis in a business asset is the capitalized

---

[37]*Noyce*, 97 TC 670 (1991).

cost that the firm has not yet deducted. Adjusted basis conveys no information concerning the fair market value of the asset.

> ***Depreciation for an Appreciating Asset?***   Richard and Fiona Simon purchased two 100-year old antique violin bows for a total cost of $51,500. The couple used the bows in their business as professional violinists and claimed depreciation deductions based on a five-year recovery period. The IRS denied the deductions because the bows were treasured works of art that had actually appreciated in value since they were acquired by the Simons. A federal court concluded that the violin bows met the definition of depreciable property because they suffered "wear and tear" in the taxpayers' business activity. Thus, the Simons could recover their cost and reduce their tax basis in the violin bows to zero even though the bows continued to increase in value.[38]

The Limited Expensing Election

Objective 6
Explain the benefit of and the limitations on the limited expensing election.

The tax law allows firms to elect to expense (rather than capitalize) a limited dollar amount of the cost of tangible personalty placed in service during the taxable year.[39] The dollar amount is based on the following schedule:

For Taxable Years Beginning In:	The Dollar Amount Is:
1997	$18,000
1998	18,500
1999	19,000
2000	20,000
2001 or 2002	24,000
2003 or thereafter	25,000

By making the **limited expensing election,** many small firms can simply deduct the cost of new assets and avoid the burden of maintaining MACRS depreciation schedules. Firms that purchase assets with an aggregate cost in excess of the annual dollar amount may expense part of the cost of a specific asset or assets. The unexpensed cost is capitalized and recovered through MACRS.

> ***Expensing Election and MACRS.***   In July 1998, Firm B purchased two items of heavy equipment: item 1 ($29,000 cost) and item 2 ($23,000 cost). Both items have a seven-year recovery period. These are the only items of tangible personalty that Firm B placed in service during 1998. The firm elects to expense $18,500 of the cost of item 1. The MACRS deduction on the capitalized cost of the items is computed as follows:

---

[38]*Simon,* 103 TC 247 (1994).
[39]§179.

	Initial Cost	Amount Expensed	Depreciable Basis	Table Percentage	MACRS Depreciation
Item 1	$29,000	$18,500	$10,500	14.29%	$1,500
Item 2	23,000	–0–	23,000	14.29	3,287
		$18,500			$4,787

Firm B's 1998 depreciation deduction for the equipment is $23,287 ($18,500 expense + $4,787 MACRS depreciation). At the close of the year, the adjusted basis of item 1 is $9,000, and the adjusted basis of item 2 is $19,713.

The expensing election has two limitations. First, if a firm purchases more than $200,000 of tangible personalty during a year, the annual dollar amount is reduced dollar for dollar by the excess over $200,000. For instance, if a firm buys $213,000 of personalty during 1999, it may elect to expense only $6,000 of the cost ($19,000 annual dollar amount − $13,000 excess cost). The firm must capitalize the remaining $207,000 and recover the cost through normal MACRS depreciation.

Second, the deductible expense is limited to the firm's taxable business income for the year computed without regard to the expense. Suppose a firm's only asset acquisition for the year is a $15,000 computer system. If the firm's taxable income (before consideration of the $15,000 expenditure) is more than $15,000, it may deduct the entire cost of the computer. If the firm's taxable income is less than $15,000, it may deduct only that portion of the computer's cost that reduces taxable income to zero.[40]

Incorporating Depreciation into the Net Present Value Calculation: Purchase versus Leasing Decision

Objective 7
Incorporate depreciation deductions into the computation of net present value.

Business managers routinely make decisions relating to the acquisition of operating assets. One of the more common decisions is whether the firm should purchase an asset or lease that asset from another company. Both options provide the firm with the use of the asset over time, but the cash flows associated with each option are very different. To make the choice that maximizes the value of the acquisition, the manager must compare the after-tax cost of each option in present value terms. The following example of such a comparison illustrates how depreciation deductions are incorporated into a cash flow analysis:

Purchase versus Leasing.   SGM Corporation needs to acquire a piece of heavy machinery for use in its construction business. SGM could purchase the machine for $75,000 cash. The machine would be seven-year recovery property. SGM's engineers estimate that the machine would actually last for 10 years, after which

---

[40]In this case, the firm can carry forward the nondeductible portion of the $15,000 cost to subsequent taxable years. The firm's use of this carryforward will be subject to the various limitations on the expensing election. Alternatively, the firm can capitalize the nondeductible cost and claim MACRS depreciation. See Reg. §1.179-3.

time it would have no residual value. Alternatively, SGM could lease the machine for 10 years for an annual rent of $11,000. SGM is in a 35 percent marginal tax bracket and uses a 9 percent discount rate to compute net present value. To decide whether to purchase or to lease the machine, SGM must calculate and compare the after-tax cost of each option.

Purchase Option

Purchase price in year 1				$(75,000)
Present value of tax savings from depreciation (see following table)				21,262
After-tax cost of purchase option				$(53,738)

Year	MACRS Depreciation	Tax Savings at 35%	Discount Factor	Present Value of Tax Savings
1	$10,717	$3,751	—	$ 3,751
2	18,367	6,428	.917	5,894
3	13,118	4,591	.842	3,866
4	9,367	3,278	.772	2,531
5	6,698	2,344	.708	1,660
6	6,690	2,342	.650	1,522
7	6,698	2,344	.596	1,397
8	3,345	1,171	.547	641
	$75,000			$21,262

Lease Option

Annual lease payment	$(11,000)
Tax savings	
($11,000 deduction × 35%)	3,850
After-tax annual payment	$ (7,150)
Present value of year 1 payment	$ (7,150)
Present value of years 2–10 payment	
($7,150 × 5.995 discount factor)	(42,864)
After-tax cost of rent option	$(50,014)

A comparison of after-tax cash flows provides SGM with the information necessary to make a rational choice. To minimize its after-tax cost and maximize the value of the transaction, SGM should lease the machine (after-tax cost $50,014) rather than buy it (after-tax cost $53,738).

Amortization of Intangible Assets

Objective 8
Explain how a firm recovers the cost of purchased intangibles through amortization.

Firms may own a variety of assets with no physical substance but that represent a valuable property right or economic attribute. The tax basis in such intangible assets may be recoverable under some type of **amortization** method authorized by the Internal Revenue Code. As a general rule, amortization is permitted only if the intangible asset has a determinable life.[41] For instance, the capitalized costs that went into the

---

[41]Reg. §1.167(a)-3.

development of a patent or copyright may be deducted ratably over the duration of years that the patent or copyright conveys an exclusive legal right to its owner. In contrast, a firm's tax basis in an intangible asset with an indeterminable life is not amortizable but can be recovered only when the firm disposes of the asset.

> ***Intangible Assets with Indeterminable Life.***   During the current year, Firm FG purchased 16,000 shares of common stock in ABC Inc. The firm also bought a 10 percent interest in the KLM Partnership. Firm FG must capitalize the cost of both these intangible equity interests. Because the interests represent a permanent investment, Firm FG cannot recover the capitalized cost through amortization.

In the following paragraphs, we will analyze three types of intangible assets subject to cost recovery through amortization: organizational and start-up costs, leasehold costs, and purchased intangibles.

Organizational and Start-Up Costs

The tax law stipulates that the **organizational costs** of forming a partnership or corporation are capital expenditures because these costs create an intangible asset (the organizational form) that lasts as long as the entity exists. Accordingly, legal and accounting fees attributable to the formation of a partnership or corporation and any filing or registration fees required under state or local law must be capitalized rather than deducted. However, the tax law allows newly formed entities to elect to amortize their organizational costs over a 60-month period, starting with the month in which business begins.[42]

For tax purposes, every new business venture, regardless of organizational form, must capitalize its **start-up expenditures.** Start-up expenditures include both the up-front costs of investigating the creation or purchase of a business and the routine expenses incurred during the preoperating phase of a business. This preoperating phase ends only when the business has matured to the point that it can generate revenues. Firms may elect to amortize their start-up expenditures over 60 months, beginning with the month in which the business becomes operational.[43]

> ***Organizational and Start-Up Costs.***   Mr. D and Mrs. G go into partnership to operate a day care center. Their first step is to engage an attorney to draft a partnership agreement; the entrepreneurs pay $800 to the attorney for her services and another $160 to register their new partnership with the state. The partners spend the next two months locating and renting a suitable facility for their center, hiring and training staff, publicizing the new business, and applying for the operating license required under local law. Their expenses with respect to these activities total $3,840. The DG partnership receives its operating license in late August, and the day care center enrolls its first student on September 3.

---

[42]§709 and §248.

[43]§195. According to §195(c)(1), interest expense, taxes, and research and experimentation costs are not considered start-up expenditures and may be deducted even if incurred during the preoperating phase of a business venture.

The DG partnership must capitalize $960 of organizational costs and $3,840 of start-up expenditures. On the first Form 1065 (U.S. Partnership Return of Income), the partnership makes a written election to amortize these costs over 60 months.[41] If the partnership reports on a calendar year basis, it may claim a current year amortization deduction of $320:

Amortizable costs:	
Organizational costs	$ 960
Start-up expenditures	3,840
	$4,800

$4,800 ÷ 60 months = $80 monthly amortization
$80 × 4 months (September through December) = $320

The DG partnership will amortize the remaining $4,480 capitalized organizational and start-up costs over the next 56 months.

The capitalization requirement for start-up expenditures does not apply to the **expansion costs** of an existing business.[45] Once the DG partnership in the above example begins operating its first day care center, it has established an active business. If Mr. D and Mrs. G decide to open a second center at a different location, they will repeat the process of renting a facility, hiring and training additional staff, and advertising the new location. Although the expenses with respect to these activities are functionally identical to the $3,840 of start-up expenditures, the DG partnership can deduct these expenses because they are incurred in the conduct of an existing business.

Leasehold Costs and Improvements

When a firm rents tangible property for use in its business, it may incur up-front costs to acquire the lease on the property. Such **leasehold costs** must be capitalized and amortized over the term of the lease.[46] In contrast, if a firm pays for physical improvements to leased property, the cost of the **leasehold improvements** must be capitalized to an asset account, assigned to a MACRS recovery period, and depreciated under the normal MACRS rules. This cost recovery rule applies even when the term of the lease is shorter than the MACRS recovery period.[47]

Leasehold Costs and Improvements.   Early in the year, VB Corporation entered into a lease agreement for commercial office space. VB's cost of negotiating the lease was $3,120. The corporation also spent $28,000 to construct built-in

---

[44]The two partners, not the partnership itself, will pay tax on the income generated by the day care center. Nevertheless, the partnership is required to file an information return on which any elections that affect the computation of taxable income are made. See §703(b).

[45]§195(c)(1)(B). See IRS Letter Ruling 9331001 (April 23, 1993).

[46]§178.

[47]§168(i)(8).

cabinets, bookshelves, and lighting fixtures to conform the leased space to its needs. The term of the lease is 48 months, beginning on May 1. VB Corporation must capitalize the $3,120 lease acquisition cost and amortize it over 48 months ($65 per month for a current year amortization deduction of $520). The corporation must also capitalize the $28,000 cost of the leasehold improvements. These improvements are seven-year recovery property, and VB will recover its cost basis through MACRS depreciation.[48]

Purchased Intangibles

A firm that purchases an established business enterprise is usually buying more than just the monetary and tangible operating assets recorded on the business's balance sheet. A substantial portion of the value of the business may consist of intangible assets that contribute to the profitability of the enterprise. If the firm pays a lump-sum price for the entire business, it must allocate a portion of the price to each monetary and tangible asset acquired. The price allocated to each asset equals that asset's fair market value and becomes the firm's cost basis in the asset.[49] If the asset is inventory or MACRS property, the firm can recover its basis as cost of good sold or through depreciation.

If the lump-sum price exceeds the value of the monetary and tangible assets, the excess is allocated to the intangible assets of the business. Such assets include **goodwill** (value created by the expectancy that customers will continue to patronize the business) and **going-concern value** (value attributable to the synergism of business assets working in coordination). Other common purchased intangibles are:

- Information-based intangibles such as accounting records, operating systems or manuals, customer lists, and advertiser lists.
- Customer-based or supplier-based intangibles such as favorable contracts with major customers or established relationships with key suppliers.
- Know-how intangibles such as designs, patterns, formulas, certain patents and copyrights, and other intellectual properties.
- Workforce intangibles such as the specialized skills, education, or loyalty of company employees and favorable employment contracts.
- Covenants not to compete and similar arrangements with prior owners of the business.
- Franchises, trademarks, trade names, licenses, and permits.

For tax purposes, firms recover the cost of purchased intangibles over a 15-year period, regardless of the actual length of time during which the firm expects the intangible to yield any commercial benefit.[50] Amortization begins in the month in which the intangible asset is acquired. The tax treatment of purchased intangibles may differ from the treatment of such intangibles under GAAP. For instance, capitalized goodwill is generally amortizable over a 40-year period for financial statement purposes.

---

[48]Unless VB Corporation renews its lease on the commercial office space after 48 months, it will not have recovered its entire cost basis in the leasehold improvements when it surrenders the space back to the lessor. The tax consequences of this situation are discussed in the next chapter.

[49]Reg. §1.1060-1T.

[50]§197. The 15-year amortization rule does not apply to equity interests in other businesses, debt instruments, existing leases of tangible property, and computer software available for purchase by the general public. Under §167(f)(1), the cost of such off-the-shelf software is amortizable over 36 months.

Amortization of Purchased Intangibles. On March 9, the BV Company (a calendar year taxpayer) paid $2 million to buy a business enterprise from Mr. L. The sales contract stated that $1.7 million of the lump-sum price was attributable to the appraised value of monetary and tangible operating assets. An additional $100,000 was attributable to the business's trade name, and $200,000 was attributable to a convenant not to compete. Under this covenant, Mr. L agreed not to engage in a similar business for the next three years. The BV Company must capitalize the $300,000 cost of the purchased intangibles and amortize the cost over 15 years at a rate of $1,667 per month. BV Company's amortization deduction in the year of purchase is $16,670 ($1,667 for 10 months).

The purchaser of a business must determine the cost basis of each tangible and intangible asset included in the purchase as well as any cost recovery method allowed with respect to each asset. The next example illustrates this important process.

Comprehensive Example. Firm RT purchased the business operated by SW Inc. for a lump-sum price of $1 million. At date of purchase, the appraised values of the business assets were:

	Appraised Value
Accounts receivable	$120,000
Supplies	25,000
Inventory	325,000
Furniture and fixtures	360,000
Lease on real property (8-year remaining term)	40,000
	$870,000

Firm RT was willing to pay $1 million because the business has such an excellent reputation in the local community. The firm's cost basis in each of its newly acquired business assets is:

	Initial Cost Basis
Accounts receivable	$ 120,000
Supplies	25,000
Inventory	325,000
Furniture and fixtures	360,000
Lease on real property	40,000
Purchased goodwill	130,000
	$1,000,000

- Firm RT will recover its basis in the accounts receivable as the receivables are collected.
- It will recover its basis in the supplies as a deduction when the supplies are consumed.
- It will recover its basis in the inventory through cost of goods sold.

- It will recover its basis in the furniture and fixtures through MACRS depreciation.
- It will recover its basis in the lease through amortization deductions over the eight-year remaining term of the lease.
- It will recover its basis in the goodwill through amortization deductions over 15 years.

Depletion of Natural Resources

Firms engaged in the business of extracting minerals, oil, gas, and other natural deposits from the earth incur a variety of up-front costs to locate, acquire, and develop their operating mines and wells. Many of these costs must be capitalized and recovered over the period of years during which the mine or well is productive.[51] The method for recovering a firm's investment in an exhaustible natural resource is called **cost depletion.** The annual cost depletion deduction is based on the following formula:

$$\frac{\text{Units of production sold during the year}}{\substack{\text{Estimated total units of production at} \\ \text{the beginning of the year}^{49}}} \times \text{Unrecovered basis in the mine or well}$$

Cost Depletion. Company M, which operates a mining business, spent $500,000 for geological surveys, mineral rights, and excavation costs, all of which were capitalized as the basis of a new copper mine. At the beginning of year 1 of production, the company's engineers estimated that the mine should produce 80,000 tons of copper ore. During year 1, 20,000 tons of ore were extracted and sold. The company's cost depletion deduction for year 1 was $125,000:

$$\frac{20,000 \text{ tons}}{80,000 \text{ tons}} \times \$500,000 \text{ initial basis} = \$125,000$$

At the beginning of year 2, the engineers revised their estimate of the mine's remaining productivity to 65,000 tons; during year 2, 32,000 tons of copper ore were extracted and sold. The cost depletion deduction for year 2 was $184,615:

$$\frac{32,000 \text{ tons}}{65,000 \text{ tons}} \times \$375,000 \text{ unrecovered basis} = \$184,615$$

By the year in which the copper deposit is exhausted and the mine is no longer productive, Company M will have recovered its entire $500,000 tax basis through cost depletion deductions.

---

[51]Oil and gas producers may deduct many intangible drilling and development costs, thereby minimizing the capitalized basis of productive wells.

[52]§611.

Percentage Depletion

Objective 9
Distinguish between cost depletion and percentage depletion.

To encourage the high-risk activity of mineral exploration and extraction, Congress invented **percentage depletion,** an annual deduction based on the gross income generated by a depletable property multiplied by an arbitrary depletion rate. For instance, the statutory depletion rate for sulfur and uranium is 22 percent; the rate for gold, silver, copper, iron ore, natural gas, and crude oil is 15 percent, and the rate for asbestos, coal, and lignite is 10 percent. In any year, a firm is allowed to deduct the *greater* of the cost depletion or percentage depletion attributable to its properties.[53]

Let's highlight the relationship of cost depletion and percentage depletion by returning to our example of Company M and its copper mine.

> **Percentage Depletion.**   Company M can sell its copper ore for $40 per ton in each year of production. The company's percentage depletion deduction equals 15 percent of gross income from sales of the ore. The following table shows the computation of the company's annual depletion deduction (indicated by bold type):

Year	Estimated Tons/ Beginning of Year	Tons Sold during Year	Gross Income	Unrecovered Basis/ Beginning of Year	Cost Depletion	Percentage Depletion*
1	80,000	20,000	$ 800,000	$500,000	**$125,000**	$120,000
2	65,000	32,000	1,280,000	375,000	184,615	**192,000**
3	30,000	17,000	680,000	183,000	**103,700**	102,000
4	15,000	18,500	740,000	79,300	79,300	**111,000**
5	5,000	4,000	160,000	–0–	–0–	**24,000**
6	2,500	2,000	80,000	–0–	–0–	**12,000**

*15 percent of Gross Income.

> Note that in years 1 through 4, Company M deducted the *greater* of cost depletion or percentage depletion and reduced the tax basis in the mine accordingly, But in year 4, a curious thing occurred. Company M claimed a $111,000 depletion deduction that exceeded its unrecovered basis in the mine by $31,700! And in years 5 and 6, the firm deducted $36,000 of percentage depletion even though it had a zero basis in the copper mine.

The magic of the percentage depletion deduction is that it is not limited to the capitalized cost of the mineral property. Percentage depletion is available in every year in which the property generates gross income, regardless of the fact that the tax basis in the property has been reduced to zero. In such cases, percentage depletion is not a cost recovery deduction at all but an indirect method of providing a preferential tax rate on the income earned by the extractive industries.

Not surprisingly, this highly beneficial deduction is subject to restrictions. Annual percentage depletion may not exceed 50 percent of the taxable income from the depletable property (100 percent for oil and gas property).[54] In the oil and gas industry, only independent producers and royalty owners are entitled to percentage depletion; this tax break is denied to the giant integrated companies that extract, refine, and sell oil and gas

---

[53]§613(a) and (b).
[54]Ibid.

EXHIBIT 6–1

Tax treatment of business expenditures

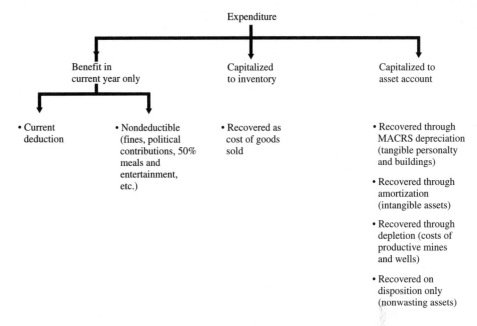

to retail customers.[55] Even with these restrictions, percentage depletion represents a valuable government subsidy. According to the Tax Expenditures Budget, this preference costs the government almost $1 billion each year.

Conclusion

The after-tax cost of a business expenditure is a function of the time period over which the firm can claim the expenditure as a tax deduction. If an expenditure is not deductible in the current year but must be capitalized to an asset account, its after-tax cost depends on the method (if any) by which the firm can compute cost recovery deductions with respect to the asset. Exhibit 6–1 summarizes the tax treatment of business expenditures and should help you appreciate the key roles that cost of goods sold, depreciation, amortization, and depletion play in the tax planning process.

[55]§613A(c).

Key Terms

Adjusted basis   130
Amortization   144
Capitalization   126
Cost basis   130
Cost depletion   149
Cost of goods sold   133
Depreciation   135
Expansion costs   146
FIFO   154
Going-concern value   147
Goodwill   147
Half-year convention   137

Intangible drilling and development costs
   (IDC)   129
Leasehold costs   146
Leasehold improvements   146
Leverage   131
LIFO   134
Limited expensing election   142
Midmonth convention   138
Midquarter convention   137
Modified Accelerated Cost Recovery System
   (MACRS)   135
Organizational costs   145

Questions and Problems for Discussion

1. How is the principle of conservatism reflected in the tax law's premise concerning the deductibility of business expenditures?

2. Assume that Congress enacted legislation requiring firms to capitalize advertising costs and amortize them over 20 years. Discuss the potential effects of such legislation on the amount of advertising that firms purchase and the price that advertising businesses charge for their product.

3. Discuss the relationship between cost recovery deductions and cash flows.

4. To what extent do cost recovery deductions with respect to the capitalized cost of a tangible business asset reflect a decline in the economic value of that asset?

5. Can a firm have a negative tax basis in an asset?

6. If the tax law did not allow farming businesses to deduct soil and water conservation expenditures but required capitalization of these costs, in what year or years would businesses recover these costs?

7. Corporation J is engaged in the manufacture of electrical appliances. Corporation K provides architectural services. During the year, both corporations paid $56,000 of annual premiums to carry fire and casualty insurance on their tangible assets. Corporation J was required to capitalize the $56,000 cost for tax purposes while Corporation K was allowed a $56,000 deduction. Can you explain this difference in tax treatment between the two corporations?

8. Identify the tax and nontax considerations that firms must consider in adopting the LIFO method of accounting for inventories.

9. Identify four possible differences in the computation of depreciation expense for financial statement purposes and MACRS depreciation.

10. What is the purpose of the MACRS half-year, midquarter, and midmonth conventions?

11. Why do the MACRS tables published by the IRS incorporate a depreciation convention for the first year during an asset's recovery period but not for the year of disposition?

12. Discuss the reasons why the limited expensing election is more valuable to small firms than to large firms.

13. Firm O purchased two items of business personalty during the year. The first item cost $35,000 and has a five-year recovery period, and the second item cost $48,000 and has a seven-year recovery period. Firm O wants to make the limited expensing election for one of its new assets. Which asset should the firm choose and why?

14. Do the following tax items result in a temporary or a permanent difference between book income and taxable income?

    a. MACRS depreciation deduction.

    b. Percentage depletion in a year in which the tax basis of the depletable asset is zero.

    c. Fifteen-year amortization of purchased goodwill.

15. Describe the difference in tax treatment between the start-up costs of a new business and the expansion costs of an existing business.

16. On February 1, Mr. B purchased a business from Mr. and Mrs. S for a lump-sum price of $750,000. The business consisted of the following balance sheet assets:

	Appraised Fair Market Value
Accounts receivable	$ 27,600
Inventory	195,000
Office supplies (4 month's worth)	8,500
Furniture and fixtures	395,000

By buying the business, Mr. B acquired a very favorable lease on office space with a remaining term of 31 months; Mr. B estimates that the value of this lease is $20,000. The purchase contract stipulates that Mr. and Mrs. S will not engage in a competitive business in the immediate geographic location for the next 36 months. Discuss how Mr. B can recover the cost of each of the business assets acquired in this purchase.

17. Firm W and Firm X both have goodwill and going-concern value worth approximately $1 million. However, only Firm X reports an amortization deduction with respect to its goodwill and going-concern value on its tax return. Can you explain this difference in tax treatment between the two firms?

18. Under what circumstances is percentage depletion not a true cost recovery deduction?

Application Problems

1. Firm L purchased only one business asset during its current calendar taxable year. The asset cost $250,000 and has a three-year recovery period. Compute Firm L's MACRS depreciation deductions with respect to this asset over the recovery period assuming that:
   a. The asset was placed in service on September 29.
   b. The asset was placed in service on October 2.

2. Company K, a calendar year taxpayer, acquired and placed in service only one business asset during 1998: equipment costing $75,000. The equipment has a seven-year MACRS recovery period. What is the maximum amount of depreciation the company may deduct for 1998 if the asset was placed in service on March 18? Company K's 1998 taxable income before depreciation exceeds $1 million.

3. At the beginning of its 1998 taxable year, Firm HG owned the following business assets:

	Date Placed in Service	Initial Cost	Accumulated Depreciation	Recovery Period	Depreciation Convention
Office furniture	6/19/96	$25,000	$ 9,696	7-year	Half-year
Office equipment	5/2/95	70,000	49,840	5-year	Half-year
Printing equipment	9/30/95	58,000	41,296	5-year	Half-year

On July 8, Firm HG sold its printing equipment. On August 18, the firm purchased and placed in service tools costing $38,000; these tools are three-year recovery property. These were the firm's only capital transactions for 1998. Based on these facts, compute Firm HG's 1998 depreciation deduction.

In making your computation, assume that the firm's 1998 taxable income before depreciation is over $1 million.

4. BTN Inc., a calendar year taxpayer, paid $89,000 for machinery (seven-year recovery property) that was placed in service on September 9, 1998.
   a. Assuming that the machinery was the only tangible property placed in service during 1998, compute BTN's maximum cost recovery deduction.
   b. How would your computation change if BTN paid $215,000 for the machinery?
   c. How would your computation change if BTN paid $250,000 for the machinery?

5. AP Inc. constructed a new manufacturing plant for a total cost of $7,615,000 and placed it in service on March 2. To finance the construction, AP took out a $6 million, 30-year mortgage on the property. Based on these facts, compute AP's depreciation deductions for the manufacturing plant for the first, second, and third years of its operation.

6. On April 23, Mrs. Y purchased a taxi business from Mr. M for a lump-sum price of $60,000. The business consists of a two-year-old taxicab worth $19,000, Mr. M's license to operate a taxi business in City C, and Mr. M's list of regular clients. The cab license has no expiration date. Mrs. Y projects that the customer list will be valuable for only about six months, after which time she will have established her own client base. Based on these facts, compute the total amount of Mrs. Y's cost recovery deductions for the current year. In making the computation, assume that Mrs. Y does not elect to expense any of the cost of the taxi.

7. In 19X8, A&Z Inc. incurred $450,000 of capitalized costs to develop a uranium mine. When the mine opened, the corporation's geologists estimated that 900,000 tons of ore would eventually be extracted. During 19X8, 215,000 tons were mined and sold. A&Z's gross revenues from the sales totaled $689,000, and its operating expenses for the mine were $200,000. Based on these facts, calculate A&Z's depletion deduction for 19X8.

8. EDI Company, a calendar year taxpayer, purchased new business equipment for $800,000 and placed it in service on March 1, 19X8. EDI's chief engineer determined that the equipment had an estimated useful life of 120 months and a $50,000 residual value to the company. For financial statement purposes, EDI uses the straight-line method to compute depreciation.
   a. Compute EDI's book depreciation expense for 19X8.
   b. Assuming that the equipment has a seven-year recovery period and is subject to the half-year convention, compute EDI's MACRS depreciation deduction for 19X8.
   c. Compute EDI's book basis and tax basis in the equipment at the beginning of 19X9.

9. ZEJ Company, a calendar year taxpayer, reported $619,300 net income before tax on its 19X9 financial statements prepared in accordance with GAAP. The corporation's records reveal the following information:
   - ZEJ incurred $75,000 of research and experimentation costs that directly resulted in a new patent for the company. ZEJ capitalized these costs on its financial statements and will amortize them over the patent's 17-year life.

The current year amortization expense per books was $1,471.
   - ZEJ's depreciation expense per books was $98,222, and its MACRS depreciation deduction was $120,000.
   - ZEJ was organized two years ago. During its first taxable year, the company capitalized $27,480 organizational costs for tax purposes and elected to amortize the cost over 60 months. For book purposes, the company expensed the costs in the year incurred.

Based on the above facts, compute ZEJ Company's 19X9 taxable income.

10. Mr. and Mrs. FB, a retired couple, decided to try their hand at operating a family restaurant. During the months of March and April, they incurred the following expenses:

Prepaid rent on commercial real estate	
($2,100 per month from April through December)	$18,900
Prepaid rent on restaurant equipment	
($990 per month from April through December)	8,910
Advertising of upcoming "grand opening"	900
Staff hiring and training	11,500
	$40,210

Mr. and Mrs. FB served their first meal to a customer on May 1. Based on these facts, determine the proper tax treatment of the above expenses on the couples' current year tax return.

Issue Recognition Problems

Identify the tax issue or issues suggested by the following situations and state each issue in the form of a question.

1. Mr. R lived in a two-bedroom, one-bath residence until August when he moved to a new home and converted his old residence into residential rent property. He had no trouble finding tenants who signed a one-year lease and moved in on September 1. As of this date, the market value of the old residence was

$120,000. Mr. R purchased the residence six years ago for $180,000.

2. Mrs. K owns and operates her own consulting firm, and her husband, Mr. K, owns and operates a printing business. During the current year, Mrs. K's consulting business generated $89,000 of taxable income. Mr. K's business operated at a loss. In July, Mr. K bought new office furniture for $16,000. This was the only purchase of tangible business personalty by either spouse for

the year. Mr. and Mrs. K always file a joint tax return.

3. ROJ Inc. recently purchased a 20-acre industrial complex consisting of three warehouses and two office buildings surrounded by parking lots. About 12 acres of the land is undeveloped. ROJ paid a lump-sum purchase price of $19.4 million.

4. Firm PY purchased industrial equipment from a Canadian vendor. The firm paid $12,800 to transport the equipment to its manufacturing plant in Florida. It paid a single premium of $1,700 for insurance against casualty or theft of the equipment while in route.

5. WRT Inc. owns and operates a chain of retail bookstores. The company recently decided to add coffee bars in each of the stores to sell gourmet coffee drinks and pastries to the bookstore customers. The company has not yet obtained the necessary licenses required under local law to serve food to the public. However, it has incurred almost $30,000 in up-front expenditures on the coffee bars.

6. Mr. Q is a professional musician. During the current year, he paid $50,000 for an antique bass viol made by the famed instrument maker Francesco Ruggieri in the 17th century. Mr. Q uses the viol for both daily practice and performances. The price of a good-quality bass viol in a music store is about $2,200.

7. Company JJ, a calendar year corporation, bought an airplane for use in its mining exploration business in December. The manufacturer delivered the plane to the company's hangar on December 19. Because of severe winter weather, JJ's pilot was unable to fly the plane on company business until February 16 of the next year.

8. TCJ Inc. bought a 10-acre tract of undeveloped land that it intends to improve and subdivide for sale to real estate customers sometime during the next three years. During the current year, TCJ paid $4,300 to a local company to clean up the land by hauling away trash, cutting down dead trees, and spraying for poison ivy.

9. Firm D paid a lump-sum price of $500,000 for a small commercial office building. A local consulting company approached Firm D with a proposal. For a flat fee of $15,000, the firm will analyze the components of the building (shelving, lighting fixtures, floor coverings, plumbing, etc.) to determine how much of the $500,000 price is attributable to five-year or seven-year recovery property rather than to the building itself.

Tax Planning Cases

1. MRT Corporation, a calendar year taxpayer, placed the following business assets in service during 19X5:

Asset	Initial Cost	Recovery Period	Date Placed in Service
Manufacturing equipment	$119,000	7 years	April 23
Furniture and fixtures	16,000	7	May 2
Transportation equipment	195,000	5	September 3
Office equipment	120,000	7	December 1

  a. Compute MRT Corporation's MACRS depreciation deduction with respect to the assets placed in service during 19X5.

  b. Late in 19X5, MRT decided to purchase $200,000 of additional equipment. The corporation could buy the equipment and place it in service before year-end or it could postpone the acquisition until the first week in January. What impact does this decision have on MRT Corporation's depreciation deduction with respect to the assets already acquired during 19X5?

2. Company C has a marginal tax rate of 34 percent and uses an 8 percent discount rate to compute NPV. The company plans to buy a business asset costing $100,000. The asset is three-year recovery property, and the company can use the half-year convention in year 1. The company could use existing funds to buy the asset or it could borrow the entire $100,000 purchase price. The repayment schedule for the debt is as follows:

	Amount Borrowed	Interest Payment	Principal Repayment
Year 1	$100,000		
Year 2		$(12,000)	
Year 3		(12,000)	
Year 4		(12,000)	
Year 5		(12,000)	$(100,000)

Based on the above facts, should Company C buy the asset with existing funds or leverage the purchase by borrowing?

3. MG Inc., a corporation in the 34 percent marginal tax bracket, uses duplicating equipment in its home office. The corporation's current equipment was purchased several years ago and is fully depreciated. This old equipment is still operating and should continue to do so for four years (years 1, 2, 3, and 4). MG's chief financial officer estimates that repair and maintenance costs for the old equipment will be $1,400 in year 1, $1,400 in year 2, $1,500 in year 3, and $1,600 in year 4. At the end of year 4, the equipment will have no residual value to MG.

MG could junk the old equipment and buy new equipment for $5,000 cash. The new equipment would have three-year MACRS recovery period with a half-year convention. The new equipment should not require any repairs or maintenance during years 1 through 4 and will have no residual value to MG at the end of year 4.

a. Assume MG may not elect to expense the $5,000 cost of the new equipment. Which option (keep old or buy new) minimizes MG's after-tax cost? In making your calculations, use a 10 percent discount rate.

b. Assume MG does elect to expense the entire $5,000 cost of the new equipment. Under this change in facts, which option (keep old or buy new) minimizes MG's after-tax cost?

7 Property Dispositions

Learning Objectives

After studying this chapter, you should be able to:

1. Distinguish between the concepts of gain or loss realization and gain or loss recognition.

2. Describe the installment sale method and its effect on the timing of gain recognition.

3. Explain why the law prevents taxpayers from recognizing losses realized on sales of property to related parties.

4. Identify the two components of the definition of capital gain or loss.

5. List the five categories of noncapital assets.

6. Define the limitation on the deductibility of capital losses.

7. Differentiate between the carryback and carryforward rules for net capital losses incurred by individuals and by corporations.

8. Apply the Section 1231 netting process to characterize gains and losses.

9. Incorporate the loss recapture and depreciation recapture rules into the Section 1231 netting process.

10. Describe the tax consequences of property dispositions that don't involve a sale or exchange.

Chapter 7 continues our investigation of the tax consequences of property transactions. In this chapter, we will discuss how firms account for gains or losses resulting from property dispositions. This discussion centers on three basic tax questions:

- What is the gain or loss recognized on the disposition of property?
- In what taxable year does the recognition occur?
- What is the tax character of the recognized gain or loss?

The answers to these questions determine the tax cost or savings and, in turn, the after-tax cash flows resulting from the property disposition.

Computation of Gain or Loss Recognized

Realization and Recognition of Gains or Losses

The Internal Revenue Code specifies that gross income includes "gains derived from dealings in property."[1] The law allows a deduction for "any loss sustained during the taxable year and not compensated for by insurance or otherwise."[2] These two rules mean that firms must account for gains and losses from property transactions in the computation of taxable income. The computation of **realized gain or loss** from the disposition of property is based on the following formula:[3]

$$\begin{array}{r} \text{Amount realized on disposition} \\ \underline{\text{(Adjusted basis of property)}} \\ \text{Realized gain or (loss)} \end{array}$$

    This formula reflects the realization principle of accounting introduced in Chapter 5. Under this principle, increases or decreases in the value of assets over time do not enter into the computation of income. Such increases or decreases are not taken into account until an asset is converted to a different asset through some type of external transaction with another party. As a simple illustration of this principle, suppose that Firm F bought an asset four years ago for $25,000. Although the market value of the asset has steadily increased over the past four years, the firm has not reported any of this accrued economic gain on either its financial statements or tax returns for those years. In the current year, Firm F sells the asset for $60,000 cash, finally realizing a $35,000 gain.

Objective 1
Distinguish between the concepts of gain or loss realization and gain or loss recognition.

    A third general rule of law is that the entire gain or loss realized on a property disposition is taken into account for tax purposes.[4] In other words, realized gain or loss becomes **recognized gain or loss** for the year, as shown in the expanded formula.

$$\begin{array}{c} \text{Amount realized on disposition} \\ \underline{\text{(Adjusted basis of property)}} \\ \text{Realized gain or (loss)} \\ \downarrow \\ \underline{\text{Recognized gain or (loss)}} \end{array}$$

    This rule means that Firm F will report the $35,000 gain realized on the asset sale as income on both its current year financial statements and its tax return. Most of the property transactions examined in Chapter 7 reflect this linkage between realization and recognition. In Chapter 8, we will explore the exceptions to the general rule: transactions in which realized gain or loss is not recognized in the same year.

    The realization principle has important tax planning implications because it gives property owners a measure of control over the timing of gain or loss recognition. A firm owning property that has appreciated in value can defer paying tax on the accrued gain by continuing to hold the property. In contrast, a firm with a low marginal tax rate in the current year can sell appreciated property so that the entire accrued gain is taxed at the low rate. A firm owning property that has declined in value can

---

[1] §61(a)(3).
[2] §165(a).
[3] §1001(a).
[4] §1001(c).

plan to realize the loss in the year in which it will derive the most benefit from the tax deduction. By maximizing the tax savings generated by the deduction, the firm can reduce its economic loss on the property.

Sales and Exchanges

The most common property disposition is a sale for cash (or the buyer's promise to pay cash at some future date) or an exchange of property for a different noncash asset. The **amount realized** by the seller equals the sum of any money plus the fair market value of any property received.[5] For example, if Company J exchanges equipment for marketable securities and the securities are worth $50,000, Company J's amount realized is $50,000. While the amount realized is determined by reference to the value of the cash and/or property received by the seller, the amount realized presumably equals the value of the property surrendered. In our example, both parties to the transaction must believe that the equipment is also worth $50,000. Why is this so? In an economic setting, no rational person would sell property for less than its value, nor would any purchaser pay more for property than its value. The private market created between seller and purchaser establishes the equal values of the properties changing hands.

Relief of Debt as Amount Realized.   In Chapter 6, we learned that the tax basis of property includes any amount that the owner borrowed from another party to acquire the property. In other words, tax basis encompasses both the owner's equity in the property and any debt to which the property is subject. If the owner sells the property and is relieved of debt as part of the transaction, the owner must include the debt relief in the amount realized on sale.

> ***Relief of Debt.***   The TG Corporation purchased investment land 15 years ago for $450,000. TG put $100,000 of its own money into the investment and borrowed the remaining $350,000 from a bank, which took a mortgage on the property. TG's cost basis in the land is $450,000. Each year as TG paid down the principal of the mortgage, the payments increased TG's equity in the land but had no effect on TG's basis. In the current year, TG sold the land for $875,000. The purchaser assumed the $200,000 principal balance of the mortgage and paid the $675,000 remaining sales price in cash. TG's realized gain is computed as follows:
>
> | | |
> |---|---:|
> | Amount realized on sale: | |
> | Cash received | $ 675,000 |
> | Relief of debt | 200,000 |
> | | $ 875,000 |
> | Basis of land | (450,000) |
> | Realized gain | $ 425,000 |

---

[5]§1001(b).

Tax-Free Recovery of Basis and Cash Flow.   In a sale or exchange of property, only the excess of amount realized over adjusted basis is taxable income. Accordingly, sellers recover their investment in the property at no tax cost.

> ***Realized Gain and Basis Recovery.***   Firm R owns an asset with a basis of $5,000. If the firm sells the asset for $8,000 cash, it realizes a taxable gain of only $3,000. The first $5,000 of the cash received represents a nontaxable recovery of Firm R's investment in the asset. Assuming that Firm R has a 35 percent marginal tax rate, the sale generates $6,950 of cash flow.
>
> | | Tax Result | Cash Flow |
> |---|---|---|
> | Amount realized on sale | $ 8,000 | $ 8,000 |
> | Basis | (5,000) | |
> | Gain realized | $ 3,000 | |
> | | .35 | |
> | Tax cost of gain | $ 1,050 | (1,050) |
> | After-tax cash flow | | $ 6,950 |

If a seller realizes a loss on a sale or exchange, the entire amount realized is a tax-free recovery of the seller's investment. Moreover, the seller may be allowed to deduct the *unrecovered* investment (the realized loss) in the computation of taxable income.

> ***Realized Loss and Basis Recovery.***   Refer to the facts in the preceding example. If Firm R sells the asset for only $4,000, it realizes a $1,000 loss. *Assuming that this loss is fully deductible,* the firm recovers its $5,000 investment in the asset in the form of $4,000 cash plus a $1,000 deduction.
>
> | | Tax Result | Cash Flow |
> |---|---|---|
> | Amount realized on sale | $ 4,000 | $4,000 |
> | Basis | (5,000) | |
> | Loss realized | $(1,000) | |
> | | .35 | |
> | Tax savings from loss | $ (350) | 350 |
> | After-tax cash flow | | $4,350 |

Note that in these two examples, the realized gain or loss does not enter into the computation of Firm R's net cash flow. Only the tax cost or savings resulting from the gain or loss are cash items.

Taxation of Inflationary Gains.   As the preceding examples demonstrate, taxpayers who sell property can recover their basis at no tax cost. In financial terms, a return of investment does not represent income. Only the amount realized in excess of the investment—a return *on* investment—should be recognized as income. This return is overstated if the value of the dollar has changed between the date an asset is purchased and the date that asset is sold. In a period of inflation, the dollars that the taxpayer invested in the asset were worth more in terms of purchasing power than the dollars the taxpayer receives from the asset's sale.

> ***Inflationary Gain.***   Refer to the first example in which Firm R sells an asset with a cost basis of $5,000 for an amount realized of $8,000. Because of inflation, a dollar in the year the firm acquired the asset was worth $1.25 of today's dollars. In current dollar terms, Firm R's investment in its asset is $6,250 ($5,000 basis × $1.25). The firm's economic gain on sale is only $1,750 ($8,000 amount realized − $6,250 inflation-adjusted basis). However, because the tax system fails to account for changes in the dollar's purchasing power over time, Firm R pays tax on a gain of $3,000, $1,250 of which is not economic income but a return of the firm's original investment.[6]

The Installment Sale Method of Reporting Gain

Objective 2
Describe the installment sale method and its effect on the timing of gain recognition.

When some or all of the amount realized on the sale of property consists of the buyer's note (a debt obligation to pay cash at some future date), the seller may be entitled to use a special method of accounting for gain realized on the transaction. The **installment sale method** provides that the realized gain is not recognized in the year of sale.[7] Instead, gain recognition is linked to the seller's receipt of cash over the life of the note.

Under the installment sale method, the seller determines the gain recognized in the year of sale and each subsequent year by multiplying the cash received each year by a **gross profit percentage.** This percentage is calculated by dividing the gain realized on sale by the total contract price.

> ***Installment Sale Method.***   During year 1, Firm B sold land with a basis of $150,000 for a contract price of $214,500. The purchaser paid $14,500 down and gave Firm B a note for the $200,000 balance of the contract price. The note provides for annual principal payments of $20,000 in years 2 through 11 plus 10 percent annual interest on the unpaid balance. Firm B's gain realized and gross profit percentage are computed as follows:

---

[6]Congress and the Treasury are well aware of this problem. The theoretically sound solution is to allow taxpayers to adjust the basis in their assets for inflation. Lawmakers have been reluctant to enact this solution into law because of the potential revenue loss and the enormous complexity it would add to the computation of basis, cost recovery deductions, and recognized gains and losses.
   [7]§453.

Amount realized on sale:	
Cash received	$ 14,500
Purchaser's note	200,000
	$ 214,500
Basis of land	(150,000)
Realized gain	$ 64,500

$$\frac{\$64,500 \text{ realized gain}}{\$214,500 \text{ contract price}} = 30.07 \text{ gross profit percentage}$$

Firm B will recognize the following taxable gain each year:

Year	Cash Received	Gross Profit Percentage	Taxable Gain Recognized
1	$14,500	30.07%	$ 4,360
2	20,000	30.07	6,014
3	20,000	30.07	6,014
4	20,000	30.07	6,014
5	20,000	30.07	6,014
6	20,000	30.07	6,014
7	20,000	30.07	6,014
8	20,000	30.07	6,014
9	20,000	30.07	6,014
10	20,000	30.07	6,014
11	20,000	30.07	6,014
			$64,500

Note that the annual interest payments that Firm B receives on the installment note do not enter into the computation of recognized gain. The firm must recognize these payments as ordinary income under its regular method of accounting.

Temporary Book/Tax Difference.   A taxpayer must use the installment sale method to account for gain recognized on qualifying sales of property unless the taxpayer makes a written election *not* to use the method.[8] (The method has no application to loss transactions.) The installment sale method does not affect the *amount* of gain recognized. In the preceding example, Firm B will eventually recognize the entire $64,500 gain realized on the land sale. The method affects only the *timing* of the gain recognition and, consequently, results in a temporary difference between book and taxable income. In Firm B's case, book income in year 1 includes a $64,500 gain, only $4,360 of which is included in taxable income. In years 2 through 11, this difference will reverse as the firm reports $6,014 of taxable income that is not reported on its financial statements.

---

[8] §453(d).

The book/tax difference from the installment sale method is in the taxpayer's favor. Specifically, the method allows sellers to defer the tax cost of the realized gain, thereby decreasing the cost in present value terms. If Firm B's marginal tax rate is 35 percent, its tax liability on the $64,500 gain is $22,575. Because of the installment sale method, the firm will pay this tax over an 11-year period. Assuming a 9 percent discount rate, the tax in present value terms is only $15,036.

Basis Implications.   When a seller receives the purchaser's note as part of the amount realized on a property sale, the seller generally takes a basis in the note equal to the note's face value. This basis represents the dollars that the seller will recover as tax-free principal payments as the note is paid off.

Note Receivable Basis.   Company Q sold land with a basis of $245,000 for a contract price of $300,000. The purchaser gave Company Q a six-year, interest-bearing note for the entire contract price. Company Q elected out of the installment sale method and, therefore, recognized its $55,000 realized gain in the year of sale. Company Q's basis in the note receivable is the note's face value of $300,000. The principal payments that Company Q will receive over the next six years will reduce both the face value and the tax basis in this note to zero.

In the case of an installment sale, the seller is not entitled to a tax-free recovery of the dollars represented by the purchaser's note. Instead, the seller will recognize a percentage of every dollar received as taxable income. Consequently, the seller's tax basis in the installment note is reduced by the deferred gain represented by the note.[9]

Installment Note Receivable Basis.   Refer back to the previous example in which Firm B deferred the recognition of $60,140 gain realized under the installment sale method. Firm B's initial basis in the note received from the purchaser is $139,860 ($200,000 face value − $60,140 deferred gain). After Firm B receives the first $20,000 principal payment and recognitizes $6,014 of deferred gain, the basis in the note is reduced to $125,874 ($180,000 face value − $54,126 remaining deferred gain). Firm B's receipt of each subsequent principal payment will reduce the face value of the note, the note's tax basis, and Firm B's deferred gain until all three amounts are reduced to zero.

Limitations on the Installment Sale Method.   Since the enactment of the original installment sale rules in 1926, Congress has been concerned that taxpayers might exploit the tax deferral opportunity inherent in this accounting method. Over the years, Congress has narrowed the scope of the method through a series of limitations on its use. One set of limitations applies to the type of property eligible for installment sale treatment. Stocks or securities traded on an established market are ineligible.[10] Real or

---

[9] §453B(b).

[10] §453(k)(2)(A). Established securities markets include the New York Stock Exchange (NYSE), the American Stock Exchange (AMEX), and NASDAQ.

personal property held as inventory for sale to customers in the regular course of business is also ineligible.[11] Thus, retailers that normally extend credit to their customers, such as Sears and JCPenney, can't use the installment sale method to recognize ordinary income from inventory sales.

A second set of limitations applies if a taxpayer converts an installment obligation to cash.[12] In such case, the taxpayer must immediately recognize the entire deferred gain represented by the obligation. Refer back to the Firm B example and assume that after collecting the first principal payment in year 2, the company sold the installment note to a local financial institution for its face value of $180,000. Because Firm B accelerated its receipt of cash from the installment sale, it must recognize the remaining $54,126 deferred gain in year 2. What if Firm B tried the more subtle technique of pledging the note as collateral for a $180,000 loan from the financial institution? In this case, Firm B still owns the note but has used it indirectly to obtain cash. Nonetheless, Firm B must still recognize the $54,126 deferred gain; the installment sale rules stipulate that a pledge of an installment note is considered a disposition of the note for cash.[13]

Disallowed Losses on Related Party Sales

Objective 3
Explain why the law prevents taxpayers from recognizing losses realized on sales of property to related parties.

Earlier in the chapter, we focused on the general rule that the entire gain or loss realized on a property disposition is recognized for tax purposes. Consequently, firms can usually deduct losses realized on the sale of business assets. One important exception to the general rule is that losses realized on the sale or exchange of property between related parties are nondeductible.[14] For purposes of this exception, the Internal Revenue Code defines related parties as people who are members of the same family, an individual and a corporation if the individual owns more than 50 percent of the value of the corporation's outstanding stock, and two corporations controlled by the same shareholders.[15]

> **Disallowed Loss.**   Firm M sold a business asset to Purchaser P for $75,000. Firm M's basis in the asset was $90,000. The firm reported the $15,000 realized loss on its financial statements. Firm M and Purchaser P are related parties for federal tax purposes. Consequently, Firm M may not recognize the $15,000 loss as a deduction in the computation of taxable income. Even though Firm M's loss is disallowed, Purchaser P takes a $75,000 cost basis in the asset.

This disallowance rule is based on the theory that a related party loss may not represent an economic loss to the seller. For instance, when a corporation realizes a loss on the sale of an asset to an unrelated purchaser, the loss corresponds to the unrecovered investment in the asset—a permanent reduction in the corporation's net worth. If the corporation sells that asset to its controlling shareholder, the underlying ownership of the asset doesn't change. If the value of the asset increases subsequent to the sale, the

---

[11]§453(b)(2).
[12]§453B.
[13]§453A(d).
[14]§267(a)(1).
[15]§267(b)(1),(2), and (3). A person's family includes a spouse, brothers and sisters, ancestors, and lineal descendants. §267(c)(4).

shareholder may eventually recover the corporation's entire investment. In this case, the corporation's loss on sale has no economic substance and should not be deductible in computing taxable income.

A second explanation for the disallowance rule is that related party transactions occur in a fictitious market in which buyer and seller may not be negotiating at arm's length. Because of this possibility, the government has no assurance that the selling price of the asset equates to the market value at which the asset would change hands between unrelated parties. If the selling price is unrealistically low, the seller's loss is inflated and results in an unwarranted tax deduction. Because of this possibility, the loss disallowance rule applies to every related party sale, regardless of the actual bargaining stance between the parties. For instance, if a brother realizes a loss on the sale of a business asset to his sister, the loss is nondeductible, even if the brother can prove that the siblings have been estranged for years and that the transaction between them was strictly at arm's length.

Offset of Gain by Previously Disallowed Loss.   From the seller's perspective, the loss disallowance rule causes a permanent difference between loss realized and loss recognized on the sale of property. Thus, the seller never receives the benefit of a tax deduction for the disallowed loss. However, in the right set of circumstances, the *purchaser* may receive some or all of the benefit. If the purchaser subsequently sells the property acquired in the related party transaction and realizes a gain, the purchaser can offset this gain by the previously disallowed loss.[16]

Use of Seller's Disallowed Loss by Purchaser.   Refer to the preceding example in which Firm M realized a $15,000 disallowed loss on the sale of an asset to Purchaser P. Assume that the asset was nondepreciable in P's hands. Several years after the related party transaction, Purchaser P sells the asset to an *unrelated* buyer. The tax consequences of the sale based on three different assumptions as to the selling price are presented in the following table:

	Assumption 1	Assumption 2	Assumption 3
Amount realized	$ 93,000	$ 81,000	$ 70,000
Basis of asset	(75,000)	(75,000)	(75,000)
Gain (loss) realized	$ 18,000	$ 6,000	$ (5,000)
Previously disallowed loss	(15,000)	(6,000)	–0–
Gain (loss) recognized	$ 3,000	$ –0–	$ (5,000)

This example demonstrates that Purchaser P can use Firm M's previously disallowed loss only to *reduce* the gain recognized on a subsequent sale of the asset. The disallowed loss cannot *create* a recognized loss or *increase* the recognized loss on a subsequent sale.

---

[16]§267(d).

Tax Character of Recognized Gains and Losses

Taxpayers that dispose of property must compute the gain or loss realized on the disposition and determine the taxable year (or years) in which the gain or loss is recognized. In addition, they must determine the character of the recognized gain or loss. In the tax world, every gain or loss is ultimately characterized as either ordinary or capital. A **capital gain or loss** results from the sale or exchange of a capital asset.[17] Any gain or loss that does not meet this definition is **ordinary** in character.[18]

Objective 4
Identify the two components of the definition of capital gain or loss.

The capital gain/loss definition has two distinct components. First, the transaction resulting in the gain or loss must be a sale or exchange. Second, the asset surrendered must be a capital asset. If a firm disposes of a capital asset in some way other than a sale or exchange, the realized gain or loss from the transaction is ordinary in character. Several of these dispositions are discussed later in the chapter. At this point, let's focus our attention on the second component of the capital gain/loss definition: the capital asset requirement.

Capital Asset Defined

Objective 5
List the five categories of noncapital assets.

The Internal Revenue Code defines the term **capital asset** by exception.[19] For tax purposes, *every* asset is a capital asset unless it falls into one of five categories:

1. Inventory items or property held by the taxpayer primarily for sale to customers in the ordinary course of business.
2. Accounts or notes receivable acquired in the ordinary course of business (i.e., acquired through the sale of inventory or the performance of services).
3. Real or depreciable property used in a business (including rental real estate) and intangible business assets subject to amortization.[20]
4. A copyright, literary, musical, or artistic composition, a letter or memorandum, or similar property held by a taxpayer whose personal efforts created the property or a person to whom the property was gifted by the creator.
5. Certain publications of the U.S. government.

Capital asset status is not determined by the intrinsic nature of the asset itself but by the use for which the asset is held by its owner.

> *Capital Asset Defined.*   Ms. H, a professional sculptor, purchased $50 worth of clay and created a work of art that she sold for $5,000 to BVC Corporation. BVC uses the sculpture as decoration in the lobby of its corporate headquarters. The work of art is not a capital asset in the hands of its creator, so Ms. H's $4,950 gain recognized on the sale is ordinary income. In contrast, the sculpture is a capital asset to BVC Corporation because it is not a *depreciable* business asset. As a result, if the corporation were to sell the sculpture, its recognized gain or loss would be capital in character.

---

[17]§1222.
[18]§64 and §65.
[19]§1221.
[20]Reg. §1.167(a)-3 and §197(f)(7).

Capital Loss Limitation

Objective 6
Define the limitation on
the deductibility of
capital losses.

The federal income tax system contains a subset of rules applying to capital gains and losses. One logical way to analyze these rules is to begin with the limitation on capital losses: *capital losses can be deducted only to the extent of capital gains.*[21] This limitation has a major impact on the tax savings generated by a capital loss. The next three examples demonstrate this impact.

Fully Deductible Capital Loss.   Firm SD sold a capital asset with a $100,000 basis for an amount realized of $25,000. If the firm's marginal tax rate is 25 percent, how much tax savings does this $75,000 capital loss generate for the firm? If Firm SD recognized at least $75,000 of capital gain during the year, the capital loss generates $18,750 of current tax savings and the firm's after-tax loss on the sale is $56,250:

Loss on sale of capital asset	$(75,000)
Current tax savings	
($75,000 deductible loss × 25%)	18,750
After-tax loss	$(56,250)

Partially Deductible Capital Loss.   Assume that Firm SD recognized only $40,000 capital gain during the year. In this case, the firm can deduct only $40,000 of its capital loss; its $35,000 **net capital loss** (excess of current year capital loss over capital gain) is nondeductible.[22] The tax savings generated by the capital loss decreases to $10,000, and the after-tax loss increases to $65,000:

Loss on sale of capital asset	$(75,000)
Current tax savings	
($40,000 deductible loss × 25%)	10,000
After-tax loss	$(65,000)

Nondeductible Capital Loss.   In the worst case scenario, Firm SD recognized no capital gains during the year. Consequently, none of the firm's $75,000 net capital loss is deductible, and the firm's before-tax and after-tax loss are both $75,000.

---

[21]§1211. This strict limitation is relaxed very slightly for individual taxpayers. See the discussion of individual capital losses in Chapter 15.

[22]Net capital losses are reported for financial statement purposes and result in a difference between book income and taxable income.

Loss on sale of capital asset	$(75,000)
Current tax savings	–0–
After-tax loss	$(75,000)

Loss Carrybacks and Carryforwards.   The above examples are incomplete in that they show the effect of the capital loss limitation only for an isolated year. If a taxpayer has a net capital loss for the year, the law provides a mechanism by which the loss can be used as a deduction in a previous or future year. For no obvious policy reason, the tax law differentiates between capital losses incurred by individuals and those incurred by corporations.

- A net capital loss incurred by an individual is carried forward indefinitely.[23] In any future year in which the individual recognizes net capital gain (excess of current year capital gain over capital loss), the loss carryforward is deductible to the extent of such gain.

Objective 7
Differentiate between the carryback and carryforward rules for net capital losses incurred by individuals and by corporations.

- A net capital loss incurred by a corporation is carried back three years and forward five years, but only for use as a deduction against net capital gains recognized during this eight-year period.[24]

Let's look at an example of the operation of the corporate rule.

Capital Loss Carryback.   RO Inc., a corporation facing a 35 percent marginal tax rate, sold two capital assets during 19X4, recognizing a $50,000 gain on the first sale and an $85,000 loss on the second. RO deducted $50,000 of the loss on its 19X4 tax return; its nondeductible net capital loss is $35,000. The corporation's taxable income for the three previous years is as follows:

	19X1	19X2	19X3
Ordinary income	$600,000	$400,000	$730,000
Net capital gain	–0–	10,000	12,000
Taxable income	$600,000	$410,000	$742,000

- Because it had no net capital gain in the earliest year of its carryback period, RO can't deduct any of its 19X4 net capital loss against 19X1 income.
- RO may deduct $10,000 and $12,000 of the 19X4 loss against the taxable income reported in 19X2 and 19X3, recompute its tax liability accordingly, and file for a refund of tax.
- RO will carry the $13,000 remaining net capital loss forward as a potential deduction against future capital gains.

---

[23]§1212(b)(1).
[24]§1212(a)(1).

Taxation of Capital Gains

Under the federal income tax system, capital gains have the unique capacity to absorb capital losses. This valuable characteristic is analogous to a preferential tax rate on capital gains.

> **The Value of Capital Gains.**   KLJ Inc. recognized $100,000 of income and incurred an $80,000 capital loss during the current year. If the income is all ordinary, the capital loss is nondeductible. If KLJ's marginal tax rate is 34 percent, its tax liability for the year is $34,000. If the income is capital gain, the loss is deductible. In such case, the corporation's tax liability drops to $6,800 ($20,000 taxable income × 34 percent). Consequently, KLJ's $100,000 capital gain is taxed at only 6.8 percent.

Preferential Rates for Individuals.   In a year in which a taxpayer recognizes a net capital gain (excess of capital gain over capital loss), the net gain is included in taxable income. If the taxpayer is a corporation, this net gain is taxed at the same rates as ordinary income. If the taxpayer is an individual, the net capital gain may be taxed at a preferential rate of 10, 20, 25, or 28 percent.[25] Given that the highest marginal rate for individuals is currently 39.6 percent, the preferential rates on capital gains are extremely valuable to high-income individuals. The details of the preferential rate structure are discussed in Chapter 15.

Capital Asset Definition Revisited

The characterization of gains and losses recognized on sales or exchanges of property can be a high-stakes game. As a general rule, taxpayers prefer capital gains to ordinary income and they prefer ordinary losses to capital losses. As we discussed earlier in this section, the characterization of gain and loss depends on whether the property was a noncapital or a capital asset in the hands of the seller. More specifically, does the property fit into one of the five explicit categories of noncapital assets listed in the Internal Revenue Code? If the property does not fall into one of these five categories, the statute states that the property is a capital asset. This classification scheme is presented in the following diagram:

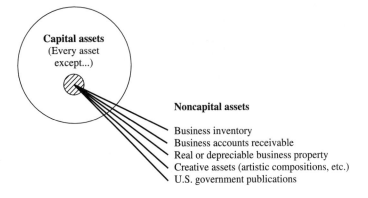

---

[25]§1(h). These rates apply only to long-term capital gains, which are derived from the sale of assets held for more than one year. See §1222.

The Rise and Fall of the *Corn Products* Doctrine.   In 1955, the Supreme Court concluded that the literal language of the statute was not reflective of the congressional intent behind the definition of capital assets. The case was *Corn Products Refining Co.* v. *Commissioner*[26] and the assets under scrutiny were corn futures contracts. The plaintiff was a corporation that maintained an inventory of raw corn, which it used in the manufacture of a variety of food products. To guarantee its future supply of corn at a favorable price, the corporation routinely purchased corn futures—contracts to purchase a fixed amount of grain on a future date for a stipulated price. If the corporation decided not to take delivery on a particular contract, the contract was sold. The corporation reported its net gain from these sales as capital gain, eligible for the highly preferential tax rate on corporate capital gains then in effect.

The IRS contended that the net gain should be taxed as ordinary income because the futures contracts were not capital assets. While the IRS conceded that the contracts did not fall into any of the five noncapital asset categories, it argued that the corporation did not purchase the contracts for speculative or investment reasons but solely to guarantee a source of inventory. Because the contracts were of vital importance to the operation of the corporation's business, they should be classified as noncapital. The Supreme Court was persuaded by this argument, concluding that "Congress intended that profits and losses arising from the everyday operation of a business be considered as ordinary income or loss rather than capital gain or loss."[27]

This relaxed judicial definition of capital assets was an open invitation to firms confronted with potentially nondeductible capital losses resulting from the sale of assets. If a firm could tell a plausible story as to why the asset was an integral component of its business operation, it could invoke the *Corn Products* doctrine and claim the loss as an ordinary deduction. This subjective method of converting capital loss to ordinary loss was part of the tax law for three decades.

In 1988, the IRS challenged the doctrine in the case of *Arkansas Best Corp.* v. *Commissioner.*[28] The corporation in this case owned a controlling stock interest in a subsidiary corporation. When the subsidiary encountered severe financial difficulties, its parent purchased additional stock to provide much-needed cash to the subsidiary's foundering business. When the parent corporation eventually sold this stock, it reported an ordinary loss because the stock had been purchased "exclusively for business purposes and subsequently held for the same reasons."[29] The IRS insisted that the stock was a capital asset and that the loss recognized on its sale was a capital loss. In an opinion that amounted to a reversal of the *Corn Products* decision and a deathblow to the *Corn Products* doctrine, the Supreme Court held for the government, concluding that a taxpayer's motivation in purchasing an asset is irrelevant to the question of whether such asset is capital in character. Because of the decision in *Arkansas Best,* the definition of capital asset is once more dependent on a literal reading of the law. If an asset does not fall within one of the five statutory exceptions, it is a capital asset—period.

Dispositions of Noncapital Assets

The expansive definition of a capital asset as every asset except for those specifically listed in the Internal Revenue Code may be misleading. In the business context, capital

---

[26]350 U.S. 46 (1955).
[27]Ibid., p. 50.
[28]485 U.S. 212 (1988).
[29]Ibid., p. 215.

assets are the exception rather than the rule. Most properties listed on a firm's balance sheet fall into one of first three categories of noncapital assets. In this section of the chapter, we will analyze the tax consequences of the dispositions of these noncapital business assets.

What types of business properties are capital in character? Any asset held by a firm for long-term investment rather than for active business or commercial use is a capital asset. Similarly, equity and creditor interests in other firms, such as stocks, bonds, and partnership interests, are capital in character. Self-created patents are given explicit capital asset status in the Internal Revenue Code.[30] Finally, the goodwill and going-concern value created by a well-established and profitable business operation is a capital asset.[31]

Inventory

The first category of noncapital assets includes any property that firms carry as inventory or hold for sale to customers. When firms sell inventory assets as part of their everyday operations, the recognized gain or loss is the quintessence of ordinary business income or loss. For firms engaged in the manufacture, production, wholesaling, distribution, or retailing of tangible goods, the identification of inventory assets is fairly straightforward. Disputes between taxpayers and the IRS concerning the status of property as inventory most frequently arise when the asset in question is land.

Real Estate Sales.   If a taxpayer sells a tract of land at a profit, the taxpayer usually prefers to categorize the tract as an investment asset and the profit as capital gain. The IRS might challenge this result if it believes that the taxpayer acquired and held the land primarily for sale to customers rather than as a long-term investment. From this perspective, the profit from the sale is ordinary income. The federal courts have been called on many times over the years to resolve this particular difference of opinion. In cases in which the land sale was an unusual or isolated occurrence, the courts have tended to side with the taxpayer. In cases in which the taxpayer sold other tracts of land on a regular and continuous basis, subdivided and improved the land prior to sale, or advertised the availability of the land to the general public, the courts have tended to agree with the IRS that the land was an inventory asset in the hands of the taxpayer.

Accounts Receivable

The second category of noncapital assets includes business accounts receivable. Normally, firms dispose of their accounts receivable through collection or by writing off uncollectible receivables as bad debts. Occasionally, firms sell an account receivable to another party as a quick means of raising cash. The difference between the cash received and the firm's tax basis in the receivable represents ordinary income or loss.

Section 1231 Assets

The third category of noncapital assets includes real or depreciable property used in a business (including rental real estate) and intangible business assets subject to amortization. This category comprises the core operating assets reported on a firm's bal-

---

[30]§1235.

[31]*Purchased* goodwill/going-concern value is not a capital asset to the purchaser. Purchased intangibles fall into the third category of noncapital assets, and the tax consequences of their disposition are subject to the specialized rules of §197(f)(1).

ance sheet. The tax consequences of a sale of an operating asset depends on the length of time the seller held the asset prior to sale. If the holding period is a year or less, gain or loss recognized on sale is ordinary in character. If the holding period exceeds one year, the gain or loss is subject to a favorable (if rather complex) set of characterization rules.

Objective 8
Apply the Section 1231 netting process to characterize gains and losses.

These rules are found in Section 1231 of the Internal Revenue Code; consequently, the assets subject to the rules are called **Section 1231 assets.** The basic rule of Section 1231 is simple. If the *combined result* of all sales and exchanges of Section 1231 assets during the year is a net loss, the loss is an ordinary business loss. On the other hand, if the result is a net gain, the gain is treated as a capital gain.[32] The following diagram depicts the Section 1231 netting process and the two possible results:

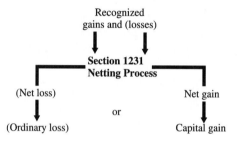

Note that this asymmetric rule offers the best of both worlds to the business community—ordinary loss or capital gain on the sale of operating assets. Let's work through two examples of the basic Section 1231 netting process.

Section 1231 Net Loss.   During 19X8, Company RC sold three Section 1231 assets with the following result:

	Gain or (Loss) Recognized
Asset sale 1	$ 45,000
Asset sale 2	(35,000)
Asset sale 3	(16,000)
Section 1231 net loss	$ (6,000)

Company RC's $6,000 Section 1231 net loss is an ordinary loss, fully deductible in the computation of 19X8 taxable income.

Section 1231 Net Gain.   Assume that asset sale 2 generated only a $5,000 (rather than a $35,000) loss for Company RC. In this case, the company has a net gain on the sale of its Section 1231 assets:

[32]§1231(a)(1).

	Gain or (Loss) Recognized
Asset sale 1	$ 45,000
Asset sale 2	(5,000)
Asset sale 3	(16,000)
Section 1231 net gain	$ 24,000

Under the basic rule of Section 1231, Company RC can treat the $24,000 gain as a capital gain. Consequently, the company can claim up to $24,000 of capital losses or capital loss carryforwards as 19X8 deductions. If the company's capital loss deduction is less than $24,000, the excess Section 1231 gain is considered net capital gain. If the company's income is taxed at the individual rates (for example, if Company RC is a sole proprietorship), this gain is taxed at the preferential capital gains rates.

Objective 9
Incorporate the loss recapture and depreciation recapture rules into the Section 1231 netting process.

Recapture of Previous Year Ordinary Losses.   Before Company RC can treat its 19X8 Section 1231 net gain as a capital gain, it must consider an exception to the basic characterization rule. This exception applies if a taxpayer has a Section 1231 net gain in the current year but had a Section 1231 net loss in any of the five previous taxable years. In such case, the taxpayer must **recapture** the previous year loss (which was deductible as ordinary loss) by treating an equivalent amount of current year gain as ordinary income.[33] The next diagram incorporates this recapture rule.

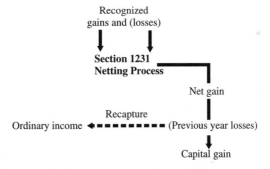

Recapture of Previous Year Loss.   Company RC did not sell any Section 1231 assets in 19X3 through 19X5 or in 19X7. However, in 19X6, it recognized a $7,100 Section 1231 net loss, which was an ordinary deduction in the computation of 19X6 taxable income. In 19X8, Company RN must recapture the 19X6 loss by reporting $7,100 of its $24,000 Section 1231 net gain as ordinary income. The $16,900 remaining Section 1231 net gain is treated as capital gain.

Once a taxpayer has recaptured a previous year Section 1231 net loss, the loss is not recaptured again. If Company RC has a Section 1231 net gain in 19X9, the entire gain is

---

[33]§1231(c).

treated as capital gain because the company has no *unrecaptured* Section 1231 losses for the previous five-year period.

Depreciation Recapture

The pro-taxpayer rule of Section 1231 is modified when applied to gains recognized on the sale of depreciable or amortizable property. The modification requires that gain attributable to previous year depreciation or amortization deductions be characterized as ordinary income rather than Section 1231 gain.[34] This **depreciation recapture** rule has three components: full recapture, partial recapture, and 20 percent recapture. Before analyzing each component, let's add the basic recapture rule to our diagram.

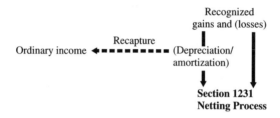

Full Recapture Rule.   The full recapture rule applies to gains recognized on sales of depreciable personalty and amortizable intangibles. Under this rule, an amount of gain equal to accumulated depreciation or amortization through date of sale is recharacterized as ordinary income.[35] The rationale for this recapture requirement can best be explained through a numeric example.

> ***Depreciation Deductions Converted to Capital Gain.***   Firm D purchased a tangible asset several years ago for $100,000 and has accumulated $40,000 of MACRS depreciation through date of sale. As a result, the firm's adjusted basis in the asset is $60,000. If the firm sells the asset for $100,000, it recognizes a $40,000 gain. Absent a recapture requirement, this gain is a Section 1231 gain with the potential (subject to the Section 1231 netting process) for capital gain treatment. However, the entire gain is attributable to previous years' cost recovery deductions, which reduced the firm's *ordinary income* in those years by $40,000.

The recapture requirement prevents this conversion of ordinary income into capital gain. In our example, Firm D must characterize its $40,000 gain as ordinary income. If we modify the example by changing the amount realized on sale, the amount of recaptured ordinary income also changes. The following table illustrates the recapture computation based on four different sales prices:

---

[34]The ordinary income created by any of the depreciation recapture rules is not eligible for installment sale treatment and must be recognized in the year of sale. §453(i).

[35]§1245.

Calculation of Depreciation Recapture

		Assumption 1	Assumption 2	Assumption 3	Assumption 4
Sales price		$100,000	$ 90,000	$105,000	$ 48,000
Cost of asset	$100,000				
Depreciation	(40,000)				
Adjusted basis		(60,000)	(60,000)	(60,000)	(60,000)
Gain (loss) recognized		$ 40,000	$ 30,000	$ 45,000	$(12,000)
Gain recaptured as ordinary income		$ 40,000	$ 30,000	$ 40,000	$ –0–
Section 1231 gain (loss)		–0–	–0–	5,000	(12,000)
		$ 40,000	$ 30,000	$ 45,000	$(12,000)

- Assumption 1 reflects the original facts in the Firm D example: the $40,000 gain recognized equals the $40,000 accumulated depreciation, and the entire gain is recaptured as ordinary income.
- Under Assumption 2, the $30,000 gain recognized is less than accumulated depreciation. In this case, the entire gain is recaptured as ordinary income.
- Under Assumption 3, the $45,000 gain exceeds accumulated depreciation. In this case, only $40,000 of the gain (an amount equal to accumulated depreciation) is recaptured and the remaining $5,000 gain (the actual appreciation in the value of the asset) is Section 1231 gain.
- Under Assumption 4, Firm D recognizes a $12,000 loss on the sale of the asset. This is a Section 1231 loss; the recapture rules don't apply to losses.

Partial Recapture Rule for Realty.   The recapture rule applying to depreciable realty (buildings, improvements, and other permanent attachments to land) is less stringent than the full recapture rule.[36] Although Congress has changed the details of this rule many times over the past decades, the essential concept is that only *accelerated depreciation in excess of straight-line depreciation* is recaptured. In the preceding chapter, we learned that real property placed in service after 1986 and subject to MACRS must be depreciated under the straight-line method. Therefore, the partial recapture rule applies only to realty placed in service before 1987.

Partial Depreciation Recapture.   Company NB sold a residential apartment complex for a total price of $1 million: $200,000 for the underlying land and $800,000 for the building itself. The company purchased the property 15 years ago for $1,120,000 and allocated $170,000 and $950,000 of this cost basis to the land and building, respectively. Company NB has deducted $600,000 of accelerated depreciation with respect to the basis of the building through date of sale. Straight-line depreciation over the 15-year period would have been only

---

[36]§1250. Nonresidential realty (commercial buildings, warehouses, and so on) placed in service after 1980 and before 1987 and depreciated under an accelerated method, is subject to the full recapture rule. See §1245(a)(5) prior to its amendment by the Tax Reform Act of 1986.

$325,000; consequently, the company has deducted $275,000 of excess accelerated depreciation. The computation of Company NB's recognized gain on sale and characterization of that gain is as follows:

	Land		Building	
Sales price		$ 200,000		$ 800,000
Cost of asset	$170,000		$ 950,000	
Depreciation	–0–		(600,000)	
Adjusted basis		(170,000)		(350,000)
Gain recognized		$ 30,000		$ 450,000
Gain recaptured as ordinary income				
(excess accelerated depreciation)		$ –0–		$ 275,000
Section 1231 gain		30,000		175,000
		$ 30,000		$ 450,000

Twenty Percent Recapture by Corporations.   Corporate taxpayers must contend with a special recapture rule applying to gain recognized on the sale of depreciable realty.[37] Corporations must compute the excess of the gain that would have been converted to ordinary income under the full recapture rule over the gain converted to ordinary income under the partial recapture rule. The corporation must then recapture 20 percent of this excess as additional ordinary income.

Twenty Percent Recapture for Corporations.   If Company NB in the preceding example is a corporation, the 20 percent rule has the following result:

	Land	Building
Ordinary income under full recapture		
(entire gain recognized)	$ –0–	$450,000
Ordinary income under partial recapture		
(excess accelerated depreciation)	–0–	(275,000)
Excess	–0–	$175,000
		.20
Additional recapture	–0–	$ 35,000
Summary of Gain Characterization		
Ordinary income under full recapture rule	$ –0–	$ –0–
Ordinary income under partial recapture rule	–0–	275,000
Ordinary income under 20% rule	–0–	35,000
Section 1231 gain	30,000	140,000
	$30,000	$450,000

---

[37]§291(a)(1).

The 20 percent recapture rule has particular significance with respect to real property placed in service after 1986. Because firms must use the straight-line method to compute MACRS depreciation for these properties, the partial recapture rule is inapplicable. Even so, corporations that sell these properties must recapture 20 percent of the amount that would have been ordinary income if the property were subject to the full recapture rule.

Comprehensive Example

The tax rules governing the character of the gains and losses recognized on the sale or exchange of business operating assets are enormously complex. Before leaving this subject, let's review the rules by working through a comprehensive example.

Characterizing Gains and Losses.   In 19X8, BC Inc., a calendar year corporation, recognized a $145,000 capital loss on the sale of marketable securities. The corporation did not sell any other capital assets during the year. Therefore, BC cannot deduct any of the capital loss on its 19X8 tax return *unless* it recognized a Section 1231 net gain for the year.

BC Inc. recognized the following gains and losses on sales of operating assets. The column headed *Accumulated Depreciation* reflects the correct MACRS depreciation claimed through date of sale.

	Date Placed in Service	Date Sold	Initial Basis	Accumulated Depreciation	Selling Price	Gain (Loss)
Office equipment	11/3/X7	2/14	$ 8,200	$ 2,300	$ 5,100	$ (800)
Duplicating equipment	8/16/X4	5/14	4,000	3,650	2,350	2,000
Furniture	12/19/X6	5/31	18,000	4,900	20,400	7,300
Hauling equipment	2/12/X7	8/28	32,000	12,000	19,250	(750)
Real property:						
Land	4/12/X4	11/3	100,000	–0–	125,000	25,000
Building	4/12/X4	11/3	500,000	62,000*	550,000	112,000

*Straight-line.

These gains and losses are characterized as follows:

	Gain (Loss)	Ordinary Income or (Loss)	Section 1231 Gain or (Loss)
Office equipment	$ (800)	$ (800)	
Duplicating equipment	2,000	2,000	
Furniture	7,300	4,900	$ 2,400
Hauling equipment	(750)		(750)
Real property:			
Land	25,000		25,000
Building	112,000	12,400	99,600
		$18,500	$126,250

- BC Inc. owned the office equipment for less than a year. Therefore, this asset is neither a capital asset nor a Section 1231 asset, and the loss recognized on the sale is ordinary.
- The gain recognized on the sale of the duplicating equipment is less than accumulated depreciation. Therefore, the entire gain is recaptured as ordinary income.
- The gain recaptured as ordinary income on the sale of the furniture is limited to the accumulated depreciation. The rest of the gain is Section 1231 gain.
- The loss recognized on the sale of the hauling equipment is Section 1231 loss.
- The gain recognized on the sale of the land is Section 1231 gain.
- The gain recognized on the sale of the building is subject to the 20 percent recapture rule. Therefore, $12,400 (20 percent of $62,000 accumulated depreciation) is recaptured as ordinary income. The rest of the gain is Section 1231 gain.

BC Inc.'s tax returns for the previous five years show $8,400 of unrecaptured Section 1231 net losses. Thus, the final step in characterizing the corporation's current gains and losses is to recapture this loss.

	Ordinary Income or (Loss)	Section 1231 Gain or (Loss)
Current year totals	$18,500	$126,250
Previous loss recapture	8,400	(8,400)
	$26,900	$117,850

Based on the final characterization, BC Inc. has $117,850 Section 1231 net gain that is treated as capital gain for 19X8. As a result, the corporation may deduct $117,850 of its $145,000 capital loss from the security sale. The $27,150 nondeductible loss can be deducted only on a carryback or carryforward basis.

Other Property Dispositions

Objective 10
Describe the tax consequences of property dispositions that don't involve a sale or exchange.

To this point in the chapter, our consideration of the tax consequences of property dispositions has been limited to the consequences of sale or exchange transactions. While sales and exchanges are certainly the most common ways for firms to dispose of assets, they are not the only ways. In this section, we consider three other property dispositions and their effect on taxable income.

Abandonment and Worthlessness

If a firm formally relinquishes its ownership interest in an asset or property right, the unrecovered basis in the asset represents an **abandonment loss.**[38] Firms are allowed to claim abandonment losses as ordinary deductions; this result holds even if the abandoned property was a capital asset because the loss was not realized on a sale or exchange. To claim a loss, a firm must take overt action to indicate that it has no intention of reviving its interest or reclaiming the property in the future.[39]

> ***Abandonment Loss.*** Firm WB occupied leased office space for several years. During this time, the firm made various leasehold improvements, the cost of which were capitalized to an asset account. In the current year, Firm WB had a serious dispute with its landlord, broke its lease, and relocated to a new office. Unfortunately, the firm's leasehold improvements were not portable so that the firm had to leave them behind. Firm WB's adjusted basis in these improvements was $28,200. The firm can claim a $28,200 abandonment loss as an ordinary deduction on its current year tax return.

Firms typically don't abandon property unless the property no longer has any value, or is worthless, to the firm. The Internal Revenue Code contains a specific rule for securities that become worthless during the taxable year.[40] The owner must treat the securities as if they were sold on the last day of the year for a price of zero. This fictitious sale triggers a realized loss equal to the owner's basis in the securities. If the securities were capital assets in the owner's hands, the loss is characterized as a capital loss because it resulted from a deemed sale. For purposes of this rule, securities include (1) corporate stocks and (2) bonds, debentures, or other forms of corporate or government debt that bear interest coupons or are in registered form.

An important modification to the worthless securities rule applies if a corporation owns worthless securities in an affiliated corporation.[41] An **affiliated corporation** is any 80 percent or more controlled domestic subsidiary that has always derived more than 90 percent of its annual gross receipts from the conduct of an active business. In this case, the law allows the corporation to treat the securities as a noncapital asset. Accordingly, the corporation's loss is not subject to the capital loss limitation but is fully deductible.

> ***Worthless Securities.*** BGH Inc., a calendar year taxpayer, owns XYZ Corporation registered bonds with a tax basis of $290,000. BGH owns no equity stock in XYZ. BGH also owns 90 percent of the outstanding stock of Subsidiary S, a domestic corporation deriving all its gross receipts from a manufacturing business. BGH's basis in this stock is $500,000. Both the bonds and the stock are capital assets.
>
> During 19X9, BGH's chief financial officer determined that the XYZ bonds and the Subsidiary S stock are worthless. For tax purposes, BGH recognizes a loss

---

[38]Regs. §1.165-1(b), §1.165-2, and §1.167(a)-8.

[39]*Echols* v. *Commissioner,* 950 F.2d 209 (CA-5, 1991).

[40]§165(g)(1).

[41]§165(g)(3).

> as if it sold both securities on December 31 for an amount realized of zero. The $290,000 loss from the deemed bond sale is a capital loss. However, the $500,000 loss from the deemed stock sale qualifies as an ordinary loss.

Foreclosures

If a firm owns property that serves as the collateral for a debt, the firm stands to lose the property if it fails to service the debt and the creditor forecloses. In this property disposition, the tax consequences depend on whether the debt is recourse or nonrecourse in nature. A **recourse debt** is one for which the debtor is personally liable and must be paid out of any and all assets owned by the debtor. A **nonrecourse debt** is secured by only the specific property that the debtor pledged as collateral; the debtor is not personally liable for repayment of the debt.

> **Recourse Debt Foreclosure.**   Company T owned a tract of land for which it paid $400,000 and which was subject to a $275,000 recourse mortgage. The company is in financial difficulty and failed to make the interest and principal payments on the mortgage. The creditor foreclosed and took title to and possession of the land. As part of the foreclosure proceedings, Company T and the creditor agreed that the fair market value of the land was $240,000. Consequently, Company T paid $35,000 cash to the creditor in full settlement of the $275,000 recourse mortgage.[42]

In Company T's situation, the tax law treats the foreclosure as if the company sold the property for its $240,000 value.[43] If Company T operates a real estate business and the land was part of its inventory, the $160,000 loss recognized on this deemed sale is ordinary. If Company T used the land in the conduct of its business, the loss is a Section 1231 loss. If Company T held the land as an investment, the loss is a capital loss.

What would be the tax implications if Company T was in such poor financial condition that after the foreclosure, the creditor decided not to pursue its legal claim to an additional $35,000 from the company? In this case, Company T would recognize $35,000 of ordinary cancellation-of-debt income.[44] This subsequent development does not affect the tax consequences of the foreclosure itself.

> **Nonrecourse Debt Foreclosure.**   Refer to the facts in the preceding example but assume that the $275,000 mortgage on the Company T's land was a nonrecourse debt. The creditor's only right when the company defaulted on the debt was to foreclose on the land. From the creditor's perspective, it received an asset worth only $240,000 in full settlement of a $275,000 debt and, as a result, incurred a

---

[42]This value is frequently established by the creditor's subsequent sale of the property at public auction.
[43]Reg. §1.1001-2(c) Example 8.

[44]§61(a)(12). If Company T is insolvent, only the cancellation-of-debt income in excess of the insolvency is taxable. If Company T is involved in bankruptcy proceedings, none of the cancellation-of-debt income is taxable. §108(a).

$35,000 bad debt loss. Company T treats the foreclosure as a deemed sale for an amount realized of $275,000—the full amount of the nonrecourse debt—and recognizes a $125,000 loss.[45]

Casualties and Thefts

In this uncertain world, firms often discover that they have disposed of assets involuntarily because of a sudden, destructive event such as a fire, flood, earthquake, or other act of nature, or through some human agency such as theft, vandalism, or riot. If a firm is adequately insured, the reimbursement from the insurance company should compensate for the economic loss from such disasters. If the insurance reimbursement is less than the adjusted basis of the destroyed property, the firm can claim the unrecovered basis as an ordinary deduction.[46] If the insurance proceeds exceed the adjusted basis, the firm must recognize the excess as taxable income unless it takes advantage of a gain deferral opportunity discussed in the next chapter.

Casualty Loss.   During the current year, Firm JBJ suffered a casualty loss: a flood destroyed four automobiles used in the firm's business. The firm carried property insurance and received $42,000 after filing a claim with its insurance company. The adjusted basis of the four automobiles was $53,800. Firm JBJ can deduct its $11,800 unrecovered basis as an ordinary loss in the computation of taxable income.

Conclusion

The rules governing the tax consequences of property transactions are among the most complicated in the tax law. Nevertheless, business managers must understand how these rules operate to determine the taxable gain or deductible loss triggered by sales, exchanges, and other dispositions of assets. The rules relate both to the timing of gain or loss recognition and the character of the gain or loss. The critical distinction between ordinary and capital gain or loss can result in significant differences in tax cost or tax savings. Business managers who fail to consider this distinction may miss tax planning opportunities that can dramatically improve after-tax cash flows attributable to asset dispositions. In the next chapter, we continue our discussion of property transactions by examining still another asset disposition—a nontaxable exchange.

[45]Reg. §1.1001-2(c) Example 7 and *Commissioner* v. *Tufts,* 461 U.S. 300 (1983).
[46]Reg. §1.165-7(b).

Key Terms

Abandonment loss   179
Affiliated corporation   179
Amount realized   159
Capital asset   166

Capital gain or loss   166
Depreciation recapture   174
Gross profit percentage   161
Installment sale method   161

Net capital loss 167	Recapture 173
Nonrecourse debt 180	Recognized gain or loss 158
Ordinary gain or loss 166	Recourse debt 180
Realized gain or loss 158	Section 1231 asset 172

Questions and Problems for Discussion

1. BBB Company, which manufactures industrial plastics, owns the following assets. Characterize each asset as either a capital, ordinary, or Section 1231 asset.
   a. A computer system used in the company's main office.
   b. A 50 percent interest in a business partnership organized to conduct a mining operation in Utah.
   c. Heavy equipment used to mold the company's best-selling plastic item.
   d. The company's customer list developed over the 12 years it has been in existence.
   e. The company's inventory of raw materials used in the manufacturing process.
   f. An oil painting of the company's founder and first president that hangs in the corporate board room.
   g. A patent developed by the company's research and development department.
   h. The corporate airplane.

2. For tax purposes, what is the difference between a sale of property and an exchange of property?

3. Under what circumstances could a taxpayer have an amount realized on the disposition of an asset without any corresponding inflow of cash or property?

4. Under what circumstances would a taxpayer elect not to use the installment sale method of reporting gain?

5. Does the characterization of gain or loss as either ordinary or capital have any effect on the computation of a firm's net income per books?

6. Distinguish between a firm's tax basis in an asset and its equity in that asset.

7. Corporation A and Corporation Z both have business goodwill worth approximately $1 million. The goodwill is a capital asset to Corporation A and a Section 1231 asset to Corporation Z. Can you explain this apparently inconsistent tax characterization?

8. Company W, a calendar year, cash basis business, paid $2,700 for office supplies in November 19X1 and properly deducted the cost on its 19X1 tax return. In March 19X2, the company moved its office location. Rather than transport the office supplies still on hand, it sold them to a neighboring business for $500 cash. What is the amount and character of the gain or loss recognized on this sale?

9. Two years ago, Firm OP bought a tract of land for $600,000, paying $50,000 down and borrowing the balance of the purchase price from a commercial lender. The land is the collateral for OP's debt. To date, Firm OP has not repaid any of the loan.
   a. If the debt is recourse, to what extent do Firm OP and the commercial creditor bear the risk of loss if the value of the land decreases to $475,000?
   b. How does your answer change if the debt is nonrecourse?

10. Mr. K realized a loss on the sale of an asset to Mr. P. Mr. K and Mr. P have been best friends since they were college roommates in 1968. Does this sale represent an arm's-length transaction? Are Mr. K and Mr. P related parties for tax purposes?

11. Define the *Corn Products* doctrine and explain its relevance to the definition of capital assets.

12. Why do both corporate and noncorporate taxpayers prefer capital gains to ordinary income? Why is the preference stronger for noncorporate taxpayers?

13. Why is the partial recapture rule inapplicable to sales of realty subject to MACRS depreciation?

14. Does a taxpayer always realize a loss on the involuntary disposition of property because of a casualty or a theft?

15. Firm F's adjusted basis in operating asset A is $75,000. If the firm carries $75,000 of property insurance on this asset, is it adequately protected against risk of loss?

Application Problems

1. During the current year, Firm CS performed consulting services for Company P. The two parties agreed that Company P would pay for the services by transferring investment securities to Firm CS. At date of transfer, the securities had a market value of $50,000. Company P's tax basis in the securities was $47,000.
   a. How much income must Firm CS recognize on the receipt of the securities? What is the character of this income? What is Firm CS's tax basis in the securities?
   b. How much income must Company P recognize on the transfer of the securities? What is the character of the income?
   c. Does the transfer of the securities result in a tax deduction for Company P? If so, what is the amount of the deduction?

2. In 1993, TYR Inc. purchased a warehouse for $295,000. During the current year, the corporation sold the warehouse to Firm D for a cash payment of $80,000. The warehouse is subject to a $225,000 nonrecourse mortgage. Consequently, the bank holding the mortgage had to approve the sale before legal title could be transferred from TYR to Firm D. Through date of sale, TYR claimed $72,000 of straight-line depreciation on the warehouse.
   a. Compute the gain recognized on TYR's sale of the warehouse.
   b. What is the character of this gain?
   c. Would your answers change if TYR is a noncorporate business?

3. During 19X1, LM Inc. sold investment land with a tax basis of $50,000 for $95,000. Payment consisted of $15,000 cash down and the purchaser's note for $80,000. The note will be paid in 10 annual installments of $8,000, beginning in 19X2.
   a. Compute LM Inc.'s recognized gain under the installment sale method in 19X1 and 19X2.
   b. In 19X4, LM pledges the note as partial collateral for a $75,000 bank loan. The unpaid principal at date of pledge is $56,000. Determine the tax consequences of this transaction to LM Inc.

4. Corporation S sold investment land to Corporation P for $100,000 cash. Corporation S's basis in the land was $167,000. Mr. and Mrs. J own 100 percent of the stock of both corporations.
   a. What is Corporation P's tax basis in the investment asset purchased from Corporation S?
   b. Corporation P holds the land as an investment for seven years before selling it to an unrelated buyer. Compute the gain or loss recognized by Corporation P if the amount realized on sale is (1) $175,000, (2) $120,000, or (3) $95,000.

5. Firm GH, a calendar year taxpayer, generated $430,000 of 19X8 net income from its routine business operations. In addition, the firm sold the following assets during 19X8. Based on this information, compute the firm's taxable income for 19X8.

	Date Placed in Service	Date Sold	Initial Basis	Acc. Depr.	Selling Price
Office equipment	1/13/X3	1/20	$ 22,400	$ 18,600	$ 4,500
Construction equipment	5/19/X4	3/24	175,000	121,700	50,000
Furniture	9/19/X7	5/31	6,000	1,500	4,750
Transportation equipment	2/12/X6	9/29	83,200	26,000	55,000

6. Corporation JK, a calendar year taxpayer, generated $980,000 of 19X9 net income from its routine business operations. In addition, the corporation sold the following assets during 19X9:

	Date Acquired/ Placed in Service	Date Sold	Initial Basis	Acc. Depr.	Selling Price
Investment securities	8/12/X2	3/23	$144,000	$ –0–	$ 64,000
Production equipment	2/19/X3	9/30	76,000	76,000	13,000
Business realty:					
Land	4/15/X0	11/13	85,000	–0–	100,000
Building	4/15/X0	11/13	200,000	58,300	210,000

a. Based on this information, compute JK's taxable income for 19X9. In making your computation, assume the corporation used the straight-line method to calculate depreciation on the building.

b. How would your answer change if Corporation JK sold the securities for $150,000 rather than $64,000?

7. Corporation Q, a calendar year taxpayer, has incurred the following Section 1231 net gains and losses since its formation in 19X1:

	19X1	19X2	19X3
Section 1231 gains	$ 15,000	$ 7,600	$ –0–
Section 1231 losses	(13,000)	(9,000)	(5,000)
Net gain or (loss)	$ 2,000	$(1,400)	$(5,000)

a. In 19X4, Corporation Q sold only one asset and recognized a $3,900 Section 1231 gain. How much of this gain is treated as capital gain?

b. In 19X5, Corporation Q recognized a $16,700 Section 1231 gain on the sale of one asset and a $3,000 Section 1231 loss on the sale of a second asset. How much of the $13,700 net gain is treated as capital gain?

8. Firm P, a noncorporate taxpayer, purchased residential realty in 1982 for $1 million. The firm sold the realty in the current year for $450,000. Through date of sale, the firm claimed $814,000 of accelerated depreciation on the realty. Straight-line depreciation would have been $625,000.

a. Compute the amount and character of Firm P's recognized gain on sale.

b. How would your answer change if Firm P was a corporation?

9. Firm R owned depreciable real property subject to a $300,000 nonrecourse mortgage. The firm's financial officer determined that the property's current market value was only $250,000. Consequently, the firm surrendered the property to the creditor rather than continue to service the mortgage. At date of surrender, Firm R's adjusted basis in the property was $195,000. Based on these facts, determine the cash flow consequences of the transaction to Firm R, assuming that the gain recognized is taxed at 28 percent.

10. ZEJ Inc., a calendar year taxpayer, reported $270,000 net income before tax on its 19X9 financial statements prepared in accordance with GAAP. The corporation's records reveal the following information:

During 19X9, ZEJ realized a $70,000 book gain on the sale of business equipment for $100,000 cash. Book depreciation through date of sale was $48,000 while MACRS depreciation through date of sale was $63,000.

In 19X6, ZEJ realized a $140,000 gain on the sale of investment land. The corporation accepted a $200,000 installment note from the purchaser as part of the sales price. In 19X9, ZEJ received a $12,300 interest payment and a $20,000 principal payment on this note. ZEJ is using the installment sale method to recognize gain from the 19X6 sale; its gross profit percentage is 71 percent.

During 19X9, ZEJ sold marketable securities to a shareholder who owns 81 percent of the corporation's outstanding stock. The amount realized on sale was $60,000, and the corporation's basis in the securities was $42,000.

Based on the above facts, compute ZEJ Inc.'s 19X9 taxable income.

11. Ms. D sold a business that she had operated as a sole proprietorship for 18 years. On date of sale, the business balance sheet showed the following assets:

	Tax Basis
Accounts receivable	$ 32,000
Inventory	125,000
Furniture and equipment:	
Cost	45,800
Accumulated depreciation	(38,000)
Leasehold improvements:	
Cost	29,000
Accumulated depreciation	(5,100)

The purchaser paid a lump-sum price of $300,000 cash for the business. The sales contract stipulates that the fair market value of the business inventory is $145,000 and the value of the remaining balance sheet assets equals adjusted tax basis. Assuming that Ms. D's marginal tax rate on ordinary income is 39.6 percent, compute the net cash flow from the sale of her business.

12. In 19X0, Firm SJ purchased land for $100,000 with $10,000 of its own funds and $90,000 borrowed from a commercial bank. The bank holds a recourse mortgage on the land. For each of the following independent transactions, compute the firm's positive or negative cash flow. Assume that (1) Firm SJ is solvent, (2) any recognized loss is fully deductible, and (3) Firm SJ's marginal tax rate is 35 percent.
    a. Firm SJ sells the land for $33,000 cash and the buyer's assumption of the $80,000 principal balance of the mortgage.
    b. Firm SJ sells the land for $113,000 cash and pays off the $80,000 principal balance of the mortgage.
    c. Firm SJ sells the land for $82,000 cash and pays off the $80,000 principal balance of the mortgage.
    d. Firm SJ defaults on the $80,000 mortgage. The bank forecloses and sells the land at public auction for $64,000. The bank notifies Firm SJ that it will not pursue collection of the firm's remaining debt.
    e. Firm SJ defaults on the $80,000 mortgage. The bank forecloses and sells the land at public auction for $64,000. The bank requires Firm SJ to make a $16,000 cash payment to pay off the remaining debt.

Issue Recognition Problems

Identify the tax issue or issues suggested by the following situations and state each issue in the form of a question.

1. On March 1, DS Company, a calendar year taxpayer, recognized a $15,000 loss on the sale of marketable securities. On May 12, the company recognized an $85,000 Section 1231 gain on the sale of an office building. In forecasting the company's current year taxable income, the company's chief financial officer plans to deduct the $15,000 loss against the $85,000 gain.
2. Firm LD, a calendar year taxpayer, owns 20,000 shares of stock in M Inc. LD's basis in the shares is $160,000. In November, LD's chief financial officer learned that M Inc. had just declared bankruptcy. The CFO was unable to determine if M Inc. was solvent or whether the corporation's board of directors intended to try to save the corporation or dissolve it under state law.
3. A fire damaged, but did not destroy, industrial equipment used by Firm L in its manufacturing process. Immediately before the fire, the equipment was worth $40,000. After the fire, the equipment was worth only $15,000. Firm L's adjusted basis in the equipment was $14,000. The firm received only $10,000 of insurance proceeds in reimbursement for its loss.
4. Company LR owns a commercial office building. Four years ago, LR entered into a long-term lease with Lessee M for 2,400 square feet of office space. Company LR spent $13,600 to finish out the space to meet Lessee M's requirements. The leasehold improvements included several interior walls and special purpose electrical wiring. During the current year, Lessee M terminated the lease and moved out of the office space. To make the space more marketable, Company LR tore down the interior walls and removed the special purpose wiring.
5. In 19X6, Corporation M, a manufacturing company, loaned $80,000 to its employee Mr. E. The corporation received Mr. E's properly executed and written note in which he promised to repay the corporation at the end of seven years and to pay annual interest of 12 percent (the market interest rate on the date of the loan). In 19X8, when interest rates were 8 percent, Corporation M sold the $80,000 note to an unrelated party for $92,700.
6. In 19X4, Corporation NM generated a $25,000 net operating loss and recognized an $8,000 net capital loss. The corporation's tax return for 19X3 (the corporation's first taxable year) reported $15,000 of taxable income, $10,000 of which was capital gain.
7. In 19X7, Firm WD, a calendar year taxpayer, sold depreciable realty for an amount realized of $225,000. The firm purchased the realty 12 years earlier for $350,000 and had deducted $155,000 of MACRS depreciation through date of sale. During an audit of the firm's 19X7 tax return, the IRS agent determined that the firm had

incorrectly computed its annual depreciation with respect to the realty. The correct depreciation through date of sale should have been $200,000.

8. Corporation AD operates four antique dealerships. In 19X7, the corporation sold a 200-year-old desk to its sole shareholder, Mr. C, for $35,000. The corporation reported its $2,700 realized gain as ordinary income from the sale of inventory on its 19X7 tax return. In 19X8, Mr. C sold the desk to an unrelated collector for $60,000 and reported a $25,000 capital gain on his 19X8 tax return.

9. During the current year, Mr. V sold his sole proprietorship business to an unrelated party for a lump-sum price of $900,000. The contract of sale specifies that $100,000 is for a covenant not to compete—Mr. V's promise not to operate a similar business anywhere in the state for the next four years.

10. Corporation TJ ceased business operations and was dissolved under state law in 19X9. On the last day of its existence, the corporation's balance sheet showed $2,200 of unamortized organizational costs and $12,000 of unamortized goodwill.

11. At the beginning of the year, Firm GH owned 8,200 shares of common stock in LSR Inc., a publicly traded corporation. The firm's basis in these shares was $290,000. On a day when the LSR stock was trading at $1.14 per share, Firm GH delivered the 8,200 shares to its broker with a letter stating that the firm was formally abandoning its ownership of its equity interest in LSR Inc.

Tax Planning Cases

1. Firm Z, a corporation in the 39 percent tax bracket, has $100,000 to invest in year 1 and two investment choices. Investment 1 will generate $12,000 of taxable cash flow each year for years 2 through 6. In year 6, the firm should be able to sell the investment for $100,000. Investment 2 will not generate any taxable income in years 2 through 6. However, in year 6, Firm Z should be able to sell Investment 2 for $165,000.
   a. Assuming a 6 percent discount rate, which investment has the greater net present value to Firm Z?
   b. Would your answer change if Firm Z is a noncorporate taxpayer in the 39.6 percent tax bracket and the gain on sale of Investment 2 is eligible for the 20 percent capital gains rate?

2. Mr. RH, a businessman in the 39.6 marginal tax bracket, purchased 30 acres of undeveloped ranch land 10 years ago for $935,000. This year Mr. RH is considering subdividing the land into one-third acre lots and improving the land by adding streets, sidewalks, and utilities. He plans to advertise the 90 lots for sale in a local real estate magazine. Mr. RH projects that the improvements will cost $275,000 and that he can sell the lots for $20,000 each. Mr. RH is also considering an offer from a local corporation that wants to purchase the 30-acre tract in its undeveloped state for $1.4 million. Assuming that Mr. RH makes no other property dispositions during the year, which alternative (develop or sell as is) maximizes his cash flow?

3. Corporation Y began business operations in 19X1. For its first four years of operations, the corporation reported the following taxable income:

	19X1	19X2	19X3	19X4
Ordinary income	$12,000	$ 6,000	$150,000	$600,000
Net capital gain	–0–	19,000	4,000	–0–
Taxable income	$12,000	$25,000	$154,000	$600,000

During 19X5, Corporation Y generated $900,000 ordinary income and recognized a $20,000 loss on the sale of a capital asset. The corporation's chief financial officer is considering selling a second capital asset before the end of the year. This sale would generate a $21,000 capital gain that would allow the corporation to deduct its entire current year loss. Alternatively, the corporation could just carry its $20,000 net capital loss back to 19X2 and 19X3 and receive a refund of tax paid in those years. Which course of action do you recommend and why?

8 Nontaxable Exchanges

Learning Objectives

After studying this chapter, you should be able to:

1. Explain how nontaxable exchange provisions make the tax law neutral for certain exchanges of business or investment assets.
2. Compute the substituted basis of qualifying property received in a nontaxable exchange.
3. Compute gain recognized when boot is received in a nontaxable exchange.
4. Identify the types of property that qualify for like-kind exchange treatment.
5. Describe the effect of the relief and assumption of debt in a like-kind exchange.
6. Compute gain recognized and the basis of replacement property in an involuntary conversion.
7. Explain the tax consequences of the transfer of property in exchange for an equity interest in a corporation or a partnership.
8. Describe the tax consequences of a wash sale.

In our analysis of the tax consequences of property dispositions thus far, we've been working under the premise that any realized gain or loss is recognized (taken into account for tax purposes) in the year of disposition. In Chapter 8, we will examine a number of business transactions that trigger gain or loss realization but do not result in current recognition of some or all of that gain or loss. These transactions are called **nontaxable exchanges,** and each one is authorized by a specific provision of the Internal Revenue Code. Congress enacted these provisions for particular tax policy reasons, which we will discuss as we look at the details of selected provisions.

Tax-Free Conversions of Wealth

Objective 1
Explain how nontaxable exchange provisions make the tax law neutral for certain exchanges of business or investment assets.

The nontaxable exchange provisions are extremely useful because they allow taxpayers to convert wealth from one form to another without a current tax cost. In other words, a nontaxable exchange provision makes the tax law *neutral* with respect to certain business and investment decisions.

Neutrality of Nontaxable Exchange. Firm T, which has a 39.6 percent marginal tax rate, owns an investment asset with a basis of $50,000 and a fair market value of $110,000. The asset generates $6,600 of annual income, which represents a 6 percent return on value. Firm T is evaluating a transaction that involves selling this asset and reinvesting the proceeds in a new business venture that promises a 7.5 percent return on capital. If the sale of the investment asset is taxable, Firm T will have only $86,240 of after-tax proceeds to invest:

Amount realized on sale	$110,000
Basis in investment asset	(50,000)
Gain realized and recognized	$ 60,000
	.396
Tax cost	$ 23,760
After-tax cash	
($110,000 − $23,760)	$ 86,240

The annual income generated by an investment of $86,240 at a 7.5 percent rate of return is only $6,468. Therefore, Firm T should reject the transaction because of the front-end tax cost.

On the other hand, if the conversion of the investment to an equity interest in the new business venture can be accomplished with no front-end tax cost, the new investment is superior to the old and Firm T should undertake the transaction.

Unfortunately for taxpayers in the same strategic position as Firm T, tax neutrality for asset exchanges is the exception rather than the rule. Asset exchanges are taxable events unless the exchange meets the requirements of one of a handful of nontaxable exchange provisions scattered throughout the Internal Revenue Code. These requirements vary substantially across provisions. Some nontaxable exchange provisions are mandatory in their application if the requirements are met. Other provisions are elective on the part of the taxpayer. Some apply only to realized gains, while others apply to both realized gains and losses. Certain provisions require a direct exchange of noncash assets, and others allow the taxpayer to be in a temporary cash position. Nevertheless, all the nontaxable exchanges share several characteristics. We begin our study of nontaxable exchanges by analyzing these common characteristics in the context of a generic exchange. By doing so, we can focus on the fundamental structure of nontaxable exchanges before considering the details of any particular exchange.

A Generic Nontaxable Exchange

Exchanges of Qualifying Property

Every nontaxable exchange transforms one property interest into another. The precise type of property that can be swapped tax free depends on the unique qualification requirements of the operative statutory provision. But only the disposition and receipt of **qualifying property** can result in a nontaxable exchange. Consider the diagram of a nontaxable exchange between Firm A and Firm B in Exhibit 8–1. Given that the exchange involves only qualifying property, it is nontaxable to both firms. What else do we know about this exchange? Assuming that Firms A and B are unrelated parties dealing at arm's length, they must have agreed that the properties are of equal value.

EXHIBIT 8–1

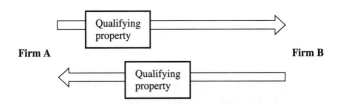

To quantify the respective tax consequences of the exchange to each firm, we must know the dollar value of the qualifying properties and the tax basis in the property each firm is surrendering. This information is presented in Exhibit 8–2. Because Firm A disposed of property with an adjusted basis of $140,000 in return for property worth $200,000, Firm A realized a $60,000 gain. Because the exchange involved qualifying property and was therefore nontaxable, Firm A does not recognize any gain in the current year.[1] Similarly, Firm B's disposition of qualifying property with an adjusted basis of $185,000 in return for qualifying property worth $200,000 resulted in a $15,000 realized but unrecognized gain.

EXHIBIT 8–2

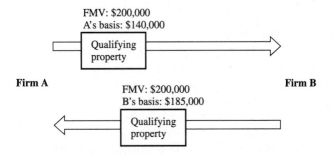

The Substituted Basis Rule

Objective 2
Compute the substituted basis of qualifying property received in a nontaxable exchange.

The nontaxable exchange label is really a misnomer. The tax law does not intend that gains and losses realized on nontaxable exchanges should escape recognition permanently. Instead, the exchange provisions are designed so that unrecognized gains and

---

[1]For financial reporting purposes, gain or loss realized on an asset exchange is generally included in income.

losses are merely deferred until some future year in which the qualifying property is disposed of in a taxable transaction. This deferral is accomplished through the rule for calculating the tax basis of qualifying property acquired in the exchange: the basis of this property equals the basis of the qualifying property surrendered. In the Firm A/ Firm B exchange, each firm paid $200,000 (the value of the property surrendered) to acquire their new properties. Because the exchange was nontaxable, the firms did not take a cost basis in their new properties. Instead, Firm A's basis in its new property is $140,000, while Firm B's basis in its new property is $185,000.

This **substituted basis** rule causes the unrecognized gain or loss on a nontaxable exchange to be embedded in the basis of the qualifying property acquired. The gain or loss remains dormant as long as the participant in the exchange continues to hold the property. If and when a participant makes a taxable disposition of the property, the deferral ends and the unrecognized gain or loss attributable to the nontaxable exchange is finally recognized.

To demonstrate this important concept, return to the facts in the Firm A/Firm B exchange. If Firm A eventually sells its new property for $200,000 cash, the firm will recognize a $60,000 gain, even though the property has not appreciated in value since Firm A acquired it in the exchange. Similarly, if Firm B sells its new property for $200,000, the firm will recognize the $15,000 gain deferred on the exchange. This observation suggests a second method for computing the basis of qualifying property acquired in a nontaxable exchange: that basis equals the property's fair market value minus deferred gain or plus deferred loss realized on the exchange. The substituted basis rule for nontaxable exchanges is summarized as follows:

Basis of Qualifying Property Acquired in a Nontaxable Exchange

Substituted basis rule: Basis of property surrendered = <u>Basis of qualifying property acquired</u>

Fair market value method: FMV of qualifying property acquired
− Deferred gain on exchange or
<u>+ Deferred loss on exchange</u>
<u>Basis of qualifying property acquired</u>

The Effect of Boot

Objective 3
Compute gain recognized when boot is received in a nontaxable exchange.

To this point, the facts of our generic exchange are contrived in that the market values of the properties that Firms A and B swapped were equal. A more realistic scenario is that the values of the properties qualifying for nontaxable exchange treatment are unequal. In this case, the party to the exchange owning the qualifying property of lesser value must transfer additional value in the form of cash or nonqualifying property to make the exchange work.

In tax parlance, any cash or nonqualifying property included in a nontaxable exchange is called **boot.** The presence of boot does not disqualify the entire exchange. Instead, the party receiving the boot must recognize a portion of realized gain equal to the value of the boot. Refer to Exhibit 8–3 in which the value of the property surrendered by Firm B was only $192,000. For Firm A to agree to the exchange, Firm B had to throw in $8,000 cash so that Firm A received $200,000 total value in exchange for its asset worth $200,000. In this case, Firm A received $8,000 of boot and must recognize $8,000 of its $60,000 realized gain.

Because Firm A must recognize and pay tax on $8,000 of gain, the firm can increase its basis in the newly acquired property by this amount. In other words, the

EXIBHIT 8–3

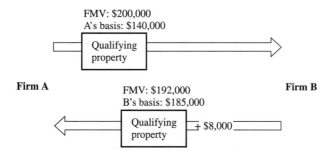

FMV: $200,000
A's basis: $140,000

Qualifying property

Firm A

FMV: $192,000
B's basis: $185,000

Qualifying property   + $8,000

Firm B

investment that Firm A should recover tax free with respect to the property equals the firm's $140,000 investment in the surrendered property plus $8,000 on which the firm has already paid tax. Firm A must allocate this basis between the two assets acquired—$8,000 cash and the qualifying property. Cash always takes a basis equal to face value. Consequently, only $140,000 of basis is allocated to the qualifying property. This $140,000 basis number can also be derived by subtracting Firm A's $52,000 deferred gain from the $192,000 value of the qualifying property. The modification to the substituted basis rule when boot is received in a nontaxable exchange is summarized as follows:

Basis of Qualifying Property Acquired in a Nontaxable Exchange: Boot Received

Substituted basis rule: Basis of qualifying property surrendered
+ Gain recognized
− FMV of boot received
Basis of qualifying property acquired

The fact that Firm B paid $8,000 boot in the Firm A/Firm B exchange did not cause gain recognition to the firm. Firm B surrendered property with an aggregate basis of $193,000 ($8,000 cash + $185,000 basis of surrendered property) and acquired property worth $200,000. As a result, Firm B realized a $7,000 gain, none of which is recognized. Firm B's basis in the newly acquired property is $193,000, the aggregate basis of the cash and property surrendered. This $193,000 basis equals the $200,000 market value of the new property less Firm B's $7,000 deferred gain on the exchange. The substituted basis rule when boot is paid in a nontaxable exchange is summarized as follows:

Basis of Qualifying Property Acquired in a Nontaxable Exchange: Boot Paid

Substituted basis rule: Basis of qualifying property surrendered
+ FMV of boot paid
Basis of qualifying property acquired

Two more facts concerning the inclusion of boot in a nontaxable exchange should be mentioned. First, the receipt of boot can never trigger recognition of more gain than the recipient realized on the exchange. For example, if Firm A received $70,000 of cash and qualifying property worth $130,000 in the Firm A/Firm B exchange, the receipt of $70,000 boot would trigger recognition of the entire $60,000 gain realized. (After all, Firm A would recognize only a $60,000 gain if it sold the property for $200,000 cash!) In this case, Firm A's basis in the qualifying property would be $130,000 ($140,000 basis of qualifying property surrendered + $60,000 gain recognized − $70,000 boot received).

Exhibit 8–4

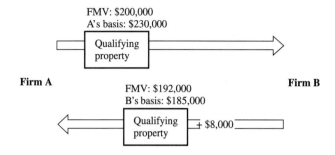

Second, the receipt of boot does not trigger recognition of realized loss. Consider the new set of facts in Exhibit 8–4 in which Firm A surrendered qualifying property with a basis of $230,000 in exchange for $8,000 cash and qualifying property worth $192,000. As a result, Firm A realized a $30,000 loss, none of which is recognized. Firm A's $230,000 basis in the surrendered property must be allocated between the $8,000 cash received and the new property. Because the cash absorbed $8,000 of the substituted basis, Firm A's substituted basis in the qualifying property is $222,000 ($230,000 basis of qualifying property surrendered − $8,000 boot received). This basis number can also be derived by adding Firm A's $30,000 deferred loss to the $192,000 market value of the property.

Summary

The Internal Revenue Code contains an assortment of nontaxable exchange provisions with distinctly different definitional and operational rules. Nonetheless, these provisions share the following generic characteristics.

- The exchange must involve qualifying property, as defined in the provision.
- The gain or loss realized on the exchange is deferred.
- The basis of the qualifying property received equals the basis of the qualifying property surrendered (substituted basis rule).
- The receipt of boot triggers gain recognition to the extent of the boot's fair market value.

The remainder of the chapter focuses on four nontaxable exchanges with particular relevance in the business world: like-kind exchanges, involuntary conversions, formations of business entities, and wash sales. Before proceeding with our discussion, refer back to the formula on page 158 that illustrates the link between gain or loss realization and gain or loss recognition. Let's expand the formula to include the possibility of gain or loss deferral resulting from a nontaxable exchange.

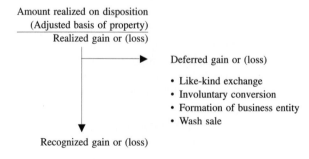

Like-Kind Exchanges

Objective 4
Identify the types of property that qualify for like-kind exchange treatment.

No gain or loss is recognized by a taxpayer that exchanges business or investment property for property of a like kind.[2] This rule allows firms to convert one asset to another asset with the same function or purpose at no tax cost. The rule's scope, however, is limited: it does not apply to exchanges of inventory property, equity or creditor interests (stocks, bonds, notes, etc.), or partnership interests.

Like-Kind Personalty.   The definition of **like-kind property** for tangible personalty is determined by reference to a detailed IRS classification system.[3] Under this system, automobiles and taxis constitute one class of like-kind property, while buses constitute another. Accordingly, the exchange of a business automobile for another automobile is nontaxable, while the exchange of an automobile for a bus is a taxable transaction. Airplanes and helicopters are like-kind properties, while airplanes and tugboats are not. The logic of the classification system is not always apparent: office furniture and copying equipment are like-kind properties, while copying equipment and computers are not. Livestock of the same sex are like-kind properties, while livestock of different sexes are not.[4] If a rancher swaps a bull held for breeding purposes for another bull, the exchange is nontaxable, but if he swaps the bull for a breeding heifer, the exchange is a taxable event. Clearly, firms that want to dispose of business personalty through a nontaxable exchange should consult their tax advisors to determine exactly which assets qualify as like-kind.[5]

Like-Kind Realty.   In contrast to the narrow rules defining like-kind personalty, virtually all types of business and investment real estate are considered like-kind. As a result, any swap of realty for realty can be structured as a tax-free exchange.[6]

> ***Like-Kind Realty Exchange.***   An Arizona firm that owned undeveloped investment land in Tucson negotiated with a New York firm that owned an apartment complex in Manhattan to trade their properties. This exchange is diagrammed in Exhibit 8–5. The investment land has an appraised value of $800,000, while the apartment complex is worth $925,000. As a result, the Arizona firm paid $125,000 cash to the New York firm to equalize the values exchanged.

Exhibit 8–5 suggests a practical question: How did the Arizona firm and the New York firm find each other? The probable answer is that they worked through a real estate broker (called a facilitator) who specializes in putting together like-kind exchanges. What are the tax consequences of the exchange?

---

[2]§1031.

[3]Reg. §1.1031(a)-2(b)(1) and Rev. Proc. 87-56, 1987-2 CB 674.

[4]§1031(e).

[5]There are no published IRS guidelines for intangible assets. Whether intangible assets are like-kind depends on the nature of the legal right represented by the asset. For example, copyrights on two different novels are like-kind, but a copyright on a novel and a copyright on a song are not. Reg. §1.1031(a)-2(c)(3), Examples 1 and 2.

[6]Reg. §1.1031(a)-1(b).

EXHIBIT 8–5

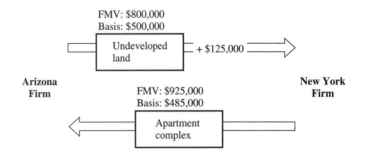

Tax Consequences of Exchange

	Arizona Firm	*New York Firm*
Amount realized:		
Value of realty acquired	$ 925,000	$ 800,000
Boot received	–0–	125,000
	$ 925,000	$ 925,000
Basis of property surrendered:		
Realty	(500,000)	(485,000)
Boot paid	(125,000)	–0–
Gain realized	$ 300,000	$ 440,000
Gain recognized*	$ –0–	$ 125,000
Gain deferred	300,000	315,000
	$ 300,000	$ 440,000

*Lesser of FMV of boot received or gain realized.

The final step in the analysis of this like-kind exchange is to determine each party's basis in its newly acquired realty.

Basis Computation

	Arizona Firm	*New York Firm*
Basis of realty surrendered	$ 500,000	$ 485,000
Boot paid	125,000	–0–
Gain recognized	–0–	125,000
Boot received	–0–	(125,000)
Basis of realty acquired	$ 625,000	$ 485,000

Note that the Arizona firm's basis in its Manhattan property equals the $925,000 value of the property less the $300,000 gain deferred in the nontaxable exchange. The New York firm's basis in its Tucson property equals the $800,000 value of the property less the $315,000 gain deferred in the nontaxable exchange.

Exhibit 8–6

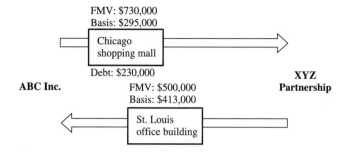

FMV: $730,000
Basis: $295,000

Chicago
shopping mall

Debt: $230,000

ABC Inc.

FMV: $500,000
Basis: $413,000

St. Louis
office building

**XYZ
Partnership**

Exchanges of Mortgaged Properties

Objective 5
Describe the effect of the relief and assumption of debt in a like-kind exchange.

Many real property interests involved in like-kind exchanges are subject to mortgages that are transferred along with the property and become the legal liability of the new owner. As we learned in Chapter 7, a taxpayer that is relieved of debt on the disposition of property must treat the relief as an amount realized from the disposition. In the like-kind exchange context, a party that surrenders mortgaged property receives boot equal to the debt relief. In other words, the relief of debt is treated exactly like cash received in the exchange, while the assumption of debt is treated as additional cash paid.

> **Exchange of Mortgaged Property.** ABC Inc. and the XYZ Partnership exchanged a Chicago shopping mall and a commercial office building in St. Louis. This exchange is diagrammed in Exhibit 8–6. The net value of the shopping mall is $500,000 ($730,000 appraised value – $230,000 mortgage), and the unencumbered value of the office building is $500,000.

Tax Consequences of Exchange

	ABC Inc.	*XYZ Partnership*
Amount realized:		
Value of realty acquired	$ 500,000	$ 730,000
Boot received (debt relief)	230,000	–0–
	$ 730,000	$ 730,000
Basis of property surrendered:		
Realty	(295,000)	(413,000)
Boot paid (debt assumed)	–0–	(230,000)
Gain realized	$ 435,000	$ 87,000
Gain recognized*	$ 230,000	$ –0–
Gain deferred	205,000	87,000
	$ 435,000	$ 87,000

*Lesser of FMV of boot received or gain realized.

Basis Computation

	ABC Inc.	XYZ Partnership
Basis of realty surrendered	$ 295,000	$ 413,000
Boot paid	–0–	230,000
Gain recognized	230,000	–0–
Boot received	(230,000)	–0–
Basis of realty acquired	$ 295,000	$ 643,000

In a like-kind exchange in which both properties are subject to a mortgage so that both parties are relieved of debt, only the *net* amount of debt is considered boot given and boot received.[7]

Net Debt Relief as Boot. Firm O and Firm R entered into a like-kind exchange of realty. The property surrendered by Firm O was subject to a $120,000 mortgage, and the property surrendered by Firm R was subject to a $100,000 mortgage. Firm O was relieved of a $20,000 net amount of debt and therefore received $20,000 of boot in the exchange. Firm R assumed a $20,000 net amount of debt and therefore paid $20,000 of boot in the exchange. Consequently, Firm O must recognize up to $20,000 of realized gain, while Firm R has a totally nontaxable exchange.

Tax Planning with Like-Kind Exchanges

The like-kind exchange provision offers firms an opportunity to reduce the tax cost of dispositions of appreciated property. By deliberately structuring a transaction to qualify as a like-kind exchange, the parties to the transaction can create tax savings to share between them.

A Tax Planning Proposal. Company P wants to acquire a tract of undeveloped land from Firm S. Company P plans to build a shopping mall on the land, a development that should increase property values in the surrounding geographic area. Firm S owns other acreage in the area and will benefit considerably from Company P's construction of the mall. Nevertheless, Firm S is reluctant to sell the tract because of the tax cost. The tract has an appraised value of $1 million, and Firm S's tax basis is only $120,000. By selling the land, Firm S will recognize an $880,000 gain taxed at 35 percent.

Company P is quite willing to purchase the tract of land from Firm S for cash. However, both firms understand that if they can structure the transaction as a like-kind exchange, Firm S will avoid current year tax. Therefore, Company P

[7]Reg. §1.1031(b)-1(c).

proposes to exchange a commercial office building, which it recently purchased for $900,000, for the undeveloped land owned by Firm S.

Why would Firm S agree to accept a $900,000 asset in exchange for a tract of land worth $1 million? To answer this question, let's focus on the after-tax value of the transaction to Firm S. If Firm S sells the land for $1 million cash, the after-tax value is $692,000.

After-Tax Value of Sale	
Amount realized on sale	$1,000,000
Basis of land	(120,000)
Gain recognized	$ 880,000
	.35
Tax cost	$ 308,000
Amount realized on sale	$1,000,000
Tax cost	(308,000)
After-tax value of sale transaction	$ 692,000

If Firm S exchanges the land for like-kind property worth $900,000, the tax cost with respect to the disposition is deferred. If the deferral period is long enough, the decrease in the tax cost could exceed the decrease in the amount realized on the disposition. For example, if Firm S projects that it will hold the realty acquired in the exchange for at least four years, the present value of the future tax cost at a 9 percent discount rate is only $193,284 and the after-tax value of the transaction increases to $706,716.

After-Tax Value of Exchange	
Amount realized on exchange	
(value of commercial office building)	$ 900,000
Basis of land	(120,000)
Gain deferred on nontaxable exchange	$ 780,000
	.35
Tax deferred on nontaxable exchange	$ 273,000
Present value of tax cost deferred for four years	
($273,000 × .708 discount factor)	$ 193,284
Amount realized on exchange	$ 900,000
Tax cost	(193,284)
After-tax value of exchange	$ 706,716

If Firm S accepts Company P's proposal, the two firms share the tax savings attributable to the like-kind exchange. Company P receives its share in the form of a $100,000 discount in the cost of the land acquired from Firm S. Of course, from Firm

S's perspective, the after-tax value of the transaction would be maximized if Company P would agree to locate, purchase, and exchange real property worth $1 million in exchange for Firm S's tract of land. In this case, Firm S would capture the entire tax savings and Company P would not benefit from structuring the transaction as a like-kind exchange. The extent to which the firms ultimately share the tax savings depends on their relative negotiating talents and the final terms of the transaction between them.

Involuntary Conversions

Objective 6
Compute gain recognized and the basis of replacement property in an involuntary conversion.

Firms generally control the circumstances in which they dispose of property. Occasionally, a disposition is involuntary; property may be stolen or destroyed by a natural disaster such as a flood or a fire. If the property is not insured or if the insurance proceeds are less than the property's adjusted basis, the owner can deduct the unrecovered basis as an ordinary casualty loss. However, if the property is insured and the insurance proceeds exceed the adjusted basis, the disposition actually results in a realized gain. Another example of an **involuntary conversion** is a condemnation of private property by a government agency that takes the property for public use. If a government has the right of eminent domain, it can compel a property owner to sell property to the agency for its fair market value. If the condemnation proceeds exceed the basis of the condemned property, the owner has a realized gain.

The tax law allows a taxpayer that realizes a gain on the involuntary conversion of property to elect to defer the gain if two conditions are met.[8] First, the taxpayer must reinvest the amount realized on the conversion (the insurance or condemnation proceeds) in **property similar or related in service or use.** This condition essentially requires taxpayers to replace their original property to avoid paying current tax on the realized gain.[9] Both the IRS and the courts have been very strict in their interpretation of the concept of similar or related property. For instance, the IRS ruled that a taxpayer who owned a bowling alley that was destroyed by fire and who used the insurance proceeds to purchase a billiard parlor was ineligible for nonrecognition treatment because the properties were not similar in function.[10]

The second condition is that replacement of the involuntarily converted property must occur within the two taxable years following the year in which the conversion took place. Thus, taxpayers making the deferral election usually have ample time to locate and acquire suitable replacement property.

If the cost of qualifying replacement property equals or exceeds the amount realized on an involuntary conversion, none of the taxpayer's realized gain is recognized. If the taxpayer does not reinvest the entire amount realized in replacement property (i.e., the taxpayer uses some of the insurance or condemnation proceeds for other purposes), the amount not reinvested is treated as boot and the taxpayer must recognize gain accordingly. In either case, the basis of the replacement property is its cost less unrecognized gain. As a result, unrecognized gain is deferred until the taxpayer disposes of the replacement property in a future taxable transaction.

---

[8]§1033.

[9]If real property held for business or as an investment is condemned by a government agency, the owner may replace it with like-kind property (any realty held for business or as an investment) rather than realty similar or related in service or use to the property so condemned. §1033(g).

[10]Rev. Rul. 83-93, 1983-1 CB 364.

Gain Realized on Involuntary Conversion. Company UL owned business equipment that was completely destroyed in the most recent California earthquake. The equipment's adjusted basis was $80,000. The company collected $100,000 of insurance proceeds because of the destruction of its property, thereby realizing a $20,000 gain on the involuntary conversion. Company UL purchased identical equipment in the year after the disaster. The following table shows the tax consequences under four different assumptions about the cost of the replacement property:

Insurance Proceeds	Cost of Replacement Property	Unreinvested Proceeds	Gain Recognized	Gain Deferred	Basis of Replacement Property*
$100,000	$135,000	$ –0–	$ –0–	$20,000	$115,000
100,000	100,000	–0–	–0–	20,000	80,000
100,000	92,000	8,000	8,000	12,000	80,000
100,000	77,000	23,000	20,000	–0–	77,000

*Cost less gain deferred.

The involuntary conversion rule provides relief to taxpayers deprived of property through circumstances beyond their control and who want nothing more than to return to the status quo by replacing that property. The rule applies to the involuntary conversion of any type of asset.[11] Moreover, the rule is elective; taxpayers that would benefit by recognizing the entire gain realized on an involuntary conversion may choose to do so.

Formations of Business Entities

Objective 7
Explain the tax consequences of the transfer of property in exchange for an equity interest in a corporation or a partnership.

In the early days of the federal income tax, Congress decided that the tax law should be neutral with respect to the formation of business entities. If entrepreneurs wanted to organize a new business venture as a corporation or partnership for legal or financial reasons, they should not be discouraged from doing so because of a front-end tax cost. Congress achieved this neutrality by enacting a pair of nontaxable exchange provisions that the business community has relied on for decades. These provisions allow organizers to transfer assets to either a corporate or a partnership entity in exchange for an ownership interest in the entity without the recognition of gain or loss. In this section of the chapter, we will examine the basic operation of these two extremely useful nontaxable exchanges.

Corporate Formations

No gain or loss is recognized when property is transferred to a corporation solely in exchange for that corporation's stock if the transferors of property are in control of the corporation immediately after the exchange.[12] In this context, the term *property* is defined very broadly to include cash and both tangible and intangible assets. Personal

---

[11] The involuntary conversion rules apply to business and investment assets, as well as assets owned by individuals and used for personal enjoyment and consumption.

[12] §351.

Exhibit 8–7

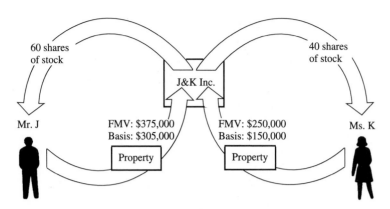

services are not property; individuals who perform services for a corporation in exchange for that corporation's stock must recognize the value of the stock as compensation income. To satisfy the control requirement for this nontaxable exchange, the transferors of property in the aggregate must own at least 80 percent of the corporation's outstanding stock.[13]

> ***Corporate Formation.*** Mr. J and Ms. K each owned and operated a business enterprise. The two decided to combine forces by transferring their respective operating assets to newly incorporated J&K Inc. Based on recent appraisals, Mr. J's assets have a fair market value of $375,000 and Ms. K's assets have a fair market value of $250,000. Therefore, the corporation's beginning balance sheet reflected operating assets with a total value of $625,000. The articles of incorporation authorize J&K Inc. to issue 100 shares of voting common stock. These shares were issued in proportion to the value of the contributed assets: 60 shares to Mr. J and 40 shares to Ms. K. This corporate formation is diagrammed in Exhibit 8–7.

> ***Tax Consequences of Formation.*** Mr. J's adjusted basis in the business assets he transferred to J&K Inc. is $305,000. Ms. K's adjusted basis in the business assets she transferred to J&K Inc. is $150,000. Consequently, the two transferors realized the following gain on the exchange of property for stock:

	Mr. J	Ms. K
Amount realized on exchange (value of stock received)	$ 375,000	$ 250,000
Basis of property transferred	(305,000)	(150,000)
Gain realized	$ 70,000	$ 100,000

---

[13]More precisely, the transferors must own stock possessing at least 80 percent of the voting power represented by all outstanding voting shares and at least 80 percent of the total number of shares of all nonvoting classes of stock. §368(c) and Rev. Rul. 59-259, 1959-2 CB 115.

Because Mr. J and Ms. K in the aggregate own 100 percent of J&K Inc.'s outstanding stock immediately after the exchange, neither recognizes any taxable gain. Each takes a substituted basis in the shares of stock ($305,000 stock basis for Mr. J and $150,000 stock basis for Ms. K).[14] Thus, their unrecognized gains on the corporate formation are deferred until they dispose of the stock in a taxable transaction.

The corporate formation is also nontaxable to J&K Inc. The corporation does not recognize gain on the exchange of 100 shares of newly issued stock for operating assets worth $625,000.[15] J&K Inc.'s basis in the assets equals their adjusted basis in the hands of the transferors.[16] Under this **carryover basis** rule, the corporation's basis in the assets transferred by Mr. J is $305,000, and its basis in the assets transferred by Ms. K is $150,000.[17]

The nontaxable exchange provision governing corporate formations applies to transfers of property to an existing corporation. However, if the transferor fails to meet the 80 percent control requirement, the exchange of property for stock is a taxable event.

Taxable Exchange of Property for Stock. Two years after J&K is formed, a third individual, Mr. L, contributes real property with a fair market value of $285,000 and an adjusted basis of $240,000 to the corporation in exchange for 50 shares of newly issued stock. Immediately after the exchange, Mr. L (the only transferor involved in the transaction) holds only 33 percent of the corporation's outstanding stock. Because he does not meet the control requirement, Mr. L must recognize the $45,000 gain realized on the exchange. Because the exchange is taxable, Mr. L takes a $285,000 cost basis in the J&K shares.

Even though the transaction is taxable to Mr. L, the corporation does not recognize gain on the issuance of stock in exchange for the real property.[18] Nevertheless, because Mr. L recognized his entire realized gain, J&K's tax basis in the real property is its $285,000 fair market value.

Partnership Formations

The tax law treats partnership formations in the same way it treats corporate formations. Specifically, neither the partners nor the partnership recognizes gain or loss when property is transferred to a partnership in exchange for an equity interest therein.[19] If Mr. J and Ms. K in our earlier example had decided to become partners in an unincorporated business, they could have transferred their appreciated assets to J&K Partnership in exchange for a 60 percent and 40 percent interest in partnership capital without recognizing gain. Mr. J's basis in his partnership interest would be a substituted basis of

---

[14]§358(a)(1).

[15]§1032.

[16]§362.

[17]For financial reporting purposes, contributed assets are booked at fair market value.

[18]Corporations never recognize gain or loss when they exchange newly issued or treasury stock for either property or services. Reg. §1.1032-1(a).

[19]§721.

$305,000, and Ms. K's basis in her partnership interest would be a substituted basis of $150,000.[20] The partnership would take a carryover basis in their contributed assets of $305,000 and $150,000, respectively.[21]

While this nontaxable exchange provision is clearly a first cousin to the corporate provision, it lacks any control requirement and is more flexible. For example, if our third individual, Mr. L, wants to become a partner in some future year, he can do so without recognizing gain. If he contributes appreciated real property (fair market value $285,000 and adjusted basis $240,000) for a one-third equity interest in the J&K Partnership, the transaction qualifies as a nontaxable exchange and his $45,000 realized gain escapes current taxation. Of course, Mr. L's basis in his new interest and the partnership's carryover basis in its new real property would be only $240,000.

Wash Sales

Objective 8
Describe the tax consequences of a wash sale.

The **wash sale** rule is an atypical nontaxable exchange provision because it defers only the recognition of *losses* realized on certain sales of marketable securities.[22] A wash sale occurs when an investor sells securities at a loss and reacquires substantially the same securities within 30 days after (or 30 days before) the sale. This rule inhibits investors from selling securities for no other reason than to generate a tax loss, then immediately buying the stock back to keep their original investment portfolio intact. If the wash sale rule applies, the cost of the reacquired securities is increased by the unrecognized loss realized on the sale of the original securities.

> **Wash Sale.**   BNJ Company owns 10,000 shares of Acme common stock with a basis of $85,000. The stock is currently trading at $6 per share so that the company's holding is worth only $60,000. The company believes that the stock is an excellent long-term investment and that the depression in the market price is temporary. Nonetheless, BNJ sells the stock on July 13 to trigger a $25,000 tax loss. If BNJ repurchases 10,000 shares of Acme stock before August 13, the company cannot recognize the $25,000 realized loss. If BN paid $61,000 for the replacement shares, its basis in these shares is $86,000 ($61,000 cost + $25,000 unrecognized loss).

Taxpayers can easily avoid the wash sale rule by waiting for more than 30 days to reestablish their investment position. The risk, of course, is that in the time between sale and repurchase, the market value of the securities rebounds and the taxpayer must pay a higher price for the same securities. This additional cost could easily exceed the tax benefit of the recognized loss on sale.

Conclusion

Business managers may defer the recognition of gain realized on the conversion of capital from one form to another by structuring the conversion as a nontaxable exchange. The gain deferral reduces the present value of the tax cost of the conversion

---

[20]§722.
[21]§723.
[22]§1091.

and increases the value of the transaction. While the advantages offered by the various nontaxable exchange provisions are considerable, these transactions require careful planning and a respect for the technical nuances differentiating one from the other.

Chapter 8 is the final chapter in Part Three of the text. In Part Three, we focused on the measurement of taxable income from business operations. You've learned how firms account for their routine income-generating activities and how that accounting can differ under generally accepted accounting principles (GAAP) and the tax law. You've been introduced to the tax consequences of asset acquisitions and dispositions and determined how property transactions affect taxable income. In Part Four of the text, we turn to the next issue: how the tax liability on that income is calculated and paid to the federal government.

Key Terms

Boot   190
Carryover basis   201
Involuntary conversion   198
Like-kind property   193
Nontaxable exchange   187

Property similar or related in service
   or use   198
Qualifying property   189
Substituted basis   190
Wash sale   202

Questions and Problems for Discussion

1. Four years ago, Company PJ acquired 1,000 acres of undeveloped land in a like-kind exchange. On the date of the exchange, the land's fair market value was $700,000. During the past four years, the land appreciated in value by $600,000; a recent appraisal indicated that it is worth $1.3 million today. However, if Company PJ sells the land for its current fair market value, the taxable gain will be $825,000. Can you explain this result?

2. In a nontaxable exchange between unrelated parties, are the amounts realized by the parties always equal?

3. In a nontaxable exchange, do the tax consequences to one party in any way depend on the tax consequences to the other party?

4. Is the substituted basis of the qualifying property received in a nontaxable exchange more or less than the cost of that property?

5. Determine if each of the following transactions qualifies as a nontaxable exchange:

   a. Firm A exchanges a 2 percent interest in the MG Partnership for a 10 percent interest in the KLS Partnership.

   b. Mr. B exchanges investment land for common stock in RV Inc. Immediately after the exchange, Mr. B owns 42 percent of RV's outstanding stock.

   c. Corporation C exchanges business equipment for a 25 percent interest in a residential apartment complex.

   d. Company D exchanges 15,000 units of inventory for a new computer system.

6. Firm Q, a real estate broker and developer, exchanged 16 acres of land for a commercial warehouse owned and operated by Company M. Company M, a light industrial business, plans to hold the land as a long-term investment. Is this exchange nontaxable to Firm Q and Company M?

7. Company W exchanged the following assets for Blackacre, investment land worth $2 million:

	Company W's Basis	Fair Market Value
Real property used in Company W's business	$800,000	$1,750,000
Marketable securities	30,000	250,000

Does Company W recognize any gain on this exchange?

8. Under what conditions can the destruction of property by casualty or theft result in an economic loss but a realized gain?

9. Why is the nontaxable exchange rule applying to partnership formations more flexible than the nontaxable exchange rule applying to corporate formations?

10. Explain the difference between a substituted basis in an asset and a carryover basis in an asset.

11. If a corporation engages in a nontaxable exchange of assets, could the transaction result in a book/tax difference? Is this difference a permanent or a temporary difference?

12. When a taxpayer transfers appreciated property to a corporation in exchange for newly issued stock and the exchange is nontaxable, the gain deferred on the exchange actually doubles. Can you explain this?

13. Why doesn't Congress extend the wash sale rule to apply to realized gains?

14. During the current year, Firm B recognized a $100,000 capital gain on the sale of investment land. Toward the end of the year, the firm plans to sell stock from its investment portfolio to generate a $100,000 capital loss. The firm has two blocks of stock that are candidates for sale (basis exceeds current market price by $100,000). However, the firm plans to reacquire whichever block it sells on the 31st day after the sale. How should the firm decide which block of stock to sell and reacquire?

15. Why is the label "nontaxable exchange" a misnomer?

Application Problems

1. Firm A exchanged an old asset with a tax basis of $20,000 for a new asset with a fair market value of $32,000. Under each of the following assumptions, apply the generic rules to compute A's realized gain, recognized gain, and tax basis in the new asset.
   a. Old asset and new asset are not qualified property for nontaxable exchange purposes.
   b. Old asset and new asset are qualified property for nontaxable exchange purposes.
   c. Old asset and new asset are not qualified property for nontaxable exchange purposes. To equalize the values exchanged, Firm A paid $1,700 cash to the other party.
   d. Old asset and new asset are qualified property for nontaxable exchange purposes. To equalize the values exchanged, Firm A paid $1,700 cash to the other party.
   e. Old asset and new asset are not qualified property for nontaxable exchange purposes. To equalize the values exchanged, Firm A received $4,500 cash from the other party.
   f. Old asset and new asset are qualified property for nontaxable exchange purposes. To equalize the values exchanged, Firm A received $4,500 cash from the other party.

2. Firm Q exchanged old property with a tax basis of $80,000 for new property with a fair market value of $65,000. Under each of the following assumptions, apply the generic rules to compute Q's realized loss, recognized loss, and tax basis in the new property.
   a. Old property and new property are not qualified property for nontaxable exchange purposes.
   b. Old property and new property are qualified property for nontaxable exchange purposes.
   c. Old property and new property are not qualified property for nontaxable exchange purposes. To equalize the values exchanged, Firm Q paid $2,000 cash to the other party.
   d. Old property and new property are qualified property for nontaxable exchange purposes. To equalize the values exchanged, Firm Q paid $2,000 cash to the other party.
   e. Old property and new property are not qualified property for nontaxable exchange purposes. To equalize the values exchanged,

Firm Q received $8,000 cash from the other party.

f. Old property and new property are qualified property for nontaxable exchange purposes. To equalize the values exchanged, Firm Q received $8,000 cash from the other party.

3. Company T exchanged an old asset with a tax basis of $30,000 and a fair market value of $40,000 for a new asset worth $37,500 and $2,500 cash.

   a. If the old asset and the new asset are qualified property so that the exchange is nontaxable, compute Company T's realized and recognized gain and tax basis in the new asset.

   b. How would your answers change if the new asset were worth only $26,000 and Company T received $14,000 cash in the exchange?

4. XYZ Inc. exchanged old duplicating equipment for new duplicating equipment. The corporation's adjusted basis in the old equipment was $13,000 ($30,000 initial cost − $17,000 accumulated depreciation), and its value was $20,000. Because the new equipment was worth $28,500, XYZ Inc. paid $8,500 cash in addition to the old equipment.

   a. Compute the corporation's realized gain on the exchange and determine the amount and character of any recognized gain.

   b. Compute the corporation's basis in its new equipment.

5. RTY Inc. exchanged old furniture for new furniture. The corporation's adjusted basis in the old furniture was $41,000 ($60,000 initial cost − $19,000 accumulated depreciation), and its value was $55,000. Because the new furniture was worth only $52,500, RTY Inc. received $2,500 cash in addition to the new furniture.

   a. Compute the corporation's realized gain on the exchange and determine the amount and character of any recognized gain.

   b. Compute the corporation's basis in its new furniture.

6. Firm ML, a noncorporate taxpayer, exchanged residential rental property plus $15,000 cash for 20 acres of investment land with an appraised value of $200,000. The firm used the straight-line method to compute depreciation on the residential rental property.

   a. Assuming that Firm ML's exchange was negotiated at arm's length, what is the value of the residential rental property?

   b. If the adjusted basis of the residential rental property is $158,000, compute Firm ML's realized and recognized gain on the exchange. What is the character of the recognized gain?

   c. Compute Firm ML's basis in the 20 acres of investment land.

7. Refer to the facts in Problem 6, but assume that Firm ML exchanged the residential rental property for the 20 acres of investment land plus $22,000 (i.e., Firm ML *received* cash in the exchange).

   a. Assuming that Firm ML's exchange was negotiated at arm's length, what is the value of the residential rental property?

   b. If the adjusted basis of the residential rental property is $158,000, compute Firm ML's realized and recognized gain on the exchange. What is the character of the recognized gain?

   c. Compute Firm ML's basis in the 20 acres of investment land.

8. Firm PO and Corporation QR exchanged the following business real estate:

	Marvin Gardens (Exchanged by PO)	Boardwalk (Exchanged by QR)
Market value	$ 800,000	$250,000
Mortgage	(550,000)	–0–
Equity	$ 250,000	$250,000

   a. If Firm PO's adjusted basis in Marvin Gardens was $310,000, compute the firm's realized gain, recognized gain, and basis in Boardwalk.

   b. If Corporation QR's adjusted basis in Boardwalk was $60,000, compute the corporation's realized gain, recognized gain, and basis in Marvin Gardens.

9. Company B and Firm W exchanged the following business real estate:

	Blackacre (Exchanged by B)	Whiteacre (Exchanged by W)
Market value	$ 400,000	$ 525,000
Mortgage	(100,000)	(225,000)
Equity	$ 300,000	$ 300,000

   a. If Company B's adjusted basis in Blackacre was $240,000, compute the company's realized gain, recognized gain, and basis in Whiteacre.

   b. If Firm W's adjusted basis in Whiteacre was $100,000, compute the company's realized gain, recognized gain, and basis in Blackacre.

10. RP Inc. owned residential real estate with an adjusted tax basis of $680,000 that was condemned by City Q because the city needed the land for a new convention center. RP received $975,000 of condemnation proceeds for the real estate.

   a. What are the tax consequences if RP spent $200,000 of the proceeds to expand its inventory and the remaining $775,000 to purchase new residential real estate? What is the corporation's basis in the inventory and the new real estate?

   b. How would your answer change if RP's basis in the condemned real estate was $850,000 rather than $680,000?

   c. How would your answer change if RP invested the entire condemnation proceeds plus an additional $100,000 cash in new residential real estate?

11. PV Inc. transferred the operating assets of one of its business activities into newly incorporated SV Inc. in exchange for 100 percent of SV's common stock. PV's adjusted basis in the operating assets was $4 million, and their fair market value was $10 million.

   a. Discuss the business reasons why a parent corporation like PV operates a business through a wholly owned subsidiary like SV.

   b. Compute PV's realized gain, recognized gain, and basis in its SV common stock.

12. ZEJ Inc., a calendar year taxpayer, reported $500,000 net income before tax on its 19X9 financial statements prepared in accordance with GAAP. The corporation's records reveal the following information:

During 19X9, ZEJ received an $80,000 reimbursement from its insurance company for the theft of equipment with a book basis of $62,000 and an adjusted tax basis of $58,000. The corporation used $75,000 of the reimbursement to replace the equipment and the remaining $5,000 to pay for the corporation's Christmas party.

   During 19X9, ZEJ exchanged investment real estate with a book and tax basis of $250,000 for commercial real estate with a fair market value of $600,000.

Based on the above facts, compute ZEJ Inc.'s 19X9 taxable income. In making your computation, assume that the corporation defers the recognition of taxable gain whenever possible.

13. Corporation A and Corporation Z go into partnership to develop, produce, and market a new product. The two corporations contribute the following properties in exchange for equal interests in the AZ Partnership:

	Corporation A	Corporation Z
Cash	$100,000	$ 50,000
Business equipment (fair market value)	30,000	80,000

Corporation A's adjusted basis in the contributed equipment is $34,000, and Corporation Z's adjusted basis in the contributed equipment is $12,000.

   a. Compute each corporation's realized and recognized gain or loss on the formation of the partnership.

   b. Compute each corporation's basis in its half interest in the AZ Partnership.

   c. Compute the partnership's basis in the equipment contributed by each corporate partner.

Issue Recognition Problems

Identify the tax issue or issues suggested by the following situations and state each issue in the form of a question.

1. ST Inc. and Firm WX are negotiating an exchange of the following business properties:

	Office Building (Owned by ST)	Warehouse (Owned by WX)
Market value	$2,000,000	$1,700,000
Mortgage	(450,000)	–0–

ST Inc. has agreed to pay $150,000 cash to Firm WX to equalize the values of the properties exchanged. ST's adjusted basis in the office building is $700,000 and WX's adjusted basis in the warehouse is $500,000.

2. Company JK disposed of the following two items of business equipment in a like-kind exchange:

	Inital Cost	Acc. Depr.	Fair Market Value
Item 1	$75,000	$38,000	$45,000
Item 2	30,000	16,000	10,000

In exchange for the two items, JK received like-kind equipment worth $50,000 and $5,000 cash.

3. NBV Inc., a California corporation, exchanged commercial real estate located in San Francisco for commercial real estate located in Tokyo, Japan. NBV's gain realized was $16.3 million.

4. FM Inc. operates a dairy farm. The local government required the corporation to destroy 150 head of cattle because the herd had been exposed to "mad cow" disease. None of the cattle displayed any symptoms of the disease before they were destroyed. The local government paid $150,000 to FM Inc. as compensation for the loss. The corporation's adjusted basis in the herd was $105,000.

5. Company T owned and operated a drive-in movie theater from 1980 through 1995. The company ceased operations because so few people were attending the outdoor facility. In the current year, the entire facility (movie screen, projection building, snack bar, 15 picnic tables, and playground equipment) was destroyed by a tornado. Company T received an insurance reimbursement for $360,000. The company's aggregate adjusted basis in the destroyed properties was $200,000. Four months after the twister, Company T purchased a new four-screen movie theater complex located in an urban shopping mall.

6. In 19X7, an office building owned by Firm F was completely destroyed by fire. Firm F's adjusted basis in the building was $485,000, and the firm received a $550,000 reimbursement from its insurance company. On its 19X7 tax return, the firm elected to defer the $65,000 gain realized on the involuntary conversion. In early 19X8, Firm F invested $560,000 in another office building. In 19X9, the firm settled a dispute with its insurance company concerning the 19X7 claim; pursuant to the settlement, Firm F received an additional reimbursement of $25,000.

7. In 19X6, an industrial plant owned by Company C, a calendar year taxpayer, was destroyed in a flood. Company C's adjusted basis in the plant was $1.65 million, and the company received a $2 million reimbursement from its insurance company. On its 19X6 tax return, Company C elected to defer the gain realized on the involuntary conversion. The company promptly began construction of a new plant on the site of the old. However, because of unexpected delays, construction was not completed until January 19X9 and Company C did not place the new industrial plant into service until March 19X9. The total construction price was $3 million.

8. In 19X8, transportation equipment owned by Corporation ABC was stolen. The corporation's adjusted basis in the equipment was $105,000, and the firm received a $400,000 reimbursement from its insurance company. Corporation ABC immediately paid $440,000 for replacement transportation equipment. On its 19X8 tax return, the corporation elected to defer the $295,000 gain realized on the involuntary conversion. In 19X9, the corporation's business generated a $7 million net operating loss—the first in ABC's history. The corporation's aggregate taxable income on its 19X7 and 19X8 returns was $3.2 million.

9. Mr. P, a professional architect, entered into an agreement with Partnership M under which he (1) designed three buildings for the partnership and (2) transferred a copyright to design software to the partnership. Mr. P had no tax basis in this software. In exchange for the services and computer software, Mr. P received a 35 percent interest in Partnership M.

10. On May 19, Firm WJ realized a $48,000 loss on the sale of 10,000 shares of voting common stock in the XZY Corporation. On May 30, the firm purchased 3,200 shares of nonvoting preferred stock in XZY Corporation.

Tax Planning Cases

1. Firm NS owns 90 percent of the outstanding stock of Corporation T. The firm owns business realty that the corporation needs for use in its business. The appraised value of the realty is $4 million. Firm NS's adjusted basis in the realty is $5.6 million. Both Firm NS and Corporation T are in the 35 percent marginal tax bracket. Based on these facts, discuss the tax implications of each of the following courses of action and decide which course you would recommend to Firm NS.
   a. Firm NS could exchange the realty for newly issued shares of Corporate T stock worth $4 million.
   b. Firm NS could sell the realty to Corporate T for $4 million cash.
   c. Firm NS could lease the realty to Corporation T for its annual fair rental value of $600,000.

2. Firm K, a noncorporate taxpayer, has owned nondepreciable business realty with a $600,000 basis for four years. Two unrelated parties want to acquire the realty from Firm K. Party A has offered $770,000 cash for the realty. Party B has offered to exchange undeveloped land with a fair market value of $725,000 for the realty. If Firm K accepts this offer, it would hold the land for no more than two years before selling it. The value of the undeveloped land has appreciated 10 percent annually for the last eight years. Firm K's marginal tax rate on ordinary income is 39.6 percent, and it uses a 7 percent discount rate to compute net present value. Based on these facts,

which offer should Firm K accept to maximize the net present value of the transaction?

3. In the current year, Corporation EF decides to replace old, outmoded business equipment (adjusted basis $50,000) with new, improved equipment. The corporation has two options:
   • *Option 1:* Sell the old equipment for $120,000 cash and use the cash to purchase the new equipment. This option has no transaction cost.
   • *Option 2:* Exchange the old equipment for the new equipment. This exchange has a $6,000 transaction cost that the corporation could deduct in the current year.
   The new equipment has a MACRS recovery period of five years, and Corporation EF will use the half-year convention. Based on these facts, which option should the corporation choose? In making your computations, assume a 35 percent tax rate and a 10 percent discount rate.

4. DM Inc. incurred a $25,000 net capital loss in 19X3 that has carried forward into 19X8. During 19X8, a hurricane destroyed business assets in which DM Inc. had a $120,000 basis. The corporation received an insurance reimbursement of $150,000 which the corporation immediately used to purchase replacement assets. The new assets have a three-year MACRS recovery period. Should DM Inc. make an election to defer the gain recognized on the involuntary conversion?

Comprehensive Problems for Part Three

1. Croyden Company is a calendar year, accrual basis corporation. Mr. and Mrs. Croyden are the sole corporate shareholders. Mr. Croyden is president and Mrs. Croyden is vice president of the corporation. Croyden's financial records, which are prepared in accordance with GAAP, show the following information for the current year.

Revenues from sales of goods	$12,900,000
Cost of goods sold (LIFO)	(9,260,000)
Gross profit	$ 3,640,000
Bad debt expense	$ 24,000
Administrative salaries and wages	612,000
State and local business taxes; employment taxes	135,000
Interest expense	33,900
Advertising	67,000
Property insurance premiums	19,800
Life insurance premiums	7,300
Depreciation expense	148,800
Repairs, maintenance, utilities	81,000

Croyden's records reveal the following facts concerning its current year business operation.

- Because of the UNICAP rules, Croyden's cost of goods sold for tax purposes exceeds cost of goods sold for financial statement purposes by $219,000.
- Bad debt expense equals the addition to the corporation's allowance for bad debts. Actual write-offs of uncollectible accounts during the year totaled $31,200.
- Administrative salaries include an accrued $50,000 year-end bonus to Mr. Croyden and an accrued $20,000 year-end bonus to Mrs. Croyden. These bonuses were paid on January 17 of the following year.
- The life insurance premiums were on key-person policies for Mr. and Mrs. Croyden. The corporation is the policy beneficiary.
- Croyden disposed of two assets during the year. (These dispositions are *not* reflected in the financial statement information shown above.)

The corporation sold office furnishings for $45,000. The original cost of the furnishings was $40,000 and accumulated MACRS depreciation through date of sale was $12,700. The corporation exchanged transportation equipment for a 15 percent interest in a newly formed business partnership. The original cost of the transportation equipment was $110,000 and accumulated MACRS depreciation through date of exchange was $38,900.

- The correct MACRS depreciation for business assets placed in service prior to the current

year (including the office furnishings and transportation equipment disposed of during the year) is $187,600. The only operating asset acquired during the year was an item of heavy equipment costing $275,000. The equipment has a seven-year recovery period and was placed in service on February 11.
- Croyden's prior year tax returns reveal that the corporation has no unrecaptured Section 1231 losses and a $7,400 capital loss carryforward into the current year.

Based solely on the above facts, compute Croyden Company's current year taxable income.

2. LN Consulting is a calendar year, cash basis unincorporated business. The business is not required to provide audited financial statements to any external user. LN's accounting records show the following cash receipts and disbursements for the current year.

Revenues from service contracts	$292,000
Proceeds from sale of mutual fund shares	18,000
Insurance reimbursement for fire loss	7,000
Administrative salaries	$ 32,000
Professional fees	800
Business meals and entertainment	1,090
State and local business taxes; employment taxes	5,000
Interest expense	7,600
Advertising	970
Office expense	1,200
Office rent	14,400
New office equipment	8,300

LN's records reveal the following facts concerning its current year business operation.

- The firm was organized two years ago when $1,280 of start-up costs were capitalized for federal tax purposes.
- In December, the bookkeeper prepaid $1,500 of interest on a business debt. This interest is related to the following taxable year.
- LN disposed of three assets during the year.

The firm exchanged computer equipment for used modular office furniture. (These assets are not like-kind for federal tax purposes.) The original cost of the computer equipment was $13,000 and accumulated

MACRS depreciation through date of exchange (July 10) was $9,700. The office furniture has a market value of $6,000. Office furniture has a seven-year recovery period.

The firm sold 1,200 shares in a mutual fund for $18,000. LN purchased the shares as a short-term investment of excess working capital. The cost of the shares was $16,600.

An electrical fire completely destroyed a company car. The adjusted basis of the car prior to its destruction was $9,100 and LN's property insurance company paid $7,000 to LN in complete settlement of its damage claim. LN used the insurance money to pay various operating expenses.

- The correct MACRS depreciation for business assets placed in service prior to the current year (including the computer equipment and company car disposed of during the year) is $4,600. The only operating asset purchased during the year was an item of office equipment costing $8,300. The equipment has a seven-year recovery period and was placed in service on August 19.

Based solely on the above facts, compute the taxable income generated by LN Consulting's current year activities.

PART FOUR

The Taxation of Business Income

9

Sole Proprietorships, Partnerships, and S Corporations

Learning Objectives

After studying this chapter, you should be able to:

1. Explain how the net profit or loss from a sole proprietorship affects the owner's taxable income.
2. Describe the legal requirements for the home office deduction.
3. Compute the FICA payroll taxes and describe the employer's responsibility for remitting these taxes to the federal government.
4. Describe the tax base and the tax rate for the federal self-employment tax.
5. Distinguish between a general partnership and a limited partnership.
6. Differentiate between a partner's distributive share of partnership income and cash flow from the partnership.
7. Adjust the basis in a partnership interest to reflect the information reported on the partner's Schedule K-1.
8. Apply the basis limitation rule to determine the current year deduction for distributive shares of partnership loss.
9. Explain how limited liability companies (LLCs) are treated for federal tax purposes.
10. Determine if a corporation is eligible to be an S corporation.
11. Contrast the basis limitation rule for S corporation losses with the basis limitation rule for partnership losses.

In Part Three of *Principles of Taxation for Business and Investment Planning*, we learned that taxable income from business operations is conceptually equivalent to net profit because firms can subtract operating expenses from revenues in calculating taxable income. More formally, taxable income equals gross income minus allowable deductions.[1] In Part Four of the text, we will analyze the rules governing the computation of the tax liability on business income. Throughout

---

[1] §63(a).

EXHIBIT 9–1

Categories of business organization

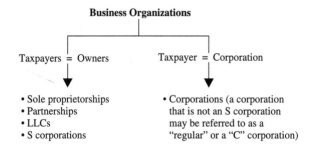

Part Three, we used the labels *firm* and *company* to refer to organizations conducting business operations. We could get by with these generic labels because we were concentrating on the *measurement of taxable income*. The measurement process does not depend on the specific type of legal entity operating the business. As stated in Chapter 4, the tax law is essentially neutral across business entities with respect to the tax base. But to make the actual *tax computation*, we must focus on the specific organizational form of the business.

For tax purposes, business organizations fall into one of two categories. The first category consists of organizations that are not taxable entities. The income generated by the organization is taxed directly to the owners. This category includes sole proprietorships, partnerships, limited liability companies (LLCs), and S corporations, all of which are discussed in Chapter 9. The second category consists of corporations, which are both persons under the law and taxpayers in their own right. Corporations pay tax on their income at the entity level. If a corporation distributes after-tax earnings to its owners, the distributed income is taxed a second time at the owner level. This potential for double taxation, as well as the other unique characteristics of corporate taxpayers, is examined in detail in Chapter 10. Exhibit 9–1 contrasts the two categories of business organizations in terms of the identity of the taxpayer.

Part Four includes two more chapters that complete our discussion of the taxation of business income. Chapter 11 compares the tax advantages and disadvantages of the various business entities and identifies tax planning strategies unique to each. Finally, Chapter 12 introduces the complexities that develop when business entities operate in more than one taxing jurisdiction.

Sole Proprietorships

The simplest form of business organization is a **sole proprietorship,** defined as an unincorporated business activity owned by one individual.[2] A sole proprietor owns the assets of the business in his or her own name and is personally liable for the debts incurred by the business. In other words, the business has no legal identity separate and apart from that of its owner. Sole proprietorships are the most common form of business entity in the United States. According to recent Internal Revenue Service data, over 18 million nonfarm sole proprietorships operate in this country, and three of every four businesses that report to the IRS are operated by sole proprietors.[3]

---

[2]This definition includes businesses in which the owner's spouse has an equity interest in the business under state property law.

[3]IRS Statistics of Income Bulletin, Summer 1997.

Overview of Schedule C

Objective 1
Explain how the net profit or loss from a sole proprietorship affects the owner's taxable income.

The taxable income generated by a sole proprietorship is reported on Schedule C (Profit and Loss From Business) of the proprietor's Form 1040 (U.S. Individual Income Tax Return).[4] This schedule is essentially the proprietorship's income statement for the current year. Gross income from the sale of goods to customers or performance of services for clients is accounted for in Part I. The proprietorship's operating expenses and cost recovery deductions are listed in Part II. An excess of gross income over allowable deductions is reported as net profit, while an excess of allowable deductions over gross income is reported as net loss.

Once More With Feeling—Sold Proprietorship.   Mr. Tom Owen owns and operates a firm that manufactures reproductions of antique furniture. The business name for this sole proprietorship is Once More With Feeling. For 1997, the business records reflect the following items of revenue and expense.

Revenue from furniture sales	$1,117,300
Sales returns	(21,000)
Expenses: Advertising	$ 6,200
Accounts written off as uncollectible	8,800
Attorney and CPA fees	2,150
Business license tax	2,500
Cost of goods sold	599,700
Fire, casualty, and liability insurance	5,600
Interest to Credit Union	7,300
MACRS depreciation	3,600
Payroll taxes	9,250
Rent on workroom	23,200
Repairs to tools and equipment	17,900
Supplies	18,000
Utilities	14,000
Wages	73,200

Mr. Owen used the above information to prepare the Schedule C included in his 1997 Form 1040. Page 1 of this Schedule C is shown as Exhibit 9–2. The $304,900 net profit reported on Schedule C was included in Mr. Owen's 1997 taxable income.

Note that the tax liability on net profit is not computed on Schedule C. Instead, the net profit carries to the first page of Form 1040 as ordinary income and is combined with all other income items recognized during the year. Consequently, the individual's business income is just one component of total income on which tax is computed. Similarly, if the sole proprietorship operated at a loss, the loss carries to the first page of Form 1040 to be deducted against the individual's other income for the year. If the business loss exceeds other income, the individual can carry the excess loss back 2 years and forward 20 years as a net operating loss (NOL) deduction.

---

[4]Agricultural business operations are reported on Schedule F (Profit and Loss From Farming).

EXHIBIT 9–2

SCHEDULE C (Form 1040)	**Profit or Loss From Business** (Sole Proprietorship)	OMB No. 1545-0074
Department of the Treasury Internal Revenue Service (99)	▶ Partnerships, joint ventures, etc., must file Form 1065. ▶ Attach to Form 1040 or Form 1041. . ▶ See Instructions for Schedule C (Form 1040).	**1997** Attachment Sequence No. **09**

Name of proprietor	Social security number (SSN)
Tom G. Owen	497 45 9058

A Principal business or profession, including product or service (see page C-1)
Retail Sales — Furniture
B Enter principal business code (see page C-6) ▶ | 3 | 9 | 7 | 0 |

C Business name. If no separate business name, leave blank.
Once More With Feeling
D Employer ID number (EIN), if any
8 | 1 | 1 | 1 | 3 | 8 | 4 | 1 | 9 |

E Business address (including suite or room no.) ▶ *1017 East Main*
City, town or post office, state, and ZIP code   *Widner, Kentucky 40506*

F Accounting method: (1) ☐ Cash   (2) ☒ Accrual   (3) ☐ Other (specify) ▶
G Did you "materially participate" in the operation of this business during 1997? If "No," see page C-2 for limit on losses. ☒ Yes ☐ No
H If you started or acquired this business during 1997, check here . . . . ▶ ☐

Part I   Income

1	Gross receipts or sales. **Caution:** If this income was reported to you on Form W-2 and the "Statutory employee" box on that form was checked, see page C-2 and check here . . . . ▶ ☐	**1**	1,117,300
2	Returns and allowances	**2**	21,000
3	Subtract line 2 from line 1	**3**	1,096,300
4	Cost of goods sold (from line 42 on page 2)	**4**	599,700
5	**Gross profit.** Subtract line 4 from line 3	**5**	496,600
6	Other income, including Federal and state gasoline or fuel tax credit or refund (see page C-2) . . .	**6**	-
7	**Gross income.** Add lines 5 and 6 . . . . ▶	**7**	496,600

Part II   Expenses. Enter expenses for business use of your home only on line 30.

8	Advertising	**8**	6,200	19 Pension and profit-sharing plans	**19**	
9	Bad debts from sales or services (see page C-3) . .	**9**	8,800	20 Rent or lease (see page C-4):		
10	Car and truck expenses (see page C-3)	**10**		a Vehicles, machinery, and equipment .	**20a**	
11	Commissions and fees . .	**11**		b Other business property . .	**20b**	23,200
12	Depletion	**12**		21 Repairs and maintenance . .	**21**	17,900
13	Depreciation and section 179 expense deduction (not included in Part III) (see page C-3) . .	**13**	3,600	22 Supplies (not included in Part III)	**22**	18,000
				23 Taxes and licenses . . .	**23**	11,750
				24 Travel, meals, and entertainment:		
14	Employee benefit programs (other than on line 19) . . .	**14**		a Travel	**24a**	
15	Insurance (other than health) .	**15**	5,600	b Meals and entertainment .		
16	Interest:			c Enter 50% of line 24b subject to limitations (see page C-4) .		
a	Mortgage (paid to banks, etc.) .	**16a**		d Subtract line 24c from line 24b	**24d**	
b	Other	**16b**	7,300	25 Utilities	**25**	14,000
17	Legal and professional services	**17**	2,150	26 Wages (less employment credits) .	**26**	73,200
18	Office expense	**18**		27 Other expenses (from line 48 on page 2)	**27**	
28	**Total expenses** before expenses for business use of home. Add lines 8 through 27 in columns . ▶				**28**	191,700
29	Tentative profit (loss). Subtract line 28 from line 7				**29**	304,900
30	Expenses for business use of your home. Attach Form 8829				**30**	
31	**Net profit or (loss).** Subtract line 30 from line 29.					
	• If a profit, enter on Form 1040, line 12, and ALSO on Schedule SE, line 2 (statutory employees, see page C-5). Estates and trusts, enter on Form 1041, line 3.				**31**	304,900
	• If a loss, you MUST go on to line 32.					
32	If you have a loss, check the box that describes your investment in this activity (see page C-5).					
	• If you checked 32a, enter the loss on **Form 1040, line 12,** and ALSO on **Schedule SE, line 2** (statutory employees, see page C-5). Estates and trusts, enter on Form 1041, line 3.				**32a** ☐ All investment is at risk.	
	• If you checked 32b, you MUST attach **Form 6198.**				**32b** ☐ Some investment is not at risk.	

For Paperwork Reduction Act Notice, see Form 1040 instructions.   Cat. No. 11334P   Schedule C (Form 1040) 1997

Individual Net Operating Loss.   Mr. Y reported the following items on his Form 1040 for 19X9:

Salary from employer	$ 21,600
Interest and dividend income from investments	1,200
Business loss from sole proprietorship	(26,810)
Net operating loss	$ (4,010)

Mr. Y can use his $4,010 net operating loss as a carryback deduction (to 19X7 and 19X8) or as a carryforward deduction for the next 20 years.[5]

Cash Flow Implications.   The after-tax cash generated by a profitable sole proprietorship belongs to the individual owner. The individual can retain the cash for use in the business, spend it for personal consumption, or invest it in other income-producing property. In the latter case, earnings from the owner's investments (interest, dividends, rents, etc.) are not considered business income and are not reported on Schedule C.[6]

Dispositions of Business Assets.   Only the results of the sole proprietorship's routine business operations are reported on Schedule C. If the owner disposes of assets used in the operation of the sole proprietorship, recognized gains and losses are reported on Form 4797 (Sales of Business Property). The tax consequences of the disposition are based on the rules discussed in Chapters 7 and 8. For instance, if the owner sells business equipment at a gain, he must report depreciation recapture as ordinary income and any additional gain as Section 1231 gain. If he sells the equipment at a loss, the loss is a Section 1231 loss.

Interest Expense.   If an individual borrows money for a business purpose relating to her sole proprietorship, the interest paid on the debt is deductible on Schedule C. The deductibility of business interest is in sharp contrast to the tax treatment of other types of interest expense. For example, individuals can't deduct the interest paid on debt incurred to purchase consumer goods such as a family car or a new wardrobe. If the sole proprietorship fails to generate enough cash to service the business debt, the individual owner is personally liable for its repayment and the sole proprietorship's creditors can look to the owner's nonbusiness assets for satisfaction.

The Home Office Deduction.   If an individual uses a portion of his personal residence as an office for his sole proprietorship, the expenses allocable to the home office may qualify as a business deduction.

Home Office Deduction.   Mrs. HB, a self-employed consultant, uses one room of her home as a business office. This room represents 15 percent of the home's square footage. During the current year, Mrs. HB incurred the following expenses in connection with her home:

Home mortgage interest	$18,000
Property tax on residence	4,300
Homeowner's insurance	2,950
Utilities	3,600
House cleaning service	2,400
Repairs	1,900
	$33,150

---

[5]This example ignores many technical details that can make computation of the individual NOL deduction extremely complicated.

[6]Chapter 15 discusses the taxation of investment income earned by an individual taxpayer.

> If Mrs. HB's office meets the tax law requirements, she can deduct $4,973 (15 percent of the total expenses) as a business deduction on her Schedule C. She can also claim a MACRS depreciation deduction based on 15 percent of the cost of the residence.

Objective 2
Describe the legal requirements for the home office deduction.

The possibility of transforming some percentage of monthly household expenses into tax deductions might prompt the conversion of many a spare bedroom into a home office—even if the use of such office is extraneous to the conduct of the homeowner's business. The tax law limits the potential for abuse through a set of tough requirements for qualifying a portion of a residence as a home office. Essentially, the office must be *exclusively* used on a regular basis as the principal place of any business operated by the homeowner or as a place to meet with patients, clients, or customers.[7] The requirement that the home office is the *principal* place of business is particularly strict: the office must be the most important and significant location compared to any other locations at which the individual conducts business.[8]

> ***Principal Place of Business.*** Mr. K is a self-employed obstetrician who treats patients at three different urban hospitals. Although Mr. K spends more than 12 hours during an average week at each hospital, he does not maintain an office in any of the hospitals. He does all his medical reading, patient billing and record keeping, and other administrative tasks in his home office where he spends two to three hours each day. Patient treatment is the most significant aspect of Mr. K's business, and he spends more hours working at the hospitals than in his home office. Consequently, the home office is not the principal place of his medical practice, and the expenses allocable to the office are not deductible.

The Tax Reform Act of 1997 relaxed the strict principal place of business requirement for a home office. Beginning in 1999, a home office used exclusively for administrative or management activities qualifies as a principal place of business if the taxpayer has no other fixed location where such activities are conducted. Under this new standard, Mr. K's office described in the above example qualifies as a home office and the expenses allocable to the office will be deductible on Mr. K's 1999 Schedule C.

Even when an individual meets the qualification requirements for a home office, the home office deduction is limited to the taxable income of the business before consideration of the deduction.[9] In other words, the home office deduction can't create or increase a net loss. A sole proprietor who claims a home office deduction must isolate the deduction on line 30, Schedule C, and attach a separate Form 8829 to show the detailed computation of the deduction. Clearly, the IRS is very sensitive about home office deductions. Sole proprietors who are entitled to the deduction should carefully document the various expenses on which the deduction is based and be prepared to justify the necessity of a home office if their tax return is selected for audit.

---

[7] §280A(c)(1).
[8] *Commissioner* v. *Soliman*, 506 U.S. 168 (1993).
[9] §280A(c)(5).

Employment Taxes

In a sole proprietorship, the owner may be the only person working in the business or the proprietorship may have any number of employees. In the latter case, the sole proprietor must obtain an **employer identification number** from the IRS and comply with the state and federal employment tax requirements imposed on every business organization.

Objective 3
Compute the FICA payroll taxes and describe the employer's responsibility for remitting these taxes to the federal government.

Unemployment and FICA tax.   Employers must pay both a state and federal unemployment tax based on the compensation paid to their employees during the year.[10] As we discussed in Chapter 1, these taxes fund the national unemployment benefits program. Employers must also pay the tax authorized by the Federal Insurance Contribution Act (FICA) that funds our national Social Security and Medicare systems. This **employer payroll tax** has two components: a Social Security tax of 6.2 percent of a base amount of compensation paid to each employee plus a Medicare tax of 1.45 percent of the employee's total compensation.[11] Congress adjusts the Social Security base amount each year; in 1998, the base is $68,400.

> **Employer Payroll Tax.**   Mr. B has a full-time employee, Mrs. Z, who manages Mr. B's sole proprietorship. Mrs. Z's 1998 salary was $80,000, and Mr. B's employer payroll tax on this salary was $5,401.
>
> | | |
> |---|---|
> | Social Security tax (6.2% of $68,400) | $4,241 |
> | Medicare tax (1.45% of $80,000) | 1,160 |
> | Employer payroll tax | $5,401 |

In addition to paying unemployment and payroll taxes, employers are responsible for collecting the FICA tax levied on their employees.[12] This **employee payroll tax** is computed in exactly the same manner as the employer payroll tax.

> **Employee Payroll Tax Withheld by Employer.**   Based on the facts in the preceding example, Mrs. Z's employee payroll tax for 1998 was also $5,401.[13] As Mrs. Z's employer, Mr. B withheld this tax from Mrs. Z's salary and remitted it along with his own FICA tax liability to the government for a total payment of $10,802. Thus, with respect to the employee payroll tax, Mr. B acts as the collection agent for the federal government.

Employers should take their responsibility to collect and remit employee payroll tax very seriously. If an employer fails to remit the proper FICA tax for an employee, the federal government may collect both halves of the tax (the employer and the employee portions) from the employer.[14]

---

[10]§3301.
[11]§3111.
[12]§3102.
[13]§3101. The employee payroll tax is nondeductible for federal income tax purposes.
[14]The employer is not technically liable for an employee's payroll tax. However, an employer that fails to "collect, truthfully account for, and pay over" this tax is subject to a penalty equal to 100 percent of such tax. In other words, the penalty on the employer equals the uncollected employee tax. §6672. This penalty has been described as the "iron fist" of the FICA tax system.

Income Tax Withholding on Employee Compensation. Employers are required by law to withhold federal income tax (and possibly state income tax) from the compensation paid to their employees.[15] Employers must remit the withholding to the Treasury periodically throughout the year. The withholding for each employee is based on the information provided on the employee's Form W-4 (Employee's Withholding Allowance Certificate) and computed by reference to withholding tables provided by the IRS.

Gross and Net Compensation. During 1998, Mr. B withheld $16,000 of federal income tax from Mrs. Z's $80,000 gross salary. Therefore, Mrs. Z received only $58,599 of after-tax (net) compensation:

Gross salary	$ 80,000
FICA tax withheld	(5,401)
Federal income tax withheld	(16,000)
Net salary received	$ 58,599

At the end of each year, employers are required to provide information to each employee concerning the gross wages or salary paid to that employee during the year and the payroll and income tax withheld from that gross income. This information is summarized on the familiar Form W-2 (Wage and Tax Statement).

Income Tax Consequences to the Employer. Business organizations can deduct the gross amount of current compensation paid to their employees.[16] They are also allowed to deduct state and federal unemployment taxes and the employer payroll tax; these taxes are ordinary and necessary expenses incurred in the conduct of an active business.[17] Let's summarize the relationship between these deductible expenses, the employer's withholding requirements, and the net compensation paid to employees by referring back to Mr. B's sole proprietorship.

Compensation and Cash Disbursements. For 1998, Mr. B paid $80,000 of compensation to Mrs. Z and $5,401 of employer payroll tax on that compensation. He withheld $21,401 of employee payroll tax and income tax from Mrs. Z's compensation and remitted a total of $26,802 in tax to the federal government.

---

[15]§3402.

[16]Unless some or all the compensation must be capitalized to inventory under the uniform capitalization (unicap) rules.

[17]See Rev. Rul. 80-164, 1980-1 CB 109.

	Deductible Business Expense	Cash Disbursed To:	
		Mrs. Z	U.S. Treasury
Salary	$80,000	$58,599	$21,401
Employer FICA tax	5,401		5,401
	$85,401	$58,599	$26,802

Self-Employment Tax

Objective 4
Describe the tax base and the tax rate for the federal self-employment tax.

While sole proprietors are responsible for collecting both payroll and income taxes from their employees and remitting the taxes to the government, sole proprietors themselves are not employees and do not receive a salary from the business. Sole proprietors are self-employed and, as such, must pay the federal **self-employment (SE) tax** on their business income.[18] Refer to Schedule C in Exhibit 9–2 and note how line 31 instructs the sole proprietor to carry net profit to Schedule SE. The self-employment tax on net profit is computed on this schedule and paid along with the individual's income tax for the year.

The SE tax has two components: a Social Security tax of 12.4 percent of a base amount of net earnings from self-employment plus a Medicare tax of 2.9 percent of total net earnings. The Social Security base amount for 1998 is $68,400. Note that the SE tax rates equal the *combined* employer/employee payroll tax rates. Furthermore, the annual base amounts for the SE tax and the payroll tax are the same number. The SE tax was enacted to complement the FICA tax; the federal government collects the same tax on a sole proprietor's self-employment income as it would collect on an identical amount of compensation income. To complete the parallel, sole proprietors can claim one-half of their SE tax (the equivalent of the employer payroll tax) as an income tax deduction.[19]

In calculating after-tax business income, sole proprietors must factor in both the income tax and the SE tax levied on that income.

Self-Employment Tax.   Mr. B's sole proprietorship generated $200,000 of net profit in 1998. If his marginal income tax rate is 36 percent, the after-tax income from the business is $116,653:

Schedule C net profit		$200,000
Self-employment tax:		
Net earnings from self-employment	$184,700[20]	
Social Security tax (12.4% of $68,400)	8,482	
Medicare tax (2.9% of $184,700)	5,356	

---

[18]§1401. Self-employed individuals are not eligible to receive unemployment benefits and, therefore, are not subject to state and federal unemployment taxes.

[19]§164(f).

[20]The statutory base for the SE tax is "net earnings from self-employment." Net earnings equals net profit minus a deduction equal to 7.65 percent of such profit. §1402(a)(12). Schedule SE builds this

Total SE tax		(13,838)
Income tax:		
Schedule C net profit	$200,000	
One-half SE tax	(6,919)	
	$193,081	
	.36	
		(69,509)
After-tax business income		$116,653

Note that the SE tax is not a progressive tax; the combined 15.3 percent rate applies to the very first dollar of self-employment income. For sole proprietors who earn modest incomes, the SE tax can be a heavier burden than the income tax.

Partnerships

Entrepreneurs who pool their resources by becoming co-owners of a business can organize the business as a partnership. **Partnerships** are unincorporated entities created by contractual agreement among two or more business associates.[21] Such associates can include individuals, corporations, and even other partnerships. All 50 states and the District of Columbia have enacted statutes (generally patterned after the Uniform Partnership Act and the Uniform Limited Partnership Act) to define the characteristics and requirements for partnerships operating within their jurisdiction.

Forming a Partnership

Objective 5
Distinguish between a general partnership and a limited partnership.

The first step in the formation of a partnership is the drafting of a partnership agreement by the prospective partners.[22] A partnership agreement is a legal contract stipulating both the rights and obligations of the co-owners of the business and the percentage of profits and losses allocable to each. The partnership form gives the co-owners the flexibility to customize their business arrangement to suit their unique situation. The partners can agree to share all profits and losses equally or they can decide on different sharing ratios for special items of income, gain, deduction, or loss. Ideally, a partnership agreement should be drafted by an attorney, should be in writing, and should be signed by all the partners. However, even oral partnership agreements between business associates have been respected as binding contracts by the courts.[23]

A partnership can be a **general partnership** in which all partners have unlimited personal liability for the debts incurred by the partnership. Alternatively, a partnership can be a **limited partnership** in which one or more partners are liable for partnership debt only to the extent of their capital contributions to the partnership. Limited partnerships must have at least one general partner. A limited partner's role is restricted to that

---

deduction into its computation of net earnings by defining that number as 92.35 percent of Schedule C income.

[21]The term *partnership* encompasses syndicates, groups, pools, joint ventures, or any other unincorporated business organization. §761(a).

[22]The organizational and start-up costs of a new partnership must be capitalized and amortized over 60 months. See the discussion of organizational and start-up costs in Chapter 6.

[23]See, for example, *Elrod*, 87 TC 1046 (1986) and *Kuhl* v. *Garner*, 894 P.2d 525 (Oregon, 1995).

of a passive investor; state law prohibits limited partners from active involvement in the partnership business. Limited partners who violate this prohibition may forfeit their limited liability for the partnership's debts.

Tax Basis in Partnership Interests.   Partnerships are both legal entities (title to property can be held and conveyed in the partnership name) and accounting entities (financial books and records are maintained by the partnership). An equity interest in a partnership entity is an intangible asset, the value of which depends on the underlying value of the partnership business. Partnership interests are considered illiquid assets; partnership agreements typically prevent partners from disposing of their interests without the consent of the other partners. A partner's initial tax basis in a partnership interest equals the cash plus the adjusted basis of any property transferred to the partnership in exchange for the equity interest.[24]

As legal entities, partnerships can borrow money in their own name. Nonetheless, general partners have unlimited liability for repayment of the debt to the partnership's creditors. If the partnership business does not generate enough cash to service its debts, the general partners must contribute funds to satisfy any unpaid liabilities.[25] As a result, a partner's economic investment in a partnership consists of the initial investment of cash or property *plus* the share of partnership debt for which the partner may ultimately be held responsible. The tax law acknowledges this responsibility by providing that a partner's share of partnership debt is included in the basis in her partnership interest.[26]

> ***Basis in Partnership Interest.***   Three individuals each contributed $10,000 cash to a new business partnership in which they are equal general partners. The partnership immediately borrowed $24,000 from a local bank, which it used to purchase equipment and supplies. Each partner's basis in his partnership interest is $18,000: the initial cash contribution plus a proportionate share of the partnership debt.[27]

Partnership Reporting Requirements

The Internal Revenue Code states that "a partnership as such shall not be subject to the income tax . . . Persons carrying on a business as partners shall be liable for income tax only in their separate or individual capacities."[28] Although partnerships are not taxable entities, they are required to file an annual Form 1065 (U.S. Partnership Return of Income) with the IRS.[29]

---

[24]The exchange of property for a partnership interest is nontaxable to both the partner and the partnership. §721.

[25]In this respect, a general partner's risk with respect to the partnership business is equivalent to a sole proprietor's business risk.

[26]§752(a).

[27]The regulatory rules for calculating a partner's apportioned share of partnership debt are extremely complex. The simplest summary of these rules is that recourse debt is allocated only to general partners based on their relative loss-sharing ratios and nonrecourse debt is allocated to all partners based on their profit-sharing ratios. Reg. §1.752-2.

[28]§701.

[29]As a general rule, partnerships are required to use the same taxable year as that used by their partners. Under this rule, a partnership consisting of individual partners who are calendar year taxpayers files its Form 1065 on a calendar year basis. §706(b).

The taxable income generated by partnership activities is measured and characterized at the entity level. All items of gross income and deduction relating strictly to the operation of the partnership business are reported on page 1 of Form 1065; the net of these items is reported on line 22 as ordinary income or loss. This income or loss is allocated among the partners according to the sharing ratio specified in the partnership agreement. The partners report their share of income or loss on their respective returns and include it in the calculation of taxable income. Accordingly, net profit from a business organized as a partnership is taxed directly to the partners; the tax rate depends on whether the partner is an individual or a corporation.[30] Because partnerships serve only as conduits of income, they are described as **passthrough entities.**

> ***Once More with Feeling—Partnership.***   Refer back to our earlier example in which Mr. Tom Owen operates a furniture business (Once More With Feeling) as a sole proprietorship. Let's change the facts by assuming that Mr. Owen and two co-owners organized Once More With Feeling as a partnership. Mr. Owen owns a 60 percent equity interest as a general partner. Once More With Feeling generated $304,900 of ordinary business income for 1997. Page 1 of the partnership's Form 1065 is shown as Exhibit 9–3.

Partnerships frequently recognize items of income or gain and incur expenses or losses that don't relate to ordinary business operations. For example, a partnership might invest excess cash in marketable securities that pay dividends and interest. The partnership might recognize a gain or loss on the sale of one of these securities. Or the partnership could make a cash contribution to a local charity. These items are not included in the calculation of ordinary business income or loss. Instead, they are reported on Schedule K of Form 1065 and allocated to the partners for inclusion on the partners' returns.[31] These **separately stated items** retain their tax character as they pass through to the partners.[32]

> ***Separately Stated Items.***   For several years, the Once More With Feeling partnership has invested any excess cash in a mutual fund. During 1997, the partnership received a $1,680 dividend from the fund. The partnership made a $2,500 donation to the United Way during 1997. Neither the dividend nor the donation was included in the computation of the partnership's ordinary income. As a 60 percent partner, Tom Owen was allocated a $1,008 share of the dividend and a $1,500 share of the donation. Because these shares retained their tax character, Mr. Owen reported his share of the dividend as investment income (instead of business income) and his share of the donation as a personal charitable contribution (instead of a business expense) on his 1997 Form 1040.

---

[30]If partnership income is allocated to a partner that is a passthrough entity (another partnership, LLC, or S corporation), the income is passed through again until it is finally allocated to a taxable entity (an individual or corporation).

[31]More specifically, Reg. §1.702-1(a)(8)(ii) explains that each partner must be able to take into account separately his or her distributive share of any partnership item that results in an income tax liability different from that which would result if the item were not accounted for separately.

[32]§702(b).

EXHIBIT 9–3

Form **1065**		U.S. Partnership Return of Income		OMB No. 1545-0099	

Department of the Treasury
Internal Revenue Service

For calendar year 1997, or tax year beginning .... , 1997, and ending .... , 19 .... .
▶ **See separate instructions.**

1997

A Principal business activity	Use the IRS label. Otherwise, please print or type.	Name of partnership ONCe MoRe with Feeling	D Employer identification number
Retail Sales			81 7138419
B Principal product or service		Number, street, and room or suite no. If a P.O. box, see page 10 of the instructions.	E Date business started
Furniture		1012 East Main	1990
C Business code number		City or town, state, and ZIP code	F Total assets (see page 10 of the instructions)
3970		Widner, Kentucky 40506	$ N/a

G Check applicable boxes: (1) ☐ Initial return (2) ☐ Final return (3) ☐ Change in address (4) ☐ Amended return
H Check accounting method: (1) ☐ Cash (2) ☒ Accrual (3) ☐ Other (specify) ▶ ....
I Number of Schedules K-1. Attach one for each person who was a partner at any time during the tax year ▶ ....3...............

Caution: *Include only trade or business income and expenses on lines 1a through 22 below. See the instructions for more information.*

Income

1a	Gross receipts or sales	**1a**	1,117,300		
b	Less returns and allowances.	**1b**	21,000	**1c**	1,096,300
2	Cost of goods sold (Schedule A, line 8)			**2**	599,700
3	Gross profit. Subtract line 2 from line 1c.			**3**	496,600
4	Ordinary income (loss) from other partnerships, estates, and trusts *(attach schedule)*. . .			**4**	
5	Net farm profit (loss) *(attach Schedule F (Form 1040))*			**5**	
6	Net gain (loss) from Form 4797, Part II, line 18.			**6**	
7	Other income (loss) *(attach schedule)*			**7**	
8	**Total income (loss)**. Combine lines 3 through 7			**8**	496,600

Deductions (see page 11 of the instructions for limitations)

9	Salaries and wages (other than to partners) (less employment credits)			**9**	73,200
10	Guaranteed payments to partners			**10**	
11	Repairs and maintenance			**11**	17,900
12	Bad debts			**12**	8,800
13	Rent			**13**	23,200
14	Taxes and licenses			**14**	11,750
15	Interest			**15**	7,300
16a	Depreciation (if required, attach Form 4562)	**16a**	3,600		
b	Less depreciation reported on Schedule A and elsewhere on return	**16b**		**16c**	3,600
17	Depletion **(Do not deduct oil and gas depletion.)**			**17**	
18	Retirement plans, etc.			**18**	
19	Employee benefit programs			**19**	
20	Other deductions *(attach schedule)* professional Fees 2,150 advertising 6,200 utilities 14,000 insurance 5,600 supplies 18,000			**20**	45,950
21	**Total deductions.** Add the amounts shown in the far right column for lines 9 through 20 .			**21**	191,700

22	**Ordinary income (loss)** from trade or business activities. Subtract line 21 from line 8 . .			**22**	304,900

Please Sign Here

Under penalties of perjury, I declare that I have examined this return, including accompanying schedules and statements, and to the best of my knowledge and belief, it is true, correct, and complete. Declaration of preparer (other than general partner or limited liability company member) is based on all information of which preparer has any knowledge.

▶ Signature of general partner or limited liability company member		▶ Date	

Paid Preparer's Use Only	Preparer's signature ▶		Date	Check if self-employed ▶ ☐	Preparer's social security no.
	Firm's name (or yours if self-employed) and address ▶			EIN ▶	
				ZIP code ▶	

For Paperwork Reduction Act Notice, see separate instructions.   Cat. No. 11390Z   Form **1065** (1997)

Tax Consequences to Partners

Objective 6
Differentiate between a partner's distributive share of partnership income and cash flow from the partnership.

Distributive Shares and Cash Flows.   After the close of its taxable year, a partnership issues a Schedule K-1 (Partner's Share of Income, Credits, Deductions, etc.) to each partner. Schedule K-1 provides detailed information concerning the partner's **distributive share** of the partnership's ordinary income or loss from its business activities and all separately stated items. The schedule tells individual partners how and where to include each item on their tax return. For instance, a partner's distributive share of ordinary income or loss is reported on Schedule E of Form 1040.

Partners must pay tax on their distributive share of partnership income, regardless of the cash flow from the partnership during the year. In an extreme case, partners may decide to retain all available cash in the partnership business; as a result, each partner must find another source of funds to pay the tax on his distributive share of partnership income. Alternatively, partners may decide to withdraw just enough cash from the business to pay their tax liabilities. Another possibility is that the partners withdraw all the cash generated by the business for personal consumption. The important point is that the cash flow is irrelevant in determining the partners' tax liability on their partnership's business income.

> ***Partnership Schedule K-1.***   Each partner in Once More With Feeling received a Schedule K-1 reporting that partner's distributive share of ordinary business income, dividend income, and charitable donation for 1997. Tom Owen's Schedule K-1 is shown as Exhibit 9–4. Based on the information on this schedule, Mr. Owen included $182,940 (60 percent of the partnership's $304,900 business income) and $1,008 (60 percent of the partnership's $1,680 dividend income) in his 1997 taxable income. He included a $1,500 donation (60 percent of the $2,500 partnership donation) in his total charitable contributions for the year.[33] According to Line 22 of Schedule K-1, the partnership distributed $150,000 cash to Mr. Owen during 1997. This cash flow from the business is irrelevant to the computation of Mr. Owen's 1997 taxable income.

Guaranteed Payments.   The personal involvement of individual partners in the business operated by their partnership can vary greatly across partners. Limited partners, by definition, do not actively participate in the day-to-day operation of the business and, at most, may take part in major management decisions. General partners may have different levels of participation; some may be sporadically involved, while others may devote 100 percent of their workweek to the business.

Partners who contribute their time and talent to the partnership on a continuous basis expect to be compensated for their work. These partners typically receive a special allocation of income based on the value of the personal service rendered to the business. This compensatory allocation is called a **guaranteed payment** and usually is distributed to the recipient in the form of regular cash payments throughout the year.

Guaranteed payments to partners are analogous to the salaries paid to employees of the partnership. The partnership deducts guaranteed payments in computing ordinary income, and partners report guaranteed payments as ordinary income.[34] However, partners can't be employees of their partnerships any more than individuals can be employees of their sole proprietorships. Because a guaranteed payment is not a salary, neither the partnership nor the partner pays the FICA payroll tax on the payment. Nor does the partnership withhold any federal income tax from the payment. If a partner is entitled to a monthly guaranteed payment of $10,000, that partner receives a $10,000 cash distribution. At the end of the year, the partnership does not issue a Form W-2 to the partner. Instead, the total guaranteed payments are reported as an ordinary income item on the partner's Schedule K-1.

---

[33]The tax consequences of personal charitable contributions are discussed in Chapter 16.
[34]§707(c).

EXHIBIT 9–4

SCHEDULE K-1 (Form 1065)	Partner's Share of Income, Credits, Deductions, etc.	OMB No. 1545-0099
Department of the Treasury Internal Revenue Service	► See separate instructions. For calendar year 1997 or tax year beginning , 1997, and ending , 19	1997

Partner's identifying number ► 497-45-9058   Partnership's identifying number ► 81 : 1138419

Partner's name, address, and ZIP code	Partnership's name, address, and ZIP code
Tom G. Owen 330 Aspen Lane Widner, Kentucky 40506	Once More With Feeling 1012 East Main Widner, Kentucky 40506

A This partner is a ☒ general partner ☐ limited partner
☐ limited liability company member

B What type of entity is this partner? ► *individual*

C Is this partner a ☒ domestic or a ☐ foreign partner?

D Enter partner's percentage of:

	(i) Before change or termination	(ii) End of year
Profit sharing	60 %	60 %
Loss sharing	60 %	60 %
Ownership of capital	60 %	60 %

E IRS Center where partnership filed return: Cincinnati, OH

F Partner's share of liabilities (see instructions):
Nonrecourse . . . . $ 42,000
Qualified nonrecourse financing . $ ....
Other . . . . $ ....

G Tax shelter registration number . ► ....

H Check here if this partnership is a publicly traded partnership as defined in section 469(k)(2) . . . . ☐

I Check applicable boxes: (1) ☐ Final K-1 (2) ☐ Amended K-1

J Analysis of partner's capital account:

(a) Capital account at beginning of year	(b) Capital contributed during year	(c) Partner's share of lines 3, 4, and 7, Form 1065, Schedule M-2	(d) Withdrawals and distributions	(e) Capital account at end of year (combine columns (a) through (d))
25,000		182,448	(150,000)	57,448

		(a) Distributive share item		(b) Amount	(c) 1040 filers enter the amount in column (b) on:
Income (Loss)	**1**	Ordinary income (loss) from trade or business activities . . .	**1**	182,940	See page 6 of Partner's Instructions for Schedule K-1 (Form 1065).
	2	Net income (loss) from rental real estate activities	**2**		
	3.	Net income (loss) from other rental activities	**3**		
	4	Portfolio income (loss):			
	a	Interest	**4a**		Sch. B, Part I, line 1
	b	Dividends . *mutual fund*	**4b**	1,008	Sch. B, Part II, line 5
	c	Royalties	**4c**		Sch. E, Part I, line 4
	d	Net short-term capital gain (loss)	**4d**		Sch. D, line 5, col. (f)
	e	Net long-term capital gain (loss):			
		(1) 28% rate gain (loss)	**e(1)**		Sch. D, line 12, col. (g)
		(2) Total for year.	**e(2)**		Sch. D, line 12, col. (f)
	f	Other portfolio income (loss) *(attach schedule)*	**4f**		Enter on applicable line of your return.
	5	Guaranteed payments to partner	**5**		See page 6 of Partner's Instructions for Schedule K-1 (Form 1065).
	6	Net section 1231 gain (loss) (other than due to casualty or theft):			
	a	28% rate gain (loss)	**6a**		
	b	Total for year.	**6b**		
	7	Other income (loss) *(attach schedule)*	**7**		Enter on applicable line of your return.
Deductions	**8**	Charitable contributions (see instructions) *(attach schedule)* . .	**8**	1,500	Sch. A, line 15 or 16
	9	Section 179 expense deduction.	**9**		See page 7 of Partner's Instructions for Schedule K-1 (Form 1065).
	10	Deductions related to portfolio income *(attach schedule)* . . .	**10**		
	11	Other deductions *(attach schedule)*.	**11**		
Credits	**12a**	Low-income housing credit:			
		(1) From section 42(j)(5) partnerships for property placed in service before 1990	**a(1)**		Form 8586, line 5
		(2) Other than on line 12a(1) for property placed in service before 1990	**a(2)**		
		(3) From section 42(j)(5) partnerships for property placed in service after 1989	**a(3)**		
		(4) Other than on line 12a(3) for property placed in service after 1989	**a(4)**		
	b	Qualified rehabilitation expenditures related to rental real estate activities	**12b**		See page 8 of Partner's Instructions for Schedule K-1 (Form 1065).
	c	Credits (other than credits shown on lines 12a and 12b) related to rental real estate activities.	**12c**		
	d	Credits related to other rental activities	**12d**		
	13	Other credits	**13**		

For Paperwork Reduction Act Notice, see Instructions for Form 1065.   Cat. No. 11394R   Schedule K-1 (Form 1065) 1997

Self-Employment Income. Individual general partners are considered to be self-employed. Consequently, any guaranteed payments plus their distributive share of ordinary business income are net earnings from self-employment subject to SE tax.[35] Limited partners are not considered self-employed and are not required to pay self-employment tax on their distributive share of ordinary income.[36]

---

[35]§1402(a).
[36]§1402(a)(13).

EXHIBIT 9–4

(concluded)

Schedule K-1 (Form 1065) 1997   Page **2**

	(a) Distributive share item		(b) Amount	(c) 1040 filers enter the amount in column (b) on:
Investment Interest	**14a** Interest expense on investment debts	**14a**		Form 4952, line 1
	b (1) Investment income included on lines 4a, 4b, 4c, and 4f . .	**b(1)**		See page 8 of Partner's Instructions for Schedule K-1 (Form 1065).
	(2) Investment expenses included on line 10.	**b(2)**		
Self-employment	**15a** Net earnings (loss) from self-employment	**15a**	*182,940*	Sch. SE, Section A or B
	b Gross farming or fishing income.	**15b**		See page 9 of Partner's Instructions for Schedule K-1 (Form 1065).
	c Gross nonfarm income.	**15c**		
Adjustments and Tax Preference Items	**16a** Depreciation adjustment on property placed in service after 1986	**16a**		
	b Adjusted gain or loss	**16b**		See page 9 of Partner's Instructions for Schedule K-1 (Form 1065) and Instructions for Form 6251.
	c Depletion (other than oil and gas)	**16c**		
	d (1) Gross income from oil, gas, and geothermal properties . .	**d(1)**		
	(2) Deductions allocable to oil, gas, and geothermal properties	**d(2)**		
	e Other adjustments and tax preference items *(attach schedule)*	**16e**		
Foreign Taxes	**17a** Type of income ▶			Form 1116, check boxes
	b Name of foreign country or possession ▶			
	c Total gross income from sources outside the United States *(attach schedule)*	**17c**		Form 1116, Part I
	d Total applicable deductions and losses *(attach schedule)* .	**17d**		
	e Total foreign taxes (check one): ▶ ☐ Paid ☐ Accrued . .	**17e**		Form 1116, Part II
	f Reduction in taxes available for credit *(attach schedule)* . .	**17f**		Form 1116, Part III
	g Other foreign tax information *(attach schedule)*	**17g**		See Instructions for Form 1116.
Other	**18** Section 59(e)(2) expenditures: a Type ▶			See page 9 of Partner's Instructions for Schedule K-1 (Form 1065).
	b Amount	**18b**		
	19 Tax-exempt interest income	**19**		Form 1040, line 8b
	20 Other tax-exempt income.	**20**		See page 9 of Partner's Instructions for Schedule K-1 (Form 1065).
	21 Nondeductible expenses	**21**		
	22 Distributions of money (cash and marketable securities) . . .	**22**	*150,000*	
	23 Distributions of property other than money	**23**		
	24 Recapture of low-income housing credit:			
	a From section 42(j)(5) partnerships	**24a**		Form 8611, line 8
	b Other than on line 24a.	**24b**		
Supplemental Information	**25** Supplemental information required to be reported separately to each partner *(attach additional schedules if more space is needed):*			

⊛

Self-Employment Income.   Refer to page 2 of Mr. Owen's Schedule K-1 from the Once More With Feeling partnership (Exhibit 9–4). Line 15(a) shows that Mr. Owen's $182,940 distributive share of the partnership's business income represents net earnings from self-employment. Mr. Owen must report this amount on a Schedule SE and compute his 1997 SE tax accordingly.

Comprehensive Example.   To summarize our discussion of the tax consequences of operating a business as a partnership, consider the case of the ABC Partnership. This business is owned by three individuals, general partners A and B and limited partner C. The partnership agreement specifies that A and B are each allocated 40 percent of partnership profit or loss, while C is allocated 20 percent. Partner A works full time managing the business, while Partner B devotes about 800 hours a year to the business. During 1997, A and B received monthly guaranteed payments of $3,000 and $1,100, respectively. These were the only cash distributions made by the partnership during the year. The ABC Partnership generated $140,000 of ordinary business income *before* deducting the guaranteed payments. It also earned $3,300 of interest income on an investment in a mutual fund. These income items were allocated to each partner and reported on their Schedule K-1s as follows:

Partnership ABC 1997 Schedule K-1s

	Partner A	Partner B	Partner C	Total
Guaranteed payments	$36,000	$13,200	$ –0–	$ 49,200
Ordinary business income				
($140,000 – $49,200)	36,320	36,320	18,160	90,800
Total ordinary income	$72,320	$49,520	$18,160	$140,000
Interest income	1,320	1,320	660	3,300
Net earnings from self-employment	$72,320	$49,520	$ –0–	

The partners included their respective shares of ordinary income and interest income in their 1997 taxable income. Partners A and B paid self-employment tax on their net earnings from self-employment. If Partner A is in a 28 percent marginal tax bracket and Partners B and C are in a 31 percent marginal tax bracket, their after-tax cash flows with respect to the partnership are computed as follows:

Partnership ABC Cash Flows

		Partner A		Partner B		Partner C
Guaranteed payments		$ 36,000		$ 13,200		$ –0–
SE tax[37]		(10,047)		(6,997)		–0–
Income tax:						
Ordinary income	$72,320		$49,520		$ 18,160	
Interest income	1,320		1,320		660	
One-half SE tax	(5,024)		(3,499)		–0–	
Taxable income	$68,616		$47,341		$ 18,820	
	.28		.31		.31	
		(19,212)		(14,676)		(5,834)
After-tax cash flow		$ 6,741		$ (8,473)		$(5,834)

---

[37]Self-employment tax liability for 1997 based on 92.35 percent of net earnings from self-employment. See fn. 20.

Partner A had a modest positive cash flow with respect to the partnership business, while Partners B and C had negative cash flows. The cash flow information reflects the fact that the three partners paid tax on 1997 partnership income that they did not withdraw as cash from the business during the year.

Adjusting the Basis of a Partnership Interest

Objective 7
Adjust the basis in a partnership interest to reflect the information reported on the partner's Schedule K-1.

When a partner pays tax on partnership income but does not receive a cash distribution of that income, the partner is making an additional investment in the partnership—an investment that the partner is entitled to recover tax free at some future date. When a partner receives a cash distribution from the partnership, the distribution is a nontaxable return of investment.[38] These increases and decreases in the investment are captured as positive or negative year-end adjustments to the tax basis in the partner's interest in the partnership.[39] Let's continue our comprehensive example involving Partners A, B, and C to illustrate these adjustments.

Partnership ABC Basis Adjustments for 1997. The following table shows the adjustments to each partner's basis in his interest in the ABC Partnership for 1997:[40]

	Partner A	Partner B	Partner C
Adjusted basis at beginning of year	$ 35,000	$ 60,000	$100,000
Increased by:			
Total ordinary income	72,320	49,520	18,160
Interest income	1,320	1,320	660
Decreased by:			
Cash distributions (guaranteed payments)	(36,000)	(13,200)	–0–
Adjusted basis at end of year	$ 72,640	$ 97,640	$118,820

When a partnership generates an ordinary business loss or incurs a separately stated loss, each partner is allocated a distributive share of the loss to include in the computation of taxable income. Such loss allocations represent a decrease in the partner's investment in the partnership that is captured as a negative basis adjustment. This year-end adjustment is made *after* any adjustments for income items or cash distributions.[41]

To illustrate the negative basis adjustment for losses, assume that in 1998, the ABC Partnership generated a $50,000 operating loss *before* deducting a $36,000 guaranteed payment to Partner A and a $13,200 guaranteed payment to Partner B. The partnership earned $2,400 of interest income and recognized a $19,600 capital loss on the sale of mutual fund shares. These items were allocated to each partner and reported on their Schedule K-1s as follows:

---

[38] §731(a) and §733. If a partner receives a cash distribution that exceeds the partner's basis, the excess distribution is recognized as a capital gain.

[39] §705(a). Basis is also increased for a partner's distributive share of tax-exempt income.

[40] This example and all subsequent examples of basis adjustments ignore any changes in partnership debt included in the partner's basis.

[41] Reg. §1.705-1(a). Basis is also decreased for a partner's distributive share of any nondeductible expense.

Partnership ABC 1998 Schedule K-1s

	Partner A	Partner B	Partner C	Total
Guaranteed payments	$ 36,000	$ 13,200	$ –0–	$ 49,200
Ordinary business loss				
($50,000 + $49,200)	(39,680)	(39,680)	(19,840)	(99,200)
Net ordinary loss	$ (3,680)	$(26,480)	$(19,840)	$(50,000)
Interest income	960	960	480	2,400
Capital loss	(7,840)	(7,840)	(3,920)	(19,600)
Net earnings from self-employment	$ (3,680)	$(26,480)	$ –0–	

Partnership ABC Basis Adjustments for 1998.   The following table shows the adjustments to each partner's basis in his interest in the ABC Partnership for 1998:

	Partner A	Partner B	Partner C
Adjusted basis at beginning of year	$ 72,640	$ 97,640	$118,820
Increased by:			
Interest income	960	960	480
Decreased by:			
Cash distributions (guaranteed payments)	(36,000)	(13,200)	–0–
Net ordinary loss	(3,680)	(26,480)	(19,840)
Capital loss	(7,840)	(7,840)	(3,920)
Adjusted basis at end of year	$ 26,080	$ 51,080	$ 95,540

Objective 8
Apply the basis limitation rule to determine the current year deduction for distributive shares of partnership loss.

Basis Limitation on Loss Deductions.   As a general rule, partners recognize their distributive share of partnership losses in the current year. In the preceding example, each partner deducted his share of ABC's ordinary business loss in the computation of 1998 taxable income.[42] Similarly, each partner deducted his share of ABC's capital loss, subject to the capital loss limitation.[43] The tax law provides that partners can recover their entire basis in a partnership in the form of tax deductions but cannot deduct losses in excess of basis.[44] In other words, the basis in an intangible partnership interest can never fall below zero, just as the basis in tangible business property can never be depreciated below zero. If a partner's distributive share of loss exceeds the basis in his partnership interest, the partner carries the excess loss forward indefinitely and can deduct it in any year in which sufficient basis in the partnership interest is restored.

---

[42]This example assumes that the §465 at-risk limitation and the §469 passive activity loss limitation are inapplicable for all three partners.
[43]See the discussion of the capital loss limitation in Chapter 7.
[44]§704(d).

Suppose that in 1999, the ABC Partnership had a very bad year. The partnership business generated a $160,000 operating loss, and Partners A and B did not receive any guaranteed payments. The partnership did earn $3,000 of interest income from its mutual fund.

Partnership ABC 1999 Schedule K-1s

	Partner A	*Partner B*	*Partner C*	*Total*
Guaranteed payments	$ –0–	$ –0–	$ –0–	$ –0–
Ordinary loss	(64,000)	(64,000)	(32,000)	(160,000)
Interest income	1,200	1,200	600	3,000
Net earnings from self-employment	$(64,000)	$(64,000)	$ –0–	

The ordinary loss that each partner may deduct in 1999 is limited to the adjusted basis in his partnership interest immediately before the negative basis adjustment for the loss.

Partnership ABC Basis Adjustments for 1999

	Partner A	*Partner B*	*Partner C*
Adjusted basis at beginning of year	$ 26,080	$ 51,080	$ 95,540
Increased by:			
Interest income	1,200	1,200	600
	$ 27,280	$ 52,280	$ 96,140
Decreased by:			
Deductible ordinary loss	(27,280)	(52,280)	(32,000)
Adjusted basis at end of year	$ –0–	$ –0–	$ 64,140
Summary:			
Ordinary loss for 1999	$(64,000)	$(64,000)	$(32,000)
Deductible loss	27,280	52,280	32,000
Loss carryforward	$(36,720)	$(11,720)	$ –0–

All three partners include their distributive share of interest income in 1999 taxable income. Partners A and B can deduct only $27,280 and $52,280 of their distributive shares of ordinary loss. Partner C, who had sufficient basis, can deduct his entire $32,000 distributive share. Partners A and B must restore basis in their partnership interests before they can deduct their loss carryforwards from 1999. Partners A and B could create basis by investing more money in the partnership. If the business is failing (as the $160,000 operating loss suggests), the partners could lose any additional investment. In such case, Partners A and B would make the mistake of throwing good money after bad to secure a tax deduction. Of course, if the partnership business becomes profitable again, the distributive shares of future income will create basis against which Partners A and B can deduct their loss carryforwards.

Let's complete our comprehensive example by examining one more year of the ABC Partnership's business operation. In 2000, the partnership generated $89,000 of ordinary business income *before* deducting an $18,000 guaranteed payment to Partner A and a $6,600 guaranteed payment to Partner B. The partnership earned $3,400 of interest income and recognized a $11,000 capital gain on the sale of mutual fund shares. These items were allocated to each partner and reported on their Schedule K-1s as follows:

Partnership ABC 2000 Schedule K-1s

	Partner A	Partner B	Partner C	Total
Guaranteed payments	$18,000	$ 6,600	$ –0–	$24,600
Ordinary business income ($89,000 – $24,600)	25,760	25,760	12,880	64,400
Total ordinary income	$43,760	$32,360	$12,880	$89,000
Interest income	1,360	1,360	680	3,400
Capital gain	4,400	4,400	2,200	11,000
Net earnings from self-employment	$43,760	$32,360	$ –0–	

Partnership ABC Basis Adjustments for 2000

	Partner A	Partner B	Partner C
Adjusted basis at beginning of year	$ –0–	$ –0–	$64,140
Increased by:			
Ordinary income	43,760	32,360	12,880
Interest income	1,360	1,360	680
Capital gain	4,400	4,400	2,200
Decreased by:			
Cash distributions (guaranteed payments)	(18,000)	(6,600)	–0–
	$ 31,520	$ 31,520	$79,900
Loss carryforward from 1999	(31,520)	(11,720)	–0–
Adjusted basis at end of year	$ –0–	$ 19,800	$79,900

The 2000 distributive shares of ordinary income, interest income, and capital gain created $31,520 of basis for Partner A, which allowed him to deduct an equivalent amount of loss carryforward from 1999. The distributive shares created enough basis for Partner B to allow him to deduct his entire 1999 loss carryforward. Consequently, Partner A will include only $12,240 and Partner B will include only $20,640 of ordinary partnership income (plus their entire distributive shares of interest and capital gain) in their 2000 taxable income. Partner A still has a $5,200 loss carryforward into subsequent years.

2000 Ordinary Partnership Income			
	Partner A	*Partner B*	*Partner C*
Ordinary income	$ 43,760	$ 32,360	$12,880
Loss carryforward from 1999	(31,520)	(11,720)	–0–
Ordinary taxable income	$ 12,240	$ 20,640	$12,880
Loss carryforward	$ (5,200)		

Limited Liability Companies

Objective 9
Explain how limited liability companies (LLCs) are treated for federal tax purposes.

The co-owners of a business often prefer the partnership form to the corporate form because partnership income is not subject to an entity level tax but is taxed only once at the owner level. The partnership form also provides the greatest flexibility in the manner in which business income can be divided among the co-owners. The major disadvantage of the partnership form is the unlimited personal liability of the co-owners (general partners) for the business's debt obligations.

Over the last decade, every state (and the District of Columbia) has enacted legislation authorizing an innovative form of business organization called a **limited liability company (LLC).** An LLC is an unincorporated legal entity owned by one or more *members.* In contrast to a partnership, every member of an LLC has limited liability for the LLC's debts and obligations. This limited liability protects even those members who are actively involved in the LLC's business operation. State laws do not limit the number of members nor the type of entity that can be a member in an LLC. Thus, an LLC's membership can include individuals, partnerships, corporations, and even other LLC's.

Under Treasury regulations that classify business entities for federal tax purposes (the check-the-box regulations), an LLC with two or more members is classified as a partnership.[45] Consequently, business income earned by an LLC is not taxed at the entity level but passes through to the various members. An LLC with only one member (i.e., one owner) is classified as a sole proprietorship for federal tax purposes.

LLCs offer business owners as terrific combination: a single, owner-level tax on business income and limited liability for business debt. Moreover, this new form of business is not subject to many of the bothersome tax rules and restrictions that apply to S corporations (our next topic). As a result, LLCs are an attractive option for newly formed business ventures. However, because LLCs are such a new form of business, many tax questions concerning their operation have yet to be resolved. Business owners and their advisers must consider this element of uncertainty in making the decision to organize an LLC.

Subchapter S Corporations

Before the advent of LLCs, entrepreneurs who wanted to organize their business to avoid both the corporate income tax and the risk of unlimited personal liability had only one choice: the subchapter S corporation. This form of business organization is legally a

---

[45]Reg. §301.7701-3(b)(1). Under this regulation, an LLC can elect to be classified as a corporation for federal tax purposes. There is no obvious reason why a domestic LLC would ever make such an election.

corporate entity, organized as such under state law.[46] A predominant characteristic of corporations is the limited liability of their shareholders. If a corporate business gets into financial trouble and can't satisfy its debt obligations, the corporate creditors have no claim against the personal assets of the shareholders. Thus, the shareholders' risk is limited to their investment in the corporation.

For federal tax purposes, a **subchapter S corporation** is a passthrough entity; the corporation's business income is allocated and taxed directly to the corporation's shareholders.[47] The statutory rules providing for this passthrough are almost identical to the partnership rules. The ordinary income or loss generated by an S corporation's business is reported on page 1 of Form 1120S (U.S. Income Tax Return for an S Corporation). This income or loss is allocated among the shareholders based on their percentage ownership of the corporation's outstanding stock.[48]

> ***Once More with Feeling—S Corporation.*** Refer back to our earlier example involving Mr. Tom Owen and his antique furniture restoration business. Let's change the facts again by assuming that Mr. Owen and his two co-owners incorporated the business as Once More With Feeling, Inc., which is an S corporation for federal tax purposes. Tom Owen owns 60 percent of the S corporation's outstanding stock. Once More With Feeling, Inc. generated $304,900 of ordinary business income for 1997. Page 1 of the S corporation's Form 1120 is shown as Exhibit 9–5.

If an S corporation recognizes items of income, gain, deduction, or loss that don't relate to ordinary business operations, these items are separately stated on Schedule K of Form 1120S and retain their tax character as they flow through to the shareholders.

> ***Separately Stated Items.*** Once More With Feeling, Inc. received a $1,680 dividend and made a $2,500 United Way donation during 1997. (These are the two separately stated items included in the earlier partnership example.) Assume also that the S corporation recognized a $3,710 gain on the sale of mutual funds shares acquired four years ago. None of these items is included in the computation of the corporation's ordinary business income.

Eligible Corporations

Objective 10
Determine if a corporation is eligible to be an S corporation.

Individuals who organize their business as an S corporation must form a domestic corporation eligible to be an S corporation for federal tax purposes. Eligibility is based on three statutory requirements:[49]

---

[46]While a partnership must have at least two co-owners as partners, a corporation may be owned by a single shareholder.

[47]§1363(a) and §1366.

[48]§1377(a).

[49]§1361. Corporations that have been operating as regular corporations and that meet the eligibility requirements can be converted to S corporations. Converted S corporations are subject to several troublesome corporate level taxes that don't apply to original S corporations. See §1374 and §1375.

EXHIBIT 9–5

Form **1120S**	**U.S. Income Tax Return for an S Corporation**	OMB No. 1545-0130
Department of the Treasury Internal Revenue Service	▶ Do not file this form unless the corporation has timely filed Form 2553 to elect to be an S corporation. ▶ See separate instructions.	**1997**

For calendar year 1997, or tax year beginning _____ , 1997, and ending _____ , 19 _____

A. Date of election as an S corporation **1990**	Use IRS label. Other-wise, please print or type.	Name **Once More With Feeling, Inc.**	C Employer Identification number **81 : 1138419**
B Business code no. (see Specific Instructions) **3970**		Number, street, and room or suite no. (If a P.O. box, see page 9 of the instructions.) **1012 East Main**	D Date incorporated **1990**
		City or town, state, and ZIP code **Widner, Kentucky 40506**	E Total assets (see Specific Instructions) $ **N/a**

F Check applicable boxes: (1) ☐ Initial return   (2) ☐ Final return   (3) ☐ Change in address   (4) ☐ Amended return
G Enter number of shareholders in the corporation at end of the tax year . . . . ▶ **3**

Caution: Include only trade or business income and expenses on lines 1a through 21. See the instructions for more information.

Income

1a	Gross receipts or sales **1,117,300**	b Less returns and allowances **21,000**	c Bal ▶	1c **1,096,300**
2	Cost of goods sold (Schedule A, line 8)			2 **599,700**
3	Gross profit. Subtract line 2 from line 1c			3 **496,600**
4	Net gain (loss) from Form 4797, Part II, line 18 (attach Form 4797) .			4
5	Other income (loss) (attach schedule)			5
6	Total income (loss). Combine lines 3 through 5 . . . . . . ▶			6 **496,600**

Deductions (see page 10 of the instructions for limitations)

7	Compensation of officers			7
8	Salaries and wages (less employment credits)			8 **73,200**
9	Repairs and maintenance			9 **17,900**
10	Bad debts			10 **8,800**
11	Rents			11 **23,200**
12	Taxes and licenses			12 **11,750**
13	Interest			13 **7,300**
14a	Depreciation (if required, attach Form 4562)	14a **3,600**		
b	Depreciation claimed on Schedule A and elsewhere on return .	14b		
c	Subtract line 14b from line 14a			14c **3,600**
15	Depletion (Do not deduct oil and gas depletion.)			15
16	Advertising			16 **6,200**
17	Pension, profit-sharing, etc., plans			17
18	Employee benefit programs . . . *utilities 14,000 Supplies 18,000*			18
19	Other deductions (attach schedule) *prof. fees 2,150, insurance 5,600*			19 **39,750**
20	Total deductions. Add the amounts shown in the far right column for lines 7 through 19 . ▶			20 **191,700**
21	Ordinary income (loss) from trade or business activities. Subtract line 20 from line 6 . .			21 **304,900**

Tax and Payments

22	Tax: a Excess net passive income tax (attach schedule) . .	22a	
	b Tax from Schedule D (Form 1120S)	22b	
	c Add lines 22a and 22b (see pages 12 and 13 of the instructions for additional taxes) . . .		22c
23	Payments: a 1997 estimated tax payments and amount applied from 1996 return	23a	
	b Tax deposited with Form 7004	23b	
	c Credit for Federal tax paid on fuels (attach Form 4136) . . .	23c	
	d Add lines 23a through 23c		23d
24	Estimated tax penalty. Check if Form 2220 is attached . . . . ▶☐		24
25	Tax due. If the total of lines 22c and 24 is larger than line 23d, enter amount owed. See page 4 of the instructions for depository method of payment . . . . ▶		25
26	Overpayment. If line 23d is larger than the total of lines 22c and 24, enter amount overpaid ▶		26
27	Enter amount of line 26 you want: Credited to 1998 estimated tax ▶ _____ Refunded ▶		27

Please Sign Here

Under penalties of perjury, I declare that I have examined this return, including accompanying schedules and statements, and to the best of my knowledge and belief, it is true, correct, and complete. Declaration of preparer (other than taxpayer) is based on all information of which preparer has any knowledge.

▶ _____   _____   _____
   Signature of officer   Date   Title

Paid Preparer's Use Only	Preparer's signature ▶		Date		Check if self-employed ☐	Preparer's social security number
	Firm's name (or yours if self-employed) and address ▶				EIN ▶	
					ZIP code ▶	

For Paperwork Reduction Act Notice, see the separate instructions.   Cat. No. 11510H   Form **1120S** (1997)

- Only individuals, estates, and certain trusts may be shareholders of the corporation; nonresident aliens (persons who are neither citizens nor permanent residents of the United States) cannot be shareholders. This requirement ensures that the S corporation's business income will be taxed at the individual rates.
- The number of shareholders is limited to 75. A married couple is considered a single shareholder, even if both spouses own shares.
- The corporation can have only a single class of outstanding common stock; an S corporation cannot include preferred stock in its capital structure. Because of this requirement, shares of stock in an S corporation carry identical rights with respect to corporate profits and assets. This requirement is not violated if the outstanding shares have different voting rights.

There are no statutory limits on an S corporation's invested capital, volume of sales, or number of employees. Consequently, S corporations can be very large corporate enterprises.

Subchapter S Election.   An eligible corporation becomes an S corporation by the unanimous election of its shareholders.[50] The election is permanent for the life of the corporation unless shareholders owning a majority of the stock agree to revoke the election.[51] The election is immediately terminated if the corporation loses its eligibility. For example, if a shareholder sells shares to a partnership (an ineligible shareholder), the corporation's S status ends on the day of the sale.[52] The corporation is no longer a passthrough entity but is subject to the corporate income tax.

The inadvertent termination of an S election can be a disaster for shareholders whose long-term financial strategies are based on the assumption that the future income from their business will be taxed directly to them. Moreover, the shareholders of a corporation that has lost its S election generally cannot make a new election for five years.[53] Because of the potential severity of the problem, the tax law provides a relief measure. If shareholders discover that an inadvertent termination has occurred and take immediate steps to correct the situation (repurchase the corporate stock from the partnership in our example), the IRS may allow the original S election to remain in effect.[54]

Tax Basis in S Corporation Stock.   A shareholder's initial tax basis in stock issued by an S corporation equals the cash plus the adjusted basis of any property transferred to the corporation in exchange for the stock.[55] When an S corporation incurs a debt, no shareholder has any personal liability for the debt. Accordingly, no S corporation debt is included in a shareholder's stock basis, even if the shareholder has personally guaranteed the debt.

> ***Basis in S Corporation Stock.***   Three individuals each contributed $10,000 cash to form a new S corporation. Each individual received 100 shares of the corporation's 300 shares of outstanding stock. The S corporation immediately borrowed $24,000 from a local bank, which the corporation used to purchase equipment and supplies. The bank required the shareholders to personally guarantee repayment of the loan. Each shareholder's basis in her S corporation stock is $10,000: the initial cash contribution to the corporate entity.

Tax Consequences to Shareholders

After the close of its taxable year, an S corporation issues a Schedule K-1 (Shareholder's Share of Income, Credits, Deductions, etc.) to each shareholder. The S corporation Schedule K-1 serves the same function as a partnership Schedule K-1; it informs

---

[50]§1362(a). To document consent to the election, each shareholder must file a signed Form 2553 with the IRS.
[51]§1362(d)(1).
[52]§1362(e)(1).
[53]§1362(g).
[54]§1362(f).
[55]The transfer of property to a corporation in exchange for stock in that corporation is nontaxable to the transferors if they have at least 80 percent control of the corporation immediately after the transfer. §351.

the owners of their respective shares of business income or loss as well as their shares of any separately stated item.

The S corporation shareholders must incorporate the information on Schedule K-1 into their individual tax returns. Thus, the income from the corporation's business is taxed at the individual rates and the shareholders pay the tax. The cash (if any) that the shareholders received from the corporation during the year is irrelevant in determining their tax liability on the S corporation's income.

S Corporation Schedule K-1.   Each shareholder in Once More With Feeling, Inc. received a Schedule K-1 reporting that shareholder's proportionate share of ordinary business income, dividend income, charitable donation, and capital gain. As a 60 percent shareholder, Tom Owen was allocated a $182,940 share of the S corporation's ordinary business income, a $1,008 share of the dividend, a $1,500 share of the donation, and a $2,226 share of the capital gain. Mr. Owen's 1997 Schedule K-1 reflecting these passthrough items in shown as Exhibit 9–6. According to line 20 of Schedule K-1, the S corporation distributed $150,000 cash to Mr. Owen during 1997. This cash from the business is irrelevant to the computation of Mr. Owen's 1997 taxable income.

Salary Payments.   A significant difference between partnerships and S corporations is that an individual who owns stock in an S corporation can be an employee of the corporation. Shareholders who work in the corporate business receive salaries as compensation for their service. Both the corporation and the employee pay the FICA payroll tax on the salary, and the corporation withholds federal income tax. At the end of the year, the corporation issues a Form W-2 to any shareholder/employee, as well as a Schedule K-1. S corporation shareholders are not considered to be self-employed. Therefore, their allocated share of business income is not subject to self-employment tax.

Adjusting the Basis of S Corporation Stock

Shareholders make positive and negative adjustments to the basis in their S corporation stock in much the same way as partners adjust the basis in their partnership interests.[56] Specifically, shareholders increase the basis in their S corporation stock by their share of the corporation's income and gain for the year. Conversely, shareholders reduce stock basis by their share of any corporate losses. Cash distributed by an S corporation to a shareholder is a nontaxable return of investment that reduces stock basis.[57]

Objective 11
Contrast the basis limitation rule for S corporation losses with the basis limitation rule for partnership losses.

Basis Limitation on Loss Deductions.   The tax law imposes the same general limitation on S corporation losses as it does on partnership losses: such losses are currently deductible only to the extent of the owner's investment. Under the limitation rule for S corporations, a shareholder can deduct an amount of loss that reduces his stock basis to zero.[58] If a shareholder also has basis in any debt obligation from the S corporation, the shareholder may deduct additional loss to reduce the debt basis to zero.[59] In other

[56]§1367(a).
[57]Salary payments to shareholder/employees have no effect on stock basis. If a shareholder receives a cash distribution that exceeds stock basis, the excess distribution is recognized as a capital gain. §1368.
[58]§1366(d)(1)(A).
[59]§1366(d)(1)(B).

EXHIBIT 9–6

SCHEDULE K-1 (Form 1120S)	Shareholder's Share of Income, Credits, Deductions, etc.	OMB No. 1545-0130
Department of the Treasury Internal Revenue Service	► See separate instructions. For calendar year 1997 or tax year beginning _____ , 1997, and ending _____ , 19 ___	**1997**

Shareholder's identifying number ► *497-45-9058*   Corporation's identifying number ► _____

Shareholder's name, address, and ZIP code	Corporation's name, address, and ZIP code
Tom G. Owen *330 Aspen Lane* *Widner, Kentucky 40506*	*Once More With Feeling Inc.* *1012 East Main* *Widner, Kentucky 40506*

A Shareholder's percentage of stock ownership for tax year (see Instructions for Schedule K-1) . . . . . . ► *60* %
B Internal Revenue Service Center where corporation filed its return ► *Cincinnati, OH*
C Tax shelter registration number (see instructions for Schedule K-1) . . . . ►
D Check applicable boxes: **(1)** ☐ Final K-1   **(2)** ☐ Amended K-1

		(a) Pro rata share items		(b) Amount	(c) Form 1040 filers enter the amount in column (b) on:
Income (Loss)	1	Ordinary income (loss) from trade or business activities . . .	1	*182,940*	See pages 4 and 5 of the Shareholder's Instructions for Schedule K-1 (Form 1120S).
	2	Net income (loss) from rental real estate activities	2		
	3	Net income (loss) from other rental activities	3		
	4	Portfolio income (loss):			
	a	Interest	4a		Sch. B, Part I, line 1
	b	Dividends . *mutual fund*	4b	*1,008*	Sch. B, Part II, line 5
	c	Royalties	4c		Sch. E, Part I, line 4
	d	Net short-term capital gain (loss)	4d		Sch. D, line 5, col. (f)
	e	Net long-term capital gain (loss):			
		(1) 28% rate gain (loss)	e(1)		Sch. D, line 12, col. (g)
		(2) Total for year	e(2)	*2,226*	Sch. D, line 12, col. (f)
	f	Other portfolio income (loss) *(attach schedule)*	4f		*(Enter on applicable line of your return.)*
	5	Net section 1231 gain (loss) (other than due to casualty or theft):			
	a	28% rate gain (loss)	5a		See Shareholder's Instructions for Schedule K-1 (Form 1120S).
	b	Total for year	5b		
	6	Other income (loss) *(attach schedule)*	6		*(Enter on applicable line of your return.)*
Deductions	7	Charitable contributions *(attach schedule)*	7	*1,500*	Sch. A, line 15 or 16
	8	Section 179 expense deduction	8		See page 6 of the Shareholder's Instructions for Schedule K-1 (Form 1120S).
	9	Deductions related to portfolio income (loss) *(attach schedule)* .	9		
	10	Other deductions *(attach schedule)*	10		
Investment Interest	11a	Interest expense on investment debts	11a		Form 4952, line 1
	b	**(1)** Investment income included on lines 4a, 4b, 4c, and 4f above	b(1)		See Shareholder's Instructions for Schedule K-1 (Form 1120S).
		(2) Investment expenses included on line 9 above	b(2)		
Credits	12a	Credit for alcohol used as fuel	12a		Form 6478, line 10
	b	Low-income housing credit:			
		(1) From section 42(j)(5) partnerships for property placed in service before 1990.	b(1)		Form 8586, line 5
		(2) Other than on line 12b(1) for property placed in service before 1990	b(2)		
		(3) From section 42(j)(5) partnerships for property placed in service after 1989	b(3)		
		(4) Other than on line 12b(3) for property placed in service after 1989	b(4)		
	c	Qualified rehabilitation expenditures related to rental real estate activities	12c		
	d	Credits (other than credits shown on lines 12b and 12c) related to rental real estate activities	12d		See pages 6 and 7 of the Shareholder's Instructions for Schedule K-1 (Form 1120S).
	e	Credits related to other rental activities.	12e		
	13	Other credits	13		

For Paperwork Reduction Act Notice, see the Instructions for Form 1120S.   Cat. No. 11520D   Schedule K-1 (Form 1120S) 1997

words, an individual's investment in an S corporation that can be recovered through tax deductions includes both his equity investment and his investment as a corporate creditor.

EXHIBIT 9–6

(concluded)

Schedule K-1 (Form 1120S) (1997)		Page **2**
(a) Pro rata share items	**(b) Amount**	**(c)** Form 1040 filers enter the amount in column (b) on:

Adjustments and Tax Preference Items

14a Depreciation adjustment on property placed in service after 1986	**14a**	See page 7 of the Shareholder's Instructions for Schedule K-1 (Form 1120S) and Instructions for Form 6251
b Adjusted gain or loss	**14b**	
c Depletion (other than oil and gas)	**14c**	
d (1) Gross income from oil, gas, or geothermal properties	**d(1)**	
(2) Deductions allocable to oil, gas, or geothermal properties	**d(2)**	
e Other adjustments and tax preference items *(attach schedule)*	**14e**	

Foreign Taxes

15a Type of income ▶		Form 1116, Check boxes
b Name of foreign country or U.S. possession ▶		
.c Total gross income from sources outside the United States *(attach schedule)*	**15c**	Form 1116, Part I
d Total applicable deductions and losses *(attach schedule)*	**15d**	
e Total foreign taxes (check one): ▶ ☐ Paid ☐ Accrued	**15e**	Form 1116, Part II
f Reduction in taxes available for credit *(attach schedule)*	**15f**	Form 1116, Part III
g Other foreign tax information *(attach schedule)*	**15g**	See Instructions for Form 1116

Other

16 Section 59(e)(2) expenditures: **a** Type ▶		See Shareholder's Instructions for Schedule K-1 (Form 1120S).
b Amount	**16b**	
17 Tax-exempt interest income	**17**	Form 1040, line 8b
18 Other tax-exempt income	**18**	See page 7 of the Shareholder's Instructions for Schedule K-1 (Form 1120S).
19 Nondeductible expenses	**19**	
20 Property distributions (including cash) other than dividend distributions reported to you on Form 1099-DIV	**20** *150,000*	
21 Amount of loan repayments for "Loans From Shareholders"	**21**	
22 Recapture of low-income housing credit:		
a From section 42(j)(5) partnerships	**22a**	Form 8611, line 8
b Other than on line 22a	**22b**	

23 Supplemental information required to be reported separately to each shareholder *(attach additional schedules if more space is needed)*:	

....

....

Nondeductible S Corporation Loss. Ms. J owns 25 percent of the outstanding stock of SGM Inc., a calendar year S corporation. At the beginning of 19X7, Ms. J's basis in her stock was $81,000. Two years ago, Ms. J loaned the corporation $30,000 and received a written note from SGM as evidence of the debt. For 19X7, SGM incurred a $500,000 operating loss. Although Ms. J's Schedule K-1 reflects a $125,000 passthrough loss, Ms. J can deduct only $111,000 of the loss on her 19X7 Form 1040:

	Stock Basis	Note Basis
Beginning of year	$ 81,000	$ 30,000
Deductible loss	(81,000)	(30,000)
End of year	$ –0–	$ –0–
Nondeductible loss	$(14,000)	

Ms. J's $14,000 nondeductible loss is carried forward into subsequent years. If she creates basis by making an additional investment in SGM Inc. as either a shareholder or a creditor, she can deduct the loss to the extent of the additional basis. Alternatively, if SGM generates future income, Ms. J's share of this income will first increase the basis in her note to its original face value of $30,000.[60] Any additional income will increase her stock basis. Ms. J can then deduct her loss carryforward to the extent of her restored basis.

Basis Restoration.   Ms. J's 25 percent share of SGM's income for 19X8 is $50,000. The corporation made no cash distributions during the year. Her income allocation restores Ms. J's investment basis and allows her to deduct her $14,000 loss carryforward on her 19X8 return:

	Stock Basis	Note Basis
Beginning of year	$ –0–	$ –0–
Allocated share of income:		
Increase to note basis		30,000
Increase to stock basis	20,000	
	$ 20,000	$30,000
Loss carryforward from 19X7	(14,000)	
End of year	$ 6,000	$30,000

Because of the deduction for her loss carryforward, Ms. J's 19X8 taxable income includes only $36,000 of ordinary income from SGM Inc.

If SGM Inc. were to repay the $30,000 loan from Ms. J before her basis in the note was restored to its face amount, the repayment is considered an amount realized on the sale of the note. Because the note is a capital asset to Ms. J, she would recognize a capital gain equal to the excess of the repayment over her basis.[61]

Conclusion

In this chapter, we've examined the tax consequences of organizing and operating a business as a sole proprietorship or as a passthrough entity. In the case of a sole proprietorship, the business income is included in the owner's taxable income for the year and is subject to tax at the individual rates. In the case of a general or limited partnership, LLC, or S corporation, the business income is allocated to the owners of the entity. The income is taxed directly to the partners, members, or shareholders at their marginal rate. Many taxpayers deliberately use these organizational forms to avoid paying an entity level tax on business income. This tax strategy is one of the topics covered in Chapter 11. Before we can evaluate this strategy, we must examine the tax consequences of organizing and operating a business as a regular corporation.

---

[60]§1367(b)(2).

[61]§1232 and Rev. Rul. 64-162, 1964-1 CB 304.

Key Terms

Distributive share 225	Partnership 222
Employee payroll tax 219	Passthrough entity 224
Employer identification number 219	Self-employment (SE) tax 221
Employer payroll tax 219	Separately stated item 224
General partnership 222	Sole proprietorship 214
Guaranteed payment 226	Subchapter S corporation 235
Limited liability company (LLC) 234	
Limited partnership 222	

Questions and Problems for Discussion

1. Can a sole proprietorship be described as a passthrough entity?

2. Mrs. L owns and operates a business as a sole proprietor. Near the end of her taxable year, she is evaluating a new opportunity that would generate $25,000 of additional income for her business. What marginal tax rate should Mrs. L use to compute the tax cost of this opportunity?

3. During the current year, Mr. P's sole proprietorship generated a $17,000 net loss. Discuss the extent to which Mr. P can use this loss as an net operating loss carryback deduction.

4. During the current year, Firm Q, a cash basis taxpayer, remitted $26,800 of FICA payroll tax to the federal government. However, the firm deducted only $13,400 FICA tax on its income tax return. Can you explain this apparent inconsistency?

5. Critique the employee payroll tax on the normative standards of (*a*) convenience to the taxpayer and (*b*) vertical equity.

6. Define the tax base for the self-employment tax. When do sole proprietors pay the self-employment tax to the federal government?

7. Why is only half of a sole proprietor's self-employment tax liability deductible in the computation of taxable income?

8. Mrs. G, Mr. Y, and Ms. N want to become co-owners of a business enterprise. Compare the extent of their personal liability for the debts incurred by the enterprise if they organize as:
   a. A general partnership.
   b. A limited partnership.
   c. An LLC.
   d. An S corporation.

9. Why are certain items of income, gain, deduction, or loss separately stated on a partnership or an S corporation tax return?

10. Four years ago, Mr. JB purchased 1,000 shares of UPF Inc. for $10,000. These shares represent a 30 percent equity interest in the corporation. UPF is an S corporation for federal tax purposes. During the current year, UPF defaulted on a $120,000 debt to a major creditor.
    a. To what extent can the creditor demand repayment of the debt from Mr. JB?
    b. Would your answer change if UPF is a partnership in which Mr. JB is a 30 percent general partner?
    c. Would your answer change if UPF is a partnership in which Mr. JB is a 30 percent limited partner?
    d. Would your answer change if UPF is an LLC in which Mr. JB is a 30 percent member?

11. Mr. Y sold his interest in a business to an unrelated purchaser for $500,000 cash. How does Mr. Y determine his adjusted basis for purposes of computing gain or loss realized on the sale if the business is:
    a. A sole proprietorship.
    b. A partnership.
    c. An S corporation.

Application Problems

1. During the current year, Ms. W's sole proprietorship, the WW Bookstore, generated $120,000 of net profit. In addition, Ms. W recognized a $17,000 gain on the sale of business furniture and shelving, all of which was recaptured as ordinary income. The savings account in which Ms. W temporarily invests her excess working capital earned $3,900 of interest income.
   a. Which of these income items are subject to self-employment tax?
   b. Assuming that Ms. W's self-employment tax for the year is $11,300 and her marginal income tax rate is 31 percent, compute the after-tax income from her bookstore activities.

2. Mr. C, a self-employed consultant, uses a room of his home as a business office, which meets all tax law requirements for a home office. This room represents 10 percent of the home's square footage. During the current year, Mr. C incurred the following expenses in connection with his home:

Home mortgage interest	$12,980
Property tax on residence	2,200
Homeowner's insurance	1,475
Utilities	2,100
Furnace repairs	300

   Mr. C purchased the home in 1992 for $225,000. For MACRS depreciation purposes, he allocated $185,000 to the building and $40,000 to the land.
   a. If Mr. C's gross business income for the year exceeded his operating expenses by $75,000, compute his net profit for the year.
   b. If Mr. C's gross business income for the year exceeded his operating expenses by $1,800, compute his net profit for the year.

3. Ms. JC recently graduated from veterinary school and opened her own professional practice. For the current year, her net profit from the practice was $32,000. Compute Ms. JC's after-tax income from her practice assuming:

   a. Her self-employment tax for the year is $4,522 and her marginal income tax rate is 28 percent.
   b. What percentage of the federal tax burden on Ms. JC's business income is represented by the self-employment tax?

4. Ms. J is a self-employed attorney. During the current year, the net profit from her practice was in excess of $300,000. Consequently, she is in the 39.6 percent tax bracket. Early in the year, Ms. J hired Mr. B as a paralegal and paid him a salary of $33,000.
   a. Compute the employer payroll tax on Mr. B's salary.
   b. In addition to the employer payroll tax, Ms. J paid $400 of unemployment tax on Mr. B's salary. Mr. B's salary and related taxes reduced Ms. J's net earnings from self-employment, thereby saving $962 in self-employment tax. Based on these facts, compute the after-tax cost of the salary payment to Ms. J.

5. KLMN Partnership's financial records show the following:

Gross receipts from sales	$ 670,000
Cost of goods sold	(460,000)
Operating expenses	(96,800)
Business meals and entertainment	(6,240)
Realized loss on equipment sale	(13,500)
Charitable contribution	(1,500)
Distributions to partners	(10,000)

   The cash distributions helped the partners pay their previous year individual tax liabilities. Based on these facts, compute KLMN's ordinary business income for the year.

6. Refer to the facts in the preceding problem. Mr. T is a 10 percent general partner in the KLMN Partnership. During the year, Mr. T received a $1,000 cash distribution from KLMN to help him pay his previous year tax liability.

a. Compute Mr. T's distributive shares of partnership ordinary income and separately stated items.

b. If Mr. T's adjusted basis in his interest in KLMN was $45,000 at the beginning of the year, compute his adjusted basis at the end of the year. Assume that partnership debt did not change during the year.

c. How would your basis computation change if the partnership debt at the end of the year was $28,000 more than its debt at the beginning of the year?

7. Early in the year, individual X and individual Y formed the XY General Partnership. X contributed $50,000 cash, and Y contributed depreciable business assets with a fair market value of $50,000. Y's adjusted basis in these assets was only $10,000. The partnership agreement provides that partnership income and loss will be divided equally between the two partners. Partnership operations for the year generated a $42,000 loss. Based on these facts, how much loss may each partner deduct currently and what basis will each partner have in her interest at the beginning of the next year?

8. AV Inc. is a member of an LLC that is a partnership for federal tax purposes. During the current year, the corporation received a Schedule K-1 from the LLC reporting a $1,200 distributive share of capital loss and a $4,000 distributive share of Section 1231 gain. During the year, AV Inc. recognized a $5,000 capital loss on the sale of marketable securities and a $17,000 Section 1231 loss on the sale of business equipment. Based on these facts, what effect do the partnership losses have on AV's taxable income?

9. Mr. B and Ms. G are equal general partners in the BG Partnership. Mr. B manages the partnership business and receives a monthly guaranteed payment of $4,000. Ms. G does not perform any services for the partnership and therefore receives no guaranteed payment.

a. If the BG Partnership generated $75,000 ordinary income before consideration of the monthly payment to Mr. B, calculate each partner's distributive share of this income.

b. Calculate each partner's net earnings from self-employment.

c. How would your calculations change if the partnership's ordinary income before consideration of Mr. B's guaranteed payment was only $32,000?

10. Mrs. Z owns a 60 percent general interest in the YZ Partnership. At the beginning of 19X8, Mrs. Z's adjusted basis in her partnership interest was $95,000. For 19X8, the partnership generated a $210,000 business loss, earned $14,600 of dividend and interest income on its investments, and recognized a $6,200 gain on the sale of a capital asset. The partnership made no distributions during 19X8 to its partners and had no debt.

a. Based on these facts, how much of her distributive share of YZ's loss can Mrs. Z deduct on her 19X8 return?

b. Compute Mrs. Z's adjusted basis in her partnership interest at the end of 19X8.

c. Would your answers change if Mrs. Z received a $5,000 cash distribution from the partnership during 19X8?

11. Refer to the facts in the preceding problem. In 19X9, YZ Partnership generated $7,000 of ordinary business income and $18,000 of dividend and interest income. The partnership made no distributions during 19X9. At the end of the year, the partnership had $21,000 of debt.

a. Based on these facts, how much partnership income will Mrs. Z report on her 19X9 return?

b. Compute Mrs. Z's adjusted basis in her partnership interest at the end of 19X9.

12. At the beginning of 19X1, Ms. P purchased a 20 percent interest in the PPY Partnership for $20,000. Ms. P's Schedule K-1 for 19X1 reported that her share of the partnership debt at year-end was $12,000 and her distributive share of 19X1 ordinary loss was $28,000. On January 1, 19X2, Ms. P sold her interest to another partner for $2,000 cash.

a. What amount of her distributive share of PPY's 19X1 loss can Ms. P deduct on her 19X1 tax return?

b. Based on these facts, compute Ms. P's recognized gain on the sale of her partnership interest.

13. In 19X7, Mr. L paid $15,000 for 5 percent of the stock in BLS Inc., an S corporation. In November 19X7, he loaned $8,000 to the corporation. BLS gave Mr. L a promissory note to repay the debt on demand and to pay interest at 11 percent a year. For 19X7, BLS generated a $600,000 operating loss.
    a. What amount of Mr. L's allocated share of the loss can he deduct on his 19X7 individual tax return?
    b. Compute Mr. L's basis in his BLS stock and his BLS note at the beginning of 19X8.

14. Refer to the facts in the preceding example. For 19X8, BLS generated $408,000 of ordinary business income.
    a. What amount of Mr. L's allocated share of this income is included in his 19X8 taxable income?
    b. Compute Mr. L's basis in his BLS stock and his BLS note at the beginning of 19X9.
    c. How would your answers change if the corporation's 19X8 ordinary business income was only $220,000?

15. Refer to the facts in part *c* of the preceding problem. In July 19X9, BLS repaid its $8,000 debt to Mr. L. What are the consequences of the loan repayment to Mr. L?

Issue Recognition Problems

Identify the tax issue or issues suggested by the following situations and state each issue in the form of a question.

1. Mrs. E has operated a sole proprietorship for six years. Over this period of time, net profit has been stable and Mrs. E's marginal tax rate has been a constant 28 percent. Mrs. E projects that her profit next year will be the same as this year. Consequently, she estimates her tax cost for next year based on a 28 percent rate. Late in the current year, Mrs. E's husband graduated from law school and accepted an excellent offer of employment from a local firm.

2. Mr. J is a full-time employee of B Inc. and also operates a sole proprietorship. In the current year, Mr. J's salary from B Inc. was $70,000 and his net earnings from self-employment were $60,000.

3. Mrs. V is a concert violinist. She maintains a business office in one room of her personal residence. She often spends the entire day in the office, either practicing with one of her three violins, listening to tapes of her performances, or working on her business correspondence. Mrs. V gives approximately 25 concerts a year in cities around the world. Consequently, she is away from home and living in hotels for days, and even weeks, at a time.

4. Mr. T is a professional writer who maintains his business office in one room of his personal residence. The office contains Mr. T's desk, filing cabinets, personal computer and printer, copying machine, phone system, and fax machine. It also contains his family's library of video tapes, music CDs, popular novels, and the set of encyclopedias used by his three children for their schoolwork.

5. Ms. Y owns a 15 percent limited interest in the AF Partnership, which uses a calendar year for tax purposes. On April 12 of the current year, Mrs. Y sold her entire interest to the R Corporation; consequently, she was a partner for only 102 days during the year. For the current year, AF generated $845,000 of ordinary business income and recognized a $70,000 capital gain on the November 13 sale of marketable securities.

6. Nine years ago, Mr. L paid $20,000 for a 2 percent limited interest in a very profitable partnership. Every year Mr. L has properly included his distributive share of partnership income in taxable income. In the current year, Mr. L sold his interest to an unrelated party for $80,000 and included a $60,000 gain recognized on sale in his taxable income.

7. The 18 partners in the KT Limited Partnership unanimously voted to convert their partnership to an LLC because of the attractive legal characteristics of this new type of passthrough entity. To make the conversion, each partner will exchange his interest in KT for a membership interest in the newly formed LLC.

8. Four individual investors are evaluating the tax cost of operating their business as an S corporation. They assume that the corporation itself will pay no tax on its annual business income. They plan to incorporate the business in a state with a 7 percent corporate income tax.

9. Mr. Y just sold his entire 20 percent interest in the DK Partnership to an unrelated purchaser for $7,500. Mr. Y's adjusted basis in the interest was zero, and he had a $12,000 ordinary loss carryforward from DK's previous tax year.

10. Mrs. P received her Schedule K-1 from an LLC which reported a $12,000 distributive share of ordinary loss and a $1,900 distributive share of capital loss. Mrs. P's adjusted basis in her LLC interest before consideration of these losses was $6,200.

11. Mr. M, a cash basis individual, is a general partner in the MNOP Partnership. Both Mr. M and MNOP use a calendar year for tax purposes. According to the partnership agreement, MNOP pays a $10,000 guaranteed payment to Mr. M on the last day of every calendar month. However, because of a bookkeeping error, the partnership did not pay (and Mr. M did not receive) his final guaranteed payment for 19X8 until January 10, 19X9.

12. Mr. D received his Schedule K-1 from DES Inc., an S corporation, which showed allocations of $8,900 of tax-exempt interest and $4,700 of ordinary loss. Mr. D's adjusted basis in his stock before consideration of these allocations was $2,000.

13. Mr. and Mrs. W are the only shareholders in WW Inc., an S corporation. During the year, the corporation paid $21,000 to the caterers who provided food for the couple's silver wedding anniversary celebration.

14. The 100 shares of NS Inc.'s outstanding stock are owned by seven unrelated individuals. NS Inc. has an valid S corporation election in effect. Late in the year, one individual announces to his fellow shareholders that he intends to give his NS shares to his son-in-law, who is a citizen and resident of Canada.

15. BR Inc. owns a 20 percent interest in a limited partnership. All the other partners are individual shareholders in BR. During the current year, BR sold land to the partnership for use in the partnership's business activity. BR's basis in the land was $400,000, and the selling price was $275,000. This price was determined by an independent appraiser.

16. The JKL Partnership uses the calendar year for tax purposes. For 19X8, the partnership generated $1 million of ordinary business income. Corporation L, a 10 percent limited partner in JKL, uses a fiscal year ending June 30 as its tax year.

17. FG Inc. owned a 3 percent limited interest in a partnership that has been unprofitable for several years. The partnership recently informed its partners that they must contribute additional capital if the partnership business is to survive. FG Inc. decided not to contribute any more money to the partnership and sent written notification to the general partner relinquishing its equity interest. On the date of notification, FG's adjusted basis in the interest was $15,500.

Tax Planning Cases

1. Mr. and Mrs. JW own and operate a restaurant business as a sole proprietorship. The couple has decided to purchase $85,000 of new kitchen equipment for the restaurant. They also want to buy two new automobiles—one for their personal use and one for their 19-year-old son's personal use. The two automobiles will cost $65,000. Mr. and Mrs. JW have $70,000 in a savings account that they can use to partially fund these purchases. They intend to borrow the additional $80,000 from a local bank at 10 percent annual interest. What steps should the couple take to minimize the after-tax cost of the borrowed funds?

2. Mr. E and Mrs. F began a new partnership venture at the beginning of 19X8. They each contributed $30,000 cash to the EF General Partnership in exchange for a 50 percent partnership interest. The partnership immediately borrowed $50,000 from an unrelated creditor, a debt that the partnership does not have to repay for two years. In November 19X8, the partners estimate with reasonable certainty that the partnership's operating loss for 19X8 will be $100,000. However, the partnership business has started to generate positive cash flow, and the partners also estimate that EF will be profitable in 19X9, perhaps generating as much as $125,000 of ordinary income. In anticipation of these future profits, Mr. E and Mrs. F are considering withdrawing their initial cash contributions from the partnership before Christmas. Mr. and Mrs. F are both in the 39.6 percent tax bracket for 19X8. Based on these facts, what tax planning advice can you offer the partners?

10   The Corporate Taxpayer

Learning Objectives

After studying this chapter, you should be able to:

1. Identify the four primary legal characteristics of the corporate form of business organization.
2. Compute the corporate dividends-received deduction.
3. Prepare a Schedule M-1 reconciliation of a corporation's book and tax income.
4. Compute the regular tax on corporate taxable income.
5. Explain why the value of a tax credit is greater than the value of a deduction of the same amount.
6. Discuss the purpose of the alternative minimum tax.
7. Describe the corporate tax payment and return filing requirements.
8. Explain why corporate profits distributed as dividends to shareholders are double taxed.
9. Identify the circumstances in which the incidence of the corporate tax falls on consumers, suppliers, labor, or capital.

In the previous chapter, we studied business organizations that are not taxable entities: sole proprietorships, partnerships, limited liability companies (LLCs), and S corporations. These organizations serve as conduits of income to the business owners who are taxed directly on such income. In Chapter 10, we turn to the rules governing the taxation of business income earned by corporations.[1] In contrast to sole proprietorships and passthrough entities, corporations are taxpayers in their own right. The tax liability on corporate profits is determined without reference to the tax situations of the shareholders who own the corporation.

Chapter 10 begins with a discussion of the legal characteristics of the corporate form of organization. The discussion then shifts to the computation of taxable income on the corporate tax return and the reconciliation of that income with the corporation's financial statement income. The corporate tax rate structure is examined, the function of tax credits is explained, and the alternative minimum tax is

---

[1]Corporations for which a subchapter S election is not in effect are referred to as regular corporations or C corporations. In this text, any reference to a corporation means the taxable, rather than the passthrough, variety.

introduced. The chapter concludes by analyzing the tax consequences of distributions of earnings to corporate investors.

Legal Characteristics of Corporations

Objective 1
Identify the four primary legal characteristics of the corporate form of business organization.

A corporation is an entity formed under state law to conduct a business operation. Ownership of the entity is embodied in the outstanding shares of the corporation's stock. **Closely held corporations** are privately owned by a relatively small number of shareholders. These shareholders are often personally involved in the operation of the corporate business, and their ownership is stable over time. In contrast, the stock in **publicly held corporations** is traded on established securities markets such as the New York Stock Exchange or NASDAQ. The ownership of these corporations may be diffused over thousands of shareholders and may change on a daily basis.

Many entrepreneurs operate in the corporate form because of the advantageous legal and financial characteristics of this business entity. Perhaps the most important legal characteristic is the **limited liability** of shareholders. The rights of corporate creditors and other claimants extend only to corporate assets and not to the personal assets of the corporation's owners. While this characteristic protects shareholders against many types of business risk, the scope of the protection is narrowed by two facts. First, financial institutions may refuse to lend money to small, closely held corporate businesses unless the shareholders personally guarantee repayment of the debt. Second, licensed professionals, such as physicians, attorneys, and CPAs, cannot avoid personal liability for their negligence or misconduct by operating in the corporate form. Even if they offer their services to the public as employees of a personal service corporation, professionals typically must protect themselves by carrying malpractice insurance.

A second attractive characteristic is the **unlimited life** of a corporation. Under state and federal law, corporations are persons separate and distinct from their owners. Consequently, their legal existence is not affected by changes in the identity of their shareholders. This characteristic gives corporations the vitality and stability so conducive to the operation of a successful enterprise. A related characteristic is the **free transferability** of equity interests in corporations. Stock in publicly traded corporations is a highly liquid asset; investors can buy and sell this stock with maximum convenience and minimal transaction cost. Because their stock is traded on an established securities market, public corporations have access to millions of potential investors and can raise large amounts of venture capital.

In the context of closely held corporations, the characteristic of free transferability may be conspicuously absent. Shareholders are often family members or colleagues who want to protect the ownership of the business from outsiders. To this end, the stock in closely held corporations is usually subject to some type of **buy-sell agreement.** The agreement may prohibit the owner from disposing of the stock without approval of the other shareholders, or it may restrict the owner from transferring the stock to anyone but the existing shareholders or the corporation itself.

A fourth characteristic of the corporate form of business organization is **centralized management.** Unlike a sole proprietorship or a general partnership, the owners of a corporation do not directly supervise the business. Instead, managerial decisions are made by a board of directors appointed by and acting on behalf of the shareholders and by the officers of the corporation who are hired by the board of directors. This characteristic is crucial to the efficient management of publicly traded corporations with thousands of shareholders. In contrast, the shareholders of closely held corporations usually serve on the board of directors and frequently are employed as corporate officers. In such case, the characteristic of centralized management has little significance.

Affiliated Groups

For various legal, financial, and managerial reasons, a single corporate entity may not be the best organizational form for a multifaceted business enterprise. The enterprise may operate more efficiently if it is compartmentalized into several corporate entities that form an **affiliated group.** Affiliated groups consist of a parent corporation that directly owns 80 percent or more of at least one subsidiary corporation plus all other subsidiaries that are 80 percent owned within the group.[2] Only taxable, domestic corporations are included in an affiliated group. The following diagram illustrates an affiliated group consisting of four corporations:

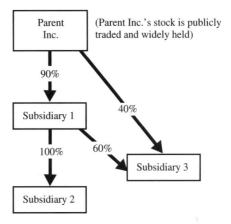

Parent Inc. is the parent corporation of the affiliated group because of its direct 90 percent ownership of Subsidiary 1. Subsidiaries 2 and 3 are also included in the Parent Inc. group because 100 percent of each corporation's outstanding stock is owned within the group.

An affiliated group may consist of just two corporations or a conglomerate with hundreds of subsidiaries. Regardless of its size, the tax law basically regards an affiliated group as a single entity. For instance, affiliated groups may elect to file a **consolidated tax return**—a single return reporting the combined results of the operations of all corporations in the group.[3] The major advantage of consolidated filing is that a net loss generated by one corporation within the group can offset the taxable income generated by other group members.

> ***Consolidated Return Filing.***   Refer to the affiliated group illustrated in the above diagram. For the current year, the separate operations of the group members resulted in the following:

---

[2]§1504 (a)(1).
[3]§1501.

	Net Income (Loss)
Parent Inc.	$ 960,000
Subsidiary 1	(750,000)
Subsidiary 2	225,000
Subsidiary 3	114,000

If the corporations file on a separate basis, Parent Inc., Subsidiary 2, and Subsidiary 3 report their incomes on their respective tax returns and pay tax accordingly. Subsidiary 1 reports a $750,000 net operating loss. This loss would generate an immediate tax benefit only to the extent that Subsidiary 1 could deduct it as a net operating loss (NOL) carryback. If the group files a consolidated return, the taxable income on the return is $549,000 (combined net income and loss for the four members). Consequently, Subsidiary 1's loss generates an immediate tax benefit by reducing the affiliated group's taxable income by $750,000.

Nonprofit Corporations

Many corporations are formed to conduct philanthropic, rather than profit-motivated, activities. As a general rule, these **nonprofit corporations** are nontaxable entities. Specifically, any corporation formed exclusively for "religious, charitable, scientific, testing for public safety, literary, or educational purposes, or to foster national or international amateur sports competition" is exempt from federal income taxation.[4] The IRS is generous in granting tax-exempt status to thousands of organizations devoted to some aspect of the public good. Nonetheless, a tax-exempt corporation that conducts a profitable sideline activity unrelated to its philanthropic purpose may find itself liable for the corporate tax on unrelated business taxable income.[5]

Unrelated Business Taxable Income.   Phi Delta Theta is a national fraternity organized as a tax-exempt corporation. The fraternity published a quarterly magazine *The Scroll* that featured articles concerning the achievements of fraternity members and alumni. The costs of publication were paid from the earnings from an endowment fund. This fund generated over $100,000 of annual investment income. The IRS determined that publication of *The Scroll* was incidental to the educational purpose that was the basis for Phi Delta Theta's tax-exempt status. Consequently, the annual income from the endowment fund was unrelated business income on which the fraternity must pay tax.[6]

---

[4]§501(a) and (c)(3).
[5]§511 and §512.
[6]*Phi Delta Theta Fraternity* v. *Commissioner,* 887 F.2d 1302 (CA-6, 1989).

Computing Corporate Taxable Income

Corporations report their taxable income and calculate the federal tax liability on that income on Form 1120 (U.S. Corporation Income Tax Return). The information on page 1, Form 1120 is essentially the corporation's income statement for tax accounting purposes.

Form 1120.   Movement Plus Inc., a calendar year, accrual basis corporation, operates aerobics and dance studios. The first page of Movement's 1997 Form 1120 is reproduced as Exhibit 10–1. During the year, the corporation recognized $822,000 gross profit from fees and memberships (lines 1a and 3) and $13,800 interest income from short-term investments of excess working capital (line 5). These two items represent Movement Plus total income of $835,800 on line 11. The corporation's deductible operating expenses are listed on lines 12 through 26 and totaled to $510,860 on line 27. Movement Plus had a $6,700 NOL carryforward from 1996 reported as a current year deduction on line 29c. The corporation's 1997 taxable income of $318,240 is reported on line 30.

Corporations are allowed a deduction for charitable contributions made during the year. The annual deduction is limited to 10 percent of taxable income *before* the deduction. Contributions in excess of this limit are carried forward for five years as a deduction against future taxable income.[7]

Limit on Contribution Deduction.   During 1997, Movement Plus Inc. contributed $40,000 to local charities. However, the corporation's deduction for the contribution is limited to $35,360, as shown on line 19 of Form 1120. This limitation is computed as follows:

Total income (line 11)	$835,800
Deductions *excluding* line 19 charitable contribution deduction and *including* NOL deduction	(482,200)
Taxable income *before* charitable contribution deduction	$353,600
	.10
Charitable contribution deduction	$ 35,360

Movement Plus Inc. has a $4,640 contribution carryforward ($40,000 contribution – $35,360 contribution deduction) into 1998.

---

[7]§170(b)(2) and (d)(2). For purposes of this limitation, taxable income is computed without any dividend-received deduction or loss carrybacks into the year.

Exhibit 10–1

Form **1120**		U.S. Corporation Income Tax Return		OMB No. 1545-0123
Department of the Treasury Internal Revenue Service		For calendar year 1997 or tax year beginning .... , 1997, ending .... , 19 ... ▶ Instructions are separate. See page 1 for Paperwork Reduction Act Notice.		**1997**

A Check if a:			Name	*Movement Plus Inc.*	B Employer identification number 28 : 4288317
1 Consolidated return (attach Form 851) ☐		Use IRS label. Other- wise, print or type.	Number, street, and room or suite no. (If a P.O. box, see page 5 of instructions.) *4800 Sun Valley Road*		C Date incorporated *1988*
2 Personal holding co. (attach Sch. PH) ☐			City or town, state, and ZIP code *Albuquerque NM 87131*		D Total assets (see page 5 of instructions) *N/A*
3 Personal service corp. (as defined in Temporary Regs. sec. 1.441-4T— see instructions) ☐					$
E Check applicable boxes:	(1) ☐ Initial return	(2) ☐ Final return	(3) ☐ Change of address		

Income

	1a	Gross receipts or sales *822,000*	b Less returns and allowances			c Bal ▶	1c	*822,000*
	2	Cost of goods sold (Schedule A, line 8)					2	
	3	Gross profit. Subtract line 2 from line 1c					3	*822,000*
	4	Dividends (Schedule C, line 19)					4	
	5	Interest					5	*13,800*
	6	Gross rents					6	
	7	Gross royalties					7	
	8	Capital gain net income (attach Schedule D (Form 1120))					8	
	9	Net gain or (loss) from Form 4797, Part II, line 18 (attach Form 4797)					9	
	10	Other income (see page 6 of instructions—attach schedule) . . .					10	
	11	**Total income.** Add lines 3 through 10 . . . . ▶					11	*835,800*

Deductions (See instructions for limitations on deductions.)

	12	Compensation of officers (Schedule E, line 4)					12	*40,000*
	13	Salaries and wages (less employment credits)					13	*255,100*
	14	Repairs and maintenance					14	*16,900*
	15	Bad debts					15	
	16	Rents					16	*43,300*
	17	Taxes and licenses					17	*24,750*
	18	Interest					18	
	19	Charitable contributions (see page 8 of instructions for 10% limitation) .					19	*35,360*
	20	Depreciation (attach Form 4562)	20	*42,600*				
	21	Less depreciation claimed on Schedule A and elsewhere on return . . .	21a				21b	*42,600*
	22	Depletion					22	
	23	Advertising					23	*12,200*
	24	Pension, profit-sharing, etc., plans					24	
	25	Employee benefit programs					25	
	26	Other deductions (attach schedule) *Insurance 19,250, utilities 21,400*					26	*40,650*
	27	**Total deductions.** Add lines 12 through 26 . . . . ▶					27	*510,860*
	28	Taxable income before net operating loss deduction and special deductions. Subtract line 27 from line 11					28	*324,940*
	29	**Less:** a Net operating loss deduction (see page 9 of instructions) . . .	29a	*6,700*				
		b Special deductions (Schedule C, line 20)	29b				29c	*6,700*

Tax and Payments

	30	**Taxable income.** Subtract line 29c from line 28					30	*318,240*
	31	**Total tax** (Schedule J, line 10)					31	*107,364*
	32	Payments: a 1996 overpayment credited to 1997	32a					
	b	1997 estimated tax payments	32b	*110,000*				
	c	Less 1997 refund applied for on Form 4466	32c	(	d Bal ▶	32d	*110,000*	
	e	Tax deposited with Form 7004				32e		
	f	Credit for tax paid on undistributed capital gains (attach Form 2439) . .				32f		
	g	Credit for Federal tax on fuels (attach Form 4136). See instructions . .				32g		32h	*110,000*
	33	Estimated tax penalty (see page 10 of instructions). Check if Form 2220 is attached . . ▶ ☐					33	
	34	**Tax due.** If line 32h is smaller than the total of lines 31 and 33, enter amount owed . .					34	
	35	**Overpayment.** If line 32h is larger than the total of lines 31 and 33, enter amount overpaid					35	*2,636*
	36	Enter amount of line 35 you want: **Credited to 1998 estimated tax ▶** *2,636* Refunded ▶					36	

Sign Here	Under penalties of perjury, I declare that I have examined this return, including accompanying schedules and statements, and to the best of my knowledge and belief, it is true, correct, and complete. Declaration of preparer (other than taxpayer) is based on all information of which preparer has any knowledge.		
	▶ Signature of officer	Date	▶ Title

Paid Preparer's Use Only	Preparer's signature ▶		Date		Check if self-employed ☐	Preparer's social security number
	Firm's name (or yours if self-employed) and address ▶				EIN ▶	
					ZIP code ▶	

Cat. No. 11450O

The Dividends-Received Deduction

Objective 2
Compute the corporate dividends-received deduction.

The last deduction listed on the first page of Form 1120 (and described on line 29b as a special deduction) is the **dividends-received deduction.**[8] Corporations that receive dividends from other taxable, domestic corporations are entitled to this deduction. The basic dividends-received deduction equals a percentage of the total dividends included in gross income. The percentage depends on the recipient corporation's investment in the corporation paying the dividend, as shown in the following schedule:

[8] §243.

Dividends-Received Deduction

- If the recipient corporation owns *less than 20 percent* of the stock of the paying corporation → the deduction equals 70 percent of the dividends received.

- If the recipient corporation owns *at least 20 percent but less than 80 percent* of the stock of the paying corporation → the deduction equals 80 percent of the dividends received.

- If the recipient corporation owns *80 percent or more* of the stock of the paying corporation → the deduction equals 100 percent of the dividend received.

Dividends-Received Deduction.   ABC Inc. owns 5 percent of the stock of Corporation X, 50 percent of the stock of Corporation Y, and 83 percent of the stock of Corporation Z. The three corporations in which ABC invested are taxable, domestic entities. ABC's gross income includes the following dividends:

Corporation X	$ 24,000
Corporation Y	8,000
Corporation Z	90,000
	$122,000

ABC's dividends-received deduction is $113,200:

Corporation X dividend ($24,000 × 70%)	$ 16,800
Corporation Y dividend ($8,000 × 80%)	6,400
Corporation Z dividend ($90,000 × 100%)	90,000
	$113,200

Because of the dividends-received deduction, only $8,800 of ABC's gross dividend income is included in taxable income. If ABC's marginal tax rate is 35 percent, the tax on this income is $3,080 and the corporation's tax rate on its dividend income is only 2.5 percent ($3,080 ÷ $122,000). This low rate is not as generous as it first may seem. The dividends that ABC included in gross income represent after-tax dollars. In other words, Corporations X, Y, and Z already paid federal income tax on the business earnings distributed as dividends to their investors (including ABC). As we will discuss in a later section of this chapter, ABC's dividends-received deduction simply prevents most of these earnings from being taxed again at the corporate level.

Objective 3
Prepare a Schedule M-1 reconciliation of a corporation's book and taxable income.

Reconciling Book Income and Taxable Income

Because of the many differences between the measurement of income for federal tax purposes and the measurement of income under generally accepted accounting principles (GAAP), the taxable income reported on page 1, Form 1120, is usually not the same as the net income reported on the corporation's financial statements. The corporation must reconcile the two numbers on Schedule M-1, page 4, Form 1120, so that the IRS can see the differences between financial statement income and taxable income. Let's work through an example of this important book/tax reconciliation.

Schedule M-1 Reconciliation.   In 19X6, Company SB, a calendar year, accrual basis corporation, reported $3,430,928 of net income on its audited financial statements and $4,743,800 of taxable income on its Form 1120. The following Schedule M-1 reconciles these numbers.

Schedule M-1	Reconciliation of Income(Loss) per Books With Income per Return (See page 18 of instruction					
1	Net income (loss) per books	3,430,928	7	Income recorded on books this year not included on this return (itemize):		
2	Federal income tax	1,900,872		Tax exempt interest $		
3	Excess of capital losses over capital gains	205,000		*deferred income*		
4	Income subject to tax not recorded on books this year (itemize): *prepaid rent*	81,000		*on like-kind exchange*	700,000	
5	Expenses recorded on books this year not deducted on this return (itemize):		8	Deductions on this return not charged against book income this year (itemize):		
	a Depreciation . . . . . $			a Depreciation . . . . . $ 433,000		
	b Contributions carryover $			b Contributions carryover $		
	c Travel and entertainment $ 246,000 *bad debt expense* 13,000	259,000	9	Add lines 7 and 8	433,000 1,133,000	
6	Add lines 1 through 5	5,876,800	10	Income (line 28, page 1)-line 6 less line 9	4,743,800	

- The corporation's net income per books is entered on line 1, and the federal income tax expense per books is entered on line 2.[9] This expense is not deductible in the computation of taxable income.
- Company SB realized a $205,000 net capital loss on the sale of investment securities and included the loss in the computation of financial statement income. This nondeductible loss is entered on line 3.
- Company SB received $81,000 of prepaid rent that was credited to a liability account as unearned revenues for financial statement purposes. This taxable income is recorded on line 4.
- Company SB incurred $492,000 of meal and entertainment expense. The nondeductible half of this expense is entered on line 5(c).
- Company SB's annual addition to its allowance for bad debts exceeded its actual write-off of uncollectible accounts receivable by $13,000; this nondeductible excess is detailed on line 5.

The total on line 6 is financial statement income increased by (1) taxable income items not included in book income and (2) expense items not deducted on the tax return.

- Company SB realized a $700,000 gain on an exchange of commercial real estate. The exchange involved like-kind properties so the realized gain was not recognized for tax purposes. The deferred gain is entered on line 7.
- Company SB's MACRS depreciation deduction exceeded its depreciation expense per books by $433,000. This excess is reflected on line 8(a).

---

[9]See the discussion of tax expense versus tax payable in Chapter 5.

> The total on line 9 equals (1) book income items not included in taxable income and (2) allowable deductions not reported as expenses for book purposes.
>
> Line 10 is the final number in the reconciliation: taxable income reported on page 1, Form 1120, *before* any NOL deduction and dividends-received deduction. Company SB had neither of these special deductions in 19X6. Consequently, the company paid federal tax based on $4,743,800 of income.

Computing the Regular Corporate Tax

Objective 4

Compute the regular tax on corporate taxable income.

The final section on the first page of Form 1120 (Exhibit 10–1) is labeled "Tax and Payments." After the corporation has computed taxable income, it must calculate the federal tax due on that income. The first step in the calculation is to determine the corporation's regular tax liability, which is based on the following rate schedule:[10]

If Taxable Income Is:		The Tax Is:			Of the Amount Over-
Over-	*But Not Over-*				
$ –0–	$ 50,000			15%	$ –0–
50,000	75,000	$ 7,500	+	25%	50,000
75,000	100,000	13,750	+	34%	75,000
100,000	335,000	22,250	+	39%	100,000
335,000	10,000,000	113,900	+	34%	335,000
10,000,000	15,000,000	3,400,000	+	35%	10,000,000
15,000,000	18,333,333	5,150,000	+	38%	15,000,000
18,333,333		6,416,667	+	35%	18,333,333

Technically, this rate structure is progressive: observe the 15 percent, 25 percent, and 34 percent rates on the first $100,000 of corporate taxable income. The marginal rate increases to 39 percent on taxable income in excess of $100,000 but drops back to 34 percent for taxable income from s$335,000 to $10 million. The additional 5 percent on income between $100,000 and $335,000 is actually a **surtax,** or extra tax, designed to recoup the benefit of the 15 percent and 25 percent rates on the first $75,000 of taxable income. This benefit equals $11,750, computed as follows:

Tax on $75,000 at 34%		$ 25,500
Tax on $50,000 at 15%	$7,500	
Tax on $25,000 at 25%	6,250	
		(13,750)
Benefit of 15% and 25% rates		$ 11,750

---

[10]§11(b)(1).

The maximum 5 percent surtax is $11,750 ($235,000 × 5 percent). Accordingly, corporations with taxable income between $335,000 and $10 million actually pay tax at a flat 34 percent rate.

Regular Tax Calculation.   Corporation M's taxable income is $4 million. Based on the corporate rate schedule, the regular tax liability on this income is $1,360,000.

Taxable income	$4,000,000
	(335,000)
Taxable income in excess of $335,000	$3,665,000
Marginal rate on excess	.34
	$1,246,100
Plus tax on $335,000 (from rate schedule)	113,900
	$1,360,000

Because Corporation M's taxable income is between $335,000 and $10 million, its regular tax liability can be calculated by simply multiplying $4 million by 34 percent.

Corporate taxable income in excess of $10 million is taxed at 35 percent. A second surtax of 3 percent is levied on taxable income from $15 million to $18.33 million. The maximum 3 percent surtax is $100,000 ($3.33 million × 3 percent), which equals the difference between a 34 percent and a 35 percent rate on the first $10 million of taxable income. Because of this second surtax, corporations with taxable income in excess of $18.33 million pay 35 percent of their total taxable income to the federal government.

Regular Tax Calculation.   Corporation R's taxable income is $40 million. Based on the corporate rate schedule, the regular tax liability on this income is $14 million.

Taxable income	$ 40,000,000
	(18,333,333)
Taxable income in excess of $18,333,333	$ 21,666,667
Marginal rate on excess	.35
	$ 7,583,333
Plus tax on $18,333,333 (from rate schedule)	6,416,667
	$ 14,000,000

Because Corporation R's taxable income exceeds $18.33 million, its regular tax liability can be calculated by simply multiplying $40 million by 35 percent.

Personal Service Corporations.   Closely held corporations that are owned by individuals who perform services in the fields of health, law, engineering, architecture, accounting, actuarial science, performing arts, or consulting for the corporation's clientele are denied even the minimal progressivity of the corporate rate schedule. The income earned by these **personal service corporations** is taxed at a flat 35 percent rate.[11]

Tax Credits

Objective 5
Explain why the value of a tax credit is greater than the value of a deduction of the same dollar amount.

A corporation's regular tax liability is offset by any tax credits for which the corporation is eligible. A **tax credit** is a direct reduction in tax liability. As a result, the value of a credit is greater than the value of a deduction of the same amount.

> *Deduction versus Credit.*   JHG Inc.'s taxable income is $600,000, and its regular tax liability (at 34 percent) is $204,000. If the corporation is allowed an additional $50,000 deduction, the tax liability decreases to $187,000 and the tax savings from the deduction is $17,000 (34 percent of $50,000). In comparison, if the corporation is entitled to a $50,000 tax credit, the tax liability decreases to $154,000 and the tax savings from the credit is $50,000.
>
> | | *Deduction* | *Credit* |
> | -------------------------- | ----------- | --------- |
> | Taxable income | $600,000 | $600,000 |
> | Additional deduction | (50,000) | |
> | Recomputed taxable income | $550,000 | $600,000 |
> | | .34 | .34 |
> | Precredit tax | $187,000 | $204,000 |
> | Tax credit | | (50,000) |
> | Recomputed tax liability | $187,000 | $154,000 |

Tax credits are generally nonrefundable, which means they can reduce current year tax liability to zero, but any credit in excess of precredit tax liability does not generate a refund from the Treasury. However, the tax law may provide that an excess credit can be carried back or forward to reduce the corporation's tax liability in a different year.

Because tax credits reduce the regular tax liability on corporate income, they are equivalent to a preferential tax rate. To be eligible for a particular credit, corporations must engage in very specific activities or transactions that Congress believes are worthy of government support. From this perspective, tax credits are instruments of fiscal policy and are enacted by Congress to increase the efficiency of the tax system as an agent of economic change. Currently, the tax law provides a **general business credit,** which is the sum of the following 12 credits for the tax year.[12]

---

[11]§11(b)(2) and §448(d)(2).

[12]§38. The general business credit that a firm can use each year is limited to $25,000 plus 75 percent of the firm's precredit tax liability in excess of $25,000. §38(c). Any amount of unused credit can be carried back 1 year and forward 20 years. §39(a).

- Investment and rehabilitation credit.
- Work opportunity credit.
- Alcohol fuels credit.
- Research credit.
- Low-income housing credit.
- Enhanced oil recovery credit.
- Disabled access credit.
- Renewable electricity production credit.
- Empowerment zone employment credit.
- Indian employment credit.
- Employer social security credit.
- Orphan drug credit.

Most of these credits are narrow in scope and are available to relatively few corporations. Moreover, the list of credits changes as Congress experiments with new credits and discards those that fail to produce the intended behavioral result. To learn how a tax credit can induce a certain corporate behavior, we will look at the mechanics of just one credit.

Rehabilitation Credit

Corporations that renovate or reconstruct commercial buildings originally placed in service before 1936 or buildings certified as historic structures by the U.S. Department of the Interior are entitled to a **rehabilitation credit.**[13] The credit equals 10 percent of the rehabilitation costs of a qualifying commercial building and 20 percent of the rehabilitation costs of a certified historic structure. Congress designed this credit to encourage businesses to undertake urban renewal projects that might be financially unfeasible without the tax savings from the credit.

> **Rehabilitation Credit.**   Corporation QT must locate a suitable facility to house one of its regional offices and has narrowed its search to two buildings. One building is newly constructed and ready for occupancy. The second building was constructed in 1925 and is in need of extensive renovation. The purchase price of the first building is $10 million, while the purchase price of the second building is only $3 million. The corporation estimates that the rehabilitation costs with respect to the second building would be $7.5 million. For tax purposes, the corporation's cost basis in either building ($10 million for the new building or $10.5 million for the old building) can be depreciated over the same 39-year recovery period.
>
> Without the rehabilitation credit, the cost of the new building is less than that of the old building and the company has no reason to invest in the older structure. The credit reduces the cost of the old building to $9,750,000:

---

[13]§47.

Purchase price	$ 3,000,000
Rehabilitation cost	7,500,000
	$10,500,000
Tax savings from credit	
($7,500,000 × 10%)	(750,000)
After-tax cost	$ 9,750,000

Because of the rehabilitation credit, Corporation QT minimizes its cost by purchasing the old building. Note that the tax savings from the credit is not a function of the corporation's marginal tax rate. But the savings calculation is based on the assumption that Corporation QT's precredit tax liability is sufficient to allow full use of the credit in the current year. If this is not the case and the corporation must carry forward some of the credit for use in a future year, the present value of the carryforward might be insufficient to tip the scale in favor of the rehabilitation project.

Alternative Minimum Tax

Objective 6
Discuss the purpose of the alternative minimum tax.

The **alternative minimum tax (AMT) system** is a second federal tax system parallel to the regular income tax system described throughout the text. Congress enacted the corporate AMT primarily for political reasons. Under the regular tax system, corporations with substantial economic income can occasionally take advantage of tax exclusions, deductions, or credits to dramatically reduce, or even eliminate, their tax liabilities. In past years, these occasions received a great deal of publicity and caused people to lose respect for a tax system so riddled with "loopholes" that huge companies escape taxation altogether. In response to this embarrassing public perception, Congress created a backup system to ensure that every corporation with significant income pays a "fair share" of the federal tax burden.

In the Tax Reform Act of 1997, Congress carved out an exception to the AMT for certain small corporations. For 1998 (or a tax year beginning in 1998), a corporation with average annual gross receipts of $5 million or less for its three prior tax years is exempt from the AMT. To maintain its exemption for tax years after 1998, the corporation's average annual gross receipts for the prior three-year period cannot exceed $7.5 million.[14]

Alternative Minimum Taxable Income

The base for the corporate AMT is **alternative minimum taxable income (AMTI).**[15] The computation of AMTI begins with taxable income for regular tax purposes. This income number is increased or decreased by a series of complicated **AMT adjustments** and increased by specific **tax preferences.** The computation of AMTI is presented in the following formula:

---

[14]§55(e).
[15]§55(b)(2).

$$\begin{array}{r}
\text{Taxable income for regular tax purposes} \\
+ \text{ or } - \text{ AMT adjustments} \\
\underline{+ \text{ AMT tax preferences}} \\
\text{Alternative minimum taxable income}
\end{array}$$

To get a sense of the nature of AMT adjustments and preferences, let's examine three of the more common: the depreciation adjustment, excess percentage depletion, and the NOL adjustment.

Depreciation Adjustment.   Under MACRS, business assets with a 3-year, 5-year, 7-year, or 10-year recovery period are depreciated under the 200 percent declining balance method. For AMT purposes, depreciation on these assets is computed under a 150 percent declining balance method.[16] Consequently, the MACRS depreciation deduction with respect to these assets is greater than its AMT counterpart in the early years of an asset's life and the excess MACRS becomes a positive adjustment in the computation of AMTI. Of course, at some point in the asset's life, the situation reverses and AMT depreciation exceeds MACRS depreciation. At this point, the annual AMT adjustment becomes negative. Over the life of the asset, MACRS and AMT depreciation are equal and the positive and negative AMT adjustments zero out.

AMT Depreciation.   Corporation JS has two depreciable assets. During the current year, the MACRS depreciation, AMT depreciation, and AMT adjustment for each asset is:

	MACRS	AMT Depreciation	AMT Adjustment
Asset 1	$17,800	$12,000	$5,800
Asset 2	2,100	4,300	(2,200)
	$19,900	$16,300	$3,600

Corporation JS has a $5,800 positive AMT adjustment for Asset 1 (excess MACRS over AMT depreciation) and a $2,200 negative AMT adjustment for Asset 2 (excess AMT depreciation over MACRS). The corporation must add its $3,600 aggregate positive adjustment to regular taxable income in the computation of AMTI.

Excess Percentage Depletion.   As we discussed in Chapter 6, the percentage depletion that corporations deduct over the productive life of a mine or well is not limited to the tax basis in the mineral property. If a corporation has recovered its entire basis and continues to deduct percentage depletion with respect to the property, the depletion deduction in excess of the zero basis is an AMT tax preference.[17]

---

[16]§56(a)(1). For property placed in service before January 1, 1999, AMT depreciation is based on the extended recovery periods under the alternative depreciation system (ADS) described in §168(g).

[17]§57(a)(1).

> ***Depletion Preference.***   Corporation JS had $240,000 of unrecovered basis in a mining property at the beginning of the year and deducted $310,000 of percentage depletion. The corporation has $70,000 excess depletion and must add this preference to regular taxable income in the computation of AMTI.

NOL Deduction.   Even if a corporation's business operations generate a profit, the corporation may have no taxable income because it has a NOL carryforward or carryback into the year. For AMT purposes, the NOL deduction is limited to 90 percent of AMTI.[18]

> ***AMT NOL Deduction.***   Corporation JS's taxable income before any NOL deduction is $2 million. The corporation has a $3 million NOL carryforward into the year. For regular tax purposes, Corporation JS can deduct $2 million of the carryforward, thereby reducing taxable income to zero. The corporation's AMTI before the NOL deduction is $2.4 million. Under the AMT rules, Corporation JS can deduct only $2.16 million of its NOL carryforward (90 percent of $2.4 million), resulting in AMTI of $240,000.

Calculating AMT

Calculation of the corporate AMT is a three-step process.[19] First, AMTI is reduced by any exemption to which the corporation is entitled. The basic exemption is $40,000. This exemption is reduced by 25 percent of AMTI in excess of $150,000. Consequently, the exemption is reduced to zero for corporations with AMTI in excess of $310,000.

> ***AMTI Exemption.***   SC Inc.'s AMTI is $293,000. The corporation's exemption is $4,250.
>
> | | |
> |---|---:|
> | AMTI | $ 293,000 |
> | | (150,000) |
> | Excess AMTI | $ 143,000 |
> | | .25 |
> | Reduction in exemption | $ 35,750 |
> | Basic exemption | $ 40,000 |
> | | (35,750) |
> | SC Inc.'s exemption | $ 4,250 |

---

[18]§56(a)(4). Because the AMT NOL is calculated under the AMT system, the AMT NOL deduction can be a different amount than the NOL deduction for regular tax purposes.

[19]§55 provides the rules for the AMT computation.

In the second step of the AMT calculation, AMTI in excess of the exemption is multiplied by a flat 20 percent rate to compute **tentative minimum tax.** In the third step, the tentative minimum tax is compared to the corporation's regular tax liability. Any excess of tentative minimum tax over regular tax becomes the corporation's AMT, which it pays *in addition to* its regular tax.[20] The AMT calculation is presented in the following formula and demonstrated in the next example:

$$
\begin{array}{r}
\text{Alternative minimum taxable income} \\
\underline{\text{(exemption)}} \\
\text{AMTI in excess of exemption} \\
\underline{.20} \\
\text{Tentative minimum tax} \\
\underline{\text{(regular tax)}} \\
\overline{\underline{\text{Alternative minimum tax}}}
\end{array}
$$

AMT Computation.   In 19X8, Corporation Q has taxable income of $500,000 and AMTI of $975,000. The corporation's tax liability is computed as follows:

AMTI	$ 975,000
Exemption	–0–
	$ 975,000
	.20
Tentative minimum tax	$ 195,000
Regular tax ($500,000 × 34%)	(170,000)
AMT	$ 25,000
19X8 tax liability (regular tax + AMT)	$ 195,000

Although Corporation Q's AMTI is almost twice its taxable income, the corporation's AMT is relatively small. Because the 20 percent AMT rate is so much less than the 34 percent or 35 percent regular tax rate, tentative minimum tax can't exceed regular tax unless AMTI is significantly greater than taxable income. Therefore, corporations with modest AMT adjustments and preferences escape the AMT.[21] Nonetheless, the additional record keeping necessary to compute annual AMTI increases the tax compliance costs of these corporations.

Minimum Tax Credit

In the preceding example, the fact that Corporation Q's $195,000 tax bill for 19X8 consists of both regular tax and AMT may seem of little practical importance. Even so, corporations must keep careful track of their AMT because this tax payment is trans-

---

[20]As a general rule, none of the tax credits available under the regular tax system reduce AMT. The major exception is the foreign tax credit, which is described in detail in Chapter 12.

[21]Corporations with AMTI (computed without any NOL deduction) in excess of $2 million are liable for an environmental tax of .12 percent of such excess. §59A. The revenues for this tax are earmarked for environmental cleanup.

formed into a **minimum tax credit.** This credit carries forward indefinitely and reduces the corporation's regular tax in subsequent years. However, the credit cannot reduce regular tax to less than the corporation's tentative minimum tax for the year.[22] The logic behind this credit is that the corporate AMT is not designed as a permanent tax increase. Instead, the AMT merely accelerates the payment of income tax into years when a corporation's taxable income is dramatically less than AMTI. To demonstrate the important function of the minimum tax credit, refer back to Corporation Q's situation.

Minimum Tax Credit. In 19X9, Corporation Q has taxable income of $750,000 and AMTI of $800,000. The corporation's tax liability is computed as follows:

AMTI	$800,000
Exemption	–0–
	$800,000
	.20
Tentative minimum tax	$160,000
Regular tax ($750,000 × 34%)	$255,000
AMT (regular tax exceeds tentative minimum tax)	–0–
Minimum tax credit from 19X8	(25,000)
19X9 tax liability	$230,000

In this two-year example, the AMT affected only the timing and not the amount of Corporation Q's income tax liability. With or without the AMT, Corporation Q pays a total tax of $425,000 for the two years:

Two-Year Summary for Corporation Q

	Total Tax with AMT	*Total Tax without AMT*
19X8	$195,000	$170,000
19X9	230,000	255,000
	$425,000	$425,000

The effect of the AMT over the two-year period was to accelerate $25,000 of tax liability into 19X8, not to permanently increase that liability. Realistically, AMT liabilities may take any number of years to reverse as minimum tax credits against regular tax. For growing businesses, each successive year's tentative minimum tax may exceed regular tax. In such case, the corporation's use of its minimum tax credit is postponed indefinitely. Of course, regardless of the fact that a corporation may recoup AMT in a future year, that AMT always increases the corporation's tax cost in present value terms.

---

[22]§53.

Payment and Filing Requirements

Objective 7
Describe the corporate tax payment and return filing requirements.

Corporations are required to pay their federal income tax liability for the year in four installments.[23] Each installment is 25 percent of the liability, and the installments are due by the 15th day of the 4th, 6th, 9th, and 12th months of the taxable year. Corporations that fail to make their required installment payments on a timely basis incur a statutorily imposed **underpayment penalty.** If the total of the installment payments is less than the corporation's actual tax liability as reported on Form 1120, the corporation must pay the balance due by the 15th day of the 3rd month following the close of the taxable year.[24] If the total is more than the liability, the corporation is entitled to a refund of the overpayment.

The required installment payments must total to 100 percent of the tax reported on the corporation's return for that year. Because corporations can't know the exact tax liability until after year-end, they must base their installment payments on their best estimate of that liability. Corporations that underestimate this liability pay the statutory penalty. The law provides a measure of relief to small corporations (defined as corporations with less than $1 million of taxable income). These corporations escape the underpayment penalty if their total installment payments equal 100 percent of their tax liability reported on the *previous* year's tax return.[25] This *safe harbor* provision is very useful to newly formed corporations with rapidly growing business operations.

Safe Harbor Estimate. In 19X7, Corporation DF's taxable income was $400,000 and its tax liability was $136,000. During 19X8, the corporation made four $35,000 installment payments of 19X8 tax. Corporation DF's 19X8 taxable income was $930,000, and its tax liability was $316,200. Although Corporation DF paid only $140,000 of this liability during the year, it does not incur an underpayment penalty because the payment exceeded 100 percent of the corporation's 19X7 tax liability.

Corporations must file their annual income tax returns with the IRS by the 15th day of the 3rd month following the close of the taxable year.[26] Corporations that are unable to meet this filing deadline may request an automatic six-month extension of time to file their returns, and corporations routinely take advantage of this grace period.[27] It should come as no great surprise that corporations that file delinquent returns may incur monetary penalties imposed by the Internal Revenue Code.[28]

Distributions of Profits to Investors

The corporate form of business organization allows an unlimited number of investors to contribute capital to the business. Investors can take the role of creditor, either by lending money directly to the corporation in exchange for a promissory note or by

---

[23]§6655.

[24]Corporations do not send tax payments directly to the IRS. Instead, they deposit their payments in a government account maintained by a qualified depositary, such as a commercial bank.

[25]Large corporations with highly fluctuating patterns of annual income may look to other statutory exceptions to the strict 100 percent requirement for relief from the underpayment penalty.

[26]§6072(b).

[27]Reg. §1.6081-3.

[28]§6651 describes the penalties for late filing. These penalties are discussed in more detail in Chapter 17.

purchasing the corporation's debt instruments traded on a public bond market. Alternatively, investors can become owners by contributing money or property directly to the corporation in exchange for shares of equity stock, purchasing shares from other shareholders, or purchasing shares traded on a public stock market.

Of course, both creditors and shareholders expect a return on their investment. Creditors receive interest income on their corporate notes or bonds. On the other side of the transaction, corporations are allowed to deduct the interest paid on their debt obligations. As a result, the dollars of business profit that flow through to investors as interest are not taxed at the corporate level but only to the investors. Corporate stockholders may receive a return on their investment in the form of dividends. Corporations cannot deduct dividend payments in the computation of taxable income. The business profit flowing through to investors as dividends is taxed both at the corporate level and again to the shareholders receiving the dividends.

Objective 8
Explain why corporate profits distributed as dividends to shareholders are double taxed.

This double taxation of corporate earnings is one of the dominant characteristics of the federal income tax system. The fact that dividends are paid with after-tax dollars is a major consideration affecting the choice of organizational form—a consideration we will analyze in the next chapter. This fact also justifies the corporate dividends-received deduction. Without this deduction, business profit would be taxed over and over again as it moved through a chain of corporate investors before final distribution to individual shareholders for personal consumption.

From the corporate perspective, the nondeductibility of dividend payments creates a bias in favor of debt financing.[29] A corporation that raises capital by borrowing can deduct the interest paid on the debt. If the corporation faces a 35 percent tax rate, the after-tax cost of the capital is only 65 percent of the before-tax cost; in effect, the federal government pays 35 percent of the return on the creditors' investment. If the corporation raises capital by selling a new issue of common stock, the after-tax cost of the dividends paid on that stock equals the before-tax cost. Of course, the choice of debt financing has serious nontax implications, one of the more important of which is that interest and principal payments (unlike dividends paid on common stock) are not discretionary on the part of management. Corporations with high debt-to-equity ratios tend to have more burdensome cash flow commitments and a greater risk of insolvency than corporations with less debt in their capital structures. Companies that break faith with their creditors suffer financial distress that may even lead to bankruptcy. In many situations, the nontax costs associated with debt financing outweigh the tax savings from the corporation's interest deduction.[30]

Alternatives to Double Taxation

How could the present income tax system be reformed to eliminate the double taxation of corporate income? One alternative would be to treat corporations as pass-through entities by requiring them to allocate income to their shareholders on an annual basis. Shareholders would include their share of corporate earnings in their gross income and pay tax accordingly. This alternative would be administratively cumbersome, if not impossible, for publicly traded corporations in which stock ownership changes daily. In addition, this alternative could cause cash flow problems for investors who find themselves owing a large tax liability on their pro rata share of

---

[29]Richard A. Brealey and Stewart C. Myers, *Principles of Corporate Finance,* 5th ed. (New York: McGraw-Hill, 1996), p. 418.
[30]Ibid., p. 421.

corporate income but who did not receive a commensurate cash distribution from the corporation.

Another alternative is to make dividends nontaxable to individual investors so that the only tax levied on corporate income is at the entity level. This alternative certainly has the virtue of simplicity. But it is vulnerable to political attack as a tax break to the wealthy who earn far more dividend income than middle- and lower-income individuals. A variation on this alternative would be to allow corporations to deduct dividend payments (in the same way they deduct interest payments) so that distributed corporate income would be taxed only at the shareholder level.

Still another alternative is a system in which individuals are allowed a tax credit for the corporate tax attributable to the dividends included in their gross income. For example, if a shareholder received a dividend of $6,500, representing $10,000 of business income on which the corporation already paid $3,500 of tax, the shareholder would include the full $10,000 ($6,500 cash received grossed up by the $3,500 tax) in income and compute tax liability accordingly. The shareholder would then reduce that liability by a $3,500 credit. The end result is that the $10,000 of business income is taxed only once at the individual's marginal rate. Variations of this credit system are currently used in Canada and several western European nations.

Over the past decades, Congress and the Treasury have considered all these alternatives as solutions to the structural problem of double taxation. While the alternatives have theoretical merit, their implementation would result in significant revenue loss. Thus, it is unlikely that any of the alternatives will be enacted into law in the near future.

Incidence of the Corporate Tax

Objective 9
Identify the circumstances in which the incidence of the corporate tax falls on consumers, suppliers, labor, or capital.

Because corporations are taxpayers in their own right and yet have no human persona, they become easy political targets in any debate on tax reform. People don't enjoy paying taxes and often believe that their tax burden is too heavy because some other taxpayer's burden is too light. Impersonal corporate taxpayers become scapegoats as the hue and cry becomes "raise taxes on the corporate giants, not middle-class Americans." This sentiment ignores the fact that corporations are nothing more than a form in which people organize their business and that an increase in the corporate tax represents an additional cost of conducting that business.

Just who does pay the corporate income tax? The answer to this question varies across corporate businesses, depending on the nature of the markets in which they compete. In some markets, corporations may shift their tax costs directly to their customers as part of the price of goods and services. In markets in which price competition is fierce, management may offset tax costs by trimming production costs. In such case, the tax is passed on to the corporation's suppliers (smaller orders for materials), employees (lower compensation or workforce reductions), and even to consumers (lower quality). Still another possibility is that tax costs simply reduce the corporation's net income. In this case, the tax is paid by shareholders in the form of shrinking dividends or reduced market prices for the corporation's stock. The question of the economic incidence of the corporate tax and whether that tax falls hardest on consumers, suppliers, labor, or capital has been researched and argued for decades without a definitive answer. Nonetheless, one conclusion is inescapable: corporations do not pay taxes—people do.

Conclusion

Corporations have many legal and financial characteristics that make them the entity of choice for many enterprises and the only option for publicly traded companies. Corporations are taxable entities in their own right, paying tax at progressive rates ranging from 15 percent to 35 percent on annual income. When corporations distribute after-tax income as dividends to their shareholders, the business income is taxed a second time. In the next chapter, we will consider the impact of this potential double taxation on the choice of business entity and the entire tax planning process.

Key Terms

Affiliated group 251	Limited liability 250
Alternative minimum tax (AMT) system 261	Minimum tax credit 265
	Nonprofit corporations 252
Alternative minimum taxable income (AMTI) 261	Personal service corporation 259
	Publicly held corporation 250
AMT adjustments 261	Rehabilitation credit 260
Buy-sell agreement 250	Surtax 257
Centralized management 250	Tax credit 259
Closely held corporation 250	Tax preferences 261
Consolidated tax return 251	Tentative minimum tax 264
Dividends-received deduction 254	Underpayment penalty 266
Free transferability 250	Unlimited life 250
General business credit 259	

Questions and Problems for Discussion

1. To what extent does the corporate characteristic of limited liability protect shareholder/employees who perform professional services for corporate clients?

2. The corporate form of business is characterized by centralized management. Describe this characteristic as it applies to (*a*) publicly held corporations and (*b*) closely held corporations.

3. The corporate form of business is characterized by free transferability of equity interests. Describe this characteristic as it applies to (*a*) publicly held corporations and (*b*) closely held corporations.

4. Mr. and Mrs. D and their six children own 100 percent of the stock in three family corporations. Do these corporations qualify as an affiliated group eligible to file a consolidated corporate tax return?

5. RP Inc. owns 51 percent of the voting stock of QV Inc. RP's board of directors elects the majority of the members of QV's board of directors and thereby controls the management of QV's business. Are RP and QV an affiliated group eligible to file a consolidated corporate tax return?

6. Corporation L owns and operates a national chain of retail music stores. The corporation wants to expand into a new, extremely competitive, and highly specialized business—the composition and production of rock music videos. Can you identify any nontax reasons why Corporation L may want to operate its new business through a controlled subsidiary corporation?

7. Corporations are entitled to a dividends-received deduction with respect to dividend income from

other domestic, taxable corporations. Why is this deduction not available with respect to taxable dividends received from foreign corporations?

8. Is the dividends-received deduction a permanent or temporary difference between book income and taxable income?

9. During the current year, TV Inc. made a $25,000 charitable contribution, only $21,000 of which was deductible. Is the $4,000 nondeductible contribution a permanent or temporary difference between book income and taxable income?

10. Corporations subject to the AMT are penalized because they took advantage of certain tax preferences during the year. If Congress doesn't want corporations to take advantage of a certain tax preference, why doesn't Congress simply repeal the preference?

11. For the last six years, Corporation V's AMTI has exceeded its regular taxable income but the corporation has never paid an AMT liability. Can you explain this result?

12. In your own words, explain the conclusion that corporations do not pay tax—people do.

Application Problems

1. Corporation P owns 93 percent of the outstanding stock of Corporation T. For the current year, the corporations' records provide the following information:

	Corporation P	Corporation T
Ordinary operating income (loss)	$500,000	$(200,000)
Capital gain (loss)	(8,300)	6,000
Section 1231 gain (loss)	(1,000)	5,000

   a. Compute each corporation's taxable income if they file separate tax returns.
   b. Compute consolidated taxable income if Corporation P and Corporation T file a consolidated tax return.

2. During the current year, GHJ Inc. received the following dividends:

BP Inc. (a taxable California corporation in which GHJ holds a 2% stock interest)	$17,300
MN Inc. (a taxable Florida corporation in which GHJ holds a 52% stock interest)	80,800
AB Inc. (a taxable Canadian corporation in which GHJ holds a 21% stock interest)	17,300

Based on this information, compute GHJ Inc.'s dividend-received deduction.

3. In 19X1, Corporation EF made a $100,000 contribution to a local charity. In each of the following situations, compute the after-tax cost of this contribution assuming that EF uses a 10 percent discount rate to compute net present value.
   a. Corporation EF had $8 million of 19X1 taxable income before consideration of the contribution.
   b. Corporation EF had $490,000 of 19X1 taxable income before consideration of the contribution. In 19X2, Corporation EF's taxable income was $6 million. EF made no charitable contributions in 19X2.
   c. Corporation EF had $190,000 of 19X1 taxable income before consideration of the contribution. For 19X2 through 19X6, Corporation EF's annual taxable income was $130,000. EF made no charitable contributions in these years.

4. EFG Inc., a calendar year, accrual basis taxpayer, reported $479,900 of net income after tax on its current year financial statements prepared in accordance with GAAP. The corporation's financial records reveal the following information:
   • EFG earned $10,700 on an investment in tax-exempt municipal bonds.
   • EFG's allowance for bad debts as of January 1 was $21,000. Write-offs for the year totaled $4,400, while the addition to the allowance was $3,700. The allowance as of December 31 was $20,300.

- On August 7, EFG paid a $6,000 fine to a municipal government for a violation of a local zoning ordinance.
- EFG's depreciation expense per books was $44,200, and its MACRS depreciation deduction was $31,000.
- The current year is EFG's second taxable year. In its first taxable year, the corporation recognized an $8,800 net capital loss. During the current year, EFG recognized a $31,000 Section 1231 gain on the sale of equipment. This was the corporation's only disposition of noninventory assets.
- In its first taxable year, EFG capitalized $6,900 of organizational costs for tax purposes and elected to amortize the costs over 60 months. For book purposes, the corporation expensed the costs.
- EFG's federal income tax expense for the year was $244,800.

   a. Based on the above facts, compute EFG Inc.'s taxable income and regular tax liability.

   b. Prepare a Schedule M-1, page 4, Form 1120, reconciling EFG's book and tax income for the current year.

5. Corporation AB's marginal tax rate is 15 percent and Corporation YZ's marginal tax rate is 35 percent.

   a. If both corporations are entitled to an additional deduction of $5,000, how much tax savings will the deduction generate for each corporation?

   b. If both corporations are entitled to a tax credit of $5,000, how much tax savings will the credit generate for each corporation? (Assume that each corporation's precredit tax liability exceeds $5,000.)

6. In each of the following cases, compute the corporation's regular tax liability:

   a. Corporation A, which manufactures frozen food products, has taxable income of $160,000.

   b. Corporation B, a personal service corporation providing medical care, has taxable income of $160,000.

   c. Corporation C, which develops and operates golf resorts, has taxable income of $3.91 million.

   d. Corporation D, which drills oil wells, has taxable income of $16.8 million.

   e. Corporation E, which manufactures farm equipment, has taxable income of $57 million.

7. Refer to the cases in Problem 6. In each case, identify the corporation's marginal tax rate and compute the corporation's average tax rate.

8. PT Corporation's regular taxable income for the year is $100,000. The corporation has positive AMT adjustments totaling $45,000 and a $22,000 AMT tax preference. Based on these facts, compute PT's AMT (if any) for the year.

9. RS Corporation's regular taxable income for the year is $3,590,000. The corporation has positive AMT adjustments totaling $980,000 and AMT tax preferences totaling $315,000. Based on these facts, compute RS's AMT (if any) for the year.

10. GK Inc. has taxable income of $1.25 million before any NOL deduction. The corporation has $2.8 million of NOL carryforwards but no other AMT adjustments or preferences. Based on these facts, compute GK's tax liability.

11. Corporation H was formed in 19X5. For 19X5 through 19X7, Corporation H's regular tax and tentative minimum tax were as follows:

Year	Regular Tax	Tentative Minimum Tax
19X5	$ 20,000	$ 16,000
19X6	87,000	90,000
19X7	159,000	182,000

   a. Compute Corporation H's tax liability for 19X5, 19X6, and 19X7.

   b. Compute Corporation H's tax liability in 19X8 if the corporation's regular taxable income is $900,000 and its AMTI is $1.1 million.

   c. Compute Corporation H's tax liability in 19X8 if the corporation's regular taxable income is $900,000 and its AMTI is $1.48 million.

12. In 19X8, NB Inc.'s federal income tax liability was $242,000. Compute the required installment payments of 19X9 tax in each of the following cases:

   a. NB's 19X9 taxable income is $593,000.

   b. NB's 19X9 taxable income is $950,000.

   c. NB's 19X9 taxable income is $1,400,000.

13. Mr. J, who is in the 39.6 marginal tax bracket, owns 100 percent of the stock of JJ Inc. In the

current year, JJ Inc. generates $500,000 of taxable income and pays a $100,000 dividend to Mr. J. Compute JJ Inc.'s tax liability and Mr. J's tax cost with respect to the dividend under each of the following assumptions.

a. The federal tax rules currently in effect apply to the dividend payment.

b. The federal tax system has been amended to allow corporations to deduct dividend payments to their shareholders.

c. The federal tax system has been amended to make dividend income nontaxable to individual shareholders.

d. The federal tax system has been amended to allow shareholders to (1) gross up dividend income received by the corporate tax paid with respect to the dividend and (2) credit this tax against their personal tax liability for the year.

14. LFT Inc. manufactures laundry detergent and other cleaning products. During the year, the government increased the corporate tax rate by 2 percent. The corporation's marketing department determined that LFT could not raise its prices and retain its current market share. The production department concluded that manufacturing costs cannot be reduced by another penny. Consequently, LFT's before-tax profits remain constant, while after-tax profits decline by the full tax increase. The stock market reaction to the decline in earnings is a fall in LFT's stock price.

a. Based on these facts, who bears the incidence of the increase in LFT's corporate tax?

b. How would your answer change if LFT held its after-tax profit constant by shutting down the on-site day care center for its employees' preschool children and eliminating this operating cost from its budget?

Issue Recognition Problems

Identify the tax issue or issues suggested by the following situations and state each issue in the form of a question.

1. The Greentown Foundation is a nonprofit corporation exempt from federal income tax. The corporation's stated purpose is to solicit volunteers to plant and tend public gardens and greenbelts located in inner cities. The corporation's board of directors is considering publishing a gardener's newsletter that it could sell in retail bookstores to raise money for its various projects.

2. TK Enterprises Inc., an accrual basis corporation, needs to raise capital. One idea is for the corporation to sell bonds to the public for $625 each. These bonds would have no stated rate of interest but would be redeemable from the corporation in five years for a redemption price of $1,000.

3. BB Corporation has not paid a dividend for six years. In the current year, the board of directors decides to declare a dividend. The corporation hires a consultant to review and update its shareholder records so that the dividend can be distributed in the proper amounts to the proper people. The consultant's fee for her services is $16,800.

4. M&M Inc. is a calendar year, accrual basis corporation. At its December meeting, the board of directors authorized a $50,000 contribution to a local charity. The corporation's bookkeeper mailed a $50,000 check to the charity on January 12.

5. Twenty years ago, XZ Corporation developed, manufactured, and marketed Kepone, a chemical pesticide. As a result of manufacturing practices that violated state environmental standards, harmful levels of Kepone were discharged into the soil and groundwater. A state agency sued XZ for damages, and the corporation was indicted for criminal negligence for the unlawful discharge of toxic substances. The judge imposed a $1 million fine on XZ. After extensive meetings with the judge and prosecutors, XZ created the Midwest Environment Foundation, the purpose of which is to alleviate the effects of Kepone waste. The corporation contributed $950,000 to this nonprofit organization, and the

judge promptly reduced XZ's fine to $50,000. The corporation's taxable income before consideration of the contribution or the fine is $87 million.

6. Several years ago, Corporation F purchased heavy machinery for $618,000. The corporation sold the machinery this year for $500,000. Through date of sale, MACRS depreciation on the machinery was $320,000, while AMT depreciation was $198,000. Corporation F has paid an AMT in three of its last five taxable years and expects to do so again this year.

7. In its first year of operations, Corporation TF incurred a $120,000 NOL. The director of tax projects that the corporation will generate

$40,000 of regular taxable income in each of the next three years. Consequently, the director estimates that the corporation will have no tax liability in these years because of the NOL carryforward deduction.

8. Corporation W is a calendar year taxpayer. For the past nine years, the corporation's taxable income has been stable, averaging $2 million per year. Through November of the current year, the corporation's taxable income was $1.81 million. In April, June, and September, Corporation W made a $175,000 installment payment of tax. In December, the corporation recognized a $5 million gain on the sale of investment land.

Tax Planning Cases

1. Congress recently enacted a new nonrefundable credit based on the cost of qualifying alcohol and drug counseling programs provided by any corporate employer to its employees. The credit is limited to 50 percent of the total cost of the program. If a corporation elects the credit, none of the program costs are allowed as a current year deduction. Any credit in excess of current year tax liability may not be carried back or forward to another year.
   a. TMM Corporation spent $80,000 for a qualifying counseling program during the current year. If TMM has $500,000 of taxable income before consideration of this expense, should it elect the credit or deduct the program's cost as an ordinary business expense?
   b. Would your answer change if TMM had taxable income of only $70,000 before consideration of the expense?

2. A&Z Inc. averages $4 million of taxable income a year. Because it needs a quick influx of cash, the board of directors is considering two options: selling a new issue of preferred stock to the public for a total offering price of $500,000 or borrowing $500,000 from a local bank. The market dividend rate on preferred stock is only 5.6 percent, while the bank's interest rate is 9 percent. Which option minimizes the after-tax cost of the new capital?

3. In 19X5, Corporation E paid both regular tax ($2,714,000) and AMT ($129,300). The director of tax forecasts that Corporation E will be in an AMT position for 19X6 and 19X7. However, in 19X8 the corporation's AMTI will be significantly less than regular taxable income. Based on these facts and assuming a 12 percent discount rate, calculate the cost of the AMT in present value terms.

11 The Choice of Business Entity

Learning Objectives

After studying this chapter, you should be able to:

1. Explain the advantage of operating a business with start-up losses as a passthrough entity.
2. Calculate the difference in after-tax cash flow attributable to operating a business as a passthrough entity rather than as a corporation.
3. Describe how families can use partnerships or S corporations to shift business income from individuals in a high tax bracket to individuals in a low tax bracket.
4. Identify the characteristics of partnerships and S corporations that owners should consider in choosing between the two types of passthrough entity.
5. Define the term *constructive dividend.*
6. List the three factors that can create tax savings when individuals use closely held corporations as tax shelters.
7. Identify the reasons why Congress enacted the accumulated earnings tax and the personal holding company tax.
8. Explain how the tax rates apply to income earned by members of a controlled corporate group.

In the two preceding chapters, we identified the basic forms of business organization and learned how the choice of form determines whether business income is taxed at the individual or corporate rates. These chapters concentrated on the tax rules and regulations applying to different business entities. In Chapter 11, we will build on this technical knowledge as we consider the tax planning implications of the choice of business entity. The first half of the chapter focuses on the advantages of conducting a business as a passthrough entity. The second half explains how business owners can control the tax cost of operating in the corporate form and even use corporations to shelter income from high individual rates. Throughout the chapter, we will analyze how planning strategies relating to the choice of entity affect after-tax cash flow available to the business owners.

No one organizational form is ideal for every business venture. The tax characteristics of one form may be advantageous in one case and disadvantageous in another. In some cases, a passthrough entity accomplishes the owners' tax objectives;

while in other cases, a taxable corporation is the better option. Oftentimes, owners have compelling nontax reasons for operating their business in a particular form. As the business matures and the owners' financial situations evolve, the optimal organizational form for their business may change. Finally, business owners must reevaluate the form in which they conduct their business activities every time Congress amends the Internal Revenue Code. Even minor alterations in the law can affect the tax pros and cons of passthrough entities and taxable corporations.

Tax Planning with Passthrough Entities

From Chapter 9, we know that businesses organized as partnerships (including limited liability companies [LLCs]) and S corporations are not subject to federal income tax at the entity level. Instead, income passes through the entity to be reported by and taxed directly to the owners of the business. If the business operates at a loss, the loss passes through and is reported as a deduction by the owners. Cash distributions from passthrough entities are generally nontaxable. These cash flows represent a return of the owners' investment in the business and do not affect the income or loss reported by the owners. For many individuals, this combination of rules represents their best opportunity to control tax costs and maximize the cash flows from their business activities.

Maximizing the Tax Benefit of Start-Up Losses

Objective 1
Explain the advantage of operating a business with start-up losses as a passthrough entity.

Organizers of a new business may expect the enterprise to lose money during its start-up phase. If the business is organized as a passthrough entity, these initial losses can generate an immediate tax savings to the owners. If the business is organized as a corporation, the losses do not flow through but are trapped at the entity level as net operating loss carryforwards. As a result, the tax savings from the start-up losses are deferred until the corporation can deduct them against future taxable income. The following case focuses on this important difference in timing:

Start-Up Losses.   A group of individuals owns a business that reported the following income and deductions for its first three years of operation:

Year	Gross Income	Allowable Deductions	Net Income or Loss
1	$ 420,000	$ (720,000)	$(300,000)
2	800,000	(920,000)	(120,000)
3	1,530,000	(1,000,000)	530,000

If the owners organized the business as a passthrough entity, the operating losses in years 1 and 2 were deductible in the computation of the owners' taxable incomes for each year.[1] In year 3, the owners paid tax on $530,000 of business income. If the owners

[1] If a passthrough loss exceeds the owner's other items of income for the year, the excess loss is a net operating loss. The owner can carry the NOL back as a deduction to the two preceeding years or forward as a deduction for 20 years.

organized the business as a corporation, the net operating losses in years 1 and 2 carried forward and resulted in $110,000 of corporate taxable income in year 3. To isolate the tax effect of the timing difference, let's use a hypothetical 35 percent tax rate for both the individual owners and the corporation and a 9 percent discount rate.

Tax Savings and Costs

Passthrough Entity

Year	Current (Deduction) or Taxable Income	Tax Savings or (Cost)	Discount Factor	Present Value of Tax Savings or (Cost)
1	$(300,000)	$ 105,000		$ 105,000
2	(120,000)	42,000	.917	38,514
3	530,000	(185,500)	.842	(156,191)
		$ (38,500)		$ (12,677)

Corporation

Year	(NOL Carryforward) or Taxable Income	Tax Savings or (Cost)	Discount Factor	Present Value of Tax Savings or (Cost)
1	$(300,000)	$ –0–		$ –0–
2	(120,000)	–0–		–0–
3	110,000	(38,500)	.842	(32,417)
		$ (38,500)		$ (32,417)

In this simplified case, the present value of the tax cost is minimized if the owners organized their business as a passthrough entity rather than as a corporation. The dramatic difference in tax cost is entirely attributable to the timing of the deduction for the first two years of losses. With a passthrough entity, these losses were deductible in the year incurred. Consequently, the owners received the tax savings from the deduction in years 1 and 2. With a corporate entity, the tax savings from the loss deduction were postponed until year 3 and the value of the savings decreased in present value terms.

Avoiding a Double Tax on Business Income

Objective 2
Calculate the difference in after-tax cash flow attributable to operating a business as a passthrough entity rather than as a corporation.

People who own and operate their own business often depend on the cash flow from the business to meet their family's consumption needs. Their basic financial strategy is to maximize the cash transferred from the business bank account to their personal checking account. This strategy dictates that they operate their business as a passthrough entity, rather than as a corporation, so that income is taxed only once.

Single versus Double Tax on Business Income.   Mr. and Mrs. G are the sole shareholders in an S corporation that conducts a restaurant business.[2] The restaurant generates $100,000 of taxable income annually and an equal cash flow. The

[2]To keep the example simple, assume that neither shareholder is an employee of the corporation.

corporation distributes all available cash to the shareholders each year. Assuming an individual tax rate of 28 percent, the couple's after-tax cash flow from their business is $72,000.

Annual cash from operations	$100,000
Individual tax liability	
($100,000 taxable income × 28%)	(28,000)
After-tax cash flow	$ 72,000

If Mr. and Mrs. G had not elected subchapter S status for their corporation, the $100,000 of income would be taxed at the entity level and the corporation itself would pay $22,250 of tax. The cash available for distribution to the shareholders would be $77,750. Moreover, the distribution would result in dividend income to Mr. and Mrs. G and the after-tax cash available for their personal consumption would be only $55,980:

Annual cash from operations	$100,000
Corporate tax liability	(22,250)
Cash distributed to shareholders	$ 77,750
Individual tax liability	
($77,750 dividend × 28%)	(21,770)
After-tax cash flow	$ 55,980

In Mr. and Mrs. G's case, the double taxation inherent on the corporate form would result in a 44 percent tax rate on their business income ($44,020 total tax liability ÷ $100,000 income). Clearly, these individuals are minimizing their income tax liability and maximizing the money they can spend by operating their restaurant as a pass-through entity.

Income Shifting among Family Members

Objective 3
Describe how families can use partnerships or S corporations to shift business income from individuals in a high tax bracket to individuals in a low tax bracket.

Individuals who organize a business as a passthrough entity can often save tax by making family members co-owners of the entity. The creation of a family partnership or S corporation can be an effective way to divide business income among a number of taxpayers. To the extent that this division causes any of the income to be taxed at a lower marginal rate, the total tax burden on the business shrinks. Let's illustrate this concept with a simple example.

Shift of Business Income. Mrs. A owns a sole proprietorship generating $300,000 of annual taxable income. Mrs. A is in the 39.6 percent tax bracket but has two children in the 28 percent tax bracket. If Mrs. A could convert her business into a passthrough entity in which she and her children are equal co-owners, the annual income would be allocated among three individual taxpayers. If the shift of $100,000 of business income from Mrs. A to each child decreased the tax rate on the income from 39.6 percent to 28 percent, the tax savings would be $23,200.

Tax on $200,000 at 39.6%	$ 79,200
Tax on $200,000 at 28%	(56,000)
	$ 23,200

While Mrs. A should be impressed with a strategy that reduces her business's tax bill by 30 percent, she must understand that the implementation of the strategy will not just shift income to her children—it will shift dollars to them as well. As co-owners, the children are entitled to an equal share of any cash distributions from the business. When the business eventually terminates or is sold, each child will receive one-third of any remaining property or any amount realized on sale. In other words, if Mrs. A wants to shift two-thirds of the business income, she must part with two-thirds of the wealth represented by the business.

Statutory Restrictions.   The tax savings achieved through allocations of business income to family members with low tax rates can be substantial. Not surprisingly, the Internal Revenue Code restricts the use of both partnerships and S corporations as income-shifting devices. Let's look first at the statutory rules pertaining to family partnerships.

If the income generated by a partnership is primarily attributable to the work performed by individual partners rather than to the property owned by the partnership, any allocation of that income to nonworking partners is an unjustified assignment of earned income. Accordingly, a family member cannot be a partner in a personal service business unless he or she is qualified to perform the services offered to the business's clientele.[3] In contrast, a family member can be a partner in a business in which property is a material income-producing factor.[4] Unlike a service partnership, the mere ownership of an equity interest in a capital intensive partnership entitles a partner to a share of profits.

Does a Family Partnership Exist?.   Elizabeth and Emerson Winkler, who lived on a farm in Illinois, had five children. Emerson was in poor health and was frequently hospitalized. Elizabeth and one or more of her children always drove Emerson to the hospital. During these trips, the family usually purchased three $1 lottery tickets at the gas station where they stopped for fuel. The money was contributed by any family member who happened to have a dollar bill, and Elizabeth kept all the tickets in her china cabinet. The family often joked about how they would spend their winnings from these "family" tickets. On one trip, Elizabeth

---

[3]*Commissioner* v. *Culbertson,* 337 U.S. 733 (1949).

[4]§704(e)(1). Property is a material income-producing factor if the operation of the partnership business requires substantial inventories or a substantial investment in plant, machinery, or equipment. Reg. §1.704-1(e)(1)(iv).

used her own money to purchase the three tickets. That night, one of these tickets won $6.5 million. The family agreed that Elizabeth and Emerson should each receive 25 percent of the jackpot, while each child should receive 10 percent. Consequently, when Elizabeth received the $6.5 million, she paid $650,000 to each of her five children. The IRS contended that no family partnership existed among the Winklers, and that Elizabeth and Emerson made gifts (the lottery winnings) to the children on which they owed gift tax of over $116,000. But the federal court disagreed with the IRS. The court concluded that the Winklers formed a family partnership to purchase lottery tickets. Each family member contributed capital to the partnership when he or she spent a dollar to buy a ticket and each contributed services by going into the gas station to make the purchase. Consequently, the division of the jackpot was a distribution of profits to partners rather than a taxable gift from Elizabeth and Emerson to their children.[5]

Family partnerships are often created when the owner of a business enterprise makes a gift of an equity interest to a relative, thereby creating a partnership between donor and donee. Alternatively, the owner could sell the equity interest to the relative to create the partnership. In either case, the business income must be allocated among the partners based on their proportionate interests in partnership capital.[6]

Family Partnership.   Refer to the earlier example involving Mrs. A and her two children. Mrs. A can convert her sole proprietorship to a family partnership only if capital is a material income-producing factor. In other words, if Mrs. A is a self-employed physician earning $300,000 from her medical practice, she can't make her children partners in this business unless they are qualified to provide medical services. On the other hand, if Mrs. A's business is a retail clothing store, she can transfer the assets of the business to a partnership and give her children a capital interest in the new entity. If each child receives a one-third interest, the income of the partnership can be allocated in equal shares to the partners. If Mrs. A gives each child only a 10 percent capital interest, only 10 percent of the business income can be shifted to each child.

If the partner who gave away or sold an equity interest to a family member provides valuable services to the partnership, the partner must receive a guaranteed payment in compensation for any services rendered to the business.[7] The partnership is allowed to deduct the payment, and the remaining income is allocated in proportion to the capital interests.

Compensation for Services Rendered to a Family Partnership.   Refer to the preceding example and assume that Mrs. A created a family partnership by giving a one-third equity interest in her retail clothing business to each of her two

---

[5]*Estate of Emerson Winkler,* TC Memo 1997-4.

[6]In nonfamily partnerships, the allocation of income does not have to be in proportion to each partner's ownership of capital. For example, the partnership agreement could provide that a partner who owns 50 percent of the partnership's capital is allocated 80 percent of the business income or loss.

[7]§704(e).

children. Mrs. A works 40 hours a week managing the business. If her services are reasonably worth $60,000 a year, the partnership must allocate $60,000 to Mrs. A as a guaranteed payment. If partnership income after deduction of this guaranteed payment is $240,000, the maximum allocation to each child is $80,000. Because of this allocation rule, Mrs. A can't inflate the business income shifted to her children by working for free on their behalf.

When a business is operated as an S corporation, annual income is allocated pro rata to the outstanding shares of corporate stock. Therefore, the percentage of income allocable to any one individual is based strictly on the number of shares owned by that individual. If Mrs. A converted her sole proprietorship to an S corporation and gave each child one-third of the stock, each child would be allocated one-third of the business income. If she gave each child only 10 percent of the stock, their pro rata share of the income drops to 10 percent. But before any corporate income is allocated to the shareholders, Mrs. A must receive a reasonable salary for any services performed for the family business.[8]

Transaction Costs.   Even within the confines of these statutory restrictions, partnerships and S corporations are a viable means for reducing the aggregate income tax burden on a family business. The potential income tax savings must be compared to the transaction costs of forming the entity. If an individual creates a family partnership or S corporation by giving an equity interest in an established business to a family member, the donative transfer may be subject to the federal gift tax. This tax is based on the fair market value of the transferred interest and is a liability of the donor (the individual making the gift). If the business has considerable value, the gift tax may represent a substantial transaction cost.[9] The various nontax transaction costs associated with the formation and operation of a separate legal and accounting entity should also be factored into the decision to create a family partnership or S corporation.

Transaction Costs of Partnership Formation.   Refer back to the preceding example in which Mrs. A created a family partnership by giving a one-third equity interest in her retail clothing business to each of her two children. Immediately prior to the formation of the partnership, the business had an appraised value of $950,000. Consequently, the value of Mrs. A's gift to each child was $316,667. Her federal gift tax liability on these gifts was $21,600. Mrs. A paid a professional fee of $2,750 to the attorney who drafted the partnership agreement and an $800 fee to transfer title in the business real estate to the new partnership. Thus, the transaction costs of forming the family partnership totaled $25,150. The gift tax is a nondeductible personal expense. The attorney's fee is an an organizational cost that the partnership can amortize over 60 months. The title transfer fee is capitalized to the partnership's basis in the real estate.[10]

Nontax Considerations.   Entrepreneurs should carefully determine the extent to which the creation of a family-owned entity will dilute their control of the business. Many business owners who are willing to shift income and dollars to their relatives may be

---

[8]§1366(e).
[9]The federal gift tax is discussed in more detail in Chapter 15.
[10]Reg. §1.709-2.

reluctant to give those relatives a voice in management. A limited partnership arrangement in which the entrepreneur is the sole general partner can eliminate this concern. Another option is for the entrepreneur to create an S corporation capitalized with both voting and nonvoting stock. The entrepreneur can keep the voting shares and give the nonvoting shares to his kin, thereby retaining complete control of the corporate business.

Individuals who transfer equity interests in a business to a family member should understand that the transfer must be complete and legally binding. The recipient becomes the owner of an intangible property right. Absent any restrictions, the recipient is free to dispose of this right, with or without the blessing of the other co-owners. Buy-sell agreements among the partners or shareholders in a family business are commonly used to restrict family members from selling or assigning their equity interest to an unrelated third party.

Still another important consideration is that the transfer of an equity interest must be irrevocable; the transferor can't simply change his mind and take the interest back if he becomes dissatisfied with his co-owners. If the transferor becomes estranged from his family, an income-shifting business arrangement could turn into a bitterly resented trap. A parent who has an ill-favored child can always disinherit the child. It is another matter entirely if the child owns a third of the shares in the family S corporation. A change in the relative economic circumstances of family members can also undermine an income-shifting strategy. Consider a situation in which a high-income taxpayer suffers a severe economic setback. An irreversible business arrangement that shifts income away from this taxpayer could cause a personal financial crisis. These unhappy possibilities emphasize a point made earlier in the text: tax strategies must be evaluated on the basis of flexibility. If a business owner is uneasy about her family's ability to cooperate as co-owners or to accommodate each other's changing financial needs, a family partnership or S corporation may be a bad idea.

> *A Family Partnership Gone Wrong.*   Refer one last time to the family partnership created by Mrs. A and her two children. Six years after the partnership was formed, one of the children died in an accident and his widow inherited his one-third interest in the partnership. The widow cannot get along with Mrs. A and the surviving child and bitterly contests every decision they make concerning the management of the retail clothing business. Because of the continual discord, the three partners finally discontinue the business and terminate the partnership.

Partnership or S Corporation?

Objective 4
Identify the characteristics of partnerships and S corporations that owners should consider in choosing between the two types of passthrough entity.

Entrepreneurs who organize their business as a passthrough entity must choose between some type of partnership or an S corporation. The choice depends on the tax and nontax characteristics that differentiate these two organizational forms. In the next few paragraphs, we will identify the more important of these characteristics and examine how they enter into the decision-making process. Then we will analyze two planning cases.

Characteristics of Partnerships and S Corporations

Costs of Entity Formation and Operation.   The transfer of cash or property to a new partnership or corporation in exchange for a controlling equity interest is a nontaxable exchange.[11] Consequently, creating a new business entity has no up-front income tax cost. The owners will incur various legal, accounting, and professional fees incidental to the creation of the entity under state law. If the owners form a corporation, they must bear the incremental cost of filing a timely subchapter S election with the IRS. In addition, they must incur the ongoing cost of monitoring the ownership structure to ensure that their corporation continues to meet the eligibility requirements for an S corporation. If the corporation loses its eligibility and the election terminates, the corporation automatically reverts to a taxable entity. An S corporation may be more expensive to operate than a partnership because of state tax costs. Several states, including Connecticut, Tennessee, and Texas, treat S corporations as taxable entities for purposes of the state's corporate income or franchise tax. In contrast, partnerships are typically exempt from state income tax at the entity level.

Flexibility of Income and Loss Sharing Arrangement.   The partnership form offers co-owners the maximum flexibility to tailor their business arrangement to fit their needs. The partnership agreement specifies the amount and type of capital each partner contributes to the business. The agreement can create special sharing ratios for different items of income, gain, deduction, and loss. Moreover, the partners can amend their agreement every year. S corporations offer less flexibility because of the statutory restrictions on capital structure. S corporations can have only a single class of stock outstanding, and each share of stock must represent an identical claim on the income and assets of the business.

Owner Liability.   For many years, an S corporation was the only choice for co-owners who wanted to (1) pay a single tax on their business income at the owner level and (2) avoid unlimited personal liability for claims against the business. In contrast, the traditional partnership form involved greater financial risk for general partners, who have unlimited liability for business debt. Even limited partnerships must have at least one general partner. Over the last decade, state laws have created two innovative variations of the partnership form that offer increased protection against financial risk. In a **limited liability partnership (LLP),** general partners are not personally liable for malpractice-related claims arising from the professional misconduct of another general partner. In many states, professionals such as CPAs and attorneys can organize their practices as LLPs to safeguard themselves against the negligent actions of any one partner.[12]

In a limited liability company (LLC), every member has limited liability for all debts of or claims against the business.[13] The advent of LLCs has certainly changed the business environment. This new form of organization combines the tax advantages of a passthrough entity and the legal protection of the corporate form, without the costs or complications of the latter. The number of these organizations has been growing at a phenomenal rate, and many observers believe that LLCs are now the entity of choice for new businesses.

Two Planning Cases

To complete our discussion of the relative advantages and disadvantages of partnerships and S corporations, let's develop two cases in which differences between these organizational forms are key variables in the planning process.

---

[11]See the discussion of §721 and §351 in Chapter 8.

[12]The Big Six (soon to be the Big Five) public accounting firms have reorganized themselves as LLPs.

[13]See the discussion of LLCs in Chapter 9.

Leveraged Real Property Venture.   Six individuals decide to form a company to purchase, rehabilitate, and manage a hotel. The hotel property is subject to a $3,000,000 nonrecourse mortgage, and the current owner is willing to sell his equity in the property for only $50,000. The commercial lender holding the mortgage has agreed to the conveyance of the hotel to the new company. The individuals will each contribute $20,000 cash in exchange for equal ownership interests. The company will use the cash to buy the hotel and begin the necessary renovations. The individuals forecast that the company will generate a $264,000 tax loss for its first year of operations. Most of this loss is from cost recovery deductions with respect to the hotel building and its furnishings.

The individuals intend to organize the company as a passthrough entity; consequently, each one will be allocated $44,000 of the first-year loss. The individuals can deduct the loss only to the extent of the tax basis in their equity interest in the company.[14] If the company is organized as an S corporation, each individual's stock basis is $20,000—the cash contributed to the corporation. Therefore, each can deduct only $20,000 of the first-year loss.

If the company is organized as a partnership, the tax basis in each partner's interest includes both the contributed cash *and* a portion of the partnership's debts. Because of the $3,000,000 nonrecourse mortgage on the hotel, each individual has an initial basis of $520,000 ($20,000 cash + one-sixth of the mortgage). Because the partnership debt is included in basis, the individuals can deduct their entire distributive shares of the first-year business losses.

With respect to risk of financial loss, the individuals are indifferent between the partnership and the S corporation form. In either case, the commercial lender can look only to the hotel property itself for satisfaction of the mortgage. The choice of entity should not affect the *total* business loss each individual will eventually deduct. In the S corporation case, each shareholder can carry his $24,000 disallowed loss forward as a deduction against future income from the hotel business. The disadvantage of the S corporation form is that the loss deduction is deferred. By operating their company as a partnership, the individuals can deduct the loss in the year incurred, thereby maximizing the value of the tax savings from the loss.

Transferring Equity to Successive Generations.   Mr. and Mrs. B are approaching retirement age and want to begin transferring their business to their three children and, ultimately, to their seven grandchildren. The grandchildren range from 1 year to 18 years of age, and the adults in the family agree that it would be premature to make any of the grandchildren a co-owner. Mr. and Mrs. B could certainly create a family partnership to give their children an ownership interest in the business. In this case, a legally drafted partnership agreement would create and define the equity interests of each family member. But what happens in four years when one partner wants to transfer a portion of her equity to the eldest grandchild or in six years when Mr. B wants to withdraw from the business

---

[14]This statement assumes that the at-risk and the passive activity loss limitations are inapplicable. The passive activity loss limitation is discussed in Chapter 15.

entirely and divide his equity among his three children? Every time the family desires to modify the ownership structure of the business, the partnership agreement must be amended and the partnership interests redefined—a procedure that may be both inconvenient and costly.

As an alternative, Mr. and Mrs. B could incorporate their business as an S corporation with a specified number of shares of outstanding common stock. Each share would represent a pro rata interest in the business. Mr. and Mrs. B, and eventually their children, can modify the ownership structure of the corporation by simply giving shares to another relative. By choosing an S corporation rather than a partnership, Mr. and Mrs. B can minimize the transactions costs associated with a systematic transfer of the ownership of the business to their offspring.

Tax Planning with Closely Held Corporations

At some point in the life of a small business, the owners may decide to operate as a corporation rather than as a passthrough entity. Perhaps the business organization has become so complex that the partnership form is unwieldy. Or perhaps the business has grown to the extent that the owners want to sell stock to the public and the corporate form becomes a legal necessity. Regardless of the size or nature of the enterprise or the number of shareholders, the double taxation of business income is the predominant tax problem associated with the corporate form. In this section of the chapter, we will discuss how the owners of closely held corporations cope with the problem.

Getting Cash Out of the Corporation

Owners of closely held corporations are aware that any cash dividends have an extremely high tax cost. Consequently, they can become very aggressive and very creative in devising ways to bail cash out of their corporations. The standard tactic is for an individual shareholder to assume an additional role with respect to the corporate entity. For instance, shareholders commonly serve as corporate officers or executives. In their role as employees, they are entitled to salaries, the payment of which creates cash flow to the recipient and a deduction to the corporation. As a result, the business dollars paid as compensation are taxed only once at the individual level.[15] Similarly, shareholders can become creditors by lending money to their corporations; the interest paid by the corporation to the shareholder is a deductible expense. Shareholders may lease property to their corporations for rent payments that the corporation is allowed to deduct. In all these cases, the cash received by the shareholder, whether as salary, interest, or rent, is taxable as ordinary income. The critical difference is at the corporate level where dividends are paid with after-tax dollars but salaries, interest, and rents are paid with before-tax dollars.

Objective 5
Define the term
constructive dividend.

Constructive Dividends.   The IRS has no quarrel with shareholders who transact with their corporations if the transaction is based on reasonable terms comparable to the terms that would be negotiated between unrelated parties. Still, the IRS understands that the owners of closely held corporations have a strong incentive to violate this arm's-length standard. When revenue agents audit these corporations, they pay special atten-

---

[15]This statement ignores the employer and employee payroll tax levied on the salary.

tion to any deductions based on payments to shareholders. If an agent concludes that the payment is unreasonable in light of the facts and circumstances, the IRS may conclude that the unreasonable portion is a **constructive dividend.**

> ***Unreasonable Compensation.***   Mr. C, sole shareholder and chief executive officer of C Inc., receives an annual salary of $450,000. If other companies comparable in size and function to C Inc. pay salaries to their CEOs ranging from $400,000 to $500,000 and if Mr. C has the talent and experience to merit such handsome compensation, his salary appears reasonable and C Inc. can deduct it as a legitimate business expense. Conversely, if the CEO salaries paid by comparable firms average only $300,000 a year and Mr. C spends more time each week on the golf course than at corporate headquarters, the IRS may conclude that some portion of his salary is unreasonable.[16]

Let's build on the preceding example by assuming that the revenue agent who audited C Inc. decides that $150,000 of Mr. C's annual salary was unreasonable and should be treated as a dividend. What are the tax consequences of this decision?

> ***Constructive Dividend.***   C Inc.'s current taxable income *before* consideration of the $450,000 payment to Mr. C is $1 million. The following table compares the tax consequences at the corporate and individual level if the entire payment is a salary or if only $300,000 is a salary and $150,000 is a dividend.
>
> | | Salary | Salary/ Dividend |
> | --- | --- | --- |
> | C Inc.'s taxable income *before* salary deduction | $1,000,000 | $1,000,000 |
> | Salary deduction | (450,000) | (300,000) |
> | C Inc.'s taxable income | $ 550,000 | $ 700,000 |
> | | .34 | .34 |
> | C Inc.'s tax cost | $ 187,000 | $ 238,000 |
> | Mr. C's taxable income: salary | $ 450,000 | 300,000 |
> | dividend | –0– | 150,000 |
> | | $ 450,000 | $ 450,000 |
> | Mr. C's marginal tax rate | .396 | .396 |
> | Mr. C's tax cost | $ 178,200 | $ 178,200 |

While the tax cost of the payment at the individual level is the same in both columns, the tax cost at the corporate level increases by $51,000 if $150,000 of Mr. C's purported salary is a constructive dividend. The additional tax cost reduces the value of the corporate stock by $51,000 and the economic incidence of the tax increase falls squarely on Mr. C as the sole shareholder.

---

[16]The topic of reasonable compensation is discussed in detail in Chapter 14.

These next two examples illustrate constructive dividends from corporation to shareholder in two other contexts.

Unreasonable Rent Payments.   Mr. Serednesky rented office space from an unrelated third party for $8,000 annual rent, then subleased the office space to his wholly owned corporation for $16,604. The corporation deducted the $16,604 payment as rent expense on its tax return for the year. The IRS determined that only $8,000 of the payment represented a reasonable, arm's-length rent and that $8,604 of the payment was a nondeductible dividend.[17]

Shareholder Expenses.   Mr. Leonard was the sole shareholder and employee of a personal service corporation. The corporation paid $1,663 of Mr. Leonard's personal travel and entertainment expenses and deducted the payment as a business expense. The IRS treated the payment as a nondeductible constructive dividend that Mr. Leonard had to include in his taxable income. The federal court agreed with the IRS's evaluation of the transaction. When Mr. Leonard protested that the tax consequences unfairly penalized him for operating a business in corporate form, the court replied, "The corporate bed may have lumps; once chosen, however, a taxpayer must endure a sleepless night every now and then."[18]

Thin Capitalization.   The organizers of closely held corporations usually understand that if they invest funds in exchange for a corporate debt obligation, the corporation can deduct the interest paid on the debt. Moreover, a loan is temporary in that the organizers can receive a return of their investment according to a fixed repayment schedule or even on demand. On the other hand, if they contribute funds in exchange for equity stock, the duration of their investment is indeterminate and any dividends the corporation pays on the investment are nondeductible. As a result, organizers are motivated to include as much debt as possible in their corporation's capital structure.

If the debt held by shareholders is excessive, the IRS may contend that some or all of the debt is disguised equity. As a result, the interest payments on the debt are actually nondeductible dividends. Even worse, any principal repayments may be reclassified as constructive dividends.[19] Because these repayments were nondeductible to the corporation, their reclassification doesn't affect the corporation's taxable income or tax liability. However, the shareholders who believed they were receiving a nontaxable return of investment must recognize the repayments as ordinary income.

---

[17]*Social Psychological Services, Inc.,* TC Memo 1993–565.

[18]*Leonard,* TC Memo 1989–432.

[19]This is typically the case when the debt held by the shareholders is in proportion to their stock interests. As a result, principal repayments are treated as distributions under §302(d) and are taxable as dividends to the extent of the corporation's earnings and profits.

> ***Disguised Equity.***   Mr. and Mrs. V formed VV Inc. in 1992 by contributing
> $1,000 in exchange for 100 shares of VV common stock (the minimum capitaliza-
> tion under state law). The couple also loaned $25,000 to VV Inc. in exchange for
> the corporate's note. The note had no fixed repayment schedule but did provide
> for 9 percent annual interest. The corporation has never paid a dividend and paid
> no interest on the shareholder debt from 1992 through 1997. Late in 1997, VV
> Inc. distributed $36,250 to Mr. and Mrs. V. According to the corporate financial
> records, the distribution was a repayment of the 1992 loan plus $11,250 accrued
> interest. The corporation deducted the $11,250 interest payment on its 1997 tax
> return, and Mr. and Mrs. V reported $11,250 of interest income on their 1997 tax
> return. The revenue agent who audited the corporation's return concluded that Mr.
> and Mrs. V's 1992 loan to the corporation was, in substance, an equity
> investment. Thus, the entire $36,250 distribution was a dividend—nondeductible
> to VV Inc. and fully taxable to Mr. and Mrs. V.

The IRS is most likely to challenge the validity of shareholder debt when a
closely held corporation is **thinly capitalized,** with an unusually high ratio of debt to
equity. From the government's perspective, the debt-equity ratio indicates the business risk borne by the corporation's creditors. A capital structure can become so top
heavy with debt that repayment depends on the corporation's continuing profitability
rather than on the security of the underlying equity base. In such case, the purported
debt has the economic characteristics of common stock. Although the tax law does
not contain a safe harbor, a debt-equity ratio of 3 to 1 or less is generally considered
immune from IRS attack.[20] Regardless of the corporation's debt-equity ratio, shareholders should take care that any loan to their corporation has all the attributes of arm's-
length debt. The loan should be evidenced by the corporation's written, unconditional
promise to repay the principal by a specified date plus a fixed market rate of interest.
Ideally, the debt should not be subordinated to other corporate liabilities and the shareholders should not hold debt in the same proportion as they own the corporate stock. By
respecting these formalities, shareholders can minimize the possibility that the IRS will
question the capital structure of their corporation.

Using Closely Held Corporations as Tax Shelters

Individuals who don't need all the cash generated by their business have a unique
opportunity. Through careful planning, they can use the corporate form to shelter business income from the high individual tax rates.

> ***Corporation as Tax Shelter.***   Mrs. X operates a travel agency that generates
> $60,000 of net income in 19X1. Mr. X is a highly compensated professional, and
> the family does not need to spend the money earned by Mrs. X for personal
> consumption. Because of Mr. X's substantial income, the couple's marginal tax

---

[20]Boris I. Bittker and James S. Eustice, *Federal Income Taxation of Corporations and Shareholders,*
6th ed. (Boston: Warren Gorham Lamont, 1994), pp. 4–35.

rate is the maximum 39.6 percent. Mrs. X organized the travel agency as a corporation. Consequently, the 19X1 tax cost with respect to her business income is $10,000 (15 percent on the first $50,000 of taxable income + 25 percent on the next $10,000). After paying this tax, the corporation has $50,000 to retain in the business or invest in other income-producing assets. The business income is taxed only once because no cash is distributed to Mrs. X as a dividend.[21]

Mrs. X is not permanently avoiding double taxation by accumulating her business's after-tax cash at the corporate level. The accumulated earnings increase the value of her equity. So long as Mrs. X continues to own the corporate stock, this unrealized appreciation is not taxable. But at some future date when Mrs. X sells the stock or liquidates the corporation, she will recognize the appreciation in value as taxable gain and indirectly pay a second tax on the corporation's accumulated income.[22] Even so, Mrs. X's strategy significantly reduces this second tax in present value terms.

Deferral of Double Tax.   Because Mrs. X's travel agency accumulated $50,000 of after-tax income in 19X1, the value of Mrs. X's stock increased by $50,000. Mrs. X operated the travel agency for seven more years before selling her stock to an unrelated purchaser. Consequently, she deferred recognition of this $50,000 increase in value until 19X8. Her $50,000 capital gain from the sale was taxed at the preferential 20 percent rate. The present value of the tax at a 10 percent discount rate is $5,130.

19X1 increase in value recognized in 19X8	$50,000
Individual tax rate on capital gains	.20
Tax on 19X1 increase in value	$10,000
Present value of tax cost ($10,000 × .513 discount factor)	$ 5,130

Mrs. X's accumulation strategy reduced the total tax cost on $60,000 of 19X1 before-tax business income to $15,130 ($10,000 corporate tax + $5,130 present value of shareholder tax). Here is the pivotal comparison: if Mrs. X operated her travel agency as a passthrough entity, the 19X1 tax bill would have been $23,760 ($60,000 passthrough income × 39.6 percent individual tax rate).

Objective 6
List the three factors that can create tax savings when individuals use closely held corporations as tax shelters.

Even with double taxation, Mrs. X saved $8,630 of tax by operating her business as a corporation. This savings is attributable to three factors. The first factor is the *spread between the corporate and individual tax rates:* in Mrs. X's case, her corporation's average tax rate is about 17 percent compared to her 39.6 percent individual rate. The second factor is *deferral:* Mrs. X postponed paying any shareholder-level tax for seven years. The third factor is *conversion:* by avoiding dividend payments, Mrs. X transformed ordinary income to capital gain eligible for a preferential tax rate.

[21]This example ignores the tax consequences of any salary that Mrs. X receives from her corporation.
[22]As we will discuss in Chapter 15, this day of reckoning never comes if Mrs. X holds the stock until her death.

Penalty Taxes on Corporate Accumulations

Objective 7
Identify the reasons why Congress enacted the accumulated earnings tax and the personal holding company tax.

The federal tax authorities have long been aware that business owners like Mrs. X who have no pressing need for cash can use a closely held corporation as a tax shelter. Decades ago, Congress attempted to discourage this tactic by enacting two penalty taxes aimed at corporations that fail to distribute at least some portion of their after-tax profit as dividends. A corporation liable for either the accumulated earnings tax or the personal holding company tax must pay the tax *in addition to* its income tax liability for the year.

Accumulated Earnings Tax.   The IRS can impose an **accumulated earnings tax** on any corporation "formed or availed of for the purpose of avoiding the income tax with respect to its shareholders by permitting earnings and profits to accumulate instead of being divided or distributed."[23] This tax avoidance purpose is presumed to exist when a corporation accumulates earnings beyond the reasonable needs of its business. The tax equals 39.6 percent of accumulated taxable income, roughly defined as taxable income net of income taxes and dividends paid. Theoretically, a corporation with $1 million taxable income that fails to pay any dividends for the year *and* has no financial justification for retaining any of its $660,000 after-tax earnings could pay accumulated earnings tax of $261,360 (39.6 percent of $660,000).

The accumulated earnings tax is designed to coerce corporations to pay dividends. It is no coincidence that the penalty rate on unjustified accumulations equals the highest marginal rate that would apply if after-tax corporate income were distributed and taxed to individual shareholders. The imposition of this tax is a very uncertain and subjective matter. Many closely held corporations have retained millions of dollars of after-tax income, and their shareholders have never worried about the accumulated earnings tax.[24] Such peace of mind is attributable to documented and compelling business reasons justifying the accumulation. These corporations' balance sheets may show that their retained earnings financed the development of a new product line, the geographic expansion of the business, the retirement of long-term debt, or the construction of a new manufacturing facility. On the other hand, corporations vulnerable to the tax display two common traits. They have a history of minimal or nonexistent dividend payments, and their balance sheets reveal an overabundance of nonbusiness liquid assets such as long-term certificates of deposit, portfolios of marketable securities, investment real estate, and most damning of all, substantial loans to shareholders.

> *No Reasonable Business Need.*   When the IRS audited the tax return filed by the Iowa School of Men's Hairstyling, Inc., it concluded that the corporation had no reasonable business need to accumulate its after-tax income for the year. The school offered four justifications for the accumulation: (1) the school planned to expand its business to the west side of Des Moines at an estimated cost of $300,000; (2) the school needed cash reserves because of a recent reduction in enrollments; (3) the federal government had proposed reductions in student loans, resulting in an uncertain financial climate for trade schools; and (4) due to a

---

[23]§532(a). Sections 531 through 537 describe the accumulated earnings tax.

[24]Publicly held corporations are normally immune to the accumulated earnings tax because their dividend policies are not controlled by their shareholders.

decline in the hair services business, the corporation was forced to enter the real estate market. The IRS was unconvinced and assessed an accumulated earnings tax of $17,123. The federal court criticized the corporation's justifications as insubstantial, vague, indefinite, and irrelevant and upheld the assessment of the penalty tax.[25]

The tax law gives newly incorporated businesses some leeway to retain after-tax income on a "no-questions-asked" basis. Specifically, every corporation can accumulate $250,000 without establishing business need for the accumulation and without exposure to the penalty tax.[26] Refer back to our previous example involving Mrs. X and her travel agency. At the rate of $50,000 a year, the corporation will take five years to accumulate $250,000 of after-tax earnings. After this point, Mrs. X may have to convince an IRS agent that any additional accumulations have a corporate business purpose.

Personal Holding Company Tax.   Corporations qualifying as personal holding companies may be liable for a **personal holding company tax.**[27] The statutory definition of a **personal holding company** is technically complex—suffice it to say that personal holding companies are owned by a small number of individual shareholders and earn primarily nonbusiness income such as dividends, interest, rents, and royalties. The personal holding company tax equals 39.6 percent of *undistributed* corporate earnings. Accordingly, a personal holding company that distributes 100 percent of its after-tax income as dividends has no liability for an additional penalty tax.[28]

Congress enacted the personal holding company tax more than 60 years ago. Its purpose was to discourage individuals from incorporating their investment portfolios to take advantage of corporate tax rates that were 45 percentage points less than individual rates. Today, the spread between the highest corporate and individual rates is much less dramatic. Nevertheless, any corporation qualifying as a personal holding company must attach a Schedule PH showing the computation of this additional penalty tax to its annual Form 1120.

Controlled Corporate Groups

Objective 8
Explain how the tax rates apply to income earned by members of a controlled corporate group.

Individual business owners can use corporations as income tax shelters only if the corporate rates are lower than the individual rates. Currently, the lowest corporate rate is 15 percent and the highest individual rate is 39.6 percent—a spread of 24.6 percentage points. However, the 15 percent rate applies to only the first $50,000 of corporate taxable income. As we learned in Chapter 10, corporations with incomes over $335,000 pay tax at a flat 34 or even 35 percent rate. Clearly, the tax-sheltering potential of the corporate form diminishes as the corporate business prospers.

The shareholders of a growing business might be tempted to fragment the business into more than one corporation. If Mrs. X in our previous examples expands her travel agency by opening a second office in a different location, she could form a

---

[25]*Iowa School of Men's Hairstyling, Inc.*, TC Memo 1992–619.

[26]Personal service corporations may accumulate only $150,000 without establishing reasonable business need.

[27]§541. Sections 541 through 547 describe the personal holding company tax.

[28]Personal holding companies are not subject to the accumulated earnings tax. §532(b)(1).

EXHIBIT 11–1

Controlled corporate groups

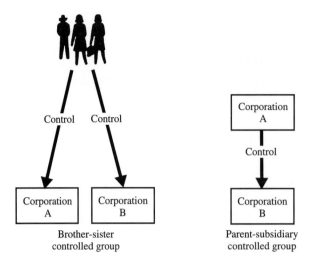

Brother-sister controlled group

Parent-subsidiary controlled group

second corporation through which to operate the new office. Mrs. X might expect this cloning strategy to double the benefit of the low corporate tax rates. She might also anticipate that each corporation could accumulate $250,000 of after-tax earnings before the accumulated earnings tax became a problem. Unfortunately, Mrs. X's strategy won't work. In the case of a **controlled group** of corporations, the progressive tax rate schedule applies to the aggregate taxable income of the group rather than to the separate incomes of each member.[29] Additionally, the group as a whole can retain only $250,000 of after-tax earnings without establishing a reasonable business need for the accumulation.[30]

A controlled group can be either a brother-sister configuration of corporations owned by the same individual shareholders or a parent-subsidiary configuration. Both types of controlled groups are pictured in Exhibit 11–1.

Individual shareholders form controlled groups of multiple corporations for many excellent nontax reasons. However, by doing so, the shareholders are not multiplying the tax-sheltering potential of the corporate form of business organization.

Conclusion

This chapter concludes our study of the four basic forms of business organization. Three of these forms—sole proprietorships, partnerships, and S corporations—are not taxable entities for federal purposes. Individuals who use these forms pay a single level of tax on their business income. Only the fourth type—corporations—are subject to federal income tax at the entity level; shareholders pay a second tax on their business income when they receive dividend distributions from the corporation. Business owners who want to engage in successful tax planning must understand the basic tax rules that differentiate sole proprietorships, passthrough entities, and corporations. By developing strategies that take advantage of these rules, the owners can control tax costs, maximize after-tax income available for personal consumption, and enhance the value of their investment in the business.

---

[29]§1561(a)(1).
[30]§1561(a)(2).

Key Terms

Accumulated earnings tax   290
Constructive dividend   286
Controlled group   292
Limited liability partnership   283

Personal holding company   291
Personal holding company tax   291
Thin capitalization   288

Questions and Problems for Discussion

1. Mr. and Mrs. V are self-employed professional musicians. Their average combined annual income from performance fees and music lessons is $130,000. The couple wants to shift income to their two children, ages 19 and 22. Can Mr. and Mrs. V organize their music business as a family partnership and give each child a 40 percent interest?

2. Mr. and Mrs. B own and operate a fast-food restaurant. This business generates average annual net profit of $160,000. The couple wants to shift some of this income to their two children, ages 19 and 22. Can Mr. and Mrs. B organize their restaurant as a family partnership and give each child a 40 percent interest?

3. Ms. J is eager to create a family partnership to generate income and cash flow for her three college-age children. Ms. J owns two businesses that could be organized as a partnership among the four family members. Ms. J established the first business 15 years ago. Currently, the business consists of operating assets with a total market value of $15 million. Ms. J established the second business only 10 months ago. This business is growing rapidly and already is generating taxable income. However, its operating assets have a total market value of only $300,000. Which business is the better candidate for a family partnership? Explain your reasoning.

4. Discuss the tax and nontax reasons why the outstanding stock in an S corporation is typically subject to a buy-sell agreement.

5. Mr. ER operates an antique store located on the first floor of a four-story office building owned by Mr. ER. The top three stories are leased to business tenants. Mr. ER is considering giving a one-third interest in both the antique store and the building to each of his two grandchildren and operating the businesses in one passthrough entity. Mr. ER wants to continue to receive 100 percent of the rent from his tenants for several years but is willing to distribute one-third of the net profit from the antique store to his grandchildren each year. Based on this objective, which form of organization should Mr. E choose?

6. Mr. Q, Mr. R, and Mr. T are dentists who practice as equal co-owners of QRT Dental Services. A patient of Mr. R's recently sued him for medical malpractice and obtained a $500,000 judgment from the court. Discuss each co-owner's personal liability for this judgment assuming that:
   a. QRT is a general partnership.
   b. QRT is a limited liability partnership.
   c. QRT is a limited liability company.

7. Refer to the facts in the previous problem. During the current year, QRT purchased $30,000 of dental equipment on credit. When QRT failed to pay its bill, the seller took the firm to court and won a judgment for $30,000. Discuss each co-owner's personal liability for this judgment assuming that:
   a. QRT is a general partnership.
   b. QRT is a limited liability partnership.
   c. QRT is a limited liability company.

8. Mrs. T and Mrs. N, who are unrelated parties, each owns and operates a small business that generates between $70,000 and $90,000 annual profit. Each woman is in the 31 percent marginal tax bracket. Mrs. T has decided to incorporate her business as a taxable corporation. Mrs. N has decided to continue to operate as a sole proprietorship. Both decisions maximize the after-tax value of the business to its owner. How can you explain this apparent contradiction?

9. BNC Inc., a closely held corporation, was organized in 1977. To date, the corporation has accumulated over $10 million of after-tax

income. During the current year, BNC's taxable income is $750,000 and its federal tax liability is $255,000. Describe two different ways that BNC can avoid exposure to the accumulated earnings tax for the year.

10. Describe the FICA payroll tax implications when the IRS classifies a portion of a corporate salary payment to a shareholder/employee as a constructive dividend.

11. When the IRS classifies a portion of a corporate salary payment to a shareholder/employee as a constructive dividend, which party (the corporation or the shareholder) bears the economic burden of the tax consequences?

12. Ms. K recently lent $20,000 to her closely held corporation, which needed the money for working capital. Ms. K sees no reason to document the loan other than as a "loan payable–shareholder" on the corporate balance sheet. She also sees no reason for her corporation to pay interest on the loan. What advice can you offer Ms. K concerning this related-party transaction?

13. Explain the logic of the 39.6 percent tax rate for both the accumulated earnings tax and the personal holding company tax.

14. In what way does a corporation's balance sheet provide information concerning the corporation's exposure to the accumulated earnings tax?

15. Why are publicly traded corporations such as General Motors generally immune from the accumulated earnings tax?

16. How would the tax shelter potential of closely held corporations be affected by:
    a. A decrease in the highest individual tax rate from 39.6 percent to 25 percent?
    b. A decrease in the preferential tax rate on individual capital gains from 20 percent to 12 percent?
    c. Repeal of the accumulated earnings tax?

17. Both brother-sister corporate groups and parent-subsidiary corporate groups are controlled groups for federal tax purposes. However, the qualification as a controlled group is much more of an issue for brother-sister groups than parent-subsidiary groups. Can you explain why?

Application Problems

1. Mrs. FB, who is in the 39.6 percent tax bracket, owns a residential apartment building that generates $80,000 of annual taxable income. Mrs. FB plans to create a family partnership by giving each of her two children a 20 percent equity interest in the building (Mrs. FB will retain a 60 percent interest). Mrs. FB will continue to manage the building. The value of her services is $15,000 per year. If Mrs. FB's children are in the 15 percent tax bracket, compute the tax savings attributable to this income-shifting arrangement.

2. WRT Inc., a calendar year S corporation, has 100 shares of stock outstanding. At the beginning of the year, Mr. W owned all 100 shares. On September 30, he gave 25 shares to his brother B and 40 shares to his daughter D. WRT's ordinary income for the year was $216,000. Based on these facts, what portion of this income must each shareholder include in income?

3. Mr. T, who is in the 39.6 percent tax bracket, is the sole shareholder of T Inc., which manufactures greeting cards. The corporation's average annual net profit (before deduction of Mr. T's salary) is $200,000. For each of the following cases, compute the tax burden on this profit.
   a. Mr. T's salary is $100,000. The corporation pays no dividends.
   b. Mr. T's salary is $100,000, and the corporation distributes its after-tax income as a dividend to Mr. T.
   c. T Inc. is an S corporation. Mr. T's salary is $100,000. The corporation makes no cash distributions to Mr. T.
   d. T Inc. is an S corporation. Mr. T draws no salary. The corporation makes no cash distributions to Mr. T.
   e. T Inc. is an S corporation. Mr. T draws no salary. The corporation makes cash distributions of all its income to Mr. T.

4. Mr. P and Mrs. Q are the two equal shareholders in Corporation PQ. Both shareholders have a 36 percent marginal tax rate. The corporation's financial records show the following:

Gross income from sales of goods	$ 880,000
Operating expenses	(410,000)
Interest paid on debt to Mr. P and Mrs. Q	(62,000)
Dividend distributions:	
Mr. P	(50,000)
Mrs. Q	(50,000)

a. Based on these facts, compute the income tax cost for this business operation.

b. How would your computation change if the interest on the shareholder debt was $162,000 and the corporation paid no dividends?

5. Ms. X, who is in the 39.6 percent tax bracket, is the sole shareholder and president of Corporation X. The corporation's financial records show the following:

Gross income from sales of goods	$1,590,000
Operating expenses	(930,000)
Salary paid to Mrs. X	(300,000)
Dividend distributions	(200,000)

a. Based on these facts, compute the income tax cost for this business operation.

b. How would your computation change if Mrs. X's salary was $500,000 and the corporation paid no dividends?

6. Mr. Z is the sole shareholder of TZ Inc. He is also the owner of the office building that serves as corporate headquarters. In 19X5, TZ Inc. paid $180,000 annual rent to Mr. Z for the use of the building. The corporation's marginal tax rate was 34 percent, and Mr. Z's marginal tax rate was 39.6 percent. The revenue agent who audited TZ's 19X5 return concluded that the fair rental value of the office building was $125,000.

a. What effect does the revenue agent's conclusion have on Mr. Z's tax liability for 19X5?

b. What effect does the revenue agent's conclusion have on TZ Inc.'s tax liability for 19X5?

7. In 19X1, Mr. and Mrs. AD formed AD Inc. by transferring $50,000 cash in exchange for 100 shares of common stock and a note from the corporation for $49,000. The note obligated the corporation to pay 10 percent annual interest and to repay the $49,000 principal on demand. AD Inc. has never declared a dividend nor made any interest payments on the debt to its shareholders. However, in 19X7, the corporation distributed $25,000 cash to Mr. and Mrs. AD and recorded the payment on its books as a principal repayment. When the IRS audited the corporation in 19X9, the revenue agent determined that this payment was a constructive dividend.

a. What is the effect of the constructive dividend on AD Inc.'s 19X7 tax liability if the corporation's marginal tax rate was 34 percent?

b. What is the effect of the constructive dividend on Mr. and Mrs. AD's 19X7 tax liability if the couple's marginal tax rate was 36 percent?

8. During a recent IRS audit, the revenue agent decided that in 19X8 the FP family used their closely held corporation, FP Inc., to avoid tax at the shareholder level by accumulating earnings beyond the reasonable needs of the business. FP Inc.'s 19X8 taxable income was $900,000, and it paid no dividends for the year. The corporation had no business need to retain any of this income. Compute FP's accumulated earnings tax for 19X8 assuming that:

a. The corporation had accumulated $4 million of after-tax income through 19X7.

b. The corporation had accumulated $129,000 of after-tax income through 19X7.

Issue Recognition Problems

Identify the tax issue or issues suggested by the following situations and state each issue in the form of a question.

1. Mr. and Mrs. KK have a 39.6 percent marginal tax rate. Their son, a freshman in college, earned minimal income from his summer job, and his marginal tax rate on his last Form 1040 was only 15 percent. Mr. and Mrs. KK are considering making their son an equal co-owner in a family business that generates over $200,000 of taxable

income each year. The couple believes that every dollar of income shifted to their son will save 24.6 cents of tax for the family.

2. Mr. J owns a 40 percent interest in the newly formed JKL Partnership. The partners organized their business as a passthrough entity so that the start-up loss would generate an immediate tax savings. Mr. J, however, had a substantial loss from another business and has no taxable income against which to deduct his 40 percent share of the JKL loss.

3. Mr. and Mrs. B own 100 percent of the stock of BB Inc., which operates a temporary employment business. Late last year, Mr. B was short of cash in his personal checking account. Consequently, he paid several personal bills by writing checks on the corporate account and recorded the payments as miscellaneous expenses. Eight months later he repaid the corporation in full.

4. REW Inc. is closely held by six members of the REW family. The corporation owns two vans that employees use for various business transportation purposes. However, for at least eight weeks during each year, the shareholders use the vans to take their families on extended vacation trips.

5. Eight years ago, Mr. and Mrs. L created a family partnership with their son, the son's wife, their daughter, and the daughter's husband. Each of these six individuals owns an equal interest in the partnership. In the current year, the son and his wife decide to divorce.

6. LSN Inc., a calendar year S corporation, has 13 shareholders. Since its incorporation, LSN has retained over $800,000 of income and reinvested it in the corporate business. Because LSN is a passthrough entity, the shareholders have paid tax on this undistributed income and increased their stock basis accordingly. The shareholders want to revoke their corporation's S election and operate LSN as a taxable corporation. The corporation currently has only $69,000 cash in its corporate bank account.

7. Last year, Mrs. K and Mrs. T, unrelated individuals, each contributed the business assets

of their respective sole proprietorships to a newly formed corporation. The shareholders believed that by combining their businesses and operating in corporate form, they could substantially increase profitability. They were encouraged to do so because they could transfer their assets in exchange for stock without recognizing gain. Unfortunately, Mrs. K and Mrs. T discovered that they couldn't work together effectively. They agreed to part company by dissolving the corporation and taking back the ownership of their respective business assets (essentially just reversing the incorporation process).

8. TY Inc. is closely held by eight members of the TY family. The corporation purchased investment land 12 years ago for $100,000. The land was recently appraised at a value of $3 million. A buyer has offered to pay cash for the land. Because the shareholders need the cash, they plan to have the corporation distribute the land to them as a dividend. They will then sell the land themselves, and recognize a $2.9 million capital gain, taxable at the preferential individual rate of 20 percent.

9. Mr. and Mrs. CR own 100 percent of the stock in CR Inc. The corporation recently hired Mr. N, the couple's nephew, in an executive position at an annual salary of $30,000. The nephew, age 20, has been in several scrapes with the law and needs financial help, and the CR family agreed that a low stress job with the family business is just what he needs for a year or two.

10. The WQ Corporation, a closely held family business, has not paid a dividend for the last seven years. Each year the minutes of the board of director's December meeting state that the corporation must accumulate after-tax income to pay for a new manufacturing facility. Until plans for construction are finalized, the corporation has been investing its excess cash in marketable securities. In the current year, the corporation curtails its manufacturing business and abandons its plan for the new facility.

Tax Planning Cases

1. Mr. and Mrs. TE own a sizable investment portfolio of stock in publicly traded corporations. The couple has four children, ages 20, 22, 25, and 27, with whom they want to share their wealth. Unfortunately, none of the children has demonstrated any ability to manage money. As a result, Mr. and Mrs. TE plan to transfer their portfolio to a new corporation in exchange for 20 shares of voting stock and 400 shares of nonvoting stock. They will then give 100 nonvoting shares to each child. The couple plans to serve as the directors of the corporation, continue to manage the investment portfolio, and distribute cash dividends to the shareholders when their children need money. They estimate that the portfolio will generate $72,000 of annual dividend income.

   a. If the TE Family Corporation is operated as an S corporation, compute the annual income tax burden on the dividend income generated by the investment portfolio. Assume that Mr. and Mrs. TE are in the 39.6 percent tax bracket and each child is in the 15 percent tax bracket. To simplify the case, ignore any value of the couple's management service to the corporation.

   b. Compute the tax burden for the first year if (1) TE Family Corporation does not have a subchapter S election in effect and (2) the corporation distributes a dividend of $100 per share of stock.

2. Mr. Y operates a photography studio as a sole proprietorship. His average annual income from the business is $100,000. Because Mr. Y does not need the entire cash flow generated by the business for personal consumption, he is considering incorporating the business. He will work as a corporate employee for a $40,000 annual salary. The corporation will accumulate its after-tax income to fund future business expansion (the corporation will not distribute dividends to Mr. Y). For purposes of this case, assume that Mr. Y's marginal income tax rate is 31 percent and ignore any employment tax consequences.

   a. Assuming that the new corporation would not be a personal service corporation for federal tax purposes, would Mr. Y decrease the annual tax burden on the business by incorporating?

   b. How would your answer change if the new corporation would be a personal service corporation?

3. Three individuals plan to invest a total of $75,000 in a new commercial venture in 19X1. The group plans to hold the venture for four years, then sell it. They must decide whether to organize the venture as a passthrough entity or as a taxable corporation. If the venture is a passthrough entity, the owners will reinvest the *entire annual income* at the entity level and pay the individual tax on their share of the income from other sources of funds. If the venture is a corporation, it will not pay dividends and will reinvest *after-tax* income at the corporate level. Because of the greater level of reinvestment, the venture should generate more annual income if organized as a passthrough entity. The income projections are as follows:

	Passthrough Entity	Corporation
Year 1 taxable income	$30,000	$30,000
Year 2 taxable income	40,000	39,000
Year 3 taxable income	50,000	48,000
Year 4 taxable income	55,000	50,000

The individuals are confident they can sell their equity in the venture at the end of year 4 for cash. If the venture is a passthrough entity, they project that the value of the equity will be $300,000. If the venture is a corporation, the value of the stock will be $275,000. (The difference in value is attributable to the greater accumulation of earnings in the passthrough entity.) Each individual has a 31 percent marginal tax rate and uses a 12 percent discount rate to compute net present value. Based on these facts, should they organize the venture as a passthrough entity or a corporation?

12 Jurisdictional Issues in Business Taxation

Learning Objectives

After studying this chapter, you should be able to:

1. Define the term *nexus* and differentiate between physical presence nexus and economic nexus.

2. Apportion corporate taxable income among states with jurisdiction to tax the income using the Uniform Division of Income for Tax Purposes Act (UDITPA) three-factor formula.

3. Explain the significance of a permanent establishment for determining jurisdiction under an income tax treaty.

4. Describe the U.S. global system of taxation as it applies to U.S. firms conducting international business operations.

5. Compute a foreign tax credit.

6. Explain how firms operating in high-tax and low-tax foreign jurisdictions can cross credit to maximize their foreign tax credit.

7. Identify the difference in tax consequences between a foreign branch operation and a foreign subsidiary.

8. Compute a deemed paid foreign tax credit.

9. Explain how corporations can defer U.S. tax on their foreign source income by operating through foreign subsidiaries.

10. Define a controlled foreign corporation (CFC) and explain how subpart F income earned by a CFC is constructively repatriated to the U.S. parent.

11. Describe the role of Section 482 in the international transfer pricing area.

Chapter 12 introduces the issues that arise when firms operate in more than one taxing jurisdiction. Firms conducting business activities that span territorial boundaries must confront the possibility that more than one government has authority to tax the activity and that an overlap in jurisdictions will cause the same income to be taxed more than once. In this chapter, we will learn how business managers can minimize the burden of such double taxation. We will also discover how the differences in tax costs across jurisdictions create planning opportunities. Managers can implement many effective strategies to shift income away from those jurisdictions with high tax costs. These strategies relate back to our basic maxim that tax costs decrease and cash flows increase when income is generated in a jurisdiction with a low tax rate.

Chapter 12 begins with an overview of state and local taxes as a cost of doing business, then focuses on the key issues involving state income taxation. The first issue concerns the states' right to tax interstate commerce and the federal restrictions on such right. The concept of income apportionment is introduced, and basic strategies for reducing the aggregate tax burden on multistate business activities are discussed. The remainder of the chapter deals with the taxation of international business ventures. We will learn that the United States has a global tax system that can result in the double taxation of foreign source income. The major role of the foreign tax credit in mitigating double taxation and the limitations on its use are covered in some detail. We will consider how U.S. firms can organize overseas operations to control the federal tax consequences of those operations. Finally, we will discuss how U.S. corporations use foreign subsidiaries to defer income recognition and reduce the tax cost of international business.

State and Local Taxation

In the United States, even the smallest firm is typically subject to three taxing jurisdictions: local government, state government, and the federal government. Historically, firms concentrated their tax planning efforts at the federal level and devoted less attention to controlling state and local tax costs. Over the past decade, companies have become more aware of the increasing burden of state and local taxes.[1] In response to demand by the business community, public accounting firms have developed specialized state and local tax (SALT) practices to provide expert professional help. More than ever before, firms and their tax advisors are formulating strategies to minimize real and personal property taxes, unemployment taxes, and sales and use taxes.

In the first section of this chapter, we focus on planning opportunities in the area of state income taxation. As we learned in Chapter 1, most states impose both a personal (individual) and a corporate income tax. Consequently, the net income generated by business activities in these states is subject to state tax whether the business is organized as a passthrough entity or a corporation. For federal purposes, corporations are allowed to deduct state income tax in the computation of taxable income.[2] The tax savings from this deduction reduces the cost of the state tax.

> ***Federal Deduction for State Income Tax.***   ZT Inc. paid $45,000 of state income tax during the current year. If ZT's federal tax rate is 34 percent, the after-tax cost of the payment is only $29,700:

---

[1]According to a recent survey of America's fastest growing companies, state and local taxes represent their most rapidly growing tax burden, with a 15.3 percent average increase during 1995. *Growing Your Own Business,* Coopers & Lybrand LLP, July/August 1996.

[2]For individual taxpayers, the state tax liability on both business and nonbusiness income is allowed as an itemized deduction. See Chapter 16.

State tax paid	$(45,000)
Federal tax savings	
($45,000 deduction × 34%)	15,300
After-tax cost	$(29,700)

Nonetheless, ZT Inc.'s aggregate tax burden is increased because the corporation must pay income tax at both the state and federal level. If ZT's taxable income before consideration of any income tax payments is $900,000 and the state tax rate is 5 percent, ZT's combined tax rate for the year is 37.3 percent.

State tax liability	
($900,000 taxable income[3] × 5%)	$ 45,000
Federal tax liability	
($855,000 taxable income × 34%)	290,700
Total income tax liability	$335,700
$335,700 ÷ $900,000 before-tax income = 37.3%	

Constitutional Restrictions on State Jurisdiction

A state's taxing jurisdiction applies to all individuals who reside in the state and all corporations formed under the laws of the state. This jurisdiction extends to nonresident individuals and corporations conducting a business activity within the state. Thus, firms engaged in interstate commerce may be subject to the taxing authority of any number of states. Given that thousands of U.S. companies conduct business in more than one state, if not all 50 states, some degree of national coordination of state income tax systems is necessary to avert fiscal anarchy.

Article 1 of the U.S. Constitution grants the federal government the power to "regulate commerce with foreign nations, and among the several states, and with the Indian tribes." This **Commerce Clause** empowers Congress and the federal courts to establish ground rules for state tax laws. For a state tax to be constitutional, it must not discriminate against interstate commerce. For instance, an income tax with a 3 percent rate for resident corporations and a 6 percent rate for nonresident corporations would be blatantly illegal. In addition, state taxes can be levied only on business enterprises having nexus with the state. **Nexus** means the degree of contact between a business and a state necessary to establish jurisdiction.

Objective 1
Define the term *nexus* and differentiate between physical presence nexus and economic nexus.

The Issue of Nexus.   Let's examine the concept of nexus by considering the regional operation conducted by Show-me Inc., which is incorporated in Missouri. Show-me's

---

[3]State income tax payments are not deductible in the computation of taxable income for state purposes. Five states (Alabama, Iowa, Louisiana, Missouri, and North Dakota) allow corporations to deduct a limited amount of federal tax in the computation of taxable income for state purposes.

Exhibit 12–1

Show-me Inc.

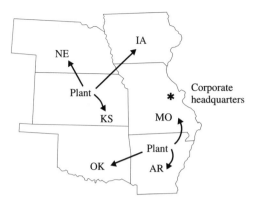

corporate headquarters are in St. Louis, and its two manufacturing plants are situated in Kansas and Arkansas. The corporation uses a common carrier to ship its products to customers in Missouri, Kansas, Arkansas, Iowa, Nebraska, and Oklahoma. Show-me's operations are illustrated in Exhibit 12–1.

Because Show-me Inc. is formed and protected under Missouri law and is commercially domiciled in the state, the corporation has nexus with Missouri. Show-me has employees and owns real and personal property located in Kansas and Arkansas, and these states provide public benefits (fire and police protection, roads and highways, etc.) that add value to the corporation's business. Thus, Show-me's physical presence in these two states creates nexus allowing both Kansas and Arkansas to tax the corporation.

But what about the other three states in Show-me's region? According to the facts, Show-me has no physical presence in Iowa, Nebraska, or Oklahoma. Under a long-standing federal statute, Public Law 86-272, firms do not establish nexus by simply selling tangible goods to customers residing in a state. Firms can even send traveling salespeople into a state to solicit orders for such goods without creating nexus.[4] Because of this federally mandated immunity, Show-me Inc. is not subject to income tax in Iowa, Nebraska, and Oklahoma.

P.L. 86-272 does not pertain to business activities other than the sale of tangible goods. As a result, nonresident firms providing services (including the leasing of tangible property) or marketing intangible property to in-state residents are not immune to the state's taxing jurisdiction. Currently, the issue of nexus with respect to these in-state activities is unsettled. Several states have taken the aggressive position that any firm conducting a regular commercial activity within the state has established *economic* nexus. Accordingly, the state has jurisdiction to tax the firm regardless of the lack of physical presence in the state.[5] To date, Congress and the federal courts have remained silent on this controversial issue.[6]

> ***Economic Nexus.***   Show-me Inc.'s research division recently developed a manufacturing process that the corporation patented with the federal government.

---

[4]15 U.S.C. 381-384 (1959).

[5]The landmark case in this area is *Geoffrey, Inc.* v. *South Carolina Tax Commission,* 437 SE.2d 13 (1993), *cert. denied,* 510 U.S. 992 (1993).

[6]A KPMG Peat Marwick survey of corporate tax directors and CFOs reveals that nexus is the top state and local tax issue. "The uncertainty surrounding when an out-of-state corporation has sufficient contacts with a state to be subject to tax thwarts the compliance and planning effort and inhibits business." *The Tax Adviser,* June 1996, p. 324.

Show-me licensed this patent to a number of companies, three of which operate in South Carolina. The companies pay an annual royalty for the use of the patent. Although Show-me Inc. has no physical presence (tangible property or employees) in South Carolina, it does earn revenue from marketing an intangible asset to South Carolina customers. On the basis of this economic nexus, South Carolina claims jurisdiction to tax Show-me's royalty income.

The nexus issue is particularly uncertain for firms that sell goods and services over the Internet. Traditional nexus concepts make little sense when applied to business activities conducted in cyberspace. Consequently, many firms are hesitant about expanding their Internet operations for fear of inadvertently creating nexus with states that currently lack taxing jurisdiction. In turn, state governments are concerned that the anticipated growth in electronic commerce will result in a loss of sales tax and income tax revenues from traditional commercial activities. The business community, the Internet industry, and state governments all acknowledge the need for a workable tax policy with respect to electronic commerce. Such policy should "facilitate, not impede, the growth of new technologies, while ensuring that no unfair tax advantage accrues to companies that develop or utilize such technologies."[7]

Internet Tax Freedom Act.   A bill is before the U.S. Congress that prohibits the imposition of new or existing state taxes on Internet transactions. The Internet Tax Freedom Act (S. 442) calls for an in-depth study of both domestic and international electronic commerce and the development of tax policy guidelines by a consortium of government, business, and consumer groups. For obvious reasons, the Internet industry is extremely supportive of this bill. Critics claim that enactment of the bill would establish the Internet as a giant tax shelter and that "for a bunch of nerds, computer types have proven to be very effective lobbyists."[8]

Apportionment of Business Income

The federal courts have established the principle that states may tax only the income attributable to a firm's in-state business activities; the state may not tax income attributable to the firm's *extraterritorial value.* To comply with this principle, state law must provide a rational and fair method for determining the portion of a firm's total income subject to that state's tax.

In 1957, a National Conference of Uniform State Laws drafted the **Uniform Division of Income for Tax Purposes Act (UDITPA)** as a recommended method for apportioning a firm's income among multiple state jurisdictions. Today, most states authorize an apportionment formula conforming to or modeled after UDITPA. Firms use these formulas to derive an **apportionment** percentage, which determines the income subject to tax in each state. The UDIPTA formula is based on three equally weighted factors: the sales factor, the payroll factor, and the property factor.

---

[7]Houghton and Friedman, "Lost in [Cyber] Space?" 97 *State Tax Notes* 174-25.

[8]Lee Sheppard, "What Does 'No New Internet Taxes' Mean?" 97 *State Tax Notes* 141-51.

$$\frac{\text{Sales factor + Payroll factor + Property factor}}{3} = \text{State apportionment percentage}$$

Objective 2
Apportion corporate taxable income among states with jurisdiction to tax the income using the Uniform Division of Income for Tax Purposes Act (UDITPA) three-factor formula.

Each factor itself is a percentage:

• The sales factor is the ratio of gross receipts from sales to in-state customers divided by total gross receipts from sales.
• The payroll factor is the ratio of compensation paid to employees working in-state divided by total compensation.
• The property fraction is the ratio of the cost of real or tangible personal property located in-state divided by the total cost of such property.

To demonstrate the mechanics of income apportionment, let's examine the following data for Duo Inc., a corporation conducting business in just two states, Georgia and Alabama.

Apportionment Formulas.   For the current taxable year, Duo Inc.'s financial records provide the following information. (All numbers are in thousands of dollars.)

	Georgia	*Alabama*	*Total*
Gross receipts from sales	$ 8,200	$ 6,800	$15,000
Payroll expense	1,252	697	1,949
Property costs	18,790	10,004	28,794

Because both states use a three-factor UDITPA formula, each state's apportionment percentage is computed as follows:

	Georgia	*Alabama*
Sales factor	54.67% ($8,200 ÷ $15,000)	45.33% ($6,800 ÷ $15,000)
Payroll factor	64.24% ($1,252 ÷ $1,949)	35.76% ($697 ÷ $1,949)
Property factor	65.26% ($18,790 ÷ $28,794)	34.74% ($10,004 ÷ $28,794)

Georgia: $$\frac{54.67\% + 64.24\% + 65.26\%}{3} = 61.39\%$$

Alabama: $$\frac{45.33\% + 35.76\% + 34.74\%}{3} = 38.61\%$$

If Duo's average annual income is $40 million, the income subject to Georgia's tax is $24,556,000 (61.39 percent of $40 million) and the income subject to Alabama's tax is $15,444,000 (38.61 percent of $40 million). Under these simple assumptions, exactly 100 percent of Duo Inc.'s business income is subject to state taxation. No income is taxed twice or escapes taxation altogether.

Realistically, state apportionment methods never achieve this mathematical precision. One major reason is that about one-half of the states that levy an income tax use a modified three-factor formula in which sales are *double-weighted* (the sales factor is counted twice and the factor total is divided by four). Another reason is that the definitions of the factors vary from state to state. For instance, the payroll factor under Virginia law includes compensation paid to corporate executive officers, while this compensation is excluded from North Carolina's payroll factor. Similarly, the measurement of apportionable business income is inconsistent across states. For instance, New Jersey law excludes interest and dividend income from the apportionment base, while New York law includes both as apportionable business income. Clearly, states do not conform to a strictly uniform method of apportionment, and the federal courts have declined to require them to do so.[9] As a result, the division of a firm's taxable income among states inevitably results in some overlap or omission.

Tax Planning Implications

Multistate businesses can reduce their overall tax cost to the extent they can shift income from a high-tax state to a low-tax state. This strategy often involves the manipulation of the state apportionment formulas. Let's refer back to our example involving Duo Inc., the corporation conducting business in both Georgia and Alabama. Currently, Georgia's tax rate on corporate income is 6 percent, while Alabama's tax rate is 5 percent. Because of this rate differential, every $100 of income that Duo can shift from Georgia's jurisdiction to Alabama's jurisdiction saves one dollar of tax.

Revised Apportionment.   Duo's management plans to build a new manufacturing plant at an estimated cost of $17 million. If the plant is built in Alabama, the corporation's property factors will be revised as follows. (All numbers are in thousands of dollars.)

	Georgia	*Alabama*	*Total*
Property costs	$18,790	$10,004	$28,794
New manufacturing plant	–0–	17,000	17,000
Revised property costs	$18,790	$27,004	$45,794
Revised property factors	41.03%	58.97%	

Consequently, Georgia's apportionment percentage will decrease, while Alabama's apportionment percentage will increase:

Georgia: $\dfrac{54.67\% + 64.24\% + 41.03\%}{3} = 53.31\%$

Alabama: $\dfrac{45.33\% + 35.76\% + 58.97\%}{3} = 46.69\%$

Because Duo's decision to build a new plant in Alabama increases that state's apportionment percentage, the decision results in a favorable income shift from Georgia to Alabama and a tax savings of $32,320.[10]

---

[9]*Moorman Manufacturing Co.* v. *Bair, Director of Revenue of Iowa,* 437 U.S. 267 (1978).

[10]The Alabama apportionment percentage will also reflect any increase in the Alabama payroll factor attributable to the new manufacturing facility.

	Original Apportionment	
	Georgia	Alabama
Total taxable income	$40,000,000	$40,000,000
Apportionment percentage	.6139	.3861
State taxable income	$24,556,000	$15,444,000
	.06	.05
State tax	$ 1,473,360	$ 772,200
	Revised Apportionment	
	Georgia	Alabama
Total taxable income	$40,000,000	$40,000,000
Apportionment percentage	.5331	.4669
State taxable income	$21,324,000	$18,676,000
	.06	.05
State tax	$ 1,279,440	$ 933,800
Total state tax:		
Original apportionment	$ 2,245,560	
Revised apportionment	(2,213,240)	
Tax savings	$ 32,320	

Of course, the tax savings from the income shift is only one factor that Duo's management must evaluate in selecting the optimal site for the plant. Management should certainly consider how the corporation's real and personal property tax costs will be affected by the geographic location of the plant. Nontax factors, such as the local cost of construction and the availability of a skilled workforce, are key elements in the decision-making process. While Duo may minimize its state income tax cost by locating its new manufacturing facility in Alabama, this location is not necessarily the best choice for maximizing the value of the facility to the corporation.

Tax Consequences of International Business Operations

In the current business environment, firms operating on a multinational level are becoming the rule rather than the exception.[11] Increasing globalization is creating exciting opportunities for U.S. businesses to expand into the emerging markets of Eastern Europe, Africa, Asia, and South America. These opportunities are coupled with formidable obstacles. Business managers with international aspirations must cope with differences across currencies, languages, technological sophistication, and cultural and political traditions.

Managers must be aware of the foreign tax implications of international business operations. When a U.S. firm plans to expand its activities into another country, it should identify the taxes included in the country's fiscal structure. The firm's liability for these taxes will depend on the nature and extent of its activity within the country and whether such activity triggers the country's taxing jurisdiction. If the foreign country

---

[11]A recent survey indicates that 47 percent of America's fastest growing companies currently sell their products abroad and another 6 percent plan to enter the international market within the year. *Growing Your Own Business,* Coopers & Lybrand LLP, July/August 1996.

imposes a net income tax, its jurisdiction may depend on whether a tax treaty is in effect between the country and the United States.

Income Tax Treaties

Objective 3
Explain the significance of a permanent establishment for determining jurisdiction under an income tax treaty.

An **income tax treaty** is a bilateral agreement between the governments of two countries defining and limiting each country's respective tax jurisdiction. The treaty provisions pertain only to individuals and corporations that are residents of either country and override the countries' generic jurisdictional rules.[12] Under a typical treaty to which the United States is a party, a firm's profits are taxable only by the country of residence (the home country) *unless* the firm maintains a **permanent establishment** in the other country (the host country). In this case, profits attributable to the permanent establishment are taxed by the host country. A permanent establishment is a fixed location, such as an office or factory, at which the firm carries on its regular commercial operations.[13] Because of this rule, a U.S. firm conducting a business activity in a treaty country avoids that country's income tax if the firm does not maintain a fixed place of business in the host country.

> ***Permanent Establishment.***   YNK Inc., a U.S. manufacturing company, sells its products to several major customers located in Country T. The corporation frequently sends its sales representatives into Country T to meet with the customers and secure their orders. If the United States and Country T have a tax treaty in effect and if YNK has no permanent establishment in the host country, Country T lacks jurisdiction to tax any of the corporation's profits. If no treaty exists, Country T's tax law may provide that YNK's activity within the country creates jurisdiction. In such case, YNK is liable for Country T income tax on the profits derived from sales to Country T customers.

U.S. Jurisdiction to Tax Global Income

Objective 4
Describe the U.S. global system of taxation as it applies to U.S. firms conducting international business operations.

The United States has a global system of taxation under which its citizens, permanent residents, and domestic corporations are taxed on *worldwide* income. In other words, when the United States is the home country, it claims jurisdiction to tax a firm's income regardless of where the income is earned. The United States does not surrender this primary jurisdiction when a U.S. firm engages in **outbound transactions** with residents of other nations, even if the profit from the transaction is taxed by a foreign government.[14] Thus, a fundamental issue confronting U.S. companies operating abroad is the potential double taxation of their business income.

As we learned in Chapter 5, firms can deduct foreign income taxes paid or accrued during the taxable year. However, a deduction is an imperfect remedy for double taxation.

---

[12]The term *resident* includes individuals who are citizens or permanent residents of a country and corporations formed under the laws of the country or a political subdivision thereof.

[13]U.S. Treasury Department, Model Income Tax Treaty, article 5.

[14]The United States also taxes business income earned in this country by nonresident aliens and foreign corporations. §871(b) and §882. Any discussion of the tax rules applying to these *inbound transactions* is beyond the scope of this text.

Deduction of Foreign Income Tax.   Corporation Q, which pays a 35 percent U.S. income tax, generates $1 million of profit subject to another nation's 22 percent income tax. Even with a deduction for the foreign income tax (and disregarding state tax), Corporation Q's combined tax rate on this income is 49.3 percent.

Foreign tax liability	
($1 million taxable income × 22%)	$220,000
U.S. tax liability	
($780,000 taxable income × 35%)	273,000
Total income tax liability	$493,000

$493,000 ÷ $1 million before-tax income = 49.3%

The federal government understands that U.S. firms facing this tax burden could be at a competitive disadvantage in the global marketplace. Therefore, the tax law contains the powerful mechanism of a foreign tax credit to alleviate double taxation at the international level.

The Foreign Tax Credit

U.S. citizens, residents, and domestic corporations may elect to credit foreign income tax paid or accured during the year against their U.S. tax liability.[15] Taxpayers electing the credit are not allowed a deduction for foreign income taxes.[16] The **foreign tax credit** is available only for income taxes; foreign excise, value-added, sales, property, and transfer taxes are not creditable.[17] Let's refer back to the example involving Corporation Q to demonstrate the power of the foreign tax credit.

Credit for Foreign Income Tax.   If Corporation Q forgoes a deduction for its $220,000 foreign tax payment and elects the tax credit, its U.S. tax liability decreases to $130,000 and its combined tax rate decreases to 35 percent.

Precredit U.S. tax	
($1 million taxable income × 35%)	$ 350,000
Foreign tax credit	(220,000)
U.S. tax liability	$ 130,000

---

[15]§901(a). The election to claim a foreign tax credit is made annually so that taxpayers can choose between the credit or the deduction on a year-to-year basis.

[16]§275(a)(4)(A).

[17]Firms either deduct or capitalize their noncreditable taxes relating to their foreign business activities.

Foreign tax liability	
($1 million taxable income × 22%)	$ 220,000
U.S. tax liability	130,000
Total income tax liability	$ 350,000

$350,000 ÷ $1 million before-tax income = 35%

By permitting Corporation Q to claim the foreign tax credit, the United States effectively relinquished its taxing jurisdiction to the extent that another nation exercised its jurisdiction. In other words, the United States reduced its 35 percent rate by the 22 percent foreign rate so that Corporation Q paid only a 13 percent U.S. tax on its foreign income.

Limitation on the Annual Credit

Objective 5
Compute a foreign tax credit.

The foreign tax credit is subject to a major limitation: the annual credit cannot exceed a specific percentage of the precredit U.S. tax for the year. This percentage is based on the ratio of the taxpayer's **foreign source income** divided by taxable income.[18]

Foreign Tax Credit Limitation.   In 19X9, Corporation R had $800,000 of taxable income, $300,000 of which was generated by the corporation's business activities in Country M. Country M has a 40 percent income tax; consequently, Corporation R paid $120,000 of foreign tax during the year.[19] The corporation's U.S. income tax liability is computed as follows:

U.S. source income	$500,000	
Foreign source income	300,000	
Taxable income		$ 800,000
U.S. tax rate		.34
Precredit U.S. tax		$ 272,000
Foreign tax credit		(102,000)
U.S. tax liability		$ 170,000

Corporation R's foreign tax credit is *limited* to the precredit U.S. tax of $272,000 multiplied by the ratio of the corporation's foreign source income to taxable income.

$$\$272,000 \times \frac{\$300,000 \text{ foreign source income}}{\$800,000 \text{ taxable income}} = \$102,000$$

---

[18]§904(a). The Internal Revenue Code contains elaborate and lengthy rules for distinguishing between foreign source and U.S. source income. See §861 through §865.

[19]The statement assumes that Country M and the United States use the same definition of taxable income. Actually, the definition of taxable income varies considerably from country to country.

Even though Corporation R paid $120,000 of foreign income tax, only $102,000 of this payment is creditable against 19X9 U.S. tax. Note that the limited credit equals the *entire precredit U.S. tax* on the corporation's foreign source income ($300,000 × 34 percent = $102,000). Note also that the corporation's U.S. tax liability equals 34 percent of its $500,000 of U.S. source income. Because of the foreign tax credit, Corporation R pays no U.S. tax on its foreign source income. Because of the limitation on that credit, the corporation pays the full U.S. tax on its domestic income.

Excess Credit Carrybacks and Carryforwards.   When a firm is subject to the foreign tax credit limitation, the **excess foreign tax credit** (foreign tax paid but not credited) can be carried back two years and forward five years.[20] The firm can use its excess credits in a carryback or carryforward year, subject to the annual limitation.

Excess Credit Carryback.   In the preceding example, Corporation R had an excess credit of $18,000 ($120,000 foreign tax paid – $102,000 limited credit) in 19X9. The corporation's U.S. tax return for 19X7 showed the following:

U.S. source income	$350,000
Foreign source income	250,000
Taxable income	$ 600,000
U.S. tax rate	.34
Precredit U.S. tax	$ 204,000
Foreign tax credit (actual tax paid)	(77,500)
U.S. tax liability	$ 126,500

The credit limitation did not apply because the $77,500 foreign tax paid was less than the $85,000 limitation.

$$\$204,000 \times \frac{\$250,000 \text{ foreign source income}}{\$600,000 \text{ taxable income}} = \$85,000$$

Consequently, Corporation R had a $7,500 *excess limitation* in 19X7 ($85,000 limitation – $77,500 credited foreign tax). Because of the excess limitation, the corporation can carry back $7,500 of its 19X9 excess credit and obtain a $7,500 refund of 19X7 tax. The remaining $10,500 excess credit is available as a carryback to 19X8. If the corporation had no excess limitation in 19X8, it carries the excess credit forward to the next five taxable years.

Objective 6
Explain how firms operating in high-tax and low-tax foreign jurisdictions can cross-credit to maximize their foreign tax credit.

Cross-Crediting.   If a firm's foreign source income is taxed by a foreign jurisdiction at a rate *lower* than the U.S. rate, the firm's combined rate on such income is the higher U.S. rate. In such case, the firm has an excess limitation equal to the U.S. tax paid on its foreign source income. If the foreign source income is taxed by a foreign jurisdiction at a rate *higher* than the U.S. rate, the combined rate is the higher foreign rate. In this case, the firm pays no U.S. tax on its foreign source income. It will, however, have an excess foreign tax credit.

---

[20]§904(c).

In a year in which a firm earns income in both low-tax and high-tax foreign jurisdictions, the excess credit from the high-tax income can be used to the extent of the excess limitation from the low-tax income. This **cross-crediting** reduces the firm's overall tax rate on its foreign source income. Let's develop a case to illustrate this important result.

Cross-Crediting.   CVB Inc. has the following taxable income:

U.S source income	$350,000
Foreign source income:	
Country L	100,000
Country H	100,000
Taxable income	$550,000

CVB paid $15,000 of income tax to Country L and $42,000 of income tax to Country H. The corporation's U.S. tax liability is $130,000.

Taxable income	$550,000
U.S. tax rate	.34
Precredit U.S. tax	$187,000
Foreign tax credit (actual tax paid)	(57,000)
U.S. tax liability	$130,000

The credit limitation does not apply because the $57,000 foreign tax paid is *less* than the $68,000 limitation.

$$\$187,000 \times \frac{\$200,000 \text{ foreign source income}}{\$550,000 \text{ total taxable income}} = \$68,000$$

In this example, CVB pays only $11,000 of U.S. tax on its $200,000 of foreign source income:

Foreign source income	$200,000
U.S. tax rate	.34
	$ 68,000
Foreign tax credit	(57,000)
U.S. tax on foreign source income	$ 11,000

Therefore, the corporation's combined rate on this income is 34 percent, even though the $100,000 earned in Country H was subject to a 42 percent foreign tax rate. Because CVB blended low-tax and high-tax income in computing its foreign tax credit limitation, the corporation reduced its U.S. tax bill by every dollar of foreign tax paid during the year.

AMT Foreign Tax Credit

In Chapter 10, we discussed the possibility that a corporation may pay an alternative minimum tax (AMT) in addition to its regular federal tax. The AMT equals any excess of the corporation's tentative minimum tax over regular tax. Corporations can reduce tentative minimum tax by a foreign tax credit.[21] The AMT credit is subject to the same basic limitation as the regular credit: the AMT credit is limited to the percentage of tentative minimum tax attributable to foreign source alternative minimum taxable income (AMTI). The AMT credit is subject to a *second* limitation: the credit can't exceed 90 percent of tentative minimum tax.

> **AMT Foreign Tax Credit.**   Corporation T has taxable income of $500,000, all of which is foreign source, and paid $190,000 of foreign income tax during the year. The corporation has no AMT adjustments or preferences; therefore, its AMTI is also $500,000. Corporation T's U.S. tax liability is computed as follows:
>
> | | |
> |---|---|
> | Precredit regular tax | |
> | ($500,000 taxable income × 34%) | $ 170,000 |
> | Foreign tax credit | (170,000) |
> | Regular tax | $ –0– |
>
> Corporation T's foreign tax credit is limited to the precredit U.S. tax of $170,000 multiplied by the ratio of foreign source income to taxable income.
>
> $$\$170,000 \times \frac{\$500,000 \text{ foreign source income}}{\$500,000 \text{ taxable income}} = \$170,000$$
>
> Corporation T's AMT is computed as follows:
>
> | | |
> |---|---|
> | Precredit tentative minimum tax | |
> | ($500,000 AMTI × 20%) | $ 100,000 |
> | AMT foreign tax credit | (90,000) |
> | Tentative minimum tax | $ 10,000 |
> | Regular tax | –0– |
> | AMT | $ 10,000 |
>
> Corporation T's AMT foreign tax credit is limited to the precredit tentative minimum tax of $100,000 multiplied by the ratio of foreign source AMTI to AMTI.

---
[21]§59.

$$\$100,000 \times \frac{\$500,000 \text{ foreign source AMTI}}{\$500,000 \text{ AMTI}} = \underline{\underline{\$100,000}}$$

However, the AMT credit is also limited to 90 percent of tentative minimum tax. Consequently, the AMT credit is limited to $90,000.

Because of the 90 percent limit on the AMT foreign tax credit, Corporation T must pay $10,000 of U.S. tax. This result accords with the underlying policy objective of the AMT: to ensure that every U.S. corporation pays at least a nominal U.S. tax. But the result subverts the function of the foreign tax credit as a mechanism for mitigating the double taxation of worldwide income.

Organizational Forms for Overseas Operations

U.S. firms expanding internationally must decide on the form in which to operate their overseas activities. This section of the chapter surveys the basic organizational choices for foreign business ventures.

Foreign Sales Corporations

Corporations that export goods manufactured in this country for sale in foreign markets can reduce their U.S. tax burden by channeling the sales through a wholly owned **foreign sales corporation (FSC).** The statutory rules governing the operation and taxation of FSCs are exceptionally complicated.[22] In the most conceptual terms, the income channeled through a FSC is taxed at a maximum rate of 29.75 percent. This preferential rate represents a subsidy for U.S. companies competing in the world marketplace. As a tax expenditure, the FSC preference costs the federal government more than $1.5 billion each year. FSCs are completely artificial entities with no independent business purpose; corporations use FSCs for the sole purpose of obtaining the preferential tax rate for their export sales.

Branch Operations and Foreign Partnerships

Objective 7
Identify the difference in tax consequences between a foreign branch operation and a foreign subsidiary.

U.S. firms wanting to establish a presence in a foreign country can open a branch office in the host country. A branch operation is not a separate legal entity but is merely an extension of the U.S. firm. Any income or loss generated by the foreign branch is commingled with income and losses from the firm's other business activities. To the extent the branch is profitable, its income is subject to U.S. tax. Any foreign tax paid on branch income is included in the computation of the foreign tax credit. The same tax consequences result if a U.S. firm becomes a partner in a foreign partnership. The firm reports its distributive share of the partnership's foreign source income or loss and is entitled to a tax credit for its distributive share of foreign income taxes paid by the partnership.

---

[22]See §921 through §927.

Domestic Subsidiaries

U.S. corporations often create wholly owned subsidiaries to house foreign business operations. Because of the corporate parent's limited liability as a shareholder, this strategy confines the risks inherent in the foreign operation to the subsidiary corporation. If the subsidiary is a domestic corporation, the tax consequences are virtually identical to a branch operation. The parent and subsidiary can file a consolidated U.S. tax return so that profits and losses generated by the overseas business activity are combined with those of the parent and any other domestic subsidiaries.[23] The group can elect a consolidated foreign tax credit for income taxes paid by the subsidiary and any other corporation in the group.

Foreign Subsidiaries

Another alternative is for a U.S. corporation to create a subsidiary under the laws of the foreign jurisdiction. In such case, the subsidiary is a foreign corporation, although it is completely controlled by a U.S. parent. Similarly, the foreign jurisdiction is both home and host country to the subsidiary even though a U.S. shareholder owns the corporation. Multinational corporations typically have cogent political and legal reasons for using foreign subsidiaries, such as the public image of the business in the host country or prohibitions against foreign ownership of real property located in the host country. When a U.S. corporation conducts a business operation through a foreign subsidiary, the tax consequences of the subsidiary's activities cannot be combined with those of the parent; foreign subsidiaries are ineligible to be included in a U.S. consolidated tax return.[24] Operating losses incurred by the subsidiary are isolated; the parent can't use these losses to shelter its own income from U.S. taxation. Depending on the tax laws of the foreign jurisdiction, the corporation may be allowed to carry the loss back or forward as a net operating loss deduction.

The income generated by the foreign subsidiary's local business activity may be taxed by its home country but is not directly subject to U.S. tax. When the subsidiary distributes a dividend to its U.S. parent, the dividend is fully included in the parent's taxable income; dividends from foreign corporations are ineligible for a dividends-received deduction.[25]

Objective 8
Compute a deemed paid foreign tax credit.

Deemed Paid Foreign Tax Credit.   When a foreign subsidiary pays a dividend to its U.S. parent, the issue of double taxation again takes center stage. These dividends represent after-tax income to the extent the subsidiary paid tax to its home country in the year the income was earned. The dividends are subject to U.S. tax in the hands of the recipient parent. While these dividends are foreign source income, the parent corporation itself has not paid any foreign tax. To solve this dilemma, the Internal Revenue Code authorizes a **deemed paid foreign tax credit.** This credit is available only to U.S. corporations owning 10 percent or more of the voting stock of a foreign corporation that paid dividends during the taxable year.[26]

The best way to explain the computation of the deemed paid foreign tax credit is through an example.

---

[23]See the discussion of consolidated corporate returns in Chapter 10.
[24]§1504(b)(3).
[25]§245 contains several exceptions to this general rule.
[26]§902(a).

Deemed Paid Credit.   YNK Inc., a U.S. corporation, formed FC Inc. under the laws of Country K. In its first year of operation, FC generated $100,000 of income and paid $25,000 of tax to Country K. The foreign subsidiary distributed its $75,000 after-tax income to YNK as a dividend.[27] The preliminary step in the computation of YNK's deemed paid credit is to increase (gross-up) this dividend by the foreign tax that FC paid. Because FC distributed its entire after-tax income, the $75,000 dividend is grossed up by the entire $25,000 Country K tax. Therefore, YNK reports a $100,000 grossed-up dividend as foreign source income.[28] YNK is now entitled to a credit for the $25,000 foreign tax deemed paid on YNK's behalf by FC. Because of this credit, YNK's U.S. tax on the dividend is only $10,000.

Foreign source income (grossed-up dividend)	$100,000
U.S. tax rate	.35
Precredit U.S. tax	$ 35,000
Deemed paid foreign tax credit	(25,000)
U.S. tax	$ 10,000

YNK's $25,000 credit is not limited because the 25 percent foreign tax rate is *less* than the U.S. tax rate. Because of the deemed paid credit, the combined tax on the $100,000 of foreign source income earned by YNK through FC is 35 percent: $25,000 foreign tax paid by FC and $10,000 U.S. tax paid by YNK.

Deferral of U.S. Tax on Foreign Source Income

Objective 9
Explain how corporations can defer U.S. tax on their foreign source income by operating through foreign subsidiaries.

Foreign source business income earned by a foreign corporation is not subject to U.S. tax unless and until the corporation pays a dividend to a U.S. shareholder. Accordingly, U.S. corporations that don't *repatriate* (bring home) the earnings of their foreign subsidiaries are deferring U.S. tax on such earnings. If a U.S. parent has no pressing need for cash from its overseas operations, this deferral can go on indefinitely. Let's develop a case that quantifies the value of such deferral.

Deferral of U.S. Tax.   RWB Inc., a California corporation with a 35 percent U.S. tax rate, has two foreign business operations, one organized as a branch and the other organized as a foreign subsidiary. In year 1, both the branch and the subsidiary earned $500,000 of income subject to a 20 percent foreign tax. Both operations reinvested their after-tax earnings in their respective businesses.

In year 1, RWB's U.S. tax on the $500,000 of foreign source income earned by the branch is $75,000.

---

[27]The simplifying assumption in this example is that Country K does not impose a withholding tax on dividends paid to foreign parent corporations.

[28]§78.

Taxable income	$500,000
U.S. tax rate	.35
Precredit U.S. tax	$175,000
Foreign tax credit	(100,000)
U.S. tax	$ 75,000

RWB's combined tax on the branch income is $175,000 ($100,000 foreign tax + $75,000 U.S. tax). In contrast, RWB's combined tax in year 1 on the $500,000 earned by its foreign subsidiary is only $100,000, the foreign income tax paid by the subsidiary to its home country.

Note that RWB pays U.S. tax on the foreign branch's income even though it did not withdraw any cash from the branch operation. If and when RWB does withdraw cash from the foreign branch, the withdrawal will have no tax consequences. In contrast, RWB pays no U.S. tax on the income earned by the subsidiary until it withdraws cash (i.e., receives a dividend) from the subsidiary.

Tax Savings from Deferral.   RWB's foreign subsidiary pays no dividends until year 7, when it distributes $400,000 to its parent. This distribution equals the after-tax income earned by the subsidiary in year 1. RWB's U.S. tax on this dividend is $75,000:

Dividend received	$400,000	
Gross-up for tax paid by subsidiary	100,000	
Foreign source income		$500,000
U.S. tax rate		.35
Precredit U.S. tax		$175,000
Deemed paid tax credit		(100,000)
U.S. tax		$ 75,000

At a 12 percent discount rate, the present value of this tax is $38,025 and the present value of RWB's combined tax on the $500,000 of income earned by its subsidiary in year 1 and repatriated in year 7 is $138,025.

Foreign tax paid by subsidiary in year 1	$100,000
Present value of U.S. tax paid in year 7	
($75,000 × .507 discount factor)	38,025
NPV of combined tax	$138,025

This cost is $36,975 less than the combined tax on the year 1 income of the branch operation: a tax savings resulting entirely from the deferral of U.S. tax on foreign source income.

EXHIBIT 12–2

Tax haven subsidiary

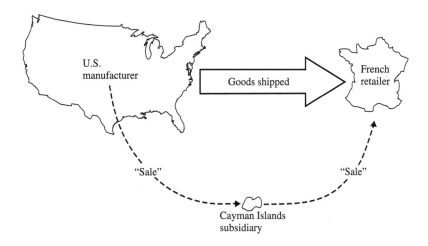

Tax deferral through the use of foreign subsidiaries is possible only if the subsidiary's income is subject to a foreign tax rate *less* than the U.S. rate. If a subsidiary operating in a high-tax country repatriates after-tax income as a dividend, the deemed paid credit reduces the domestic parent's U.S. tax on the dividend to zero. Thus, the parent's only tax cost on the foreign source income is the foreign income tax paid by the subsidiary in the year the income was earned.

Controlled Foreign Corporations

U.S. corporations with foreign subsidiaries operating in low-tax countries (countries with tax rates less than the U.S. rate) can minimize tax by shifting as much income as possible to those subsidiaries. Before 1962, U.S. companies routinely created subsidiaries in **tax haven** jurisdictions—countries with minimal or no corporate income tax. In many cases, the tax haven subsidiary existed only on paper, performing no function other than providing tax shelter for the company's business income. Consider the case of a U.S. manufacturer exporting its goods through a French subsidiary for retail sale in the European market. If the U.S. parent sold its goods directly to this marketing subsidiary at an arm's-length price, it would pay U.S. tax on the net income from the outbound transaction. Furthermore, the subsidiary would pay French income tax on the profits from its retail sales of the goods. If, however, the U.S. parent also owned a subsidiary incorporated in the Cayman Islands, a Caribbean nation with no corporate income tax, the parent could sell its goods to this subsidiary for a very low price. The Cayman subsidiary could then sell the goods to the French subsidiary for a very high price. This three-party transaction is diagrammed in Exhibit 12–2.

Even though the U.S. parent sold its goods to the Cayman subsidiary, it shipped the goods directly to the French subsidiary's warehouse outside of Paris. The Cayman subsidiary was not involved in the actual production or distribution process. Nevertheless, the subsidiary's intermediate legal title to the goods shifted most of the income from the outbound transaction to the Cayman corporation. Until such time as this corporation paid a dividend to its U.S. parent, no income taxes at all were levied on the business income.

Objective 10
Define a controlled foreign corporation (CFC) and explain how subpart F income earned by a CFC is constructively repatriated to the U.S. parent.

This classic tax avoidance scheme is just one example of the creative strategies used by international firms to divert income to tax haven jurisdictions. In 1962, Congress ended the most abusive strategies by enacting a set of rules applying to controlled foreign corporations. A **controlled foreign corporation (CFC)** is a foreign corporation in which U.S. shareholders own more than 50 percent of the voting power or stock value.[29] If a CFC earns certain types of income, the law treats such income as if it were currently distributed to the CFC's shareholders.[30] Any U.S. shareholder with a 10 percent or more interest must recognize and pay tax on its pro rata share of this constructive dividend. These shareholders are entitled to increase the tax basis in their CFC stock by their constructive dividend.[31] If the CFC subsequently makes cash distributions to its shareholders, the distributions are nontaxable to the extent of any prior year constructive dividends and reduce the tax basis in the recipient shareholder's CFC stock.[32]

CFC Constructive Dividends.   In year 1, ABC Inc. incorporated FL Inc. under the laws of Country B. For 19X1, FL earned $20,000 and paid $3,000 tax to Country B. FL did not distribute a dividend to its parent in 19X1. However, in 19X2, FL distributed $17,000 of 19X1 after-tax income as a dividend to ABC. The following table contrasts the consequences if ABC can defer recognition of FL's 19X1 income with the tax consequences of a constructive dividend from FL:

	Deferral	*Constructive Dividend*
Year 1:		
Cash received from FL	$ –0–	$ –0–
Dividend recognized	–0–	17,000
Gross-up for foreign tax paid	–0–	3,000
Foreign source income	–0–	20,000
Increase (decrease) in FL stock basis	–0–	17,000
Year 2:		
Cash received from FL	17,000	17,000
Dividend recognized	17,000	–0–
Gross-up for foreign tax paid	3,000	–0–
Foreign source income	20,000	–0–
Increase (decrease) in FL stock basis	–0–	(17,000)

Note that the constructive dividend treatment affects only the *timing* of ABC's recognition of the income earned by its foreign subsidiary. In this simple two-year example, the constructive dividend treatment for FL's 19X1 after-tax income accelerated ABC's U.S. tax liability on such income by one year.

Subpart F Income.   Not all foreign source income earned by a CFC must be constructively repatriated to its U.S. shareholders. Only narrowly defined categories of income (labeled **subpart F income** in the Internal Revenue Code) are subject to this treatment. Conceptually, Subpart F income is artificial income in that it has no commercial or economic connection to the country in which the CFC is incorporated. Subpart F income has many complex components, one of the more important of which is income derived from the sale of goods if (1) the CFC either buys the goods from or sells the goods to a related

---

[29]§957(a)
[30]§951(a)(1)(A).
[31]§961.
[32]§959.

party and (2) the goods are neither manufactured nor sold for use within the CFC's home country.[33] In our Cayman Island example, the Cayman CFC is related to both the U.S. manufacturer and the French distributor because all three corporations are members of one controlled group. Moreover, the goods described in the example never touched Cayman soil and have no connection to the country. Quite clearly, the Cayman subsidiary's entire taxable income is subpart F income on which the U.S. parent must pay current U.S. tax.

Investment of CFC Earnings in U.S. Parent.   Corporations can use CFCs to defer U.S. tax if three conditions are satisfied:

- The CFC generates foreign source income in a jurisdiction with a tax rate *less* than the U.S. rate.
- The foreign source income is not subpart F income.
- The CFC accumulates after-tax earnings instead of paying dividends.

If the U.S. parent is content to reinvest the CFC's earnings in foreign business activities, the third condition may not be an obstacle. But if the parent needs cash from its overseas operations, it may try to maneuver around this condition. An obvious strategy is for the parent to borrow money from or sell shares of its own stock to the CFC. Neither transaction results in taxable gain to the parent but both result in positive cash flow. Unfortunately, this strategy doesn't work. The tax law treats a CFC's debt or equity investment in its U.S. parent as a repatriation of earnings: a constructive dividend on which the parent must pay current U.S. income tax.[34]

U.S. Investment of CFC Earnings.   DEF Inc. owns 100 percent of the stock of FV Inc., a foreign corporation operating in a country with a 20 percent income tax. During the current year, FV earned $100,000 of income (none of which was subpart F income) and paid no dividends. However, FV paid $40,000 cash to DEF for 160 shares of newly issued DEF stock. Because of this "back door" repatriation of FV's earnings, DEF must recognize $50,000 of foreign source income.

Cash received from FV as payment for stock	$40,000
Constructive dividend recognized	$40,000
Gross-up for foreign tax paid by FV	10,000
Foreign source income	$50,000

Transfer Pricing and Section 482

Objective 11
Describe the role of Section 482 in the international transfer pricing area.

While the subpart F rules are potent, they do not extend to many types of foreign source income earned by CFCs. Consequently, U.S. parents benefit when they shift business income to their foreign subsidiaries operating in low-tax jurisdictions. If a U.S. parent has subsidiaries in high-tax jurisdictions (such as Japan, France, Germany, and the

---

[33]Such income constitutes foreign base company sales income per §954(d)(1). Subpart F income is defined in §952 through §954.

[34]§951(a)(1)(B) and §956.

United Kingdom), the tax strategy can be reversed. In such case, the parent wants to use its domestic subsidiaries as tax shelters.

Controlled groups of corporations can shift income among the members through their pricing structure for intercompany transactions. Consider the possibilities for income shifting if a U.S. parent owns an Irish subsidiary actively engaged in the manufacture of consumer goods for worldwide export sale. Although the Irish subsidiary is a CFC, its profit from sales of goods manufactured in Ireland and sold to unrelated purchasers is not subpart F income. As a result, the income is subject only to the 10 percent Irish corporate tax until the CFC pays dividends to its parent. If the parent (or any domestic subsidiary) sells raw materials to the Irish corporation, the lower the price charged for the materials, the greater the income shifted to Ireland. If the U.S. parent provides administrative, marketing, or financial services to the Irish corporation, the parent could further inflate the foreign subsidiary's profits (and diminish its own) by charging a nominal fee for the services rendered. Similarly, if the parent owns patents, copyrights, licenses, or other intangible assets that add value to the Irish manufacturing process, the parent could forgo royalty payments for the subsidiary's use of the intangible.

All the above pricing strategies shift income to the Irish subsidiary. Not surprisingly, the United States and most foreign countries, mindful of the income distortion resulting from artificial **transfer prices,** demand that related business entities deal with each other in the same arm's-length manner as they deal with unrelated parties. Under federal tax law, Section 482 gives the IRS the authority to apportion or allocate gross income, deductions, or credits between related parties to correct any perceived distortion resulting from unrealistic transfer prices.[35]

Over the past decades, the IRS has not hesitated to use its Section 482 power to ensure that domestic corporations pay U.S. tax on an appropriate amount of their international income. While corporations certainly can challenge the IRS in court, the prevailing judicial attitude is that the IRS's determination of an arm's-length transfer price should be upheld unless the corporation can demonstrate the determination is "arbitrary, capricious, or unreasonable."[36] Clearly, multinational corporations are in a defensive posture in disputes concerning their transfer pricing practices and must be constantly aware of any Section 482 exposure created by their intercompany transactions.

Transfer Pricing—An Issue of Global Proportion.   In 1997, Ernst & Young conducted a survey of the tax directors of over 450 multinational companies concerning transfer pricing issues. The survey results led to the following observations:

- Companies throughout the world regard transfer pricing as the most important international tax issue they will face over the next two years.
- Fiscal authorities in both developed and emerging markets are paying increased attention to transfer pricing compliance.
- Intercompany services are the transactions most susceptible to transfer pricing disputes.

---

[35]§482 was introduced in Chapter 5.
[36]*Liberty Loan Corp.* v. *U.S.,* 498 F.2d 225 (CA-8, 1974), *cert. denied,* 419 U.S. 1089.

> - Nearly two-thirds of the companies surveyed report that their intercompany transactions have already been the target of a transfer pricing examination.
> - Eight in ten multinationals expect to face a transfer pricing examination within the next two years.

Conclusion

In the preceding chapter, we discussed the tax implications when firms select a particular entity through which to conduct their business activities. In this chapter, we added a new tax planning variable—the jurisdiction in which the entity is taxed. To the extent that firms can manipulate this variable by locating business activities in low-tax jurisdictions, tax costs can be controlled. When a business enterprise stretches across jurisdictions, the owners run the risk that double taxation will erode their after-tax profits. If the competing jurisdictions are state governments, business income is divided according to each state's respective apportionment rule. Managers can often take advantage of anomalies in these rules and differences in state tax rates to reduce their firm's tax burden. If the competing jurisdictions are the United States and a foreign government, the foreign tax credit is an invaluable mechanism for moderating double taxation.

Multinational U.S. companies can achieve substantial tax savings by incorporating foreign subsidiaries in low-tax jurisdictions. As a general rule, the income earned by these subsidiaries is not subject to U.S. tax until it is repatriated. To take advantage of this deferral, U.S. parent corporations must carefully avoid the subpart F rules and be content with reinvesting their foreign earnings in overseas ventures. They must steer clear of transfer pricing disputes with the IRS and the enforcement agencies of other nations with jurisdictional interests. Certainly, international tax planning is a complex and challenging specialty that will become more valuable as the global economy continues to develop.

Key Terms

Apportionment   303
Commerce Clause   301
Controlled foreign corporation
 (CFC)   317
Cross-crediting   311
Deemed paid foreign tax credit   314
Excess foreign tax credit   310
Foreign sales corporation (FSC)   313
Foreign source income   309
Foreign tax credit   308

Income tax treaty   307
Nexus   301
Outbound transaction   307
Permanent establishment   307
Subpart F income   318
Tax haven   317
Transfer price   320
Uniform Division of Income for Tax
 Purposes Act (UDITPA)   303

Questions and Problems for Discussion

In the questions, problems, and cases for Chapter 12, corporations are U.S. corporations unless otherwise stated.

1. Why does a corporation's state income tax cost depend on the corporation's marginal income tax rate for federal purposes?

2. Corporation NY is a New York corporation that manufactures office equipment in a factory located in New York. In which of the following cases does Corporation NY have nexus with Pennsylvania?

   a. Corporation NY owns and operates two retail outlets for its products in Pennsylvania.

   b. Corporation NY owns no tangible property in Pennsylvania. It employs two salespeople who travel throughout Pennsylvania soliciting orders for office equipment from Corporation NY's regular customers. The corporation fills the orders out of its New York factory and ships the equipment to the customers by common carrier.

   c. Corporation NY owns no tangible property in Pennsylvania and does not have any employees who work in the state. It does have Pennsylvania customers who order equipment directly from the New York factory by telephone or fax.

   d. Refer to the facts in *c* above. Corporation NY employs two technicians who travel throughout Pennsylvania. These technicians provide repair and maintenance services to NY's customers.

3. Distinguish between the concepts of physical presence nexus and economic nexus.

4. Does the federal government require states to use a three-factor formula to apportion the income of an interstate commercial activity for state income tax purposes?

5. BNJ Inc. conducts a business activity that spans four states. BNJ's taxable income for the year was $32 million. However, the total of the taxable income numbers reported on BNJ's four state income tax returns was $34.8 million. Discuss the possible reasons for such discrepancy.

6. In what situation would a multistate business deliberately create nexus with a certain state so that the state has jurisdiction to tax a portion of the business income?

7. Distinguish between a home country and a host country in the international tax context.

8. What is the purpose of a bilateral income tax treaty between two countries?

9. LF Inc. sells its products to customers residing in Country X and Country Y. Both foreign jurisdictions have a 20 percent corporate income tax. During the year, LF made more than $30 million of sales in both Country X and Country Y. However, it paid income tax only to Country X. What factors could account for this result?

10. Both the corporate NOL deduction and foreign tax credit are limited for AMT purposes. The NOL deduction can't exceed 90 percent of AMTI, and the foreign tax credit can't exceed 90 percent of tentative minimum tax. Which limitation is more likely to eliminate (rather than defer) the tax savings from an NOL deduction or foreign tax credit?

11. Corporation PY plans to form a foreign subsidiary through which to conduct a new business venture in Country J. Corporation PY projects that this venture will operate at a loss for several years.

    a. To what extent will the foreign subsidiary's operating losses generate U.S. tax savings?

    b. To what extent will the foreign subsidiary's operating losses generate a savings of Country J income tax?

12. HD Inc. operates its business activities in Country U through a subsidiary incorporated under Country U law. The subsidiary has never paid a dividend and has accumulated over $10 million.

    a. Country U has a 45 percent corporate income tax. Describe the tax consequences to HD Inc. if it repatriates $5 million cash by instructing the foreign subsidiary to pay a $5 million dividend.

    b. How would the tax consequences of the dividend change if Country U's corporate income tax rate is only 20 percent?

13. TJ Inc. has a subsidiary incorporated under Country H law. Country H does not have a corporate income tax. Which of the following activities carried on by the subsidiary generates subpart F income?

a. The subsidiary buys woolen and leather clothing products manufactured by a Swedish company and sells the products to unrelated wholesalers in the United States. TJ Inc. owns the Swedish company.

b. The subsidiary buys coffee beans grown on plantations located in Country H and sells the beans to TJ Inc., which makes coffee products.

c. The subsidiary buys building materials from a Mexican company and sells the materials to construction companies operating in Country H. TJ Inc. owns the Mexican company.

14. Corporation BC has a subsidiary operating exclusively in Country A and a subsidiary operating exclusively in Country Z.

a. Both subsidiaries were incorporated under Delaware law and are therefore U.S. corporations. Can Corporation BC use the operating losses generated by the subsidiary operating in Country A to reduce the income generated by the subsidiary operating in Country Z?

b. Would your answer change if both subsidiaries are foreign corporations formed under the laws of the countries in which they operate?

15. DF Partnership carries on business activities in the United States and four other countries. Explain why the ordinary income generated by the foreign business activities is a separately stated item on the partnership's Schedule K, Form 1065.

16. KS Inc. owns 100 percent of the stock of Sub 1 (a CFC operating in a country with a 50 percent corporate tax) and 90 percent of the stock of Sub 2 (a CFC operating in a country with a 10 percent corporate tax). KS sells goods and services to both CFCs. Is the IRS more interested in KS's transfer pricing for sales to Sub 1 or sales to Sub 2?

17. In what situation is the United States a tax haven for an international business operation?

Application Problems

1. OP Inc. conducts business in State M and State N. Both states use the UDITPA three-factor formula to apportion income for state tax purposes. State M's corporate tax rate is 4.5 percent, and State N's corporate tax rate is 7 percent. For the current year, OP had the following sales, payroll, and property (in thousands of dollars) in each state:

	State M	State N	Total
Gross receipts from sales	$ 3,000	$7,500	$10,500
Payroll expense	800	1,200	2,000
Property costs	900	1,000	1,900

OP Inc.'s income for the year was $3 million. Based on these facts, compute the corporation's State M and State N tax liability.

2. Refer to the facts in the preceding problem. Compute OP's State M and State N tax liability if State N uses an apportionment formula in which the sales factor is double-weighted.

3. ZX Inc. has the following taxable income:

U.S. source income	$1,900,000
Foreign source income	240,000
Taxable income	$2,140,000

The corporation paid $33,000 of foreign income tax during the year. Based on these facts, compute ZX's U.S. income tax liability.

4. JHG Inc. has the following taxable income:

U.S. source income	$ 8,800,000
Foreign source income	2,690,000
Taxable income	$11,490,000

The corporation paid $1,040,000 of foreign income tax during the year. Based on these facts, compute JHG's U.S. income tax liability.

5. Corporation ABC has the following taxable income:

U.S. source income	$1,620,000
Foreign source income:	
Country A	550,000
Country B	2,000,000
Country C	2,900,000
Taxable income	$7,070,000

During the year, the corporation paid $600,000 income tax to Country B and $1.3 million income tax to Country C. Country A does not have a corporate income tax. Based on these facts, compute ABC's U.S. income tax liability.

6. CC Inc. operates solely within the United States. CC owns two subsidiaries conducting business in the United States and several foreign countries. Both subsidiaries are U.S. corporations. For the current year, the three corporations report the following:

	Foreign Source Income	U.S. Source Income	Foreign Income Tax Paid
CC Inc.	$ –0–	$600,000	$ –0–
Sub 1	3,500,000	150,000	380,000
Sub 2	4,700,000	410,000	2,350,000

  a. Assuming that CC Inc. and its two subsidiaries file a consolidated U.S. tax return, compute consolidated tax liability.
  b. How would the aggregate tax liability of the group change if the three corporations file separate U.S. tax returns?
  c. Identify the reason for the difference in the tax liability in *a* and *b* above.

7. VL Inc. began operations in 19X1. For its first two taxable years, VL's records show the following:

	19X1	19X2
U.S. source income	$300,000	$270,000
Foreign source income	200,000	630,000
Taxable income	$500,000	$900,000
Foreign income tax paid	$ 82,000	$151,000

Based on these facts, compute VL's U.S. tax liability for both years.

8. Corporation E's records show the following results for the corporation's first three years of operations:

	19X1	19X2	19X3
U.S. source income	$180,000	$350,000	$ 800,000
Foreign source income	92,000	500,000	680,000
Taxable income	$172,000	$850,000	$1,480,000
Foreign income tax paid	$ 21,000	$152,000	$ 224,400

In 19X4, Corporation E generated $2 million of taxable income ($900,000 of which was foreign source) and paid foreign income tax of $370,000.
  a. Compute Corporation E's U.S. tax liability for 19X1, 19X2, and 19X3.
  b. Compute Corporation E's U.S. tax liability for 19X4.
  c. Compute the refund generated by Corporation E's carryback of its 19X4 excess credit.

9. For the current year, BLF Inc.'s tax records show the following:

U.S. source income	$ 300,000
Foreign source income	4,900,000
Taxable income for regular purposes	$5,200,000
AMT adjustments and preferences	700,000
AMTI	$5,900,000
Foreign income tax paid	$1,900,000

All the AMT adjustments and preferences relate to BLF's foreign source income. Therefore, $5,600,000 of AMTI is foreign source AMTI. Based on these facts, compute BLF's U.S. tax liability.

10. For the current year, Corporation WM's tax records show the following:

U.S. source income	$ 250,000
Foreign source income	800,000
Taxable income for regular purposes	$1,050,000
AMT adjustments and preferences	800,000
AMTI	$1,850,000
Foreign income tax paid	$ 330,000

Because $600,000 of the AMT adjustments and preferences relate to WM's foreign source income, $1,400,000 of AMTI is foreign source AMTI. Based on these facts, compute WM's U.S. tax liability.

11. CS Inc. owns 100 percent of the stock in FS Inc., a foreign corporation. All FS's income is foreign source, and its foreign income tax rate is 20 percent. In the current year, FS distributed a $50,000 dividend to CS.
    a. Assuming that CS is in the 35 percent tax bracket and has no foreign tax credit carryforwards, compute CS's U.S. tax on the $50,000 dividend from FS.
    b. How would your computation change if CS has a $5,000 foreign tax credit carryforward into the current year?

12. JMT Inc., which has a 34 percent marginal tax rate, owns 40 percent of the stock of a CFC. At the beginning of 19X7, JMT's basis in its stock was $660,000. The CFC's net income for 19X7 was $1 million, $800,000 of which was subpart F income. The CFC paid no foreign income tax and distributed no dividends in 19X7.

    a. Does JMT have any 19X7 tax consequences with respect to its investment in the CFC?
    b. Compute JMT's basis in its CFC stock at the beginning of 19X8.

13. Refer to the facts in the preceding problem. In 19X8, the CFC's net income was $600,000, none of which was subpart F income. The CFC distributed a $300,000 dividend to its shareholders ($120,000 to JMT). What is the tax consequence to JMT of its receipt of the 19X8 dividend from the CFC?

14. Corporation YZ, which has a 35 percent marginal tax rate, owns 100 percent of the stock of Corporation Q, a foreign corporation. Corporation Q operates in Country Q, which has a 15 percent corporate income tax. Corporation Q has never paid a dividend and has accumulated $18 million of after-tax income (none of which is subpart F income). During the current year, Corporation Q lends $1 million to Corporation YZ. What is the tax consequence to Corporation YZ of this loan?

Issue Recognition Problems

Identify the tax issue or issues suggested by the following situations and state each issue in the form of a question.

1. State E wants to encourage the development of a local wine industry. Consequently, it recently decreased its excise tax rate on retail sales of locally produced wines to 3 percent. The state's excise tax on wines produced out-of-state but sold in-state is 10 percent.

2. ABC Inc. operates a meat and poultry business. The corporation distributes its products in six states and pays income tax to each, based on the meat and poultry income apportionable to each. Last year, ABC invested in a motion picture. The picture was a commercial success, and ABC recently received a royalty check for $1,800,000 from the movie's producer.

3. Corporation NW is incorporated and has its commercial domicile in State N. For the current year, the corporation sold its manufactured products to customers in State N (61 percent of sales), State O (28 percent of sales), and State P (11 percent of sales). Corporation NW has nexus

with State N and State O. However, the corporation has no physical presence in State P and therefore is not subject to income tax in that state. Both State N and State O use the three-factor UDITPA formula to apportion business income for state income tax purposes.

4. The United States has a tax treaty with the United Kingdom that provides certain tax benefits to U.K. corporations conducting business in the United States. The United States does not have an income tax treaty with Chile. SA Company, a Chilean firm that exports good to the United States, decides to operate its export business through a shell corporation formed under U.K. law.

5. BK Inc. is a consulting firm with its headquarters in New York City. During the current year, the firm entered into a consulting contract with a multinational corporation. Mrs. K, an employee of the firm, spent 33 days working at firm headquarters, 28 days in London, 50 days in Paris, and 14 days in Hong Kong performing the professional services specified in the contract.

The firm received a $1 million fee upon completion of Mrs. K's work.

6. Corporation HS operates a fleet of ocean-going cargo vessels. During the past year, one HS vessel was docked at its home port in New Orleans for 55 days, on the high seas for 120 days, and docked at various foreign ports of call for the remaining 190 days. The corporation's net income attributable to operation of this vessel was $620,000.

7. Corporation B conducts business in a foreign jurisdiction that imposes a 1 percent tax on gross receipts from sales occurring within the jurisdiction. In the current year, Corporation B paid $750,000 of gross receipts tax to the jurisdiction.

8. TY Inc. manufactures paper products in the United States and sells the products internationally. Because most of its foreign sales are in high-tax jurisdictions, TY has excess foreign credits with respect to its paper business. During the current year, TY earned $8 million of interest income on long-term bonds issued by Country NT, which has no income tax.

9. Corporation D has a foreign subsidiary conducting a manufacturing business in Country Z, which has a 25 percent corporate income tax. The IRS recently challenged the transfer price at which Corporation D performs managerial services for the subsidiary and used its Section 482 authority to reallocate $10 million of income from the subsidiary to Corporation D. On the other hand, the taxing authorities in Country Z maintain the transfer price was perfectly accurate.

10. CK Enterprises, a U.S. partnership, owns 4 percent of the stock in TT Inc., which is incorporated in Country T. TT declared a $1 million dividend ($40,000 of which was payable to CK Enterprises). Under Country T law, TT must withhold a 20 percent income tax on any dividend paid to a foreign shareholder and remit the withholding to Country T. Consequently, CK's bookkeeper received a check for only $32,000.

11. HG Inc. owns a foreign subsidiary with over $8 million of accumulated foreign source income (on which HG has never paid U.S. tax). The subsidiary recently purchased $500,000 worth of stock in a publicly traded U.S. corporation with over 30,000 shareholders.

Tax Planning Cases

1. Corporation TN wants to open a branch operation in eastern Europe and must decide between locating the branch in either Country R or Country S. Labor costs are substantially lower in Country R than in Country S. For this reason, the Country R branch would generate $700,000 of annual net profit, while the Country S branch would generate only $550,000 of annual net profit. However, Country R has a 20 percent corporate income tax, while Country S has a 10 percent corporate income tax. Based on these facts, in which country should Corporate TN locate its eastern European branch?

2. Corporation V, which is in the 35 percent tax bracket, wants to expand its business activities into Country J. The corporation could simply open a branch office or it could incorporate a foreign subsidiary under the laws of Country J. In either case, the new foreign operation should generate $500,000 of net profit annually.

However, Corporation V would incur $25,000 of additional yearly transaction costs by operating through a foreign subsidiary. These costs are deductible in computing the corporation's taxable income for purposes of Country J's 18 percent corporate income tax. For planning purposes, Corporation V assumes that it can avoid repatriating foreign source earnings for five years (year 1 earnings will be repatriated in year 5). Based on these facts and assuming a 10 percent discount rate, should Corporation V use a foreign branch or a foreign subsidiary to conduct business in Country J?

3. NMJ Corporation owns 100 percent of the stock of FJ Inc., a foreign corporation conducting business in Country F. FJ Inc. generates $100,000 of before-tax annual income on which it pays a 30 percent tax to Country F. FJ Inc. can reinvest its after-tax earnings for an indefinite time period in Country F and earn a 10 percent

before-tax rate of return. Alternatively, FJ could distribute its after-tax earnings to NMJ, which could invest the funds in the United States to earn a 12.5 percent before-tax rate of return.

Assuming that NMJ's U.S. tax rate is 35 percent, should NMJ repatriate its subsidiary's earnings to maximize its rate of return?

Comprehensive Problems for Part Four

1. Univex is a calendar year, accrual basis business. Univex's financial records provide the following information for the current year.

Revenues from sales of goods	$783,200
Cost of goods sold (FIFO)	(417,500)
Gross profit	$365,700
Interest income from certificates of deposit	1,300
Dividend income from IBM stock	6,720
Bad debt expense	$ 3,900
Administrative salaries and wages	153,400
Business and employment taxes	31,000
Interest expense on debt incurred to buy inventory	5,100
Advertising	7,000
Property insurance premiums	4,300
MACRS depreciation	21,240
Repairs, maintenance, utilities	39,700
Supplies	4,120
Contributions to charity	5,000

Univex's records reveal the following facts concerning its current year business operation.

- Bad debt expense equals the addition to an allowance for bad debts. Actual write-offs of uncollectible accounts during the year totaled $2,000.
- Univex made no asset dispositions during the year.
- The owners of the business did not receive any compensation or withdraw any funds from the business during the year.
- Univex is entitled to an $1,800 general business credit for the year.

Based solely on the above facts, complete the following:

a. Assume Univex is a sole proprietorship. Compute net profit from the business on Schedule C, Form 1040, and identify the items

from Univex's records that do not appear on Schedule C.

b. Assume Univex is a limited liability company. Compute ordinary income from business activities on page 1, Form 1065 and complete Schedule K, Form 1065.

c. Assume Univex is a corporation operating in a state without a corporate income tax. Assume also that Univex made estimated federal tax payments for the current year totaling $20,000. Compute taxable income on page 1, Form 1120. Calculate the corporation's federal income tax liability and complete page 1, Form 1120 accordingly.

2. Dollin Inc. is incorporated under Virginia law and has its corporate headquarters in Richmond. Dollin manufactures various goods and sells them at wholesale. It has a branch operation through which it sells goods in the United Kingdom. Dollin owns 100 percent of a French corporation (French Dollin) through which it sells goods in France. For 1998, Dollin Inc.'s financial records provide the following information.

Net income from sales (before income tax):	
Domestic sales	$ 967,900
U.K. sales (foreign source income)	415,000
Worldwide sales	$1,382,900
Dividend income:	
Brio Inc.	$ 8,400
French Dollin (foreign source income)	33,800

- Dollin Inc. pays state income tax in Virginia, North Carolina, and South Carolina. North Carolina and South Carolina tax their apportioned share of Dollin's net income from worldwide sales. Virginia taxes its apportioned share of net income only from domestic sales. Because Virginia is Dollin's commercial domicile, the state also taxes Dollin's U.S.

source dividend income net of any federal dividends-received deduction. The states have the following apportionment factors and tax rates:

	Apportionment Factor	Tax Rate
Virginia	43.19%	6.00%
North Carolina	11.02%	7.75%
South Carolina	8.52%	5.00%

- In 1998, Dollin Inc. paid $149,200 of income tax to the United Kingdom.
- Brio Inc. is a taxable U.S. corporation. Dollin owns 2.8 percent of Brio's outstanding stock.
- The $33,800 dividend from French Dollin is a distribution of after-tax earnings with respect to which French Dollin paid $17,000 of income tax to France.
- Dollin Inc. elects to claim the foreign tax credit rather than to deduct foreign income taxes.

Based solely on the above facts, compute the following:

a. Dollin Inc.'s 1998 state income tax liability to Virginia, North Carolina, and South Carolina.
b. Dollin Inc.'s 1998 federal income tax liability. In making your computation assume that (1) Dollin paid or accrued the state tax liabilities computed in (a) during 1998; and (2) no state income tax is allocable to foreign source income.

PART FIVE

The Individual Taxpayer

13

The Individual Tax Formula

Learning Objectives

After studying this chapter, you should be able to:

1. Explain how an individual's filing status affects the calculation of taxable income and determines the rates at which that income is taxed.
2. List the four steps in the computation of individual taxable income.
3. Explain the relationship between the standard deduction and itemized deductions.
4. Compute an individual taxpayer's exemption amount.
5. Compute the regular tax on ordinary income.
6. Explain why a marriage penalty exists in the federal income tax system.
7. Explain why the marginal rate indicated in the rate schedule may not be the actual marginal rate at which the next dollar of income is taxed.
8. Describe the child credit and dependent care credit.
9. Recognize the circumstances that may trigger the individual alternative minimum tax (AMT).
10. Describe the individual tax payment and return filing requirements.

Parts Three and Four of *Principles of Taxation for Business and Investment Planning* are devoted to the subject of the taxation of business income. In Part Three, we learned how income is measured for federal tax purposes, and we identified the important differences between taxable income as defined in the Internal Revenue Code and financial statement income determined under generally accepted accounting principles (GAAP). In Part Four, we discovered that the computation of taxable income does not vary significantly across business entities, but the rate at which the income is taxed does depend on the type of entity. Income generated by a sole proprietorship or an S corporation is taxed at the individual rates. Income generated by a regular corporation is taxed at the corporate rates. Income generated by a partnership is allocated to either individual or corporate partners and taxed accordingly.

In Part Four, we observed that a corporation's net business income is essentially equivalent to its taxable income. In contrast, an individual's net business income is just one component of the total tax base reported on Form 1040 (U.S. Individual

Income Tax Return). Unlike corporate taxpayers, people engage in many nonbusiness activities that have a bearing on their taxable income. If a person engages in a nonbusiness activity that results in an economic benefit, he or she may have to recognize the value of the benefit as income. If the activity involves an expense or loss, the person may be allowed to claim the expense or loss as a tax deduction. Therefore, before we can compute individual taxable income and the federal tax liability on such income, we must turn our attention to the tax consequences of nonbusiness transactions in which people commonly engage.

Part Five of the text is devoted to an in-depth study of the individual taxpayer. Chapter 13 lays the groundwork with an overview of the computation of the individual tax base and the tax liability on that base. The chapter also describes the tax payment and return filing requirements with which individuals must comply. Chapter 14 concentrates on the tax implications of compensation arrangements from the perspective of both employer and employee. Chapter 15 turns to the tax consequences of investment activities, while Chapter 16 focuses on personal activities. Throughout Part Five, we will emphasize the planning opportunities created by the tax rules under consideration, as well as the impact of those rules on cash flows.

Filing Status for Individuals

For federal tax purposes, every individual who is either a citizen or permanent resident of the United States is a taxable entity who may be required to file an income tax return.[1] One of the first items of information that must be provided on this return is **filing status.** Filing status, which is a reflection of an individual's marital and family situation, affects the calculation of taxable income and determines the rates at which that income is taxed.

Married Individuals and Surviving Spouses

Objective 1
Explain how an individual's filing status affects the calculation of taxable income and determines the rates at which that income is taxed.

An individual who is married on the last day of the taxable year can elect to file a **joint return** with his or her spouse.[2] A joint return reflects the combined activities of both spouses for the entire year. A husband and wife who file a joint return have **joint and several liability** for their tax bill. In other words, each spouse is responsible for paying the entire tax (not just one half) for the year.[3] With respect to a joint return, any reference to the taxpayer is actually a reference to two people.

Married Filing Jointly.   Ms. KB and Mr. RL were legally married under Hawaiian law on December 12, 19X0. For federal tax purposes, their marital status was determined on December 31, 19X0. The newlyweds elected to file a joint return for 19X0 that reported their combined incomes for the entire calendar year.

[1]§7701(b) distinguishes between resident aliens and nonresident aliens. The former are subject to the same tax rules as U.S. citizens. Nonresident aliens are subject to federal income tax only if they earn U.S. source income during the year.
[2]§6013.
[3]§6013(d)(3).

For the taxable year in which a married person dies, the widow or widower can file a joint return with the deceased individual.[4] If the widow or widower maintains a home for a dependent child, he or she qualifies as a **surviving spouse** for the two taxable years following the year of death.[5] As such, the individual can use the married filing jointly tax rates for these two years.

> ***Surviving Spouse.***   Refer to the facts in the preceding example. Mrs. KBL died on September 14, 19X6, and Mr. RL has not remarried. Mr. RL filed a joint return for 19X6 reflecting his deceased wife's activities from January 1 through September 14 and his activities for the entire year. The couple had two children, ages 3 and 5, who live with their father. Because Mr. RL met the definition of surviving spouse, he was entitled to compute his tax liability for 19X7 and 19X8 using the married filing jointly rates.

As an alternative to joint filing, married individuals can file **separate returns** that reflect each spouse's independent activity and personal tax liability. In a few situations, individuals can derive some tax benefit by filing separately, but most couples who file separate returns do so for nontax reasons.

> ***Married Filing Separately.***   Mr. and Mrs. Q have been legally separated for six years but have not divorced because of their religious faith. They live in different cities and have no joint financial dealings or obligations. Because they lead completely independent lives, they choose to file separate tax returns.

Unmarried Individuals

An individual who is unmarried on the last day of the year, who is not a surviving spouse, and who maintains a home that is the principal place of abode for a child or other dependent family member qualifies as a **head of household** for tax return filing purposes.[6]

> ***Head of Household.***   Refer back to our example involving Mr. RL, a widower with two dependent children living at home. In 19X7 and 19X8, Mr. RL filed his tax return as a surviving spouse. In 19X9, his filing status changed to head of household. Mr. RL will continue to qualify as a head of household until his children grow up and move out of his home or until he remarries.

An unmarried individual who is neither a surviving spouse nor a head of household files as a **single taxpayer.** Note that the tax law does not provide any special filing status for minor or dependent children. Regardless of age, children who earn income in their own name must file returns as single taxpayers, even if the income is collected and controlled by their parents.[7]

---

[4]§6013(a)(2).
[5]§2(a). A person does not qualify as a surviving spouse if he or she remarries within these two years.
[6]§2(b).
[7]§73.

Overview of the Taxable Income Computation

One pragmatic way to approach the computation of individual taxable income is to observe how the computation is presented on Form 1040. In this section of the chapter we will do just that, concentrating on the basic structure of the computation without devoting much attention to its separate elements. In subsequent chapters, we will examine the more important of these elements in detail. This overview of the taxable income computation from a compliance perspective offers a practical benefit: it will help you to read and interpret your own Form 1040. The federal tax return is, after all, a legal document to which individuals must affix their signature. By doing so, they are attesting that they have examined the return and that the information on the return is "true, correct, and complete." Therefore, every person, even if he or she uses a professional tax return preparer, should understand the flow of information on a Form 1040 and how that information culminates in taxable income.

The Four-Step Procedure

Objective 2
List the four steps in the computation of individual taxable income.

The computation of taxable income on an individual return is based on four procedural steps contained on pages 1 and 2 of Form 1040.

Step 1: Calculate Total Income

As the first step in the computation of taxable income, an individual must list all items of income recognized in the current year on page 1 of Form 1040. Based on the material in earlier chapters, we know that this list includes taxable income generated by any business activity in which the individual engaged. If the individual operated a sole proprietorship, the net profit (as computed on Schedule C) is carried to page 1. Similarly, if the individual conducted business through a partnership or owned stock in an S corporation, his or her distributive share of the passthrough entity's annual income is carried from Schedule E to page 1. The list of income items also includes any salary or wage payments that the individual earned as an employee and any income generated by the individual's investments. The listed items are added together to result in the individual's **total income**.

Mr. and Mrs. Volpe: Step 1.   In 1997, Mr. and Mrs. Volpe recognized three items of income.

Mr. Volpe's salary from his employer	$ 39,400
Interest income on certificates of deposit	8,600
Business income from Mrs. Volpe's sole proprietorship	56,730
Total income	$104,730

The first page of Mr. and Mrs. Volpe's 1997 Form 1040 on which these income items are listed is shown as Exhibit 13–1.

EXHIBIT 13–1

Form **1040**	Department of the Treasury—Internal Revenue Service	1997	
	U.S. Individual Income Tax Return	(99)	IRS Use Only—Do not write or staple in this space.

For the year Jan. 1–Dec. 31, 1997, or other tax year beginning , 1997, ending , 19 | OMB No. 1545-0074

Label
(See instructions on page 10.)
Use the IRS label. Otherwise, please print or type.

Your first name and initial: *James L.*   Last name: *Volpe*   Your social security number: 784 45 9042

If a joint return, spouse's first name and initial: *Nancy J.*   Last name: *Volpe*   Spouse's social security number: 617 38 0081

Home address (number and street). If you have a P.O. box, see page 10. *10 St. Martin Circle*   Apt. no.

For help in finding line instructions, see pages 2 and 3 in the booklet.

City, town or post office, state, and ZIP code. If you have a foreign address, see page 10. *Exeter, CN 04012*

Presidential Election Campaign (See page 10.)

	Yes	No	Note: Checking "Yes" will not change your tax or reduce your refund.
Do you want $3 to go to this fund?	✓		
If a joint return, does your spouse want $3 to go to this fund?	✓		

Filing Status

Check only one box.

1 ☐ Single
2 ✓ Married filing joint return (even if only one had income)
3 ☐ Married filing separate return. Enter spouse's social security no. above and full name here. ▶
4 ☐ Head of household (with qualifying person). (See page 10.) If the qualifying person is a child but not your dependent, enter this child's name here. ▶
5 ☐ Qualifying widow(er) with dependent child (year spouse died ▶ 19). (See page 10.)

Exemptions

If more than six dependents, see page 10.

6a ✓ Yourself. If your parent (or someone else) can claim you as a dependent on his or her tax return, do not check box 6a.

b ✓ Spouse

c Dependents:

(1) First name	Last name	(2) Dependent's social security number	(3) Dependent's relationship to you	(4) No. of months lived in your home in 1997
Sara	Volpe	249 98 1322	Child	12
Shana	Volpe	312 05 7886	Child	12

No. of boxes checked on 6a and 6b: **2**
No. of your children on 6c who:
• lived with you **2**
• did not live with you due to divorce or separation (see page 11)
Dependents on 6c not entered above
Add numbers entered on lines above ▶ **4**

d Total number of exemptions claimed

Income

Attach Copy B of your Forms W-2, W-2G, and 1099-R here.

If you did not get a W-2, see page 12.

Enclose but do not attach any payment. Also, please use Form 1040-V.

7	Wages, salaries, tips, etc. Attach Form(s) W-2	7	39,400
8a	Taxable interest. Attach Schedule B if required	8a	8,600
b	Tax-exempt interest. DO NOT include on line 8a	8b	
9	Dividends. Attach Schedule B if required	9	
10	Taxable refunds, credits, or offsets of state and local income taxes (see page 12)	10	
11	Alimony received	11	
12	Business income or (loss). Attach Schedule C or C-EZ	12	56,730
13	Capital gain or (loss). Attach Schedule D	13	
14	Other gains or (losses). Attach Form 4797	14	
15a	Total IRA distributions	15a	b Taxable amount (see page 13)	15b	
16a	Total pensions and annuities	16a	b Taxable amount (see page 13)	16b	
17	Rental real estate, royalties, partnerships, S corporations, trusts, etc. Attach Schedule E	17	
18	Farm income or (loss). Attach Schedule F	18	
19	Unemployment compensation	19	
20a	Social security benefits	20a	b Taxable amount (see page 14)	20b	
21	Other income. List type and amount—see page 15	21	
22	Add the amounts in the far right column for lines 7 through 21. This is your **total income** ▶	22	104,730

Adjusted Gross Income

If line 32 is under $29,290 (under $9,770 if a child did not live with you), see EIC inst. on page 21.

23	IRA deduction (see page 16)	23	
24	Medical savings account deduction. Attach Form 8853	24	
25	Moving expenses. Attach Form 3903 or 3903-F	25	
26	One-half of self-employment tax. Attach Schedule SE	26	4,008
27	Self-employed health insurance deduction (see page 17)	27	
28	Keogh and self-employed SEP and SIMPLE plans	28	
29	Penalty on early withdrawal of savings	29	435
30a	Alimony paid b Recipient's SSN ▶	30a	
31	Add lines 23 through 30a	31	4,443
32	Subtract line 31 from line 22. This is your **adjusted gross income** ▶	32	100,287

For Privacy Act and Paperwork Reduction Act Notice, see page 38.   Cat. No. 11320B   Form **1040** (1997)

Step 2: Calculate Adjusted Gross Income

The second step is the calculation of the individual's adjusted gross income for the year. **Adjusted gross income** (**AGI**) equals total income less a few specific nonbusiness deductions treated as **adjustments** on page 1, Form 1040.[8] One such adjustment is the deduction for one-half of any self-employment tax for which the taxpayer is liable.[9] We will identify other adjustments in subsequent discussions of transactions giving rise to

---

[8] §62. These adjustments are often described as "above-the-line" deductions.

[9] §164(f). See Chapter 9 for a discussion of SE tax.

EXHIBIT 13–1

(concluded)

Form 1040 (1997)   Page **2**

Tax Computation	33	Amount from line 32 (adjusted gross income)	33	100,287
	34a	Check if: ☐ You were 65 or older, ☐ Blind; ☐ **Spouse** was 65 or older, ☐ Blind. Add the number of boxes checked above and enter the total here . . . . ▶ **34a**		
	b	If you are married filing separately and your spouse itemizes deductions or you were a dual-status alien, see page 18 and check here . . . . . . ▶ **34b** ☐		
	35	Enter the larger of your: ⎰ **Itemized deductions** from Schedule A, line 28, **OR** ⎱ **Standard deduction** shown below for your filing status. But see page 18 if you checked any box on line 34a or 34b **or** someone can claim you as a dependent. • Single—$4,150 • Married filing jointly or Qualifying widow(er)—$6,900 • Head of household—$6,050 • Married filing separately—$3,450	35	17,070
If you want the IRS to figure your tax, see page 18.	36	Subtract line 35 from line 33	36	83,217
	37	If line 33 is $90,900 or less, multiply $2,650 by the total number of exemptions claimed on line 6d. If line 33 is over $90,900, see the worksheet on page 19 for the amount to enter .	37	10,600
	38	**Taxable income.** Subtract line 37 from line 36. If line 37 is more than line 36, enter -0- .	38	72,617
	39	**Tax.** See page 19. Check if any tax from **a** ☐ Form(s) 8814 **b** ☐ Form 4972 . . ▶	39	14,977
Credits	40	Credit for child and dependent care expenses. Attach Form 2441	40	870
	41	Credit for the elderly or the disabled. Attach Schedule R . .	41	
	42	Adoption credit. Attach Form 8839	42	
	43	Foreign tax credit. Attach Form 1116	43	
	44	Other. Check if from **a** ☐ Form 3800 **b** ☐ Form 8396 **c** ☐ Form 8801 **d** ☐ Form (specify)_____	44	
	45	Add lines 40 through 44 . . . . ▶	45	870
	46	Subtract line 45 from line 39. If line 45 is more than line 39, enter -0- . . . . ▶	46	14,107
Other Taxes	47	Self-employment tax. Attach Schedule SE	47	8,016
	48	Alternative minimum tax. Attach Form 6251	48	
	49	Social security and Medicare tax on tip income not reported to employer. Attach Form 4137	49	
	50	Tax on qualified retirement plans (including IRAs) and MSAs. Attach Form 5329 if required	50	
	51	Advance earned income credit payments from Form(s) W-2	51	
	52	Household employment taxes. Attach Schedule H	52	
	53	Add lines 46 through 52. This is your **total tax** . . . . ▶	53	22,123
Payments	54	Federal income tax withheld from Forms W-2 and 1099 . .	54	7,091
	55	1997 estimated tax payments and amount applied from 1996 return .	55	16,000
	56a	Earned income credit. Attach Schedule EIC if you have a qualifying child **b** Nontaxable earned income: amount ▶ [blank] and type ▶	56a	
Attach Forms W-2, W-2G, and 1099-R on the front.	57	Amount paid with Form 4868 (request for extension) . . .	57	
	58	Excess social security and RRTA tax withheld (see page 27) .	58	
	59	Other payments. Check if from **a** ☐ Form 2439 **b** ☐ Form 4136	59	
	60	Add lines 54, 55, 56a, 57, 58, and 59. These are your **total payments** . . . . . ▶	60	23,091
Refund Have it directly deposited! See page 27 and fill in 62b, 62c, and 62d.	61	If line 60 is more than line 53, subtract line 53 from line 60. This is the amount you **OVERPAID**	61	968
	62a	Amount of line 61 you want **REFUNDED TO YOU** . . . . ▶	62a	
	▶ b	Routing number [blank] ▶ **c** Type: ☐ Checking ☐ Savings		
	▶ d	Account number [blank]		
	63	Amount of line 61 you want **APPLIED TO YOUR 1998 ESTIMATED TAX** ▶	63	968
Amount You Owe	64	If line 53 is more than line 60, subtract line 60 from line 53. This is the **AMOUNT YOU OWE.** For details on how to pay, see page 27 . . . . ▶	64	
	65	Estimated tax penalty. Also include on line 64 . . .	65	

Sign Here
Keep a copy of this return for your records.

Under penalties of perjury, I declare that I have examined this return and accompanying schedules and statements, and to the best of my knowledge and belief, they are true, correct, and complete. Declaration of preparer (other than taxpayer) is based on all information of which preparer has any knowledge.

Your signature	Date	Your occupation
Spouse's signature. If a joint return, BOTH must sign.	Date	Spouse's occupation

Paid Preparer's Use Only

Preparer's signature ▶	Date	Check if self-employed ☐	Preparer's social security no.
Firm's name (or yours if self-employed) and address ▶			EIN
			ZIP code

nonbusiness deductions. While AGI represents an intermediate step in the computation of the tax base, it is an extremely important number in its own right. As we will soon learn, certain key nonbusiness deductions are limited by reference to the individual's AGI. As a result, the amount of these deductions is a function of AGI reported on the last line of page 1, Form 1040.

> *Mr. and Mrs. Volpe: Step 2.* Mrs. Volpe's 1997 self-employment tax liability (computed on Schedule SE, Form 1040) is $8,016. One-half of this tax is deductible in the computation of Mr. and Mrs. Volpe's 1997 AGI. In June 1997, Mr. Volpe cashed in a one-year certificate of deposit after holding it for only 10 months. Because of the early withdrawal, the bank charged a $435 penalty. The

> Volpes are allowed to deduct this penalty in computing their AGI. Both these deductions are reported on page 1, Form 1040 (Exhibit 13–1). Line 32 (the last line on page 1) shows that the couple's 1997 AGI is $100,287.

Step 3: Subtract the Standard Deduction or Itemized Deductions

Objective 3
Explain the relationship between the standard deduction and itemized deductions.

In the third step of the computation of the tax base, AGI is reduced by the *greater of* a standard deduction or the allowable itemized deductions for the year.

Standard Deduction.   The basic **standard deduction** is a function of filing status; the basic deductions for 1998 are:

Married filing jointly and surviving spouses	$7,100
Married filing separately	3,550
Head of household	6,250
Single	4,250

Any taxpayer who has reached age 65 by the last day of the taxable year is entitled to an additional deduction. Any taxpayer who is legally blind is also entitled to an additional deduction. For 1998, the additional deductions are:

Married filing jointly or separately and surviving spouse	$ 850
Head of household or single	1,050

Both the basic and the additional standard deductions are indexed for inflation and may change every year.[10]

> ***Standard Deduction.***   Mr. and Mrs. O file a joint return and are 79 and 75 years of age, respectively. Mr. O is legally blind. The couple's standard deduction for 1998 is $9,650.
>
> | | |
> |---|---|
> | Basic standard deduction | $7,100 |
> | Additional deductions for Mr. O: | |
> | Age 65 or older | 850 |
> | Legally blind | 850 |
> | Additions deduction for Mrs. O: | |
> | Age 65 or older | 850 |
> | | $9,650 |

---

[10]§63(c) and (f).

Itemized Deductions.   As a category, **itemized deductions** include any deduction allowed to an individual taxpayer that cannot be subtracted in the calculation of AGI.[11] Taxpayers report their itemized deductions on Schedule A, Form 1040. Individuals elect to itemize (i.e., subtract itemized deductions from AGI) only if their total deduction amount exceeds the standard deduction for the year. This situation is the exception rather than the rule; in 1996, only 29 percent of individual return filers elected to itemize.[12]

As a general rule, itemized deductions are allowed for expenses and losses stemming from selected, nonbusiness transactions. These deductions create a tax savings only if the individual elects to itemize. In a year in which the individual claims the standard deduction, any itemized deductions do not result in a tax benefit.

> ***Election to Itemize.***   Assume that Mr. and Mrs. O in the preceding example accumulated $9,000 of itemized deductions for 1998. Because this total is less than their $9,650 standard deduction, they use the standard deduction to compute taxable income, and their itemized deductions yield no benefit.
>
> If the couple's itemized deductions totaled $11,000, they would elect to itemize by subtracting this amount from their AGI. If the couple's marginal tax rate is 31 percent, their itemized deductions save $3,410 in tax ($11,000 × 31 percent). However, the standard deduction would have saved $2,992 ($9,650 × 31 percent). Consequently, the incremental tax savings from the itemized deductions is only $418 ($1,350 excess itemized deductions × 31 percent).

Bunching Itemized Deductions.   People can often maximize the value of their itemized deductions through a tax planning technique called **bunching.** By controlling the timing of their deductible expenses, they can concentrate the deductions into one year. By doing so, they create a critical mass of itemized deductions, the total of which exceeds their standard deduction. The following case illustrates this technique:

> ***Bunching of Itemized Deductions.***   Mr. CL, a single taxpayer with a 36 percent marginal tax rate, routinely incurs $4,000 of annual expenses qualifying as itemized deductions. This amount is less than his annual standard deduction. If his pattern of expenses is level from year to year, he will derive no benefit from the expenses. In contrast, if Mr. CL can shift $1,500 of the expenses from year 1 to year 2, he can take his standard deduction in year 1 and elect to itemize in year 2.
>
> | | *Level Pattern of Itemized Deductions* | *Bunched Deductions* |
> | --- | --- | --- |
> | Year 1: | | |
> | Itemized deductions | $4,000 | $2,500 |
> | Standard deduction | 4,250 | 4,250 |

---

[11]§63(d).

[12]"Individual Income Tax Returns: Selected Income and Tax Items for Specified Tax Years 1975–1996," Table 1, *Statistics of Income Bulletin,* Winter 1997/1998.

Year 2:		
Itemized deductions	$4,000	$5,500
Standard deduction	4,250	4,250
Itemized deductions in excess of standard deduction		$1,250
		.36
Tax savings from bunching		$ 450

How can Mr. CL shift deductible expenses from one year to another? As a cash basis taxpayer, he recognizes expenses in the year of payment. By postponing payment of an expense from December until January, he shifts the deduction from year 1 to year 2. At the end of year 2, Mr. CL may want to *accelerate* payment of deductible expenses he normally incurs early in year 3, a year in which he will take the standard deduction under his cyclical bunching strategy.

Overall Limitation on Itemized Deductions.   Individual taxpayers with AGI in excess of a threshold amount must reduce the total of certain itemized deductions by 3 percent of the excess AGI.[13] This reduction is limited to 80 percent of the total of these deductions. In other words, every individual regardless of income level is allowed to deduct at least 20 percent of the total. While this overall limitation diminishes the value of itemizing deductions to high-income taxpayers, it has no effect on the standard deduction. The technical details of the overall limitation are incorporated into an Itemized Deduction Worksheet included as Appendix 13–A to this chapter.

> *Mr. and Mrs. Volpe: Step 3.*   During 1997, Mr. and Mrs. Volpe incurred the following expenses that qualify as itemized deductions:
>
> | | |
> |---|---|
> | Connecticut personal income tax | $5,140 |
> | Real estate tax on the Volpes' personal residence | 1,920 |
> | Home mortgage interest | 8,080 |
> | Gifts to charity | 1,930 |
>
> These deductions are listed on Schedule A (shown as Exhibit 13–2) and totaled on line 28. Note that the overall limitation on itemized deductions did not affect the Volpes because their AGI was *less* than the 1997 threshold ($121,200 for married filing jointly. Because the Volpes' $17,070 total itemized deductions exceeded their 1997 standard deduction ($6,900), the couple elected to itemize by carrying the $17,070 total to line 35, page 2, Form 1040 (see Exhibit 13–1 on page 336).

Objective 4
Compute an individual taxpayer's exemption amount.

Step 4: Subtract Total Exemption Amount

The fourth and last step in the computation of taxable income is a reduction of AGI by the individual's exemption amount. This amount equals the annual **personal exemption**

---

[13]§68.

EXHIBIT 13–2

SCHEDULES A&B (Form 1040)	Schedule A—Itemized Deductions	OMB No. 1545-0074

Department of the Treasury Internal Revenue Service (99)

(Schedule B is on back)

► Attach to Form 1040. ► See Instructions for Schedules A and B (Form 1040).

1997

Attachment Sequence No. **07**

Name(s) shown on Form 1040 *James L. and Nancy J. Volpe*

Your social security number 784 45 9042

Medical and Dental Expenses		Caution: Do not include expenses reimbursed or paid by others.			
	1	Medical and dental expenses (see page A-1)	1		
	2	Enter amount from Form 1040, line 33. ⌊ 2 ⌋			
	3	Multiply line 2 above by 7.5% (.075)	3		
	4	Subtract line 3 from line 1. If line 3 is more than line 1, enter -0-		4	
Taxes You Paid (See page A-2.)	5	State and local income taxes	5	5,140	
	6	Real estate taxes (see page A-2)	6	1,920	
	7	Personal property taxes	7		
	8	Other taxes. List type and amount ►	8		
	9	Add lines 5 through 8		9	7,060
Interest You Paid (See page A-2.) **Note:** Personal interest is not deductible.	10	Home mortgage interest and points reported to you on Form 1098	10	8,080	
	11	Home mortgage interest not reported to you on Form 1098. If paid to the person from whom you bought the home, see page A-3 and show that person's name, identifying no., and address ►	11		
	12	Points not reported to you on Form 1098. See page A-3 for special rules .	12		
	13	Investment interest. Attach Form 4952 if required. (See page A-3.)	13		
	14	Add lines 10 through 13		14	8,080
Gifts to Charity If you made a gift and got a benefit for it, see page A-3.	15	Gifts by cash or check. If you made any gift of $250 or more, see page A-3	15	1,930	
	16	Other than by cash or check. If any gift of $250 or more, see page A-3. You **MUST** attach Form 8283 if over $500	16		
	17	Carryover from prior year	17		
	18	Add lines 15 through 17		18	1,930
Casualty and Theft Losses	19	Casualty or theft loss(es). Attach Form 4684. (See page A-4.)		19	
Job Expenses and Most Other Miscellaneous Deductions (See page A-5 for expenses to deduct here.)	20	Unreimbursed employee expenses—job travel, union dues, job education, etc. You **MUST** attach Form 2106 or 2106-EZ if required. (See page A-4.) ►	20		
	21	Tax preparation fees	21		
	22	Other expenses—investment, safe deposit box, etc. List type and amount ►	22		
	23	Add lines 20 through 22	23		
	24	Enter amount from Form 1040, line 33. ⌊ 24 ⌋			
	25	Multiply line 24 above by 2% (.02)	25		
	26	Subtract line 25 from line 23. If line 25 is more than line 23, enter -0- . . .		26	
Other Miscellaneous Deductions	27	Other—from list on page A-5. List type and amount ►		27	
Total Itemized Deductions	28	Is Form 1040, line 33, over $121,200 (over $60,600 if married filing separately)? **NO.** Your deduction is not limited. Add the amounts in the far right column for lines 4 through 27. Also, enter on Form 1040, line 35, the **larger** of this amount or your standard deduction. **YES.** Your deduction may be limited. See page A-5 for the amount to enter.	►	28	17,070

For Paperwork Reduction Act Notice, see Form 1040 instructions.   Cat. No. 11330X   Schedule A (Form 1040) 1997

($2,700 for 1998) multiplied by the number of people in the individual's family.[14] The family consists of the taxpayer (two taxpayers on a joint return) plus any person qualifying as the taxpayer's **dependent.** Qualification is based on five requirements:

- The person must have a familial relationship with the taxpayer (lineal ancestor, descendant, sibling, aunt or uncle, niece or nephew, or in-law) *or* reside in the taxpayer's home for the entire year.
- The taxpayer must provide over half the financial support of the person for the year.

---

[14]§151 and §152 contain the personal exemption rules.

- The person's gross income for the year must be less than the personal exemption. This requirement is waived for a child under age 19 or a child who is a full-time student under age 24.
- The person must not file a joint return with a spouse.
- The person must be a U.S. citizen or a resident of the United States, Mexico, or Canada.

An individual may claim an exemption for any person meeting these five requirements. If a person who is claimed as a dependent on another return is required to file his or her own tax return, the person may not claim an exemption on this return.

Personal Exemptions.   In 1998, Mr. and Mrs. J provided 100 percent of the financial support of their three children who all live at home. The oldest child, age 18, has a part-time job and earned $4,800 during the year, which she saved for college. Although the child's gross income exceeded the exemption amount, she qualified as Mr. and Mrs. J's dependent because she is under age 19. Consequently, Mr. and Mrs. J's exemption amount on their 1998 Form 1040 was $13,500 ($2,700 × five family members).

The oldest child filed her own 1998 Form 1040 as a single taxpayer. She reported $4,800 of wages and deducted a $4,250 standard deduction.[15] However, because her parents claimed her as a dependent on their return, she could not claim a personal exemption on her return. Consequently, her 1998 taxable income was $550.

Exemption Phaseout.   The total exemption amount is gradually phased out for individuals with AGI in excess of a threshold amount.[16] This phaseout mechanism is conceptually similar to the reduction of itemized deductions because it diminishes the value of personal exemptions to high-income taxpayers. The major difference between the two mechanisms is that the exemption amount can be decreased to zero. The details of this phaseout mechanism are incorporated into an Exemption Amount Worksheet included as Appendix 13–B to this chapter.

Mr. and Mrs. Volpe: Step 4.   Mr. and Mrs. Volpe have two daughters (ages 7 and 10) who live with their parents and are entirely dependent on them for financial support. Mr. and Mrs. Volpe also provide about 80 percent of the annual financial support for Annie Jarvis, Mrs. Volpe's widowed mother (age 80). Mrs. Jarvis received $2,800 of taxable interest from several savings accounts during 1997. On line 6, page 1, Form 1040 (Exhibit 13–1), the Volpes claimed exemptions for themselves and their two children. They could not claim Annie Jarvis as a dependent because her $2,800 gross income exceeded the $2,650 exemption amount for 1997. The Volpes' total exemption amount of $10,600 ($2,650 × 4) is reported on

---

[15]An individual who is claimed as a dependent on another person's return is entitled to a standard deduction on his or her own tax return. However, the standard deduction is limited to the *greater* of the person's earned income plus $250 or an inflation adjusted base. The 1998 base is $700. §63(c)(5).

[16]§151(d)(3).

line 37, page 2, Form 1040 (Exhibit 13–1). The exemption phaseout did not affect the Volpes because their AGI was *less* than the 1997 threshold ($181,800 for married filing jointly).

The Taxable Income Formula

The four-step procedure for computing individual taxable income can be summarized by the following formula:

$$
\begin{array}{r}
\text{Total income} \\
\underline{\text{(Adjustments)}} \\
\text{Adjusted gross income} \\
\text{(Standard or itemized deductions)} \\
\underline{\text{(Exemption amount)}} \\
\underline{\text{Taxable income}}
\end{array}
$$

The AGI reported on Form 1040 is the closest gauge of the individual's disposable income for the year. The standard deduction and exemption amount are not based on monetary expenses or economic losses and are unrelated to specific cash flows. The purpose of these two subtractions from AGI is to shelter a base amount of disposable income from tax. If a person's AGI is less than the tax-free threshold represented by the combined standard deduction and exemption amount, his taxable income is zero. Evidently, the government believes that such person must spend every dollar of AGI to buy the necessities of life and has no financial ability to pay income tax.

Mr. and Mrs. Volpe: Taxable Income.   Pages 1 and 2 of Mr. and Mrs. Volpe's Form 1040 (Exhibit 13–1) reflect the following computation of the couple's 1997 taxable income.

Total income (line 22)	$104,730
Adjustments (line 31)	(4,443)
Adjusted gross income (line 32)	$100,287
Itemized deductions (line 35)	(17,070)
Exemption amount (line 37)	(10,600)
Taxable income (line 38)	$ 72,617

Computing Tax Liability

The tax liability on individual taxable income is computed under the rate schedule determined by the taxpayer's filing status.[17] These rate schedules are adjusted annually for inflation. The 1998 rate schedules are as follows:

---

[17]Form 1040 instructions require individuals with taxable incomes less than $100,000 to use a Tax Table to compute tax. These tables are derived from the rate schedules and eliminate the arithmetic required to use the schedules.

Individual Tax Rate Schedules

Married Filing Jointly and Surviving Spouses

If Taxable Income Is:		The Tax Is:			Of the Amount Over-
Over-	But Not Over-				
$ –0–	$ 42,350			15%	$ –0–
42,350	102,300	$ 6,352.50	+	28%	42,350
102,300	155,950	23,138.50	+	31%	102,300
155,950	278,450	39,770	+	36%	155,950
278,450		83,870	+	39.6%	278,450

Married Filing Separately

If Taxable Income Is:		The Tax Is:			Of the Amount Over-
Over-	But Not Over-				
$ –0–	$ 21,175			15%	$ –0–
21,175	51,150	$ 3,176.25	+	28%	21,175
51,150	77,975	11,569.25	+	31%	51,150
77,975	139,225	19,885	+	36%	77,975
139,225		41,935	+	39.6%	139,225

Head of Household

If Taxable Income Is:		The Tax Is:			Of the Amount Over-
Over-	But Not Over-				
$ –0–	$ 33,950			15%	$ –0–
33,950	87,700	$ 5,092.50	+	28%	33,950
87,700	142,000	20,142.50	+	31%	87,700
142,000	278,450	36,975.50	+	36%	142,000
278,450		86,097.50	+	39.6%	278,450

Single

If Taxable Income Is:		The Tax Is:			Of the Amount Over-
Over-	But Not Over-				
$ –0–	$ 25,350			15%	$ –0–
25,350	61,400	$ 3,802.50	+	28%	25,350
61,400	128,100	13,896.50	+	31%	61,400
128,100	278,450	34,573.50	+	36%	128,100
278,450		88,699.50	+	39.6%	278,450

Objective 5
Compute the regular tax on ordinary income.

Each rate schedule consists of five income brackets with progressively higher tax rates. To compute the tax on a given amount of income, refer to the first two columns to identify the correct bracket. Then determine the portion of income in that bracket (the excess of total income over the bracket floor). The tax liability equals this excess multiplied by the bracket rate plus a base tax (the third column). This base tax is the cumulative tax on the income in the lower brackets.

Tax Computation on Ordinary Income.   Mr. and Mrs. A who file a joint return, Mr. B who files as a head of household, and Ms. C who files as a single taxpayer each reports $90,000 taxable income on Form 1040 for 1998. Their tax liability (rounding up to whole dollars) is computed as follows:

	Mr. and Mrs. A (Married Filing Jointly)	Mr. B (Head of Household)	Ms. C (Single)
Taxable income	$ 90,000	$ 90,000	$ 90,000
Bracket floor	(42,350)	(87,700)	(61,400)
Excess over floor	$ 47,650	$ 2,300	$ 28,600
Bracket rate	.28	.31	.31
	$ 13,342	$ 713	$ 8,866
Base tax	6,353	20,143	13,897
Tax liability	$ 19,695	$ 20,856	$ 22,763

Preferential Rate on Capital Gain.   The tax computation must take into account any preferential rate applying to capital gains included in taxable income. The complicated capital gains rate structure is discussed in detail in Chapter 15. This next example illustrates the basic effect of a preferential rate on the computation of an individual's annual tax liability.

Tax Computation on Ordinary Income and Capital Gain.   Assume that Ms. C in the preceding example recognized a $25,000 capital gain as part of her 1998 taxable income. This gain is eligible for a 20 percent preferential tax rate. Consequently, Ms. C's 1998 tax liability is computed as follows:

Taxable income	$90,000
Capital gain	(25,000)
Ordinary income portion of taxable income	$65,000
Bracket floor	(61,400)
Excess over floor	$ 3,600
Bracket rate	.31
	$ 1,116
Base tax	13,897
Tax on ordinary income	$15,013
Tax on capital gain ($25,000 × 20%)	$ 5,000
Tax liability	$20,013

The 20 percent capital gains rate reduced Ms. C's 1998 tax liability from $22,763 to $20,013 for a tax savings of $2,750.

The Marriage Penalty Dilemma

Objective 6
Explain why a marriage penalty exists in the federal income tax system.

A comparison of the four rate schedules reveals that the married filing jointly schedule has the widest brackets and therefore results in the smallest tax liability for any given income. This fact suggests that the tax rates are biased in favor of married couples: In our previous example in which a married couple (Mr. and Mrs. A) and a single taxpayer (Ms. C) both had $90,000 of ordinary taxable income, the couple's tax was $19,695, while the single's tax was $22,763. The rationale for this difference is straightforward: two people can't live as well as one on the same income. Mr. and Mrs. A presumably have less financial ability to pay than Ms. C and thus should pay less tax.

But now suppose that Mr. and Mrs. A are both employed and earn identical salaries. Assume that their separate returns would each reflect $45,000 of taxable income (half their combined income).[18] If they could use the rate schedule for single taxpayers, each would have tax liability of $9,305 and their combined tax burden would be only $18,610. Based on a comparison of this number to their $19,695 joint liability, the couple could complain that they are paying a $1,085 penalty for being married.[19]

These examples show that the federal income tax system is not marriage neutral. This lack of neutrality is characteristic of a system combining progressive tax rates and joint filing for married taxpayers. To demonstrate this point, assume that four people, A, B, C, and D, are taxed under a hypothetical system consisting of a 20 percent rate on income up to $30,000 and a 30 percent rate on income in excess of $30,000. The following table presents the relevant information if A, B, C, and D each file their own tax return:

Taxpayer	Taxable Income	Tax
A	$30,000	$ 6,000
B	30,000	6,000
C	10,000	2,000
D	50,000	12,000

Now assume that A marries B and C marries D. If the system requires the couples to file joint returns, the result is as follows:

Taxpayer	Taxable Income	Tax
AB	$60,000	$15,000
CD	60,000	15,000

As married couples, AB and CD have equal taxable incomes and equal tax liabilities. For couple AB, this liability is $3,000 more than their combined tax as two single people. Because A and B aggregated their respective incomes on the joint return, $30,000 of that income was boosted out of the 20 percent bracket into the 30 percent

---

[18] This example ignores the difference in the standard deduction for married and single taxpayers.

[19] The couple can't avoid the marriage penalty by filing separately. Because of the married filing separately rate structure, the combined liabilities of the spouses basically equals their liability on a joint return.

bracket. As a result, the tax increased by $3,000. For couple CD, the liability on their joint return is $1,000 more than their combined single liabilities. In CD's case, the aggregation of their respective incomes boosted only $10,000 into the higher tax bracket.

The marriage penalties imposed on AB and CD disappear if each spouse could file as a single taxpayer. Couple AB would file two returns, each showing a $6,000 tax. Couple CD would do the same; C's return would show $2,000 tax, while D's return would show $12,000 tax. While this solution makes the tax system marriage neutral, CD could certainly complain that the solution is unfair. To the extent that married couples operate as an economic unit, their financial ability to pay tax is a function of their aggregate income. Accordingly, couples with the same aggregate income (such as AB and CD) should pay the same total tax, regardless of how many returns they file. Based on this premise, the obvious solution to the marriage penalty—giving married couples the choice to file as single taxpayers—violates the horizontal equity of the tax system.

The Elusive Marginal Tax Rate

Objective 7
Explain why the marginal rate indicated in the rate schedule may not be the actual marginal rate at which the next dollar of income is taxed.

The marginal tax rate is the percentage applying to the *next* dollar of taxable income. Obviously taxpayers must know their marginal rate to compute tax costs and the after-tax cash flows from any income-generating transaction. Individuals can determine their apparent marginal rate by comparing their projected taxable income for the year to the applicable rate schedule. For instance, if a single taxpayer estimates that his 1998 income will be $140,000, he can refer to the 1998 rate schedule and observe that his statutory marginal rate is 36 percent. However, this apparent rate is not necessarily the actual marginal rate.

When an individual recognizes an additional dollar of income, AGI generally increases by one dollar. This increase changes the calculation of any deduction limited by reference to AGI. In this chapter, we learned that both allowable itemized deductions and the exemption amount shrink as AGI climbs above a threshold level. In subsequent chapters, we will encounter more of these AGI-sensitive deductions. If an additional dollar of AGI triggers a decrease in one or more deductions, taxable income will increase by *more* than one dollar.

> **Increased AGI and Marginal Tax Rate.**   Ms. G, a single individual with an apparent marginal rate of 36 percent, needs to calculate her after-tax cash flow from a transaction expected to generate $10,000 of taxable cash flow. The $10,000 increase in Ms. G's AGI will cause several deductions to decrease by an aggregate amount of $700. Consequently, the $10,000 of incremental income will result in a $10,700 increase in taxable income and $3,852 of additional tax ($10,700 × 36 percent). Ms G's actual marginal tax rate on the incremental income is 38.52 percent, and her after-tax cash flow from the transaction would be $6,148 ($10,000 cash −$3,852 tax cost).

The lesson of this example is that the individual marginal tax rate can be an elusive number. The inverse relationship between AGI and allowable deductions can result in a hidden surtax not reflected by the apparent statutory rate. Because of the complex interaction between AGI and allowable deductions, the only sure way to calculate the incremental tax liability from a proposed transaction is to "run the numbers"—incorporate the tax consequences of the transaction into a complete calculation of taxable income.

Individual Tax Credits

Individual taxpayers can reduce their tax liability by any tax credits for which they are eligible. People who conduct business as a sole proprietorship or in a passthrough entity are entitled to the general business credit discussed in Chapter 10. People who pay foreign income tax are entitled to the foreign tax credit discussed in Chapter 12. In addition to these credits, individuals may qualify for a number of other credits, four of which are described in the following paragraphs.

Child Credit

Objective 8
Describe the child credit and dependent care credit.

The Tax Reform Act of 1997 introduced a new credit for families with dependent children. In 1998, individual taxpayers can claim a $400 credit for each dependent child under age 17 at the close of the year.[20] In 1999 and subsequent years, the **child credit** increases to $500 per child. This credit phases out for high-income taxpayers. On a joint return, the total credit is reduced by $50 for every $1,000 increment (or portion thereof) of AGI in excess of $110,000. For single individuals and heads of households, the credit phaseout begins when AGI exceeds $75,000. For married individuals filing separate returns, the phaseout begins when AGI exceeds $55,000.

Child Credit. Mr. and Mrs. W reported $117,890 AGI on their 1998 Form 1040. The couple has four dependent children who were ages 18, 14, 12, and 10 on December 31, 1998. Mr. and Mrs. W's 1998 child credit is $800.

Adjusted gross income	$117,890
AGI threshold	(110,000)
Excess AGI	$ 7,890
Excess AGI divided by $1,000 and rounded up to nearest whole number	8
Maximum total credit:	
($400 × three children under age 17)	$ 1,200
Phaseout ($50 × 8)	(400)
Child credit	$ 800

Dependent Care Credit

Individuals who maintain a home for one or more dependents either under age 13 or physically or mentally incapable of caring for themselves may be eligible for a **dependent care credit.**[21] The credit is based on the cost of caring for these children or dependents. Such costs include compensation paid to caregivers who work in the home (nannies, housekeepers, and babysitters) and fees paid to child care or day care centers. The purpose of the credit is to provide tax relief to people who must incur these costs to be gainfully employed. Consequently, the annual cost on which the credit is based is limited to the

---

[20]§24.
[21]§21.

taxpayer's earned income for the year. On a joint return, the limit is based on the *lesser* of the husband's or wife's earned income. The cost is further limited to $2,400 if the taxpayer has only one dependent and $4,800 if the taxpayer has two or more dependents.

The credit equals a percentage of dependent care costs (subject to the two limitations described in the preceding paragraph). The percentage is determined by reference to AGI for the year.

Credit Percentage	AGI Range
30%	$ –0– to $10,000
29	10,001 to 12,000
28	12,001 to 14,000
27	14,001 to 16,000
26	16,001 to 18,000
25	18,001 to 20,000
24	20,001 to 22,000
23	22,001 to 24,000
22	24,001 to 26,000
21	26,001 to 28,000
20	Over 28,000

Mr. and Mrs. Volpe: Dependent Care Credit. Refer back to page 2 of Mr. and Mrs. Volpe's 1997 Form 1040 (Exhibit 13–1). Line 18 reports taxable income of $72,617 and line 39 reports $14,977 of tax computed on that income. During 1997, Mr. and Mrs. Volpe paid $4,350 to an after-school camp program for their two young daughters. The dependent care cost was less than Mr. Volpe's $39,400 salary (the lesser of either spouse's earned income). The cost was also less than $4,800 (the dollar limit for two dependents). Consequently, Mr. and Mrs. Volpe are entitled to an $870 dependent care credit ($4,350 dependent care cost × 20 percent). This credit is reported on line 40 and is the couple's only tax credit for the year. (In 1998, the Volpes should be eligible for the new child credit.) Thus, Mr. and Mrs. Volpe's 1997 income tax liability is reduced to $14,107 on line 46.

Earned Income Credit

Many individuals pay no federal income tax because of the shelter provided by the standard deduction and the exemption amount. However, low-income families are not sheltered from the employee payroll tax, which is levied on the first dollar of wages or salary earned during the year. In 1975, Congress enacted the **earned income credit** to offset the impact of the payroll tax on low-income workers and to encourage individuals to seek employment rather than to depend on welfare.

The credit is based on a percentage of the taxpayer's earned income.[22] The percentage depends on whether the taxpayer has no children, one child, or more than one child. For 1998, the maximum credit available to a family with two or more children is $3,756. If earned income exceeds a dollar threshold, the credit is phased out. For a family with

---

[22]§32.

two or more children, the 1998 phaseout threshold is $12,260 and the credit is reduced to zero when earned income reaches $30,095. The earned income credit differs from most other credits because it is *refundable:* taxpayers may receive a refund of the credit that exceeds precredit income tax liability.

Refund of Earned Income Credit.   Mr. and Mrs. BV's precredit income tax for the year was $2,200. Based on the number of their children and their earned income, Mr. and Mrs. BV claimed an earned income credit of $3,000. This credit reduced their income tax liability to zero and entitled them to an $800 refund from the government.

The government estimates that 20 million families, the poorest fifth of this country's workforce, qualify for the earned income credit. The IRS computes the credit for those taxpayers who request such assistance when filing their income tax returns.

Earned Income Credit or Higher Minimum Wage?   According to a recent *Business Week* editorial, the earned income credit is a better alternative than a higher minimum wage to subsidize low-income families. An increase in the minimum wage raises the labor costs for companies that employ workers with limited skills. Thus, an increased minimum wage may reduce the number of entry-level jobs available. In contrast, the earned income credit does not adversely affect business costs and encourages people to accept entry-level jobs because they must work in order to receive the credit. The minimum wage does not always help improverished families because workers who earn the minimum (such as teenagers) may belong to households with income well above the poverty line. The earned income credit, however, is a function of family, rather than individual, income.[23]

Excess Payroll Tax Withholding

The federal employee payroll tax equals 6.2 percent of an annual base amount of compensation plus 1.45 percent of total compensation. Employers are required to withhold this tax from their employees' paychecks and remit the withholding to the Treasury. When an employee changes jobs during the year, the new employer must withhold payroll tax without regard to any tax withheld by any former employer. As a result, the employee may indirectly overpay his or her payroll tax for the year.

Excess Payroll Tax Withholding.   Mrs. V worked for FM Inc. during the first nine months of 1998, then resigned to take a new position with CN Company. Mrs. V's 1998 salary from FM was $80,000 from which the corporation withheld $5,401 employee payroll tax (6.2 percent of $68,400 base + 1.45 percent of $80,000). Her salary from CN was $42,000 from which the company withheld $3,213 (7.65 percent of $42,000). In computing this withholding, CN ignored the fact that FM had already withheld 6.2 percent on the annual base. Consequently, CN withheld $2,604 of excess payroll tax from Mrs. V's salary:

---

[23]Gary Becker, "How to End Welfare As We Know It—Fast," *Business Week,* June 3, 1996.

Mrs. V's 1998 payroll tax liability:	
$68,400 × 6.2%	$4,241
$122,000 total salary × 1.45%	1,769
	$6,010
Payroll tax withheld:	
FM Inc.	$5,401
CN Company	3,213
	$8,614
Excess withholding ($8,614 − $6,010)	$2,604

Mrs. V may claim this **excess payroll tax withholding** as a credit against her income tax liability.[24] Mrs. V's tax credit has no effect on the two firms that employed her during the year. Neither FM nor CN is entitled to any refund of the employer payroll tax on Mrs. V's compensation.

Alternative Minimum Tax

Objective 9
Recognize the circumstances that may trigger the individual alternative minimum tax (AMT).

Individuals are subject to the alternative minimum tax (AMT) system and may owe AMT in addition to their regular income tax.[25] The individual AMT is based on alternative minimum taxable income (AMTI), which is computed under the formula introduced in Chapter 10.

$$\begin{array}{r} \text{Taxable income for regular tax purposes} \\ \text{+ or − AMT adjustments} \\ \underline{\text{+ AMT tax preferences}} \\ \overline{\overline{\text{Alternative minimum taxable income}}} \end{array}$$

Many AMT adjustment and preference items are common to both corporate and individual taxpayers. However, several items are unique to individuals. For instance, the standard deduction and exemption amount are AMT adjustments that must be added back to taxable income in the AMTI computation.[26] The overall limitation on itemized deductions does not apply in the AMT world. Consequently, any reduction of itemized deductions pursuant to this limitation is a negative AMT adjustment.[27] We will identify other individual items in subsequent chapters when we discuss the transaction triggering the AMT adjustment or preference.

Individuals can reduce their AMTI by an exemption determined by reference to their filing status. However, the basic exemption is reduced by 25 percent of AMTI in excess of a threshold. The basic exemption, the AMTI threshold, and the AMTI at which the exemption is reduced to zero (AMTI maximum) are presented in the following table:

---

[24]§31. The excess payroll tax withholding credit is refundable.
[25]§55.
[26]§56(b)(1)(E).
[27]§56(b)(1)(F).

	Basic Exemption	AMTI Threshold	AMTI Maximum
Married filing jointly and surviving spouses	$45,000	$150,000	$330,000
Married filing separately	22,500	75,000	165,000
Head of household or single	33,750	112,500	247,500

AMTI Exemption.   Ms. X, a head of household, has AMTI of $91,000. Because her AMTI is below the threshold, her exemption is $33,750.

Mr. and Mrs. Y, who file a joint return, have AMTI of $351,600. Because their AMTI is greater than the AMTI maximum, their exemption is reduced to zero.

Mr. and Mrs. Z, who file a joint return, have AMTI of $215,000, which falls in the phaseout range. Consequently, their exemption is $28,750, computed as follows:

AMTI	$ 215,000
AMTI threshold	(150,000)
AMTI in excess of threshold	$ 65,000
	.25
Reduction in exemption	$ 16,250
Basic exemption for married filing jointly	$ 45,000
Reduction	(16,250)
Exemption	$ 28,750

An individual's tentative minimum tax is based on a rate structure consisting of two brackets:

- 26 percent on the first $175,000 of AMTI in excess of the exemption ($87,500 for married filing separately).
- 28 percent of any additional excess AMTI.[28]

Tentative AMT.   Refer to the three taxpayers in the preceding example. Their tentative minimum tax is calculated as follows:

	Ms. X	Mr. and Mrs. Y	Mr. and Mrs. Z
AMTI	$ 91,000	$351,600	$215,000
Exemption	(33,750)	–0–	(28,750)
AMTI in excess of exemption	$ 57,250	$351,600	$186,250

---

[28]Individuals who can use the 20 percent capital gains rate in computing regular tax can use the rate in computing tentative minimum tax. §55(b)(3).

26% of first $175,000 of excess AMTI	$ 14,885	$ 45,500	$ 45,500
28% of additional excess AMTI	–0–	49,448	3,150
Tentative minimum tax	$ 14,885	$ 94,948	$ 48,650

Any excess of tentative minimum tax over regular tax becomes the individual's AMT for the year. Because the top AMT rate is 11.6 percentage points less than the 39.6 percent top marginal rate for regular tax purposes, AMTI must be significantly greater than regular taxable income for tentative minimum tax to exceed regular tax.

> **Individual AMT.**   Mr. C, a single individual with $600,000 of taxable income, has regular tax liability of $216,613. Mr. C does not owe AMT unless his AMTI exceeds $786,118.
>
> | | |
> |---|---|
> | Tentative minimum tax on $786,118 AMTI: | |
> | $175,000 × 26% | $ 45,500 |
> | ($786,118 − $175,000) × 28% | 171,113 |
> | | $ 216,613 |
> | Regular tax liability | (216,613) |
> | AMT | $ –0– |

While most individual taxpayers have some AMT adjustments or tax preferences every year, few have enough to trigger an AMT liability. But when unusual circumstances converge to create a critical mass of adjustments and preferences, the result can be a greatly inflated AMTI and an unexpected and unwelcome AMT.[29]

Payment and Filing Requirements

Objective 10
Describe the individual tax payment and return filing requirements.

Individual taxpayers are required to pay their income and self-employment tax to the federal government periodically over the course of the year. The income tax with respect to compensation is paid automatically; employers are required to withhold income tax from each wage or salary payment and remit this withholding to the Treasury on their employees' behalf.[30] The tax with respect to other income items, such as net profit from a sole proprietorship, distributive shares of partnership income, or investment income must be paid in four equal installments.[31] The first three of these installments are due on April 15, June 15, and September 15 of the current year, while the fourth installment is due on January 15 of the following year.

Individuals who fail to make timely payments of at least 90 percent of their current year tax liability in the form of withholding and quarterly installments may incur an

---

[29]A portion of AMT becomes an AMT credit that the individual can carry forward to reduce regular tax liability in subsequent years. §53.

[30]§3402. The withholding is based on the information concerning marital and family status provided by the employee to the employer on Form W-4. Employees can also specify a dollar amount of income tax to be withheld during the year.

[31]§6654(c).

underpayment penalty.[32] Because of the uncertainty inherent in estimating the tax owed for the year in progress, the law provides a **safe-harbor estimate.** Individuals with AGI of $150,000 or less in the preceding year may pay current year estimated tax equal to 100 percent of the preceding year's liability.[33] By doing so, they avoid any underpayment penalty, regardless of their actual current year liability. The safe-harbor estimate for individuals with AGI in excess of $150,000 in the preceding year jumps to 110 percent of the preceding year's tax liability.[34]

> *Safe-Harbor Estimate.*   Mrs. G works for a local corporation and knows that her income tax withholding for the current year will be at least $14,000. Mr. G recently started a new business venture and is uncertain as to how much income the business might generate. The couple knows that in the previous year their AGI was $92,000 and they paid $25,116 of income and self-employment tax. Therefore, they can make a safe-harbor estimate for the current year by paying in $25,116. If they make four installment payments of $2,779 each, their total installments plus Mrs. G's withholding will equal $25,116, and they are immune to penalty regardless of their actual current year tax liability.

Form 1040 must be filed by the 15th day of the 4th month following the close of the taxable year; for calendar year taxpayers, this is the familiar April 15 due date.[35] If the tax paid throughout the year (withholding and quarterly installments) is *less* than the tax computed on the return, the taxpayer must pay the balance due with the return. If the prepayment is *more* than the tax, the return serves as a claim for refund of the overpayment. Individuals who are not ready to file a completed return by the due date may request an automatic extension of the filing deadline for four months (August 15 for a calendar year taxpayer).[36] This extension applies only to the return filing requirement; individuals who estimate that they still owe tax should pay the estimated balance due with the extension request to avoid interest and penalties.[37] If the four-month extension isn't enough extra time, individuals may request a second extension for two more months (until October 15). This second extension is not automatic, and the IRS grants approval only if unusual circumstances justify further delay.[38]

> *Mr. and Mrs. Volpe: Tax Refund.*   Refer back to page 2 of Mr. and Mrs. Volpe's 1997 Form 1040 (Exhibit 13–1). Mrs. Volpe's 1997 self-employment tax of $8,016 is reported on line 47. The couple's $22,123 total tax (income and self-employment) is reported on line 53. During 1997, Mr. Volpe's employer withheld

---

[32]§6654(a) and (d)(1)(B)(i).

[33]§6654(d)(1)(B)(ii).

[34]§6654(d)(1)(C). The Taxpayer Relief Act of 1997 changed the safe-harbor estimate percentage for individuals with AGI in excess of $150,000. For 1998, a safe-harbor estimate equals 100 percent of 1997 tax. For 1999, 2000, and 2001, the percentage increases to 105 percent of the preceeding year's tax. For 2002, the percentage increases to 112 percent. For 2003 and subsequent years, the percentage reverts to 110 percent.

[35]§6072(a).

[36]See Form 4868 (Application for Automatic Extension of Time to File U.S. Individual Income Tax Return).

[37]Reg. §1.6081-4T.

[38]See Form 2688 (Application for Additional Extension of Time to File U.S. Individual Income Tax Return).

$7,091 income tax from Mr. Volpe's salary (line 54) and the couple made installment payments of estimated tax totaling $16,000 (line 55). Because the Volpes' total payments ($23,091 on line 60) exceeded their total tax by $968, the government owed them a refund of this amount. The entry on line 63 shows that Mr. and Mrs. Volpe decided to apply their $968 refund to their 1998 estimated tax rather than to receive a cash refund.

Conclusion

Chapter 13 provides the "big picture" with respect to individual taxpayers. In this chapter, we developed the basic formula for the computation of taxable income and discussed the significance of AGI in this formula. You learned how to compute the regular tax on individual income, identified the most common credits that reduce regular tax, and considered the threat of the alternative minimum tax. The chapter closed with a synopsis of the payment and filing requirements for individual taxpayers.

In the next three chapters, we will explore the incredible variety of transactions that affect the computation of individual taxable income. Our discussions of the tax consequences of many specific transactions will reinforce your understanding of the individual tax formula and will lead to many new tax planning ideas. Hopefully, the material in these chapters will also give you a real appreciation of the complexities and nuances that make the study of individual taxation so challenging and yet so fascinating.

Key Terms

Adjusted gross income (AGI) 335	Itemized deduction 337
Adjustments 335	Joint and several liability 332
Bunching 338	Joint return 332
Child credit 347	Personal exemption 339
Dependent 339	Safe-harbor estimate 353
Dependent care credit 347	Separate return 333
Earned income credit 348	Single taxpayer 333
Excess payroll tax withholding 350	Standard deduction 337
Filing status 332	Surviving spouse 333
Head of household 333	Total income 334

Questions and Problems for Discussion

1. Discuss the extent to which adjusted gross income (AGI) is actually a net income number.
2. Describe the effect of an increase in AGI on a taxpayer's:
   a. Total itemized deductions.
   b. Standard deduction.
   c. Exemption amount.
   d. Alternative minimum taxable income (AMTI).
   e. Dependent care credit.

3. Discuss possible tax policy reasons why individuals who are age 65 or older receive an additional standard deduction.
4. Individuals who are legally blind receive an additional standard deduction, while individuals with other disabilities, such as deafness or paralysis, are not entitled to an additional deduction. Is there a tax policy justification for the different treatment?

5. The overall limitation on itemized deductions and the exemption phaseout increase the tax burden on high-income individuals. Why does the tax law contain these two complicated provisions instead of a higher marginal tax rate for such individuals?

6. Identify the reasons why individual taxpayers benefit more from deductions that reduce AGI than from itemized deductions.

7. While checking the computations on his Form 1040, Mr. G realized he had misclassified a $2,700 expense as a business deduction on Schedule C. The expense should have been an itemized deduction on Schedule A. Mr. G did not correct the error because he assumed the correction would not affect taxable income. Is this assumption correct?

8. Individuals who plan to bunch itemized deductions into one year can either postpone the payment of expenses from an earlier year or accelerate the payment of expenses from a later year. Which technique is preferable from a cash flow standpoint?

9. Is AGI or taxable income a closer gauge of an individual's disposable income for the year?

10. Under the current rate structure, a single person pays more tax than a married couple on the same taxable income. What economic circumstances might a single person cite to argue that his ability to pay tax is not necessarily greater than a married couples' ability to pay tax on the same income?

11. Single individuals S and Z were married this year and filed their first joint return. To what extent did this change in filing status affect the following:
    a. S and Z's aggregate standard deduction.
    b. S and Z's aggregate exemption amount.
    c. S and Z's aggregate dependent care credit.
    d. S and Z's aggregate AMTI exemption.

12. Explain why an individual's combined standard deduction and exemption amount can be considered a bracket of income taxed at a zero rate.

13. Why is the formula for computing individual taxable income so much more complicated than the formula for computing corporate taxable income?

14. The tax law provides for both refundable and nonrefundable credits. What is the difference between the two types of credit?

15. Congress enacted the earned income credit to offset the impact of the payroll tax on low-income workers. Why did Congress not accomplish this goal by providing a payroll tax exemption for a base amount of annual compensation paid by an employer to an employee?

16. When he accepted his current job, Mr. MG instructed his employer to withhold substantially more federal income tax from his monthly paycheck than was indicated by his marital and family situation. As a result, Mr. MG routinely overpays his tax and receives a refund each spring, which he invests in a mutual fund. Mr. MG views this strategy as an efficient means of enforced savings. Do you agree?

17. Ms. JR has been very ill since the beginning of the year and unable to attend to any financial matters. Her CPA advised that she request an automatic extension of time to file her prior year Form 1040. Ms. JR likes this idea because she believes the balance of tax due with the return will be at least $20,000 and she wants to avoid paying this tax for as long as possible. By requesting the extension, how long can Ms. JR delay paying the $20,000 to the Treasury?

Application Problems

1. In 1998, Mr. and Mrs. A had the following income items:

Mr. A's salary	$36,000
Mrs. A's Schedule C net profit	41,800
Interest income	1,300

Mrs. A's self-employment tax for the year was $5,906. The couple had $4,150 of itemized deductions. Mr. and Mrs. A have no children or other dependents. Based on these facts, compute the couple's 1998 income tax liability on a joint return.

2. In 1998, Mr. and Mrs. B had the following income items:

Mr. B's salary	$112,000
Mrs. B's salary	82,800
Distributive share of ordinary partnership income	13,500

The couple had $19,700 of itemized deductions (none of which were medical expense, investment interest expense, casualty, theft, or gambling loss). Mr. and Mrs. B have two dependent children over age 17. Based on these facts and using the worksheets in Appendixes 13–A and 13–B, compute the couple's 1998 income tax liability on a joint return.

3. In 1998, Mr. C, an unmarried individual, had the following income items:

Interest income	$ 14,200
Distributive share of ordinary loss from an S corporation	(5,500)
Distributive share of ordinary partnership income	179,000

Mr. C had $13,600 of itemized deductions (none of which were medical expense, investment interest expense, casualty, theft, or gambling loss) and no dependents. Based on these facts and using the worksheets in Appendixes 13–A and 13–B, compute Mr. C's 1998 income tax liability.

4. In 1998, Mr. and Mrs. D had the following income items:

Dividend income	$ 3,400
Capital gain eligible for 10% preferential rate	2,900
Mrs. D's salary	28,000

Mr. D is age 66 and Mrs. D is age 58. The couple's itemized deductions totaled $5,200. The couple has no dependents. Based on these facts, compute Mr. and Mrs. D's 1998 income tax liability on a joint return.

5. In 1998, Mr. RG, an unmarried individual, had the following income items:

Salary	$270,000
Interest income	9,700
Dividend income	31,000

Mr. RG had $34,000 of itemized deductions (none of which were medical expense or casualty, theft, or gambling loss). Mr. RG did have $5,200 of investment interest expense in 1998. Mr. RG has four dependent children (ages 5 through 15) and two dependent parents who live in his home. Based on these facts and using the worksheets in Appendixes 13–A and 13–B, compute Mr. RG's 1998 income tax liability.

6. For 1998, Mrs. E, who qualifies as a head of household, had $115,000 of taxable income. Compute Mrs. E's tax liability assuming that:
   a. Taxable income includes no capital gain.
   b. Taxable income includes $22,000 capital gain eligible for the 20 percent preferential rate.

7. On March 4, 1998, Mr. and Mrs. SP celebrated the birth of their third child. What is the impact of this event on the couple's 1998 tax liability, assuming that AGI on their 1998 joint return was:
   a. $72,000.
   b. $200,000.
   c. $450,000.

8. In 1998, Mr. M's salary was $60,000 and Mrs. M's salary was $70,000. The couple had no other income items, no deductions, and no dependents.
   a. Compute the couple's tax liability on a joint return.
   b. Compute the couple's combined tax liability if they file separate returns.
   c. Compute the couple's marriage penalty (excess of tax on a joint return over combined tax liability on two returns filed as single taxpayers).

9. Ms. NM, a single taxpayer, projects that she will incur $3,800 of expenses qualifying as itemized deductions in both 19X1 and 19X2. Assuming that the standard deduction for single taxpayers is $4,250, compute the effect on Ms. NM's 19X1 and 19X2 taxable income if she can shift $800 of expenses from 19X1 to 19X2.

10. Mrs. A is an unmarried taxpayer with one dependent child living in her home. Mrs. A's AGI for 1998 is $40,000, and she does not itemize deductions. During 1998, the 18-year-old

child earned $5,000 from a part-time job and incurred no deductible expenses.

a. Compute Mrs. A's 1998 tax liability.

b. Compute her child's 1998 tax liability.

11. In 1998, Mr. LK had the following income items:

Salary	$35,000
Net income from a rental house	3,000

Mr. LK has custody of his four-year-old son, who attends a day care center while Mr. LK is at work. During 1998, Mr. LK paid $2,100 to this center. Mr. LK has no itemized deductions for the year. Based on these facts, compute Mr. LK's 1998 tax liability.

12. Mr. and Mrs. OP have two dependent children. During the year, the couple paid $7,200 of wages to a housekeeper whose primary responsibility was to care for the children. The couple paid $549 of employer payroll tax on the housekeeper's wages. Mr. and Mrs. OP file a joint return. In each of the following cases, compute the couple's dependent care credit.

a. One child is age 10 and the other is age 15. Mr. OP's earned income is $75,000, and Mrs. OP does not have earned income. Their AGI is $81,300.

b. One child is age 2 and the other is age 6. Mr. OP's earned income is $45,000, and Mrs. OP's earned income is $28,000. Their AGI is $81,300.

13. On March 31, 1998, Mr. R quit his job with MT Inc. and began a new job with PK Company. His salary from MT Inc. was $53,900, and his salary from PK Company was $70,000. Based on these facts, compute Mr. R's excess payroll tax withholding credit for 1998.

14. In 1998, Mr. and Mrs. K's AGI was $14,000. Their federal income tax withholding was $850. They had no itemized deductions and two dependent children. The couple is entitled to a $3,400 earned income credit. Based on these facts, compute Mr. and Mrs. K's 1998 tax refund.

15. In each of the following cases, compute the taxpayer's AMT (if any) for 1998. For all cases, assume that taxable income does not include any capital gain.

a. Mr. and Mrs. BH's taxable income on their joint return was $200,000 and their AMTI before exemption was $345,000.

b. Mr. CK's taxable income on his single return was $76,000 and his AMTI before exemption was $104,000.

c. Ms. W's taxable income on her head of household return was $123,000 and her AMTI before exemption was $190,000.

16. In January 1999, Ms. NW projects that her employer will withhold $25,000 from her salary. However, she has income from several other sources and must make quarterly installments of tax with respect to such income. Compute the total quarterly installments that result in a safe-harbor estimate of her 1999 tax assuming that:

a. Ms. NW's AGI was $176,000 and the tax liability was $47,200 on her 1998 Form 1040.

b. Ms. NW's AGI was $139,000 and the tax liability was $36,800 on her 1998 Form 1040.

Issue Recognition Problems

Identify the tax issue or issues suggested by the following situations and state each issue in the form of a question.

1. Mr. LR died on April 16 of the current year. Mr. and Mrs. LR had been married for 29 years and had always filed a joint return. Mrs. LR remarried on December 21 of the current year.

2. Mr. and Mrs. JC were married in 1985. This year the couple traveled to Reno, Nevada, immediately after Christmas and obtained a quick divorce on December 29. They spent two weeks vacationing in California, returned to their home in Texas on January 13, and remarried the next day.

3. Mr. GS, an unmarried individual, provides the entire financial support for his invalid mother. Until the current year, she lived with Mr. GS. However, in March, Mr. GS moved his mother to a nursing home so that she could receive full-time care.

4. Mr. T is a 20-year-old college student. This year he lived on campus for nine months and in his parents' home during the summer. His parents paid for all Mr. T's living expenses, but a scholarship paid for his $22,000 college tuition.

5. Mr. and Mrs. TB have an 11-year old child. The couple is divorced, and Mrs. TB has sole custody of the child. However, Mr. TB pays his former wife $1,200 child support each month.

6. Mr. G, age 90, lives in a nursing home. He has no gross income and is financially dependent on his four adult children, each of whom pays 25 percent of the cost of the home.

7. Mr. and Mrs. WQ both have full-time jobs. They employ Mrs. WQ's 18-year-old sister as an after-school babysitter for their 10-year-old son.

8. Mr. TJ, a self-employed attorney, has sole custody of his nine-year-old daughter. This year she spent eight weeks during the summer at a recreational camp. The total cost to Mr. TJ was $3,800.

9. During the first eight months of the year, Ms. V was self-employed and earned $40,000 of net income. In September, she accepted a full-time job with MW Company and earned $51,000 of salary through the end of the year.

10. Mr. and Mrs. P own and operate a sole proprietorship that generates approximately $60,000 of annual net profit. This business is the couple's only source of income. In April, June, and September, Mr. and Mrs. P paid their quarterly installments of current year tax. In December, the couple won $250,000 in a state lottery.

11. In November, Mr. K discovered that his combined income tax withholding and quarterly installment payments would be less than his prior year tax liability and, therefore, would not be a safe-harbor estimate. He immediately requested that his employer withhold enough tax from his December paycheck to result in a safe harbor estimate.

12. Mr. P's AGI includes a $8,700 dividend paid by a German corporation and $11,600 of interest paid by a Canadian bank. Mr. P paid $3,000 of foreign income tax during the year.

13. Mr. and Mrs. CD engage a CPA to prepare their Form 1040. For the last two years, the itemized deductions on their return totaled $8,000 and $8,200. The CPA estimates that $750 of the couple's fee relates to the preparation of the Schedule A on which the itemized deductions are detailed.

Tax Planning Cases

1. Mr. and Mrs. WG's AGI averages $425,000 annually, and they are in the 39.6 percent tax bracket. They support their 22-year-old son who is a full-time college student. Mr. and Mrs. WG are considering giving their son a portfolio of marketable securities that generates $20,000 of annual income. He could support himself with this income stream (he would be financially independent) and would file his own tax return. Compute the tax savings to the family resulting from this plan.

2. Mr. and Mrs. TP estimate that their current year AGI will be $260,000 and their itemized deductions will be $40,000. The couple has the opportunity to invest in a new business activity that should generate $20,000 of additional ordinary income this year. Before they can make a decision concerning the investment, they must know the income tax cost with respect to the additional income. Compute the tax cost assuming that the couple files a joint return, has three dependent children, and no AMT adjustments or preferences for the year.

3. Assume that the tax law allows individuals to claim an itemized deduction for the cost of music lessons for the taxpayer or any member of his family. Instead of this deduction, individuals may claim the first $1,000 of the cost as a nonrefundable tax credit (no carryforward or carryback of any excess credit). In each of the following situations, advise the taxpayer as to whether she should take the deduction or credit in 1998. In each situation the taxpayer is single.

   a. Ms. M has AGI of $95,000. Before consideration of the $5,000 cost of her music lessons, she has no itemized deductions.

b. Ms. N has AGI of $28,000. Before consideration of the $5,000 cost of her music lessons, she has $4,200 of itemized deductions.

c. Ms. O has AGI of $95,000. Before consideration of the $5,000 cost of her music lessons, she has $7,200 of itemized deductions.

APPENDIX 13–A
ITEMIZED DEDUCTION WORKSHEET

Total itemized deductions listed on Schedule A		. . . . .	
Less deductions for:			
Medical expense	. . . .		
Investment interest expense	. . . .		
Casualty, theft, or gambling loss	_____		
Total		(_____)	
Total itemized deductions subject to overall limitation		. . . . .	
		.80	
Maximum reduction		══════	
Adjusted gross income (AGI)		. . . . .	
Annual inflation adjusted AGI threshold*		(_____)	
Excess AGI		. . . . .	
		.03	
Tentative reduction		══════	
Total itemized deductions listed on Schedule A		. . . . .	
Less the *smaller* of the maximum or tentative reduction		(_____)	
Total itemized deductions allowed		══════	

Total itemized deductions listed on Schedule A			$ 22,875
Less deductions for:			
Medical expense		$–0–	
Investment interest expense		4,289	
Casualty, theft, or gambling loss		–0–	
Total			(4,289)
Total itemized deductions subject to overall limitation			$ 18,586
			.80
Maximum reduction			$ 14,869
Adjusted gross income (AGI)			$ 173,681
1998 AGI threshold			(124,500)
Excess AGI			$ 49,181
			.03
Tentative reduction			$ 1,475
Total itemized deductions listed on Schedule A			$ 22,875
Less the *smaller* of the maximum or tentative reduction			(1,475)
Total itemized deductions allowed			$ 21,400

*The 1998 threshold is $124,500 ($62,250 for married filing separately).

> ***Example.*** In 1998, Mr. M's total itemized deductions listed on his Schedule A were $22,875 and his AGI was $173,681. Mr. M had no medical expense deduction and no casualty, theft, or gambling loss. He did, however, have investment interest expense of $4,289. Based on these facts, Mr. M's total itemized deductions allowed in 1998 were $21,400, computed as follows:

APPENDIX 13–B
EXEMPTION AMOUNT WORKSHEET

Annual inflation adjusted personal exemption	. . . . . .	1998 personal exemption	$ 2,700
Multiply by number of exemptions (taxpayers and dependents) on return	×	Multiply by number of exemptions (taxpayers and dependents) on return	× 6
Tentative exemption amount		**Tentative exemption amount**	$ 16,200
Adjusted gross income (AGI)	. . . . . .	Adjusted gross income (AGI)	$ 211,777
Annual inflation adjusted AGI threshold*	( )	1998 AGI threshold for married filing jointly	(186,800)
Excess AGI		**Excess AGI**	$ 24,977
Excess AGI divided by $2,500 (*rounded up to whole number*) (if 50 or more, the exemption amount is –0–)	. . . . . .	Excess AGI divided by $2,500 (*rounded up to whole number*) (if 50 or more, the exemption amount is –0–)	10
Multiply by 2	× 2	Multiply by 2	× 2
Percentage (%) reduction in tentative exemption amount		**Percentage (%) reduction in tentative exemption amount**	20
Tentative exemption amount	. . . . . .	Tentative exemption amount	$ 16,200
Percentage reduction		Percentage reduction	.20
Reduction in exemption amount		**Reduction in exemption amount**	$ 3,240
Exemption amount (Tentative exemption − reduction)		**Exemption amount** ($16,200 − $3,240)	$ 12,960

*1998 thresholds are:

MFJ $186,800
MFS   93,400
HH   155,650
S   124,500

> *Example.* In 1998, Mr. and Mrs. K filed a joint return on which they reported six exemptions. Their AGI was $211,777. Based on these facts, Mr. and Mrs. K's 1998 exemption amount is $12,960, computed as follows:

14 Compensation and Retirement Planning

Learning Objectives

After studying this chapter, you should be able to:

1. Distinguish between employees and independent contractors and explain the tax implications of each classification.
2. List the important factors determining reasonable compensation for a shareholder/employee of a closely held corporation.
3. Compute the tax savings when a family member in a low tax bracket works as an employee of a family business.
4. Identify the most common nontaxable employee fringe benefits.
5. Explain how employers and employees can share tax savings by including nontaxable fringe benefits in a compensation package.
6. Describe the tax consequences to both employers and employees of stock options and incentive stock options (ISOs).
7. Contrast the tax treatment of reimbursed and unreimbursed employment-related expenses.
8. Compare the after-tax accumulation of wealth in a qualified retirement plan to the accumulation in a nonqualified savings plan.
9. Calculate the tax cost of a premature withdrawal from a qualified retirement plan.
10. Explain why employers use nonqualified deferred-compensation plans to provide retirement benefits to highly compensated employees.
11. Describe the tax benefit of a Keogh plan to a self-employed individual.
12. Describe the tax consequences of IRA contributions and withdrawals.

The first item of income listed on page 1 of Form 1040 and the most important (if not the only) item of income recognized by millions of individuals is the compensation they earn as employees.[1] Such compensation can consist of an hourly wage, an annual salary, sales commissions, tips, fees, fringe benefits, bonuses, severance pay, or any other economic benefit received for services

---

[1] According to a 1997 report by the Congressional Joint Committee on Taxation, wages and salaries comprise 74 percent of the total income reported by individual taxpayers.

rendered in the course of employment.[2] In the first part of Chapter 14, we will concentrate on this broad category of income by describing a variety of popular compensation techniques and analyzing the tax and cash flow implications of each. In the second part of the chapter, we will consider the arrangements through which people convert current compensation into retirement income. Through long-range tax planning, individuals can maximize the cash flow available for consumption and enjoyment during their post-employment years.

The Compensation Transaction

The payment of compensation is a transaction with tax consequences to two parties: the employer making the payment and the employee receiving the payment. The nature and amount of the compensation is determined by contractual agreement between these parties. The employer's objective in negotiating the contract is to minimize the after-tax cost of the compensation paid; the employee's objective is to maximize the after-tax value of the compensation received. High-ranking employees can usually negotiate with their employers on a personal basis. Because they are transacting in a private market, employer and employee can work together to achieve their respective objectives. Specifically, they can compare different compensation arrangements and evaluate the tax consequences to both parties. By doing so, employer and employee can design a package offering the greatest overall tax savings and dividing the savings between them on a mutually satisfactory basis. In contrast, rank-and-file employees typically transact with their employers in an impersonal, public market. These employees can only accept or reject the compensation arrangement offered by the employer. In such case, both employee and employer must pursue their tax planning objectives independently.

Employee or Independent Contractor?

Objective 1
Distinguish between employees and independent contractors and explain the tax implications of each classification.

The employer/employee relationship is characterized by the employer's right to direct and control how, when, and where the employee's duties are performed.[3] The relationship is continuous; an **employee** works according to a regular schedule in return for periodic payments from the employer. The relationship is also exclusive; an employee provides services for a single employer rather than to the general public.

As an alternative to hiring an employee to perform a certain service, a firm can engage an independent contractor to do the job. An **independent contractor** is a self-employed individual who performs services for valuable consideration and who retains control over the manner in which the services are performed. The independent contractor's clients don't oversee his work but can only accept or reject the final results of the contractor's efforts. The relationship between client and independent contractor is impermanent, and the contractor can work for any number of clients during the same time period.

Tax Consequences of Worker Classification

For tax purposes, the distinction between employee and independent contractor is critical. As you learned in Chapter 9, employers are liable for federal and state payroll taxes based on the compensation paid to their employees during the year. In addition, employ-

---

[2] Reg. §1.61-2.
[3] Reg. §31.3401(c)-1(b).

ers are required to withhold both employee payroll tax and federal, state, and local income tax from their employees' wages and salaries. At the end of the calendar year, employers must issue a Form W-2 (Wage and Tax Statement) to each employee.[4] These forms provide detailed information about total compensation paid during the year as well as the various taxes withheld by the employer on the employee's behalf.

When clients engage independent contractors, the fees paid to the contractors are not subject to FICA payroll taxes and clients are not required to withhold income tax. At the end of the year, clients must issue a Form 1099-MISC (Miscellaneous Income) to each independent contractor stating the annual compensation paid. Independent contractors who operate as sole proprietors (rather than in partnership with other individuals) report this compensation as business income on their Schedule C, Form 1040. Independent contractors pay self-employment tax on the net profit from their business and make quarterly installments of both self-employment and federal income tax.

Business versus the IRS: The Worker Classification Controversy

The classification of a worker as either employee or independent contractor is a subjective determination, based on the facts and circumstances of each case.[5] In most cases, the classification is clear. But occasionally, the nature of the relationship between the party paying the compensation and the worker does not clearly indicate whether the worker is an employee or an independent contractor.

The Firm's Viewpoint.   When a firm hires a worker whose classification is ambiguous, the firm has a financial incentive to treat the worker as an independent contractor. By doing so, the firm avoids both the employer payroll tax and the administrative cost of the various withholding requirements. Moreover, the firm doesn't have to provide independent contractors with the fringe benefits available to its permanent workforce. A firm's payroll cost for an employee includes both base compensation (wage or salary) plus the incremental cost of any benefits (medical and life insurance, paid vacation, sick leave, retirement pensions, etc.) for which the employee is eligible. If the firm can engage an independent contractor for the same base compensation, it eliminates this incremental cost.

The IRS's Viewpoint.   In theory, the federal government should be indifferent as to whether firms classify workers as employees or independent contractors. The IRS should collect the same employment tax on the worker's compensation, either in the form of payroll tax or self-employment tax. Similarly, the compensation is subject to income tax regardless of whether the recipient is an employee or is self-employed. Realistically, the IRS has a higher probability of collecting these taxes if the firm classifies the individual as an employee. In this case, the firm is legally responsible for remitting both the employment tax and the income tax on the compensation to the government.

If the firm classifies the individual as an independent contractor, the entire responsibility for payment of these taxes shifts to the individual. The IRS has determined that

---

[4]§6051(a). Employers must issue Form W-2s by January 31. If an employee who terminates employment during the year submits a written request for a Form W-2, the employer must issue the form within 30 days of receipt of the request.

[5]In Rev. Rul. 87-41, 1987-1 CB 296, the IRS lists 20 factors for determining whether an individual is an employee or an independent contractor.

self-employed individuals as a group have a relatively low level of compliance with the tax laws, either because they fail to file a tax return or because they understate their business income.[6] For this reason, the IRS takes an aggressive stance with respect to worker classification. Firms that classify workers as independent contractors must be aware of the risk that a revenue agent may challenge this classification on audit. If the agent concludes that facts and circumstances tip the scales in favor of employee status, the firm may find itself liable for unpaid taxes, interest, and penalties because it failed to carry out its responsibilities as an employer.[7]

Wage and Salary Payments

Tax Consequences to Employees.   As cash basis taxpayers, employees recognize gross wage or salary payments as income in the year in which the payments are actually or constructively received. In terms of cash flow, the payments are net of the employee payroll tax and income tax withheld by the employer. While the payroll tax withholding usually equals the individual's payroll tax liability for the year, the income tax withholding is an approximate number. If the annual withholding exceeds the individual's actual income tax liability, the IRS owes the individual a refund. Alternatively, the withholding may be less than the actual liability, in which case the individual pays the balance of tax due when she files her tax return or extension request.

Tax Consequences to Employers.   From the employer's perspective, the income tax consequences of wage or salary payments depend on the nature of the services performed by the employee. If the employer is an individual and the services do not relate to such individual's trade or business, the payment for such services is a nondeductible personal expense. For instance, people who employ private housekeepers, or gardeners, or nannies for their children can't deduct the compensation paid to these household employees. Of course, the fact that employees are performing domestic services does not excuse employers from their payroll tax obligations with respect to the compensation paid.[8]

For sole proprietorships, partnerships, and corporations that hire employees to perform business services, the compensation is either a deductible expense or a capitalized cost. This distinction depends on the nature of the service and the employer's method of accounting.

Accounting for Compensation Paid.   During the current year, Corporation BF paid a $90,000 salary to its in-house attorney, an expense that the corporation deducted in the computation of taxable income. Corporation BF paid

---

[6]See "Self-Employed Nonfilers, Post-Audit, Tax Year 1988," *Statistics of Income Bulletin,* Fall 1994, p. 123.

[7]From 1988 through 1995, the IRS reclassified 527,000 workers as employees and assessed their employers $830 million in back taxes, interest, and penalties. "Independent Contractor Legislation: Opportunity Knocks for Small Businesses," *Journal of Accountancy,* September 1996, p. 34.

[8]In 1998, household employers are not required to pay or withhold payroll tax unless they pay $1,100 or more in wages to an employee during the year. §3121(a)(7)(B) and (x). Household employers are not required to withhold federal income tax unless the employee requests it and the employer agrees. §3401(a)(3).

$2,679,000 of wages to workers on its production line, a direct labor cost that the corporation capitalized to manufactured inventory.

If a compensatory payment is deductible, a cash basis firm is allowed the deduction in the year the compensation is paid, while an accrual basis firm takes the deduction in the year the liability for the compensation is incurred.[9]

Reasonable Compensation

The tax law stipulates that only *reasonable* compensation for services rendered is deductible as a business expense. This stipulation is subjective: "reasonable and true compensation is only such amount as would ordinarily be paid for like services by like enterprises under like circumstances."[10] As a general rule, the IRS assumes that compensation resulting from an arm's-length negotiation between employer and employee is reasonable. In other words, the IRS does not usually challenge compensation determined in the competitive marketplace. This tolerance is subject to a statutory restriction applying to publicly held corporations.[11] These corporations can deduct no more than $1 million of the annual remuneration paid to their chief executive officer or to any of the four other most highly paid officers. This limitation is subject to a major exception: it does not apply to **performance-based compensation** paid solely because the corporate officer attained a performance goal established by a compensation committee consisting of outside members of the corporation's board of directors. The terms of the compensation arrangement, including the performance goal, must be disclosed to the corporation's shareholders who must approve the arrangement by a majority vote.

Closely Held Corporations.   The payment of compensation by a closely held corporation to an individual who is both an employee and a shareholder may not be an arm's-length transaction. To the extent the individual influences or even controls corporate policy in his capacity as a shareholder, salary negotiations between the individual and the corporation reflect a fictitious market.[12] As a result, the IRS tends to look very closely to determine if the compensation is reasonable. If the IRS concludes that the compensation is unreasonably high, it will reclassify the unreasonable portion as a constructive dividend.[13]

The determination of reasonable compensation is based on the facts and circumstances of each particular employer/employee relationship. Consequently, the federal courts have been called on to decide thousands of cases in which the IRS and a corporate employer disagreed on this issue. In a recent decision, the Second Circuit Court of Appeals described five broad categories of factors relevant in evaluating the reasonableness of employee compensation.

- The shareholder/employee's role in the corporate business, including the number of hours worked and the duties performed.

---

[9]An accrual basis firm that pays compensation to a related party who uses the cash method of accounting is not allowed a deduction until the year in which payment is made and the recipient recognizes the payment as income. §267(a)(2).

[10]Reg. §1.162-7(a)(3).

[11]§162(m).

[12]See the discussion of fictitious markets involving related parties in Chapter 3.

[13]See the discussion of constructive dividends in Chapter 11.

- External comparisons with other companies: specifically, the compensation paid to the employee relative to the compensation paid to comparable employees by unrelated employers in a similar business.
- The financial condition of the corporate employer, including sales, net income, capital value, and general economic fitness.
- The employee's degree of control over dividend policy in his or her capacity as shareholder.
- The internal consistency of the corporation's compensation system throughout the employee ranks.[14]

Objective 2
List the important factors determining reasonable compensation for a shareholder/employee of a closely held corporation.

The appellate court pointed out that no single factor determines the issue and that it must "assess the entire tableau from the perspective of an independent investor—that is, given the dividends and return on equity enjoyed by a disinterested stockholder, would that stockholder approve the compensation paid to the employee?"[15] In other words, if unrelated shareholders acting in their economic self-interest would agree to the compensation paid to a shareholder/employee, that compensation should be considered reasonable.

S Corporations.   The IRS views the issue of reasonable compensation in an entirely different light when the employment relationship is between an S corporation and its sole shareholder. In this case, the entire net profit from the corporate business is taxable as ordinary income to the individual who owns the corporation. With respect to the income tax, the individual is indifferent as to the salary he receives (and the corporation deducts) during the year. But the individual is not indifferent with respect to the federal payroll tax. Every dollar of salary is subject to the combined 15.3 percent FICA tax rate, while cash distributions of net profits are not subject to FICA tax at all.[16] Therefore, the individual has an incentive for his corporation to pay an unreasonably *low* salary to minimize payroll tax cost. In several recent cases, the IRS successfully challenged this tax avoidance tactic by convincing the court that a portion of an S corporation's annual cash distributions should be reclassified as salary to the corporation's sole shareholder.[17]

Objective 3
Compute the tax savings when a family member in a low tax bracket works as an employee of a family business.

Family Members as Employees.   While the tax law doesn't prohibit closely held business organizations from hiring employees who are related to the organization's owners, the compensation paid to these relatives must be reasonable for the services actually performed. Subject to this constraint, business owners can effectively shift income to family members who work in the business.

Family Members as Employees.   Mrs. Y, who owns and operates a sole proprietorship, is in the 31 percent tax bracket. Mrs. Y has two dependent children, ages 14 and 17, who work for her after school and during the summer. The younger child performs clerical chores and runs errands for her mom, while the older child drives a delivery van. Mrs. Y pays her children a reasonable wage based on the

---

[14]*Rapco, Inc.* v. *Commissioner,* 85 F.3d 950 (CA-2, 1996).
[15]Ibid., p. 955.
[16]S corporation shareholders do not pay self-employment tax on their allocated share of the corporation's business income.
[17]See *Spicer Accounting, Inc.* v. *Commissioner,* 918 F.2d 90 (CA-9, 1990).

actual number of hours worked each week. In 1998, the younger child earned $3,100, the older child earned $5,950, and the family saved $2,551 of income tax.

Tax savings of business deduction to Mrs. Y ($9,050 wages paid × 31%)	$ 2,806	
Tax consequences to:	*Younger Child*	*Older Child*
Wage income	$ 3,100	$ 5,950
Standard deduction (single)	(3,100)	(4,250)
Taxable income	$ –0–	$ 1,700
Tax rate (single)		.15
Tax cost of compensation to children		255
Tax savings to family		
Mrs. Y's savings	$ 2,806	
Older child's cost	$ (255)	
	$ 2,551	

The income shift in this example had a second beneficial tax effect. The $9,050 deduction for the wages paid to her children reduced Mrs. Y's net earnings from self-employment and, therefore, her self-employment tax. However, wages paid to an employer's child under age 18 are not subject to federal FICA or unemployment tax.[18] Consequently, the wage payments to the two children did not create an additional payroll tax cost to the family.

Foreign Earned Income Exclusion

Before leaving the topic of wage and salary payments, we should consider the special case of individuals who are U.S. citizens but who reside and work on an extended basis in another country. These individuals, referred to as **expatriates**, may face a higher cost of living because of their overseas assignment or may incur additional costs such as foreign income taxes on the compensation earned in the foreign jurisdiction. Because of these financial concerns, U.S. firms with international business operations may have difficulty staffing their foreign offices. To help U.S. firms compete in the labor market and to encourage them to employ U.S. citizens to work abroad, the tax law allows expatriates to exclude an annual amount of their foreign earnings from taxable income. In 1998, this **foreign earned income exclusion** is limited to $72,000.[19] Expatriates may not claim a foreign tax credit for any foreign income tax paid on the excluded income.[20]

> ***Foreign Earned Income Exclusion.***   PBG Inc. maintains a branch office in Portugal, which is managed by Mr. S. Although Mr. S is a U.S. citizen, he has been a resident of Lisbon since 1994. Mr. S's salary from PBG is $95,000, on which he

[18]§3121(b)(3)(A) and §3306(c)(5).
[19]§911(a).
[20]§911(d)(6).

paid $14,280 of Portuguese income tax. In preparing his 1998 Form 1040, Mr. S may exclude $72,000 of his foreign earned income from taxable income. Consequently, only $23,000 of his salary is subject to U.S. tax. Mr. S may also claim a foreign tax credit based on the portion of his Portuguese income tax attributable to his *taxable* salary.

Employee Fringe Benefits

As a general rule, individuals are taxed on any economic benefit received in return for services rendered to their employers, even if the benefit does not result in any direct cash flow.[21] However, the tax law allows employees to exclude the value of certain statutorily defined **fringe benefits** from income. These fringe benefits not only escape the income tax but also are exempt from payroll tax. Firms that provide fringe benefits account for the cost of the benefits in the same manner as they account for the base compensation paid. If the salary or wage paid to an employee is currently deductible, the cost of the employee's fringe benefits is also deductible.[22] This section of the chapter describes several of the more important nontaxable fringe benefits and discusses how employers and employees include these benefits in their compensation arrangements to mutual advantage.

Objective 4
Identify the most common nontaxable employee fringe benefits.

Health and Accident Insurance.   The Internal Revenue Code allows employees to exclude the value of health and accident insurance coverage provided by their employer.[23] Hence, premiums that employers pay directly to insurance carriers on behalf of their employees are not taxable to the employees. Similarly, if an employer has a self-insured medical reimbursement plan, participating employees do not recognize the imputed value of their coverage under the plan as income. This fringe benefit has tremendous significance to the U.S. workforce. Millions of employees can't afford private medical insurance and rely on their employers for insurance protection. A worker's decision to accept or reject a job offer may depend on whether the prospective employer provides a comprehensive health and accident insurance plan. The tax law encourages employers to do so by making this form of compensation nontaxable. Such preferential treatment is costly; the Treasury loses over $50 billion of annual tax revenues because of the exclusion for employer-provided medical insurance, making it one of the largest items in the government's tax expenditures budget.

Group Term Life Insurance.   Employees may exclude the value of term life insurance coverage provided under a group policy carried by their employers, but only to the extent the life insurance coverage does not exceed $50,000. If the coverage exceeds $50,000, the employee is taxed on the cost of the excess. This cost is determined by reference to a uniform premium table provided by the Treasury rather than by reference to the actual insurance premiums paid by the employer.[24]

---

[21]Reg. §1.61-21.

[22]Reg. §1.263A-1(e)(3)(ii)(D).

[23]§106. For taxable years beginning after 1996, this exclusion extends to the value of employer-provided long term care insurance. §213(d)(1)(D).

[24]Reg. §1.79-3. The employer's actual cost of group term life insurance is a §162 expense. Reg. §1.162-10 and Rev. Rul. 69-478, 1969-2 CB 29.

Group Term Life Insurance.   Mr. K, a 46-year-old employee of the ABC Corporation, has life insurance coverage of $90,000 under ABC's group term plan. According to the Treasury's table, the cost of $1,000 of life insurance to a 46-year-old person is 29 cents a month. The annual cost of Mr. K's $40,000 excess coverage is $139.20 (40 × $.29 × 12 months). This amount is a taxable fringe benefit to Mr. K; accordingly, ABC Inc. must report $139.20 as part of Mr. K's compensation on his Form W-2.

Dependent Care Assistance Programs.   Employees may exclude amounts paid or incurred by their employer for dependent care assistance.[25] Thus, employers may provide on-site day care for their employees' children (or other dependents) as a nontaxable fringe benefit. Alternatively, employers may contract with a third party to provide dependent care or may reimburse employees directly for their dependent care expenses. The annual exclusion is limited to $5,000 ($2,500 in the case of a separate return filed by a married individual). If the value of employer-provided dependent care exceeds $5,000 for the taxable year, the employee must recognize the excess as taxable income.

Other Nontaxable Fringe Benefits.   Most firms provide their employees with a variety of fringe benefits. The benefits that a particular firm chooses to offer depends on the nature of its business activities and the composition of its workforce. The list of possible benefits includes employee use of company cars, on-premise dining facilities, employer-provided parking and public transportation, moving expense reimbursements, business club memberships, professional dues and subscriptions, and even company-sponsored picnics and Christmas parties. Each item on this list (as well as many other employee perks) can qualify as a nontaxable fringe benefit, but only if the item meets the detailed, and sometimes strict, requirements specified in the Internal Revenue Code and Treasury regulations.[26]

Fringe Benefits and Self-Employed Individuals

While the Internal Revenue Code confers nontaxable status on many fringe benefits provided by employers to their employees, it generally does not extend this preferential status to benefits that a self-employed individual provides for himself. As a result, certain commodities that employees can obtain with before-tax dollars (as nontaxable compensation), self-employed persons must obtain with after-tax dollars. For instance, if a sole proprietor spends $600 of net profit from her business to purchase a $50,000 term life insurance policy to protect her family, the $600 is a nondeductible personal expense. Individuals who operate a business partnership are subject to a similar rule of law. If the partnership covers both partners and employees under a group term life insurance plan, the cost of a partner's coverage is a guaranteed payment that the partner must recognize as taxable income.[27] Even shareholder/employees of S corporations may fall victim to this rule. Any shareholder who owns more than 2 percent of an S corporation's outstanding stock is treated as a nonemployee for fringe-benefit purposes.[28]

---

[25]§129.
[26]See §132 and accompanying regulations.
[27]Rev. Rul. 91-26, 1991-1 CB 184.
[28]§1372.

Therefore, if such 2 percent shareholder is covered under the S corporation's group term life insurance plan, the shareholder must treat the cost of the coverage as taxable compensation rather than as a nontaxable employee fringe benefit.

In 1996, Congress took a major step toward redressing the uneven treatment of employees and the self-employed by enacting a statutory provision that eventually will allow self-employed individuals to deduct 100 percent of the cost of health and accident insurance for themselves and their families in computing adjusted gross income (AGI) (see line 27, page 1, Form 1040).[29] This provision applies to sole proprietors as well as to partners and 2 percent shareholders in S corporations. Consequently, owners of passthrough entities who must recognize taxable income because the entity purchased medical insurance on their behalf eventually will be allowed a deduction equal to the amount of such income.

Compensation Planning with Fringe Benefits

Objective 5
Explain how employers and employees can share tax savings by including nontaxable fringe benefits in a compensation package.

Fringe benefits are an extremely popular form of compensation. One reason is that the employer's cost of providing the benefit is usually less than the benefit's value to the employee. This differential is attributable to the employer's economy of scale: the cost per person of providing a commodity such as health insurance or child care to a large population is less than the cost of the commodity to one individual.

Cost versus Value of Fringe Benefit.   Corporation X, which has 1,200 employees, maintains a group medical plan with a commercial insurance company. Employee Y participates in this plan; the annual cost of Y's coverage is $2,400. If Employee Y were not a participant, he would pay $3,600 per year for comparable private medical insurance. Corporation X operates an on-premise day care facility in which employees can enroll their preschool children at no charge. The firm's annual operating cost for the facility is $1,750 per child. Employee Y's son attends this facility. If the facility were not available, Y would pay $2,100 per year to enroll his son in private day care. The aggregate value of these two fringe benefits to Employee Y is $5,700. Corporation X's cost to provide the benefits is only $4,150.

Cafeteria Plans.   Because employees have varying financial needs and consumption preferences, each one places a different value on any noncash benefit offered by his or her employer.

Valuing Fringe Benefits.   In the preceding example, employee Y placed a $2,100 value on the child care provided by Corporation X because he is willing to pay $2,100 for this commodity. Employee Z, another corporate employee, has no children. Therefore, employee Z places a zero value on employer provided child care. She would prefer a different fringe benefit or even additional salary from Corporation X rather than a worthless fringe benefit.

[29]§162(l). The 100 percent deduction is being phased in gradually and won't be fully effective until the year 2007. In 1998, only 45 percent of health and accident insurance costs are deductible.

Employers such as Corporation X can maximize the aggregate value of their fringe-benefit programs to their employees through a **cafeteria plan.** Under a cafeteria plan, each employee may select noncash benefits from a menu of benefit choices. In lieu of noncash benefits, employees may simply select additional taxable salary.[30] By participating in a cafeteria plan, employees can combine both nontaxable and taxable benefits to result in the greatest after-tax compensation based on their individual needs and preferences.

Negotiating with Nontaxable Fringe Benefits.   Employers are certainly aware that employees may enjoy substantial tax savings because of nontaxable fringe benefits. By substituting nontaxable benefits for taxable compensation, employers can capture some portion of this savings for themselves and reduce the after-tax cost of the compensation. The examples that follow demonstrate this important point.

Salary Payment.   Corporation L is negotiating a one-year employment contract with Mrs. K, who begins the negotiation by requesting a $60,000 salary. Corporation L's marginal tax rate is 34 percent, and Mrs. K's marginal tax rate is 31 percent. The after-tax cost of this salary to Corporation L and the after-tax value of this salary to Mrs. K are computed as follows:

	Corporation L	*Mrs. K*
Salary payment	$(60,000)	$ 60,000
Employer/employee payroll tax	(4,590)	(4,590)
Income tax savings (cost):		
Salary deduction × 34%	20,400	
Payroll tax deduction × 34%	1,561	
Salary income × 31%		(18,600)
After-tax (cost) value	$(42,629)	$ 36,810

Now assume that Corporation L makes a counteroffer to Mrs. K: the corporation will pay a $50,000 salary and provide complete medical and dental insurance coverage for her and her family, free parking in a convenient garage, and a membership in the corporation's on-premise health spa. The value of these nontaxable fringe benefits to Mrs. K and their incremental cost to Corporation L is $7,000.[31]

Reduced Salary Plus Fringe Benefits.   The after-tax cost of the compensation package (salary plus fringe benefits) to Corporation L and the after-tax value of this package to Mrs. K are computed as follows:

---

[30]Cafeteria plans are described in §125.

[31]Employer-provided parking and on-premise athletic facilities can qualify as nontaxable fringe benefits. §132(f) and (j)(4).

	Corporation L	Mrs. K
Salary payment	$(50,000)	$ 50,000
Fringe-benefit (cost) value	(7,000)	7,000
Employer/employee payroll tax	(3,825)	(3,825)
Income tax savings (cost):		
Salary deduction × 34%	17,000	
Fringe-benefit deduction × 34%	2,380	
Payroll tax deduction × 34%	1,301	
Salary income × 31%		(15,500)
After-tax (cost) value	$(40,144)	$ 37,675

The substitution of $7,000 of nontaxable fringe benefits for $10,000 of salary decreased Corporation L's after-tax cost of obtaining Mrs. K's services by $2,485 and increased Mrs. K's after-tax compensation by $865.[32] Thus, both parties to this negotiation benefited from the nontaxable status of the employee fringe benefits.

Employee Stock Options

Corporate employers often include stock options as a major component of the compensation package offered to key employees. A **stock option** is the right to purchase the corporation's stock for a stated price (the strike price) for a given period of time. From the employee's perspective, stock options are an opportunity to acquire equity at a bargain price. From the employer's perspective, stock options are a form of compensation that requires no cash outlay and, in fact, may eventually result in an infusion of capital. In addition, the option gives the employee a financial interest in the corporation's long-term success and a powerful incentive to contribute to that success in every way possible.

Stock Options for Everyone!   According to a recent *Business Week* article, stock options (once reserved for top executives and workers with high-tech startup firms that couldn't afford to pay competitive salaries) are filtering down to an increasing number of rank-and-file corporate employees. Since 1989, when pioneer PepsiCo Inc. granted every employee bonus options worth 10 percent of their salary, over 2,000 companies have instituted broad-based option plans. "Options are a productivity factor for booksellers at newly public Borders, tellers at NationsBank, box packers at Pfizer, chemists at Monsanto, baggage handlers at Delta Airlines, and expresso servers at Starbucks."[33]

To analyze the tax consequences of compensatory stock options, consider the case of BRT Inc. and its employee, Mr. B. In year 1, BRT pays a bonus to Mr. B by granting

---

[32]Corporation L's cost decrease would be greater if the incremental cost of providing the fringe benefits is less than $7,000.

[33]Kerry Capell, "Options for Everyone," *Business Week*, July 22, 1996.

Exhibit 14–1

Tax consequences of Mr. B's stock option

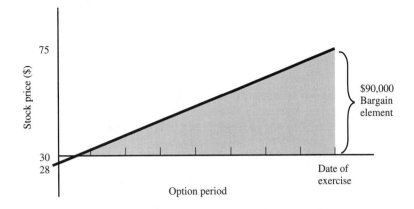

Objective 6
Describe the tax consequences to both employers and employees of stock options and incentive stock options (ISOs).

him an option to buy 2,000 shares of BRT common stock for a strike price of $30 per share at any time during the next eight years. On the date of grant, BRT common is selling for $28 per share. Because the strike price exceeds the market price, the option has no readily ascertainable value and Mr. B does not recognize income on receipt of the option.[34] The risk that Mr. B assumes in accepting the option is that the market price of BRT common will not climb above $30 per share over the term of the option. In this case, Mr. B will let the option lapse and his year 1 bonus in retrospect was worthless.

Mr. B's expectation is that the market price of BRT stock will increase over the option period. Suppose that by year 8, the stock is selling at $75 per share. Mr. B exercises the option by paying $60,000 cash to the corporation for 2,000 shares of stock with a market value of $150,000. Mr. B must recognize the $90,000 **bargain element** (the excess of market value over cost) as ordinary income in year 8. These results are shown in Exhibit 14–1 in which the vertical axis is BRT stock price and the horizontal axis is the eight-year option period.

The shaded area in Exhibit 14–1 represents the value of Mr. B's option, which increased over time as the BRT share price climbed from $28 to $75. Mr. B defers recognition of income until he realizes this value by converting the option to actual shares of stock. Mr. B's tax basis in his 2,000 shares is $150,000: $60,000 out-of-pocket cost plus $90,000 income recognized on the exercise of the option.

Note that in year 8, Mr. B has *negative* cash flow; he must pay $60,000 for the stock plus both income and payroll tax on $90,000 of compensation. Mr. B can generate cash by selling some of his BRT shares. This sale will not trigger additional income unless the selling price exceeds Mr. B's $75 per share basis. On the other hand, BRT Inc. received $60,000 cash as paid-in capital when Mr. B exercised his stock option. The corporation can deduct the $90,000 bargain element as compensation paid in year 8.[35]

Incentive Stock Options

The tax law creates a special type of employee stock option called an **incentive stock option (ISO).** The qualification requirements for ISOs are numerous and complex, but the preferential treatment of ISOs as compared to nonqualifying options is straightforward.[36] When an employee exercises an ISO, he does not recognize the bargain element

---

[34]Reg. §1.83-7.
[35]Reg. §1.83-6.
[36]Incentive stock options are defined in §422(b).

as taxable income.[37] The tax basis in the purchased shares is the employee's out-of-pocket cost, and the employee recognizes no income with respect to these shares unless and until he disposes of them in a taxable transaction. Furthermore, any gain recognized on disposition is capital gain.

Refer back to the facts concerning Mr. B's option to purchase 2,000 shares of BRT common stock and assume that the option qualified as an ISO. In year 8, Mr. B does not recognize any income when he purchases 2,000 shares of stock worth $150,000 for only $60,000. Suppose that Mr. B holds these shares until year 15, when he sells them for $225,000. Mr. B's capital gain on sale is $165,000 ($225,000 amount realized – $60,000 basis), $90,000 of which represents the untaxed bargain element on exercise of the option. The following table contrasts Mr. B's income tax cost from this sequence of transactions to the tax cost if the stock option had not qualified as an ISO. The table assumes a 36 percent rate on ordinary income and a 20 percent rate on capital gain.

ISO versus Nonqualified Option		
	ISO	Nonqualified Option
Year 8 (exercise of option):		
Ordinary income recognized	$ –0–	$ 90,000
Tax cost at 36%	**–0–**	**32,400**
Basis in 2,000 shares	60,000	150,000
Year 15 (sale of stock):		
Selling price	$225,000	$ 225,000
Basis	(60,000)	(150,000)
Capital gain recognized	$165,000	$ 75,000
Tax cost at 20%	**33,000**	**15,000**

This table reflects the dual advantage of ISOs as compared to nonqualified stock options: the extension of the tax *deferral* period until the year of sale and the *conversion* of the option's bargain element from ordinary income to capital gain. However, individuals who are planning to exercise ISOs must be cautious. The untaxed bargain element is an individual alternative minimum tax (AMT) adjustment added to taxable income in the computation of alternative minimum taxable income (AMTI).[38] Accordingly, individuals may want to avoid exercising ISOs in a year in which they have any exposure to the AMT.

An additional negative feature of ISOs is that employers never receive a tax deduction for the option's bargain element. Consequently, employers derive no tax benefit when an employee exercises an ISO.

Corporate Deduction for Stock Options. The following table compares the cash flow consequences to BRT Inc. of compensating Mr. B with an ISO rather than with a nonqualified stock option.

[37] §421(a).
[38] §56(b)(3).

	ISO	Nonqualified Option
Year 8 (Mr. B's exercise of option):		
Paid-in capital from issuance of shares	$60,000	$60,000
Deduction for bargain element	–0–	$90,000
BRT's marginal tax rate		.35
Tax savings from deduction	–0–	31,500
Net cash flow in year 8	$60,000	$91,500

Mr. B's sale of his stock in year 15 has no effect on BRT Inc.

Employment-Related Expenses

Objective 7
Contrast the tax treatment of reimbursed and unreimbursed employment-related expenses.

It is not unusual for individuals to incur out-of-pocket expenses relating to their employment. Common examples are union dues, subscriptions to professional or trade journals, uniforms, continuing education courses that maintain or improve job skills, and transportation costs incurred while conducting business for an employer. Many employers routinely reimburse employees for employment-related expenses, thereby assuming the economic burden of the expense. In such case, the employee neither reports the cash reimbursement as income nor claims the expense as a deduction. The whole expense/reimbursement transaction is a wash and has no impact on the employee's taxable income for the year.

The tax consequences of unreimbursed employment-related expenses are much less benign. Congress has expressed its belief that individuals should not be allowed to deduct such expenses. If the expenses are truly necessary to the successful performance of an employee's duties, the employer should be willing to provide reimbursement. Acting on this belief, Congress put employment-related expenses into the category of **miscellaneous itemized deductions,** which are deductible only to the extent that their total exceeds 2 percent of AGI.[39] Because of this limitation, many individuals derive no tax benefit from their unreimbursed employment-related expenses.

Unreimbursed Employment-Related Expenses.   Ms. J, who is employed by an advertising firm, spent $1,500 to attend a seminar on computer graphics. This unreimbursed employment-related expense is Ms. J's only miscellaneous itemized deduction for the year. If Mrs. J's AGI is $69,400, she can deduct only $112 of the cost of the seminar.

Miscellaneous itemized deductions	$1,500
AGI threshold ($69,400 × 2%)	(1,388)
Allowable deduction	$ 112

[39] §67.

If Ms. J's AGI equals or exceeds $75,000, her total miscellaneous itemized deductions fall short of the 2 percent AGI threshold. In such case, none of the employment-related expense is deductible and Ms. J's *after-tax* cost of the seminar is $1,500.

Moving Expenses

The tax law allows individuals to deduct unreimbursed moving expenses incurred in connection with "the commencement of work by the taxpayer as an employee or as a self-employed individual, at a new principal place of work."[40] **Moving expenses** include the cost of transporting household goods and personal belongings from the taxpayer's former residence to a new residence. The costs of traveling to the new residence (with the exception of the cost of meals en route) also qualify as moving expenses. The moving expense deduction is an adjustment in the computation of AGI (see line 25, page 1, Form 1040).

If an employee receives a moving expense reimbursement from his employer, the reimbursement is nontaxable to the extent of the moving expenses qualifying for the deduction. Any excess reimbursement is taxable compensation to the employee.

Moving Expenses.   Corporation BV transferred employee C from its San Diego office to its San Antonio office. Employee C paid $3,800 to the moving company that transported his household goods from his California home to his new home in Texas. He also paid $2,400 to fly his family from California to Texas.

- If employee C did not receive any reimbursement from Corporation BV, he may deduct $6,200 from total income in the computation of AGI.
- If employee C received a $5,000 reimbursement from Corporation BV, he may deduct $1,200 from total income in the computation of AGI.
- If employee C received a $7,000 reimbursement from Corporation BV, he must recognize the $800 excess reimbursement as additional compensation.

Retirement Planning

At some point in their lives, most people confront the need to plan for retirement. Given the current life expectancy for the average American, individuals who want to retire by age 65 know that they can anticipate living 20 years after leaving the workforce. These

---

[40]§217. To qualify for the deduction, individuals must meet both a distance test and a duration-of-new-employment test.

individuals also know that they should take action now to maintain their standard of living during this postemployment period. Specifically, they must invest some portion of their current income in financial assets that will be the source of future income. In this section of the chapter, we will learn how the tax laws encourage people to save for retirement. By taking advantage of tax-favored retirement plans, individuals can maximize the future value of their investments and enhance their prospects for long-term security.[41]

> ***Retirement Planning Is Top Priority.***   Based on a survey of employee benefit specialists, retirement planning has replaced health care as the top priority for today's labor force. The "tidal wave of Baby Boomers" approaching retirement age is recognizing the need to evaluate the adequacy of retirement savings. Many firms have initiated investment education programs to help their employees assess their investment options and develop strategies to increase their retirement income.[42]

Tax Advantages of Qualified Retirement Plans

Objective 8
Compare the after-tax accumulation of wealth in a qualified retirement plan to the accumulation in a nonqualified savings plan.

The tax law confers a generous set of tax advantages on an array of retirement savings plans, which are described generically as **qualified retirement plans.** While the statutory requirements and the financial and legal structures of the plans vary considerably, they all offer two basic benefits to the individuals who participate in the plans:

- Current dollars of earned income contributed to the plan (or contributed by an employer on an employee's behalf) are not subject to current tax.
- The plan itself is tax exempt, so that the earnings generated by the contributed dollars are not taxed currently.

The impact of these two benefits on the rate at which the contributed dollars grow over time is tremendous. The next example highlights this impact.

> ***Qualified Retirement Plan Contributions.***   Mr. Q and Mrs. R, who are both in the 39.6 percent marginal tax bracket, have decided to contribute $20,000 of annual compensation to a retirement fund. Both funds earn an annual 9 percent rate of return and involve the same financial risk. The only difference is that Mr. Q's fund is a qualified retirement plan while Mrs. R's fund is not. The following table shows the calculation of the balances in the two funds after 25 years:

---

[41]While many people anticipate that they will receive federal Social Security benefits during their retirement years, they can't undertake any type of individualized tax planning to increase these benefits. Consequently, we will address the tax consequences of Social Security in Chapter 16 as part of our discussion of government transfer payments.

[42]"Benefit Specialists Identify Priorities for 1998," *Deloitte & Touche Review*, December 22, 1997.

	Mr. Q	Mrs. R
Annual compensation contributed to fund	$ 20,000	$ 20,000
Income tax cost of compensation	–0–	(7,920)
After-tax annual contribution	$ 20,000	$ 12,080
Before-tax rate of return on contributions	.09	.09
After-tax rate of return on contributions	.09	.0544
Fund balance after 25 years	$1,694,018	$612,781

The balance in Mr. Q's fund does not represent the disposable wealth available to him on retirement. The tax law allows Mr. Q to *defer* the tax on his retirement savings—not to escape taxation entirely. When Mr. Q withdraws money from the fund, the withdrawals are fully taxable. In contrast, Mrs. R's fund balance consists of after-tax dollars that she may withdraw and spend at no further tax cost. The next example provides a final comparison of the two funds.

> ### *Qualified Retirement Plan Withdrawals.*   At the end of 25 years, both Mr. Q and Mrs. R withdraw the balance from their retirement funds. Mr. Q pays a 39.6 percent tax on the entire withdrawal.
>
> | | Mr. Q | Mrs. R |
> |---|---|---|
> | Fund balance after 25 years | $1,694,018 | $612,781 |
> | Income tax cost of withdrawal | (670,831) | –0– |
> | After-tax disposable wealth | $1,023,187 | $612,781 |

This comparison of after-tax wealth is dramatic testimony to the power of tax deferral. Moreover, Mr. Q can prolong the deferral by liquidating his retirement fund gradually over a number of years rather than in a single lump sum. Depending on the type of plan, he may have the option of receiving the fund balance in the form of an annuity, a series of fixed payments over a specific period of time.[43] In such case, Mr. Q will pay tax on the retirement dollars received each year. The tax law does limit the duration of the tax deferral that people can achieve by investing in qualified retirement plans. Plan participants must begin receiving a statutorily defined **minimum distribution** no later than April 1 of the year following the year in which they reach the age of 70½.[44]

---

[43]An annuity can last for a specified number of months or years or for the lifetime (or lifetimes) of the annuitant (annuitants).

[44]§401(a)(9) and §408(a)(6). Participants who fail to receive the minimum distribution must pay a 50 percent excise tax on the undistributed amount. §4974. In the case of employer-sponsored retirement plans, employees who continue to work after reaching age 70½ may postpone receiving distributions until they retire.

Premature Withdrawals

Objective 9
Calculate the tax cost of
a premature withdrawal
from a qualified
retirement plan.

When Congress decided to allow individuals to defer income tax through participation in qualified plans, the intent was that participants use the plans to save for retirement. To discourage people from withdrawing funds before retirement, the Internal Revenue Code imposes a 10 percent penalty on any **premature withdrawal** from a qualified plan.[45] Generally, a withdrawal is premature unless the participant has reached the age of 59½ by the date of withdrawal. This rule is subject to a number of important exceptions. For instance, the penalty is waived if the owner is totally or permanently disabled or if the withdrawal is made by the owner's estate or beneficiary subsequent to the owner's death.

The 10 percent penalty applies only to the portion of a withdrawal included in the participant's current income. Individuals who withdraw funds from a qualified plan can avoid both the income tax and any premature withdrawal penalty by contributing the funds to another qualified plan within 60 days of the withdrawal.

Rollover of Withdrawal. Mrs. H, age 48, participated for 14 years in a qualified retirement plan sponsored by her employer, Company A. In the current year, she resigned from Company A to accept a new job with Company Z. Because of her termination of employment, she received a cash distribution of the $35,000 balance in her Company A plan. Mrs. H spent $12,000 of this money to buy a new car and made a **rollover contribution** of the $23,000 remainder to the qualified retirement plan sponsored by Company Z. Consequently, Mrs. H recognized only $12,000 of the distribution as taxable income subject to her 31 percent marginal tax rate. The total tax cost of the withdrawal was $4,920.

Income tax ($12,000 × 31%)	$3,720
Premature withdrawal penalty ($12,000 × 10%)	1,200
Total tax cost	$4,920

Types of Qualified Plans

The qualified retirement plans authorized by the Internal Revenue Code fall into three categories:

- Plans that employers provide for their employees.
- Plans available to self-employed individuals (Keogh plans).
- Individual retirement accounts (IRAs) available to any person who recognizes compensation or earned income.

This section of the chapter describes the plans included in each category. As you will observe, qualified plans come in a variety of shapes and sizes. But regardless of the

[45]§72(t).

differences in structure or operation, qualified retirement plans share a common characteristic: they all are vehicles for tax-deferred savings.

Employer-Provided Plans

One of the more common fringe benefits that firms offer to employees is participation in one or more retirement plans sponsored and maintained by the firm. For an **employer-provided plan** to be a qualified plan for federal tax purposes, the plan must satisfy a formidable list of statutory requirements.[46] These requirements reflect two underlying congressional objectives. The first objective is that *employer-provided plans should carry minimum risk for participating employees.* To meet this objective, the law requires that:

- Qualified plans must be written, permanent arrangements and must be administered in trust form so that the plan assets are invested by an independent trustee for the exclusive benefit of the employees and their families.
- Qualified plans must be funded; annual contributions made to a plan by an employer on behalf of the employees must consist of cash or other valuable property.
- Employees must have a nonforfeitable (vested) right to 100 percent of their retirement benefits under a qualified plan after no more than seven years of service with the employer.

The second objective is that *employer-provided plans should provide benefits in an equitable manner to all participating employees.* Accordingly, plans may not discriminate in favor of the firm's officers, owner-employees, or highly compensated employees. In other words, rank-and-file employees must be entitled to participate in qualified retirement plans on essentially the same basis as the firm's chief executive officer.

Defined-Benefit Plans.   Employer-provided plans may take the form of a pension plan under which participating employees are promised a targeted or defined benefit when they retire from the firm. Firms make annual contributions to their pension plans based on the actuarially determined cost of funding the future retirement benefits to which the current workforce is entitled.[47] These contributions are deductible payroll expenses, even though the employees do not recognize the contributions as income.[48] For tax purposes, firms must comply with a minimum funding standard for their qualified pension plans.[49] Because of this standard, a firm may be required to make contributions in years in which it operates at a loss or experiences cash flow difficulties. For this

---

[46]§401 through §415.

[47]In 1974, Congress created the Pension Benefit Guaranty Corporation (PBGC) to insure defined benefit plans and to guarantee that participating employees receive their promised pension, even if the plan is underfunded or is terminated by the employer. Qualified plans must pay annual premiums to the PBGC for such insurance. One in every four workers in the United States has a pension protected by the PBGC. *Pension Insurance Data Book 1996: PBGC Single Employer Program.*

[48]Employer contributions to qualified plans are not subject to FICA payroll tax. §3121(a)(5).

[49]§412 contains the minimum funding standards that employers must satisfy every year for qualified defined-benefit plans.

reason, employers should regard employee pension plans as long-term financial obligations.

> ***Funding a Defined-Benefit Plan.***   BN Inc. provides a qualified defined-benefit plan for its employees. In 1998, an independent actuary determined that BN Inc. must contribute $4.28 million to the plan to fund the future pension benefits to which BN's workforce is entitled. The contribution does not represent current compensation to the employees participating in the plan. However, BN Inc. can deduct the $4.28 million contribution on its 1998 Form 1120.

The annual pension that employers can provide through a qualified **defined-benefit plan** is limited to the *lesser* of 100 percent of the retiree's average compensation for her three highest compensation years or an inflation-adjusted base amount.[50] In 1998, the base amount is $130,000. Firms wanting to provide more generous pensions must do so through nonqualified retirement plans. The tax consequences of nonqualified plans are discussed later in this section.

> ***Contribution Limit on Defined-Benefit Plan.***   Mr. U, a corporate officer of BN Inc., earns a $150,000 salary and anticipates a salary increase every year until his retirement. Mr. U is a participant in BN's qualified pension plan. Although Mr. U's average compensation for his three highest compensation years is projected to be at least $180,000, BN's 1998 plan contribution on Mr. U's behalf is limited to the amount necessary to fund an annual pension benefit of only $130,000.

Defined-Contribution Plans.   Employer-provided plans may be structured as **defined-contribution plans** under which the employer pays a specified annual amount into each participating employee's retirement account. The yearly contribution for each employee is limited to the *lesser* of 25 percent of annual compensation or an inflation-adjusted base amount.[51] In 1998, this base amount is $30,000. Employers may deduct their yearly contributions even though these contributions are not taxable to the employees.

> ***Contribution Limit on Defined-Contribution Plan.***   Ms. L, a midlevel manager with Corporation JH, earned a $110,000 salary in 1998. Ms. L is a participant in JH's qualified defined-contribution plan. Corporation JH's 1998 contribution to Ms. L's plan account is limited to $27,500 (25 percent of annual compensation).

Profit-sharing plans under which firms contribute a percentage of current earnings to an employee trust are a common type of defined-contribution plan. In a year in which the firm operates at a loss, it has no obligation to contribute to the plan. As a result, profit-sharing plans are favored by newly formed companies with volatile earnings and uncertain cash flows. From the employees' perspective, these plans

---

[50]§415(b).
[51]§415(c).

require them to share the risk associated with their employer's business. The retirement savings available to each employee depends in large part on the long-term success of that business.

Section 401(k) plans, also described as *salary reduction plans* or *cash-or-deferred arrangements,* are another popular qualified plan. Under these plans, each participating employee defines his or her own contribution by authorizing the employer to divert some amount of current salary or wage to the employee's retirement account. The compensation diverted to the account is tax deferred to the employee even though it is deductible by the employer.[52] In 1998, the maximum compensation that employees can elect to contribute to a Section 401(k) plan is $10,000. Employers often agree to make additional contributions or even match their employees' contributions to Section 401(k) plans.

> *Section 401(k) Plan Contribution.*   Mrs. T, a financial analyst with Company PW, received a $75,000 salary in 1998. She elected to contribute the maximum $10,000 to PW's Section 401(k) plan. Consequently, only $65,000 of her salary is taxable. PW's policy is to match each employee's elective contribution (subject to the annual contribution limit). In Mrs. T's case, the 1998 limit is $18,750 (the lesser of 25 percent of Mrs. T's $75,000 salary or $30,000) and PW's additional contribution is limited to $8,750 ($18,750 − $10,000).

Objective 10
Explain why employers use nonqualified deferred-compensation plans to provide retirement benefits to highly compensated employees.

Nonqualified Deferred-Compensation Plans.   Qualified retirement plans seem to offer a win-win situation to U.S. businesses. Employers can deduct contributions made to the plans on their employees' behalf, while employees defer recognition of income with respect to these contributions until they receive distributions from the plans at retirement. But as we learned in our discussion of pension plans, profit-sharing plans, and Section 401(k) plans, the amount of compensation that employers can offer on a tax-deferred basis is limited. Moreover, because of the nondiscrimination requirements, employers can't be overly selective as to the employees who may participate in a qualified retirement plan. Finally, most employers need professional help to cope with the morass of federal rules and regulations governing qualified plans; hence, these plans can be expensive to maintain, even for the smallest employer.

These negative aspects of qualified plans have prompted many employers to establish nonqualified retirement plans. Employers can use these plans to offer unlimited **deferred compensation** to key employees, such as highly paid corporate executives, without extending the benefits of the plan to other employees. In their simplest form, deferred-compensation plans are nothing more than contractual arrangements under which an employer agrees to pay some portion of the employee's compensation at a specified future date. The arrangement is unfunded; the employer accrues its liability for the deferred compensation but does not set aside any cash or property to secure the liability.

Employees who agree to this arrangement don't recognize income with respect to their deferred compensation because they are not in actual or constructive receipt of any payment from their employer.[53] These employees will recognize income in the future

---

[52]This compensation is subject to payroll tax in the year of contribution. §3121(v)(1)(A).
[53]Rev. Rul. 60-31, 1960-1 CB 174.

year in which their employer makes good on its contractual obligation to pay the deferred compensation. On the employer's side of the arrangement, the accrued liability for deferred compensation is a current expense for financial statement purposes. However, employers are not allowed a tax deduction for deferred compensation until the year of payment when the employee includes the compensation in income.[54]

> ***Deferred Compensation.***   Mr. J, age 49 and the chief operating officer of NY Inc., received a $300,000 salary in 1998. At its December meeting, NY's board of directors awarded him a $150,000 bonus to be paid in three annual installments, beginning in the year Mr. J retires at age 60. NY does not set aside any cash or property to fund Mr. J's deferred compensation but accrues a $150,000 liability on its financial records. Mr. J does not recognize the deferred compensation as 1998 income nor does NY Inc. deduct the deferred compensation on its 1998 Form 1120. Mr. J will recognize income and the corporation will claim a deduction over the three years when the compensation is actually paid.

Employees who consider saving for retirement through a deferred-compensation plan must weigh the tax advantages against the financial risk inherent in the plan. In the case of an unfunded plan, the employee is an unsecured creditor of the employer with respect to the deferred compensation. If the employer is financially secure, the employee's retirement is equally secure. But if the employer's business should fail and the employer defaults on its liabilities, the employee may discover that her right to deferred compensation has little or no value as a source of retirement income.

Keogh Plans for Self-Employed Individuals

Objective 11
Describe the tax benefit of a Keogh plan to a self-employed individual.

Individuals who earn self-employment income can make annual payments to a **Keogh plan** (named after the congressman who sponsored the legislation that created this qualified plan).[55] These payments are deductible as an adjustment in the computation of AGI (see line 28, page 1, Form 1040). Thus, individuals pay no income tax on the business earnings invested in their Keogh plans.[56] Because Keogh plans are qualified retirement plans, the earnings generated by the financial assets held in the plan are tax exempt. Accordingly, sole proprietors and partners can take advantage of Keogh plans to accumulate tax-deferred savings in the same way that employees take advantage of their employer-provided plans.

Like employer-provided plans, Keogh plans must be administered by an independent trustee. Commercial banks, credit unions, brokerage firms, and other financial institutions typically serve as trustees for the prototype Keogh plans they maintain and manage for their individual clients. While Keogh plans can be either defined-benefit or defined-contribution plans, the latter type are more popular. Individuals who own defined-contribution Keogh plans can invest the *lesser* of 20 percent of earned income from self-

---

[54]§404(a)(5). Deferred-compensation plans typically require the employer to accrue interest on its liability to the employee. Employers may not deduct this interest until the year it is actually paid to the employee. *Albertson's Inc.* v. *Commissioner,* 42 F.3d 537 (CA-9, 1994), *cert. denied,* 116 S. Ct. 51 (1995).

[55]§401(c) and §404(a)(8).

[56]They do, however, pay self-employment tax on this income. *Gale* v. *United States,* 768 F. Supp. 1305 (ND Ill., 1991).

employment or an inflation-adjusted base amount ($30,000 in 1998) each year.[57] For purposes of computing this limitation, earned income from self-employment is reduced by the deduction for one-half of the individual's self-employment tax.

Keogh Plan Contribution.   In 1998, Mr. L's earnings from his sole proprietorship were $63,000 and his self-employment tax was $8,902. Mr. L deducted $4,451 (one-half of his self-employment tax) as an adjustment to AGI. His maximum contribution to his Keogh plan for 1998 is:

Net earnings from self-employment	$63,000
Self-employment tax deduction	(4,451)
	$58,549
	.20
Maximum contribution	$11,710

This contribution is deductible as an adjustment in computing Mr. L's AGI.

Keogh plans have a potentially serious downside for self-employed individuals who hire employees to work in their business: the plan must provide retirement benefits to such employees on a nondiscriminatory basis. In other words, the owner of the business can't use a Keogh plan to defer tax on her own earnings unless the plan allows her employees to do the same with respect to their compensation. The owner's tax savings from the Keogh plan is eroded by the incremental cost of including employees in the plan. Clearly, the self-employed person with no employees is the ideal candidate for a Keogh plan.

Individual Retirement Accounts

Objective 12
Describe the tax consequences of IRA contributions and withdrawals.

Every person who receives compensation as an employee or earns self-employment income may save for retirement on a tax-deferred basis through an **Individual Retirement Account (IRA).** People establish IRAs with commercial banks or other financial institutions that serve as trustee of the account.[58] IRAs are tax exempt: the income generated by the financial assets in the account is not taxed until the owner withdraws the income at retirement. Individuals can contribute the *lesser* of $2,000 or 100 percent of compensation/earned income to their IRAs each year. For married couples who file a joint return, each spouse may contribute $2,000 to an IRA if their *combined* compensation/earned income is at least $4,000.[59]

Deduction of IRA Contributions.   Annual contributions to an IRA may be fully deductible as an adjustment in the computation of AGI (see line 23, page 1, Form 1040),

---

[57]Individuals who want to contribute the maximum 20 percent must maintain a combined profit-sharing plan (with discretionary contributions) and a money-purchase pension plan (with required contributions of a stated percentage of self-employment income). See Sally M. Jones, "Maximizing Deductible Contributions to a One-Participant Plan," *Journal of Taxation*, February 1998.

[58] §408 contains the qualification requirements for Individual Retirement Accounts.

[59]§219(c).

nondeductible, or partially deductible. If the individual making the contribution is an active participant in any other qualified retirement plan (an employer-provided or Keogh plan), the deduction is computed by reference to AGI before adjustment for the deduction. The 1998 computational rules can be summarized as follows:[60]

If AGI is less than:

    $50,000 (married filing jointly)

    $30,000 (single or head of household)

    → IRA contributions are fully deductible

If AGI is more than:

    $60,000 (married filing jointly)

    $10,000 (married filing separately)[61]

    $40,000 (single or head of household)

    → IRA contributions are nondeductible

If AGI is between:

    $50,000 and $60,000 (married filing jointly)

    $–0– and $10,000 (married filing separately)

    $30,000 and $40,000 (single or head of household)

    → IRA contributions are partially deductible. The deduction is phased out proportionally as AGI increases through the $10,000 phaseout range.

Phaseout of Deduction for IRA Contribution.   In 1998, Mr. and Mrs. S each made the maximum $2,000 contribution to their respective IRAs. Both spouses are active participants in their respective employer's profit-sharing plan. Before consideration of any deduction for their IRA contributions, the AGI on this couple's joint return is $53,890. Because this AGI falls in the phaseout range, their IRA contributions are partially deductible.

AGI before IRA deduction	$ 53,890
Phaseout threshold for married filing jointly	(50,000)
AGI in phaseout range	$ 3,890

$$\$3{,}890 \div \$10{,}000 = .389 \text{ phaseout percentage}$$

Each spouse's IRA contribution	$ 2,000
	.389
Deduction phaseout	$ 778

---

[60]§219(g). The AGI thresholds in these rules are scheduled to increase every year through 2007.

[61]Married individuals filing separate returns who live apart at all times during the year are considered single taxpayers under the IRA rules. §219(g)(4).

According to statute, this phaseout is *rounded down* to the nearest $10. Consequently, Mr. and Mrs. S can deduct $1,230 of each IRA contribution, and their AGI for the year is $51,430.

AGI before IRA deduction		$53,890
Each spouse's IRA contribution	$2,000	
Deduction phaseout (rounded down)	(770)	
Deductible contribution	$1,230	
	2	
IRA deduction		(2,460)
AGI		$51,430

IRA Deduction for Nonparticipants.   If an individual who contributes to an IRA is *not* an active participant in any other qualified retirement plan, the contribution is fully deductible, subject to one major exception. If that individual's *spouse* on a joint return is an active participant in another plan, the individual's deduction is phased out proportionally as AGI increases through a $10,000 phaseout range that begins at $150,000.

IRA Deduction for a Nonparticipant Spouse.   In 1998, Mr. and Mrs. D each make the maximum $2,000 contribution to an IRA. Mr. D is an active participant in a Keogh plan, but Mrs. D is not an active participant in any other qualified plan.

- Assuming that the couple's AGI on their 1998 joint return is $42,000 before consideration of their IRA contributions, each spouse's contribution is fully deductible. Consequently, their 1998 AGI is $38,000.
- Assuming that the couple's AGI is $92,000 before consideration of their IRA contributions, Mr. D's contribution is nondeductible, but Mrs. D's contribution is fully deductible. Consequently, their 1998 AGI is $90,000.
- Assuming that the couple's AGI is $200,000 before consideration of their IRA contributions, neither spouse's contribution is deductible and their 1998 AGI is $200,000.

Withdrawals from IRAs.   High-income individuals who are active participants in other qualified plans can't deduct their IRA contributions. Such individuals invest in IRAs to take advantage of the tax deferral on the earnings generated by the account. When a person retires and begins to withdraw funds from an IRA, any portion of the withdrawal attributable to nondeductible contributions is a nontaxable return of investment rather than tax-deferred income. The nontaxable withdrawal is based on the ratio of the person's unrecovered investment at the beginning of the year to the current year value of the IRA. The *current year value* is defined as the year-end IRA balance *plus* current year withdrawals.[62]

---

[62]§408(d).

IRA Withdrawals.   Mr. J owns an IRA to which he made $44,000 of contributions, $19,000 of which were nondeductible. In 19X1, Mr. J retired at age 63 and made his first withdrawal of $15,000 from his IRA. The account balance at the end of 19X1 was $73,220. In 19X2, Mr. J withdrew $17,500 from the IRA. The account balance at the end of 19X2 was $60,200. (Note that during both 19X1 and 19X2, the IRA continued to generate tax-exempt earnings.) The yearly withdrawals that Mr. J must recognize as taxable income are computed as follows:

		19X1		19X2
Year-end balance in IRA		$73,220		$60,200
Plus withdrawals during the year		15,000		17,500
Current year value of IRA		$88,220		$77,700
Nondeductible contributions	$19,000		$19,000	
Prior year recoveries	(–0–)		(3,231)	
Unrecovered investment	$19,000		$15,769	
Ratio of unrecovered investment				
to current year value	.2154		.2029	
Withdrawal during the year		$15,000		$17,500
		.2154		.2029
Nontaxable recovery of investment		$ 3,231		$ 3,551
Taxable income:				
(Withdrawal – Nontaxable recovery)		$11,769		$13,949

As Mr. J continues to withdraw funds from his IRA, he will treat a portion of each withdrawal as a nontaxable return of investment. By the time he completely liquidates the account, he will have recouped his $19,000 of nondeductible contributions on a tax-free basis.

As a general rule, owners who make withdrawals from their IRAs before reaching age 59½ are subject to the 10 percent penalty described earlier in the chapter. However, this penalty is waived in a number of situations. For instance, an individual can withdraw funds from an IRA to pay higher education expenses (tuition, fees, books, supplies, and equipment). An individual who qualifies as a "first-time homebuyer" can withdraw up to $10,000 to finance the acquisition of a home. While some or all of the withdrawal must be included in the owner's taxable income, the taxable portion escapes the premature withdrawal penalty.[63]

Roth IRAs.   The Tax Reform Act of 1997 created a new type of savings vehicle labeled a **Roth IRA** (named for Senator William V. Roth, Jr., who championed the legislation in Congress).[64] Basically, a Roth IRA works like a regular IRA with two major differences. First, contributions to a Roth IRA are nondeductible. Second, *qualified* withdrawals from a Roth IRA are completely tax free. To qualify, a withdrawal must be made:

---

[63] §72(t)(2)(E) and (F).

[64] §408A contains the tax rules governing Roth IRAs.

- On or after the date on which the owner reaches age 59½ (or after the owner's death or permanent disability) or
- To finance the acquisition of a home by a first-time homebuyer (subject to the $10,000 maximum).

In addition, a qualified withdrawal must occur after the five-year period beginning with the year in which the owner made the initial contribution to the Roth IRA.

This new tax-favored investment is not available to everyone. The maximum $2,000 annual contribution to a Roth IRA is reduced proportionally over an AGI phase-out range. For married individuals filing jointly, the phaseout range is between $150,000 and $160,000 of AGI. For married individuals filing separately, the phaseout range is between zero and $15,000 of AGI.[65] For single individuals or heads of household, the phaseout range is between $95,000 and $110,000 of AGI.

Roth IRA.   Mr. T, a single individual, is an active participant in his employer's qualified pension plan. In 1998, he wants to contribute $2,000 to some type of IRA.

- If Mr. T's 1998 AGI is *less* than $30,000, he can make a fully deductible contribution to a regular IRA or a nondeductible contribution to a Roth IRA.
- If Mr. T's 1998 AGI is *more* than $40,000 but *less* than $95,000, he can make a nondeductible contribution to a regular IRA or a nondeductible contribution to a Roth IRA.
- If Mr. T's 1998 AGI is *more* than $110,000, he can make a nondeductible contribution to a regular IRA. He cannot contribute to a Roth IRA.

If Mr. T makes a contribution to a regular IRA, tax on the IRA earnings is deferred until Mr. T withdraws the earnings at retirement. If Mr. T makes a contribution to a Roth IRA, the IRA earnings are nontaxable when Mr. T withdraws them at retirement.

Individuals who are eligible to make deductible contributions to a regular IRA or nondeductible contributions to a Roth IRA must determine which investment vehicle will maximize their after-tax retirement income. The comparison of these investment options is complicated and requires assumptions about the individual's tax situation at retirement. However, individuals who cannot make *deductible* contributions to a regular IRA should contribute to a Roth IRA to take advantage of the tax-exempt (rather than tax-deferred) earnings.[66]

---

[65]See footnote 61.

[66]In certain circumstances, individuals can roll over a regular IRA into a Roth IRA. For details concerning the tax consequences of such rollovers, see Stanley D. Baum, "IRA Planning after the Taxpayer Relief Act of 1997—More Choices Than Ever," *Journal of Taxation*, October 1997.

Conclusion

In Chapter 14, we've explored the tax consequences of compensation arrangements between employer and employee. These arrangements can consist of a mix of cash payments and noncash fringe benefits, many of which are excluded from the recipient's income. Corporate employers frequently include stock options and ISOs in the compensation packages offered to key employees. By understanding both the economic implications and the tax consequences of the various forms of current compensation, employers and employees can negotiate to improve their respective after-tax positions.

No area of the tax law offers a better opportunity for effective long-term planning than qualified retirement plans. The tax deferral available through these plans is one of the surest routes toward wealth maximization. Young adults who are just beginning their careers should take immediate advantage of any pension or profit-sharing plans sponsored by their employers. Entrepreneurs who own and operate their own businesses should consider making regular contributions to a qualified Keogh plan. And every working person, regardless of age, who can afford to save even a few dollars each year toward retirement should consider an IRA.

Key Terms

Bargain element 373	Keogh plan 383
Cafeteria plan 371	Minimum distribution 378
Deferred compensation 382	Miscellaneous itemized
Defined-benefit plan 381	deductions 375
Defined-contribution plan 381	Moving expenses 376
Employee 362	Performance-based compensation 365
Employer-provided plan 380	Premature withdrawal 379
Expatriate 367	Profit-sharing plan 381
Foreign earned income exclusion 367	Qualified retirement plans 377
Fringe benefits 368	Rollover contribution 379
Incentive stock option (ISO) 373	Roth IRA 387
Independent contractor 362	Section 401(k) plan 382
Individual Retirement Account (IRA) 384	Stock option 372

Questions and Problems for Discussion

1. Discuss how the presence of a strong labor union may change the nature of the market in which rank-and-file employees and their employer negotiate.
2. Discuss the difference in the relationship between an employer and employee and a client and an independent contractor.
3. Mr. U accepted an engagement to perform consulting services for the MK Company. The engagement will last at least 18 months. Identify any reasons why Mr. U might prefer to be classified as an MK employee rather than as an independent contractor.
4. Discuss the practical reasons why the tax law authorizes the IRS to collect unwithheld employee payroll tax from the employer rather than the employees who were liable for the tax.
5. A reasonable compensation problem for the sole shareholder of a regular corporation is quite different from the reasonable compensaton

problem for the sole shareholder of an S corporation. What is the difference?

6. Mr. B owns 10 percent of the stock of ABC Inc. and is the corporation's director of marketing. The corporation has a medical insurance plan for its employees. During the current year, the corporation paid $1,400 of premiums to the insurance carrier for Mr. B's coverage. Contrast the treatment of this payment to Mr. B if ABC Inc. is a regular corporation or an S corporation.

7. In the current year, publicly held Corporation DF paid its chief executive officer a $1.4 million salary, only $1 million of which was deductible. It also accrued a $200,000 liability for deferred compensation payable to the CEO in the year 2006 (when the CEO must retire). To what extent does either transaction result in a difference between DF's financial statement income and its taxable income? Is the difference a permanent or a temporary difference?

8. Discuss how employees who routinely incur unreimbursed employment-related expenses can maximize the tax benefit of the expenses by bunching them into one year.

9. Mr. Z was recently promoted to an executive position by his corporate employer. The corporation now requires him to entertain clients much more frequently, and Mr. Z expects to incur at least $800 of out-of-pocket business entertainment expenses each month. The corporation will either reimburse him directly for these expenses or give him a salary bonus at year-end that indirectly covers his annual expenses. Which option should Mr. Z insist on and why?

10. Six years ago, Corporation AT granted a stock option to employee N giving her the right to purchase 1,000 shares of AT stock for $15 per share. At date of grant, AT stock was selling for $14.10 per share. Over the last six years, the market price has steadily declined to $11.80 per share. What are the tax consequences to employee N in the current year when the option lapses?

11. Two years ago, Corporation WZ granted a stock option to employee R giving him the right to purchase 2,500 shares of WZ stock for $30 per share. Since the date of grant, the market price of the stock has risen steadily and reached $31 just days ago. However, the option period is 10 years. Should R exercise the option immediately to minimize the income he must recognize or should he wait for eight more years before exercising the option?

12. Explain the basic difference between a defined-benefit retirement plan and a defined-contribution retirement plan.

13. How does the fact that employees have a vested right to their benefits reduce the risk of participating in an employer-sponsored qualified retirement plan?

14. How does the fact that an employer-sponsored qualified retirement plan is administered by an independent trustee reduce the employees' risk of participating in the plan?

Application Problems

1. Mr. and Mrs. SW are the sole shareholders of SW Inc. For the last three years, SW has employed the couple's son as a sales representative and paid him an annual salary of $30,000. During a recent IRS audit, the revenue agent discovered that the son has never made a sale for SW Inc. and spends most of his time playing saxophone in a jazz band. Compute the potential tax cost of this discovery to Mr. and Mrs. SW under the following assumptions. In making your calculations, ignore any payroll tax implications.

   a. Mr. and Mrs. SW are in the 36 percent tax bracket and SW Inc. is an S corporation.

   b. Mr. and Mrs. SW are in the 36 percent tax bracket and SW Inc. is a taxable corporation in the 34 percent tax bracket.

2. Mrs. ST's corporate employer recently adopted a cafeteria plan under which its employees can receive a $3,000 year-end Christmas bonus or enroll in a qualified medical reimbursement plan that pays up to $3,000 of the employee's annual medical bills. Mrs. ST is in a 31 percent tax

bracket, and her medical bills average $2,300 each year.

a. Based on these facts, should Mrs. ST choose the cash bonus or the nontaxable fringe benefit?

b. Does your answer change if Mrs. ST is in the 15 percent tax bracket?

3. Mr. N and Mr. R are employed by HD Inc. The corporation provides its employees with free parking. If the parking were not available, Mr. N would pay $35 a month to a city garage. Mr. R, however, uses public transportation to commute to and from work. HD Inc. offers a complete family medical plan to its employees. Both Mr. N and Mr. R participate in this plan. Mr. N's family consists of five people, while Mr. R is single. Consequently, Mr. N's annual cost of comparable medical insurance would be $9,000, while Mr. R's cost would be just $4,100.

a. Based on the above facts, compute the value of the two fringe benefits to Mr. N assuming he has a 28 percent marginal tax rate.

b. Compute the value of the two fringe benefits to Mr. R assuming he has a 39.6 percent marginal tax rate.

4. Ms. A, an employee of WQR Company, paid $300 of union dues and $235 for small tools and supplies used on the job. In each of the following cases, compute Ms. A's after-tax cost of these employment-related expenses.

a. Ms. A's employer paid her a $535 reimbursement for the expenses.

b. Ms. A received no reimbursement from her employer. Her AGI is $13,000, she does not itemize deductions, and her marginal tax rate is 15 percent.

c. Ms. A received no reimbursement from her employer. Her AGI is $36,000, she does itemize deductions, and her marginal tax rate is 28 percent.

d. Ms. A received no reimbursement from her employer. Her AGI is $16,900, she does itemize deductions, and her marginal tax rate is 15 percent.

5. Mr. and Mrs. JN moved from Lincoln, Nebraska, to Kansas City, Missouri, so that Mr. JN could take a job with the HM Company. As part of his employment agreement with HM, Mr. JN received a $7,500 moving expense allowance.

What is the effect of this $7,500 cash receipt on Mr. and Mrs. JN's AGI assuming that:

a. Their deductible moving expense was $5,200.

b. Their deductible moving expense was $9,000.

6. In 19X3, BT Inc. granted a nonqualified stock option to Ms. P giving her the right to buy 500 shares of BT stock at $20 per share for the next six years. At date of grant, BT stock was trading on NASDAQ for $18.62 per share. In 19X9, Ms. P exercised the option when BT's stock was trading at $37.10 per share.

a. How much income must Ms. P recognize in 19X3 and 19X9 because of the stock option?

b. Compute Ms. P's basis in the 500 shares purchased in 19X9.

c. What are the tax consequences of the stock option to BT Inc. in 19X3? In 19X9?

7. In 19X0, Corporation BB granted an incentive stock option (ISO) to Mr. Y giving him the right to buy 8,000 shares of BB stock at $7 per share for the next five years. At date of grant, BB stock was trading on the AMEX for $6.23 per share. In 19X5, Mr. Y exercised the option when BB's stock was trading at $19.92 per share.

a. How much income must Mr. Y recognize in 19X0 and 19X5 because of the ISO?

b. Compute Mr. Y's basis in the 8,000 shares purchased in 19X5.

c. What are the tax consequences of the stock option to BB Inc. in 19X0? In 19X5?

8. Two years ago, Mrs. EL was granted a stock option from her corporate employer. At date of grant, the employer's stock was selling at $14 per share and the option strike price was $18 per share. This year Mrs. EL sold the option to an unrelated party for $26,000. How much gain does Mrs. EL recognize on this transaction?

9. In 19X2, Mrs. L exercised a stock option by paying $100 per share for 225 shares of ABC Inc. stock. The market price of the stock at date of exercise was $312 per share. In 19X9, Mrs. L sold the 225 shares for $480 per share. Assuming that Mrs. L is in the 36 percent tax bracket and using a 12 percent discount rate, compute the net present value of the cash flows from the exercise and sale if:

a. The stock option was nonqualified.

b. The stock option was an ISO.

10. In 1998, Mr. T (a 45-year-old single taxpayer) exercised an ISO and purchased $265,000 worth

of his corporate employer's stock for only $113,000. Mr. T's only other income was his $168,000 salary, and he does not itemize deductions. Based on these facts, compute Mr. T's 1998 tax liability.

11. During 1998, Mr. and Mrs. WD had the following income items:

Mr. WD's salary from IMR Inc.	$62,000
Mrs. WD earnings from self-employment	50,000

Mr. WD elected to contribute the maximum salary to IMR's Section 401(k) plan, and Mrs. WD contributed the maximum amount to her Keogh plan. Both spouses contributed $2,000 to their IRAs. Mrs. WD's self-employment tax for the year was $7,065. Based on these facts, compute Mr. and Mrs. WD's AGI.

12. Mr. and Mrs. DM file a joint tax return. During 1998, each spouse contributed $2,000 to a regular IRA. In each of the following cases, compute the couple's deduction for these contributions.

    a. Neither spouse is an active participant in a qualified retirement plan, and their AGI is $72,000.

    b. Mr. DM is an active participant in his employer's qualified retirement plan, but Mrs. DM is not. The couple's AGI is $70,000.

    c. Both spouses are active participants in their respective employer's qualified retirement plan, and their AGI is $39,000.

    d. Mr. DM is self-employed and does not have a Keogh plan. Mrs. DM is an active participant in her employer's qualified retirement plan. The couple's AGI is $57,900.

    e. Neither spouse is an active participant in his or her respective employer's qualified retirement plan; the couple's AGI is $48,000, and their contributions are to a Roth IRA.

13. Mrs. LU retired in 19X7 at age 63 and made her first withdrawal of $18,000 from her IRA. At the end of 19X7, the IRA balance was $89,200. In 18X8, Mrs. LU withdrew $22,000 from the IRA. At the end of 19X8, the account balance was $73,900. Based on these facts, determine how much of the 19X7 and 19X8 withdrawals were included in Mrs. LU's taxable income assuming that:

    a. Mrs. LU's contributions to her IRA were fully deductible.

    b. Mrs. LU made $21,000 of nondeductible contributions to the IRA.

    c. Mrs. LU made $49,000 of nondeductible contributions to the IRA.

    d. Mrs. LU's IRA is a Roth IRA that she opened more than five years prior to 19X7.

Issue Recognition Problems

Identify the tax issue or issues suggested by the following situations and state each issue in the form of a question.

1. Early this year, Mrs. C's employer reassigned her from its Chicago office to its Memphis office. In May, Mrs. C spent $1,100 on a house-hunting trip to Memphis. She located a new home and moved her family in September. Along with her direct moving expenses, Mrs. C's employer reimbursed her for the cost of the house-hunting trip.

2. Ms. X is an executive with GG Inc., an international business operation. She flies over 150,000 business miles each year and accumulates considerable "frequent-flier" points from the airlines by doing so. GG Inc. allows its employees to use their frequent-flier points for personal travel. In March, Ms. X used 100,000 points to obtain two first-class round-trip tickets to Paris, which she gave to her daughter as a wedding gift. The value of the tickets was $12,000.

3. Mr. K is a professor at a private university. The university waives the tuition for a faculty member's child who meets the entrance requirements. Mr. K's two children are currently enrolled in degree programs at the university. If

not for the waiver, Mr. K would pay $16,000 of annual tuition for each child.

4. Mr. DW has the full-time use of an automobile owned and maintained by his employer. During the current year, Mr. DW drove this company car 48,000 miles on business and 12,000 for personal reasons. He is not required to report this information to his employer. The employer included the $17,000 imputed value of the full-time use of the car as additional compensation on Mr. DW's Form W-2. Mr. DW's AGI was $196,000.

5. Ms. L is employed at the corporate headquarters of VD Inc. and often works late hours. The headquarters building is located in a high-crime urban area. As a result, corporate policy is that any employee leaving the premises after 7:00 P.M. must take a cab home rather than walk or use the subway. The corporation pays the cab fare. However, it does not pay employee commuting expenses under any other circumstances. During this past year, VD Inc. spent $1,080 on cab fare for Ms. L.

6. Mr. G is employed by a closely held corporation that gave him a year-end bonus of 50 shares of the corporation's stock worth $200 per share. However, Mr. G's ownership of the stock is conditional. If he resigns from his job at any time during the next four calendar years, he forfeits the stock back to the corporation. During this four-year period, he can't sell the stock or pledge it as collateral for a loan. After four years, this restriction lapses and his ownership of the 50 shares is unrestricted.

7. Mr. and Mrs. SK are both CPAs. Mr. SK is an employee of a national accounting firm, while Mrs. SK operates her own professional practice. Each year, the couple pays approximately $1,300 to subscribe to professional publications and research services that they both read and use in their work.

8. In the current year, TT Corporation agreed to defer $100,000 of compensation owed to Ms. B, the corporation's director of research. The corporation funded its obligation by transferring $100,000 cash to a trust administered by a local bank. TT cannot reclaim these funds. However, the trust fund is subject to the claims of the corporation's general creditors. Ms. B has no right to the funds until and unless she works for

TT until age 59, the corporation's mandatory retirement age.

9. Mr. T and Mr. V founded the TV Corporation six years ago and have devoted every waking hour to the corporate business. During the first four years, neither shareholder received any salary from the struggling firm. During the last two years, each shareholder received an annual salary of $200,000, which is 180 percent of the average salary paid by comparable businesses to their unrelated corporate officers.

10. Ms. J recently moved from Boston to Pittsburgh to take a job with OP Inc. Ms. J sold her home in Boston, and OP Inc. paid the $14,500 realtor's commission on the sale.

11. Mr. S was recently fired from his job because of unprofessional conduct. He believed that his reputation in the local business community was damaged and that he should make a new start in a different state. Consequently, he relocated his family to Phoenix and started to look for suitable employment, which he had not found by the end of the year. His personal moving expenses totaled $3,820.

12. Corporation GHK recently granted a stock option to employee O giving him the right to purchase 20,000 shares of GHK stock for $11 per share. On the date of grant, GHK stock was selling for $12 on a publicly traded market.

13. Six years ago, Ms. PL paid $20 per share for 1,000 shares of her corporate employer's stock. This stock is currently worth $58 per share. This year, Ms. PL wants to exercise a stock option to buy 1,000 more shares at a strike price of $29 per share. Because she does not have $29,000 cash readily available, she has requested that the corporation allow her to exchange 500 of her original shares (valued at $29,000) for the 1,000 new shares.

14. Corporation J sponsors a qualified profit sharing plan for its employees. Three years ago, Ms. PQ, a participant in the plan for over 12 years, quit her job and left town without leaving any forwarding address. The corporation has tried to locate Ms. PQ to send the Form W-2 for her last year of employment and a final paycheck she failed to collect. So far, the corporation's efforts have been unsuccessful.

15. Mr. MC, age 50, is a self-employed writer who published 11 novels in the last 20 years. Each

year, he makes the maximum allowable contribution to his Keogh plan. This year, he borrowed $200,000 from the plan to finance the construction of a new home. Under the borrowing agreement, he pays a market interest rate and must repay the debt in five years.

16. Mr. and Mrs. VC are the sole shareholders of VC Enterprises, Inc. They are also employed by the corporation and participate in VC's qualified pension plan. This year the corporation is experiencing cash flow difficulties. To ease the strain on the business, Mr. and Mrs. VC voluntarily forfeited their vested benefits under the plan and instructed the plan administrator to transfer the $219,000 value of such benefits back to the corporation.

17. Mr. X, age 53, owns an IRA with a current balance of $215,000. Mr. X recently divorced his wife and transferred this IRA to her as part of the property settlement.

Tax Planning Cases

1. At the beginning of the year, Mr. JO (age 26 and in a 28 percent marginal tax bracket) accepted a job with BL Inc. JO intends to work for BL for only eight years, after which he plans to start his own business. He has two options for accumulating the money he will need for this venture.

   • *Option 1:* JO is eligible to participate in BL's qualified Section 401(k) plan. He can afford to save $5,000 of his salary each year by diverting it to this plan. The plan earns 10 percent a year. Consequently, Mr. JO's plan balance in eight years will be $57,179 ($5,000 for eight years compounded at 10 percent).

   • *Option 2:* JO can take his entire salary in cash, pay income tax, and save $3,600 ($5,000 less $1,400 tax) in an investment fund that earns 10 percent a year. Because the annual earnings are taxable to Mr. JO, his savings in the fund will grow at only 7.2 percent a year. Consequently, his fund balance in eight years will be $37,202 ($3,600 for eight years compounded at 7.2 percent).

   Based on these facts and assuming a constant 28 percent tax rate, which option results in the greatest after-tax cash for JO to begin his business?

2. Mr. and Mrs. B, ages 64 and 65, are both retired and live on Social Security plus the interest and dividends from several investments. Their taxable income averages $20,000 a year. Mrs. B owns an IRA that she funded entirely with deductible contributions. The couple plans to withdraw $45,000 from the IRA to make some much needed improvements to their home. How should they time the withdrawal (or series of withdrawals) to maximize the cash available from the IRA?

3. Based on his corporate employer's annual bonus plan, Mr. RS is entitled to a $5,000 bonus this year. The employer gives Mr. RS two options. He can either take his $5,000 bonus in cash or the employer will credit him with $4,000 of deferred compensation. Under the deferral option, the employer will compound its $4,000 obligation to Mr. RS by 12 percent a year. Consequently, when Mr. RS retires in 10 years at age 63, the corporation will pay him $12,423 ($4,000 compounded at 12 percent for 10 years). Mr. RS can only earn 10 percent a year on his investments. Based on these facts, should Mr. RS take the current or the deferred compensation, assuming that:

   a. His current year marginal tax rate is 31 percent and his marginal tax rate at retirement will be 15 percent.

   b. His current year marginal tax rate is 31 percent and his marginal tax rate at retirement will be 31 percent.

15 Investment and Personal Financial Planning

Learning Objectives

After studying this chapter, you should be able to:

1. Distinguish between an individual taxpayer's business activities and investment activities.
2. Determine the year in which a cash basis individual must recognize interest income.
3. Explain the tax-deferral benefit of investments in life insurance policies and annuity contracts.
4. Compute capital gain or loss recognized on the disposition of assets.
5. Compute the tax on short-term and long-term capital gain.
6. Determine the deduction for a net capital loss.
7. Describe the tax benefit associated with qualified small business stock and Section 1244 stock.
8. Determine the deduction for investment interest expense.
9. Apply the passive activity loss limitation and the exception for rental real estate loss.
10. Describe the structure of the federal gift and estate tax.
11. Explain the role of the annual gift tax exclusion and the lifetime transfer tax exclusion.
12. Calculate the income tax savings from a gift of property.
13. Identify the major components of a deceased individual's taxable estate.
14. Determine the basis of property received from a decedent.

Chapter 15 focuses on the tax consequences of investment activities in which individuals commonly engage. Investment activities involve the acquisition, holding, and disposition of income-producing property. Individuals enter into investment activities expecting them to be profitable. In financial terms, they expect the investment to yield a positive return on the capital committed to the investment. This return can take the form of current income (and cash flow) generated by the property or appreciation in the property's value. This chapter explores the tax consequences of both types of returns. Of course, not every investment activity is profitable, and Chapter 15 also deals with the tax consequences of investment losses.

Many individuals who accumulate significant property through their business and investment activities want their children and grandchildren to benefit from their good fortune. These individuals must develop personal financial planning strategies to achieve this goal in the most cost-effective manner. In the final section of this chapter, we will discover that the federal gift and estate taxes are serious impediments in this planning process. However, we will also consider some basic techniques by which people can minimize these taxes and maximize the wealth available to their younger-generation family members.

Distinguishing between Business and Investment Activities

Objective 1
Distinguish between an individual taxpayer's business activities and investment activities.

For individuals, the tax consequences of investment activities can be very different from the tax consequences of business activities. But people engage in the two types of activities for exactly the same purpose: to make a profit. The distinction between business and investment activities lies in the nature of the individual's personal involvement in the activity. An individual engaging in a business activity commits time and talent to the activity on a regular basis, and the profit from the business is at least partially attributable to this personal involvement.[1] In contrast, an individual engaging in an investment activity takes a passive role as the owner of income-producing property. The profit from the activity is primarily attributable to the invested capital rather than to the owner's personal involvement. For tax purposes, this distinction holds true even when individuals devote substantial time to managing income-producing property. "A taxpayer who merely manages his investments seeking long-term gain is not carrying on a trade or business. This is so irrespective of the extent or continuity of the transactions or the work required in managing the portfolio."[2]

Investments in Financial Assets

Financial assets are legal claims on the real assets owned by a business enterprise or other organization. Financial assets include equity interests such as common and preferred corporate stock and creditor interests such as savings accounts, certificates of deposit, notes, bonds, and other debt instruments. These types of financial assets are commonly referred to as **securities.** Financial assets are intangible property rights. They have no intrinsic value; their worth depends on the underlying value of the real assets subject to their claim. Financial assets may be publicly traded on an established market or may be privately placed.

A financial asset that has gained tremendous favor over the last few decades are shares in mutual funds. Currently, U.S. taxpayers have invested over $3 trillion in

---

[1] In capital-intensive businesses, profit is attributable to the assets used in the business as well as to the personal involvement of the business owners.

[2] *Moller v. United States,* 721 F.2d 810, 814 (CA-FC, 1983).

mutual funds, making them the most popular investment vehicle on the market.[3] A **mutual fund** is a diversified portfolio of securities owned and managed by a regulated investment company. These companies sell shares in their funds to the public—specifically to purchasers wanting to diversify their financial holdings and take advantage of the professional expertise of the fund managers. A mutual fund portfolio can consist of equity stocks, debt instruments, or a combination of both, depending on the investment objectives of the particular fund.

Dividend and Interest Income

Individuals who invest in securities normally expect a return on their investment in the form of dividends or interest. As cash basis taxpayers, individuals recognize these returns as ordinary income in the year they actually or constructively receive payment. Companies or other organizations that pay dividends or interest issue annual Forms 1099-DIV (Dividends and Distributions) and Forms 1099-INT (Interest Income) to their investors to inform them of the total payments for the year. The IRS receives copies of these forms and cross-checks to make sure that the payment reported on each form matches the income reported on Schedule B of the investor's Form 1040.

Investors in stocks and mutual funds often have a dividend reinvestment option under which dividend income is used to purchase additional shares for the investor's account. Even though shareholders who elect this option receive no cash payments during the year, they are in constructive receipt of the dividends reinvested on their behalf. Occasionally, shareholders may receive a cash payment from a corporation that is not a dividend at all but a tax-free return of capital. These nontaxable distributions are labeled as such on Form 1099-DIV. Shareholders in mutual funds may receive a capital gains distribution, which is attributable to the net long-term capital gain recognized by the fund on sales of securities from its portfolio. Shareholders do not report these distributions as ordinary income dividends but as long-term capital gain on their Schedule D.

> ***Mr. and Mrs. David: Schedule B.***   Mr. and Mrs. David, who file a joint return, own a $75,000 certificate of deposit with Second Union Bank and a $100,000 bond issued by Tryton Inc. During 1997, the couple earned $4,712 interest on the CD and $6,200 interest on the bond. Shortly after year end, Mr. and Mrs. David received a Form 1099-INT from each payor on which their annual interest income was reported. The couple entered this information on Part I of their 1997 Schedule B (shown as Exhibit 15–1.) The couple's total interest of $10,912 (line 4) was carried as an income item to page 1 of their 1997 Form 1040.
>
> At the beginning of 1997, Mr. and Mrs. David owned 5,122 shares of Prime Growth mutual fund. The couple elected to have their annual dividends and capital gain distributions reinvested in additional Prime Growth shares. Consequently, they received no cash from the mutual fund during 1997. Mr. and Mrs. David received a Form 1099-DIV from Prime Growth containing the following information.

---

[3]The number of mutual funds available to investors currently exceeds the number of companies listed on the New York Stock Exchange.

Gross distribution	$12,474
Ordinary dividend	7,091
Capital gains distribution	5,383
Shares owned on January 1, 1997	5,122
Additional shares credited to investor's account (198 shares purchased at $63 per share = $12,474)	198
Shares owned on December 31, 1997	5,320

Mr. and Mrs. David also own 16,780 shares of Mortimer Industries, Inc. common stock. At the beginning of 1997, their cost basis in these shares was $59,000. During 1997, the couple received cash distributions totaling $19,000 from Mortimer. Their 1997 Form 1099-DIV from Mortimer contained the following information.

Gross distribution	$19,000
Ordinary dividend	17,980
Nontaxable distribution	1,020

Mr. and Mrs. David entered their gross distributions from Prime Growth and Mortimer on Part II, Schedule B. The capital gains distribution was reported on line 7 and entered on Schedule D for inclusion with the couple's other capital gains and losses for the year. The nontaxable distribution was reported on line 8 and reduced the tax basis in the Mortimer Industries stock to $57,980. The couple's ordinary dividends of $25,071 (line 10) was carried as an income item to page 1, Form 1040.

Tax-Exempt Interest

The public security markets offer thousands of financial assets in which people can invest. Individuals can select securities that meet their particular investment needs. In making their selection, investors should consider their overall tax situation for the year, as well as any preferential tax characteristics of the assets under consideration. One such characteristic is the tax-exempt status of the interest on certain debt instruments.

State and Local Bonds.   For federal tax purposes, interest income earned on investments in debt instruments issued by state and local governments, including the District of Columbia, is excluded from the recipient's income.[4] The interest rate on these tax-exempt bonds is typically lower than the rate on taxable bonds with a comparable degree of risk; investors who purchase tax-exempt bonds pay an implicit tax equal to this rate differen-

---

[4] §103. This exclusion extends to any portion of a mutual fund dividend attributable to the fund's investment in tax-exempt bonds.

EXHIBIT 15–1

Schedules A&B (Form 1040) 1997   OMB No. 1545-0074   Page **2**

Name(s) shown on Form 1040. Do not enter name and social security number if shown on other side. | Your social security number

Ronald and Janice David   498 31 1240

Schedule B—Interest and Dividend Income   Attachment Sequence No. **08**

			Amount
Part I **Interest** **Income** (See pages 12 and B-1.)	**Note:** *If you had over $400 in taxable interest income, you must also complete Part III.*		
	1 List name of payer. If any interest is from a seller-financed mortgage and the buyer used the property as a personal residence, see page B-1 and list this interest first. Also, show that buyer's social security number and address ▶		
	Certificate of Deposit - Second Union		4,712
	6.2% Tryton Inc. bonds		6,200
Note: If you received a Form 1099-INT, Form 1099-OID, or substitute statement from a brokerage firm, list the firm's name as the payer and enter the total interest shown on that form.		**1**	
	2 Add the amounts on line 1	**2**	10,912
	3 Excludable interest on series EE U.S. savings bonds issued after 1989 from Form 8815, line 14. You MUST attach Form 8815 to Form 1040	**3**	
	4 Subtract line 3 from line 2. Enter the result here and on Form 1040, line 8a ▶	**4**	10,912

			Amount
Part II **Dividend** **Income** (See pages 12 and B-1.)	**Note:** *If you had over $400 in gross dividends and/or other distributions on stock, you must also complete Part III.*		
	5 List name of payer. Include gross dividends and/or other distributions on stock here. Any capital gain distributions and nontaxable distributions will be deducted on lines 7 and 8 ▶		
	Prime Growth Mutual Fund		12,474
	Mortimer Industries Inc.		19,000
Note: if you received a Form 1099-DIV or substitute statement from a brokerage firm, list the firm's name as the payer and enter the total dividends shown on that form.		**5**	
	6 Add the amounts on line 5	**6**	31,474
	7 Capital gain distributions. Enter here and on Schedule D **7** 5,383		
	8 Nontaxable distributions. (See the inst. for Form 1040, line 9.) **8** 1,020		
	9 Add lines 7 and 8	**9**	6,403
	10 Subtract line 9 from line 6. Enter the result here and on Form 1040, line 9 ▶	**10**	25,071

		Yes	No
Part III **Foreign** **Accounts** **and** **Trusts** (See page B-2.)	You must complete this part if you **(a)** had over $400 of interest or dividends; **(b)** had a foreign account; or **(c)** received a distribution from, or were a grantor of, or a transferor to, a foreign trust.		
	11a At any time during 1997, did you have an interest in or a signature or other authority over a financial account in a foreign country, such as a bank account, securities account, or other financial account? See page B-2 for exceptions and filing requirements for Form TD F 90-22.1		
	b If "Yes," enter the name of the foreign country ▶		
	12 During 1997, did you receive a distribution from, or were you the grantor of, or transferor to, a foreign trust? If "Yes," you may have to file Form 3520 or 926. See page B-2		

For Paperwork Reduction Act Notice, see Form 1040 instructions.   ⊕   Schedule B (Form 1040) 1997

tial.[5] Moreover, state and local bond interest may be taxed by the state or locality in which the investor resides. Finally, the interest on tax-exempt **private activity bonds** issued by any state or local government after August 7, 1986, is a preference item for alternative minimum tax (AMT) purposes.[6] Because of these variables, even individuals in high marginal tax brackets can't assume that they will benefit by buying tax-exempt bonds until they evaluate the investment on an after-tax basis.

---

[5]See the discussion of implicit tax in Chapter 4.

[6]§57(a)(5). The proceeds from private activity bonds are used for nongovernmental purposes, such as industrial development.

U.S. Debt Obligations.   The U.S. government issues a variety of debt instruments for investors. Treasury bills are issued on a discount basis and are payable without interest at a fixed maturity date not exceeding one year from date of issue. Treasury notes have maturity periods ranging from 2 to 10 years, while Treasury bonds have maturity periods in excess of 10 years. Both are issued at face value and bear a stated rate of interest, generally payable at six-month intervals. **Series EE savings bonds** are long-term debt instruments issued at a discount. The interest on all these debt instruments is subject to federal income tax. However, the interest is completely exempt from income tax levied by any state or local government. Because state and local tax rates are generally much lower than federal rates, exemption from such taxes may result in only a modest benefit. Nonetheless, investors should be aware of this preferential tax characteristic of U.S. debt obligations.

Deferred Interest Income

Objective 2
Determine the year in which a cash basis individual must recognize interest income.

The tax law offers investors a few narrow opportunities to defer the recognition of interest income. For instance, cash basis taxpayers who purchase short-term debt obligations at a discount do not recognize income until the obligation matures.[7]

> *Interest Deferral.*   In February 19X8, Mrs. W bought a $50,000 U.S. Treasury bill for $47,000; the bill matured 52 weeks after date of issue.[8] Mrs. W reported no 19X8 income from this investment, even though most of the interest on the bill accrued during 19X8. When she redeemed the bill in February 19X9 for $50,000, she recognized the entire $3,000 of interest income.

Individuals can achieve the same type of deferral if they purchase Series EE savings bonds. Even though these discount bonds may have maturity periods of 10 years or longer, the tax law allows individuals to postpone recognition of any interest income until they cash in the bonds. In the unusual case in which an investor prefers to take the discount into annual income on an accrual basis, he may elect to do so by reporting the accrued interest on Schedule B.

Market Discount.   Cash basis investors who purchase bonds *in a market transaction* at a price lower than the bond's stated redemption value at maturity are not required to accrue the **market discount** as interest income over the life of the bond.[9] Instead, they recognize the discount as interest in the future year in which they sell the bond or the bond is redeemed.[10]

> *Deferral of Market Discount.*   Mr. B bought a publicly traded corporate bond through his broker for $21,300. Although the bond is redeemable at maturity for $25,000, it traded at a discounted price because the stated interest rate (6 percent)

---

[7]See §454 and §1271(a)(3) and (4). Short-term debt obligations have fixed maturity periods of one year or less.

[8]Treasury bills generally have 13-week, 26-week, and 52-week maturity periods.

[9]§1278(a). However, investors may elect to do so under §1278(b).

[10]This recognition rule extends to any market discount on state and local bonds. While the periodic interest payments on these bonds are tax exempt, the accrued discount is fully taxable as ordinary income.

is below the current market rate (8 percent). Each year that he holds the bond, Mr. B will include the 6 percent interest payments in current income but will not include any portion of the market discount. If he holds the bond until maturity, he will recognize the entire $3,700 excess of the $25,000 redemption proceeds over his $21,300 cost basis as ordinary income in the year of redemption.[11]

Original Issue Discount.   Investors who purchase *newly issued* long-term corporate debt instruments at a discount can't defer recognition of the interest income represented by the original issue discount. **Original issue discount (OID)** equals the excess of the bond's stated redemption value at maturity (face value) over the issue price. Even cash basis investors must recognize accrued income by amortizing this discount over the life of the bond.[12]

Amortization of OID.   Corporation J made a new public offering of 15-year bonds with a stated interest rate of only 3 percent of face value. Mr. B, our investor in the previous example, bought $50,000 of these bonds for their discounted issue price of $27,000. Mr. B's return on his investment consists of the $1,500 yearly interest payments *plus* the $23,000 difference between his cost and the cash he will collect when the bonds mature. Every year Corporation J sends Mr. B the following:

- Form 1099-INT reporting the $1,500 interest payment to Mr. B.
- Form 1099-OID reporting the amortized discount Mr. B must recognize as additional interest income.[13]

Over the 15-year term of the bonds, Mr. B will recognize $23,000 of OID income with no corresponding cash flow. However, he will not recognize any additional income when he redeems the bonds at maturity for $50,000.

Deferral Opportunities with Life Insurance Policies and Annuity Contracts

Objective 3
Explain the tax deferral benefit of investments in life insurance policies and annuity contracts.

Life Insurance Policies.   A life insurance policy is a legal contract between a purchaser (the owner of the policy) and a commercial insurance company. The owner pays a premium or series of premiums for the company's commitment to pay a specific sum of money (death benefit) on the death of the person whose life is insured. The owner has the right to name the beneficiary (the person or organization that will receive the death benefit). An individual purchases insurance on his or her own life primarily to provide financial protection for dependent family members. However, many life insurance contracts offer both protection against premature death and an investment element. The invest-

---

[11]While the tax law permits Mr. B to defer the recognition of the discount, this discount is not converted to capital gain. See §1276.

[12]§1272(a). This income recognition rule does not apply to tax-exempt state and local obligations.

[13]The annual OID income on debt instruments issued after July 1, 1992, is based on the instrument's constant yield to maturity. §1272(a)(3). This calculation results in increasing annual OID income over the life of the instrument. Corporations may take an annual interest deduction for amortized OID. §163(e)(1).

ment element is called the policy's **cash surrender value,** which increases every year that the policy remains in effect. The owner does not recognize this annual increase in value, called the **inside buildup,** as taxable income. If the owner eventually decides that his family no longer needs insurance protection, he may liquidate the policy for its cash surrender value. In this case, the owner recognizes the excess of the surrender proceeds over his investment in the policy (the aggregate premiums paid) as ordinary income.[14]

> ***Liquidation of Life Insurance Policy.*** Twenty years ago, Mr. X purchased an insurance policy on his own life. The policy provided a $350,000 death benefit payable to Mr. X's wife and children. To date, Mr. X has paid $33,000 of premiums on this policy. Because his wife predeceased him and his children are financially independent, Mr. X liquidated the policy for its $42,800 cash surrender value. The insurance company sent Mr. X a Form 1099-R reporting $9,800 of ordinary income.[15]

The deferral of tax on the inside buildup certainly makes life insurance contracts a tax-preferred investment. The tax consequences are even more favorable if the policy is held until it matures on the death of the insured. In this case, the beneficiary excludes the death benefit from income and the accumulated return on the owner's investment in the life insurance contract escapes income taxation entirely.[16]

> ***Life Insurance Proceeds.*** Twenty years ago, Mrs. M purchased an insurance policy on her own life. The policy provided a $350,000 death benefit payable to Mrs. M's children. Mrs. M paid $33,000 of premiums on this policy, and its cash surrender value at the beginning of the year was $42,800. Mrs. M died on May 4 with the policy still in effect. On September 3, her children received $350,000 from the insurance company and excluded the entire payment from their taxable income.

This highly advantageous tax treatment also applies to **accelerated death benefits**: payments made under the terms of the contract to insured individuals who are terminally or chronically ill.[17] Such individuals may be forced to draw against or even liquidate their life insurance policies to pay the substantial medical expenses resulting from an extended illness. The tax law alleviates this financial hardship by classifying these premature payments as nontaxable death benefits.

Annuity Contracts. Individuals purchase annuity contracts from commercial insurance companies to provide themselves with a fixed stream of income for a future period of time. The owner pays a premium or series of premiums that the insurance company invests on the owner's behalf. The owner is not taxed on the yearly inside buildup in the

---

[14] §72(e)(2).

[15] Form 1099-R reports distributions from insurance contracts, annuities, and pension, profit-sharing, IRA and other retirement plans.

[16] §101.

[17] §101(g). Accelerated death benefits include the proceeds of the sale or assignment of a contract to a *viatical settlement provider,* which is a company licensed to engage in the business of purchasing life insurance contracts from the terminally or chronically ill.

value of her investment; instead, tax is deferred until the owner begins receiving periodic payments under the contract. The portion of each annuity payment representing a distribution of accumulated earnings is taxed as ordinary income, while the portion representing a return of the owner's investment is nontaxable.

Annuity Payments.   Mrs. M purchased an annuity for a single premium of $75,000 when she was 51 years old. This year Mrs. M reached age 65 and began receiving annuity payments. Under the terms of her contract, she will receive $1,100 per month for the rest of her life; during the current year, she received eight payments. The portion of these payments representing a return of Mrs. M's investment is based on the ratio of that investment to her expected return under the contract.[18] Based on life expectancy tables provided in Treasury regulations, Mrs. M can expect to receive 240 payments ($264,000). Consequently, her exclusion ratio is 28.41 percent:

$$\frac{\$75,000 \text{ investment (single premium)}}{\$264,000 \text{ expected return}} = .2841$$

Mrs. M's nontaxable return of investment is $2,500.

Total annuity payments received	$8,800
Exclusion ratio	.2841
	$2,500

Mrs. M must recognize the remaining $6,300 of the annuity payments as ordinary income.

Each year Mrs. M will apply the exclusion ratio to determine the nontaxable portion of her annuity payments until she recovers her entire $75,000 investment. Any additional payments will be fully taxable.[19] If Mrs. M dies before recovering her investment, the unrecovered portion is allowed as an itemized deduction on her final Form 1040.[20]

Nontax Considerations.   People buy life insurance policies to protect against dying too soon and annuity contracts to protect against living too long. In addition to their protection element, both assets represent financial investments with tax-deferred returns. However, life insurance policies and annuity contracts frequently offer lower before-tax rates of return and involve higher transaction costs than investment opportunities that are not tax favored. For instance, life insurance policies have the highest commission charges of any financial product—typically more than 50 percent of the first-year premium paid by the investor. Annuity contracts routinely charge an annual fee and impose early-surrender penalties on individuals who liquidate their investment in the contract before the annuity starting date. These nontax costs can

---

[18] §72(b)(1).

[19] §72(b)(2).

[20] §72(b)(3) and §67(b)(11).

overwhelm the benefit of tax deferral, particularly for individuals in the lower tax brackets or who aren't prepared to commit to these investments for the long haul.

Gains and Losses from Security Transactions

A defining principle of federal tax law is that unrealized gains and losses are not subject to current taxation. Increases or decreases in the value of property over time are not recognized until an external transaction triggers the realization of gain or loss. Accordingly, individuals who purchase financial assets offering a return in the form of long-term appreciation defer paying tax on such return until they dispose of the asset in a taxable transaction. In this section of the chapter, we will examine the tax rules that apply to dispositions of securities. By paying close attention to these rules, individuals can control their tax costs and greatly enhance the after-tax return on such investments.

Computing Gains and Losses

Objective 4
Compute capital gain or loss recognized on the disposition of assets.

Realized gain from the sale of securities equals the excess of the amount realized over the seller's basis in the security. Realized loss equals the excess of basis over amount realized. Amount realized is the sum of any money plus the fair market value of any property received by the seller. Investors who sell securities through a broker receive a Form 1099-B (Proceeds from Broker and Barter Exchange Transactions) reporting the gross sales price. If the investor incurred any selling expenses, such as brokerage fees and commissions, these expenses are netted against the gross sales price in the computation of amount realized on sale. A seller's basis in a security depends on the transaction in which the security was acquired. Securities acquired by purchase have a cost basis including both the price of the securities plus any front-end fees or load charges.

Tracking Security Basis.   Individuals should keep careful record of the initial cost of the securities in their investment portfolios and the effect of any subsequent transactions on such basis. For instance, if an investor elects to have dividends on corporate stock or mutual funds reinvested in additional shares, the dividend amount becomes the cost basis in the new shares. If an investor receives a nontaxable distribution with respect to shares of stock or mutual funds, the basis in the shares must be reduced by this return of capital. Investors who own long-term debt instruments with original issue discount should increase their basis in the securities by the OID income accrued each year. Failure to keep track of these common basis adjustments results in overstatement or understatement of gain or loss realized on the eventual disposition of the securities.

> ***Basis Adjustments for Reinvested Dividends.***   Nine years ago, Ms. F paid $25,000 for 3,400 shares of Fastrack mutual fund. She elected to have her annual dividends reinvested in additional shares. As of June 4 of the current year, Mrs. F had recognized $19,100 of dividend income without any corresponding cash flow and acquired 2,816 additional shares with her reinvested dividends. On June 4, she sold all 6,216 shares for $58,000. Her realized gain is computed as follows:
>
> | | | |
> |---|---|---|
> | Amount realized on sale | | $58,000 |
> | Adjusted basis: cost of 3,400 shares | $25,000 | |

cost of 2,816 shares (reinvested dividends)	19,100	
		(44,100)
Gain realized on sale		$13,900

Identifying Basis on Sale.   When an investor sells a specific security with an identifiable basis, gain or loss is determined with reference to such basis. However, investment portfolios often contain blocks of identical securities acquired at different times and for different prices. If the investor sells some of the securities in the block but can't identify which securities were sold, the basis is determined by a first-in, first-out (FIFO) method.[21] In other words, the investor is presumed to have sold the securities with the earliest acquisition date. Individuals who sell mutual fund shares can also use an average basis method for calculating gain or loss. Under the simplest version of this method, the basis of each mutual fund share equals the aggregate basis of all shares divided by the total number of shares.

Worthless Securities and Nonbusiness Bad Debts.   Securities are capital assets in the hands of individual investors. Therefore, gains and losses realized on security sales are capital gains and losses subject to the special tax rules presented in the next section of the chapter. According to the general statutory definition, capital gains and losses result from the sale or exchange of capital assets.[22] The Internal Revenue Code provides that two other investment events result in capital loss. If an individual owns a security that becomes worthless during the year, the event is treated as if the individual sold the security on the last day of the year for an amount realized of zero.[23] In other words, the individual recognizes his unrecovered basis in the security as a capital loss. A similar event occurs when an individual who has lent money to another party determines that the debt is uncollectible. In such case, the individual recognizes the unpaid balance of the **nonbusiness bad debt** as a capital loss.[24]

> *Nonbusiness Bad Debt.*   Two years ago, Mr. J lent $25,000 to the PT Partnership in exchange for the partnership's interest-bearing note. PT has repaid $9,000 of the debt. However, Mr. J recently learned that PT is hopelessly insolvent and cannot pay any of its creditors. Mr. J can recognize his $16,000 bad debt as a capital loss.

Nontaxable Exchanges of Securities.   As a general rule, the exchange of a security in one business for a security in another business is a taxable event. For instance, if Mr. P owns stock in Corporation A and exchanges the stock for a long-term bond issued by Corporation Z, he recognizes the difference between his amount realized (the value of the bond) and the basis of the stock as capital gain or loss. The tax law does contain several narrow nontaxable exchange rules applying to security transactions. No gain or loss is recognized on the

---

[21]Reg. §1.1012-1(c).

[22]§1222.

[23]§165(g).

[24]§166(d). If an individual lends money or extends credit *as part of his business,* any resulting bad debt is a deductible business expense.

exchange of one class of common stock for a different class of common stock *in the same corporation.* Similarly, preferred stock can be exchanged for preferred stock *in the same corporation* at no current tax cost.[25] If a taxpayer exchanges stock or securities in one corporation for stock or securities in a different corporation, no gain or loss is recognized if the exchange is pursuant to a **reorganization** involving the two corporations.[26] In each of these nontaxable transactions, the taxpayer's basis in his newly acquired security equals the basis of the security surrendered in the exchange. Because of this substituted basis rule, gain or loss realized on the exchange is merely deferred, not eliminated.[27]

Exchange of Securities.   The shareholders of LG Inc. recently agreed to merge their corporation into SM Inc. under Missouri law. Pursuant to the merger, Ms. G exchanged her 813 shares of LG common stock for 12,300 shares of SM common stock. Her realized gain on the exchange is computed as follows:

Amount realized (fair market value of SM stock received)	$945,200
Basis in LG stock surrendered	(550,300)
Gain realized on exchange	$394,900

   If the merger of LG Inc. and SM Inc. qualifies as a reorganization for federal tax purposes, Ms. G does not recognize any of her realized gain. In this case, the basis in her 12,300 shares of SM stock is $550,300 (the basis of the LG stock surrendered in the nontaxable exchange). If the merger does not qualify as a reorganization, Ms. G must recognize a $394,900 taxable gain on the exchange. In this case, the basis in her 12,300 shares of SM stock is their $945,200 cost (the value of the LG stock surrendered).

Tax Consequences of Capital Gains and Losses

Objective 5
Compute the tax on short-term and long-term capital gain.

Individuals who recognize capital gains and losses during the taxable year can deduct the losses to the extent of the gains. In other words, individuals can combine their capital gains and losses to result in either a net gain or a net loss for the year. A net gain is included in adjusted gross income and may be taxed at a preferential rate (or rates). A net loss results in a limited deduction in the AGI computation. Before we can focus on these outcomes, we must examine the complicated rules governing the netting of capital gains and losses.

Netting Capital Gains and Losses

Capital gains and losses are reported on Schedule D, Form 1040. Each gain and loss is initially classified as short-term or long-term.[28]

---

[25]§1036.

[26]Corporate reorganizations are a set of very precisely defined transactions in which one corporation acquires another, one corporation divides into two corporations, or one corporation changes its capital structure. §368.

[27]See the discussion of generic nontaxable exchanges in Chapter 8.

[28]See §1222.

- **Short-term capital gains or losses** result from the sale or exchange of capital assets owned for one year or less. The capital loss from a nonbusiness bad debt is classified as a short-term loss, regardless of the time period of the debt.

- **Long-term capital gains or losses** result from the sale or exchange of capital assets owned for more than one year. The Tax Reform Act of 1997 created a new subcategory of long-term gains and losses, described as **28 percent rate gains or losses.** This category includes recognized gains and losses from the sale or exchange of **collectibles** (tangible assets such as works of art, antiques, gems, stamps, and coins) and any other capital asset owned for more than one year but not more than 18 months.[29]

The gains and losses in each class are combined to result in a net gain or loss for that class.

Mr. and Mrs. Dixon: Schedule D.   During 1997, Mr. and Mrs. Dixon made the following three sales:

	Date Acquired	Date Sold	Tax Basis	Selling Price
110 shares of BN Inc. stock	11/8/94	10/2/97	$ 4,200	$13,900
42 shares of EF Inc. stock	6/29/96	10/14/97	19,000	17,100
118 shares of VV Mutual Fund	2/14/97	12/6/97	15,000	16,400

Shortly after year-end, the Dixons received a 1997 Form 1099-DIV from VV Mutual Fund. The form reported a $7,800 long-term capital gain distribution, $5,300 of which was a 28 percent rate gain. Mr. and Mrs. Dixon recorded their capital transactions on Schedule D (shown as Exhibit 15–2). This schedule provides the following information:

Net short-term capital gain (line 7)	$ 1,400
Net long-term capital gain (line 16)	15,600

The $15,600 net long-term gain includes a $3,400 net 28 percent rate gain (line 15).

The next step in the netting process is to combine the short-term and long-term positions to result in the individual's total capital gain or capital loss for the year. In the previous example, Mr. and Mrs. Dixon had a total capital gain of $17,000 ($1,400 net short-term

---

[29]§1(h)(5) and (6). When an individual sells or exchanges a collectible held for personal use or enjoyment, a realized gain is recognized (taxable) but a realized loss is not recognized (nondeductible). For further discussion, see Chapter 16.

EXHIBIT 15–2

SCHEDULE D
(Form 1040)

Department of the Treasury
Internal Revenue Service   (99)

Capital Gains and Losses

► Attach to Form 1040.   ► See Instructions for Schedule D (Form 1040).

► Use Schedule D-1 for more space to list transactions for lines 1 and 8.

OMB No. 1545-0074

1997

Attachment
Sequence No. **12**

Name(s) shown on Form 1040   *Mark and Sue Dixon*

Your social security number   512 22 4061

Part I   Short-Term Capital Gains and Losses—Assets Held One Year or Less

(a) Description of property (Example: 100 sh. XYZ Co.)	(b) Date acquired (Mo., day, yr.)	(c) Date sold (Mo., day, yr.)	(d) Sales price (see page D-3)	(e) Cost or other basis (see page D-4)	(f) GAIN or (LOSS) FOR ENTIRE YEAR. Subtract (e) from (d)	
1 *118 shares VV Fund*	*2·14·97*	*12·6·97*	*16,400*	*15,000*	*1,400*	

2 Enter your short-term totals, if any, from Schedule D-1, line 2	**2**	
3 **Total short-term sales price amounts.** Add column (d) of lines 1 and 2 . . .	**3** *16,400*	
4 Short-term gain from Forms 2119 and 6252, and short-term gain or (loss) from Forms 4684, 6781, and 8824	**4**	
5 Net short-term gain or (loss) from partnerships, S corporations, estates, and trusts from Schedule(s) K-1	**5**	
6 Short-term capital loss carryover. Enter the amount, if any, from line 9 of your 1996 Capital Loss Carryover Worksheet	**6** ( )	
7 **Net short-term capital gain or (loss).** Combine lines 1 through 6 in column (f) . . . . ►	**7** *1,400*	

Part II   Long-Term Capital Gains and Losses—Assets Held More Than One Year

(a) Description of property (Example: 100 sh. XYZ Co.)	(b) Date acquired (Mo., day, yr.)	(c) Date sold (Mo., day, yr.)	(d) Sales price (see page D-3)	(e) Cost or other basis (see page D-4)	(f) GAIN or (LOSS) FOR ENTIRE YEAR. Subtract (e) from (d)	(g) 28% RATE GAIN or (LOSS) * (see instr. below)
8 *110 shares BN Inc.*	*11·8·94*	*10·2·97*	*13,900*	*4,200*	*9,700*	
42 shares EF Inc.	*6·29·96*	*10·14·97*	*17,100*	*19,000*	*(1,900)*	*(1,900)*

9 Enter your long-term totals, if any, from Schedule D-1, line 9	**9**		
10 **Total long-term sales price amounts.** Add column (d) of lines 8 and 9 . . .	**10** *31,000*		
11 Gain from Form 4797, Part I; long-term gain from Forms 2119, 2439, and 6252; and long-term gain or (loss) from Forms 4684, 6781, and 8824 . .	**11**		
12 Net long-term gain or (loss) from partnerships, S corporations, estates, and trusts from Schedule(s) K-1.	**12**		
13 Capital gain distributions	**13** *7,800*	*5,300*	
14 Long-term capital loss carryover. Enter in both columns (f) and (g) the amount, if any, from line 14 of your 1996 Capital Loss Carryover Worksheet . . .	**14** ( )	( )	
15 Combine lines 8 through 14 in column (g)	**15**	*3,400*	
16 **Net long-term capital gain or (loss).** Combine lines 8 through 14 in column (f) . . . . ►	**16** *15,600*		

*****28% Rate Gain or Loss** includes all gains and losses in Part II, column (f) from sales, exchanges, or conversions (including installment payments received) **either:** • **Before** May 7, 1997, **or**
• **After** July 28, 1997, for assets held more than 1 year but **not** more than 18 months.
It also includes **ALL** "collectibles gains and losses" (as defined on page D-4).

For Paperwork Reduction Act Notice, see Form 1040 instructions.   Cat. No. 11338H   Schedule D (Form 1040) 1997

gain + $15,600 net long-term gain) included in 1997 taxable income. The following examples illustrate two other combinations that result in total capital gain.

> ***Total Short-Term Capital Gain.*** Mr. B's Schedule D reflects a $12,200 net short-term gain and a $4,700 net long-term loss. Because the loss can be deducted (netted) against the gain, Mr. B has a $7,500 total short-term capital gain included in taxable income.

Total Long-Term Capital Gain.   Ms. C's Schedule D reflects an $8,500 net short-term loss and a $20,000 net long-term gain ($12,000 of which is a 28 percent rate gain). Because the loss can be deducted (netted) against the gain, Ms. C has a $11,500 total long-term capital gain included in taxable income. Under the netting rules, a short-term loss reduces 28 percent rate gain *before* other long-term gain. Consequently, Ms. C's $11,500 total gain consists of a 28 percent rate gain of $3,500 ($12,000 28 percent rate gain − $8,500 short-term loss) and $8,000 other long-term gain.

Preferential Rates on Long-Term Capital Gains

If an individual's taxable income includes capital gain, any short-term component of the gain is taxed at the ordinary rates, while any long-term component is taxed at the following preferential rates.[30]

- A 28 percent rate gain is taxed at a *maximum* rate of 28 percent. Thus, this rate is beneficial only if the ordinary tax rate that would apply to such gain exceeds 28 percent.
- Other long-term gain is taxed at a 20 percent rate. However, any portion of such gain that would be taxed at 15 percent under the ordinary rate structure is taxed at only 10 percent. This dual rate structure ensures that every individual benefits from the preferential long-term capital gains rate, regardless of his or her marginal rate on ordinary income.[31]

Let's refer back to the preceding three examples to illustrate how these various tax rates apply.

Mr. and Mrs. Dixon: Short-Term and Long-Term Gain.   Mr. and Mrs. Dixon's 1997 taxable income included $17,000 capital gain consisting of the following:

Short-term gain	$ 1,400
Long-term gain:	
28 percent rate gain	3,400
Other long-term gain	12,200
Total capital gain included in taxable income	$17,000

In 1997, the Dixon's marginal rate on ordinary income was 36 percent. Consequently,

---

[30]§1(h)(1) as amended by the Tax Reform Act of 1997.

[31]Further reductions in the dual long-term rate structure are scheduled to take effect in 2001. See §1(h)(2).

- $1,400 of their capital gain was taxed at 36 percent.
- $3,400 of their capital gain was taxed at 28 percent.
- $12,200 of their capital gain was taxed at 20 percent.

Short-Term Gain.   Mr. B's taxable income includes $7,500 short-term capital gain. This gain is taxed at the ordinary rates that apply to Mr. B's other income items.

Long-Term Gain.   Ms. C's taxable income includes $11,500 long-term capital gain consisting of the following:

28 percent rate gain	$ 3,500
Other long-term gain	8,000
Long-term gain	$11,500

Assume that Ms. C's marginal rate on oridnary income is 31 percent. Consequently,

- $3,500 of her capital gain is taxed at 28 percent.
- $8,000 of her capital gain is taxed at 20 percent.

Now change the facts by assuming that Ms. C's taxable income is only $34,000 and that she files as a head of household. In this case, the ordinary tax rate on her entire income is only 15 percent and the maximum rate on 28 percent rate gain is inapplicable. Consequently,

- $3,500 of her capital gain is taxed at 15 percent.
- $8,000 of her capital gain is taxed at 10 percent.

Even though Ms. C is in the lowest tax bracket, she benefits from the preferential capital gain rate, which reduces her tax bill by $400 (5 percent of $8,000).

Unrecaptured Section 1250 Gain.   Real property used in a trade or business (including rental real estate) and held for more than one year is a Section 1231 asset rather than a capital asset. When an individual sells or exchanges business or rental reallty, recognized gain is subject to the partial depreciation recapture rule discussed in Chapter 7. Any additional gain (subject to the Section 1231 netting process) is treated as long-term capital gain. Such long-term gain is taxed according to the following rules.

- If the real estate was held for more than 1 year but less than 18 months, the gain is categorized as a 28 percent rate gain.

- If the real estate was held for more than 18 months, any unrecaptured Section 1250 gain is taxed at a maximum rate of 25 percent. **Unrecaptured Section 1250 gain** is defined as Section 1231 gain that would be recaptured as ordinary income under the full depreciation recapture rule.[32]
- Any remaining gain is treated as long-term capital gain taxed at 20 percent or 10 percent.

Unrecaptured Section 1250 Gain.   During the current year, Mr. L sold two tracts of real estate, Property A and Property B, both of which he held for more than 18 months. Mr. L did not sell any other capital or Section 1231 asset during the year, and his marginal tax rate on ordinary income was 39.6 percent.

		Property A		Property B
Sales price		$800,000		$475,000
Original cost	$950,000		$440,000	
Depreciation (straight-line)	(190,000)		(32,000)	
Adjusted basis		(760,000)		(408,000)
Gain recognized		$ 40,000		$ 67,000

Because Mr. L used the straight-line method to compute depreciation, the partial recapture rule is inapplicable and the gain recognized on both sales is Section 1231 gain. However, the $40,000 gain recognized on the sale of Property A is less than the accumulated depreciation through date of sale. Consequently, the entire gain is classified as unrecaptured Section 1250 gain. With respect to the sale of Property B, only $32,000 of the $67,000 gain recognized is classified as unrecaptured Section 1250 gain. Mr. L's $72,000 total unrecaptured Section 1250 gain is taxed at 25 percent, while his $35,000 remaining Section 1231 gain is treated as long-term capital gain taxed at 20 percent.[33]

Even simple examples of the various preferential capital gains rates reflect the complexity of this tax rate structure. Individuals who must actually apply the capital gains rates to compute their tax liability can follow the 54-step procedure contained in Part IV of Schedule D. Use of this procedure is illustrated in the Comprehensive Schedule D Problem included as Appendix 15–A to this chapter.

Policy Reasons for a Preferential Capital Gains Rate

What is the theoretic justification for a preferential tax rate on capital gains? This tax policy question is relevant in assessing the vertical equity of the income tax system because capital gains are recognized most frequently by high-income individuals who engage in significant investment activities. One argument in support of the preferential

---

[32]§1(h)(7).

[33]Net short-term capital loss or net 28 percent rate loss is netted against unrecaptured Section 1250 gain before other long-term gain.

rate stems from the fact that individuals don't pay tax on capital gain each year as the gain accrues but only in the year in which the gain is realized. This bunching effect could cause the gain to be taxed at a higher rate than if it were taxed in increments over a number of years. Critics of the preferential rate point out that the bunching problem is mitigated by the deferral of tax on the capital gain until the year of realization.

A second argument is that the preferential rate on long-term gains counteracts the effect of inflation. An investor's tax basis in capital assets is not adjusted for changes in the purchasing power of the dollar. If an investor holds an asset for a long time, the dollars realized on sale may exceed the historic basis of the asset, but some or even all the realized gain may be inflationary rather than real. The counterargument is that a preferential rate on all long-term gains, regardless of the actual duration of the investor's holding period, is a crude solution to this problem. Congress periodically considers the idea of indexing the tax basis of assets to reflect changes in the value of the dollar but has backed away from this theoretically appealing solution because of the complexity it would add to the tax law.

Many economists contend that the preferential rate on capital gains encourages the mobility of capital. Without a tax break on realized gains, individuals owning appreciated assets might be unduly reluctant to liquidate or convert such assets because of the tax cost. This locking-in effect distorts financial decision making and retards the efficiency of the stock and bond markets. A variation on this argument is that the preferential rate reduces the risk associated with many financial investments and thereby increases the supply of venture capital to the nation's economy. The counterargument is that the rate applies to all capital gains irrespective of the degree of risk inherent in the underlying investment.

Capital Loss Limitation

Objective 6
Determine the deduction for a net capital loss.

If an individual's capital losses exceed his capital gains for the year, only $3,000 of the net capital loss can be entered on page 1, Form 1040, as a deduction against other income items in the computation of AGI.[34] The nondeductible portion of the loss is carried forward indefinitely to be combined with the individual's future capital gains and losses. Carryforwards retain their character as short-term or long-term loss. A long-term capital loss carryforward is netted against 28 percent rate gain before other long-term gain.

Net Capital Loss.   Ms. N sold four blocks of securities this year with the following result:

Sale #1:	Short-term capital loss	$ (4,000)
Sale #2:	Short-term capital gain	6,100
Sale #3:	Long-term capital loss	(11,500)
Sale #4:	Long-term capital gain	1,250

---

[34]§1211(b). If the net capital loss consists of both short-term and long-term loss, the $3,000 deduction is attributed to the short-term loss first. §1212(b).

> Ms. N has a net short-term gain of $2,100 and a net long-term loss of $10,250 that sum to a net loss of $8,150. She can deduct $3,000 of this loss in the computation of AGI; the $5,150 nondeductible portion becomes a long-term capital loss carryforward.

The netting of capital gains and losses on Schedule D reflects the basic rule that capital losses are deductible to the extent of capital gains. Thus, the tax savings resulting from a capital loss depend on the amount of capital gain recognized during the year.

> ***Tax Savings from Capital Losses.*** Refer to the facts in the preceding example. Ms. N's current year capital losses sheltered $6,100 of short-term capital gain, $1,250 of long-term capital gain, and $3,000 of ordinary income from tax. If Ms. N's marginal tax rate is 39.6 percent, the losses saved $3,854 of current tax.
>
> | Tax savings on: | |
> | --- | --- |
> | Short-term gain (6,100 × 39.6%) | $2,416 |
> | Long-term gain (1,250 × 20%) | 250 |
> | Ordinary income (3,000 × 39.6%) | 1,188 |
> | | $3,854 |

Ms. N's $5,150 capital loss carryforward will generate a tax savings in future years to the extent she can deduct it against capital gains or ordinary income.

> ***Capital Loss Carryforward.*** In the following year Ms. N has only one capital transaction that generates an $1,800 short-term capital gain. Consequently, she has a net short-term gain of $1,800 and a net long-term loss of $5,150 (her carryforward) that sum to a $3,350 net capital loss. Ms. N can deduct $3,000 of this loss in computing AGI and carry the $350 nondeductible portion forward to the next year.

In present value terms, the tax savings from a capital loss diminish with each year that the investor must wait to deduct the loss. The obvious tax planning strategy for an individual who recognizes a capital loss is to generate sufficient capital gains to absorb the loss as soon as possible. Of course, even without capital gains, individuals can deduct their capital losses at the rate of $3,000 per year. But for investors who suffer large losses, the value of this stream of annual deductions may be negligible.

Investments in Small Corporate Businesses

Investments in small corporate businesses that are struggling to grow involve more risk than investments in well-established corporations with proven track records. To encourage individuals to accept this higher level of risk, the tax law contains two preferential provisions that apply only to investments in small corporate ventures.

Qualified Small Business Stock

Objective 7
Describe the tax benefit associated with qualified small business stock and Section 1244 stock.

Individuals who realize capital gain on the sale or exchange of **qualified small business stock** held for more than *five years* may exclude 50 percent of such gain from income.[35] The remaining capital gain is classifed as 28 percent rate gain.[36] The stock must have been issued directly to the individual in exchange for money, property, or services rendered to the issuing corporation. In other words, individuals cannot purchase qualified small business stock from other shareholders. Moreover, the stock must be issued after August 10, 1993. Because of the five-year holding requirement, 1998 is the first year in which individuals can take advantage of this preference.[37]

> ***Gain on Qualified Small Business Stock.*** In November 1993, Ms. H contributed $200,000 to QB Inc. in exchange for 1,000 shares of stock. QB Inc. is a qualified small business. In December 1998, Ms. H sold her QB shares for $560,000, realizing a $360,000 gain. She may exclude $180,000 of this gain from her 1998 income. The $180,000 long-term capital gain included in Ms. H's income is 28 percent rate gain.

A qualified small business is a regular corporation with no more than $50 million of gross assets immediately after the qualified stock was issued. The corporation must conduct an active trade or business other than a financial, leasing, real estate, farming, mining, hospitality, or professional service business.[38]

Section 1244 Stock

Individuals who realize a loss on the disposition of **Section 1244 stock** may deduct a limited portion of the loss as ordinary, rather than capital, loss. Married couples filing jointly are limited to an annual $100,000 ordinary deduction, while unmarried individuals or married individuals filing separate returns are limited to an annual $50,000 ordinary deduction. Any loss in excess of these limits retains its character as capital loss.[39]

> ***Loss on Section 1244 Stock.*** Six years ago, Mr. and Mrs. P contributed $200,000 to NW Inc. in exchange for 1,000 shares of stock, which qualified as Section 1244 stock. This year, they sold all 1,000 shares for $30,000. This was the couple's only asset sale for the year. Their salary, interest, and dividend income totaled $319,000. Based on these facts, Mr. and Mrs. P's AGI on their joint return is $216,000.

---

[35] §1202. For any tax year, the gain eligible for this exclusion is limited to the *greater* of (1) 10 times the aggregate basis in the stock disposed of during the year or (2) $10 million reduced by eligible gain recognized in prior taxable years. If an individual disposes of stock in more than one qualified small business during a year, the limitation applies separately with respect to each business.

[36] §1(h)(7).

[37] An amount equal to 42 percent of the excluded gain is an AMT tax preference that must be added to taxable income in the calculation of the individual's AMTI. §57(a)(7).

[38] See §1202(d) and (e) for the complete definition of a qualified small business.

[39] §1244(a) and (b).

Salary, interest, dividends	$ 319,000
Maximum Section 1244 loss	(100,000)
Capital loss deduction	(3,000)
AGI	$ 216,000

Mr. and Mrs. P can carry their $67,000 nondeductible long-term capital loss ($170,000 recognized loss − $100,000 Section 1244 loss − $3,000 deductible capital loss) forward to the next year.

As a general rule, the first $1 million of stock issued by a corporation that derives more than 50 percent of its annual gross receipts from the conduct of an active business qualifies as Section 1244 stock.[40] This special character applies only to stock issued directly by the corporation to an individual investor in exchange for money or property. Stock issued for services rendered to the issuing corporation does not qualify as Section 1244 stock. The Section 1244 label has no downside. If the fledgling corporate venture is a success and the investor eventually sells the stock at a gain, that gain is characterized as capital gain. On the other hand, if the investor sells the stock at a loss or if the stock becomes worthless, a significant portion (if not all) of the loss yields an immediate benefit as a deduction in the computation of AGI.

Investment Expenses

Individuals are allowed to deduct ordinary and necessary expenses paid or incurred for the management, conservation, or maintenance of investment property.[41] This rule applies to relatively few types of out-of-pocket expenses such as subscriptions to investment publications and newsletters, investment management fees, or the rental of a safety deposit box to hold securities or investment-related documents. The deduction for investment expenses is classified as a miscellaneous itemized deduction and thus often fails to result in any tax benefit.[42]

Investment Interest Expense

Objective 8
Determine the deduction for investment interest expense.

An important set of rules governs the deductibility of interest that individuals pay on funds borrowed to purchase investment property. If the property is tax-exempt state and local bonds, no deduction at all is allowed for the interest payments.[43] The logic of this rule is apparent: Congress doesn't want the tax law to subsidize the acquisition of investments yielding nontaxable income. If an individual incurs a debt and uses the proceeds to buy investment property with the potential to yield taxable income, the interest paid on the debt is an itemized deduction but only to the extent of the debtor's

---

[40]§1244(c).
[41]§212.
[42]Miscellaneous itemized deductions are allowed only to the extent that their total exceeds 2 percent of AGI. §67.
[43]§265.

net investment income for the year.[44] The nondeductible portion of the interest expense is carried forward to future taxable years.

> ***Investment Interest Expense.***   Mr. L borrowed $40,000 at 9 percent and invested the loan proceeds in a mutual fund that paid a current dividend of $5,000. Mr. L's **investment interest expense** for the year was $3,600. Because his net investment income exceeded $3,600, Mr. L can claim the entire interest payment as an itemized deduction.
>
>   Now assume that Mr. L used the loan proceeds to purchase common stock in a corporation that did not pay a current dividend. His only investment income for the year was $750 interest earned on a savings account. In this case, Mr. L can deduct only $750 of his investment interest expense. The $2,850 nondeductible expense carries forward to next year, when Mr. L can deduct it subject to the net investment income limitation.

Net Investment Income.   Investment income includes any income item generated by property held for investment purposes. Interest income, dividends, annuity payments, and short-term capital gain on the sale of investment assets fall within this definition. **Net investment income** equals the total of these items less any expenses (other than interest) directly connected with the production of investment income. If an individual recognizes a *long-term* capital gain on the sale of an investment asset, the tax law offers an interesting choice. The individual may elect to treat the gain (or any portion thereof) as investment income, thereby securing a deduction for investment interest. But by making this election, the individual forfeits any preferential tax rate on the gain.[45] This election prevents investors from deriving a double benefit from their long-term capital gains. The gains can increase the investment interest expense deduction for the year or be taxed at a preferential rate, but not both.

Investments in Real Property

As an alternative to financial assets, individuals may put their money into real estate. In this section of the chapter, we will examine the tax consequences of this broad category of investment assets.

Undeveloped Land

Individuals who invest in undeveloped land expect a return in the form of appreciation in the value of the land. Undeveloped land typically does not generate any significant current income or cash flow to the owner.[46] However, owners may incur out-of-pocket expenses with respect to their land. Real property taxes can be a significant annual expense; investors can claim these tax payments as itemized deductions.[47] If the owner financed the acquisition of the land through a mortgage, the interest and principal payments are cash outflows with respect to the investment. The interest payments are investment interest,

---

[44]§163(d).

[45]§1(h).

[46]Owners might receive revenues from grazing, hunting, mineral, or crop leases.

[47]§164(a)(1).

deductible to the extent of the owner's income from other investment activities. Instead of treating property taxes and interest as current expenses, the owner may elect to capitalize these carrying charges to the basis of the land.[48] Another important consideration is that undeveloped land may be a very illiquid asset. All in all, land may be a poor investment choice for individuals who want ready access to cash.

The tax advantage of holding investment land is that appreciation in value is not recognized as income until the owner disposes of the land in a taxable transaction.[49] Moreover, any gain recognized on the sale of land held for at least a year qualifies for a preferential tax rate. This conclusion, of course, presumes that the land was a capital asset in the owner's hands. Individuals who make periodic sales of land run the risk that the IRS may view this activity as a business and the land as an inventory asset held primarily for sale to customers. In such case, the gains recognized on the sale are ordinary business income rather than capital gain.

The question of whether an individual who occasionally sells land is engaging in an investment or a business activity is subjective; the answer depends on the facts and circumstances of each case. When called on to decide the issue, the federal courts consider the number, frequency, and regularity of the sales and the extent to which the taxpayer actively solicited buyers, either through advertising or by engaging a real estate agent. In cases in which the taxpayer added substantial improvements to the land, such as roads and drainage ditches, or subdivided a single tract of land into smaller parcels prior to sale, the courts have generally agreed with the IRS that the taxpayer engaged in a business activity.[50]

Rental Real Estate

Developed real estate consists of land with some type of building or structure permanently attached. Individuals who hold developed real estate receive a return in the form of rents paid by tenants or lessees who occupy the property. In many respects, this investment activity is treated as a business for tax purposes. The owner recognizes the rents as ordinary income and deducts expenses associated with the operation and maintenance of the real estate.[51] These items are reported on Schedule E, Form 1040. Consequently, only the net profit from the rental activity is included in the owner's AGI. Rental real estate is a Section 1231 asset and the building component is depreciable property with either a 27.5-year or a 39-year MACRS recovery period. Therefore, the owner can recoup his investment in the building through annual depreciation deductions.

Mr. and Mrs. David: Schedule E.   Mr. and Mrs. David own residential real estate that they have leased to the same tenant since 1995. In 1997, their revenue and expenses with respect to this investment were as follows:

Rents received ($2,250 per month)	$27,000
Monthly yard maintenance	1,480
Property and liability insurance	2,880

---

[48]§266.

[49]Individuals frequently enter into like-kind exchanges of investment real property. See the discussion of these nontaxable exchanges in Chapter 8.

[50]See for example, *W. R. Royster,* TC Memo 1985-258.

[51]Reg. §1.212-1.

Interest on mortgage	1,720
Repairs and painting	4,140
Local property tax	2,075
Monthly utilities	2,900
Legal fee for consultation on zoning restriction	675

MACRS depreciation for 1997 was $6,400. This information is summarized on the couple's Schedule E, shown as Exhibit 15–3. Their $4,730 net income (line 26) was carried as an income item to page 1, Form 1040.

While rental real estate activities share many of the characteristics of business activities, they actually fall into the special class of *passive activities.*[52] This classification in no way affects the tax consequences of profitable rental activities. But as we will learn in the next section, the classification has major ramifications for rental activities operating at a loss.

Investments in Passive Activities

Objective 9
Apply the passive activity loss limitation and the exception for rental real estate loss.

Individuals can own equity interests in business enterprises without rendering any personal services to the business. Many partners and shareholders have no involvement at all in the business activity conducted by their partnership or S corporation. Nevertheless, these owners are allocated a share of the operating income of such business activity. Even the owner of a sole proprietorship might choose to leave the management and operation of the business entirely in the hands of employees. But regardless of such lack of participation, net profits from the sole proprietorship belong to the owner. In these situations, the income to which the partner, shareholder, or sole proprietor is entitled is primarily a return on invested capital. Although such income retains its tax character as ordinary business income and is reported as such on the owner's individual tax return, it is economically equivalent to investment income.

For federal tax purposes, if an individual owns an interest in a business but does not materially participate in the business, the interest is a **passive activity. Material participation** means that the individual is involved in day-to-day operations on a regular, continuous, and substantial basis.[53]

> *Passive Activity.*   The JKL Partnership consists of three equal individual partners. Mr. J and Ms. K are general partners who work full time in JKL's business, while Mr. L is a limited partner who has no personal involvement in the business. For the two general partners, their interest in JKL is clearly a business activity. However, because Mr. L does not materially participate in the partnership business, his interest in JKL is a passive activity.[54]

---

[52]§469(c)(2).
[53]§469(c)(1). Reg. §1.496–5T provides several objective tests for determining material participation.
[54]The statute creates a presumption that a *limited* partnership interest is a passive activity. §469(h)(2).

EXHIBIT 15–3

SCHEDULE E (Form 1040)	Supplemental Income and Loss	OMB No. 1545-0074
Department of the Treasury Internal Revenue Service (99)	(From rental real estate, royalties, partnerships, S corporations, estates, trusts, REMICs, etc.) ▶ Attach to Form 1040 or Form 1041. ▶ See Instructions for Schedule E (Form 1040).	19**97** Attachment Sequence No. **13**

Name(s) shown on return	Your social security number
Ronald and Janice David	498 31 1240

Part I — Income or Loss From Rental Real Estate and Royalties Note: *Report income and expenses from your business of renting personal property on Schedule C or C-EZ (see page E-1). Report farm rental income or loss from Form 4835 on page 2, line 39.*

1 Show the kind and location of each **rental real estate property:**		2 For each rental real estate property listed on line 1, did you or your family use it during the tax year for personal purposes for more than the greater of: • 14 days, or • 10% of the total days rented at fair rental value? (See page E-1.)	Yes	No
A	1412 West Reeder Ave. Omaha, Nebraska		A	✓
B			B	
C			C	

Income:		Properties			Totals (Add columns A, B, and C.)
		A	**B**	**C**	
3 Rents received	3	27,000			3
4 Royalties received	4				4
Expenses:					
5 Advertising	5				
6 Auto and travel (see page E-2)	6				
7 Cleaning and maintenance	7	1,480			
8 Commissions	8				
9 Insurance	9	2,880			
10 Legal and other professional fees	10				
11 Management fees	11				
12 Mortgage interest paid to banks, etc. (see page E-2)	12	1,720			12
13 Other interest	13				
14 Repairs	14	4,140			
15 Supplies	15				
16 Taxes	16	2,075			
17 Utilities	17	2,900			
18 Other (list) ▶ *legal fee*	18	675			
19 Add lines 5 through 18	19	15,870			19
20 Depreciation expense or depletion (see page E-2)	20	6,400			20
21 Total expenses. Add lines 19 and 20	21	22,270			
22 Income or (loss) from rental real estate or royalty properties. Subtract line 21 from line 3 (rents) or line 4 (royalties). If the result is a (loss), see page E-3 to find out if you must file **Form 6198**	22	4,730			
23 Deductible rental real estate loss. **Caution:** *Your rental real estate loss on line 22 may be limited. See page E-3 to find out if you must file **Form 8582**. Real estate professionals must complete line 42 on page 2*	23	(	)(	)(	)
24 **Income.** Add positive amounts shown on line 22. **Do not** include any losses				24	4,730
25 **Losses.** Add royalty losses from line 22 and rental real estate losses from line 23. Enter total losses here				25	( )
26 Total rental real estate and royalty income or (loss). Combine lines 24 and 25. Enter the result here. If Parts II, III, IV, and line 39 on page 2 do not apply to you, also enter this amount on Form 1040, line 17. Otherwise, include this amount in the total on line 40 on page 2				26	4,730

For Paperwork Reduction Act Notice, see Form 1040 instructions.   Cat. No. 11344L   Schedule E (Form 1040) 1997

The classification of an interest as a passive activity does not affect how the income generated by the activity is taxed. Assume that the JKL Partnership in the preceding example generated current business income of $129,000. Each of the three partners received a Schedule K-1 reporting a $43,000 distributive share of this income. All three included this share as ordinary income on their Form 1040 and paid tax accordingly. The fact that Mr. L's distributive share was passive activity income had no impact on the computation of his tax on the income.

Passive Activity Loss Limitation

The classification of an interest in a business as a passive activity has profound tax consequences if the business operates at a loss. Specifically, the owner of the passive activity can deduct the loss only to the extent of income generated by other passive activities.[55] Any loss disallowed under this limitation is carried forward as a suspended passive activity loss. Suspended losses are deductible in any future year to the extent of the owner's passive activity income in that year.[56]

> **Passive Activity Loss Limitation.**   Refer to the facts in the preceding example and assume that the JKL Partnership generated a $90,000 current operating loss. Each partner received a Schedule K-1 reporting a $30,000 distributive share of this loss. Mr. J and Ms. K, the general partners who work in the partnership business, can deduct their entire loss in the computation of AGI.[57] If his limited partnership interest is Mr. L's only passive activity, he cannot deduct any of his $30,000 loss. If he owns another passive activity that generated income for the year, he can deduct the loss to the extent of such income. Any disallowed loss is carried forward as a suspended passive activity loss. Mr. L can deduct the loss in a future year to the extent he recognizes income from either the JKL Partnership or any other passive activity.

Rental Activities.   The term *passive activity* includes any **rental activity**, defined as an activity where payments are principally for the use of tangible property for an extended period of time.[58] Activities in which substantial services are provided and customer payments are principally for such services rather than for the use of property are excluded from this definition. For instance, the operation of a hotel is a business rather than a rental activity. Similarly, businesses providing short-term use of property such as automobiles, tuxedos, or videocassettes are not rental activities. If an individual owns a rental activity, that activity is passive, regardless of the extent of the owner's participation in the operation of the activity.

As mentioned earlier in the chapter, rental real estate activities are passive activities.[59] Accordingly, individuals who invest in rental real estate can deduct losses only to the extent of their passive activity income. However, the law provides an important exception under which individuals can deduct up to $25,000 of their annual loss from rental real estate without regard to the passive activity loss limitation.[60] To qualify for the full $25,000 exception, the individual's AGI (before consideration of any rental loss) must not exceed $100,000. If AGI exceeds this threshold, the $25,000 exception is

---

[55]§469(a)(1) and (d)(1).

[56]§469(b).

[57]This statement presumes that the partners have sufficient basis in their partnership interests to absorb their loss. See Chapter 9.

[58]Reg. §1.469-1T(e)(3).

[59]Real estate professionals who devote more than one-half of their work effort each year and at least 750 hours annually to a real property business are engaged in an active business rather than a passive rental activity. A real property business includes the development, redevelopment, construction, reconstruction, acquisition, conversion, rental, operation, management, leasing or brokering of real property. §469(c)(7).

[60]§469(i). The individual must also own at least a 10 percent interest in the real estate and must be significantly involved in its management.

reduced by 50 percent of the excess. Thus, the exception shrinks to zero for taxpayers with AGI over $150,000.

> ***Rental Real Estate Exception.***   Mr. and Mrs. E own and manage three duplexes which they rent to college students. Mr. and Mrs. E do not own any other passive activities. The duplexes generated a $31,000 loss this year. Before consideration of this loss, the couple's AGI was $95,000. Because of the rental real estate exception, Mr. and Mrs. E can deduct $25,000 of this loss to reduce their AGI to $70,000. The $6,000 excess loss is a nondeductible passive activity loss that they can carry forward to the next year.
>
> If Mr. and Mrs. E's AGI before consideration of their rental loss was $141,000, their exception is reduced to $4,500:
>
> | | |
> |---|---:|
> | AGI before loss | $ 141,000 |
> | AGI threshold | (100,000) |
> | Excess AGI | $ 41,000 |
> | | .50 |
> | Reduction in $25,000 exception | $ 20,500 |
>
> Consequently, the couple can deduct $4,500 of their rental loss to reduce their AGI to $136,500. The $26,500 excess loss is a nondeductible passive activity loss that they can carry forward to the next year.

Dispositions of Passive Activities

The passive activity loss limitation is not a *permanent* loss disallowance rule. When an investor disposes of her entire interest in a passive activity in a taxable transaction (generally a sale or exchange), any suspended losses with respect to the interest are fully deductible in the year of disposition. As a result, the investor finally reaps a tax benefit from every dollar of loss disallowed in an earlier year because of the limitation. Of course, in present value terms, the tax savings from the deferred deduction is less than the savings the investor would have enjoyed from a deduction in such earlier year.

Planning Strategies with Passive Activity Losses

Suppose that Mrs. Q, a practicing attorney, paid $50,000 to buy stock in a S corporation operating a chain of Mexican restaurants. Because she does not materially participate in the S corporation's business, Mrs. Q's interest is a passive activity. On her first Schedule K-1 from the corporation, Mrs. Q is allocated a $9,000 ordinary business loss. As you learned in Chapter 9, this allocation reduces the basis in her stock to $41,000.[61] Mrs. Q owns no other passive activities and therefore recognized no passive activity income this year. Consequently, she can't deduct her $9,000 loss in computing AGI. Stated another way, Mrs. Q's passive activity loss doesn't shelter the income generated by her legal practice (or any other income item) from current tax.

---

[61]§1367(a).

Sale of a Passive Activity.   What are Mrs. Q's options with respect to her $9,000 suspended loss? Given that the restaurant business apparently is losing money, her best option may be to sell the stock as quickly as possible! Suppose that early in the next year, Mrs. Q finds a buyer who offers $30,000 for her shares. If she accepts the offer, she will recognize an $11,000 capital loss on the sale.[62] Because she disposes of her entire interest in the passive activity, she is allowed to deduct her entire $9,000 suspended passive activity loss as a current business loss. The total of the two losses corresponds to Mrs. Q's $20,000 economic loss on this unfortunate investment. The only effect of the passive activity loss limitation is to defer the deduction of the ordinary portion of the loss (and the tax benefit therefrom) for one year.

Purchase of a PIG.   If Mrs. Q believes that the restaurant business is a solid long-term investment, her second option is to find a source of passive activity income. Perhaps the restaurant business itself will become profitable so that Mrs. Q eventually can deduct her suspended loss against her share of the S corporation's future taxable income. If this possibility is too uncertain, she could invest in a moneymaking passive activity (dubbed a **passive income generator (PIG)** by the financial press). For instance, if she buys an interest in a profitable commercial office building, she can deduct her suspended loss from the S corporation to the extent of her rental income from the PIG.

Wealth Transfer Planning

Individuals who engage in successful business and investment activities inevitably accumulate capital in the process. At some point in their lives, individuals begin to think about transferring capital to other parties—usually to their children and grandchildren. The decision to part with property can be intensely personal; the man or woman struggling with the decision may be more concerned with private, family issues rather than with the financial implications of the decision. However, once the decision is made, most people are eager to adopt financial strategies to maximize the wealth available to younger-generation family members. As we will learn in this final section of Chapter 15, the impact of the federal transfer taxes is a primary consideration in the development of such strategies.

Good News, Bad News for Baby Boomers.   Over the next 20 years the largest transfer of property in U.S. history will take place as baby boomers inherit their parents' wealth. Economists estimate that boomers will inherit $4.8 trillion through the year 2015. The bad news is that the majority of individuals over age 65 have not considered the impact of the federal estate tax on their accumulated wealth.[63]

---

[62]This calculation of loss is based on Mrs. Q's basis in the stock on January 1 without adjustment for any pro rata share of the corporation's income or loss for the year of sale.

[63]Douglas D. Wilson, "Providing Guidance to Executors and Trustees," *Journal of Accountancy,* October 1997.

The Transfer Tax System

The federal transfer tax system has three components: the gift tax, the estate tax, and the generation-skipping transfer tax. This section will introduce only the first two components and omit any further mention of the highly complex and narrowly focused generation-skipping transfer tax. Congress enacted the transfer tax system early in this century as a mechanism for redistributing some portion of the private fortunes owned by the nation's richest families to the public domain. Historically, these taxes have been a concern to only a small fraction of the population. Nonetheless, for affluent individuals who have amassed wealth and wish to keep it in the family, a familiarity of the basic operation of these taxes is essential.

Structure of the Gift and Estate Taxes

Objective 10
Describe the structure of the federal gift and estate tax.

The federal gift tax is imposed on gratuitous transfers of property that individuals make during life (**inter vivos transfers**), while the federal estate tax is imposed on final transfers of property occurring at death (**testamentary transfers**). In both cases, the tax base is the fair market value of the property transferred and both taxes are computed with reference to the same rate schedule. The transfer tax rate schedule is steeply progressive, with a top marginal rate of 55 percent.[64]

The gift and estate taxes have a unique feature in that they are not computed on an annual basis. Instead, the taxes are based on the *cumulative* value of taxable transfers that a person makes over a lifetime. As a result, each successive transfer (including the last transfer at death) is boosted higher in the rate brackets and becomes more expensive in terms of tax cost.

> ***Cumulative Taxable Transfers.*** Mr. K made his first taxable transfer in 1995: a $1 million cash gift to his children. He made a second taxable gift in 1996: a gift of $1 million of property to his grandchildren. Mr. D died in 1998. His taxable estate was valued at $1 million. Exhibit 15–4 shows that the three transfers of equal value were subject to progressively higher tax rates because each successive transfer was "stacked" on the cumulative amount of the earlier transfers.

Annual Gift Tax Exclusion

Objective 11
Explain the role of the annual gift tax exclusion and the lifetime transfer tax exclusion.

Any transfer of property for which the transferor does not receive adequate consideration in money or money's worth is defined as a gift for federal tax purposes.[65] The **donor** making the gift is usually motivated by generosity or affection toward the **donee** receiving the gift. In other words, a gift occurs in a personal, rather than a business, context. Not every gift is subject to the federal gift tax. Donors can give away unlimited property to qualified charities or to their spouse and can pay tuition to

---

[64]§2001(c). A 5 percent surtax applies to taxable transfers in excess of $10 million but not in excess of the amount at which the average tax rate is 55 percent. This surtax recaptures the benefits of the progressive rates on the first $3 million of taxable transfers.

[65]§2512(b).

Exhibit 15–4

Cumulative nature of federal transfer taxes

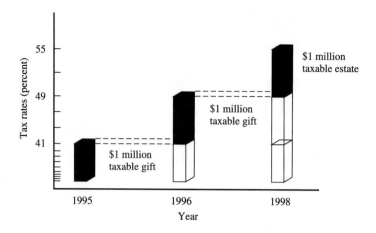

an educational institution or medical expenses for another person without incurring a gift tax.[66]

The first $10,000 of value that a donor gives to any donee during a calendar year escapes taxation; this **annual gift tax exclusion** removes most routine birthday, graduation, and Christmas presents from the gift tax base.[67] For purposes of this exclusion, married couples can elect to treat a gift made by either spouse as a gift made in equal portions by both spouses. By making this gift-splitting election, the couple doubles the exclusion to $20,000 per donee.[68] The first maxim of transfer tax planning is that individuals should take full advantage of this annual exclusion.

> *Gift Tax Exclusion.*   Mr. and Mrs. B have two adult children, who are both married, and six unmarried grandchildren. Each year Mr. and Mrs. B give $20,000 to each of 10 donees (children, children-in-law, and grandchildren), thereby transferring $200,000 of property without making a taxable gift. When the grandchildren marry and produce great-grandchildren, Mr. and Mrs. B plan to add them to their list of annual donees, systematically bestowing wealth on their younger-generation family members at no tax cost.

Lifetime Transfer Tax Exclusion

If the value of property transferred from one person to another during a calendar year exceeds $10,000 (and the donor and donee are not married), the excess value is a taxable gift. Even so, the donor still may not pay any tax on the transfer. Cumulative transfers of property that do not exceed the **lifetime transfer tax exclusion** are tax-exempt.[69] The Tax Reform Act of 1997 increased the exclusion from $600,000 (1997 and prior years) to $1 million based on the following phase-in schedule:

---

[66]§2503(e), §2522, and §2523.

[67]§2503(b). Beginning in 1999, the $10,000 exclusion will be indexed for inflation.

[68]§2513.

[69]This exemption is attributable to the unified transfer tax credit, which offsets the gift or estate tax calculated on the lifetime exclusion amount. §2505 and §2010.

For Transfers Made During	Lifetime Exclusion
1998	$ 625,000
1999	650,000
2000 and 2001	675,000
2002 and 2003	700,000
2004	850,000
2005	950,000
2006 and thereafter	1,000,000

Excluded Transfers during Life.   Ms. W made her first taxable gift in 1993 when she transferred $100,000 of marketable securities to her niece. The taxable gift was $90,000 (the excess of fair market value over the $10,000 annual exclusion); because of her $600,000 lifetime exclusion, Mrs. W's gift tax liability was zero.

In 1995, Mrs. W transferred a second block of securities worth $150,000 to her niece. The taxable gift was $140,000, and Mrs. W's *cumulative* taxable transfers equaled $230,000. Accordingly, Mrs. W paid no tax on her second gift.

In 1998, Mrs. W transferred real estate with an appraised value of $500,000 to her godchild. This transfer was a $490,000 taxable gift, only $95,000 of which was taxed.

1993 taxable gift	$ 90,000
1995 taxable gift	140,000
1998 taxable gift	490,000
Cumulative taxable transfers	$ 720,000
Lifetime exclusion	(625,000)
1998 gift subject to tax	$ 95,000

After 1998, Mrs. W will pay tax on additional taxable transfers (whether inter vivos or testamentary) to the extent the amount of the transfer exceeds the *increase* in the lifetime exclusion over $625,000.

Excluded Transfers at Death.   Assume that Mrs. W makes no gifts after 1998 and dies in 2004, leaving a taxable estate of $370,000. Because of the increased lifetime exclusion, only $145,000 of this testamentary transfer is subject to estate tax.

Taxable estate		$370,000
Lifetime exclusion in 2004	$850,000	

Lifetime exclusion used through 1988	(625,000)	
Additional lifetime exclusion		(225,000)
Estate subject to tax		$145,000

Income Tax Consequences of Gifted Property

Objective 12
Calculate the income tax savings from a gift of property.

When a donor gives property to a donee, the donor's adjusted basis in the property carries over to become the donee's basis.[70] Because of this carryover basis rule, unrealized appreciation in the value of the property is shifted from donor to donee.

Carryover Basis.   Six years ago Mr. RG transferred marketable securities with a $2,400 basis and a $10,000 market value to his 15-year-old grandson. Because of the annual exclusion, RG paid no gift tax on the transfer. Grandson's carryover basis in the securities was $2,400. Grandson received $900 of dividends each year from the securities. In the current year, he sold the securities for $16,000 and recognized a $13,600 capital gain.

Let's summarize the tax consequences of this transfer:

- Mr. RG gave valuable property to grandson without incurring any transfer tax.
- Grandson, rather than Mr. RG, recognized the income from the property subsequent to the transfer.
- Grandson, rather than Mr. RG, recognized the unrealized appreciation existing at date of gift as capital gain.

If grandson's marginal rate was less than Mr. RG's marginal rate, the income shift from the gift resulted in tax savings for the family.

Tax Savings from Income Shift.   During the six years that grandson held the securities, his marginal tax rate was 15 percent, while Mr. RG's marginal rate was 39.6 percent. The following table compares grandson's total tax on the shifted dividends and capital gain with Mr. RG's tax cost if he had not made the gift:

	Grandson	Mr. RG
Dividend income ($900 for six years)	$ 5,400	$ 5,400
Tax rate	.15	.396
Tax on dividends	$ 810	$ 2,138

---

[70]§1015 governs the income tax basis of gifted property. If the donor pays a gift tax, the carryover basis is increased by the tax attributable to the appreciation in the gifted property. If the fair market value of gifted property is *less* than the donor's basis, the donee's basis is limited to such fair market value and the donor's unrealized loss in the property disappears. Donors typically avoid giving away property that has depreciated in value.

Capital gain	$13,600	$13,600
Preferential tax rate	.10	.20
Tax on capital gain	$ 1,360	$ 2,720
Total tax liability	$ 2,170	$ 4,858

Because of the difference in marginal tax rates, Mr. RG's gift of the securities to grandson achieved an impressive $2,688 income tax savings for the family.

Kiddie Tax.   The Internal Revenue Code severely limits the tax savings resulting from a transfer of income-producing property to a child under the age of 14 years. The investment income from the property is reported on the child's tax return. However, the child's *unearned* taxable income in excess of an inflation-adjusted base amount ($700 in 1998) is taxed at the marginal rate from the child's *parents'* return.[71] Moreover, if the child is claimed as a dependent by another taxpayer, the child's standard deduction is limited to the *greater* of $700 or earned income plus $250.[72]

Kiddie Tax.   In 1995, Mr. RG, our grandfather in the preceding example, gave marketable securities to his nine-year-old granddaughter. In 1998, the grand-daughter received $4,000 of interest income from the securities, which was her only income item for the year. Her parents' marginal tax rate on their 1998 return was 36 percent. Granddaughter's 1998 tax liability is $1,041.

Interest income	$4,000
Standard deduction	(700)
Taxable income	$3,300
Unearned taxable income	$3,300
Base	(700)
Income taxed at parents' rate	$2,600
Granddaughter's tax:	
$2,600 × 36%	$ 936
$700 × 15%	105
	$1,041

While this **kiddie tax** certainly reduces the benefit of income shifts to young children, families can avoid its application by giving assets that yield deferred rather than current income. For instance, a child can be given stock in a growth corporation that doesn't pay regular dividends so that the child won't recognize any income until the year in which the stock is sold. Similarly, children can be given Series EE savings bonds that won't generate interest income until the year of redemption.

---

[71]§1(g).

[72]§63(c)(5). The $250 add-on to earned income is adjusted annually for inflation.

The Taxable Estate

Objective 13
Identify the major
components of a
deceased individual's
taxable estate.

Wealthy individuals who do not make inter vivos gifts are postponing the inevitable. No person has yet discovered a strategy to avoid the final transfer of property that must occur at death. The federal estate tax is levied on the value of this final transfer — specifically, the date-of-death value of the properties in the decedent's taxable estate.[73] The **taxable estate** includes all assets owned by the decedent and disposed of under the terms of a valid will or state intestacy statutes. These assets comprise the decedent's **probate estate.** The taxable estate may also include other property interests transferred because of the decedent's death. For instance, a decedent may have participated in a retirement plan that guarantees a death benefit to the surviving family members. Or the decedent may have owned an insurance policy on his life that pays proceeds to the beneficiary named in the policy. Neither the death benefit nor the insurance proceeds are part of the decedent's probate estate, but both amounts are included in the decedent's taxable estate.[74]

The taxable estate is reduced by outstanding debts of the decedent, the decedent's funeral expenses, and any administrative costs of settling the estate.[75] It is also reduced by any bequests to religious, charitable, educational, government, or other nonprofit organizations.[76] Thus, a person could leave her entire fortune to public causes and avoid the estate tax altogether. Lastly, the taxable estate is reduced by the property transferred to the decedent's surviving spouse.[77] Because of this **unlimited marital deduction,** the estate tax on the wealth accumulated by a married couple can be deferred until both spouses are deceased.

Taxable Estate and Federal Estate Tax.   Mr. X died in 1992 and was survived by his wife and their only child. Mr. X's will contained two specific bequests: the Metropolitan Museum of Fine Art received his art collection and his child received marketable securities with a value equal to Mr. X's lifetime transfer tax exclusion. The remainder of his probate estate went to his wife. No property interests outside Mr. X's probate estate transferred as a result of his death. Based on these facts, Mr. X's taxable estate was computed as follows:

Art collection (fair market value)		$ 800,000
Other assets owned by Mr. X (fair market value)		3,410,000
Gross estate		$4,210,000
Mr. X's outstanding debts (claims against the probate estate)		(97,600)
Funeral and administrative expenses paid from the probate estate		(78,200)
Deductible charitable bequest		(800,000)
Marital deduction:		
Other assets owned by Mr. X	$3,410,000	
Debts and expenses	(175,800)	

---

[73] §2031.
[74] §2039 and §2042.
[75] §2053.
[76] §2055.
[77] §2056.

Bequest of marketable securities to child	(600,000)
Net value of assets left to Mr. X's wife	(2,634,200)
Taxable estate	$ 600,000

Because Mr. X made no taxable gifts during his life, his $600,000 lifetime transfer tax exclusion sheltered his entire taxable estate from tax.

Mr. X's widow died in 1998. Mrs. X's will provided for a $250,000 cash bequest to her church. Her remaining estate (including the property she inherited from her husband six years earlier) was left to her child. Mrs. X's taxable estate and estate tax liability is computed as follows:

Gross estate (fair market value of assets owned by Mrs. X)	$3,181,000
Mrs. X's outstanding debts (claims against the probate estate)	(12,400)
Funeral and administrative expenses paid from the probate estate	(51,900)
Deductible charitable bequest	(250,000)
Taxable estate	$2,866,700

Because Mrs. X made no taxable gifts during her life, the federal estate tax is imposed on the $2,241,700 excess of her taxable estate over the lifetime transfer tax exclusion for 1998 ($2,866,700 taxable estate – $625,000 lifetime transfer tax exclusion). The federal estate tax on this excess is $1,018,101, which the executor of Mrs. X's estate must pay before the after-tax estate can be distributed to Mrs. X's child.

Basis Step-Up for Property Transferred at Death

Objective 14
Determine the basis of property received from a decedent.

One of the most powerful rules in the tax law concerns the basis of property transferred at death: the new owners of such property (the decedent's beneficiaries or heirs-at-law) take a basis equal to the property's fair market value at date of death.[78] The tax planning implications of this rule are tremendous. Consider the case of Mrs. Z, who purchased a tract of real estate 20 years ago for $250,000. Today, the real estate has an appraised value of $2 million. If Mrs. Z sells the property, she recognizes and pays tax on a gain of $1.75 million. If she gives the property to a family member, the donee takes a $250,000 carry-over basis and the $1.75 million appreciation will be recognized as taxable gain when the donee eventually sells the property. But if Mrs. Z dies and leaves the property to a family member in her will, the new owner's basis in the property is stepped up to $2 million. The $1.75 million potential gain with respect to the property simply vanishes.

The significance of this fair-market-value basis rule can hardly be overemphasized. Individuals who own highly appreciated assets have a strong incentive to hold the assets until death. The planning strategy becomes more complicated for an asset that *might* increase substantially in value in the future.

---

[78] §1014.

Tax Planning for Appreciating Property.   Mr. J, who is 60 years old, recently invested $50,000 in the stock of a promising new corporate venture. Mr. J anticipates that if the business is successful, the corporation could go public in 5 to 10 years. In such case, Mr. J believes that the value of his stock could skyrocket to several million dollars. Mr. J has two options with respect to this stock.

- He could give it to his various children and grandchildren as soon as possible, thereby removing any future appreciation in value from his taxable estate.
- He could plan to hold the stock until death so that such appreciation will never be subject to income tax.

In deciding which option maximizes the after-tax wealth available to his family, Mr. J must compare the projected transfer tax savings under the first option against the projected income tax savings under the second option.

Individuals who own assets that have *declined* in value should consider selling the assets to trigger a deductible loss. If they hold their depreciated assets until death, the unrealized loss (and the prospect of a deduction for such loss) will disappear when the property takes a basis equal to its fair market value.

Conclusion

Millions of individuals work conscientiously to provide financial comfort and security for themselves and their loved ones. They pay close attention to the income tax consequences of their business and investment decisions. They eagerly implement strategies to minimize their income tax costs and maximize their after-tax wealth. Unfortunately, many of these same individuals give little or no thought to long-range transfer tax planning. They have no idea of the extent of their potential taxable estate or the size of the tax bill that would fall due as a result of their death. Such shortsightedness can have disastrous financial consequences, particularly in cases of unexpected and untimely demise.[79] The moral of this story should be clear. People who engage in extensive business and investment activities should consult a tax professional to determine their exposure to the federal transfer tax. In virtually every case, the application of a few, fundamental planning principles can reduce that exposure and guarantee a brighter financial future.

---

[79]A case in point: When Joe Robbie (former owner of the Miami Dolphins) died, his estate was hit with a $47 million tax bill. The estate had insufficient liquid assets and the family was forced to sell both the football team and the Dolphins' stadium to raise cash to pay the tax.

Key Terms

Accelerated death benefits   402
Annual gift tax exclusion   424
Cash surrender value   402
Collectibles   407

Donee   423
Donor   423
Inside buildup   402
Inter vivos transfer   423

Questions and Problems for Discussion

1. Term life insurance has no investment element and no cash surrender value. Accordingly, a term policy represents pure insurance protection. What are the tax consequences in the year in which the owner lets a term policy lapse by discontinuing premium payments?

2. Mrs. SD, age 74, currently has $50,000 in a certificate of deposit paying 6 percent annual interest. In addition to this interest income, she receives Social Security and a modest pension from her former employer. Her marginal tax rate has been 15 percent for the last eight years. Mrs. SD is in reasonable health and lives independently, but she anticipates that in several years she will need to liquidate the certificate of deposit and use the money to buy into an assisted-living retirement home. Mrs. SD recently read a magazine article on the benefits of investing in tax-deferred annuities and wonders if she should transfer her $50,000 savings into an annuity. Discuss whether this tax planning strategy is advisable for Mrs. SD.

3. Describe Mr. L's tax consequences from the following exchanges:
   a. Mr. L surrenders 2,000 shares of TQJ nonvoting common stock (basis $10,000) for 1,000 shares of newly issued TQJ voting common stock (fair market value $25,000).
   b. Mr. L surrenders 2,000 shares of TQJ nonvoting common stock (basis $10,000) for 1,000 shares of newly issued Corporation Z nonvoting common stock (fair market value

$25,000). The exchange is not part of a reorganization involving TQJ Inc. and Corporation Z.
   c. Mr. L surrenders 2,000 shares of TQJ nonvoting common stock (basis $10,000) for 1,000 shares of newly issued Corporation Z nonvoting common stock (fair market value $25,000). The exchange is part of a reorganization involving TQJ Inc. and Corporation Z.
   d. Mr. L surrenders 2,000 shares of TQJ nonvoting common stock (basis $10,000) for a $25,000 30-year bond issued by AMP Corporation. The bond is worth $25,000.

4. As of November, Ms. B had $12,000 of capital losses and no capital gains for the year. She owns 4,900 shares of GG Inc. stock with a $15 basis per share and a market value of $45 per share. Ms. B plans to hold her GG stock for three more years before selling it and using the proceeds to buy a home. However, she could easily sell 400 shares to trigger a $12,000 capital gain and then immediately repurchase the shares. If Ms. B's marginal tax rate is 36 percent, should she implement this strategy?

5. What is the logic for the tax law's presumption that a limited interest in a business partnership is a passive activity?

6. Mrs. K is a shareholder in TK Inc., an S corporation. What single fact would be the strongest indicator that Mrs. K materially participates in the corporation's business?

7. Discuss the potential effect of the passive activity loss limitation on the market value of *profitable* rental real estate activities.

8. Identify the structural similarity between the investment interest expense limitation, the capital loss limitation, and the passive activity loss limitation.

9. Mr. and Mrs. FB each own 30 percent of the voting common stock of FB Inc. Four unrelated investors each own 10 percent. Based on a recent appraisal, the corporation's net worth is $10 million. Discuss the *valuation* issue suggested if:
   a. Mr. and Mrs. FB give their combined 60 percent stock interest in FB Inc. to their son.
   b. An unrelated investor gives her 10 percent stock interest in FB Inc. to her son.

10. Mr. and Mrs. T have never made a taxable gift. The couple wants their five children and dozen grandchildren to enjoy their wealth after they both are gone. However, Mr. and Mrs. T each have a will that leaves their entire property to the other. Because of the unlimited marital deduction, these transfers will eliminate any estate tax when the first spouse dies. As a result, the couple believes that their wills reflect the best tax planning strategy. Can you identify the problem with the strategy?

11. Mr. and Mrs. B earn a combined annual salary of $150,000. What two basic economic choices does the couple have with respect to this income (i.e., what can they do with their money)? Now assume that Mr. and Mrs. B have amassed property worth $2 million. What three basic economic choices does the couple have with respect to this wealth?

Application Problems

1. At the beginning of 19X7, Mrs. U paid $80,000 for a corporate bond with a stated redemption value of $100,000. Based on the bond's yield to maturity, the annual amortization of the $20,000 discount was $1,390 in 19X7 and $1,480 in 19X8. At the beginning of 19X9, Mrs. U sold the bond for $83,000. What are the tax consequences to Mrs. U in 19X7, 19X8, and 19X9 assuming that:
   a. Mrs. U bought the newly issued bond from the corporation?
   b. Mrs. U bought the bond in the public market through her broker?

2. In 19X6, Mr. DP paid $47,600 for 3,400 shares of GKL Mutual Fund and instructed the fund manager to reinvest dividends in additional shares. In 19X6 and 19X7, Mr. DP received Form 1099s from GKL reporting the following:

	Dividends Reinvested	Shares Purchased	Price per Share	Total Shares Owned
19X6	$5,070	312	$16.25	3,712
19X7	5,780	340	17.00	4,052

   a. If Mr. DP sells his 4,052 shares for $18 per share in 19X8, compute his recognized gain.

   b. If Mr. DP sells only 800 shares for $18 per share and uses the FIFO method to determine basis, compute his recognized gain.
   c. If Mr. DP sells only 800 shares for $18 per share and uses the average basis method, compute his recognized gain.

3. Fifteen years ago, Mr. F paid $50,000 for a single-premium annuity contract. This year he began receiving a $1,300 monthly payment that will continue for his life. Based on his current age, he can expect to receive $312,000. Based on these facts, how much of each monthly payment is taxable income to Mr. F?

4. Refer to the facts in the preceding problem. At the beginning of the year 2016, Mr. F's unrecovered investment in the annuity was $1,875.
   a. How much of Mr. F's total annuity payments for the year ($15,600) are taxable?
   b. Assume that Mr. F died in February 2016 after receiving only one $1,300 annuity payment. What are the tax consequences on his final Form 1040?

5. In 1992, Mr. EF, a single taxpayer, paid $45,000 to LLP Inc. for 500 shares of newly issued stock. In 1995, Mr. EF paid $40,000 to another shareholder to purchase 1,000 additional shares in LLP. To date, all of LLP's outstanding stock qualified as Section 1244 stock when it

was issued. In the current year, Mr. EF sold all 1,500 LLP shares for $16 per share. Mr. EF's only income item for the year was his $80,000 salary.

a. Based on these facts, compute Mr. EF's AGI.

b. How would the computation change if Mr. EF recognized a $20,000 capital gain on the sale of other marketable securities?

6. In 1998, Mr. J, a single individual, recognized a $70,000 long-term capital gain, a $10,000 short-term capital gain, and a $45,000 long-term capital loss. Compute J's tax liability if his taxable income before consideration of his capital transactions is $400,000.

7. In 1998, Mr. and Mrs. MS received combined salaries of $78,000 and recognized $890 of dividend income, a $1,000 short-term capital gain, and a $7,200 long-term capital gain. They incurred $6,400 of investment interest expense and $9,500 of other itemized deductions. They have no dependents and file a joint return. Based on these facts, should the couple elect to treat $4,510 of their long-term capital gain as investment income?

8. Mr. D, who is in a 36 percent marginal tax bracket, recognized a $15,000 capital loss on the sale of marketable securities in 19X1. Compute the tax savings from this loss assuming that:

a. Mr. D also recognized an $18,000 short-term capital gain in 19X1.

b. Mr. D also recognized an $18,000 long-term capital gain in 19X1.

c. Mr. D also recognized an $18,000 28 percent rate gain in 19X1.

d. Mr. D recognized no capital gains in years 19X1 through 19X5. He uses a 10 percent discount rate to compute net present value.

9. Mr. and Mrs. MH own and operate a grocery store as a sole proprietorship. Their net profit from the store and their other income and loss items for the year are:

Grocery store net profit	$44,000
Dividends and interest income	5,700
Loss from a rental house	(1,900)
Loss from a limited partnership interest	(2,600)

Based on these facts, compute Mr. and Mrs. MH's AGI.

10. Mr. V owns stock in VP Inc. and in BL Inc., both of which are S corporations. During the year Mr. V had the following income and loss items:

Salary	$ 62,300
Allocated business income from VP	19,000
Allocated business loss from BL	(25,000)

Compute Mr. V's AGI under each of the following assumptions:

a. Mr. V materially participates in VP's business but not in BL's business.

b. Mr. V materially participates in BL's business but not in VP's business.

c. Mr. V materially participates in both corporate businesses.

d. Mr. V does not materially participate in either corporate business.

11. Ms. TN owns a one-half interest in an apartment complex, which is her only passive activity. The complex operated at a $60,000 loss this year. In addition to her share of this loss, Ms. TN had the following income items:

Salary	$59,000
Interest and dividends	4,400

a. Based on these facts, compute Ms. TN's AGI.

b. How would your computation change if Ms. TN's salary were $128,000 rather than $59,000?

c. How would your computation change if Ms. TN's salary were $200,000 rather than $59,000?

12. Ms. A owns an interest in the ABCD Partnership, which is a passive activity for Ms. A. At the beginning of the year, Ms. A projected that her share of ABCD's current year business loss will be $25,000. She also projects the following income items.

Net profit from her consulting business operated as a sole proprietorship	$80,000
Interest and dividends	1,500

Ms. A is considering buying a rental house that should generate $18,000 income by the end of the year. Based on these facts, compute Ms. A's projected AGI and the tax cost of her projected rent income.

13. Mr. D earned an $85,000 salary this year. He recognized a $12,000 loss on a securities sale and a $14,000 gain on the sale of a limited partnership interest. Mr. D's share of the partnership's business income through date of sale was $2,100. (Both the gain and the business income qualify as passive activity income.) Mr. D was allocated a $13,900 business loss from an S corporation. Because he does not materially participate in the S corporation's business, his interest is a passive activity. Based on these facts, compute Mr. D's AGI.

14. Mr. JS died on June 19. At the date of his death, the total market value of his property was $10 million and he had $789,000 of outstanding debts. His executor paid $13,000 of funeral expenses and $82,600 of accounting and legal fees to settle JS's estate. In Mr. JS's will, he bequeathed $500,000 to the First Lutheran Church of Milwaukee and $1 million to Western Wisconsin College. He bequeathed his art collection (valued at $2.4 million) to his wife and the residual of his estate to his three children from a prior marriage. Based on these facts, compute Mr. JS's taxable estate.

15. Mrs. WP owns investment land with a $138,000 basis and a fair market value of $200,000. Compute the after-tax sales proceeds in each of the following cases:

   a. Mrs. WP sells the land herself. Her taxable income before considering the long-term gain on sale is $310,000.

   b. Mrs. WP gives a 25 percent interest in the land to each of her four single adult grandchildren (without incurring a gift tax). The grandchildren immediately sell the land. Each grandchild's taxable income before considering the gain on sale is $8,000.

   c. Mrs. WP dies while still owning the land. Her single daughter inherits the land and immediately sells it. The daughter's taxable income before considering the gain on sale is $79,000.

Issue Recognition Problems

Identify the tax issue or issues suggested by the following situations and state each issue in the form of a question.

1. Mr. X invests every year in Series EE savings bonds. He recently projected that his sole proprietorship will generate a sizable loss this year and he wants to accelerate income from other sources into the year to offset the loss. He could elect to recognize $28,000 of accrued interest on the savings bonds he now owns. However, he does not want to recognize current income on the Series EE bonds he will purchase in future years.

2. At the beginning of the year, Ms. A owned 2,900 shares of SBS stock with a basis of $32 per share. The corporation paid a 50 percent stock dividend during the year, and Ms. A received 1,450 additional SBS shares. Prior to this dividend, the market price per share was $90. After the dividend, the price fell to $65.

3. In 1993, Mr. L paid $18,000 to BN Inc. for a newly issued bond with a stated redemption value of $30,000. To date, Mr. L has recognized $6,000 of the original issue discount (OID) as ordinary interest income. In the current year, BN Inc. went bankrupt and informed Mr. L that his bond was worthless.

4. Mr. and Mrs. G paid $53,000 for a corporate bond with a stated redemption value of $50,000. They paid the $3,000 premium because the bond's annual interest rate is higher than the current market interest rate.

5. Three years ago, Mrs. B purchased 1,000 shares of NN Corporation stock from an unrelated party for $12 per share. Subsequent to her purchase, the value of the shares steadily declined. Two weeks ago, an unrelated party offered to buy Mrs. B's shares for 30 cents per share. She declined the offer and immediately mailed her shares to NN's secretary-treasurer with a note declaring her intention to abandon the shares.

6. Two years ago, Ms. X loaned $3,500 to her 20-year-old daughter who used the loan proceeds to buy a used car. This year, the daughter sent a letter to Ms. X informing her mother that she could not repay the debt.

7. Mr. O was a 25 percent partner in the MNOP Partnership, which operated a gift and souvenir shop. Mr. O materially participated in the partnership business. Several years ago, Mr. O lent the partnership $10,000 in return for a written note in which MNOP promised to repay $10,000 plus 12 percent interest in five years. Unfortunately, the partnership business went bankrupt before the loan was repaid.

8. At the beginning of the year, Ms. T had a $29,000 capital loss carryforward from 1997 and a $8,200 suspended passive activity loss carryforward from 1996. Ms. T died on September 12. Ms. T did not recognize any capital gain or passive activity income during the year.

9. Ms. N has $60,000 of suspended passive activity losses from her interest in the EZ Limited Partnership. In December, she sold this interest to N Inc., a regular corporation solely owned by Ms. N.

10. Mr. B has a $7,900 adjusted basis in his 5 percent limited interest in the PKO Partnership. He also has $22,000 of suspended passive activity losses from PKO. Mr. B recently sent a letter to PKO's corporate general partner formally abandoning his equity in the partnership.

11. Mr. OG, a 66-year-old divorced individual, has two children with his former wife. Mr. OG recently married a 45-year-old woman with no property of her own. Therefore, Mr. OG plans to change his will to provide that when he dies, his fortune will be placed in a trust. His current wife is entitled to the income from the trust for as long as she lives, but she has no direct ownership in the trust property. When she dies, Mr. OG's two children will inherit everything.

12. Mr. D died on March 8. His taxable estate includes an individual retirement account (IRA) with a $140,000 balance. Mr. D's contributions to this IRA were fully deductible. His son is the beneficiary of the IRA.

13. Ms. AS died on June 1. She and her surviving husband were co-owners of real property with an adjusted basis of $200,000 and a fair market value on June 1 of $1.6 million. Mr. AS inherited his wife's half of the property.

Tax Planning Cases

1. Ms. K, who is in the 39.6 percent marginal tax bracket, made the following purchases of stock in KDS Inc., a closely held corporation:

July 12, 1990	1,400 shares at $25 per share
December 3, 1995	800 shares at $46 per share
September 30, 1997	2,000 shares at $49 per share
February 2, 1998	750 shares at $53 per share

In November 1998, Ms. K agreed to sell 1,000 KDS shares to Mr. N for $60 per share. Which shares should she sell to maximize her after-tax cash from the sale?

2. Ms. EH is the owner and beneficiary of a $150,000 insurance policy on her mother's life. Ms. EH has paid $46,000 of premiums and now the policy is fully paid up (no more premiums are due). Ms. EH needs money and is considering cashing in the policy for its $80,000 cash surrender value. Alternatively, she can borrow $70,000 against the policy from the insurance company. She will pay 5 percent yearly interest (a nondeductible personal expense) and repay the loan from the death benefit. Ms. EH's mother is age 68 and in poor health. Ms. EH believes that her mother will live no more than 10 years. Ms. EH's marginal tax rate is 31 percent. Based on these facts and assuming a 10 percent discount rate, should Ms. EH cash in the policy or borrow against it?

3. Mr. and Mrs. KQ are evaluating an investment in undeveloped land. The cost of the land is $100,000, and the couple can borrow $60,000 of the purchase price at 8 percent. They will pay interest only in years 2 through 6. The annual property tax on the land will be $1,200 in years 2 through 6. Mr. and Mrs. KQ project that they can sell the land in year 6 for $160,000 and repay the $60,000 loan from the sales proceeds. The couple is in the 39.6 percent tax bracket and uses a 10 percent discount rate to compute net present value. Determine if Mr. and Mrs. KQ should make this investment under the following assumptions:

a. Mr. and Mrs. KQ have sufficient net investment income and other itemized deductions so that the $6,000 annual carrying charge (interest plus property tax) is fully deductible in years 2 through 6.

b. Because they do not have sufficient net investment income or other itemized deductions, Mr. and Mrs. KQ elect to capitalize the annual carrying charge to the basis of the land.

4. Mr. and Mrs. U's average taxable income on their joint return is $260,000. During the current year and the next several years, Mr. U plans to exercise incentive stock options with an annual bargain element of $65,000. In addition to this bargain element, the couple has approximately $10,000 of positive AMT adjustments and preferences each year. Mr. and Mrs. U want to invest $50,000 of excess funds. They could purchase either a corporate bond paying 10 percent annual interest or a newly issued private activity tax-exempt bond paying 7.5 percent annual interest. Both bonds have identical risk.

Based on these facts, which investment yields the greater after-tax cash flow?

5. Ms. ZH is evaluating two investment opportunities with identical risk. Investment A will generate $7,000 of income and cash flow in years 1 through 3. Investment P will generate a $25,000 passive activity loss in years 1 and 2 and no cash flow. In year 3, Investment P will generate $73,000 of taxable income and $23,000 of cash flow. After three years, both investments will return Ms. ZH's initial cash contribution. Ms. ZH uses an 11 percent discount rate to compute net present value. Determine the superior investment under each of the following assumptions:

a. Ms. ZH's marginal tax rate over the three-year investment period is 28 percent and she owns no other passive activities.

b. Ms. ZH's marginal tax rate over the three-year investment period is 36 percent and she owns rental property generating $40,000 annual income.

Appendix 15–A
Comprehensive Schedule D Problem

In 1997, Mr. and Mrs. Lowell made the following security sales.

	Date Acquired	Date Sold	Tax Basis	Selling Price
1,782 shares of ZT Inc. common stock	1/28/90	9/3/97	$14,900	$36,900
119 shares of MN Inc. preferred stock	2/11/94	9/12/97	9,000	7,050
2,040 shares of GG Inc. common stock	5/14/96	10/6/97	18,000	22,400
45 shares of Pluto mutual fund	8/3/97	12/30/97	3,100	3,500

Their only other property transaction for the year was the sale of a rental house for $176,000. Mr. and Mrs. Lowell purchased this property in 1991 for $172,000 and deducted $34,000 of straight-line depreciation through date of sale. They reported the sale on Form 4797 and carried their $38,000 Section 1231 gain from this form to line 11, Part II, Schedule D.

Other pertinent facts:

- Mr. and Mrs. Lowell received a 1997 Form 1099 from Pluto mutual fund reporting a $700 long-term capital gain distribution, none of which was 28 percent rate gain.

- In 1994, Mrs. Lowell loaned $3,000 to a friend who needed the money to begin a new business venture. In 1997, the friend declared personal bankruptcy and Mrs. Lowell decided not to pursue collection of the $3,000 debt in court.

- Mr. and Mrs. Lowell have a $1,200 long-term capital loss carryforward into 1997.

- Mr. and Mrs. Lowell's 1997 taxable income (as reported on line 38 of their jointly filed Form 1040) is $166,000.

The above information and the calculation of Mr. and Mrs. Lowell's regular tax liability for 1997 are reflected on the following Schedule D.

SCHEDULE D
(Form 1040)

Department of the Treasury
Internal Revenue Service   (99)

Capital Gains and Losses

▶ Attach to Form 1040.   ▶ See Instructions for Schedule D (Form 1040).

▶ Use Schedule D-1 for more space to list transactions for lines 1 and 8.

OMB No. 1545-0074

1997

Attachment
Sequence No. **12**

Name(s) shown on Form 1040   *MR. and MRS. Lowell*

Your social security number   406 | 44 | 3150

Part I   Short-Term Capital Gains and Losses—Assets Held One Year or Less

(a) Description of property (Example: 100 sh. XYZ Co.)	(b) Date acquired (Mo., day, yr.)	(c) Date sold (Mo., day, yr.)	(d) Sales price (see page D-3)	(e) Cost or other basis (see page D-4)	(f) GAIN or (LOSS) FOR ENTIRE YEAR. Subtract (e) from (d)	
1 *45 sh. Pluto MF*	*8·3·97*	*12·30·97*	*3,500*	*3,100*	*400*	
Nonbusiness bad debt					*(3,000)*	

2 Enter your short-term totals, if any, from Schedule D-1, line 2	**2**				
3 Total short-term sales price amounts. Add column (d) of lines 1 and 2 . . .	**3**	*3,500*			
4 Short-term gain from Forms 2119 and 6252, and short-term gain or (loss) from Forms 4684, 6781, and 8824			**4**		
5 Net short-term gain or (loss) from partnerships, S corporations, estates, and trusts from Schedule(s) K-1			**5**		
6 Short-term capital loss carryover. Enter the amount, if any, from line 9 of your 1996 Capital Loss Carryover Worksheet			**6** (	)	
7 Net short-term capital gain or (loss). Combine lines 1 through 6 in column (f). . . . . ▶			**7**	*(2,600)*	

Part II   Long-Term Capital Gains and Losses—Assets Held More Than One Year

(a) Description of property (Example: 100 sh. XYZ Co.)	(b) Date acquired (Mo., day, yr.)	(c) Date sold (Mo., day, yr.)	(d) Sales price (see page D-3)	(e) Cost or other basis (see page D-4)	(f) GAIN or (LOSS) FOR ENTIRE YEAR. Subtract (e) from (d)	(g) 28% RATE GAIN or (LOSS) (see instr. below)
8 *1,782 sh. ZT common*	*1·28·90*	*9·3·97*	*36,900*	*14,900*	*22,000*	*–*
119 sh. MN preferred	*2·11·94*	*9·12·97*	*7,050*	*9,000*	*(1,950)*	*–*
2040 sh. GG common	*5·14·96*	*10·6·97*	*22,400*	*18,000*	*4,400*	*4,400*

9 Enter your long-term totals, if any, from Schedule D-1, line 9	**9**				
10 Total long-term sales price amounts. Add column (d) of lines 8 and 9 . . .	**10**	*66,350*			
11 Gain from Form 4797, Part I; long-term gain from Forms 2119, 2439, and 6252; and long-term gain or (loss) from Forms 4684, 6781, and 8824 . .	**11**	*38,000*		*–*	
12 Net long-term gain or (loss) from partnerships, S corporations, estates, and trusts from Schedule(s) K-1	**12**				
13 Capital gain distributions	**13**	*700*		*–*	
14 Long-term capital loss carryover. Enter in both columns (f) and (g) the amount, if any, from line 14 of your 1996 Capital Loss Carryover Worksheet . . .	**14** (	*1,200*)	(	*1,200*)	
15 Combine lines 8 through 14 in column (g)	**15**			*3,200*	
16 Net long-term capital gain or (loss). Combine lines 8 through 14 in column (f). . . . . ▶	**16**	*61,950*			

* **28% Rate Gain or Loss** includes all gains and losses in Part II, column (f) from sales, exchanges, or conversions (including installment payments received) **either**: ● **Before** May 7, 1997, or
● **After** July 28, 1997, for assets held more than 1 year but **not** more than 18 months.
It also includes **ALL** "collectibles gains and losses" (as defined on page D-4).

For Paperwork Reduction Act Notice, see Form 1040 Instructions.   Cat. No. 11338H   Schedule D (Form 1040) 1997

Schedule D (Form 1040) 1997   Page **2**

Part III   **Summary of Parts I and II**

17	Combine lines 7 and 16. If a loss, go to line 18. If a gain, enter the gain on Form 1040, line 13	**17**	59,350

Next: Complete Form 1040 through line 38. Then, go to **Part IV** to figure your tax if:
   • Both lines 16 and 17 are gains, **and**
   • Form 1040, line 38, is more than zero.

18   If line 17 is a loss, enter here and as a (loss) on Form 1040, line 13, the **smaller** of these losses:
   • The loss on line 17; **or**
   • ($3,000) or, if married filing separately, ($1,500) . . . .   **18** (-   )

Next: Complete Form 1040 through line 36. Then, complete the **Capital Loss Carryover**
        Worksheet on page D-4 if:
   • The loss on line 17 exceeds the loss on line 18, **or**
   • Form 1040, line 36, is a loss.

Part IV   **Tax Computation Using Maximum Capital Gains Rates**

#	Description			#	Value
19	Enter your taxable income from Form 1040, line 38			**19**	166,000
20	Enter the **smaller** of line 16 or line 17	**20**	59,350		
21	If you are filing Form 4952, enter the amount from Form 4952, line 4e	**21**	-		
22	Subtract line 21 from line 20. If zero or less, enter -0-	**22**	59,350		
23	Combine lines 7 and 15. If zero or less, enter -0-	**23**	600		
24	Enter the **smaller** of line 15 or line 23, but not less than zero . . .	**24**	600		
25	Enter your unrecaptured section 1250 gain, if any (see page D-4) .	**25**	34,000		
26	Add lines 24 and 25	**26**	34,600		
27	Subtract line 26 from line 22. If zero or less, enter -0-			**27**	24,750
28	Subtract line 27 from line 19. If zero or less, enter -0-			**28**	141,250
29	Enter the **smaller** of line 19 or $41,200 ($24,650 if single; $20,600 if married filing separately; $33,050 if head of household)			**29**	41,200
30	Enter the **smaller** of line 28 or line 29			**30**	41,200
31	Subtract line 22 from line 19. If zero or less, enter -0-			**31**	106,650
32	Enter the **larger** of line 30 or line 31			**32**	106,650
33	Figure the tax on the amount on line 32. Use the Tax Table or Tax Rate Schedules, whichever applies . . . . ▶			**33**	24,718
34	Enter the amount from line 29			**34**	41,200
35	Enter the amount from line 28			**35**	141,250
36	Subtract line 35 from line 34. If zero or less, enter -0-			**36**	0
37	Multiply line 36 by 10% (.10) . . . . ▶			**37**	0
38	Enter the **smaller** of line 19 or line 27			**38**	24,750
39	Enter the amount from line 36			**39**	0
40	Subtract line 39 from line 38. If zero or less, enter -0-			**40**	24,750
41	Multiply line 40 by 20% (.20) . . . . ▶			**41**	4,950
42	Enter the **smaller** of line 22 or line 25			**42**	34,000
43	Add lines 22 and 32	**43**	166,000		
44	Enter the amount from line 19	**44**	166,000		
45	Subtract line 44 from line 43. If zero or less, enter -0-			**45**	0
46	Subtract line 45 from line 42. If zero or less, enter -0-			**46**	34,000
47	Multiply line 46 by 25% (.25) . . . . ▶			**47**	8,500
48	Enter the amount from line 19			**48**	166,000
49	Add lines 32, 36, 40, and 46			**49**	165,400
50	Subtract line 49 from line 48			**50**	600
51	Multiply line 50 by 28% (.28) . . . . ▶			**51**	168
52	Add lines 33, 37, 41, 47, and 51			**52**	38,336
53	Figure the tax on the amount on line 19. Use the Tax Table or Tax Rate Schedules, whichever applies			**53**	43,829
54	**Tax.** Enter the **smaller** of line 52 or line 53 here and on Form 1040, line 39 . . . . . ▶			**54**	38,336

16

Tax Consequences of Personal Activities

Learning Objectives

After studying this chapter, you should be able to:

1. Distinguish between gratuitous receipts that are included in taxable income and those that are nontaxable to the recipient.

2. Describe the tax consequences of property settlements pursuant to a divorce, alimony, and child support payments to both parties to the transaction.

3. Present the arguments for and against the income taxation of Social Security benefits.

4. Determine the extent to which medical expenses, local, state, and foreign tax payments, and charitable contributions are allowed as itemized deductions.

5. Compute the itemized deduction for casualty and theft losses.

6. Describe the tax treatment of revenues and expenses associated with a hobby.

7. Explain the preferential tax treatment of imputed income from owner-occupied housing.

8. Compute the itemized deduction for home mortgage interest.

9. Describe the preferential tax treatment of gain realized on the sale of a personal residence.

10. Identify the itemized deductions that are limited or disallowed in the computation of alternative minimum taxable income (AMTI).

To this point, Part Five of *Principles of Taxation for Business and Investment Planning* has focused on the consequences to individuals when they engage in profit-motivated activities. We learned how to compute taxable income derived from business, employment, and investment activities and discovered many effective techniques for reducing the tax burden on such income. Chapter 16 introduces a new topic: the tax consequences of those activities in which people engage for personal reasons. The first section of this chapter describes a number of common economic benefits that are not derived from business, employment, or investment activities and discusses the extent to which such benefits are subject to income tax. The second section of the chapter concentrates on the tax rules pertaining to personal expenses or losses and identifies the limited circumstances under which such expenses and losses result in a tax savings. The third section explains the significant tax advantages of home ownership, while the last section integrates the material introduced in Chapter 16 into the alternative minimum tax (AMT) system.

Gross Income from Whatever Source Derived

Section 61 of the Internal Revenue Code states that gross income means all income from whatever source derived. This core principle creates a presumption that any receipt of cash or property that increases an individual's net worth is subject to the income tax. The context in which the receipt occurred or the source of the receipt is irrelevant.[1] The tax law does make exceptions to the inclusive rule of Section 61, and we will identify a number of such exceptions in this chapter. Nevertheless, individuals who receive any valuable economic benefit during the year should assume such benefit is taxable, even if the benefit arose from a purely personal activity.

Gratuitous Receipts

Objective 1
Distinguish between gratuitous receipts that are included in taxable income and those that are nontaxable to the recipient.

People who receive prizes or awards must recognize the monetary value as income.[2] This general rule applies to awards based on achievement or merit such as the Nobel and Pulitzer prizes. However, students who are degree candidates at an educational institution may exclude scholarship or fellowship awards from income, but only to the extent the scholarship or fellowship pays for tuition, fees, books, supplies, and equipment required by the institution.[3] The general rule also encompasses receipts attributable entirely to good luck, such as lottery jackpots, raffle or door prizes, and gambling winnings. The prize or award need not consist of cash; the game show contestant who wins a trip to Paris must include the value of the trip in taxable income.[4]

The major exception to the rule that gratuitous receipts are taxable applies to gifts and inheritances.[5] Donees can exclude the cash or the value of property received from a donor from income. Individuals who inherit cash or property under the terms of a decedent's will or under state intestacy laws don't report the receipt as an income item on Form 1040. Similarly, life insurance proceeds are nontaxable. An individual named as beneficiary under a life insurance contract receives a gratuitous transfer of the proceeds on the death of the insured. The beneficiary may exclude the entire death benefit from income.[6]

> ***Gratuitous Receipts.*** During the current year, Ms. K received the following items:

---

[1] This principle applies to receipts derived from unlawful activities such as embezzlement or extortion. Consequently, even illegal income is subject to income tax. *James* v. *United States*, 366 U.S. 213 (1961).

[2] §74. The law provides a narrow exception for certain employee achievement awards to the extent the award consists of tangible property worth no more than $1,600. This is called *the gold watch exception.*

[3] §117.

[4] *Reginald Turner*, TC Memo 1954-38.

[5] §102.

[6] §101(a).

Birthday gift of cash from her dad	$ 1,500
Set of dishes won at a church raffle (retail value)	600
Pearl ring inherited from her grandmother (appraised value)	2,600
Insurance proceeds from a policy on her grandmother's life	50,000
Tuition scholarship to Ohio State University	12,000

The only item that Ms. K must report on her Form 1040 is the $600 value of her raffle prize.

Gift or Compensation Income?   Reverend Lloyd Goodwin received an annual salary plus the use of a parsonage from the church at which he served as pastor. The church held three "special occasion" Sundays each year when members of the congregation were invited to make anonymous cash contributions to their pastor and his family. The associate pastor collected the contributions and delivered them to Reverend Goodwin. For the three tax years in question, the contributions totaled $42,250. Reverend Goodwin did not report the contributions on his tax return. The IRS concluded that the contributions represented employment compensation to the pastor and should be included in taxable income. Members of the congregation who testified on behalf of Reverend Goodwin described the contributions as gifts made out of "love, respect, and admiration" for their pastor. The court, however, concluded that the contributions were regular payments made by persons to whom Reverend Goodwin provided professional services and, therefore, represented taxable compensation rather than nontaxable gifts.[7]

Legal Settlements

Individuals may be entitled to receive economic benefits under legal agreements or settlements. For instance, a person who has suffered an injury or detriment because of the unjustifiable actions of another party may be awarded damages by a court of law. The general rule is that legal damages are taxable income unless they represent compensation for physical injury or illness.[8]

Legal Damages.   Mrs. T was walking along a city sidewalk when she was struck by falling debris from a construction project. Mrs. T sued the construction company for negligence and was awarded a $300,000 settlement: $100,000 as com-

---

[7]*Goodwin* v. *Commissioner*, 67 F.3d 149 (CA-8, 1995).
[8]§104(a)(2).

pensation for her physical pain and trauma plus $200,000 punitive damages (damages intended to punish a defendant for extreme misconduct). Mrs. T may exclude $100,000 of this receipt from income but must report and pay tax on the $200,000 punitive damages.[9]

Objective 2
Describe the tax consequences of property settlements pursuant to divorce, alimony, and child support payments to both parties to the transaction.

Divorce.   The divorce of a married couple is a personal event that may have profound economic consequences. The divorce decree, the legal instrument specifying the rights and obligations of the divorcing parties, may require one party to transfer ownership of valuable property to the other. For *income tax* purposes, this transfer is treated as a gift, regardless of the degree of affection or animosity underlying the transfer.[10] As a result, the transferor recognizes no gain or loss on the disposition of the property. The transferee recognizes no income on receipt of the property and takes a carryover tax basis from the transferor.

The divorce decree may require one party to pay alimony to the other. Alimony consists of a series of cash payments by which a person discharges an ongoing legal obligation to support an ex-spouse. The recipient must include the alimony payments in income, while the payer may deduct them as an adjustment in computing adjusted gross income (AGI).[11] If the divorcing couple has dependent children, the parent who surrenders custody of the children may be required to pay child support to the custodial parent. Child support payments (in contrast to alimony) are not taxable income to the recipient and are nondeductible by the payer. The payment of child support raises the question of which parent can claim the personal exemption for a dependent child. Regardless of the amount of child support involved, the custodial parent is entitled to the exemption unless he or she signs a written declaration granting the exemption to the noncustodial parent.[12]

Payments Pursuant to a Divorce.   Mr. and Mrs. SV recently divorced. Under the terms of the divorce decree, Mr. SV transferred $600,000 worth of marketable securities to Mrs. SV as a property settlement. His basis in the securities was $319,000. Mr. SV is required to pay $1,500 a month to his ex-wife: $900 of alimony and $600 of child support for their five-year-old daughter, who lives with Mrs. SV.

Mr. SV did not realize gain on the surrender of the appreciated securities, and Mrs. SV did not recognize income on their receipt. She has a $319,000 basis in the securities. Mrs. SV recognizes the $900 monthly alimony payment as income, and Mr. SV is allowed a corresponding deduction. Mrs. SV is entitled to claim a personal exemption for the daughter on her Form 1040 unless she grants the exemption to Mr. SV.

[9]Mrs. T's legal fees allocable to the taxable portion of her settlement are a miscellaneous itemized deduction. See Reg. §1.212-1(k) and IRS Publication 529, *Miscellaneous Deductions.*
[10]§1041. The transfer is not subject to gift tax.
[11]§71 requires the income inclusion, while §215 and §62(a)(1) allow the deduction. The deduction is reported on line 30a, page 1, Form 1040. While legal fees paid in connection with a divorce are generally nondeductible, any fee properly attributable to the collection of alimony is a miscellaneous itemized deduction. Reg. §1.262-1(b)(7).
[12]§152(e).

Government Transfer Payments

People who receive need-based payments from a local, state, or federal government agency may exclude the payments from income.[13] Consequently, benefits provided through public assistance programs such as school lunches, food stamps, and welfare are nontaxable to the recipients. In contrast, people who are entitled to receive government transfer payments irrespective of any demonstrated economic need must include the payments in income. For instance, unemployed workers must report and pay federal income tax on unemployment compensation received from their state government.[14]

Objective 3
Present the arguments for and against the income taxation of Social Security benefits.

Social Security.   The question of whether Social Security benefits should be subject to the federal income tax is controversial. One political camp argues that these benefits should be fully taxable because they are not tied to actual financial need of the recipient. The opposing camp argues that Social Security benefits should be entirely immune to the income tax. After all, aren't retirees entitled to their benefits because they paid nondeductible employee payroll tax or self-employment tax during their working years? The federal government's complicated approach to taxing Social Security benefits reflects a cautious compromise between these polar positions. In very general terms:

- Married couples with less than $32,000 and single individuals with less than $25,000 of modified AGI are not required to pay tax on their benefits.
- Couples with modified AGI between $32,000 and $44,000 and single individuals with modified AGI between $25,000 and $34,000 may have to pay tax on 50 percent of their benefits.
- Couples with more than $44,000 and single individuals with more than $34,000 of modified AGI may have to pay tax on 85 percent of their benefits.[15]

The complete details of the computation are incorporated into a Social Security Worksheet included as Appendix 16–A to this chapter.

Gains on Sales and Exchanges of Personal Assets

Most personal assets fall into the category of *consumer durables*—tangible assets that people buy for their private use and enjoyment. Individuals can't recover the cost of these assets through depreciation. Thus, the initial cost basis of consumer durables is not adjusted downward, even though the market value of such goods invariably decreases over time. For this reason, when people sell consumer durables they usually realize a loss on the transaction. As we will discuss later in the chapter, these personal losses are nondeductible.

People occasionally hold personal assets that do not wear out, break down, or become outdated but that actually increase in value. Collectibles such as postage stamps and antiques are good examples. If an individual does realize a gain on the sale of a collectible, the gain is either short-term capital gain or 28 percent rate gain, depending on the holding period of the asset.[16]

---

[13]See Rev. Rul. 71-425, 1971-2 CB 76.

[14]§85.

[15]§86. For purposes of this general summary, modified AGI includes one-half of any Social Security benefits received and any tax-exempt income earned during the year.

[16]According to §1221(3), literary, musical, or artistic compositions, letters, and memoranda are not capital assets in the hands of either the individual who created the property or any individual who received such property as a gift from the creator. These individuals recognize ordinary income if they sell such assets at a gain.

Personal Expenses

Objective 4
Determine the extent to which medical expenses, local, state, and foreign tax payments, and charitable contributions are allowed as itemized deductions.

The Internal Revenue Code contains the unequivocal statement that no deduction is allowed for personal, living, or family expenses.[17] Accordingly, the everyday costs of managing a household, raising a family, pursuing social or civic interests, and enjoying leisure time do not result in any tax benefit to individuals. The tax law bends this rule with respect to three major categories of personal expenses: medical expenses, local, state, and foreign tax payments, and charitable contributions. Individuals who incur such expenses may be entitled to an itemized deduction on Schedule A, which is reproduced as Exhibit 16–1.

Medical Expenses

Individuals may claim an itemized deduction for the expenses of medical care for themselves and their family.[18] Deductible expenses include payments for services rendered by health care practitioners (doctors, dentists, chiropractors, etc.), payments to treatment facilities (outpatient clinics and hospitals), and the cost of medical aids (eyeglasses, hearing aids, crutches, wheelchairs, etc.) and prescription drugs. Premiums paid to purchase health and accident insurance also qualify as medical expenses. When individuals receive payments from their insurance carriers, the receipts are treated as nontaxable reimbursements of the medical expenses to which they relate.[19]

The medical expense deduction is limited to the excess of the taxpayer's total unreimbursed expenses over 7.5 percent of AGI.

Medical Expense Deduction.   Mr. and Mrs. C incurred $4,400 of qualified medical expenses (including insurance premiums) during the year. They received a $1,800 payment from their insurance company in partial reimbursement of these expenses. If the couple's AGI on this year's Form 1040 is $30,000, they can claim an itemized deduction of $350.

Qualified medical expenses	$ 4,400
Insurance reimbursement	(1,800)
Unreimbursed expenses	$ 2,600
AGI threshold ($30,000 AGI × 7.5%)	(2,250)
Medical expense deduction	$ 350

If Mr. and Mrs. C's AGI exceeds $34,667, their AGI threshold will exceed their total unreimbursed expenses and they will have no medical expense deduction for the year.

As this example demonstrates, the AGI limitation restricts the number of taxpayers who actually receive a tax benefit from their medical expenses. Only those unfortunate

---

[17] §262.

[18] §213.

[19] §105(b). Payments received under a workmen's compensation act for personal injuries or sickness are similarly nontaxable. §104(a)(1).

families that bear extraordinary health care costs receive any tax relief from this particular itemized deduction.

Local, State, and Foreign Tax Payments

Individuals may deduct income taxes and real or personal property taxes paid to local, state, or foreign governments.[20] This itemized deduction is limited in scope because it ignores many other taxes that people routinely pay. State and local sales and use taxes, gift and estate taxes, the employee payroll tax, and employment taxes paid with respect to household employees are all nondeductible personal expenses.[21] Of course, the federal income tax itself is a nondeductible expense. But interestingly, the tax law authorizes a miscellaneous itemized deduction for "expenses paid or incurred in connection with the determination, collection, or refund of any tax, whether the taxing authority be Federal, State, or municipal."[22] Because of this rule, fees paid to tax practitioners for return preparation and professional advice are deductible.

Charitable Contributions

People who give money or property to nonprofit organizations that have been granted tax-exempt status by the IRS can claim the contribution as an itemized deduction.[23] The policy rationale is that the availability of this deduction encourages private citizens to support worthy causes that benefit society as a whole. By allowing the charitable contribution deduction, the federal government indirectly subsidizes thousands of social, civic, cultural, religious, scientific, environmental, and educational institutions. In 1997, this subsidy represented a tax expenditure of over $25 billion. There are broad limits on the charitable contribution deduction that an individual may claim. In general, the annual deduction for gifts to public charities cannot exceed 50 percent of AGI. Any contribution in excess of such limit is carried forward as an itemized deduction for five years.

> ***Charitable Contribution Limitation.***   In 1996, First Lady Hilary Rodham Clinton earned $742,000 of royalties from her book, *It Takes a Village,* kept $152,000 to pay state and federal tax on the income, and donated the $590,000 remainder to charity. However, because the Clinton's AGI on their 1996 joint return was $1,065,101, their charitable contribution deduction was limited to $532,551.

When an individual donates property to charity, the amount of the deduction depends on the character of the property. If the property is a long-term capital asset, the deduction generally equals the fair market value of the property. For any other type of property, the deduction is the *lesser* of fair market value or the donor's basis.[24] Because of these rules, people who own highly appreciated capital assets enjoy a significant tax break if they give the assets to charity.

---

[20]§164. Individuals may elect to claim a credit instead of a deduction for foreign income tax paid.
[21]§275.
[22]Reg. §1.212–1(l).
[23]§170. Contributions of $250 or more to a single charity must be substantiated by a written acknowledgment from the charity. §170(f)(8).
[24]See §170(e).

Donation of Appreciated Property.   Mr. Q, who is in the 39.6 percent marginal tax bracket, owns an oil painting that he bought years ago for $50,000. The painting's value was recently appraised at $400,000. If Mr. Q gives this painting to the Metropolitan Museum of Art, his itemized deduction is $400,000 and his tax savings is $158,400 (39.6 percent of $400,000). Most of the savings is attributable to the $350,000 appreciation in the value of the painting, an unrealized gain on which Mr. Q never paid nor will pay income tax.

Tax Subsidies for Higher Education Expenses

Costs incurred by individuals for their own education or the education of their children are nondeductible personal expenses. However, Congress has become increasingly enthusiastic about subsidizing the cost of post-secondary education (college or vocational training) through federal tax incentives. The Internal Revenue Code contains a profusion of tax benefits intended to help low- and middle-income families save and pay for higher education. The most widely available of these education incentives can be summarized as follows:

- Individuals can exclude the interest earned on the redemption of qualified Series EE savings bonds to the extent of tuition and fees paid to enroll the individual or a family member in a post-secondary educational institution. In 1998, the exclusion is gradually phased out for individuals with AGI in excess of $78,350 (married filing jointly) or $52,250 (single individuals and heads of household).[25]

- Individuals can claim a **HOPE scholarship credit** based on tuition and fees paid during the first two years of post-secondary education. The maximum annual credit is $1,500 per eligible student. Individuals may also claim a **lifetime learning credit** based on 20 percent of tuition and fees paid for post-secondary education. (Tuition and fees for which a taxpayer claims a HOPE scholarship credit cannot be taken into account for a lifetime learning credit.) Currently, the lifetime learning credit is limited to $5,000 per year. Both of these credits are gradually phased out for individuals with AGI in excess of $80,000 (married filing jointly) or $40,000 (single individuals and heads of household).[26]

- Individuals can contribute a maximum of $500 every year to a tax-exempt **education IRA** established for a beneficiary (typically the individual's child or grandchild) under the age of 18. Withdrawals from the IRA are nontaxable to the extent of the beneficiary's higher education expenses. The maximum contribution is gradually phased out for individuals with AGI in excess of $150,000 (married filing jointly) and $95,000 (single individuals and heads of household).[27]

- Individuals can deduct interest paid on a qualified education loan in the computation of AGI. A **qualified education loan** is any debt incurred to pay higher education expenses. Only interest paid during the first 60 months for

[25]§135.
[26]§25A.
[27]§530.

which interest is required is eligible for deduction, and the maximum amount deductible in 1998 is $1,000. The deduction is gradually phased out for individuals with AGI in excess of $60,000 (married filing jointly) or $40,000 (single individuals and heads of household).[28]

Personal Losses

Losses on Sales and Exchanges of Personal Assets

In earlier chapters of this text, we learned that individuals are allowed to deduct losses realized on the disposition of business or investment assets. While the capital loss and passive activity loss limitations may defer recognition of such losses to future years, sooner or later the losses reduce the individual's AGI and result in a tax savings. If an individual realizes a loss on the disposition of a personal asset, the basic rule is that such loss is nondeductible. In many instances, this rule is of minimal economic significance. Suppose a person pays $1,500 for a new refrigerator for his kitchen, uses the refrigerator for eight years, then sells it at a garage sale for $200. The person's realized loss of $1,300 ($200 amount realized less $1,500 cost basis) is nondeductible, and the sale of the personal asset is a nonevent for tax purposes.

The obvious situation in which a nondeductible loss may cause real economic distress is when an individual suffers a loss on the sale of a personal residence. For many people, their residence is the most valuable asset they own, and they consider it as a long-term investment. Even so, owner-occupied housing is a personal, rather than an investment, asset for tax purposes. As a result, people who sell their home at a loss are often dismayed to discover that the loss does not reduce their taxable income.

> ***Nondeductible Personal Loss.*** Mr. Rooker purchased a membership in a private country club for $20,000. During the 13 years that he and his family were club members, they were assessed $7,000 for the cost of capital improvements to the club's swimming pool, tennis courts, and golf course. In the current year, Mr. Rooker sold his membership to an unrelated party for $15,000. The IRS acknowledged that the club membership was a capital asset and that Mr. Rooker realized a $12,000 loss on the sale ($15,000 amount realized − $27,000 original cost plus assessments). However, the IRS held that the loss was nondeductible because Mr. Rooker held the membership primarily for personal use rather than for investment purposes.[29]

Casualty and Theft Losses

Objective 5
Compute the itemized deduction for casualty and theft losses.

The tax law does allow individuals to claim an itemized deduction for personal property losses arising from casualty or theft.[30] A casualty is a sudden and unexpected event such as a fire, hurricane, earthquake, automobile accident, or vandalism that damages or destroys property. For tax purposes, the loss is the *lesser* of the individ-

---

[28]§221.
[29]This example is based on IRS Letter Ruling 8205045.
[30]§165(c)(3).

ual's tax basis in the property or the decrease in the property's value attributable to the casualty or theft.[31]

Casualty Losses.   Mrs. S owns a sailboat that suffered moderate damage during a hurricane. Her basis in the boat is $27,000, but the decrease in value because of the damage is only $5,000. Accordingly, Mrs. S's casualty loss is $5,000.[32]

     Mrs. S also owned a motorcycle that was totally destroyed in a traffic accident. Her basis in the motorcycle was $18,000, and its value immediately before the accident was $20,000. Even though the decrease in value attributable to the casualty is $20,000, Mrs. S's loss is limited to her $18,000 basis.

     A casualty or theft loss is reduced by any insurance proceeds received by the owner so that only the *unreimbursed* loss is deductible.[33] Furthermore, the loss attributable to each casualty or theft is reduced by a $100 floor. Finally, only the aggregate loss in excess of 10 percent of AGI is deductible.[34]

Casualty Loss Deduction.   Mrs. S in the preceding example received nothing from her insurance company for the damaged sailboat and $7,200 for the destroyed motorcycle. If she suffered no other casualty or theft losses for the year, Mrs. S's aggregate loss is $15,600:

	Sailboat	Motorcycle
Tax basis	$27,000	$18,000
Decrease in value	5,000	20,000
Casualty loss	$ 5,000	$18,000
Insurance proceeds	–0–	(7,200)
Unreimbursed loss	$ 5,000	$10,800
$100 floor per casualty	(100)	(100)
	$ 4,900	$10,700

Aggregate loss: $4,900 + $10,700 = $15,600

     If Mrs. S's AGI is $68,000, her itemized deduction for this loss is $8,800. If her AGI is $130,000, her deduction is only $2,600. If her AGI is $200,000, she has no itemized deduction at all.

---

[31]Reg. §1.165-7(b).

[32]The decrease in value can be determined by independent appraisal or measured by the cost of repairs necessary to restore the property to its original condition. Reg. §1.165-7(a)(2).

[33]If the insurance proceeds exceed the basis of the property, the owner may defer recognition of such gain by replacing the property. See the discussion of involuntary conversions in Chapter 8.

[34]§165(h)(1) and (2).

	AGI		
	$68,000	*$130,000*	*$200,000*
Aggregate casualty loss	$15,600	$ 15,600	$ 15,600
10% AGI threshold	(6,800)	(13,000)	(20,000)
Casualty loss deduction	$ 8,800	$ 2,600	$ –0–

Hobby and Gambling Losses

Objective 6
Describe the tax treatment of revenues and expenses associated with a hobby.

Activities in which people engage primarily for personal enjoyment may nonetheless generate revenues. Consider the case of Mr. C, a practicing physician, who breeds toy poodles as his hobby. Not only does Mr. C exhibit his own animals in local and regional dog shows but he also sells puppies and trains and shows poodles owned by other people. In a good year, Mr. C might earn as much as $3,000 from his canine-related activities. His annual expenses, such as dog food, veterinary fees, and travel to shows generally average $5,000. What are the tax consequences of Mr. C's annual **hobby loss?** Because of the inclusive rule governing income recognition, Mr. C must report his annual revenues as a miscellaneous income item (line 21, page 1, Form 1040). He is allowed a deduction for his expenses but only to the extent of his revenues.[35] Moreover, this deduction is a miscellaneous itemized deduction subject to the 2 percent AGI limitation.

Hobby Loss.   Mr. C's current year revenues from his dog-breeding activities totaled $2,980, while his related expenses totaled $5,300. His AGI (which includes the $2,980 income item) is $86,300. Mr. C may report $2,980 of his expenses as a miscellaneous item on line 22 of Schedule A. However, if this is Mr. C's only miscellaneous item, his deduction is limited to $1,254:

Total miscellaneous items	$ 2,980
AGI threshold ($86,300 × 2%)	(1,726)
Miscellaneous itemized deduction	$ 1,254

This is a very unsatisfactory result for our taxpayer. Mr. C's out-of-pocket hobby expenses exceeded his hobby revenues by $2,320, but his net taxable income from the hobby is $1,726 ($2,980 income less $1,254 itemized deduction). Furthermore, this result assumes that Mr. C can itemize deductions for the year. If he claims the standard deduction, the $2,980 of poodle income is fully taxable and he receives no tax benefit at all from the poodle expenses.

Mr. C's tax consequences would be much more favorable if he could report his dog-breeding activity as a business rather than as a hobby. In such case, he would account for

---

[35] §183.

his revenues and expenses on a Schedule C and could deduct his $2,320 net operating loss in the computation of AGI. In taking this position, Mr. C must be prepared to convince the IRS that he raises and shows his poodles with the "actual and honest objective" of making a profit rather than for recreation.[36] To this end, he should operate in a businesslike manner by maintaining a separate bank account and proper accounting records. He should actively seek out customers by advertising in the appropriate trade journals and should charge the market rate for his products and services. Of course, the best way for Mr. C to prove his intentions is to actually make a profit. The tax law establishes a presumption that any activity generating net income (gross income over deductible expenses) in three out of five consecutive years is a business. In such case, the IRS bears the burden of proof if it reclassifies the activity as a hobby; the IRS rarely, if ever, attempts to do so.

For tax purposes, gambling activities are treated very much like hobbies. Individuals must report their winnings as income and may deduct their losses only to the extent of such winnings. The deduction for gambling losses, however, is not subject to the 2 percent AGI floor on miscellaneous itemized deductions and is reported on line 27 of Schedule A.[37]

Tax Consequences of Home Ownership

Even though an owner-occupied residence is a personal asset, the Internal Revenue Code contains several preferential rules that can make such residence a fine investment. In fact, one of the greatest economic advantages of home ownership stems from the fact that the tax law treats owner-occupied real property as a nonproductive personal asset. Consider the relative economic situations of Mr. HO and Mr. FA. Neither individual owns his own home and each pays $12,000 a year to rent a dwelling. These rent payments are nondeductible personal expenses. During the current year, each man inherits $100,000. Mr. HO uses the money to buy a home, while Mr. FA invests his money in a financial asset yielding 12 percent a year. What are the cash flow implications of their respective purchases?

> **Comparative Cash Flows.**   HO now lives in his own home and no longer pays rent. Consequently, his annual after-tax cash outflow decreases by $12,000. FA continues to pay rent but also receives $12,000 of income on his $100,000 investment. If FA is in a 31 percent marginal tax bracket, his after-tax cash outflow decreases by $8,280.

	Mr. HO	Mr. FA
Cash outflow before purchase:		
Rent expense	$(12,000)	$(12,000)
Cash outflow after purchase:		
Rent expense	$ –0–	$(12,000)

---

[36]*Ronnen*, 90 TC 74, 91 (1988). For recent cases, see *De Boer*, TC Memo 1996-174 and *Holowinski*, TC Memo 1997-168.

[37]See §165(d) and §67(b)(3).

Taxable income from investment	–0–	12,000
Tax cost of income	–0–	(3,720)
	$ –0–	$ (3,720)
Decrease in cash outflow	$(12,000)	$ (8,280)

Objective 7
Explain the preferential tax treatment of imputed income from owner-occupied housing.

How can Mr. HO's decision to buy a personal asset have a better financial result than Mr. FA's decision to buy income-producing investment property? Observe that Mr. HO's personal residence provides an annual benefit worth $12,000—the rent he avoids paying because he owns a home. Economists refer to this benefit as the **imputed income from owner-occupied housing.** The federal tax system has never required homeowners to include such imputed income in their tax base. This preferential treatment creates an economic incentive for people to purchase a home. In our example, both Mr. HO and Mr. FA invested $100,000 in assets yielding a 12 percent before-tax return. Because Mr. HO's return consists of nontaxable imputed income, his after-tax return is also 12 percent, making his purchase of a personal residence the superior investment.

Home Mortgage Interest Deduction

Individuals who borrow money and use the debt proceeds to make a personal expenditure cannot deduct the interest paid on the debt.[38] The major exception to this rule applies to **qualified residence interest,** which individuals may claim as an itemized deduction.[39] Qualified residence interest consists of the interest paid on both acquisition debt and home equity debt.

Objective 8
Compute the itemized deduction for home mortgage interest.

- **Acquisition debt** is incurred to acquire, construct, or substantially improve a personal residence. Acquisition debt must be secured by the residence and is limited to $1 million ($500,000 for married filing separately).
- **Home equity debt** is any other debt secured by a personal residence to the extent the debt does not exceed the owner's equity. Home equity debt is limited to $100,000 ($50,000 for married filing separately).

In computing the deduction for qualified residence interest, individuals may take into account the interest paid with respect to their principal residence *and* one other personal residence.[40]

> ***Qualified Residence Interest.***   Mr. and Mrs. T constructed a home several years ago and financed the construction by borrowing from a local bank, a debt secured by the bank's mortgage on the residence. Last year, the couple took out a second mortgage from another lending institution which accepted their home as security. Mr. and Mrs. T used this money to purchase new furniture and to pay their three children's college tuition.

---

[38]§163(h)(1).
[39]§163(h)(3).
[40]§163(h)(4).

During the current year, the average balance of the first mortgage was $600,000 and the average balance of the second mortgage was $140,000. The couple paid $52,540 of interest on these mortgages. Only $49,700 of this interest is qualified residence interest.[41]

Acquisition debt	$600,000
Home equity debt (limited)	100,000
Qualifying debt	$700,000

$$\frac{\$700,000 \text{ qualifying debt}}{\$740,000 \text{ total debt}} \times \$52,540 \text{ total interest} = \underline{\underline{\$49,700}}$$

Therefore, Mr. and Mrs. T can claim $49,700 as an itemized deduction. Because the couple used the proceeds of the home equity debt for personal expenditures, the remainder of the interest payment is a nondeductible expense.

Vacation Homes

Many people own and maintain more than one personal residence. In addition to their **principal residence** (the home in which they reside for most of the year and which they consider their permanent address), they may own a **vacation home** for occasional use. Owners of vacation homes often rent the property to other individuals for some limited period of time. In such case, the owners can deduct the expenses of maintaining the home (utilities, homeowners insurance, repairs, etc.) allocable to the rental period on a Schedule E.[42] They are also allowed a depreciation deduction based on the number of days of rental usage. The aggregate of these deductions is limited to the gross rents less any mortgage interest or property taxes allocable to the rental period.[43]

Vacation Home.   Ms. K owns a vacation home on Cape Cod. She and her family use the home on weekends and during June and July. During August and September, Ms. K rents the home to tourists. During the current year, this rental activity resulted in the following:

Gross rents received	$ 6,400
Mortgage interest and real property tax allocable to August and September[44]	3,505
Maintenance expenses for August and September	3,760
MACRS depreciation allocable to August and September	1,200

---

[41]IRS Publication 936 contains a worksheet for computing qualified residence interest when an individual's acquisition or home equity debt exceeds the $1 million or $100,000 limit.

[42]§280A(e)(1). If an owner rents a personal residence for less than 15 days during a year, the revenue is nontaxable and the related expenses are nondeductible. §280A(g).

[43]§280A(c)(5).

[44]The mortgage interest allocable to the other 10 months of the year may be deductible as qualified residence interest. Property tax allocable to this 10-month period is an itemized deduction.

For tax purposes, Ms. K reports this rental activity on a Schedule E as follows:

Gross rents	$ 6,400
Interest and property tax deduction	(3,505)
	$ 2,895
Deductible operating expenses	(2,895)
MACRS depreciation deduction	–0–
Net rental income	$ –0–

Ms. K can carry the $865 disallowed operating expenses and the $1,200 disallowed depreciation into subsequent taxable years and include them in the future calculation of her Schedule E deductions.[45] While such deductions may decrease or even eliminate the vacation home rental income included in Ms. K's AGI, they can never generate a net rental loss.

Exclusion of Gain Realized on Sale of Principal Residence

Objective 9
Describe the preferential tax treatment of gain realized on the sale of a personal residence.

Individuals who realize gain on the sale (or exchange) of a home can exclude the gain from income if the home was owned and used as the individual's principal residence for periods aggregating at least two years during the five-year period ending on the date of sale.[46] The exclusion applies to only one sale every two years. The amount of the exclusion is limited to $250,000 for each sale. The maximum exclusion is doubled (to $500,000) for a married couple filing jointly if *either* spouse meets the two-out-of-five-year ownership requirement and *both* spouses meet the two-out-of-five-year use requirement with respect to their principal residence.

> *Maximum Exclusion.*   Mr. and Mrs. K, who file a joint tax return, purchased a principal residence as co-tenants in 1990 and have lived in the home ever since. On October 6, 1998, they realized a $618,000 gain on the sale of the residence. Because they meet the ownership/use requirement and did not sell another principal residence within the two-year period prior to the sale of this residence, they may exclude $500,000 of the gain from their 1998 income. The $118,000 recognized gain is long-term capital gain taxed at a 20 percent rate.

A person who realizes a gain on sale of a principal residence but fails to meet the ownership/use requirement or violates the two-year/one-sale rule may be eligible for a reduced exclusion. If the person sold the residence because of a change in place of employment, for health reasons, or because of unforeseen circumstances, the allowable exclusion equals the maximum exclusion multiplied by a reduction ratio. The numerator of the ratio equals the *shorter* of (1) the aggregate time period of ownership/use of the residence or (2) the time period between the earlier sale of a residence for which gain was excluded and the current sale. The denominator of the ratio is two years.

---

[45]§165(c)(5).
[46]§121 as amended by the Tax Reform Act of 1997.

> ***Reduced Exclusion.***   Refer to the facts in the preceding example and assume that Mr. and Mrs. K purchased and moved into a new principal residence on December 13, 1998. In June 1999, Mr. K suffered a major heart attack. To accommodate his physical condition, the couple sold their new residence on August 10, 1999, and moved into an assisted-living apartment. The gain realized on this sale was $15,200. Mr. and Mrs. K owned and occupied their new residence for only 240 days and sold it just 308 days after the sale of their former residence. Consequently, they fail the ownership/use requirement and violate the two-year/one-sale rule. However, because they sold the new residence for health reasons, they are eligible for a reduced exclusion of $164,384, computed as follows:
>
> $$\$500,000 \times \frac{240 \text{ days of ownership/use}}{730 \text{ days (two years)}} = \$164,384$$
>
> Consequently, they may exclude the entire $15,200 gain from their 1999 income.

Itemized Deductions as AMT Adjustments

Objective 10
Identify the itemized deductions that are limited or disallowed in the computation of alternative minimum taxable income (AMTI).

Before leaving the topic of personal activities, we should integrate the material introduced in the chapter into the alternative minimum tax (AMT) system. None of the items of income or gain derived from an individual's personal activities trigger an AMT adjustment or preference. However, certain itemized deductions resulting from these activities are limited or disallowed in the computation of alternative minimum taxable income (AMTI).[47]

- For AMT purposes, medical expenses are deductible only to the extent they exceed 10 percent of AGI.
- The itemized deduction for tax payments is disallowed.
- Miscellaneous itemized deductions (including deductible investment and employment-related expenses) are disallowed.
- Qualified residence interest paid on home equity debt is disallowed.

Our last two examples illustrate the computation of these AMT adjustments and their impact on the AMT.

> ***AMT Itemized Deductions.***   Mrs. C had 1998 AGI of $75,000 and the following itemized deductions:
>
> | | | |
> |---|---:|---:|
> | Unreimbursed medical expenses | $10,500 | |
> | AGI threshold ($75,000 × 7.5%) | (5,625) | $ 4,875 |
> | State income tax | | 4,000 |
> | Local property tax on personal residence | | 3,100 |
> | Charitable contributions | | 5,500 |
> | Qualified residence interest: | | |
> | Acquisition debt | | 9,200 |
> | Home equity debt | | 6,800 |

---

[47]§56(b)(1).

Miscellaneous itemized deductions	$ 2,400	
AGI threshold ($75,000 × 2%)	(1,500)	900
		$34,375

In computing her AMTI, Mrs. C must make the following *positive* adjustments to taxable income:

Unreimbursed medical expenses	$10,500	
AMT/AGI threshold ($75,000 × 10%)	(7,500)	
	$ 3,000	
Regular medical expense deduction	$ 4,875	
AMT medical expense deduction	(3,000)	
AMT adjustment for medical expenses		$ 1,875
Disallowed state income tax		4,000
Disallowed local property tax on personal residence		3,100
Disallowed interest on home equity debt		6,800
Disallowed miscellaneous itemized deductions		900
		$16,675

Computing AMT.   Assume that Mrs. C is a head of household with two dependents. Her 1998 tax liability is calculated as follows:

	Regular Tax	Tentative Minimum Tax
AGI	$ 75,000	
Itemized deductions	(34,375)	
Exemption amount ($2,700 × 3)	(8,100)	
Taxable income	$ 32,525	$ 32,525
AMT adjustments for:		
Itemized deductions		16,675
Exemption amount		8,100
AMTI		$ 57,300
Exemption (head of household)		(33,750)
Tax base	$ 32,525	$ 23,550
Tax rate	.15	.26
	$ 4,879	$ 6,123

Mrs. C's tax liability for the year is $6,123:

Regular tax liability	$4,879
AMT ($6,123 tentative minimum tax − $4,879)	1,244
	$6,123

Conclusion

Even when people engage in personal transactions that have no connecton to any business, employment, or investment activity, they should be sensitive to tax implications. Of course, many personal transactions are simply nonevents for tax purposes. But occasionally, a personal transaction will have economic consequences that dramatically affect tax liability. If a transaction has the potential to result in a financial benefit, the individual must consider the prospect that such benefit will be taxable. He or she should also determine if the transaction can be structured so that part or all of the benefit escapes taxation. If a transaction entails an expense or loss, the individual just might be entitled to a deduction for some portion or even the entire expense or loss. Through an awareness of this possibility, the individual can take the necessary steps to maximize the deduction and minimize his tax bill.

Key Terms

Acquisition debt   451
Education IRA   446
Hobby loss   449
Home equity debt   451
HOPE scholarship credit   446
Imputed income from owner-occupied housing   451

Lifetime learning credit   446
Principal residence   452
Qualified education loan   446
Qualified residence interest   451
Vacation home   452

Questions and Problems for Discussion

1. Contrast the basic rule pertaining to the recognition of income derived from personal activities with the basic rule pertaining to the deductibility of personal expenses and losses.

2. Discuss the tax policy reasons why people who receive gifts and inheritances are not required to recognize the value of such receipts as taxable income.

3. In what way does the tax law give preferential treatment to the divorced spouse with custody of the children from the marriage?

4. From a tax policy standpoint, why are welfare payments from a state social services agency nontaxable to the recipient while state unemployment benefits are fully taxable?

5. A basic principle of federal tax law is that a return of investment is nontaxable. Discuss the application of this principle to Social Security payments.

6. The annual premium paid by individuals to insure tangible business property used in their sole proprietorship from fire or other casualty is a deductible expense. The annual premium paid

by individuals to insure their home from fire or other casualty is nondeductible. What is the rationale for this differential treatment?

7. Mr. M is a passionate stamp collector. His current collection is so valuable that he keeps it in a safety deposit box in a local bank. This year the bank charged him $25 a month for the box. Can Mr. M deduct this expense on his Form 1040?

8. Assume that Congress amended the tax law to restrict the itemized deduction for charitable contributions to 5 percent (rather than 50 percent) of AGI. Discuss possible behavioral reactions by individuals and the incidence of the tax increase represented by this expansion of the tax base.

9. People frequently hold garage or rummage sales in which they sell used appliances, old furniture and clothing, books, toys, and other personal goods. Should these people recognize the cash proceeds from such sales as taxable income?

10. Last year, both the M family and the N family incurred $8,000 of unreimbursed medical

expenses. Mr. and Mrs. M deducted $6,000 of their expenses on Form 1040, while Mr. and Mrs. N were unable to deduct any of their expenses. How do you explain this apparently inequitable result?

11. Wealthy individuals can reduce their taxable estate by donating property to charity either during life or at death. Discuss the reasons why an inter vivos charitable donation is the preferable option for tax planning purposes.

12. Mrs. Q's profession is dentistry, but she has quite a reputation as a master gardener. Last year she won $990 in prize money from entering her roses in competitions and earned $800 in lecture fees from garden clubs around the state. Because she did not itemize deductions, none of the expenses associated with her hobby were deductible. Should Mrs. Q pay self-employment tax on her prize money and fees?

13. Discuss the similarities and differences in the structure of the hobby loss rule and the vacation home rule.

Application Problems

1. Ms. Q, age 21, is a full-time college student. She has an athletic scholarship that provides the following annual benefits:

Tuition payment	$12,800
Fees and books	3,500
Room and board	10,000

As part of her scholarship arrangement, Ms. Q works in the athletic department as a trainer and receives an annual salary of $4,200. She also receives a $2,500 annual allowance from her grandmother. Based on these facts, compute Ms. Q's AGI.

2. Mr. and Mrs. T and their family have major medical and dental insurance provided by Mrs. T's employer. During the year, the family incurred the following *unreimbursed* expenses:

Routine office visits to doctors and dentists	$940
Emergency room visits	415
Disposable contact lenses for Mr. T	360
Prescription drugs	500

Based on these facts, compute the couple's itemized deduction for medical expenses if their AGI is:

a. $25,000.
b. $50,000.

3. During the current year, Mr. AB paid the following professional fees:

To CPA for preparation of prior year Form 1040 ($2,500 related to preparation of Schedule C for Mr. AB's sole proprietorship)	$4,200
To CPA for preparation of federal gift tax return	900
To attorney for drafting of Mr. AB's will	7,800
To attorney for estate tax planning advice	3,000
To attorney for advice concerning the custody of Mr. AB's minor grandson	750
To attorney for settling a dispute with a neighbor concerning the neighbor's barking dog	400

To what extent (if any) can Mr. AB deduct these payments on his Form 1040?

4. During the current year, Mr. CC paid the following taxes:

Federal income tax	$50,789
Federal gift tax	285
Federal employer payroll tax for housekeeper	920
Indiana income tax	3,710
Indiana sales tax on consumer goods and services	2,040
Local property tax on:	
Principal residence	4,800
Vacation home	1,800
Two automobiles	900

To what extent (if any) can Mr. CC deduct these payments on his Form 1040?

5. During the current year, Mrs. PL made the following interest payments. In each case, determine the extent to which Mrs. PL can deduct the payment.

   a. $21,000 on a $280,000 mortgage incurred to construct (and secured by) Mrs. PL's personal residence.

   b. $3,000 on a $34,000 second mortgage secured by Mrs. PL's personal residence. She used the debt proceeds to pay off her credit card debt.

   c. $2,290 on credit card debt.

   d. $15,000 on a $200,000 bank loan incurred to purchase inventory for Mrs. PL's sole proprietorship.

   e. $1,610 on a bank loan incurred to purchase a car for Mrs. PL's 18-year-old son.

   f. $1,750 on a bank loan incurred to purchase mutual fund shares that generated $1,900 of dividend income this year.

6. Ms. KP has been unlucky this year. On a recent business trip to Boston, her wallet (which contained $900 of cash) was stolen. Her new automobile was completely destroyed by a fire. She paid $24,000 for the car, but its value immediately before the fire was only $18,200. She received a $14,000 reimbursement from the insurance company. A tornado wiped out a grove of ornamental trees growing near her home. She paid $6,100 to replace the trees and received no insurance reimbursement. Based on these facts, compute Ms. KP's casualty loss deduction if her AGI is:

   a. $53,000.

   b. $210,000.

7. Ms. K wants to create a scholarship in honor of her parents at the law school from which she received her degree. She could endow the scholarship with $500,000 cash or with $500,000 of marketable securities with a cost basis of $318,000. If Ms. K's AGI is $1.8 million, compare her after-tax cost of the two endowment options.

8. A burglar broke into Mr. and Mrs. V's home and stole an oil painting that the couple purchased 15 years ago for $89,000. This theft was the couple's only property loss for the year. Their AGI was $125,000. Describe the tax consequences of the theft under each of the following circumstances:

   a. The painting was insured for $200,000. Mr. and Mrs. V used the insurance proceeds to purchase another painting by the same artist.

   b. The painting was insured for $200,000. Mr. and Mrs. V used the insurance proceeds to purchase marketable securities.

   c. The painting was insured for $50,000. Mr. and Mrs. V used the insurance proceeds to purchase marketable securities.

   d. The painting was uninsured.

9. Mr. MC is a self-employed computer consultant who earns over $100,000 net profit each year. He also is an enthusiastic artist. During 19X8, Mr. MC spent $4,900 on oil paints, canvasses, supplies, and lessons at a local studio. He made several trips to the National Gallery in Washington, D.C., to attend lectures on painting technique. His total travel costs were $3,350. Describe the tax consequences of the painting activity under each of the following assumptions:

   a. During 19X8, Mr. MC earned $13,290 from sales of his paintings. This was the sixth consecutive year that the painting activity generated a net profit.

   b. During 19X8, Mr. MC earned $2,000 from sales of his paintings. The painting activity has never generated a net profit.

   c. During 19X8, Mr. MC earned $2,000 from sales of his paintings. The painting activity also generated a net loss in 19X5, but was profitable in 19X4, 19X6, and 19X7.

10. Mr. and Mrs. KG own a principal residence and a vacation home. Each residence is subject to a mortgage the couple incurred to buy the residence. For the current year, the mortgage holders provided the couple with the following information:

	Mortgage Interest Paid	Average Balance of Mortgage
Principal residence	$56,000	$890,000
Vacation home	21,700	340,000

Based on these facts, compute Mr. and Mrs. KG's qualified residence interest for the year.

11. On January 12, 1998, Mr. and Mrs. PS vacated a residence that they had owned and lived in for 16 years. They moved into a new residence that they purchased on January 3, 1998. On June 7,

1998, they realized a $278,000 gain on the sale of their former residence. On February 26, 2000, Mr. and Mrs. PS realized a $48,000 gain on the sale of the new residence.

a. How much gain must Mr. and Mrs. PS recognize on their 1998 joint return from the sale of their former residence?

b. How much gain must Mr. and Mrs. PS recognize on their 2000 joint return from the sale of their new residence? The couple sold this residence because they wanted to move to a neighborhood with better public schools for their four children.

c. Would your answer to b change if Mr. and Mrs. PS sold their new home because Mrs. PS accepted a job with an employer in another state and the family had to relocate?

12. Mrs. JM, a widow, paid $148,000 for her home in 1972. She recently sold this home and moved in with her son's family on a permanent basis. Describe the tax consequences of the sale to Mrs. JM assuming that her amount realized on sale was:

a. $140,000.

b. $250,000.

c. $500,000.

13. In 1996, Mr. B, a single taxpayer, was fired from his job with TSL Inc. for suspected embezzlement. After the police determined that Mr. B was not guilty, he sued his former employer for back wages and defamation of character. In 1998, he received a $100,000 settlement from TSL. His only other income item for the year was $6,200 of unemployment compensation. Mr. B's legal fees in connection with the litigation totaled $55,000. This fee was Mr. B's only miscellaneous itemized deduction for 1998. His only other itemized deductions were a $1,200 charitable contribution and a $1,700 state income tax payment. Based on these facts, compute Mr. B's 1998 federal income tax liability.

Issue Recognition Problems

Identify the tax issue or issues suggested by the following situations and state each issue in the form of a question.

1. A local radio station offers a $5,000 reward for information leading to the arrest of vandals and other petty criminals. Mr. J received the reward for identifying three people who spray-painted graffiti on a public building.

2. Mr. SA, a real estate broker, just negotiated the sale of a home for a wealthy client. Two days after the sale closed, Mr. SA received a beautiful leather briefcase from the client with a card reading: "In grateful appreciation of your efforts over the past year."

3. Mr. TL was a contestant on a game show and won a vacuum cleaner with a retail value of $365. Three months later, Mr. TL sold the unused appliance in a garage sale for $275.

4. The pilots of Skyway Airlines Inc. have been on strike for four months. Ms. BG, a pilot participating in the strike, recently received a $2,700 benefit from her union, the Airline Pilots Association International. The union funded the benefits for Ms. BG and her fellow pilots through a special solicitation from union members flying for other airlines.

5. Ms. LS, a bartender and aspiring actress, won a statewide beauty pageant and was awarded a $15,000 cash scholarship to be used to further her education and career goals. Ms. LS used the money to pay for private acting lessons.

6. On a recent scuba dive, Mr. UW located a shipwreck and recovered a Spanish sword inlaid with precious stones. The sword's appraised value is $11,500. Mr. UW mounted the sword over his fireplace.

7. Mrs. OP, age 60, won an age discrimination suit against her former employer. The court awarded her $100,000 in damages for mental anguish and $200,000 for the violation of her civil rights.

8. Mrs. N, who is a self-employed author working out of her home, paid $3,200 for a new computer system. She uses the system to write her books, and her two children use it for their schoolwork.

9. In honor of her 50th birthday, Mrs. VV treated herself to a complete face-lift. The $8,900 cost of the cosmetic surgery was not covered by Mrs. VV's insurance policy.

10. Mr. S suffers from severe arthritis. His physician advised him to swim for at least one hour every day in a heated pool. Because such a facility is not conveniently located in his area, Mr. S paid $25,000 to build a heated lap pool in his backyard.

11. Mrs. PM's daughter is undergoing physical therapy for severe injuries sustained in a bike accident. Every two weeks for the past year, mother and daughter drive 170 miles to a regional hospital where the daughter is treated. Then they spend the night in a motel before driving home again.

12. Mr. R, a CPA who charges $150 per hour for his professional services, keeps the financial records for a local charity. Although he spends at least 10 hours each month at this task, Mr. R does not charge the charity a fee for his services.

13. Mr. and Mrs. FP bought $500 worth of Girl Scout cookies from their godchild. Because they don't eat sweets, the couple gave away every box to various friends and family members.

14. Ms. DS owns a diamond ring worth $12,000 that she has worn on her right hand for 12 years. While washing her hands two days ago, she noticed that the ring was missing. She searched her home, her car, and her place of business but has been unable to locate the ring.

15. Mr. D recently borrowed $600,000 to purchase 62 acres of undeveloped land, a debt secured by the property. He converted a three-room log cabin on the land to his principal residence.

16. Mr. Y, age 51, realized a $79,000 gain on the sale of his principal residence. He used the proceeds to buy a sailboat on which he now lives for nine months of the year. Mr. Y spends the three winter months in his daughter's home in Miami.

17. Ms. SE paid $155,000 for a house that she occupied as her principal residence until February 1, 19X2, when she moved out and converted the house to rental property. The appraised value of the house on this date was $140,000. The house was leased to tenants who purchased the house from Ms. SE in November. Her loss realized on the sale was $24,700, computed as follows:

Amount realized		$125,000
Original cost basis	$155,000	
MACRS depreciation during rental period	(5,300)	
Adjusted basis		(149,700)
		$ (24,700)

18. Mr. and Mrs. AQ purchased their home one year ago. This year, a local government attempted to seize the home because the former residents had failed to pay their property taxes for 12 years. Mr. and Mrs. AQ paid $1,700 to an attorney who resolved the dispute in their favor.

Tax Planning Cases

1. Ms. JL is a successful attorney in the 39.6 percent marginal tax bracket. During the past several years, she provided legal services to her great uncle, who is 78 years old and in failing health. Although the uncle offered to pay Ms. JL for her work, she refused any compensation, requesting instead that her uncle remember her appropriately in his will. The uncle recently added a codicil to his will providing for a $100,000 cash bequest to Ms. JL. The remainder of his estate will pass to his two children and seven grandchildren.

   a. What tax planning objective may Ms. JL have accomplished through her request of her uncle?

   b. Can you identify both the opportunity cost and the risk inherent in Ms. JL's plan?

2. Mr. and Mrs. TB are going through an amicable divorce. Mrs. TB, who is a full-time homemaker, will have custody of the couple's two children, ages 2 and 4. She initially suggested that Mr. TB pay her $8,000 of child support each month. Mr. TB countered by offering to pay $4,000 of child support and $5,000 of alimony each month, provided that Mrs. TB allows him to claim their two children as his dependents. In either case, Mrs. TB will qualify as a head of household for federal tax purposes. Mr. TB is in a 31 percent marginal tax bracket.

a. Using 1998 data, compute Mr. TB's after-tax cost and Mrs. TB's after-tax cash flow if he pays her $8,000 of monthly child support and she claims their children as her dependents.

b. Compute Mr. TB's after-tax cost and Mrs. TB's after-tax cash flow if she accepts his counterproposal.

3. Mr. and Mrs. JM, ages 68 and 66, are a married couple who always claim the standard deduction on their joint return. The couple owns and operates a local restaurant, the Shoreline Grill, as a sole proprietorship. Mr. and Mrs. JM are both graduates of State University and make regular donations to their alma mater. Their method for doing so is a bit unusual. At the beginning and during half-time of each State University home football game, the public address system informs the crowd that the Shoreline Grill will contribute $50 to the university's athletic scholarship fund for every first down the home team makes. As a result of this commitment, Mr. and Mrs. JM contributed $4,950 to State University this year. What tax planning objective may the couple have accomplished by structuring their donation in this manner?

4. Mr. Z, who is in the 31 percent marginal tax bracket and itemizes deductions, recently inherited $30,000. He is considering three alternate uses for this windfall.

   • He could buy shares in a mutual fund paying 11 percent a year. Mr. Z would spend this income every year.

   • He could pay off a $30,000 debt to a local bank on which he currently pays 8 percent interest each year. Mr. Z used the debt proceeds for home furnishings and a new wardrobe.

   • He could pay off $30,000 of the mortgage he incurred to buy his home. This principal repayment would decrease his annual home mortgage interest expense by $2,900.

Which alternative would you recommend to Mr. Z and why?

APPENDIX 16–A
SOCIAL SECURITY WORKSHEET (ADAPTED FROM IRS PUBLICATION 915)

1. Social Security benefits received _____
2. One-half of line 1 _____
3. Adjusted gross income (AGI) (without Social Security benefits) _____
4. Tax-exempt interest income _____
5. Add lines 2, 3, and 4 _____
6. Enter:
   $32,000 (married filing jointly)
   $25,000 (single or head of household)
   –0– (married filing separately)* _____
7. Subtract line 6 from line 5 _____

If line 7 is zero or less, the Social Security benefits are nontaxable.

8. Enter:
   $12,000 (married filing jointly)
   $9,000 (single or head of household)
   –0– (married filing separately) _____
9. Subtract line 8 from line 7. If zero or less, enter zero _____
10. Enter the lesser of line 7 or line 8 _____
11. Enter one-half of line 10 _____
12. Enter the lesser of line 2 or line 11 _____
13. Multiply line 9 by 85 percent _____
14. Add line 12 and line 13 _____
15. Multiply line 1 by 85 percent _____
16. Enter the lesser of line 14 or line 15 _____

Line 16 is the taxable portion of the Social Security benefits.

1. Social Security benefits received $14,400
2. One-half of line 1   7,200
3. Adjusted gross income (AGI) (without Social Security benefits)   43,000
4. Tax-exempt interest income   600
5. Add lines 2, 3, and 4   50,800
6. Enter:
   $32,000 (married filing jointly)
   $25,000 (single or head of household)
   –0– (married filing separately)*   32,000
7. Subtract line 6 from line 5   18,800

If line 7 is zero or less, the Social Security benefits are nontaxable.

8. Enter:
   $12,000 (married filing jointly)
   $9,000 (single or head of household)
   –0– (married filing separately)   12,000
9. Subtract line 8 from line 7. If zero or less, enter zero   6,800
10. Enter the lesser of line 7 or line 8   12,000
11. Enter one-half of line 10   6,000
12. Enter the lesser of line 2 or line 11   6,000
13. Multiply line 9 by 85 percent   5,780
14. Add line 12 and line 13   11,780
15. Multiply line 1 by 85 percent   12,240
16. Enter the lesser of line 14 or line 15   11,780

Line 16 is the taxable portion of the Social Security benefits.

> **Example.** Mr. and Mrs. PB received $14,400 of Social Security benefits this year. The AGI on their joint return before considering these benefits was $43,000, and they received $600 of tax-exempt interest. Based on these facts, the taxable portion of their Social Security benefits is $11,780.

---

*Married individuals filing separate returns who live apart at all times during the year are considered single for purposes of this computation.

Comprehensive Problems for Part Five

1. Ms. Cora Yank (age 42) is an unmarried individual who has full custody of her 13-year old son William. Based on the following 1998 information, compute Mrs. Yank's 1998 federal income tax liability and the tax she must pay with her Form 1040 or the refund she should receive after filing her Form 1040.
   - Mrs. Yank works as a medical technician in a Chicago hospital. Her 1998 salary was $38,400, from which her employer withheld $5,012 of federal income tax and $2,938 employee FICA tax.
   - In 1997, Mrs. Yank was seriously injured in a traffic accident cause by another driver's negligence. During 1998, she received a $25,000 settlement from the driver's insurance company: $20,000 as compensation for her physical injuries, and $5,000 for lost wages during her convalescent period. Because she was unable to work for the first seven weeks of the year, she collected $1,400 of unemployment compensation from the state of Illinois.
   - Mrs. Yank earned $629 in interest on a savings account. She contributed $800 to a regular IRA. Mrs. Yank is not an active participant in any other qualified retirement plan.
   - Mrs. Yank paid $10,800 in rent on the apartment in which she and William live. She received $1,600 of alimony and $2,350 of child support from her former husband.
   - Mrs. Yank is covered under her employer's medical reimbursement plan. However, her 1998 medical bills exceeded her reimbursement limit by $1,630.
   - Mrs. Yank paid $2,062 in income tax to Illinois.
   - Mrs. Yank spent $470 on hospital shoes and uniforms. Her employer did not reimburse Mrs. Yank for this expense.
   - Mrs. Yank paid $1,300 for after-school child care for William.
2. Tom and Allie Benson (age 53 and 46) are residents of Fort Worth, Texas, and file a joint federal income tax return. They provide the entire support for their three children, ages 19, 18, and

14. Based on the following 1998 information, compute Mr. and Mrs. Benson's 1998 federal income and SE tax liability and the tax they must pay with their Form 1040 or the refund they should receive after filing their Form 1040.
   - Mr. Benson is an attorney who practices in partnership with 18 other attorneys. His 1998 ordinary income from the partnership was $278,300. His net earnings from self-employment for 1998 were $257,010 (92.35 percent of $278,300). During 1998, the Bensons made estimated tax payments totaling $62,600 to the IRS and a $28,500 contribution to the qualified Keogh plan maintained by the partnership.
   - The Bensons earned $10,160 of interest income and $13,790 of ordinary dividend income from their investment portfolio. They also received a $4,218 capital gains distribution from a mutual fund that was eligible for the 20 percent tax rate. According to the Bensons' 1997 tax return, they have a $9,723 capital loss carryforward into 1998.
   - The Bensons received a Schedule K-1 from an S corporation in which they own 6 percent of the outstanding stock. The S corporation operates a mink farm in Maine. The Bensons' share of the corporation's 1998 business loss was $4,930.
   - Mrs. Benson received a $50,000 cash inheritance from her great aunt who died during the year.
   - The Bensons moved from San Antonio to Fort Worth in April so that Mr. Benson could manage his partnership's office in Fort Worth. The cost of moving their household goods was $11,260. The law firm reimbursed Mr. Benson for $10,000 of this expense.
   - The Bensons paid $33,890 in interest on their home mortgage, $7,400 in property taxes on their personal residence, and $2,920 in homeowners insurance.
   - The Bensons made $21,980 in cash donations to various qualified charities.

PART SIX

The Tax Compliance Process

17

The Tax Compliance Process

Learning Objectives

After studying this chapter, you should be able to:

1. Compute a late-filing and late-payment penalty for a delinquent income tax return.
2. Describe the normal statute of limitations for a tax return and explain the circumstances that extend the statute.
3. Identify the three types of IRS audits.
4. Describe the circumstances in which the IRS imposes a negligence or a civil fraud penalty.
5. Compare the consequences of civil fraud and criminal fraud.
6. Contrast the operations of the three federal trial courts that hear tax cases.
7. Explain the role of the U.S. Circuit Courts of Appeals and the Supreme Court in the tax litigation process.
8. Define the term *transferee liability*.
9. Explain the purpose of the innocent spouse rule.

The federal income, payroll, self-employment, and transfer taxes are all self-assessed taxes. The Internal Revenue Code requires persons liable for any of these taxes to compute the tax due, file the proper return, and maintain adequate records supporting the calculations presented on the return.[1] As a practical matter, the tax laws are sufficiently complex that the majority of taxpayers engage a tax practitioner to assist in the preparation of their returns. Nevertheless, even taxpayers who rely entirely on professional help remain responsible for complying with the law and must bear the consequences of failure to comply.

This final chapter of *Principles of Taxation for Business and Investment Planning* is an overview of the federal tax compliance system. The procedural rules governing payment of tax and filing of income tax returns and the IRS's audit process are explained. Your rights as an individual taxpayer in dealing with the IRS, as well as the penalties the IRS may impose during the audit process, are described.

---

[1] See §6001 and §6011.

The chapter closes with a discussion of the judicial process by which both individuals and corporations may challenge the outcome of an IRS audit in federal court.

Filing and Payment Requirements

Most individuals report income on the basis of a calendar year and are required to file their Form 1040 for the current year by April 15 of the following year. The few individuals who have adopted a fiscal year must file their returns by the 15th day of the 4th month following the close of the taxable year. Corporations, which report on the basis of either a calendar year or a fiscal year, must file their Form 1120 by the 15th day of the 3rd month following the close of their taxable year. The law permits both individual and corporate taxpayers to request automatic extensions of time to file their annual income tax returns.[2]

As a general rule, both individuals and corporations must pay their tax for the year by the *unextended* filing date of the return for such year. From the government's perspective, taxpayers who are late in paying any portion of their tax liability received a loan from Uncle Sam. Accordingly, the IRS bills these taxpayers for interest based on the period of time from the required payment date to the date the delinquent tax is actually paid to the IRS.[3] The annual interest rate charged by the government equals the federal short-term rate plus three percentage points; interest is compounded daily, and the rate is adjusted quarterly.[4]

Millions of taxpayers overpay their annual income tax in the form of excess withholding or quarterly installment payments. In theory, these individuals and corporations loaned money to the federal government. However, the government is not required to pay interest on any overpayment of tax refunded within 45 days after the filing date for the return on which the refund is requested or the date such return is actually filed, whichever is later.[5] As a result, taxpayers who routinely receive their refund checks within this statutory grace period do not earn interest on the refund. In the rare case when the IRS fails to mail a refund check on a timely basis, the government must pay interest to the taxpayer; the annual interest rate paid by the government equals the federal short-term rate plus only two percentage points.[6]

Late-Filing and Late-Payment Penalty

Objective 1
Compute a late-filing and late-payment penalty for a delinquent income tax return.

If a taxpayer fails to file an income tax return on a timely basis, the IRS may impose a **late-filing and late-payment penalty,** the calculation of which is quite complicated. Basically, this combined penalty equals 5 percent of the balance of tax due with the return for each month (or portion thereof) that the return is delinquent. The 5 percent penalty runs only for five months (i.e., until the penalty equals 25 percent of the balance due). After five months the penalty rate drops to one-half percent of the balance of tax due with the return. This reduced penalty can run for an additional 45 months.[7]

---

[2]§6081. Individuals may request an automatic four-month extension, and corporations may request an automatic six-month extension.

[3]§6601.

[4]§6621(a)(2) and §6622.

[5]§6611(e)(1).

[6]§6611(a) and §6621(a)(1). In the case of an overpayment by a corporation that exceeds $10,000, the government's interest rate equals the short-term rate plus one-half percent.

[7]§6621.

Late-Filing and Late-Payment Penalty.   Mr. T failed to request an extension of time to file his 1997 return and didn't mail his Form 1040 to the IRS until July 29, 1998. The return showed a 1997 tax liability of $45,890 and $42,000 of tax withheld during the year by Mr. T's employer. Mr. T enclosed a check for the $3,890 balance due with his late return. Because the tax due was not paid by April 15, the IRS charged Mr. T interest on $3,890 for the period of time from April 16 through July 28. Because Mr. T's return was not filed on a timely basis, the IRS also assessed a penalty of $778.

Balance of tax due on late return		$3,890
Delinquency period:		
April 16–May 15	.05	
May 16–June 15	.05	
June 16–July 14	.05	
July 15–July 28	.05	
	.20	
		$ 778

The IRS may agree to waive this penalty (but not the interest) if Mr. T can show reasonable cause for his tardiness.

Reasonable Cause for a Delinquent Return?   David McMahan, an investment broker, engaged James Russell, an attorney with tax expertise, to file his individual income tax return. Mr. Russell filed an automatic extension and subsequently informed his client that he had also filed a second extension request for additional time to file the return. Months later, Mr. McMahan discovered that his attorney had neglected to file the second extension request. The IRS assessed a $141,028 late filing and late payment penalty against Mr. McMahan, which he contested in court. Mr. McMahan argued that his reliance on a tax professional to file an extension request was reasonable cause for the delinquent return. The court was not persuaded by his argument, observing that a "taxpayer has an affirmative nondelegable duty to ensure that the appropriate forms—whether a tax return or an extension request—are actually filed by the statutory deadline." Consequently, Mr. McMahan was liable for the penalty.[8]

One interesting feature of the late-filing penalty deserves mention. The penalty is a function of the balance of tax due with a delinquent return. If a taxpayer overpaid his income tax for the year, his return will show a refund due instead of a balance due. In this case, the government cannot assess any penalty if such return is filed after the due date. Of course, for as long as the return is delinquent, the government is enjoying an interest-free loan from the taxpayer that does not have to be repaid until the taxpayer finally decides to file.[9]

---

[8]*McMahan* v. *Commissioner*, 114 F.3d 366 (CA-2, 1997).

[9]Taxpayers who are entitled to a refund must file a return requesting such refund within two years from the original due date of their return. §6511(a).

Return Processing

Each year more than 130 million income tax returns are filed with the IRS by individuals, corporations, partnerships, and fiduciaries.[10] These returns pour into the 10 IRS service centers located throughout the country. The service centers are information-processing facilities where each tax return is checked for mathematical accuracy and logged into the IRS's computer system. This system enables the IRS to cross-check each tax return against information returns filed with respect to the taxpayer, such as Form W-2s filed by employers with respect to their employees or Form 1099s filed by payers of interest, dividend, rents, or other types of income. If a return reflects a math error or a discrepancy between the return and a corresponding information return, the service center mails a letter to the taxpayer explaining the problem and indicating that the taxpayer must pay additional tax or will receive an additional refund. The service centers are responsible for depositing personal checks or money orders attached to tax returns with the U.S. Treasury and for authorizing refund checks to be prepared and mailed.

Objective 2
Describe the normal statute of limitations for a tax return and explain the circumstances that extend the statute.

Statute of Limitations.   Many people place unjustified significance on the fact that the government promptly cashed the check included with their return or punctually mailed their refund. While these events prove that their tax return was processed, they do not mean that the IRS has accepted the accuracy of the return as filed. A **statute of limitations** gives the IRS three years from the *later* of the statutory due date (April 15th for calendar year individuals) or the date on which the return was actually filed to examine that return for mistakes and to assess any additional tax for the year.[11]

> ***Three-Year Statute of Limitations.***   Mr. and Mrs. K filed their 1997 Form 1040 on March 16, 1998. The IRS has until April 15, 2001, to audit this return and assess any additional tax. Mr. P requested an extension of time to file his 1997 return and actually filed the return on August 2, 1998. In his case, the IRS has until August 2, 2001, to audit the return and assess additional tax.

If a taxpayer files a return and omits an amount of gross income exceeding 25 percent of the gross income reported on the return, the normal three-year statute of limitations is extended to six years. If the IRS determines that a return is fraudulent (a concept discussed later in this chapter), the return remains open (subject to audit) indefinitely.

> ***Extended Statute of Limitations.***   Ms. K, a self-employed consultant, failed to include a $13,200 business receipt in the income reported on her 1997 return, which she filed on April 8, 1998. The gross income on the return was $52,000. The omitted income item was more than 25 percent of this gross income.
>
> $13,200 > $13,000 ($52,000 gross income × 25%)

---

[10]Philip Cormany, "Projections of Returns to Be Filed in Calendar Years 1997–2003," *SOI Bulletin* (Winter 1996–97), p. 102.

[11]§6501.

> Consequently, Mrs. K's 1997 return remains open until April 15, 2004. If the IRS determines that Ms. K's omission of income constituted fraud, they can audit the return and assess additional tax at any time.

Because of the possibility of audit, taxpayers should keep all supporting paperwork such as receipts and canceled checks on which the return is based for at least three years after the return is filed. Records substantiating the tax basis of property, any legal documents containing information pertinent to the return (closing statement on a property sale, divorce decree, etc.), and a copy of the return itself should be retained permanently.

The Audit Process

The IRS selects corporate tax returns for audit primarily on the basis of the magnitude of the corporation's business operations, measured in terms of taxable income and net worth as reported on the Form 1120. Individual returns are usually selected by a highly classified computer program that analyzes the contents of each return and assigns the return a **discriminate function system (DIF) score.** This score is a theoretical measure of the return's potential for generating additional tax revenue on audit. The higher the score, the greater the likelihood that the return contains an error that resulted in an understatement of tax. Obviously, returns with the highest DIF scores are chosen for examination. Although the details of the DIF selection process are a closely guarded secret, tax practitioners generally assume that highly speculative investment activities, unusually large itemized deductions, and deductions that are prone to manipulation or abuse (travel and entertainment expenses, nonbusiness bad debts, losses generated by a secondary business, etc.) inflate a return's DIF score. Similarly, high-income returns are much more likely to be selected for audit than returns reflecting modest incomes.

> *Audit Coverage.*   According to the IRS Data Book for fiscal year 1996, the IRS audited 1.94 million of the 116 million individual tax returns filed during that year, an audit coverage rate of 1.67 percent. The audit rate for returns reporting taxable income between $25,000 and $50,000 was only .95 percent, while the rate for returns with income in excess of $100,000 was 2.85 percent. The audit rate for Form 1040s containing a Schedule C with gross receipts in excess of $100,000 was 4.09 percent.

Objective 3
Identify the three types of IRS audits.

Types of Audits.   Routine audits are conducted by personnel working out of the IRS district offices which are scattered throughout the United States. The simplest audits, called **correspondence examinations,** may be handled entirely by telephone or through the mail. More complex audits take place at an IRS district office (an **office examination** conducted by a tax auditor) or at the taxpayer's place of business (a **field examination** conducted by a revenue agent). Office audits tend to focus on a few questionable items on a return. Field audits are broader in scope and involve a complete examination of the taxpayer's books and records for the year or years under investigation.

If the IRS requests a personal interview with a taxpayer or if the taxpayer requests an interview during an audit, the IRS must schedule the interview at a reasonable time and a location convenient for the taxpayer. Individuals who must deal with the IRS can represent themselves or authorize an attorney, certified public accountant, or enrolled agent to represent them. While attorneys and CPAs are licensed to practice by state boards or agencies, **enrolled agents** receive certification to practice before the IRS by passing an exam on tax law written and administered by the IRS itself.

Assessments of Deficiencies and Interest.   Individuals who are notified that their tax returns are under audit may panic unnecessarily. Any person who made a good faith effort to comply with the laws in preparing the return and has maintained adequate records has nothing to fear. In a best case scenario, the audit will be concluded promptly with no change in tax, or even with a refund (plus interest) due to the taxpayer. Of course, the return was selected for audit because of its high probability of error. Consequently, the probable outcome is that the office auditor or revenue agent will decide that the return contains a mistake that resulted in an understatement of the correct tax liability. In this case, the taxpayer is assessed a **deficiency** (the additional tax owed), plus interest based on the number of days between the time the return was originally filed and the date the deficiency is paid.

Corporations may deduct the interest paid on federal income tax deficiencies as a business expense. Currently, the IRS and the Tax Court disagree as to whether interest paid by an individual on an income tax deficiency relating to that individual's unincorporated business is deductible. Treasury regulations specifically state that interest paid by an individual on a federal income tax deficiency is nondeductible personal interest "regardless of the source of the income generating the tax liability."[12] In a recent decision, the Tax Court concluded that this regulation is invalid.[13] The court held that to the extent an income tax deficiency relates to the operation of an individual's business, the interest is a business expense deductible in the computation of adjusted gross income (AGI).

Your Rights as a Taxpayer

In 1989, Congress enacted the **Taxpayer Bill of Rights,** which requires the IRS to deal with every citizen and resident in a fair, professional, prompt, and courteous manner.[14] The Bill stipulates that the IRS must provide the technical help needed by taxpayers to comply with the law. Currently the IRS publishes over 100 free information booklets, one of which, IRS Publication 910, *Guide to Free Tax Services,* is a catalog describing the many types of assistance offered. The Taxpayer Bill of Rights ensures personal and financial confidentiality. If the IRS requests information, the taxpayer has the right to know why the IRS is asking for the information, exactly how the information will be used, and the nature of any consequences if the taxpayer refuses to provide the information. However, the Bill contains an important disclaimer: the IRS can share tax return information with state tax agencies, and under strict legal guidelines, the Department of Justice, other federal agencies, and foreign governments under tax treaty provisions.

Noncompliance Penalties

Objective 4
Describe the circumstances in which the IRS imposes a negligence or a civil fraud penalty.

Negligence.   During the course of an audit, a revenue agent may conclude that the taxpayer did not make a good faith effort to compute the correct tax for the year under examination. In such case, the IRS may impose an administrative penalty on the taxpayer. The Internal Revenue Code contains dozens of different penalties, each one

---

[12]Reg. §1.163-9T(b)(2)(i)(A).
[13]*Redlark*, 106 TC 31 (1996).
[14]In 1996, Congress enacted Taxpayer Bill of Rights 2, which expands on the original legislation.

designed to discourage a particular type of misconduct. One of the more frequently imposed is the **negligence** penalty, which equals 20 percent of any underpayment of tax attributable to the taxpayer's failure to make a reasonable attempt to comply with the law or to the taxpayer's intentional disregard of rules and regulations.[15]

> *Negligence.*   The IRS agent who audited Ms. B's 1996 Form 1040 discovered three errors that collectively resulted in a $45,000 understatement of her 1996 tax liability. The agent believed that two of the errors were attributable to Ms. B's misunderstanding of the law but that she had no legitimate excuse for the third error. The portion of the understatement attributable to the third error was $13,000. If the agent imposes a negligence penalty on Ms. B, the penalty is $2,600 (20 percent of $13,000). Ms. B must pay this penalty in addition to the $45,000 deficiency and the interest thereon.

The distinction between an honest mistake and negligence is nebulous. An individual taxpayer's exposure to the negligence penalty depends on subjective factors such as the complexity of the issue in question, the individual's level of education and business experience, the existence of supporting documentation, and the individual's degree of cooperation during the audit. When the IRS determines that a taxpayer's actions justify a negligence penalty and the taxpayer decides to challenge this determination, the burden of proof in the dispute rests on the taxpayer. In other words, the taxpayer must present a *preponderance of evidence* that the agent's finding of negligence is incorrect.[16] Individuals who follow the advice of tax practitioners in preparing their returns are much less likely to incur a negligence penalty than individuals who rely on their own judgment, although reliance on professional advice is not a guaranteed defense.

Civil Fraud.   The harshest administrative penalty that the IRS may impose is the **civil fraud** penalty, which equals 75 percent of the portion of a tax underpayment attributable to fraud.[17] Fraud can be defined as the intent to cheat the government by deliberately understating tax liability. Fraud is characterized by the systematic omission of substantial amounts of income from the tax return or by the deduction of nonexistent expenses or losses. Revenue agents often assess a fraud penalty when they discover that a taxpayer keeps two sets of financial records: one for tax purposes and one reflecting the taxpayer's true income. The fact that a taxpayer altered or destroyed business records and documents, concealed assets, or cannot account for large cash receipts or deposits is a strong indication of fraud.

> *Civil Fraud.*   The IRS agent who audited Mr. BT's 1996 Form 1040 discovered that Mr. BT made large monthly cash deposits to a bank account under a fictitious name. Mr. BT told the agent that the cash was a gift from a friend. When asked to reveal the friend's identity, Mr. BT became verbally abusive and refused to answer. After further investigation, the agent discovered that the cash represented

---

[15]§6662(a) and (b)(1).
[16]*Eric Wynn,* TC Memo 1995-609.
[17]§6663.

> $62,000 of unreported income from Mr. BT's lawn service business on which he owed $23,220 of federal tax. Because the agent concluded that Mr. BT intended to cheat the government by failing to report the income, the IRS assessed a $17,415 fraud penalty (75 percent of $23,220) on Mr. BT.

Because of the severity of the penalty, the burden of proof in establishing fraud falls on the IRS. To sustain a fraud penalty, the IRS must have more than just a preponderance of evidence; it must show by *clear and convincing evidence* that the fraud occurred.[18]

> *A Clear Case of Fraud.*   During 1992, Mr. William Tully conducted seminars in which he encouraged people to establish tax-exempt organizations through which (according to Mr. Tully) they could conduct all their financial transactions at no tax cost. While Mr. Tully did not charge for the seminars, he did charge a $3,000 fee to form a tax-exempt organization for those people who acted on his advice. Mr. Tully operated this business through his own tax-exempt organization. Thus, he did not report $620,500 of business profit on his 1992 Form 1040. The IRS discovered this omission of income, assessed a deficiency for the income tax on the business earnings, and imposed a civil fraud penalty equal to 75 percent of the deficiency. The court upheld the penalty because the facts of the case "constitute clear and convincing evidence that petitioner, fraudulently and with the intent to evade taxes known to be owing, omitted more than 90 percent of his income earned during 1992 and that the underpayment of tax required to be shown on his 1992 income tax return is due to fraud."[19]

Objective 5
Compare the consequences of civil fraud and criminal fraud.

Criminal Fraud.   If a revenue agent uncovers a particularly egregious incident of fraud, the IRS may turn the matter over to its Criminal Investigation Division. This division will assign a **special agent** to gather evidence to determine if the government has a strong enough case to indict the taxpayer for **criminal fraud,** also known as tax evasion. **Tax evasion** is a felony offense, punishable by severe monetary fines (up to $100,000 in the case of an individual and $500,000 in the case of a corporation) and by imprisonment in a federal penitentiary.[20] A person must be convicted of tax evasion in a court of law, and the prosecution must establish guilt *beyond a reasonable doubt.*[21] If the Criminal Investigation Division decides that the case against the taxpayer does not meet this strict evidential standard and therefore is too weak to prosecute, the IRS may have to settle for the civil fraud penalty.

Tax Return Preparer Penalties

The Internal Revenue Code imposes penalties on income tax return preparers who fail to comply with certain statutory rules of professional conduct.[22] The term **income tax return preparer** refers to any person who prepares returns (or who employs other people to

---

[18]*McGirl,* TC Memo 1996-313.

[19]*William J. Tully*, TC Memo 1997-310.

[20]§7201.

[21]*Bonansinga*, TC Memo 1987-586.

[22]§6694 through §6696. The American Bar Association and the American Institute of Certified Public Accountants also have standards of professional conduct for their members in tax practice.

prepare returns) for compensation, regardless of whether such person is a licensed attorney, certified public accountant, or enrolled agent. Preparers are required to:

- Sign the tax returns they fill out for their clients.
- Include their identifying number on such returns.
- Furnish clients with copies of their completed returns.
- Retain copies of all returns or a list of the names and identifying numbers of all clients.

In addition, preparers are prohibited from endorsing or negotiating any tax refund checks paid to their clients. Violation of any of these procedural rules without reasonable cause results in a monetary penalty. For instance, a preparer who fails to sign a tax return may be assessed $50 for each failure. The maximum penalty with respect to returns filed during any calendar year is limited to $25,000.

If a preparer takes a position on an income tax return resulting in an understatement of tax and the preparer knows (or should know) that such position has no realistic possibility of being sustained on its merit, the IRS may assess a $250 penalty with respect to the return. If the understatement is the result of a willful attempt to understate tax or if the position represents an intentional disregard of rules and regulations, the penalty increases to $1,000. Clearly, these penalties are intended to discourage tax advisors from taking overly aggressive positions to reduce their clients' tax liabilities. Even though the monetary penalties are modest, they can result in adverse publicity that may seriously damage an income tax return preparer's professional reputation.

Contesting the Result of an Audit

Taxpayers who disagree with all or any part of the outcome of an audit (including the imposition of administrative penalties) may appeal the disputed issue to a regional Appeals Office of the IRS. An appeal leads to an administrative conference between the taxpayer (or more typically, the taxpayer's representative) and a specially trained IRS appeals officer. The purpose of the conference is to resolve the controversy in a manner that is fair and impartial to both the government and the taxpayer. Appeal officers have broad latitude in settling disputes and may negotiate a compromise between the contestants on questionable issues. IRS Publication 5, *Appeal Rights and Preparation of Protest for Unagreed Cases,* explains a taxpayer's appeal rights and the appeals procedure in detail.

Litigation

Objective 6
Contrast the operations of the three federal trial courts that hear tax cases.

Trial Court.   When a taxpayer and the government fail to resolve their differences in an administrative conference, the taxpayer has the right to take the case to federal court for judicial review. In federal tax matters, one of three trial courts has original jurisdiction. A taxpayer may refuse to pay the deficiency determined by the IRS and file a petition with the **U.S. Tax Court** to hear the case. Alternatively, the taxpayer may pay the deficiency, then immediately sue the government for a refund in either the local **U.S. District Court** or the **U.S. Court of Federal Claims** located in Washington, D.C. The tax litigation process is illustrated in Exhibit 17–1.

The selection of the appropriate judicial forum is an important matter of strategy for the taxpayer's legal counsel. Each of the courts is different in operation, and one may be more advantageous than the others depending on the nature of the controversy. The Tax

EXHIBIT 17–1

The tax litigation process

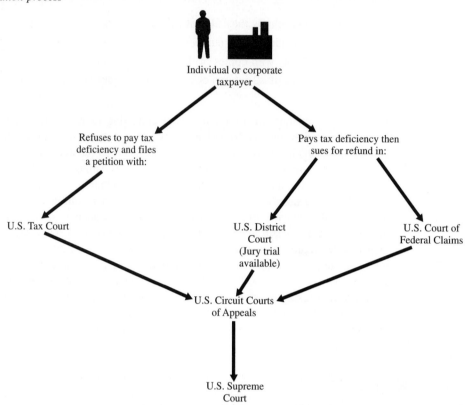

Court adjudicates only federal income, gift, and estate tax issues and is comprised of judges who are acknowledged experts in the tax law. In contrast, judges in the district courts and Court of Federal Claims preside over cases involving a wide variety of legal issues and typically have no special expertise in the tax area.

Taxpayers who want a jury trial must take their case to district court. In both the Tax Court or Court of Federal Claims, a single judge or a panel of judges tries the case and renders a verdict. If the controversy to be resolved is one of fact rather than the technical application of the law, the taxpayer's attorney may recommend that the matter be put to a jury in the hope that the jury panel (who, after all, are taxpayers themselves) may be naturally sympathetic. Of course, the viability of this strategy depends on the particular issue at hand. For instance, if the parent of a chronically ill child is arguing that the cost of a nontraditional treatment program should qualify as a deductible medical expense, a jury trial seems a wise choice. However, if a businessman is trying to prove that a $250,000 salary from his closely held corporation is reasonable compensation, he may be better off pleading his case before a Tax Court judge.

Objective 7
Explain the role of the U.S. Circuit Courts of Appeals and the Supreme Court in the tax litigation process.

Appellate and Supreme Court.   The losing party at the trial court level (taxpayer or government) may appeal the verdict to one of 13 **U.S. Circuit Courts of Appeals.** The geographic location of the trial court proceeding determines which appellate court has jurisdiction. These courts generally do not review findings of fact by a lower court, but they will consider if the lower court properly applied the relevant law to the facts.

After the appellate court has either affirmed or reversed the trial court's decision, the losing party may appeal the case to the **U.S. Supreme Court.** This Court may agree to hear the case (*grant certiorari*) or refuse to hear it (*deny certiorari*). When the Supreme Court denies certiorari, the decision of the appellate court is final. During an average term, the Supreme Court agrees to hear no more than a dozen federal tax cases, which are selected either because the Court believes that the case involves a significant and unresolved principle of law or because two or more appellate courts have rendered conflicting opinions on the proper resolution of a tax issue.

A Case History: Lori Williams v. United States

To summarize our discussion of the tax litigation process, consider the sequence of events in which Ms. Lori Williams took her case to the Supreme Court.

Facts of the Case.   During Lori Williams's marriage to Jerrold Rabin, he failed to pay $41,000 of federal employment tax related to his business. The government assessed a deficiency for the unpaid tax against Mr. Rabin and placed a lien on all his property, including the personal residence jointly owned with his wife. However, just one month before the lien was recorded, Mr. Rabin transferred his interest in the residence to Lori Williams as part of a divorce settlement. Nine months later, she contracted to sell the residence. Although Ms. Williams was not personally liable for her former husband's $41,000 tax deficiency, she paid it under protest. Her payment was the only way to remove the government's lien on the residence so that she could convey clear title to the purchasers.

Trial Court Decision.   After paying her former husband's tax bill, Ms. Williams filed a claim for refund, arguing that the government had "erroneously or illegally assessed or collected" the tax. The IRS refused to even consider her claim, responding that Ms. Williams could not seek a refund of tax assessed against another person, even though she paid the tax. Ms. Williams then brought suit against the United States for her refund in district court.[23] The district court accepted the government's argument and held that Ms. Williams lacked standing to seek a refund. In making its decision, the district court relied on precedent established in decisions by the Fifth and Seventh Circuit Courts of Appeals.[24]

Lori Williams's Appeal.   Refusing to accept defeat, Lori Williams appealed the trial court's verdict to the Ninth Circuit Court of Appeals. This court analyzed a very similar case decided in the taxpayer's favor by the Fourth Circuit Court.[25] The Ninth Circuit Court was persuaded by the Fourth Circuit Court's reasoning and decided that Lori Williams had the right to seek a refund, thereby reversing the district court's verdict.[26]

The Government's Appeal.   Now it was the government's turn to appeal the case to the Supreme Court, which granted certiorari to resolve the conflict among the appellate courts. In a decision in which six justices concurred and three justices dissented,

---

[23]*Lori Rabin Williams* v. *United States,* Civil No. 91-5286 WMB (DC CA, September 2, 1992).

[24]*Snodgrass* v. *United States,* 834 F.2d 537 (CA-5, 1987) and *Busse* v. *United States,* 542 F.2d 421 (CA-7, 1976).

[25]*Martin* v. *United States,* 895 F.2d 992 (CA-4, 1990).

[26]*Williams* v. *United States,* 24 F.3d 1143 (CA-9, 1994).

the Court affirmed the Ninth Circuit Court's decision by holding that any person who pays a tax has the right to seek a refund of such tax.[27] Justice Ruth Bader Ginsburg, writing for the majority, concluded that federal statute does not expressly restrict refund claims to those persons against which the tax was assessed. Ms. Williams had no realistic alternative to paying the tax assessed against her former husband if she ever wanted to sell the residence. Congress did not intend to leave people in Ms. Williams's predicament without legal remedy, and equity demands that the IRS consider her claim.

Making the Legal System More Taxpayer Friendly

While every taxpayer who disagrees with the IRS has a right to his day in court, many people are reluctant to bear the emotional and financial cost of litigation. To make the legal system a bit more assessable to the average person, Congress established a **Small Tax Case division** of the Tax Court.[28] A taxpayer who is disputing a deficiency of $10,000 or less for any one year may request an informal hearing presided over by an officer of the court. The current filing fee for such hearing is only $60, and the taxpayer may plead his own case without an attorney. After the presiding officer has heard the taxpayer's side of the story and rendered judgment, the matter is settled—neither taxpayer nor government may appeal the case to any other court.

Taxpayers who prevail in their litigation with the IRS may be entitled to recover litigation expenses from the government.[29] Such expenses include court costs, attorney fees, fees paid to expert witnesses, and payments for technical studies, analyses, tests, and reports necessary for the preparation of the taxpayer's case. Taxpayers who win their case are reimbursed for these expenses unless the government can convince the court that the IRS's position in the case was substantially justified. If the IRS failed to follow any of its own published rules, regulations, and procedures during the taxpayer's audit, the legal presumption is that the IRS's position was unjustified. Another factor that the courts consider in determining whether an IRS position was justifiable is whether the government pursued the litigation to harass or embarrass the taxpayer or out of political motivation.

The existence of the Small Tax Case division and the right of taxpayers to recover litigation costs from the government reflect congressional sympathy for individuals who sincerely believe that they are right and the IRS is wrong. On the other hand, Congress has little tolerance for people who waste the government's time and money by initiating foolish lawsuits against the IRS. The Internal Revenue Code authorizes the Tax Court to impose a monetary penalty up to $25,000 on a taxpayer who takes a frivolous or groundless position in a proceeding before the court or institutes a proceeding primarily for delay.[30]

IRS Collection Procedures

Taxpayers who have exhausted every avenue of appeal without success must finally pay their tax deficiency (including interest and penalties) to the government. The IRS is authorized to collect the deficiency by whatever means necessary, including seizing the

---

[27]*United States* v. *Williams,* 514 U.S. 527 (1995).

[28]§7463.

[29]§7430. Taxpayers may also be entitled to recover reasonable administrative costs incurred when dealing with the IRS.

[30]§6673.

taxpayer's assets and selling them at auction, levying bank accounts, and garnishing the taxpayer's salary or wage. Nonetheless, the IRS knows that it can't get blood out of a stone. If a taxpayer has insufficient financial means to pay a tax deficiency and is willing to cooperate, the IRS may negotiate a settlement (referred to as an **offer in compromise**) for some lesser amount. Alternatively, the IRS may allow the taxpayer to pay off the debt over time on an installment basis.

Objective 8
Define the term
transferee liability.

A question sometimes arises as to which person is legally responsible for the payment of a federal tax deficiency. If the taxpayer is a corporation, the deficiency must be satisfied with corporate assets; typically shareholders are not liable for their corporation's unpaid taxes. A major exception to this limited shareholder liability arises when the corporation is no longer in existence. In this circumstance, the shareholders have **transferee liability** for the corporation's unsatisfied debts, including federal taxes, to the extent of the value of any assets received on liquidation of the corporation.[31]

> ***Transferee Liability.***   Ms. KJ owned 30 percent of the stock of KLM Inc., which was dissolved under state law in 1996. Ms. KJ received a $55,000 cash distribution from the corporation in complete liquidation of her equity interest. The IRS audited KLM's tax returns for 1995 and 1996 and determined that the corporation underpaid its income tax by $114,800. The IRS can assess $55,000 of this deficiency against Ms. KJ.

The Innocent Spouse Rule

Objective 9
Explain the purpose of
the innocent spouse rule.

When individuals sign their Form 1040s each year, they become liable for any future tax deficiency with respect to that return. In the case of a joint return, both husband and wife must sign, thereby becoming joint and severally liable.[32] As a result, the IRS may assess either person for the entire deficiency determined on subsequent audit of the return. Occasionally this rule can work a real hardship on a person who is liable for substantial back taxes attributable to a joint return that he or she signed without any knowledge of the information included therein. Such a person may be relieved of liability for the tax deficiency under the **innocent spouse rule**.[33] Such relief is dependent on three conditions:

- The deficiency must be attributable to the omission of gross income or the claim of a bogus deduction or credit by the person's spouse.
- The person must establish that in signing the return he or she did not know, and had no reason to know, that the return understated the correct tax liability.
- Taking into account all the facts and circumstances, it is inequitable to hold the person liable for the deficiency.

One factor that the courts weigh very heavily in analyzing the third condition is whether the person significantly benefited, directly or indirectly, from any gross income omitted from the return. If a court concludes that a significant benefit existed, innocent spouse relief is denied, even if the person seeking relief was clearly ignorant of the omission. Normal spousal support is not considered a significant benefit, but an unusu-

---

[31]§6901.
[32]§6013(d)(3).
[33]§6013(e).

ally lavish or extravagant lifestyle may indicate that both spouses enjoyed the omitted income. Another factor that the courts consider is whether the person seeking relief has been deserted by or is divorced from his or her spouse.

> ***Innocent Spouse Relief.***   Mr. and Mrs. Vriner married in 1989 and divorced in 1997. The couple filed joint tax returns for 1989 through 1995 that reported no taxable income. During the marriage, Mr. Vriner worked at a restaurant owned by his parents. Mrs. Vriner never saw a paycheck from the restaurant, and her husband told her that the restaurant was none of her business. Mrs. Vriner was not employed. The couple did not have a joint checking account; Mr. Vriner paid their bills with cash or money orders. The couple resided in an old neighborhood consisting of moderate- to low-priced homes. They lived modestly, seldom dining out or traveling.
>
> In 1995, federal narcotic agents arrested Mr. Vriner for drug trafficking. Mrs. Vriner learned of her husband's illegal activities from reading the newspaper after his arrest. The IRS subsequently determined that Mr. Vriner failed to report any income from his drug trafficking and assessed a $36,417 tax deficiency for 1994 and 1995. The Tax Court decided that Mrs. Vriner was entitled to relief as an innocent spouse. She had no actual knowledge of the tax understatement and no reason to know of the understatement, given her level of education and her exclusion from family finances. The court concluded that it would be inequitable to hold Mrs. Vriner liable for the deficiency because she received very little, if any, benefit from the income that gave rise to the deficiency.[34]

Conclusion to the Text

Chapter 17 has provided a brief summary of the tax compliance process. After reading this chapter, you should have a much better sense of the rights and responsibilities of corporate and individual taxpayers. You should be aware that noncompliance with the tax laws can result in monetary penalties and, in extreme cases, criminal prosecution. Finally, you should understand the roles played by the IRS and the federal courts in administering our nation's tax laws. The information contained in this chapter, which culminates our study of the federal tax system, should serve you in good stead in your role as a taxpaying citizen or resident of the United States.

To bring *Principles of Taxation for Business and Investment Planning* to its conclusion, let's briefly revisit the three objectives established in the introduction to the text. The first objective was to familiarize readers with tax policy issues. If the text has been successful in meeting this objective, you should be confident of your ability to evaluate tax laws based on the characteristics of sufficiency, ease of administration, economic efficiency, and equity. Your study of the federal tax system should help you form rational opinions concerning the strengths and weaknesses of the system—opinions based on knowledge rather than popular misconceptions or political bombast. Perhaps you have some definite ideas as to how the tax system can be improved and are eager to work toward that improvement through the democratic process.

[34]*Barbara A. Vriner,* TC Memo 1995-465.

The second objective of the text was to bridge the gap between finance and tax. Hopefully, you now understand that these two subjects are inextricably related and that business managers cannot make good financial decisions without considering tax consequences. In our many discussions of the tax implications of business and investment transactions, we've analyzed transactions in terms of after-tax cash flows. We've observed how the net present value of cash flows can increase when tax costs are minimized or tax savings are maximized. And you've worked hard to develop an aptitude for recognizing tax planning opportunities to improve financial outcomes.

The third objective of the text was to teach the basic framework and operation of the federal income tax. Throughout the text, we've concentrated on core concepts rather than technical details. To the extent you've mastered these concepts, you understand how the income tax relates to the business, employment, investment, and even personal activities in which you will engage throughout your life. Almost certainly, you have concluded that the income tax system deserves its reputation for complexity. But if the text has achieved its third objective, you also appreciate the reasons underlying much of the complexity. In addition, you now have a theoretical framework in place. As you continue to learn about taxes and tax systems, either in the classroom or through experience, you can integrate your new knowledge into this framework. If you do this, the lessons learned from *Principles of Taxation for Business and Investment Planning* will create value for many years to come.

Key Terms

Civil fraud   473
Correspondence examination   471
Criminal fraud   474
Deficiency   472
Discriminate function system (DIF)
  score   471
Enrolled agent   472
Field examination   471
Income tax return preparer   474
Innocent spouse rule   479
Late-filing and late-payment
  penalty   468
Negligence   473

Offer in compromise   479
Office examination   471
Small Tax Case division   478
Special agent   474
Statute of limitations   470
Tax evasion   474
Taxpayer Bill of Rights   472
Transferee liability   479
U.S. Circuit Courts of Appeals   476
U.S. Court of Federal Claims   475
U.S. District Court   475
U.S. Supreme Court   477
U.S. Tax Court   475

Questions and Problems for Discussion

1. Discuss the policy reasons for a statute of limitations for tax returns.
2. Statistically, about 1 percent of the individual Form 1040s filed each year are subject to IRS audit. Why does a Form 1040 reflecting AGI of $31,000 and a standard deduction have much *less* than a 1 percent chance of audit, while a Form 1040 reflecting AGI of $235,000 and itemized deductions of $85,790 have a much *greater* than 1 percent chance of audit?
3. Which has the greater chance of audit: a Form 1040 with AGI of $200,000, all of which is salary income, or a Form 1040 with AGI of $200,000, all of which is net profit from a sole proprietorship?

4. Mrs. NM received a letter from the IRS asking her to submit written substantiation of a $1,500 charitable contribution claimed on her 1997 Form 1040 as an itemized deduction. Discuss the probable tax consequences to Mrs. NM if:
   a. She sends the IRS copies of her canceled check for $1,500 made out to the charitable organization and the thank-you letter she received in which the organization acknowledged her contribution.
   b. She ignores the IRS request because she has no substantiation.

5. Is it easier for the IRS to determine that an individual omitted an income item from a return or that the individual overstated allowable deductions?

6. Corporation VL's net worth exceeds $160 million, its stock is publicly traded, and a national CPA firm audits its financial statements. Corporation TT's net worth also exceeds $160 million. However, Corporation TT is closely held by the members of the TT family. Discuss the reasons that the IRS might choose to audit Corporation TT rather than Corporation VL.

7. NK Inc. and CS Inc. are both closely held corporations. NK's tax returns for the last five years reflect average taxable income of $90 million. CS's tax returns for the same period reflect average taxable income of $90,000. Discuss the reasons that the IRS might choose to audit NK Inc. rather than CS Inc.

8. During the IRS audit of her 1996 income tax return, Ms. H provided the revenue agent with a meticulous set of records substantiating every numeric entry on the return. The agent actually complimented Ms. H on the quality of her return preparation. Nevertheless, in computing her tax liability, Ms. H did make a $435 error in her favor. When she received formal notification that she owed an additional $435 of 1996 tax, Ms. H was dismayed that the IRS also billed her for $92 of interest on the deficiency. Ms. H doesn't understand why she must pay interest when she obviously made a good faith effort to comply with the tax law. Can you explain why?

9. Discuss the burden of proof as it relates to the taxpayer penalties for:
   a. Negligence.
   b. Civil fraud.
   c. Criminal fraud.

10. During a field examination of GNT Inc.'s income tax returns for 1995 and 1996, the revenue agent discovered that the corporation's treasurer had systematically omitted substantial income items and inflated deductions to minimize the corporation's tax liability. The agent suspects that the treasurer adopted this deliberate course of action as early as 1989. Can the IRS initiate an audit of GNT's tax returns all the way back to 1989? Explain briefly.

11. Mr. JY, a commercial artist, engaged Mr. DE, a local attorney, to prepare his 1996 income tax return. Mr. JY provided the attorney with his check register, deposit slips, receipts, and financial documents pertaining to 1996 and carefully read through the completed return before signing it. In 1998, this return was selected for audit. The IRS agent discovered that Mr. DE incorrectly deducted certain of Mr. JY's personal living expenses. Consequently, the tax shown on the return was understated by $8,900. The agent decided that the deduction represented an unrealistic position, with no reasonable basis in the law.
   a. Based on the above facts, is Mr. JY liable for payment of the $8,900 tax deficiency plus interest?
   b. Could the IRS impose a negligence penalty on Mr. JY?
   c. Could Mr. DE be penalized because of the error made in preparing Mr. JY's income tax return?
   d. Would your answer to the preceding questions change if Mr. DE were Mr. JY's brother-in-law who prepared the return as a favor rather than for compensation?

12. Mr. NG is an enrolled agent in tax practice. Last year, the IRS assessed a $750 preparer penalty on Mr. NG, who immediately hired an attorney to help him contest the penalty. Mr. NG's legal fee was $7,900. Was Mr. NG acting irrationally by spending so much money to avoid the penalty?

13. Mr. and Mrs. BL filed a joint 1995 tax return reporting $24,000 of AGI. During the year, Mr. BL was extremely ill and was hospitalized for four months. Mrs. BL, desperate for funds to pay her husband's medical bills, took a night job as a bartender. She earned approximately $7,000 of tips from this second job, none of which she

reported on the 1995 return. Mr. BL had no idea his wife had gone to such lengths on his behalf. In 1996, the couple divorced; and in 1998, the IRS notified Mr. BL that he owed a $1,100 deficiency plus interest attributable to the unreported tip income. Based on these facts, can Mr. BL avoid liability for the deficiency as an innocent spouse? Explain your conclusion.

14. Mrs. QE has decided to contest a $28,650 tax deficiency that the IRS assessed with respect to her 1996 Form 1040. She understands that she can initiate the litigation in district court or the Tax Court. Identify any reasons why Mrs. QE might prefer one trial court over the other.

Application Problems

1. Ms. CP did not request an extension of time to file her 1997 income tax return and did not mail the completed return to the IRS until July 2, 1998. She enclosed a check for $2,380, the correct balance of tax due with the return.
   a. Assuming that Ms. CP cannot show reasonable cause for filing a delinquent return, compute the late-filing and late-payment penalty.
   b. How would your answer change if Ms. CP did not mail her return until November 21, 1998?

2. Mr. DD filed a delinquent 1997 tax return on July 27, 1998. The return reflected total tax liability of $3,700, withholding of $4,000, and a $300 refund due. Based on these facts, compute the late-filing penalty for which Mr. DD is liable.

3. LZ Inc.'s taxable year is a fiscal year ending November 30. The corporate controller filed LZ's Form 1120 for the year ending November 30, 1997, on December 23, 1997.
   a. Based on these facts, what is the last day on which the IRS may assess the corporation for additional tax relating to this fiscal year?
   b. How would your answer change if LZ's return for its fiscal year ending November 30, 1997, was timely filed on its extended due date of August 15, 1998?

4. Mrs. FG, who is divorced from Mr. FG, failed to include $28,000 of alimony income on her 1996 Form 1040. The only income she reported was her $78,000 salary. Mrs. FG filed her 1996 return on January 19, 1997.
   a. What is the last date that the IRS can assess Mrs. FG with additional tax for 1996?
   b. Would your answer change if Mrs. FG also reported $37,500 of dividend and interest income on her 1996 Form 1040?

5. Ms. ER received a notice from the IRS assessing a $21,000 deficiency of 1995 income tax plus $4,300 interest on the deficiency. Ms. ER operates a sole proprietorship, and $16,800 of the deficiency relates to an incorrect method of accounting for the proprietorship's inventory. The rest of the deficiency relates to disallowed charitable contributions. If Ms. ER is in the 36 percent tax bracket, compute the after-tax cost of the $4,300 interest payment.

6. Mr. GH has an MBA degree from Stanford University and has been in business for himself for 18 years. The revenue agent who audited Mr. GH's 1995 Form 1040 discovered a glaring error resulting in a $16,200 understatement of tax. When the agent questioned him about the error, Mr. GH just shrugged his shoulders and offered no logical explanation.
   a. If the revenue agent decides that the error resulted from Mr. GH's intentional disregard of a tax rule, compute the negligence penalty the agent may impose.
   b. Should the fact of Mr. GH's education and business experience influence the agent's decision to impose the negligence penalty?

7. During the course of her audit of Mr. and Mrs. J's individual tax returns for 1995 and 1996, the revenue agent learned that the couple kept two sets of books for their sole proprietorship. The couple presented her with one set substantiating the net business income reported on their returns for the two-year period. The agent discovered the second set during a routine examination of the business's computer files. This second set indicated that Mr. and Mrs. J earned over $80,000 during 1995 and 1996 that they failed to report as taxable income. The tax deficiency on the unreported income was $32,000.

a. If the agent concludes that Mr. and Mrs. J committed fraud by deliberately underreporting income, compute the civil fraud penalty the IRS may impose.

b. Describe the procedural steps the IRS must take if it wants to charge the couple with criminal fraud.

c. Why might the IRS decide to impose a civil fraud penalty on Mr. and Mrs. J but not charge them with criminal fraud?

8. The IRS assessed a $32,800 income tax deficiency plus $4,015 interest against Mr. and Mrs. OE. The deficiency was attributable to an alleged understatement of investment income and capital gains on the couple's 1996 Form 1040. Mr. and Mrs. OE refused to pay and took their case to the U.S. Tax Court. They incurred $7,829 of attorney fees and other expenses relating to the litigation. Determine the couple's after-tax cost of this unpleasantness, assuming that:

a. They won their case and the government failed to demonstrate to the court that the IRS's position was substantially justified.

b. They won their case, but the government convinced the court that the IRS's position was substantially justified.

c. They lost their case.

9. Ms. TY is a professional tax return preparer. In 1996, she prepared the partnership return for the MK Limited Partnership, which has 42 individual partners. The IRS agent who audited this return discovered that Ms. TY had incorrectly deducted $67,000 of expenses, which resulted in an understatement of each partner's distributive share of 1996 income. Compute the preparer penalty if the IRS concludes that:

a. Ms. TY should have known that the deduction had no realistic possibility of being sustained on its merit if the partnership return was audited.

b. Ms. TY willfully attempted to understate the tax liability of the partners by claiming the erroneous deduction on the partnership return.

Issue Recognition Problems

Identify the tax issue or issues suggested by the following situations and state each issue in the form of a question.

1. On April 3, Mr. and Mrs. BR left their home in Oregon to travel to Japan. They made the trip because their son, who lives in Tokyo, was severely injured in an accident and needed their care. After nursing their son back to health, the couple returned home on June 11. On June 17, Mrs. BR mailed their delinquent Form 1040 for the prior year and remitted the $18,262 balance of tax due with the return.

2. On July 2, Mrs. N received a notice from the IRS assessing a $10,861 deficiency of 1995 and 1996 tax plus $1,900 interest (computed through the date the IRS mailed the deficiency notice). Mrs. N was temporarily short of funds, so she did not pay her tax bill within 10 days as required by the notice. Instead, she waited until September 29 to mail a check for $12,761 to the IRS.

3. On April 13, Mr. LP filed a request for an automatic extension of time to file his prior year

Form 1040. He estimated that the balance of prior year tax due was $3,800 and he paid this amount with the extension request. Mr. LP filed his return on June 20. The actual balance of tax due was $6,900, so Mr. LP paid an additional $3,100 with the return.

4. Mr. B, a self-employed consultant, charged a client a $15,000 professional fee plus $3,900 of reimbursable business expenses. The client promptly paid the $18,900 bill. At the end of the year, the client sent Mr. B a Form 1099 reporting $18,900 of income. When Mr. B prepared his Schedule C for the year, he simply reported $15,000 of income from the client. He did not report the $3,900 reimbursement nor did he deduct the expenses.

5. Mr. T has not paid income tax or filed a tax return for the last eight years. He believes that the IRS can no longer assess any back taxes for the first five of those years.

6. KP Inc., a calendar year taxpayer, filed its 1995 return on March 8, 1996. On November 19,

1998, the corporation filed an amended 1995 return reflecting $2.61 million *less* taxable income than the original return and claiming a tax refund of $913,000.

7. Corporation N, a calendar year taxpayer, incurred a net operating loss in 1997. The corporation carried the loss back as a deduction against 1994 income, thereby reducing its 1994 tax by $712,600. Corporation N's treasurer filed a claim for refund of the overpayment of 1994 tax and expects to receive a check from the government any day now.

8. Mr. MK died in 1997 and left all his property to his only relative, grandson G. After probate was completed and the estate was settled, G received his inheritance worth $942,000. Nine months later, the IRS completed an audit of Mr. MK's 1996 tax return and discovered that Mr. MK had underpaid his income tax by $18,450.

Tax Planning Cases

1. Mr. JR's tax situation for the year is very complicated. He engaged in several high-dollar investment transactions involving unresolved tax issues. He has instructed his accountant to take the most aggressive, pro-taxpayer position possible with respect to these transactions. Mr. JR also wants to take a home office deduction for one of his business activities. The deduction would be only $1,293, but Mr. JR believes he is entitled to claim this amount on his return. Can you suggest any strategic reason why Mr. JR should forego the home office deduction?

2. The IRS recently assessed a $290,800 income tax deficiency on CMP Corporation. The deficiency is attributable to a complicated accounting issue involving CMP's investment in a controlled foreign corporation. CMP plans to contest the deficiency in court. CMP is located in the Third Circuit. Neither the local district court, the Tax Court, nor the Third Circuit Court of Appeals has considered the particular tax issue in CMP's case. The Court of Federal Claims and the Eighth Circuit Court of Appeals have decided the issue in favor of the government. However, the Ninth and Tenth Circuit Courts of Appeals have taken a pro-taxpayer stand on the issue. Based on these facts, discuss CMP's litigation strategy in selecting a trial court.

Appendixes

Appendixes

APPENDIX A
PRESENT VALUE OF $1

Periods	3%	4%	5%	6%	7%	8%	9%
1	.971	.962	.952	.943	.935	.926	.917
2	.943	.925	.907	.890	.873	.857	.842
3	.915	.889	.864	.840	.816	.794	.772
4	.888	.855	.823	.792	.763	.735	.708
5	.863	.822	.784	.747	.713	.681	.650
6	.837	.790	.746	.705	.666	.630	.596
7	.813	.760	.711	.665	.623	.583	.547
8	.789	.731	.677	.627	.582	.540	.502
9	.766	.703	.645	.592	.544	.500	.460
10	.744	.676	.614	.558	.508	.463	.422
11	.722	.650	.585	.527	.475	.429	.388
12	.701	.625	.557	.497	.444	.397	.356
13	.681	.601	.530	.469	.415	.368	.326
14	.661	.577	.505	.442	.388	.340	.299
15	.642	.555	.481	.417	.362	.315	.275
16	.623	.534	.458	.394	.339	.292	.252
17	.605	.513	.436	.371	.317	.270	.231
18	.587	.494	.416	.350	.296	.250	.212
19	.570	.475	.396	.331	.277	.232	.194
20	.554	.456	.377	.312	.258	.215	.178

Periods	10%	11%	12%	13%	14%	15%	20%
1	.909	.901	.893	.885	.877	.870	.833
2	.826	.812	.797	.783	.769	.756	.694
3	.751	.731	.712	.693	.675	.658	.579
4	.683	.659	.636	.613	.592	.572	.482
5	.621	.593	.567	.543	.519	.497	.402
6	.564	.535	.507	.480	.456	.432	.335
7	.513	.482	.452	.425	.400	.376	.279
8	.467	.434	.404	.376	.351	.327	.233
9	.424	.391	.361	.333	.308	.284	.194
10	.386	.352	.322	.295	.270	.247	.162
11	.350	.317	.287	.261	.237	.215	.135
12	.319	.286	.257	.231	.208	.187	.112
13	.290	.258	.229	.204	.182	.163	.093
14	.263	.232	.205	.181	.160	.141	.078
15	.239	.209	.183	.160	.140	.123	.065
16	.218	.188	.163	.141	.123	.107	.054
17	.198	.170	.146	.125	.108	.093	.045
18	.180	.153	.130	.111	.095	.081	.038
19	.164	.138	.116	.098	.083	.070	.031
20	.149	.124	.104	.087	.073	.061	.026

APPENDIX B
PRESENT VALUE OF ANNUITY OF $1

Periods	3%	4%	5%	6%	7%	8%	9%
1	.971	.962	.952	.943	.935	.926	.917
2	1.913	1.886	1.859	1.833	1.808	1.783	1.759
3	2.829	2.775	2.723	2.673	2.624	2.577	2.531
4	3.717	3.630	3.546	3.465	3.387	3.312	3.240
5	4.580	4.452	4.329	4.212	4.100	3.993	3.890
6	5.417	5.242	5.076	4.917	4.767	4.623	4.486
7	6.230	6.002	5.786	5.582	5.389	5.206	5.033
8	7.020	6.733	6.463	6.210	5.971	5.747	5.535
9	7.786	7.435	7.108	6.802	6.515	6.247	5.995
10	8.530	8.111	7.722	7.360	7.024	6.710	6.418
11	9.253	8.760	8.306	7.887	7.499	7.139	6.805
12	9.954	9.385	8.863	8.384	7.943	7.536	7.161
13	10.635	9.986	9.394	8.853	8.358	7.904	7.487
14	11.296	10.563	9.899	9.295	8.745	8.244	7.786
15	11.938	11.118	10.380	9.712	9.108	8.559	8.061
16	12.561	11.652	10.838	10.106	9.447	8.851	8.313
17	13.166	12.166	11.274	10.477	9.763	9.122	8.544
18	13.754	12.659	11.690	10.828	10.059	9.372	8.756
19	14.324	13.134	12.085	11.158	10.336	9.604	8.950
20	14.877	13.590	12.462	11.470	10.594	9.818	9.129

Periods	10%	11%	12%	13%	14%	15%	20%
1	.909	.901	.893	.885	.877	.870	.833
2	1.736	1.713	1.690	1.668	1.647	1.626	1.528
3	2.487	2.444	2.402	2.361	2.322	2.283	2.106
4	3.170	3.102	3.037	2.974	2.914	2.855	2.589
5	3.791	3.696	3.605	3.517	3.433	3.352	2.991
6	4.355	4.231	4.111	3.998	3.889	3.784	3.326
7	4.868	4.712	4.564	4.423	4.288	4.160	3.605
8	5.335	5.146	4.968	4.799	4.639	4.487	3.837
9	5.759	5.537	5.328	5.132	4.946	4.772	4.031
10	6.145	5.889	5.650	5.426	5.216	5.019	4.192
11	6.495	6.207	5.938	5.687	5.453	5.234	4.327
12	6.814	6.492	6.194	5.918	5.660	5.421	4.439
13	7.103	6.750	6.424	6.122	5.842	5.583	4.533
14	7.367	6.982	6.628	6.302	6.002	5.724	4.611
15	7.606	7.191	6.811	6.462	6.142	5.847	4.675
16	7.824	7.379	6.974	6.604	6.265	5.954	4.730
17	8.022	7.549	7.120	6.729	6.373	6.047	4.775
18	8.201	7.702	7.250	6.840	6.467	6.128	4.812
19	8.365	7.839	7.366	6.938	6.550	6.198	4.843
20	8.514	7.963	7.469	7.025	6.623	6.259	4.870

Glossary

Abandonment loss   The unrecovered basis in an abandoned asset. Abandonment losses with respect to business assets are ordinary deductions.

Abatement   A property tax exemption granted by a government for a limited period of time.

Ability to pay   Economic resources under a person's control from which they can pay tax.

Accelerated death benefits   Payments made under a life insurance contract to insured individuals who are terminally or chronically ill.

Accrual method of accounting   An overall method of accounting under which revenues are realized in the year the earnings process is complete and expenses are matched against revenues in the year the liability for the expense is incurred.

Accumulated earnings tax   A penalty tax levied on corporations accumulating income beyond the reasonable needs of the business to avoid paying dividends to their shareholders. The tax is levied in addition to the regular income tax.

Acquisition debt   Debt incurred to acquire, construct, or substantially improve a personal residence. The debt must be secured by the residence and is limited to $1 million ($500,000 for married filing separately).

Activity-based tax   A tax imposed on the results of an ongoing activity in which persons or organizations engage.

Ad valorem tax   A tax based on the value of property.

Adjusted basis   The initial tax basis of an asset reduced by cost recovery deductions allowable with respect to the basis.

Adjusted gross income (AGI)   Total income less adjustments as computed on page 1, Form 1040. AGI is an intermediate step in the calculation of individual taxable income.

Adjustments   Deductions from total income listed on page 1, Form 1040.

Affiliated corporation   For purposes of the tax rules governing worthless securities, any 80 percent or more controlled domestic subsidiary that has always derived more than 90 percent of annual gross receipts from the conduct of an active business.

Affiliated group   A parent corporation and its 80 percent or more controlled subsidiaries.

All-events test   The test for determining if an accrued expense is deductible. For most routine accruals, the test is satisfied if the liability on which the accrued expense is based is fixed and the amount of the liability is determinable with reasonable accuracy.

Allowance method   The GAAP method for computing bad debt expense. The expense is based on the estimated losses from current year receivables.

Alternative minimum tax (AMT) system   A second federal tax system parallel to the regular tax system. Congress enacted the AMT to ensure that every individual and corporation pays at least a minimal tax every year.

Alternative minimum taxable income (AMTI)   The tax base for the AMT: regular taxable income increased or decreased by AMT adjustments and increased by AMT tax preferences.

Amortization   The ratable deduction of the capitalized cost of an intangible asset over its determinable life.

Amount realized   The sum of any money plus the fair market value of any property received by a seller on the sale or exchange of property.

AMT adjustments   Increases or decreases to regular taxable income in the computation of AMTI.

Annual gift tax exclusion   The first $10,000 of value that a donor gives to a donee during a calendar year.

Annualized income   The taxable income reported on a short-period return mathematically inflated to reflect 12 months of business operations.

Annuity   A cash flow consisting of a constant dollar amount for a specific number of time periods.

Apportionment   A method of dividing a firm's taxable income among the various states with jurisdiction to tax the firm's business activities.

Arm's-length transaction   A transaction occurring between unrelated parties who are dealing in their own self-interest.

Assignment of income doctrine   Income must be taxed to the entity that renders the service or owns the capital with respect to which the income is paid.

Average rate   The tax rate determined by dividing total tax liability by the total tax base.

Bargain element   The excess of fair market value over cost of stock acquired on exercise of a stock option.

Boot   Cash or other nonqualifying property included as part of a nontaxable exchange.

Bracket   The portion of a tax base subject to a given percentage rate in a graduated rate structure.

Bunching   A tax-planning technique to concentrate itemized deductions into one year so that the total exceeds the standard deduction for the year.

Burden of proof   The obligation of one party in a legal action to convince the court that the other party is incorrect or unjustified in its assertions of fact.

Business purpose doctrine   A transaction should not be effective for tax purposes unless it is intended to achieve a genuine and independent business purpose other than tax avoidance.

Buy-sell agreement   A binding agreement that restricts the conditions and terms under which shareholders may dispose of corporate stock.

Cafeteria plan   A compensation plan under which employees may choose among two or more benefits, including both cash and noncash items.

Calendar year   The 12-month period from January 1 through December 31.

Capital asset   Any asset that does *not* fall into one of five statutory categories: business inventory, business accounts receivable, real or depreciable business property, creative assets, and U.S. government publications.

Capital gain or loss   Gain or loss realized on the sale or exchange of a capital asset. Capital gain may be eligible for a preferential tax rate.

Capitalization   An accounting requirement that an expenditure be charged to a balance sheet account rather than against the firm's current income.

Carryover basis   The basis of transferred property in the hands of the recipient equal to the basis of the property in the hands of the transferor.

Cash method of accounting   An overall method of accounting under which revenue is accounted for when payment is received and expenses are accounted for when payment is made.

Cash surrender value   The amount paid to the owner of a life insurance policy on the liquidation of the policy.

Centralized management   A legal characteristic of the corporate form of business: corporations are managed by a board of directors appointed by and acting on behalf of the shareholders.

Child credit   A credit based on the number of the taxpayer's dependent children under age 17.

Civil fraud   The intention to cheat the government by deliberately understating tax liability.

Closely held corporations   Corporations privately owned by a relatively small number of shareholders.

Collectibles   Tangible capital assets such as works of art, antiques, gems, stamps, and coins.

Commerce Clause   Article 1 of the U.S. Constitution that grants the federal government the power to regulate interstate commerce.

Consolidated tax return   A single Form 1120 reporting the combined results of the operations of an affiliated group of corporations.

Constructive dividend   A distribution by a corporation to a shareholder that the corporation classifies as salary, interest, rent, or some other type of payment but that the IRS classifies as a dividend.

Constructive receipt   The point at which a taxpayer has unrestricted access to and control of income, even if the income item is not in the taxpayer's actual possession.

Controlled foreign corporation (CFC)   A foreign corporation in which U.S. shareholders own more than 50 percent of the voting power or stock value.

Controlled group   A brother-sister group of corporations owned by the same individual shareholders or a parent-subsidiary group of corporations.

Convenience   The second standard for a good tax. A tax should be convenient for the government to administer and for people to pay.

Correspondence examination   The simplest type of audit that can be handled entirely by telephone or through the mail.

Cost basis   The purchase price of an asset including any sales tax paid by the purchaser and any incidental costs related to getting the asset in place and into production.

Cost depletion   The method for recovering the capitalized cost of an exhaustible natural resource. Cost depletion equals unrecovered basis in the resource (mine or well) multiplied by the ratio of units of production sold during the year to the estimated total units of production at the beginning of the year.

Cost of goods sold   The capitalized cost of inventory sold during the taxable year and subtracted from gross receipts in the computation of gross income.

Criminal fraud   A felony offense involving the willful attempt to evade or defeat any federal tax.

Cross-crediting   Crediting the excess foreign tax paid in high-tax jurisdictions against the excess limitation attributable to income earned in low-tax jurisdictions.

Cumulative Bulletin (CB)   Semiannual compilation of weekly Internal Revenue Bulletins.

Declining marginal utility of income   The theory that the financial importance associated with each dollar of income diminishes as total income increases.

Deduction   An offset or subtraction in the calculation of taxable income.

Deemed paid foreign tax credit A credit available to U.S. corporations that receive dividends from a foreign subsidiary. The credit is based on foreign income tax paid by the subsidiary.

Deferred compensation A nonqualified plan under which an employer promises to pay a portion of an employee's current compensation in a future year.

Deferred taxes The balance sheet account that records the difference between tax expense for financial statement purposes and the actual liability computed on the tax return.

Deficiency An underpayment of tax determined on audit and assessed by the IRS.

Defined-benefit plan A qualified plan under which participants are promised a targeted benefit, usually in the form of a pension, when they retire.

Defined-contribution plan A qualified plan under which an annual contribution is made to each participant's retirement account.

Dependent A member of a taxpayer's family or household who receives more than half of his or her financial support from the taxpayer.

Dependent care credit A credit based on the taxpayer's cost of caring for dependents either under age 13 or physically or mentally incapable of caring for themselves.

Depreciation The systematic deduction of the capitalized cost of tangible property over a specific period of time.

Depreciation recapture Recapture computed with reference to depreciation or amortization deductions claimed with respect to property surrendered in a sale or exchange.

Direct write-off method The method for determining a bad debt deduction required by the tax law. Only receivables that are written off as uncollectible during the year are deductible.

Discount rate The rate of interest used to calculate the present value of future cash flows.

Discriminate function system (DIF) score A numeric score assigned to individual tax returns that measures the return's potential for generating additional tax on audit.

Distributive share A partner's share of any item of income, gain, deduction, or loss recognized by the partnership. Distributive shares are usually expressed as a percentage and specified in the partnership agreement.

Dividends-received deduction A corporate deduction equal to a percentage of dividend income received from other taxable, domestic corporations.

Donee An individual or organization who receives a gift

Donor An individual who makes a gift.

Dynamic forecast A projection of revenue gain or loss resulting from a tax rate change that assumes that the change will affect the tax base.

Earmarked tax A tax that generates revenues for a designated project or program rather than for the government's general fund.

Earned income credit A refundable income tax credit that offsets the impact of the payroll tax on low-income workers.

Economic performance A requirement of the all-events test for nonrecurring, extraordinary accruals. Economic performance means that all activities necessary to satisfy the accrued liability have been completed.

Education IRA An investment account through which individuals can save for higher education expenses on a tax-exempt basis.

Efficiency The third standard for a good tax. Classical economic theory holds that an efficient tax is neutral and has no effect on economic behavior. In contrast, Keynesian theory holds that an efficient tax is a fiscal policy tool by which the government can affect economic behavior.

Employee An individual who performs services for compensation and who works under the direction and control of an employer.

Employee payroll tax The FICA tax (Social Security and Medicare tax) levied on employees who receive compensaton during the year.

Employer identification number A number assigned to an employer by the IRS to identify the employer for employment tax purposes.

Employer payroll tax The FICA tax (Social Security and Medicare tax) levied on employers that pay compensation during the year.

Employer-provided plan A retirement plan sponsored and maintained by an employer for the benefit of the employees.

Employment tax A tax based on wages, salaries, and self-employment income. Federal employment taxes are earmarked to fund Social Security and Medicare.

Enrolled agent A tax practitioner certified by the IRS to represent clients in IRS proceedings.

Event or transaction-based tax A tax imposed on the occurrence of a certain event or transaction.

Excess foreign tax credit Foreign tax paid or accrued during the year but not credited against U.S. tax because of the foreign tax credit limitation.

Excess payroll tax withholding An overpayment of employee payroll tax allowed as a credit against income tax.

Excise tax A tax levied on the retail sale of specific goods or services. An excise tax may be in addition to or instead of a general sale tax.

Expansion costs Costs of enlarging the scope of operations of an existing business.

Expatriate An individual who is a U.S. citizen and resides and works for an extended period in a foreign country.

Explicit tax   An actual tax liability paid directly to the taxing jurisdiction.

Field examination   An audit conducted by a revenue agent at the taxpayer's place of business.

FIFO   The inventory costing convention under which the first goods manufactured or purchased are assumed to be the first goods sold.

Filing status   A classification for individual taxpayers reflecting marital and family situation and determining the rate schedule for the computation of tax liability.

Firm   A generic business organization. Firms include sole proprietorships, partnerships, limited liability companies, Subchapter S and regular corporations, and any other type of arrangement through which people carry on a profit-motivated activity.

Fiscal year   Any 12-month period ending on the last day of any month except December.

Flat rate   A single percentage that applies to the entire tax base.

Foreign earned income exclusion   An annual amount of foreign source earned income on which expatriates are not required to pay federal income tax.

Foreign sales corporation (FSC)   An artificial entity through which U.S. firms channel export sales to receive a preferential tax rate on export income.

Foreign source income   Taxable income attributable to a U.S. firm's business activities carried on in a foreign jurisdiction.

Foreign tax credit   A credit against U.S. tax based on foreign income tax paid or accrued during the year.

Free transferability   A legal characteristic of the corporate form of business: shareholders can buy and sell corporate stock with maximum convenience and minimal transaction cost.

Fringe benefits   Any economic benefit subject to valuation received by an employee as additional compensation.

General business credit   The aggregate of 12 different tax credits available to business enterprises.

General partnership   A partnership in which all the partners have unlimited personal liability for the debts incurred by the partnership.

Generally accepted accounting principles (GAAP)   The set of accounting rules developed by the Financial Accounting Standards Board (FASB) and adhered to by the public accounting profession.

Going-concern value   Value attributable to the synergism of business assets working in coordination.

Goodwill   Value created by the expectancy that customers will continue to patronize a business.

Graduated rates   Multiple percentages that apply to specified brackets of the tax base.

Gross income   Realized increases in wealth from whatever source derived. In the business context, gross profit from sales of goods, performance of services, and investments of capital.

Gross profit percentage   The ratio of gain realized to total contract price in an installment sale.

Guaranteed payment   A distribution from a partnership to a partner to compensate the partner for ongoing services performed for the partnership.

Half-year convention   Property placed in service on any day of the taxable year is treated as placed in service halfway through the year for MACRS purposes.

Head of household   Filing status for an unmarried individual who maintains a home for a child or dependent family member.

Hobby loss   Excess of expenses over revenue from a personal activity not engaged in for profit.

Home equity debt   Debt secured by a personal residence to the extent the debt does not exceed the owner's equity in the residence. Home equity debt is limited to $100,000 ($50,000 for married filing separately).

HOPE scholarship credit   An individual tax credit based on tuition and fees paid during the first two years of post-secondary education.

Horizontal equity   One aspect of the fourth standard of a good tax: a tax is fair if persons with the same ability to pay (as measured by the tax base) owe the same tax.

Hybrid method of accounting   An overall method of accounting that combines the accrual method for purchases and sales of inventory and the cash method for all other transactions.

Implicit tax   The reduction in before-tax rate of return that investors are willing to accept because of the tax-favored characteristics of an investment.

Imputed income from owner-occupied housing   The nontaxable economic benefit (fair rental value) derived by the owner of a home.

Incentive stock option (ISO)   A qualified stock option for federal tax purposes. Individuals do not recognize the bargain element as income on the exercise of an ISO.

Incidence   The ultimate economic burden represented by a tax.

Income effect   A behavioral response to an income tax rate increase: taxpayers engage in more income-producing activities to maintain their level of disposable income.

Income tax   A tax imposed on the periodic increases in wealth resulting from a person's economic activities.

Income tax return preparer   Any person who prepares returns (or who employs other people to prepare returns) for compensation and who is subject to tax return preparer penalties.

Income tax treaty   A bilateral agreement between the governments of two countries defining and limiting each country's respective tax jurisdiction.

Independent contractor   A self-employed individual who performs services for compensation and who retains control over the manner in which the services are performed.

Individual Retirement Account (IRA)   An investment account through which individuals with compensation or earned income can save for retirement on a tax-deferred basis.

Innocent spouse rule   The rule of law under which a person who filed a joint return with a spouse is not held liable for any deficiency of tax with respect to the return.

Inside buildup   Annual increase in value of a life insurance or annuity contract.

Installment sale method   A method of accounting for gains realized on the sale of property when some part of the amount realized consists of the buyer's note. Under the installment sale method, gain recognition is linked to the seller's receipt of cash over the life of the note.

Intangible drilling and development costs (IDC) Expenses such as wages, fuel, repairs to drilling equipment, hauling, and supplies associated with locating and preparing oil and gas wells for production. IDC are deductible for federal tax purposes.

Inter vivos transfer   A transfer of property occurring during the life of the property owner.

Internal Revenue Bulletin (IRB)   The IRS's weekly publication containing revenue rulings and revenue procedures.

Internal Revenue Code of 1986   The compilation of statutory tax laws written and enacted by the Congress of the United States.

Internal Revenue Service (IRS)   The subdivision of the U.S. Treasury Department responsible for the enforcement of the federal tax laws and the collection of federal taxes.

Investment interest expense   Interest paid by an individual on debt incurred to purchase or carry investment property.

Involuntary conversion   The receipt of insurance or condemnation proceeds with respect to property destroyed by theft or casualty or taken by eminent domain.

Itemized deduction   An allowable deduction based on an expense or loss incurred by an individual taxpayer that cannot be subtracted in the calculation of AGI.

Joint and several liability   Each spouse on a joint tax return is individually liable for the entire tax for the year.

Joint return   A return filed by husband and wife reflecting their combined activities for the year.

Jurisdiction   The right of a government to levy tax on a specific person or organization.

Keogh plan   A qualified retirement plan for self-employed individuals.

Key-man life insurance policies   Insurance purchased by a firm on the life of a high-level employee. The firm is the beneficiary of the policy.

Kiddie tax   The tax on a child's unearned income based on the child's parents' marginal rate.

Late-filing and late-payment penalty   The penalty imposed on taxpayers who fail to file their returns and pay the balance of tax due on a timely basis.

Leasehold costs   Upfront costs incurred to acquire a lease on tangible business property.

Leasehold improvements   Physical improvements made by a lessee to leased real property.

Leverage   The use of borrowed funds to create tax basis.

Lifetime learning credit   An individual tax credit based on 20 percent of tuition and fees paid for post-secondary education.

Lifetime transfer tax exclusion   The cumulative amount of property transfers that an individual can make during life or at death without incurring federal transfer tax.

LIFO   The inventory costing convention under which the last goods manufactured or purchased are assumed to be the first goods sold.

Like-kind property   Qualifying business or investment property that can be exchanged on a nontaxable basis.

Limited expensing election   The election under which firms can expense a limited dollar amount of the cost of tangible personalty placed in service during the taxable year.

Limited liability   A legal characteristic of the corporate form of business: corporate shareholders are not personally liable for the unpaid debts of the corporation.

Limited liability company (LLC)   A form of unincorporated business organization in which the members have limited liability for business debt. LLCs are generally treated as partnerships for federal tax purposes.

Limited liability partnership (LLP)   A partnership in which the general partners are not personally liable for malpractice-related claims arising from the professional misconduct of another general partner.

Limited partnership   A partnership in which one or more partners are liable for partnership debt only to the extent of their capital contributions to the partnership. Limited partnerships must have at least one general partner.

Long-term capital gain or loss   Gain or loss resulting from the sale or exchange of a capital asset owned for more than one year.

Marginal rate   The tax rate that applies to the next dollar of taxable income.

Market   A forum for commercial interaction between two or more parties for the purpose of exchanging goods or services.

Market discount   The excess of a bond's stated redemption value over the price paid for the bond in a market transaction.

Matching principle   An expense should be taken into account in the period during which the expense contributes to the generation of revenues.

Material participation   An owner's regular, continuous, and substantial involvement in the day-to-day operation of an active business.

Method of accounting   A consistent system for determining the point in time at which items of income and deduction are recognized for tax purposes.

Midmonth convention   Property placed in service on any day of a month is treated as placed in service at the midpoint of the month for MACRS purposes.

Midquarter convention   Property placed in service on any day of a quarter is treated as placed in service at the midpoint of the quarter for MACRS purposes.

Minimum distribution   The annual withdrawal an individual must make from a qualified retirement plan beginning no later than April 1 of the year following the year in which he reaches age 70½

Minimum tax credit   AMT liability carried forward indefinitely as a credit against future regular tax liability.

Miscellaneous itemized deductions   Itemized deductions that are deductible only to the extent their total exceeds 2 percent of AGI.

Modified Accelerated Cost Recovery System (MACRS)   The statutory and regulatory rules governing the computation of depreciation for tax purposes.

Moving expenses   The cost of transporting household goods and personal belongings and travel costs incurred in connection with an employment-related move. Moving expenses are an adjustment in computing AGI.

Mutual fund   A diversified portfolio of securities owned and managed by a regulated investment company.

Negative externality   An undesirable by-product of the free enterprise system.

Negligence   Failure to make a prudent attempt to comply with the tax law or the intentional disregard of tax rules and regulations.

Net capital gain   The excess of current year capital gains over capital losses.

Net capital loss   The excess of current year capital losses over capital gains.

Net cash flow   The difference between cash received and cash disbursed.

Net investment income   Income from investment assets reduced by expenses directly related to the production of investment income.

Net long-term gain or loss   Aggregate gain or loss from the sale or exchange of capital assets owned for more than a year.

Net operating loss (NOL)   An excess of allowable deductions over gross income.

Net present value (NPV)   The sum of the present values of all cash inflows and outflows relating to a transaction.

Net short-term gain or loss   Aggregate gain or loss from the sale or exchange of capital assets owned for a year or less.

Nexus   The degree of contact between a business and a state necessary to establish the state's jurisdiction to tax the business.

NOL carryback   A net operating loss allowed as a deduction in the three years prior to the year of loss.

NOL carryforward   A net operating loss allowed as a deduction in the 15 years following the year of loss.

Nonbusiness bad debt   An uncollectible debt held by an individual creditor that is unrelated to the individual's business.

Nonprofit corporations   Corporations formed for philanthropic purposes and, as a result, exempt from the federal income tax.

Nonrecourse debt   A debt secured by specific collateral for which the debtor is not personally liable.

Nontaxable exchange   A transaction resulting in realized gain or loss that is not recognized (in whole or part) in the current year.

Offer in compromise   A negotiated settlement with the IRS in which the taxpayer pays less than the entire deficiency.

Office examination   An audit conducted by a tax auditor at an IRS district office.

Ordinary gain or loss   Any realized gain or loss that is not a capital gain or loss.

Ordinary income   Any income that is not capital gain. Ordinary income is taxed at the regular individual or corporate tax rates.

Organizational costs   Expenditures incurred in connection with the formation of a partnership or corporate entity.

Original issue discount (OID)   The excess of a bond's stated redemption value over the issue price.

Outbound transaction   A transaction by which a U.S. firm engages in business in a foreign jurisdiction.

Partnership   An unincorporated association of two or more persons to conduct business as co-owners.

Passive activity   An individual's interest in (1) an active business in which the individual does not materially participate or (2) a rental activity.

Passive income generator (PIG)   An interest in a profitable passive activity.

Passthrough entities   Business entities that are not taxable entities. The income, gains, deductions, and losses recognized by a passthrough entity are reported by the entity's owners and taxed only once at the owner level.

Percentage depletion   An annual deduction based on the gross income generated by a depletable property multiplied by a statutory depletion rate.

Performance-based compensation   Compensation paid solely because the recipient employee attained a performance goal established by a compensation committee of outside members of the corporate board of directors.

Permanent difference   A difference between financial statement income and taxable income that does not reverse over time.

Permanent establishment   A fixed location at which a firm carries on its regular commercial activities. For income tax treaty purposes, a country has no jurisdiction to tax a foreign business entity unless the entity maintains a permanent establishment in the country.

Personal exemption   A dollar amount allowed as a deduction from AGI for each taxpayer and qualifying dependent. The personal exemption is indexed annually for inflation.

Personal holding company   A corporation owned by a small number of individuals that receives taxable income consisting primarily of nonbusiness income such as dividends, interest, rents, and royalties.

Personal holding company tax   A penalty tax levied on personal holding companies in addition to the regular corporate income tax.

Personal service corporations   Closely held corporations owned by individuals who perform services in the fields of health, law, engineering, architecture, accounting, actuarial science, performing arts, or consulting for the corporation's clientele. Personal service corporations are subject to a flat 35 percent tax rate.

Personalty   Any asset that is not realty.

Premature withdrawal   A withdrawal from a qualified retirement plan made before the individual reaches age 59½.

Principal residence   The home in which an individual resides for most of the year and considers his permanent address.

Private activity bonds   Tax-exempt bonds issued by state or local governments for nongovernmental purposes such as industrial development.

Private letter ruling   The IRS's written response to a taxpayer's inquiry as to how the tax law applies to a proposed transaction.

Private market   A market in which the parties deal directly with each other and can customize the terms of their agreement to meet their respective objectives.

Probate estate   Property owned by a decedent and disposed of according to the terms of a valid will or state intestacy laws.

Profit-sharing plan   A defined-contribution plan under which an employer regularly contributes a percentage of current earnings to the employees' retirement accounts.

Progressive rate structure   A graduated rate structure with rates that increase as the base increases.

Property similar or related in service or use   Qualifying replacement property in a nontaxable involuntary conversion.

Proportionate rate structure   A rate structure with a single, or flat, rate.

Public market   A market in which the parties deal indirectly through an intermediary such as a broker or a financial institution.

Publicly held corporations   Corporations with outstanding stock traded on an established securities market.

Qualified education loan   Any debt incurred to pay higher education expenses. Interest on the debt paid during the first 60 months for which interest is required is eligible for a deduction.

Qualified residence interest   Interest paid on acquisition debt or home equity debt allowed as an itemized deduction.

Qualified retirement plans   Retirement plans that meet certain statutory requirements and that allow participants to save for retirement on a tax-deferred basis.

Qualified small business stock   Stock in a corporate business that meets certain statutory requirements. Individuals who recognize gain on the sale of qualified small business stock may be eligible to exclude 50 percent of the gain from income.

Qualifying property   The specific property eligible for a particular nontaxable exchange.

Real property tax   A tax levied on the ownership of realty and based on the property's assessed market value.

Realization principle   Income is taken into account when the earnings process with respect to the income is complete and an event or transaction occurs that provides an objective measurement of the income.

Realized gain or loss   The positive or negative difference between the amount realized on the disposition of property and the adjusted basis of the property.

Realty   Land and whatever is erected or growing on the land or permanently affixed to it.

Recapture   Recharacterization of Section 1231 or capital gain as ordinary income.

Recognition   Inclusion of an item of income or deduction in the computation of taxable income.

Recognized gain or loss   Realized gain or loss taken into account for tax purposes in the current year.

Recourse debt   A debt for which the debtor is personally liable.

Recovery period   The number of years prescribed by statute over which the basis of tangible business property is depreciated under MACRS.

Regressive rate structure   A graduated rate structure with rates that decrease as the base increases.

Rehabilitation credit   A business credit equal to a percentage of the cost of rehabilitating commercial buildings placed in service before 1936 or certified historic structures.

Related party transaction   A transaction between parties who share a common economic interest or objective and who may not be dealing at arm's length.

Rental activity   An activity where payments are principally for the use of tangible property for an extended period of time. Rental activities are passive activities.

Reorganization   A statutorily defined transaction in which one corporation acquires another, one corporation divides into two corporations, or a corporation changes its capital structure.

Revenue   Total tax collected by the government and available for public use.

Revenue rulings and revenue procedures   Published pronouncements explaining how the IRS applies current tax law to a particular set of facts and circumstances.

Rollover contribution   A distribution from one qualified plan contributed to another qualified plan within 60 days.

Roth IRA   An investment account through which individuals with compensation or earned income can save for retirement on a tax-exempt basis.

Safe-harbor estimate   Estimated current year tax payments based on the preceding year's tax liability that protect the taxpayer from the underpayment penalty.

Sales tax   A general tax levied on the retail sale of goods and services.

Section   Numerically labeled subdivision of the Internal Revenue Code. Each section contains an operational, definitional, or procedural rule relating to one of the federal taxes.

Section 1231 asset   Real or depreciable property used in a trade or business (including rental real estate) and intangible business assets subject to amortization held by the owner for more than one year.

Section 1244 stock   The first $1 million of stock issued by a corporation for cash or property. Some portion of the loss on the disposition of Section 1244 stock is ordinary to individual investors.

Section 401(k) plan   A defined-contribution plan under which employees elect to contribute a portion of current year compensation to an employer-provided retirement plan.

Securities   Financial instruments including equity interests in business organizations and creditor interests such as savings accounts, notes, and bonds.

Self-employment (SE) tax   Employment tax levied on an individual's net earnings from self-employment.

Separate return   A return filed by a married individual reflecting his or her independent activity and tax liability for the year. The tax liability is based on the married filing separately rate schedule.

Separately stated item   An item of income, gain, deduction, or loss recognized by a passthrough entity that retains its character as it flows through to the owners. Separately stated items are not included in the computation of the entity's ordinary business income or loss.

Series EE savings bonds   Long-term debt instruments issued by the U.S. government at a discount.

Short-period return   A tax return for a taxable year consisting of less than 12 months.

Short-term capital gain or loss   Gain or loss resulting from the sale or exchange of a capital asset owned for one year or less.

Single taxpayer   An unmarried individual who is neither a surviving spouse nor a head of household.

Small Tax Case division   A division of the U.S. Tax Court that holds informal hearings of disputes involving tax deficiencies of $10,000 or less.

Sole proprietorship   An unincorporated business owned by one individual.

Special agent   A revenue agent who handles criminal fraud investigations.

Specific identification method   An accounting method under which cost of goods sold includes the actual cost of specific items of inventory sold during the year.

Standard deduction   A deduction from AGI based on filing status. The standard deduction amounts are indexed annually for inflation.

Start-up expenditures   Up-front costs of investigating the creation or purchase of a business and the routine expenses incurred during the preoperating phase of a business.

Static forecast   A projection of revenue gain or loss resulting from a tax rate change that assumes that the change will have no effect on the tax base.

Statute of limitations The statutory limit on the time period after a tax return is filed during which the IRS can audit the return and assess additional tax.

Step transaction doctrine The IRS can collapse a series of intermediate transactions into a single transaction to determine the tax consequences of the arrangement in its entirety.

Stock option The right to purchase corporate stock for a stated price (the strike price) for a given period of time.

Subchapter S corporation A corporation with a subchapter S election in effect. The corporation is a passthrough entity for federal tax purposes and does not pay federal income tax.

Subpart F income A category of foreign source income earned by a CFC constructively distributed to U.S. shareholders in the year earned. Conceptually, Subpart F income is artificial income in that it has no commercial or economic connection to the country in which the CFC is incorporated.

Substance over form doctrine The IRS can look through the legal formalities to determine the economic substance (if any) of a transaction and to base the tax consequences on the substance instead of the form.

Substituted basis The basis of qualifying property received in a nontaxable exchange determined by reference to the basis of the property surrendered in the exchange.

Substitution effect A behavioral response to an income tax rate increase: taxpayers engage in fewer income-producing activities and more nonincome-producing activities.

Sufficiency The first standard for a good tax. A tax should generate enough revenue to pay for the public goods and services provided by the government levying the tax.

Supply-side economic theory A decrease in the highest income tax rates should stimulate economic growth and ultimately result in an increase in government revenues.

Surtax In the corporate context, the extra 5 percent or 3 percent tax imposed to recoup the benefit of the progressive corporate tax rates.

Surviving spouse Filing status that permits a widow or widower to use the married filing jointly rate schedule for two taxable years following the death of a spouse.

Tax A payment to support the cost of government. A tax is nonpenal but compulsory and is not directly related to any specific benefit provided by the government.

Tax assessor An elected or appointed government official responsible for deriving the value of realty located within a taxing jurisdiction.

Tax avoidance The implementation of legal strategies for reducing taxes.

Tax base An item, occurrence, transaction, or activity with respect to which a tax is levied. Tax bases are usually expressed in monetary terms.

Tax basis A taxpayer's investment in any asset or property right and the measure of unrecovered dollars represented by the asset.

Tax cost An increase in tax liability for any period resulting from a transaction.

Tax credit A direct reduction in tax liability.

Tax evasion The willful and deliberate attempt to defraud the government by understating a tax liability through illegal means. Also see *Criminal fraud.*

Tax Expenditures Budget Part of the federal budget that quantifies the annual revenue loss attributable to each major tax preference.

Tax haven A foreign jurisdiction with minimal or no income tax.

Tax law The body of legal authority consisting of statutory laws, administrative pronouncements, and judicial decisions.

Tax planning The structuring of transactions to reduce tax costs or increase tax savings to maximize net present value.

Tax policy A government's attitude, objectives, and actions with respect to its tax system.

Tax preferences In the general context, provisions included in the federal tax law as incentives to encourage certain behaviors or as subsidies for certain activities. In the AMT context, specific items added to regular taxable income in the computation of AMTI.

Tax savings A decrease in tax liability for any period resulting from a transaction.

Taxable estate The aggregate fair market value of property owned by a decedent or transferred because of the decedent's death reduced by allowable deductions.

Taxable income Gross income minus allowable deductions for the taxable year.

Taxpayer Any person or organization required by law to pay tax to a governmental authority.

Taxpayer Bill of Rights Part of the federal law requiring the IRS to deal with every citizen and resident in a fair, professional, prompt, and courteous manner.

Temporary difference A difference between financial statement income and taxable income that reverses over time.

Tentative minimum tax AMTI in excess of the exemption multiplied by the AMT rates. Any excess of tentative minimum tax over regular tax is the AMT liability for the year.

Testamentary transfer A transfer of property occurring on the death of the property owner.

Thin capitalization A corporate capital structure with a high ratio of debt to equity.

Time value of money A dollar available today is worth more than a dollar available tomorrow because the current dollar can be invested to start earning interest immediately.

Total income   The sum of the income items recognized by an individual during the year and listed on page 1, Form 1040.

Transfer price   In the international area, the price at which goods or services are exchanged between controlled corporations operating in different taxing jurisdictions.

Transfer tax   A tax levied on the transfer of wealth by gift or at death and based on the market value of the transferred assets.

Transferee liability   Liability of a recipient of property (transferee) for the unpaid tax of the transferor of the property.

Treasury regulation   The official interpretation of a statutory tax rule written and published by the U.S. Treasury.

28 percent rate gain or loss   Long-term capital gain or loss from the sale or exchange of collectibles or any capital asset owned for more than one year but not more than 18 months.

U.S. Circuit Courts of Appeals   Thirteen federal courts that hear appeals of trial court decisions.

U.S. Court of Federal Claims   A federal trial court located in Washington, D.C., in which taxpayers can sue the government for a refund of tax.

U.S. District Courts   Federal trial courts in which taxpayers can sue the government for a refund of tax.

U.S. Supreme Court   The highest federal court. The Supreme Court hears appeals of circuit court decisions.

U.S. Tax Court   A federal court that tries only federal income, gift, and estate tax cases.

Underpayment penalty   The penalty imposed by the Internal Revenue Code on both individuals and corporations that fail to make required installment payments of current tax on a timely basis.

Unemployment tax   A tax levied by both the federal and state governments on compensation paid by employers to their employees. Unemployment taxes are earmarked to fund the national unemployment insurance program.

Uniform capitalization (unicap) rules   The set of tax rules governing the type of current expenditures that must be capitalized to inventory.

Uniform Division of Income for Tax Purposes Act (UDITPA)   A model act describing a recommended method for apportioning a firm's taxable income among multiple state jurisdictions.

Unlimited life   A legal characteristic of the corporate form of business: a corporation's legal existence is not affected by changes in the identity of its shareholders.

Unlimited marital deduction   A deduction in the computation of a decedent's taxable estate equal to the value of property transferred to the decedent's surviving spouse.

Unrecaptured Section 1250 gain   Section 1231 gain on the sale of business realty that would be recaptured as ordinary income under the full recapture rule.

Use tax   A tax levied on the ownership, possession, or consumption of goods if the owner did not pay the jurisdiction's sales tax when the goods were purchased.

Vacation home   A personal residence other than the owner's principal residence.

Value-added tax (VAT)   A tax levied on firms engaged in any phase of the production or manufacture of goods and based on the incremental value added by the firm to the goods.

Vertical equity   One aspect of the fourth standard of a good tax: a tax is fair if persons with a greater ability to pay (as measured by the tax base) owe more tax than persons with a lesser ability to pay.

Wash sale   A sale of marketable securities if the seller reacquires substantially the same securities within 30 days after (or 30 days before) the sale.

Index